THE GREAT DEFORMATION

THE GREAT DEFORMATION

THE CORRUPTION OF CAPITALISM IN AMERICA

DAVID A. STOCKMAN

PublicAffairs
New York

Library of Congress Cataloging-in-Publication Data is available for this book.
ISBN 978-1-58648-912-0 (HC)
ISBN 978-1-58648-913-7 (eBook)

Editorial production by Marrathon Production Services. www.marrathon.net
BOOK DESIGN BY JANE RAESE
Text set in 10-point Utopia

FIRST EDITION

10 9 8 7 6 5 4 3 2 1

To my daughters, Rachel and Victoria,
whose future inspired me to start this book,
and my wife, Jennifer,
whose patience and loving support
enabled me to complete it.

CONTENTS

INTRODUCTION

Less than two weeks before *The Great Deformation* went to press, the powers that be in Washington pulled off a "deal" that allegedly stopped the country from going over the fiscal cliff. What they did, in fact, was to permanently add nearly $5 trillion to Federal deficits over the next ten years, ensuring that the national debt will continue to surge higher and that Washington will become strangled even more deeply in a fatal paralysis of governance.

In truth, the fiscal cliff is permanent and insurmountable. It stands at the edge of a $20 trillion abyss of deficits over the next decade. And this estimation is conservative, based on sober economic assumptions and the dug-in tax and spending positions of the two parties, both powerfully abetted by lobbies and special interests which fight for every paragraph of loophole ridden tax code and each line of a grossly bloated budget.

Fiscal cliffs as far as the eye can see are the deeply troubling outcome of the Great Deformation. They are the result of capture of the state, especially its central bank, the Federal Reserve, by crony capitalist forces deeply inimical to free markets and democracy.

Why we are mired in this virtually unsolvable problem is the reason I wrote this book. It originated in my being flabbergasted when the Republican White House in September 2008 proposed the $700 billion TARP bailout of Wall Street. When the courageous House Republicans who voted it down were forced to walk the plank a second time in betrayal of their principled stand, my sense of disbelief turned into a not-inconsiderable outrage. Likewise, I was shocked to read of the blatant deal making, bribing, and bullying of the troubled big banks being conducted out of the treasury secretary's office, as if it were the M&A department of Goldman Sachs.

Most important, I had been an amateur historian on the matter of twentieth-century fiscal and monetary history, perhaps owing to my years on Capitol Hill and in the Reagan White House when they were embroiled in these topics. In fact, prior to my Washington years, while hiding out from the draft at Harvard Divinity School in 1968–1970, I had taken up serious study of the New Deal under the era's great historian Frank Freidel, and had continued the inquiry ever since. So when Fed chairman Bernanke began running around Washington shouting that the Great Depression 2.0 was at hand, I smelled a rat.

Then, when the Fed's fire hoses started spraying an alphabet soup of liquidity injections in every direction, and its balance sheet grew by $1.3 trillion in just thirteen weeks compared to $850 billion during its first ninety-four years, I became convinced that the Fed was flying by the seat of its pants, making it up as it went along. It was evident that its aim was to stop the hissy fit on Wall Street, and that the threat of a Great Depression 2.0 was just a cover story for a panicked spree of money printing that exceeded any other episode in recorded human history.

At length, the sweaty visage of Treasury Secretary Hank Paulson appeared on the TV screen yet again, this time announcing that Washington was writing a $13 billion check to bail out General Motors. That's where I lost it. I had spent the two decades since I left the White House on Wall Street in the leveraged buyout business, and at that moment I was laid up on the injured reserve list because of my own fiery mishap in Detroit. I had organized, financed, and partially owned a $4 billion auto parts supplier that I had imprudently loaded up with massive amounts of debt, and which had then been crushed by the bumbling corporate bureaucrats at GM (and Chrysler) ahead of their own crash landing.

As a consequence of my Detroit experience, I was in the midst of proving to a US prosecutor that my company's bankruptcy was due to leverage and stupidity (mine), not fraud. But three years of fighting an indictment concentrates the mind, and by then I knew one thing for certain: the Detroit-based auto industry was a debt-enfeebled house of cards that had been a Wall Street playpen of deal making and LBOs for years, including my own; it needed nothing so much as a cold bath of free market house cleaning, along with a drastic rollback of the preposterous $100,000 per year cost of UAW jobs.

Paulson's claim that the auto industry would disappear and that millions of jobs would be lost I knew to be laughable. My company had forty North American plants and I had traveled the length and breadth of the auto belt and had seen dozens of worn-out, broken-down UAW-controlled auto plants in the north that were redundant, and dozens of brand new, efficient state-of-the-art plants established by foreign automakers in the southern tier of states that could readily take up the slack. Absent the auto bailouts, there would have been no car shortage or loss of jobs—just a reallocation from the north to the South based on the rules of the free market.

By the end of the Bush administration it was starkly apparent that a Republican White House had wantonly trashed all the old-time fiscal rules, and it had been done by political neophytes: Hank Paulson and his posse of eager-beaver Goldman bankers. But I had been at the center of the most intense fiscal battle of modern times during the early Reagan era and had learned something they apparently hadn't: that the Congress is made up of representatives from 435 mini-principalities and duchies, and they reason by precedent above all else. Once Wall Street, AIG, and GM were bailed out, the state would have no boundaries: the public purse would be fair game for all.

I found this alarming in view of the long ago Reagan-era battle of the budget that had ended in dismal failure. Notwithstanding decades of Republican speech making about Ronald Reagan's rebuke to "big government," it never happened. In the interim, Republican administrations whose mantra was "smaller government" only made Big Government more corpulent, so plainly by 2008 there was no fiscal headroom left at all to plunge into "bailout nation."

After I left the White House in 1985 I wrote a youthful screed, *The Triumph of Politics,* decrying Republican hypocrisy about the evils of deficit finance. But I had also tried to accomplish something more constructive: to systematically call the roll of the spending cuts *not made* by Ronald Reagan, and thereby document that almost nobody was willing to challenge the core components that comprise Big Government.

Thus, the giant social insurance programs of Medicare and Social Security had barely been scratched; means-tested entitlements had been modestly reformed but had saved only small change because there weren't so many welfare queens after all; farm subsidies and veterans' benefits had not been cut because these were GOP constituencies; and the Education Department had emerged standing tall because middle-class families demanded their student loans and grants. In all, Ronald Reagan had left the "welfare state" barely one-half of 1 percent of GDP smaller than Jimmy Carter's, and added a massive structural deficit to boot.

But that was twenty-five years ago, and whatever fiscal rectitude had existed among the Republican congressional elders at the time had long since disappeared. During the eight years of George W. Bush, the GOP had pivoted from spending cuts not made to a spending spree not seen since the presidency of Lyndon Baines Johnson—adopting Medicare prescription drug benefits, massive growth in education spending, the monstrosity of the Homeland Security Department, sky-high farm subsidies, and pork-barrel excess everywhere. Worse still, the defense budget had doubled and the so-called Republican brand had been reduced to tax cutting for any reason and in whatever form the lobbies of K Street could concoct.

George W. Bush thus left the White House trailed by previously unthinkable bailouts and a deluge of red ink which would reach $1.2 trillion and

10 percent of GDP, even before the Obama stimulus. What was truly galling, however, was that the Wall Street satrap occupying the third floor of the Treasury Building had talked the hapless Bush into a $150 billion one-time tax rebate to "stimulate" the economy.

I had long since parted ways with the supply-siders and had left the White House with my admiration for President Reagan considerably dulled by his obdurate inflexibility on the runaway defense buildup, and his refusal to acknowledge that the giant deficits which emerged in the 1980s were his responsibility, not Jimmy Carter's. But despite all this, I thought that the Paulson tax rebate was a sharp slap in the Gipper's face. President Reagan's great accomplishment had been the burial of the Keynesian predicate: the notion that Washington could create economic growth and wealth by borrowing money and passing it out to consumers so they would buy more shoes and soda pop.

Now Paulson was throwing even that overboard. Didn't the whirling dervish from Goldman know that once upon a time all the young men and women in Ronald Reagan's crusade, and most especially the father of supply side, Jack Kemp, had ridiculed the very tax rebate that he peddled to Nancy Pelosi in February 2008 as Jimmy Carter's $50 per family folly?

At length, I saw the light, and it had nothing to do with Paulson's apparent illiteracy on the precepts of sound fiscal policy. The bailouts, the Fed's frenzied money printing, the embrace of primitive Keynesian tax stimulus by a Republican White House amounted to something terrible: a de facto coup d'état by Wall Street, resulting in Washington's embrace of any expedient necessary to keep the financial bubble going—and no matter how offensive it was to every historic principle of free markets, sound money, and fiscal rectitude.

The Obama $800 billion stimulus, which came within days of Bush's vacating the White House, removed all doubt that Keynesian policies had come roaring back in close couple with Wall Street's petulant demands for monetary juice to restart the bubble machine. This was self-evidently a deadly brew because it meant that policy action in Washington would be driven by fast-money speculators and trading robots on Wall Street, as had been so pathetically evident after the first TARP vote. And that meant, in turn, that the big spenders, the K Street lobbies, and the reflexive Republican tax cutters could all genuflect to the great god of the stock market, even as they collectively pushed the nation's fiscal accounts into a tsunami of red ink on a scale never before imagined in peacetime.

Obama's $800 billion grab bag of consumer tax-cut handouts, business loopholes, money dumps to state and local governments, highway pork barrels, green energy giveaways, and hundreds more was passed in twenty-one days with no deliberation and after an epic feeding frenzy among the K Street lobbies. Literally decades of chipping away at the federal budget monster by fiscal stalwarts like Senators Pete Domenici and Kent Conrad were flushed away in a heartbeat.

This all came tumbling down into some mind-bending questions. How did we get here? How did it happen that the nation's central bank printed nearly twice as much money in thirteen weeks as it had during the entire century before? How had fiscal prudence been thrown to the winds so completely that between TARP and the Obama stimulus program Congress had authorized $1.5 trillion in the span of 140 days based on policies that had barely been inked onto legislative parchment, let alone read or analyzed? How had the stock market index cratered from 1560 in October 2007 to 670 in a mere fifteen months? How had the top-ten Wall Street Banks been valued at $1 trillion in mid-2007 only to crash into a paroxysm of failure and bailouts twelve months later? And then there was the subprime fiasco that had not been foreseen, the flame out of the giant Washington housing finance agencies, and the thundering collapse of the derivatives market in CDOs, CDSs, and the other toxic varieties. And most unaccountable of all: the stunning and precipitous meltdown of AIG.

For me, AIG was the skunk in the woodpile. After twenty years on Wall Street I knew that the giant, globe-spanning AIG and its legendary founder, Hank Greenberg, had once been viewed as not simply the gold standard of finance, but as seated at the very right-hand of the financial god almighty. And then, in a heartbeat, AIG needed $180 billion—right now, this very day, to keep its doors open? Worse still, this staggering sum of money—the size of the Departments of Commerce, Labor, Energy, Education, and Interior combined—had been ladled out as easy as Christmas punch: Bernanke just hit the "send" key on his digital money machine.

Thus begins the inquiry that has resulted in this book. There had to be a pattern and history behind these momentous, unaccountable, and foreboding developments, I thought, because during the entire course of my career—nearly forty years in Washington and on Wall Street—none of these events would have been thought even remotely possible by most people. Zero percent interest rates? A 10 percent of GDP deficit? The bankruptcy of the $6 trillion edifice of Freddie Mac and Fannie Mae? A Great Depression 2.0 only a short time after Bernanke himself pronounced the arrival of the "Great Moderation"?

Indeed, that was the heart of the matter and it is the foil for my thesis. Bernanke said in 2004 that prosperity would be everlasting because the state and its central banking branch had perfected the art of modulating the business cycle and smoothing the natural bumps and grinds of free market capitalism. This book argues the opposite; namely, that what is at hand is the "Great Deformation." Free markets and prosperity are deeply imperiled because the state and its central banking branch have failed miserably due to overreaching, overloading, and outside capture. They have become the tools of a vicious form of crony capitalism and money politics and are in thrall to a statist policy ideology common to all three branches of today's Washington economics: Keynesianism, monetarism, and supply-side-ism.

Given the somber fiscal realities owing to the $20 trillion deficit abyss ahead, it is difficult to imagine worse, but the monetary dimension, in fact, is even more foreboding. At the heart of the Great Deformation is a rogue central bank that has abandoned every vestige of sound money. In so doing, it has enabled politicians to enjoy "deficits without tears" by monetizing massive amounts of the public debt.

It has also crushed the interest rate mechanism as an honest price signal in the financial markets; turned the treasury yield curve into a front-runner's paradise; and fueled massively leveraged carry trades which feed the 1 percent with windfalls while these trades work and generate petulant demands for bailouts when they crash. Turning Wall Street into a reckless, dangerous, and greed-riven casino, the Fed has at the same time crucified the nation's savers on a rack of ZIRP (zero interest) and fueled a global commodity bubble that erodes Main Street living standards via soaring food and energy prices—inflation that the Fed then fecklessly deletes from the CPI.

Needless to say, it took a long time to get to this lamentable state; nearly one hundred years, in fact. And that is what I now trace: a revisionist history of our era. It shows how the state-wreck ahead was fostered by FDR's repudiation of the bipartisan tradition of sound money and the New Deal's incubation of crony capitalist government. The Great Deformation was then put into brief remission during the mid-century golden era of sound money and fiscal rectitude under Dwight Eisenhower in the White House and William McChesney Martin at the Fed.

After that, the incipient state-wreck was powerfully revived by Nixon's perfidious weekend at Camp David in August 1971, where Tricky Dick blatantly and defiantly defaulted on the nation's debt obligations under the Bretton Woods gold standard. Taking the United States off the gold standard was the starting point for the present era of floating money, massive debt creation, and a dangerously unstable global money-printing spree. Nixon's malefactions were then further nourished by the final destruction of fiscal rectitude during the Reagan era, enabling both the warfare state and welfare state to balloon without the yoke of taxes weighing on the people. In the final descent into bubble finance, the Greenspan and Bernanke

Fed institutionalized the financial repression, wealth effects, and Wall Street–coddling policies that have triggered the crisis at hand.

The order of this book is not exactly chronological. It aims first to unpeel the onion of obfuscation that has emanated from Wall Street, bailout apologists, and the trio of Washington economic doctrines that assume the state can revive a failing economy when, in reality, it is a failing state that is crushing what remains of Main Street prosperity.

Part 1 on the BlackBerry Panic, that historic moment in September 2008 when Washington flooded Wall Street with bailout money, refutes the hoary urban legends that were used by the Fed and the Treasury to panic the Congress into passing TARP and to justify the Fed's balance sheet explosion. The so-called financial meltdown was purely in the canyons of Wall Street where it would have burned out on its own and meted out to speculators the losses they deserved. By contrast, the Main Street banking system was never in serious jeopardy, ATMs were not going dark, the money market industry was not imploding, and there was never any Great Depression 2.0 remotely in prospect.

That's important because it demonstrates that the September 2008 Wall Street crisis did not arrive mysteriously on a comet from deep space, thereby justifying emergency heat shields of money printing, deficits, and bailouts which broke all the rules. Instead, it grew out of decades during which Washington defied the rules, corrupting the nation's financial condition with unfinanced wars, tax cuts, and welfare state expansion, permitting rampant special interest plunder of the public purse and conducting a financial casino out of the Fed's headquarters in Washington.

Part 2, "The Reagan Era Revisited: False Narratives of Our Times," unpeels another layer of the onion that obscures a clear-eyed view of the Great Deformation's deeper history. It debunks the GOP's nostalgic claim that despite the mysterious ailment that caused the financial disasters of recent years, all would be well by simply going back to undiluted Reaganism. But "Morning in America" never happened and a fiscal disaster most surely did. Likewise, part 3 clears away the other short-circuit to comprehending the historical depth of the current crisis; namely, the claim of present-day high priests of Keynesianism that the New Deal already wrote the sacred texts and now they only need to be aggressively followed in order to clear the decks. In fact, the New Deal, despite its vaunted place in the history books, was largely a political gong show that didn't cure the Great Depression, which, in any event, was caused by a global trade and commodity collapse that is totally irrelevant to America's current traumas.

The Great Deformation is a story that evolves decade by decade after the First World War. It is a historical sketch of what happened and a polemic about what went wrong. It features a gallery of policy villains, that is, proponents of unsound finance, including Franklin Roosevelt, Richard Nixon, Arthur Burns, Walter Heller, Milton Friedman, John Connally, George Schulz, Art Laffer, Cap Weinberger, Alan Greenspan, Newt Gingrich, Bob Rubin, George W. Bush, Hank Paulson, Tim Geithner, Jeff Immelt, John Mack, Paul Krugman, Larry Summers, Barack Obama, and most especially Ben Bernanke. Alongside is a cast of policy heroes who champion the cause of sound money and fiscal rectitude at crucial times, including, in the early periods, Carter Glass, Professor H. Parker Willis, Calvin Coolidge, Herbert Hoover, Lewis Douglas, James Warburg, and later, Harry Truman, Dwight Eisenhower, George Humphrey, William McChesney Martin, Douglas Dillon, Bill Simon, Paul Volcker, Howard Baker, Pete Domenici, Bill Clinton, Paul O'Neill, Ron Paul, Richard Shelby, and Sheila Bair.

The battle turns out to be not equal. By the end of the story it will be apparent how crony capitalism won the struggle, why the fiscal cliff is insurmountable, and how a Keynesian state-wreck is at hand. The final chapter assays another road that could be taken: one that is compelling but, given the roots of the Great Deformation, difficult in the extreme.

THE GREAT
DEFORMATION

PART I

THE BLACKBERRY PANIC OF 2008

CHAPTER 1

PAULSON'S FOLLY
The Needless Rescue of AIG and Wall Street

I N THE SECOND DECADE OF THE TWENTY-FIRST CENTURY, AMERICA IS faltering under the weight of a dual crisis. Its public sector teeters on the ragged edge of political dysfunction and fiscal collapse. At the same time, its private enterprise foundation has morphed into a speculative casino which swindles the masses and enriches the few. These lamentable conditions are the Janus-faces of crony capitalism—a mutant régime which now threatens to cripple the nation's bedrock institutions of political democracy and the free market economy.

A decisive tipping point in the evolution of American capitalism and de-mocracy—the triumph of crony capitalism—took place on October 3, 2008. That was the day of the forced march approval on Capitol Hill of the $700 billion TARP (Troubled Asset Relief Program) bill to bail out Wall Street. This spasm of financial market intervention, including multitrillion-dollar support lines provided to the big banks and financial companies by the Federal Reserve, was but the latest brick in the foundation of a funda-mentally anti-capitalist régime known as "Too Big to Fail" (TBTF). It had been under construction for many decades, but now there was no turning back. The Wall Street bailouts of 2008 shattered what little remained of the old-time fiscal rules.

There was no longer any pretense that the free market should determine winners and losers and that tapping the public treasury requires proof of compelling societal benefit. Not when AAA-rated General Electric had been given $30 billion in taxpayer loans and guarantees to avoid taking modest losses on toxic assets it had foolishly funded with overnight bor-rowings that suddenly couldn't be rolled over.

Even more improbably, Goldman Sachs had been handed $10 billion to save itself from alleged extinction. Yet it then swiveled on a dime and gener-ated a $29 billion financial surplus—$16 billion in salary and bonuses on top of $13 billion in net income—for the year that began just three months later.

Even if Goldman didn't really need the money, as it later claimed, a round trip from purported rags to evident riches in fifteen months stretched the bounds of credulity. It was reminiscent of actor Gary Cooper's immortal 1950s expression of suspicion about Communism. "From what I have heard about it," he told a congressional committee, "it isn't on the level."

Nor was Washington's panicked bailout of Wall Street on the level; it was both unnecessary and targeted at the wrong problem. The so-called financial meltdown was not the real crisis; it was only the tip of the iceberg, the leading edge of a more fundamental economic malady. In truth, the US economy was heading for the wringer because a multi-decade spree of unsustainable borrowing, speculation, and financialization of the national economy was coming to an abrupt end.

In the years after 1980, America had undergone the equivalent of a national leveraged buyout (LBO). It was now saddled with $30 trillion more in combined public and private debt than would have been the case under the time-tested canons of financial discipline and prudence which prevailed during the nation's long economic ascent. This massive debt burden had fueled a three-decade prosperity party by mortgaging the nation's future. Now the bill was coming due and our national simulacrum of prosperity was over.

This rendezvous with the limits of "peak debt," however, did not mean that the Main Street economy was in danger of collapse into an instant depression. That was the specious claim of the bailsters. What did threaten was a deeper and more enduring adversity. The demise of this thirty-year debt super cycle actually meant that it was payback time. Instead of swiping growth from the future, the American economy would now face a long twilight of debt deflation and struggle to restore household, corporate, and public sector solvency.

This abrupt turn in the road should not have been surprising. America's fantastic collective binging on debt, public and private, had no historical precedent. During the century prior to 1980, for example, total public and private debt on US balance sheets rarely exceeded 1.6 times GDP. When the national borrowing spree reached its apogee in 2007, however, the $4 trillion of new debt issued by households, business, banks, and governments amounted to 6 times that year's $700 billion gain in GDP. Plain and simple, what was being recorded as GDP growth was little more than faux prosperity borrowed from the future.

In fact, by the time of the financial crisis total US debt outstanding was $52 trillion and represented 3.6 times national income of $14 trillion. Accordingly, there were now two full turns of extra debt weighing on the nation's economy. And the embedded math was forbidding: at the historic leverage ratio of 1.6 times national income, which had prevailed for most of the hundred years prior to 1980, total US public and private debt would have been only $22 trillion at the end of 2008.

So the nation's households, businesses, and taxpayers were now lugging around the aforementioned $30 trillion in excess debt. This staggering financial burden dwarfed levels which had historically been proven to be healthy, prudent, and sustainable. TARP and all its kindred bailouts and the Fed's ceaseless money printing could not relieve it. And Washington's reckless use of Uncle Sam's credit card to fund the Obama stimulus actually made it far worse by attempting to revive the false prosperity of the bubble years. The obvious question remains: Why did this plague of debt arise? Did the American people suddenly become profligate and greedy through a mysterious process of moral and social decay?

There is no evidence for the greed disease theory but plenty of reason to suspect a more foreboding cause. The real reason for the current crisis of debt and financial disorder is that public policy had veered into the ditch, permitting an unprecedented aggrandizement of the state and its central banking branch. In the process, the vital nerve center of capitalism, its money and capital markets, had been perverted and deformed. Wall Street has become a vast casino where leveraged speculation and rent seeking have displaced its vital function of price discovery and capital allocation.

The September 2008 financial crisis, therefore, was about the need to drastically deflate the Wall Street behemoths—that is, dangerous and unstable gambling houses—fostered by decades of money printing and market rigging by the Fed. Yet policy veered in the opposite direction, propping them up and thereby perpetuating their baleful effects, owing to a predicate that was dead wrong.

A handful of panic-stricken top officials, led by treasury secretary Hank Paulson and Fed chairman Ben Bernanke, proclaimed that the financial system had been stricken by a deadly "contagion" that had come out of nowhere and threatened a chain reaction of financial failures that would end in cataclysm. That proposition was completely false, but it gave rise to a fateful injunction—namely, that all the normal rules of free market capitalism and fiscal prudence needed to be suspended so that unprecedented and unlimited public resources could be poured into the rescue of Wall Street's floundering behemoths.

AIG WAS SAFE ENOUGH TO FAIL

As it happened, Washington drew the red line at AIG the day after the Lehman failure. Yet the relevant facts show that an AIG bankruptcy would not have started a chain reaction—that there never was a financial dooms-day lurking around the corner. In fact, none of the bailouts were necessary because the meltdown was strictly a matter confined to the canyons of Wall Street. It would have burned out there on its own had Washington allowed the free market to have its way with a handful of insolvent institutions that needed to be taken out: Morgan Stanley, Goldman, and Citigroup, among others.

In short, the financial "contagion" predicate, which triggered the bailout madness of the Bush White House and the Bernanke Fed, had no basis in fact. And the proof starts with AIG, the bailout poster child itself, and the alleged catalyst for the purported chain reaction. The plain fact of the matter is that AIG was structurally incapable of starting a contagion. Any modest hit to the balance sheets of a handful of its huge, global banking customers owing to the collapse of its bogus credit default insurance (CDS) would have caused a healthy purge of busted assets. At the same time, its millions of insurance policy holders were never in harms' way; they were always a pretext to obfuscate the real purposes of the Washington bailsters.

At the time of the crisis, 90 percent of AIG was solvent and no danger to the financial system or anyone else. Its $800 billion balance sheet consisted mostly of high-grade stocks and bonds that were domiciled in a manner which utterly invalidated the "contagion" theory. Indeed, this giant asset total was a statistical artifact of AIG's consolidated financial statements: its massive horde of high-grade assets was actually parceled out into scores of insurance subsidiaries subject to legal and regulatory jurisdictions scattered all over the globe. Those lockups both protected policyholders and ensured that there would be no massive asset-dumping campaign by AIG, the presumptive catalyst for the contagion.

So the crisis did not implicate AIG's vast assets. It was actually all about its hemorrhaging CDS liabilities—which could have been easily ring fenced. They were domiciled exclusively in AIG's holding company and accounted for less than 10 percent of its consolidated liabilities. These obligations could have been readily liquidated in bankruptcy without any disruption to the insurance companies, their solid assets, or their policyholders.

Nevertheless, AIG was handed a massive and wholly unwarranted taxpayer-funded infusion that ultimately totaled $180 billion. Hank Paulson, the most destructive unguided missile ever to rain down on the free market from the third floor of the US Treasury Building, later claimed, "If AIG went down, we faced real disaster. More than almost any financial firm I could think of, AIG was entwined in every part of the global system, touching businesses and consumers alike."

That was balderdash and subterfuge. A "global" firm by definition has a global footprint in the same manner as a zebra has stripes. But that obvious factoid doesn't prove that free market exchange is a transmitter of communicable economic disease, which was what Paulson and his fellow bailsters constantly implied. In fact, the unjustified largesse granted to AIG was not designed to inoculate the masses from harm, but to save the bacon of a few dozen speculators.

The paper trail uncovered by congressional investigators shows that the $400 billion (notational value) of busted CDS insurance issued by the AIG holding company was held by a very small number of the world's largest financial institutions, and virtually none of it was held by the banks of Main Street America which were allegedly being shielded from AIG's imminent collapse. Moreover, the worst-case loss faced by the dozen or so giant institutions actually exposed to an AIG bankruptcy would have amounted to no more than a few months' bonus accrual.

Yet there is not a shred of evidence that the panic-stricken amateurs surrounding Paulson ever investigated which institutions held the CDS contracts or their capacity for absorbing losses. Instead, in one of the most egregious derelictions of duty every recorded, Paulson and his posse of Goldmanite hotshots hastily and blindly shielded these behemoths from even a dollar of loss on their AIG insurance policies.

As the congressional investigators later determined, AIG's big-bank customers were actually supplied cash from a multitude of bailout spigots that aggregated to truly stunning magnitudes. This evidence also shows that each and every recipient institution had the balance sheet capacity to absorb the AIG hit, so the bailout was all about protecting short-term earnings and current-year executive and trader bonuses. That is the shocking truth of what the AIG bailout actually accomplished. Saddling innocent taxpayers with business enterprise losses generated on the free market is always an inappropriate exercise of state power, but shattering policy rules and precedent in order to vouchsafe the bonuses of a few thousand bankers is beyond the pale.

Not surprisingly, Goldman Sachs was the largest beneficiary of taxpayer largesse and was paid out nearly $19 billion on its various claims against AIG. But many of the other financial behemoths were not far behind, with a total of $17 billion going to France's second largest bank, Société Générale, while $15 billion was transferred to Deutsche Bank, $14 billion to Bank of America and Merrill Lynch, and nearly $10 billion to London-based Barclays, which also got the corpse of Lehman as a consolation prize.

It goes without saying that given the enormous balance sheet girth of these institutions—all of them were greater than $1 trillion in size—the amount of losses could have easily been absorbed without help from the taxpayers. In the case of Goldman, the largest recipient, the taxpayer funds amounted to less than eight months of profit and bonus accruals during the very next year.

In fact, at the time of the crisis the dozen or so giant international banks that got the AIG bailout money had $20 trillion in assets among them. By contrast, even in a worst-case outcome in which the banks lost twenty cents on the dollar for the mostly AAA paper (i.e., "super-senior") insured by AIG, their collective exposure to losses amounted to $80 billion at most.

Washington thus threw stupendous sums of money at AIG in a craven, discombobulated panic, yet these subventions amounted to just 0.5 percent of the elephantine balance sheets of its big global bank customers.

The September 2008 bailouts thus represented an outbreak of madness at the very top of the political system. The crisis was defined by the Paulson-Bernanke cabal in such Armageddon-like terms that all checks and balances disappeared. Every one of Washington's lesser players, including the president and the congressional leadership, stood down in the face of an immense urban legend that had materialized, as if out of whole cloth, in a matter of hours after the Lehman bankruptcy filing.

Panic-stricken Fed and Treasury officials had issued a financial ukase; namely, that an AIG bankruptcy had to be prevented at all hazards because it would bring the entire financial system tumbling down. Never in the inglorious history of Washington's financial misdeeds has such a large proposition been based on such a threadbare predicate.

The pretentious young men flitting around Secretary Hank Paulson, who was temperamentally unfit for the job and had by then seemingly come unglued, apparently did not even bother to review AIG's publicly filed financials. If they had they would have seen that its mammoth balance sheet resembled nothing so much as a clam shell. The lower half of the shell was comprised of dozens of major insurance subsidiaries and was asset rich with the previously mentioned $800 billion of mostly high-quality stocks, bonds, and other investments. They would have also recognized that the liabilities of these insurance subsidiaries were of the slow and sticky variety, consisting mainly of the current and future claims of its life, property, and casualty policyholders.

Unlike bank deposits, these insurance liabilities could not be subject to a panic "run" by retail policyholders. Instead, they would come due over years, and even decades, as eligible loss claims matured. So if they had done even a modicum of homework, they would have recognized that the balance sheet foundation of AIG was stable and was neither exposed to "contagion" nor a transmitter of it.

Had they sought out competent legal advice, they would have also discovered that in the event the parent company filed for bankruptcy, the dozens of solvent AIG insurance subsidiaries would have been pounced upon and, if necessary, legally sequestered by their regulators in the states and foreign jurisdictions where they were domiciled. These protective actions, in turn, would have paved the way for policyholders of these quarantined units to satisfy their claims in the normal course or through an orderly judicial process.

Furthermore, had they consulted knowledgeable Wall Street analysts they would have been quickly disabused of the simple-minded notion that an AIG corporate failure would trigger a global contagion. At the practical operating level, AIG was not remotely the globe-spanning octopus about which Paulson regaled frightened congressmen. Despite Hank Greenberg's fifty years of empire building, AIG was actually a late bull market concoction, a jerry-built monument to the economically senseless takeover arbitrage which emanated from the stock market bubble the Greenspan Fed had fueled in the late 1990s.

With a high-flying PE multiple of 35 times earnings, AIG had engineered a flurry of takeovers by swapping its high-value paper for the stock of its targets, which generally sported more earthbound valuations. Accordingly, between 1998 and 2001 AIG had acquired a string of large life and casualty insurers including Western National, SunAmerica, Hartford Steam Boiler, and American General. Just these four takeovers were valued at a combined $45 billion and helped boost AIG's total assets by $140 billion to nearly $450 billion over this three-year period.

The giant catch-22 embedded in this spasm of bubble-era financial engineering, however, was entirely lost on the rampaging posse on the third floor of the Treasury Building: namely, that AIG was a glorified insurance industry mutual fund. It had grown to giant size by acquisitions and investments, but it did not have automatic access to the assets sequestered in its far-flung subsidiaries.

Yes, SunAmerica alone had millions of retirement annuity customers, American General had billions of life insurance outstanding, and Hartford Steam Boiler provided fire and accident protection to a significant share of the industrial facilities in the nation. From AIG's small New York City headquarters, Greenberg and his successors could control business plans, staffing, executive compensation, underwriting standards, and much else.

But they could not extract cash or capital from any of these insurance subsidiaries without complying with state insurance commission rules designed to protect policyholders and ensure solvency.

Hank Paulson was running around Washington with his hair on fire, but contrary to the message he repeated over and over to purposely petrify congressmen his true mission was not to save middle-American annuitants and retirees; they were already being protected by insurance regulators from Connecticut to California. Instead, this alleged threat to millions of policyholders was a beard—behind which stood the handful of giant financial institutions which had purchased what amounted to wagering insurance from the AIG holding company.

To be sure, AIG's giant financial customers like Bank of America or Société Générale had not reached their tremendous girth due to their prowess as legitimate free market enterprises. They were lumbering wards of the state and, as will be seen, products of the cheap debt, moral hazard, and serial speculative bubbles being fostered by the Fed and other central banks. Not surprisingly, therefore, they were now desperately petitioning the treasury secretary for help in collecting their gambling debts from AIG.

Needless to say, Paulson did not hesitate to throw the weight of the public purse into the arena on behalf of these gamblers, because it resulted in an immediate boost to the stock price of Goldman Sachs and the remnants of Wall Street. Hank Paulson thus desecrated the rules of the free market, and for the most deplorable of reasons: namely, to make Goldman, Deutsche Bank, and the rest of the banking giants whole on gambling claims which had been incurred to carry out an end run around regulatory standards in the first place.

As previously indicated, all of the CDS gambling debts in question had been incurred at the holding company, which is to say, in the "upstairs" half of the AIG claim shell. The holding company was essentially bereft of liquidity because its assets, while massive, consisted almost entirely of the illiquid private stock of the endless string of insurance subsidiaries AIG had acquired or created over decades. And the not so secret reality was that invariably insurance regulators had imposed protective barriers, or "dividend stoppers," to protect policyholders from capital depletion by parent-company stockholders.

This meant that in the event of a bankruptcy there would be no raid on the insurance company assets to satisfy holding company liabilities. It also meant there would be no contagion—that is, the AIG holding company was in no position to engage in a fire sale of insurance subsidiary assets in order to satisfy the margin calls and loss claims against the CDS policies issued by the holding company. The insureds—the giant global banks—

would have been flat-out stiffed and have faced severe losses on the value of their CDS contracts. That would have been the end of the matter: an honest resolution under law and the rules of the free market.

The key to free market justice in this instance was the "dividend stoppers," and I had learned the everlasting truth about them during my days doing LBOs at Blackstone in the 1990s. We had come close to buying a state-regulated property and casualty (P&C) insurance company, and our plan for hitting the jackpot was to do, oddly enough, the very thing which proves there was no need to bail out AIG in September 2008. We intended to buy the target P&C insurer through an unregulated ("upstairs") holding company funded with 80 percent debt, and then strip-mine cash from the insurance subsidiary.

Stated more politely, the insurance company profits would be "up-streamed" as dividends to pay interest on the holding company debt. After collecting a generous return on the small amount of equity we had invested in the holding company, we would flip the insurance company stock to a new investor—perhaps even an insurance conglomerate like AIG—and thereby close out what promised to be a highly lucrative deal.

On the way to this easy money, however, Blackstone's pertinacious co-founder, Steve Schwarzman, became worried that an unfriendly state insurance commission could shaft us by forbidding payment of dividends in the name of "conserving assets" for the benefit of policyholders. That risk became the infamous "dividend stoppers" in our internal deliberations, and after much digging and expert advice to find a way around it, Schwarzman finally threw in the towel, pronouncing that it wasn't "safe" to plant a leveraged holding company atop a state-regulated insurance company.

Upon learning of the AIG bailout fifteen years later the salience of that episode was unmistakable. By then Steve Schwarzman was a billionaire LBO king and proven Midas. So if even he hadn't been able to find a way to get insurance company cash past a "dividend stopper," then it couldn't be done at all. In fact, AIG's holding company was massively leveraged, by way of its margin obligations under the CDS contracts, and it was now bankrupt just as Schwarzman had feared, leaving the punters who bought $400 billion of its worthless CDS insurance contracts high and dry.

AIG'S WAGERING INSURANCE WAS BOGUS

The fact that the CDS insurance underwritten by the AIG holding company was bogus embodied its own delicious irony. The big banks that got stiffed were essentially using CDS for an entirely untoward purpose in the first place; that is, it permitted banks to evade the capital requirements of their own regulators. The AIG "insurance" magically transformed high-risk assets such as collateralized debt obligations (CDOs) and other subprime mortgage bond assets into AAA-rated blue chip credits and eliminated any need for capital reserves.

While the party lasted, therefore, AIG's big-bank customers got the best of both worlds. They were able to puff up their quarterly income statements by booking fat revenues earned on higher yielding investments while paying comparatively meager amounts to AIG for the CDS insurance premiums. It amounted to found money.

At the same time, their balance sheets remained pristine because their junk assets were camouflaged as AAA credits. Since no equity capital needed to be set aside for these CDS "wrapped" assets, the banks' ROE (return on equity) was flattered enormously: it was a magical math equation in which the numerator (income) was maximized while the denominator (invested equity) was minimized.

In the trade this was known as "regulatory arbitrage," but in fact it was a giant scam under which the big banks had piled up mountains of CDOs on their balance sheets without needing a single dime of capital. The return on equity was thus infinite. Is it no wonder, then, that the Wall Street banks went into a paroxysm of hysteria—which were quickly transmitted to the third floor of the Treasury building—when the prospect suddenly materialized during the weekend of the Lehman crisis that AIG might fail and that, absent its CDS insurance wrap, their balance sheets would be exposed as buck-naked depositories of financial toxic waste.

So had AIG been required to meet its maker in bankruptcy court, insurance commissioners at home and abroad would have seized the subsidiaries, conserved the assets, and safeguarded the interests of tens of millions of policyholders. At the end of the day, grandpa's life insurance policy would have remained in force and the fire insurance on Caterpillar's factories in Peoria would have remained money good. And contrary to the blatantly misleading canard Paulson had circulated in the corridors of Washington, not one of the millions of retirement annuities written by AIG would have been jeopardized by the bankruptcy of its holding company.

In short, there was no public interest at stake in preventing AIG's demise. Indeed, the bailout's primary effect was to provide a wholly unwarranted private benefit at public expense; namely, the shielding of highly paid bank traders and executives who had exposed their institutions to embarrassing losses from taking the fall that was otherwise warranted.

Moreover, as unpleasant as it might have been for the executives and shareholders involved, such a market-driven outcome was fully aligned with the public good. The fact is, society can reap the benefits of free market capitalism only if its vital nerve center, the money and capital markets, is kept healthy and balanced by periodic purges of excess and error.

TOO BIG TO FAIL SUPPLANTS THE FREE MARKET: THE FED'S VISIBLE HAND

By the time of the September 2008 crisis, however, these long-standing rules of free market capitalism had undergone fateful erosion: traditional rules of market discipline had been steadily superseded by the doctrine of Too Big to Fail (TBTF). The latter arose, in turn, from the notion that the threat of "systemic risk" and a cascading contagion of losses from the failure of any big Wall Street institution would be so calamitous that it warranted an exemption from free market discipline.

But there was no proof of this novel doctrine whatsoever. It implied that capitalism was actually a self-destroying doomsday machine which would first foster giant institutions with wide-ranging linkages, but would then become vulnerable to catastrophe owing to the one thing that happens to every enterprise on the free market—they eventually fail.

In fact, if TBTF implied an eventual catastrophe for the system, there was an obvious solution: a "safe" size limit for banks needed to be determined, and then followed by a 1930s-style Glass-Steagall event in which banking institutions exceeding the limit would be required to be broken up or to make conforming divestitures. Yet while the TBTF debate had gone on for the better part of two decades, this obvious "too big to exist" solution was never seriously put on the table, and for a decisive reason: the nation's central bank during the Greenspan era had become the sponsor and patron of the TBTF doctrine.

This was an astonishing development because it meant that Alan Greenspan, former Ayn Rand disciple and advocate of pure free market capitalism, had gone native upon ascending to the second most powerful job in Washington. In fact, within five months of Greenspan's appointment by Ronald Reagan, who had mistakenly thought Greenspan was a hard-money gold standard advocate, the Fed panicked after the stock market crash in October 1987 and flooded Wall Street with money.

For the first time in its history, therefore, the Fed embraced the level of the S&P 500 as an objective of monetary policy. Worse still, as the massive Greenspan stock market bubble gathered force during the 1990s it had gone even further, embracing the dangerous notion that the central bank could spur economic growth through the "wealth effect" of rising stock prices.

This should have been a shocking wake-up call to friends of the free market. It implied that the state could create prosperity by tricking the people into thinking they were wealthier, thereby inducing them to borrow and consume more. Indeed, the Greenspan "wealth effects" doctrine was just a gussied-up version of Keynesian stimulus, only targeted at the prosperous classes rather than the government's client classes. Yet it went largely unheralded because Greenspan claimed to be prudently managing the nation's monetary system in a manner consistent with the profoundly erroneous floating-rate money doctrines of Milton Friedman.

Indeed, the Greenspan wealth effects doctrine sounded conservative and reassuring, especially since it was conducted behind a smokescreen of Friedmanite rhetoric about the glories of free markets and the wonders of the 1990s upwelling of new technology and productivity. In fact, Greenspan had made a Faustian bargain: once the Fed got into the stock market–propping and Wall Street–coddling business as tools of monetary policy and took on vast pretensions about its role as the nation's prosperity manager, it could not let the stock market fall back to free market outcomes.

The Greenspan Fed during the 1990s thus conducted a subtle assault on free market capitalism. The nation's level of employment, income, GDP, and general prosperity would no longer be an outcome of the invisible hand; that is, the interaction of millions of producers, consumers, and investors on the free market. Instead, the advance of the American economy now flowed from the visible ministrations of the Federal Reserve, which by the end of the decade had become the omnipotent overlord of daily economic life, influencing every nook and cranny of the nation's $14 trillion gross domestic product (GDP).

Under the maestro's wealth effects gospel, the nation's central bank orchestrated the financial markets, the stock averages, the Treasury yield curve, bank lending, housing credit, the dollar's exchange rate, the flow of merchandise trade, the movements of cross-border capital, and much more. Needless to say, this sweeping usurpation of economic power reflected a virulent outbreak of institutional hubris at the Fed and one of the greatest adventures in mission creep ever conducted by a public agency.

Under the new Greenspan doctrines, the Fed also came to believe that through deft maneuvering it could eliminate all the kinks from the business cycle and unlock virtually every dollar of "potential" GDP. But the Achilles heel to these pretensions could not be gainsaid: the keys to this exceptional macroeconomic performance were sustained financial stability and constantly rising asset prices—conditions which would generate a positive "wealth effect" and a resulting virtuous cycle of higher confidence, consumption, employment, and incomes.

Episodes of abrupt decline in the stock market averages and other financial asset prices were therefore distinctly unwelcome because they threatened to undermine the "wealth effect" that was implicit in the Fed's new modus operandi. So an embrace of "Too Big to Fail" steadily crept into the Fed's prosperity agenda. It was made official by Greenspan's panicked interest rate cutting and arrangement for a Wall Street subscribed bailout of a reckless gambling hall called Long-Term Capital Management (LTCM) during the minor financial turbulence triggered by the Russian default in August 1998.

Then and there, the "Greenspan Put" was confirmed; that is, the Fed would now pleasure Wall Street with unlimited liquidity and other interventions in order to prop up the stock market averages in the event of a deep sell-off. The road to the Wall Street meltdown of September 2008 was now guaranteed. The only question was when it would occur and what lesser bubbles and busts would occur in the interim.

After the September 1998 LTCM intervention, the insidious idea of shielding financial markets from alleged "systemic risk" contagions became an open objective of monetary policy. Yet this promise of a financial safety net under the market was ultimately self-defeating: it functioned to vastly embolden Wall Street speculators and leverage artists, meaning that the amplitude of financial bubbles and busts would now be all the greater. It also meant that if the Greenspan Put were exercised, financial losses owing to bailouts would inevitably be socialized, thereby putting the innocent American public squarely, albeit involuntarily, in harm's way.

THE FED'S HORRID BAILOUT OF LTCM

The Fed's horridly indefensible rescue of Long-Term Capital Management became the paradigm for what has become a permanent régime of bailouts and central bank rigging of the nation's money and capital markets. To be sure, unwise financial market interventions by Washington had ample precedent, reaching back to the rescue of the money-center banks during the 1994 Mexican peso crisis, the 1984 takeover of Continental Illinois Bank, the 1979 (first) bailout of Chrysler, and the early 1970s bailouts of Franklin National Bank, Penn Central, and Lockheed, among others.

But at least these had been long-standing national institutions with tens of thousands of employees. By contrast, LTCM was a Greenwich-based financial gambling shop that had been in existence less than four years, had a few hundred employees, and supplied nothing useful to the economy except easily replicable trading services. Its Fed-arranged bailout thus had an insidious implication: if in its wisdom the Fed determined that systemwide financial stability was imperiled, then the merits of the firm being rescued were irrelevant—no matter how odious its behavior might have been.

Long-Term Capital Management, in fact, was an egregious financial train wreck that had amassed leverage ratios of 30 to 1 in order to fund giant speculative bets in currency, equity, bond, and derivatives markets around the globe. The sheer recklessness and scale of LTCM's speculations had no parallel in American financial history, easily dwarfing the worst financial pyramids and gambling schemes erected before the 1929 crash by the likes of Samuel Insull, Goldman Sachs, and the American Founders Group, among many notorious others. In short, LTCM stunk to high heaven, and had absolutely no claim on public authority, resources, or even sympathy.

Its tower of leveraged speculation had been enabled by Wall Street's premier financial institutions through massive credit extensions—more than $100 billion. Through every available channel, including prime brokerage, repo desks, and over-the-counter swaps, Wall Street had raced to pump more debt into LTCM's incomprehensible trades. Given those frightful facts, any central bank worth its salt (say, one run by a Paul Volcker) would have permitted, even encouraged, LTCM to undergo a swift and harsh demise.

In pursuit of its prosperity agenda, however, the Greenspan Fed had fallen prey to the spurious doctrine that bull market speculation was evidence of general economic health. Indeed, by keeping the stock indices high and climbing, the Fed presumed it could ensure robust and unending GDP growth, a complete reversal of earlier central banking traditions that worried about "irrational exuberance" on the stock exchanges and embraced the need to timely remove the "punch bowl" before speculation got out of hand.

In a sharp rebuke to the Fed's initial 1990s exercise in bubble finance, the turmoil triggered in global financial markets by the Russian default in August 1998 took the stock averages down by nearly 20 percent in a matter of weeks. While this unexpected market swoon put LTCM and legions of lesser speculators on the ropes, such jarring corrections had previously been largely accepted as a necessary and natural check on greed, debt, and delusion in the financial markets.

In its recently acquired and purportedly superior wisdom, however, the Greenspan Fed nullified this 1998 market correction entirely by a burst of money printing and a sharp reduction in interest rates, in the context of a perfectly healthy and expanding economy (see chapter 15). When this dramatic but artificial easing of money market conditions was coupled with the $3 billion collection from Wall Street dealers arranged by the New York Fed for LTCM, it became quickly evident that the "bottom" was in and that henceforth speculators would be riding a one-way escalator ever higher.

During the next fifteen months, the S&P 500 soared by 50 percent, but not because the profit outlook for American companies had suddenly improved by half. Rather, Wall Street had come to believe that investment errors would no longer be punished and that the risk of loss and the interest expense of carrying leveraged trading positions had been dramatically reduced.

Accordingly, valuation multiples on stocks and other equities rose sharply, meaning that the same earnings were now worth a lot more. In fact, just before the dot-com bubble finally broke, the multiple on the NASDAQ had reached 100 times earnings, a level which was nearly sixfold greater than average historical valuations. These nearly lunatic stock prices reflected Wall Street's growing confidence that it had a "friend at the Fed" which could be relied upon to choke off any unwelcome downdraft in asset prices.

This financial safety net became known as the "Greenspan Put," and according to Wall Street's pitchmen it tilted the stock market toward much reward and little risk. Yet the frothy bull market which it engendered did not evidence a new era of vibrant capitalist prosperity, even if the fawning financial press endlessly proclaimed it. What had arisen, instead, was an ersatz capitalism, a financial régime in which the stock market averages reflect expected monetary juice from the central bank, not anticipated growth of profits from free market enterprises.

Worse still, by ingratiating itself to Wall Street in this manner, the Fed had broadcast an unmistakable message: namely, that there was no imaginable limit to the amount of speculative excess and reckless leverage it would tolerate and backstop if necessary. There was no other plausible inference. The financial recklessness which had been embodied in LTCM was without peer.

A few months later the dot-com bubble reached a fevered top in March 2000—the index for such issues having risen by 900 percent in a mere half decade. Even the Greenspan Put could not sustain the sheer madness that gripped large precincts of the NASDAQ at its parlous peak. Still, the Fed did not grasp how stock prices had gotten to such extreme levels in the first place, nor that its cheap money policies and TBTF promises had eviscerated the natural mechanisms by which financial market speculation is held in check.

Indeed, in response to a barely measurable downturn in the GDP metrics during 2001, the Federal Reserve unleashed a renewed torrent of money printing over the next several years, thereby driving down short-term interest rates to 1 percent, a level which had not been seen since the Great Depression. Soon the cycle of one-way speculation returned with a vengeance, fueling a boom in real estate and mortgage lending that had no precedent.

During the midst of the housing boom, of course, Fed policy makers insisted that nothing was amiss. Notwithstanding the 100 percent increase in national housing prices since the turn of the century, and the white-hot gains of 200 to 300 percent being recorded in many "sand state" markets, there simply was no visible bubble, according to both Alan Greenspan and his successor, Ben Bernanke.

By their lights, the meteoric rise in housing prices reflected nothing more than a buoyant economy and public confidence in Washington. What they neglected to note, however, was that housing prices were up in the nosebleed section of economic history precisely because the Fed had pushed interest rates down into its sub-basement.

Between early 2002 and mid-2005, the Fed had aggressively rolled out the welcome wagon for speculators, driving inflation-adjusted interest rates in the United States to patently absurd levels. During that forty-month span, when the annualized consumer price index (CPI) increase averaged about 2.6 percent, the rate on short-term borrowings was only 1.5 percent. This meant that real interest rates were negative, and not just for a month or two, but for the better part of four years. Likewise, the real rate on the 10 year Treasury bond also descended to historic lows.

In the parlance of the financial markets, the Fed's sustained spree of interest rate repression had reduced "cap rates" to all-time lows, meaning that their inverse, the price of financial assets, had been goosed to all-time highs. The Fed was thus running an out-and-out bubble machine, bloating the American economy with more cheap debt than ever before imagined.

In fact, between 2002 and 2007 total credit market debt (public and private) outstanding grew by a staggering $18 trillion, or five times more than the $3.5 trillion gain in GDP during the same period. It was only a matter of time before the American economy buckled under the load.

CHAPTER 2

FALSE LEGENDS OF DARK ATMS AND FAILING BANKS

WHEN THE GREAT FINANCIAL BUBBLE FINALLY BURST IN SEP-
tember 2008, AIG's credit default insurance was shockingly exposed as bogus. Given this evidence of utterly reckless and
massive speculation, the Fed was handed, as if on a platter, one final
chance to restore a semblance of capital market discipline.

By that late hour, however, the Fed was not even remotely interested in
financial discipline. The Greenspan Put had now been superseded by the
even more insidious Bernanke Put. In defiance of every classic canon of
sound money, the new Fed chairman had panicked in the face of the first
stock market tremors in August 2007 (see chapter 23), and thereafter the
S&P 500 had become an active and omnipresent transmission mechanism
for the execution of central bank policy. Consequently, after the Lehman
event the plummeting stock averages had to be arrested and revived at all
hazards. Accordingly, the bailout of AIG was first and foremost an exercise
in stabilizing the S&P 500.

The cover story, of course, was the threat that a financial contagion
would ripple out from the corpus of AIG, bringing disruption and job
losses to the real economy. As has been seen, however, there was nothing
at all "contagious" about AIG, so Bernanke and Paulson simply peddled
flat-out nonsense in order to secure Capitol Hill acquiescence to their dictates and to douse what they derisively called "populist" agitation; that is,
the noisy denunciation of the bailouts arising from an intrepid minority of
politicians impertinent enough to stand up for the taxpayer.

But this hardy band of dissenters—ranging from Congressman Ron
Paul to Senator Bernie Sanders—was correct. Everyday Americans would
not have lost sleep or their jobs, even if AIG's upstairs gambling patrons
had been allowed to lose their shirts. Still, the bailsters peddled a legend
which has persisted; namely, that in September 2008 the nation's financial

payments system was on the cusp of crashing, and that absent the bailouts American companies would have missed payrolls, ATMs would have gone dark, and general financial disintegration would have ensued. But this is a legend. No evidence has ever been presented to prove it because there isn't any.

Had Washington allowed nature to take its course in the days after the Lehman collapse on September 15, the only Wall Street furniture which would have been broken was the potential bankruptcy of Goldman Sachs and Morgan Stanley, the two remaining investment banks. Needless to say, the utterly myopic investment banker who was running the US government from his Treasury office wasted not a second ascertaining whether the public interest might diverge from Goldman's stock price under the circumstances at hand.

According to his memoirs, Secretary Paulson already "knew" on the very morning Lehman failed that the last two investment banks standing needed to be rescued at all hazards: "Lose Morgan Stanley, and Goldman Sachs would be next in line—if they fell the financial system might vaporize and with it, the economy."

Tendentious and sophomoric would be a more than generous characterization of that apocalyptic riff. Yet groundless as it was, the fact that Paulson and his posse treated it as truth is deeply revealing. It underscores the extent to which public policy during the bubble years had been taken captive by the satraps and princes seconded to the nation's capital by Wall Street. Such self-serving foolishness would never have been uttered in earlier times, not even by the occasional captain of industry or finance who held high financial office.

Certainly President Eisenhower's treasury secretary and doughty opponent of Big Government, George Humphrey, would never have conflated the future of capitalism with the stock price of two or even two dozen Wall Street firms. Nor would President Kennedy's treasury secretary, Douglas Dillon, have done so, even had his own family's firm been imperiled. President Ford's treasury secretary and fiery apostle of free market capitalism, Bill Simon, would have crushed any bailout proposal in a thunder of denunciation. Even President Reagan's man at the Treasury Department, Don Regan, a Wall Street lifer who had built the modern Merrill Lynch, resisted the 1984 bailout of Continental Illinois until the very end.

Once the Fed plunged into the prosperity management business under Greenspan and Bernanke, however, the subordination of public policy to the pecuniary needs of Wall Street became inexorable. No other outcome was logically possible, given Wall Street's crucial role as a policy transmission mechanism and the predicate that rising stock prices would generate a wealth effect and thereby levitate the national economy.

Not surprisingly, the Goldman Sachs "occupation" of the US Treasury coincided almost exactly with the Fed's embrace of financialization, leverage, and speculation as crucial tools of monetary management. Its legates in Washington during this era, Robert Rubin and Hank Paulson, never once agonized over violating free market rules. They simply assumed that the good of the nation depended upon keeping the Wall Street game up and running.

Nor did the Goldmanites have even the foggiest appreciation of why the old fashioned guardians of the public purse, like Bill Simon, had been so resolutely anti-bailout. To his great credit, Simon appreciated the insidious effects of bad precedent and rightly feared that once the floodgate was opened crony capitalism would flourish. He also understood that every crisis would be portrayed as a one-time exception and that once officials started chasing market-driven brush fires, the policy process would quickly degenerate into analytics-free, seat-of-the-pants ad hocery and would frequently even border on lawlessness.

In fact, that is exactly what happened in the signature bailout episodes during Goldman's occupation of the Treasury. The $20 billion bailout of the Wall Street banks during the 1994 Mexican peso crisis orchestrated by Secretary Rubin was not only unnecessary, but was done against overwhelming opposition on Capitol Hill. In the end, the American taxpayer was thrown into the breach by Treasury lawyers who tortured an ancient statute governing the Economic Stabilization Fund until it coughed up billions for a bailout of Mexico and its Wall Street lenders. In so doing, Rubin simply thumbed his nose at Congress, implying that the greater good of Wall Street trumped the democratic process.

Likewise, the entire Paulson-led campaign to bail out Wall Street during the September 2008 crisis was an exercise in pushing the limits of existing law to the breaking point. Lehman was not bailed out mainly because Washington officials had not yet found a loophole by the time of its Sunday-night filing. But as the crescendo of panic intensified, the Treasury and Fed miraculously found enough legal daylight by Tuesday to rescue AIG.

Throughout the ordeal Paulson and his posse viewed themselves as glorified investment bankers, empowered to use any expedient of law and any drain on the public purse that might be needed to ensure the survival of the remaining Wall Street firms. Rampaging around the globe and browbeating bankers and governments alike on behalf of their half-baked merger schemes, they defiled the great office of US Treasury Secretary like never before.

GOLDMAN AND MORGAN STANLEY:
THE LAST TWO PREDATORS STANDING

This was a blatant miscarriage of governance. As will be seen, at that late stage of the delirious financial bubble which had overtaken America, Goldman Sachs and Morgan Stanley had essentially become economic predators. Their bankruptcy would have resulted in no measureable harm to the Main Street economy, and possibly some gain. It would have also brought the curtains down on a generation of Wall Street speculators, and sent them packing in disgrace and amid massive personal losses—the only possible way to end the current repugnant régime of crony capitalist domination of the nation's central bank.

Goldman and Morgan Stanley helped generate and distribute hundreds of billions in toxic assets—mortgage-backed securities and CDOs based on subprime mortgages—that were now resident on the balance sheets of a wide gamut of Main Street institutions like corporate pension funds and insurance companies, along with institutional investors spread all over the planet. The TARP and Federal Reserve funds that were pumped into Goldman and Morgan Stanley, however, did nothing to ameliorate the huge losses being incurred by these gullible customers.

Instead, the Washington bailouts rescued the perpetrators, not the victims; that is, the bailout benefits were captured almost exclusively by the Wall Street insiders and fund managers who owned the common stock and long-term bonds of these two firms. Yet it was these punters who deserved to take punishing losses. It was they who enabled Goldman and Morgan Stanley—along with Bear Stearns, Lehman, and the investment banks embedded inside Citigroup and JPMorgan—to grow into giant, reckless predators.

As will be seen in chapter 20, only twenty-five years earlier these firms had been undercapitalized white-shoe advisory houses with balance sheets which were tiny and benign, but now their designation as "investment banks" reflected an entirely vestigial nomenclature. They had long ago morphed into giant ultra-leveraged hedge funds which happened to have retained relatively small-beer side operations in regulated securities underwriting and M&A advisory services.

The preponderance of their fabled profitability, however, was generated by massive trading operations which scalped spreads from elephantine balance sheets that were not only preposterously leveraged (30 to 1) but also dangerously dependent upon volatile short-term funding to carry their assets. Indeed, perched on a foundation of several hundreds of billions in debt and equity capital, these firms had become voracious consumers of "wholesale" money market funds, mainly short-term "repo" loans and unsecured commercial paper. From these sources, they had erected trillion-dollar financial towers of hot-money speculation.

On the eve of the financial crisis, Goldman had asset footings of $1.1 trillion and Morgan Stanley had also passed the trillion-dollar mark. Much of their massive wholesale funding, however, had maturities of less than thirty days, and some of that was as short as a week and even overnight. When Bear Stearns hit the wall in March 2008, for example, it was actually rolling over $60 billion of funding every morning—until, suddenly, it couldn't.

It goes without saying that these highly liquid wholesale funding markets were dirt cheap because lenders had no rollover obligation and were often fully secured. It is also obvious that on the other side of their balance sheets, these de facto hedge funds held assets which were generally more illiquid, longer term, and subject to credit and market value risk, and which therefore generated substantially higher average yields.

Due to this "duration" and "credit" mismatch, the profit spread per dollar of assets was considerable, and when harvested a trillion times over, total profits were enormous, reaching $18 billion (pre-tax) at Goldman during the year before the crisis. Since this amounted to a half million dollars of profit per employee (including secretaries and messengers) the potency of carrying a giant balance sheet on the back of cheap wholesale liabilities was self-evident.

Yet here is where the foundation of overvalued debt and equity capital came in. There were limits on the extent to which the assets of these giant "investment banks" could be funded on wholesale money. Even the frothy markets of 2008 would have viewed a balance sheet consisting mainly of slow, illiquid assets funded preponderantly with short-term liabilities as a house of cards. So the investment banks' foundation of permanent capital, in fact, was the vital linchpin beneath the whole Wall Street edifice.

Thus, Goldman's balance sheet at the time of the crisis boasted long-term debt and preferred stock of $220 billion and common stock of $60 billion, even as measured by its depressed share prices that week. Likewise, Morgan Stanley had $190 billion of long-term debt and preferred stock, and $25 billion of common stock at the current market prices of its shares. Taken together then, the last two investment banks standing rested on a half-trillion-dollar base of long-term capital.

During the boom years, this long-term capital had earned handsome returns in the form of interest and dividends, with the common stock, the most junior capital, also experiencing substantial price appreciation. Goldman's share price, for example, had peaked in late 2007 at nearly $250 per share, a level five times its May 1999 IPO price.

Yet in the matter of investments, as in the opera, it's not over until the fat lady sings. The crucial economic purpose of each firm's capital was to function as a financial shock absorber. During times of heavy economic weather, therefore, senior wholesale lenders would be spared from any losses incurred on impaired asset accounts; losses would be absorbed by the firms' more junior, permanent capital—the common equity first and ultimately the long-term debt as well.

As events unfolded in the fall of 2008, these shock absorbers were brought into play. In very short order, they had proved wanting when Lehman filed for bankruptcy and Merrill Lynch was carted-off to Bank of America on a financial stretcher. Both firms had failed because their permanent capital had been inadequate to shield the losses, thereby rendering them insolvent.

In the days after September 15, the shock absorbers of the last two investment banks left standing, Goldman and Morgan Stanley, also failed the test. Their most illiquid asset classes—such as securitized mortgages, CDOs, commercial real estate securities, and corporate junk bonds—declined in market value by between 20 percent and 50 percent during the meltdown. Even when blended with holdings of low-risk government bonds and blue chip corporate securities, the blow to capital was devastating, and they would not have survived the ordeal on their own.

THE HEALTHY RUN ON THE WHOLESALE MONEY MARKET—INTERRUPTED

In fact, as the financial meltdown gathered momentum after Lehman failed on September 15, Goldman, and especially Morgan Stanley, became the victims of a violent "run on the bank" by wholesale lenders, which in classic fashion lost confidence in the value of their collateral. Yet that "run," so much deplored by Washington officialdom, was actually a good thing—the market's mechanism for flushing out the bad assets that had piled up on Wall Street balance sheets.

Under the circumstances, these firms had no choice but to rapidly liquidate assets, even at fire sale losses, in order to generate cash to redeem the short-term funding which was coming due in a great tidal wave. Such was their just desert for engaging in the age-old folly of borrowing short and hot, and investing long and illiquid.

Had economic nature been allowed to take its course, the resulting massive destruction of capital value at the two remaining investment banks would have been profoundly therapeutic. It would have demonstrated conclusively that the combined $500 billion of long-term debt and equity capital which had been issued by Goldman and Morgan Stanley over the previous decades had been vastly overvalued and was far more vulnerable to catastrophic loss than the trend-following money managers who owned it had understood.

While the financial party fueled by the Fed's interest rate repression and "put" under risk assets roared, the Wall Street business model thrived: issuance of overvalued debt and equity enabled it to scalp gargantuan profits from balance sheets bloated with cheap wholesale money. The speculative mania on Wall Street was thus well and truly fostered in the misguided conference rooms of the Fed's Eccles Building.

When the crash came, however, the inflated prices of the Goldman and Morgan Stanley equity and bonds had come under withering attack. The fund managers who owned them should have suffered massive losses, been fired by their firms, and become an example for an entire generation of money managers, steeling them for years to come against another Wall Street swindle of such hazardous aspect.

But Paulson and Bernanke body-checked the free market before the grim reaper could complete its appointed rounds. So doing, they gave credence to the lame whining of Wall Street executives who claimed they were victims of nefarious short-sellers. But that was pettifoggery. They were actually the victims of just plain sellers: investors and traders who had belatedly recognized that the capital securities of these giant hedge funds would be soon swamped in a tidal wave of losses.

Absent Washington's bailout interventions, Goldman's stock price would likely have proven to be worth far less than its $60 book value, if anything at all. Certainly it would not have been worth even close to the ballyhooed "bargain price" of $115 per share paid by Warren Buffet (only after Uncle Sam pitched a safety net under the market) or the $250 per share it had reached during the bubble peak.

As it turned out, Washington's intervention with TARP and the Fed alphabet soup of liquidity programs stopped the wholesale bank run in its tracks. It accomplished this by the very simple expedient of replacing the hundreds of billions of private wholesale funding—short-term commercial paper and overnight repo funding—which had gone into hiding with freshly minted Federal Reserve credit. And it was this instant, cheap funding do-over which was the ultimate evil of the bailouts.

In truth, the "run" in the wholesale funding market was the market's homemade remedy for purging the speculative fevers which had overtaken Wall Street. At the time of the meltdown, the evaporation of wholesale funding was a curative agent, forcing Goldman, Morgan Stanley, and other leveraged hedge funds, including those such as Lehman and Merrill Lynch which had already been rendered insolvent, to liquidate their vast inventories of toxic assets at prices far below book value.

Moreover, this liquidation process exhibited an exceedingly precise focus that was completely inconsistent with Washington's spasmodic arm waving about "contagion." Specifically, the asset fire sales were not coming from the old-fashioned "whole loan" books (loans made to homeowners but never securitized by Wall Street) of the nation's eight thousand commercial banks and thrifts. This was because the response of conventional deposit banks to deteriorating mortgage performance was to boost loan loss reserves, not dump mortgage paper on the open market.

By contrast, the housing and real estate–based assets held by the Wall Street "investment banks" consisted preponderantly of securitized mortgages and related synthetic and derivative instruments. The book value of these "assets" had been artificially inflated from the get-go, based on implausibly optimistic default assumptions with respect to the underlying mortgage pools.

Moreover, these pools had also been drained of value time and again by the fee extractions taken at each step along the route to securitization and sale. This sequence of fee scalping included mortgage origination, packaging of these loans into mortgage-backed securities, repackaging of MBSs into CDOs, and even further repackaging of CDOs into CDOs squared.

As a consequence of the "run" in the wholesale funding market, however, this whole misbegotten edifice was being rectified. The toxic securitized mortgages and derivatives were being marked down to realistic value. Likewise, the wholesale funding market was being taught a harsh lesson on the consequences of the type of reckless lending which had permitted tiny investment banks to grow into trillion-dollar giants.

At the same time, the prices of investment bank capital securities were experiencing shocking declines, as illustrated by Goldman's stock price dive from $200 per share to less than $50 in a matter of months. In short, the dangerous business model on which these ultra-leveraged hedge funds were based was being purged from the financial system. Indeed, Lehman and Merrill were already down, and Goldman and Morgan Stanley were on the ropes.

Mr. Market was thus on the cusp of being four-for-four in eliminating these dangerous ultra-leveraged gambling operations. Unfortunately, Chairman Bernanke and Secretary Paulson drastically misconstrued this healthy run in the wholesale banking sector. Not only did they view it as a threat to the Fed's wealth effects model of monetary central planning, but they also saw it as a replay of the Great Depression–era bank runs.

As will be seen in chapter 8, however, it was nothing of the kind. Contrary to Chairman Bernanke's faulty and self-serving scholarship, the famous bank runs of 1930–1933 were not the result of monetary policy mistakes by the Fed after 1929. Instead, they were the ineluctable consequence of the wartime and postwar debt booms from 1914 to 1929 and the vast crop of insolvent borrowers which they fostered.

Likewise, Washington's massive intervention in September 2008 could not thwart a Great Depression 2.0 because the collapse of Wall Street could not have caused one. There had been no economic Armageddon looming, only a long cycle of debt liquidation, shrinking living standards, and austerity—or exactly the outcome we have experienced anyway.

The contemporary situation was nothing like the early 1930s because the United States was now a massive international debtor and importer. That condition was the opposite of the American economy's posture in 1929 when it had been the era's massive creditor, exporter, and industrial producer; that is, the US back then had played the role belonging now to the red capitalists of China.

At the end of the day, the 2008 financial panic had originated in the canyons of Wall Street; it had actually been contained there during the peak weeks of the crisis, as toxic assets were liquated and wholesale funding was withdrawn; and it would have burnt itself out there had Washington allowed the markets to have their way with errant speculators. Instead, a handful of panicked officials led by Bernanke and Paulson drove Washington into a momentary hysteria, causing it to throw the American taxpayer and the Fed's printing press into the wrong breach. So doing, they stopped a bank run that was needed and perpetuated two giant financial predators which were not.

THE MAIN STREET BANKS WERE NEVER IN DANGER

There was no logical or factual basis for the incessantly repeated claim of Washington high officials that Wall Street's losses would spill over into the nation's $12 trillion commercial banking system and from there ripple outward to infect the vitals of the Main Street economy. Owing to the composition of its asset base, the Main Street banking system was never remotely at risk, and it had no need for capital infusions from TARP.

The actual evidence shows the "run" on the wholesale money market was almost entirely confined to the canyons of Wall Street. During the heat of the fall 2008 crisis, there were no runs on the nation's eight thousand commercial banks and thrifts, save for a handful of clearly insolvent higher fliers like Indy Mac and Washington Mutual. Nor would there have been one in the absence of TARP and the Fed's aggressive Wall Street bailout actions.

The carnage on Wall Street in no way weakened the deposit guarantees of the Federal Deposit Insurance Corporation (FDIC) which reassured mom and pop that they did not need to get in line at their local bank branch. The vast bulk of assets held by the commercial banking system were either invested in safe US Treasury debt and government-guaranteed mortgage securities or whole loans to home owners, businesses, and developers which were carried on their "banking books" rather than in "trading" accounts.

There was no reason to fear a contagion of fire sale liquidations of these types of assets or a resulting flight of retail depositors. Even if the national economy plunged into recession, the commercial banking system would experience rising loan loss reserve provisions and weakened profitability. Yet this impact would play out over quarters and years, not in immediate, huge, headline-making loss events which would catalyze public fears about the safety and soundness of their local banks.

There was actually a striking note of irony in the contrast between the relatively safe commercial banking system and the bonfires on Wall Street. As it happened, the mortgage securitization machine had functioned like a giant financial vacuum cleaner, sucking the worst of the subprime and exotic mortgages off the balance sheets of local community lending institutions and into the billion dollar securitization pools assembled on Wall Street.

The main channel for this process, the nonbank mortgage broker industry, was a Wall Street instrumentality of cheap money. By the time of the final housing boom in 2003–2006, in fact, the mortgage broker channel was originating 75 percent of all mortgages. When the financial crisis came, Main Street banks were sound because, ironically, they had been driven out of the high-risk mortgage business by Wall Street and its mortgage broker agents.

When the Greenspan Fed drove short-term funding costs in the wholesale money markets down to 1 percent by the spring of 2003, it enabled Wall Street to finance massive "warehouse credit lines" to local mortgage brokers and bankers. Stocked up with Wall Street money, the latter did not need retail deposits or capital and, instead, operated as fee-based agents and were therefore free to issue risky loans. They worked out of makeshift offices and did not need vaults, tellers, or drive-through windows. With no skin in the game, they were driven entirely by mortgage production volume (see chapters 18 and 19). When the great Wall Street investment houses— including Bear Stearns, Lehman, Goldman, and Morgan Stanley along with the wholesale banking departments of JPMorgan, Citigroup, and Deutsche Bank—became aggressively involved in financing the local mortgage bankers, brokers, and boiler rooms, the planking for the subprime mortgage fiasco was laid. The Wall Street houses were able to access nearly un-limited amounts of low-cost wholesale funding by means of the commer-cial paper and repo markets and recycle it through their "warehouse lines" to local mortgage bankers and brokers. Unfortunately, the sudden avail-ability of these multibillion-dollar warehouse lines proved to be a financial poison in the world of home finance, not the socially beneficent "innova-tion" claimed by investment bankers.

Needless to say, the new army of mortgage brokers put into business by these Wall Street credit lines had not spent decades building up a franchise in local home mortgage markets, thereby acquiring the skills in prudent underwriting and borrower selection on which long-term survival in the home mortgage business inherently depends. But they did know how to organize turbo-charged boiler-rooms which cranked out prodigious num-bers of new mortgages.

These new mortgage brokers also had the capacity to grow by leaps and bounds. They had quickly discovered that salesmen currently pitching Amway products, aluminum siding, and used cars could become fully functioning mortgage bankers in a matter of days and weeks. This was es-pecially the case after the government-sponsored enterprises Fannie Mae and Freddie Mac and the big Wall Street banks introduced online comput-erized underwriting.

Like the operators of McDonald's drive-through windows, brokers sim-ply tapped the screen and another serving of home mortgage loans would instantly appear. Brokers then obtained the money for loan disbursements to homeowners simply by drawing down their warehouse lines until enough volume was achieved to facilitate a block sale of freshly minted mortgages to their Wall Street partners. The latter then completed the se-curitization and distribution process, harvesting generous fees and markups at each step along the way.

At the peak of the housing boom, outstanding warehouse lines offered by the top Wall Street houses soared to several hundred billion dollars. These huge credit lines constituted an efficient financial superhighway to transport truckloads of sketchy mortgages from Main Street America di-rectly to Wall Street.

Needless to say, the operators of these fly-by-night mortgage-stamping machines were not "bankers" in any traditional sense of the word—they had no skin in the game. Wall Street actually even went further, hiring tra-ditional banks to write subprime and other riskier mortgages. It then peri-odically bought all the resulting loans on a wholesale basis, meaning that what remained of George Bailey's Savings and Loan was enlisted in the rinse-and-repeat style of mortgage lending as well.

Accordingly, the residential loan books of the commercial banking system were surprisingly clean, even as the securitized mortgage meltdown gathered force in the fourth quarter of 2008. At that point, total commercial bank assets were $11.6 trillion. Yet only $200 billion, a tiny 1.7 percent of total assets, consisted of "toxic assets"; that is, private-label mortgage-backed securities of the type originated by the Wall Street securitization machine and which were now plummeting in value.

Furthermore, these minor holdings of toxic private-label mortgage assets were dwarfed by commercial banking system investments of nearly $1 trillion in Fannie Mae and Freddie Mac mortgage-backed securities. These "agency" backed mortgage securities had always been considered blue chip credits and a close imitation of Treasury bonds, and had officially become "risk free" upon the US government's nationalization of Freddie and Fannie.

From a big-picture perspective, then, the nation's hinterland banks had played a pretty good hand of mortgage finance poker. First, they had sold off most of their subprime originations to the Wall Street securitization machine. Next, they largely avoided reinvesting in the garbage securities Wall Street crafted from these subprime loan pools. And finally, they backfilled their investment accounts by buying mortgage securities wrapped with Uncle Sam's money-good insurance via the Freddie and Fannie guarantees, not the bogus kind sold to Wall Street and the European banks by AIG.

WHY THE MAIN STREET BANKS WERE MONEY GOOD

The commercial banks had retained on their own balance sheets about $2 trillion of residential mortgages and home equity lines of credit. But these mortgages were overwhelmingly of prime credit quality and had stayed on the books as "whole loans," rather than having been sliced and diced into tradable securities. So as the economy tumbled into recession and average home prices plunged by 35 percent, any elevation of losses would be charged to loan loss reserves and written off over years, not sold at fire-sale prices on Wall Street's crashing market for securitized paper. The commercial banking system was not vulnerable to a panic, just a slow multi-year resolution.

In short, the GSE securities plus the whole mortgage loans added up to $3.2 trillion in housing assets, but the Freddie–Fannie (GSE) paper was money good and the whole loans were higher quality and were backed by substantial loan loss reserves required by regulators. So the Main Street commercial banking system was surprisingly well insulated from the putative financial "contagion" on Wall Street.

Much the same can be said for the remaining $6 trillion of non-home mortgage assets which sat on commercial bank balance sheets at the time of the crisis. About $1.6 trillion of this was low-risk revolving and term credit to business and industry known as "C&I (commercial and industrial) loans."

Most of these business loans occupied the senior slot, or the highest payment ranking, in borrower capital structures and usually had a first lien on the operating assets of the borrower's business. So the risk of loss was modest, and the prospect of a C&I loan meltdown was essentially nonexistent. In fact, the truly risky business credit, $1.5 trillion of then-outstanding unsecured and subordinated debt, was all in junk bonds, and nearly all of these were owned by institutional investors and mutual funds, not banks.

The story was much the same in the case of the commercial real estate loan books of the Main Street banks; that is, loans on office buildings, strip malls, retail properties, and housing land acquisition and development. Once again, nearly half of the $3 trillion in outstanding commercial real estate debt had been sold to Wall Street, where it had been securitized and packaged into commercial mortgage-backed securities (CMBSs). By the time of the crisis, these hot potatoes were languishing unsold on Wall Street balance sheets or stuffed into the portfolios of pension funds and insurance companies, but they were no longer in the loan books of the Main Street banking system.

The commercial banking system had retained about $1.7 trillion of whole loans in the various commercial real estate categories, but there was little risk of a selling contagion. Most of these loans were "interest only" with a five- to ten-year bullet maturity, meaning that it would take years for borrowers to run out of cash and default on interest payments when failed strip malls and unfinished subdivisions eventually became foreclosures. That prospective slow bleed-off was irrelevant to the bonfires which raged on Wall Street in September 2008.

Indeed, busted commercial real estate loans have accounted for most of the five hundred bank closures conducted by the FDIC in the years since the crisis. Yet all of these shutdowns were orchestrated over weekends with such clockwork precision that hardly a single retail depositor anywhere in the nation was ever alarmed. Unlike Wall Street's hot money funding, Main Street loan portfolios were bedded down with high-persistency deposits. Losses would be realized over time through the bleeding cure, not a fire sale.

The remaining $2 trillion of assets on the commercial banking systems balance sheet as of October 2008 were not even remotely exposed to contagion risk. About $1 trillion of this total consisted of credit card, auto, and other consumer loans that were well secured with collateral and provisioned with deep loss reserves. The other $1 trillion consisted overwhelmingly of US Treasury securities and investment grade corporate bonds.

The workout in the commercial banking sector, therefore, has turned out to be a slow-motion write-down, not a red-hot meltdown of the type which afflicted Wall Street. There was no basis for a retail bank run and never would have been one in the absence of TARP.

This outcome was readily ascertainable in September 2008, by means of a cursory examination of the collective balance sheet of the nation's non–Wall Street banking system. There was absolutely no reason for panic about the financial "contagion" spreading to Main Street banks. Nor was there any excuse for suspending the normal rules which required the FDIC to close failed banks and to completely wipe out debt and equity security holders.

THE URBAN LEGEND OF SKIPPED PAYROLLS AND DARK ATMS

Another false vector of the contagion story centered on the panic in the money market mutual fund sector and the resulting drastic shrinkage of the commercial paper market. It was from this chain of events that the urban legend arose about ATMs going dark and business payrolls being skipped. In truth, the commercial paper market had become a giant bubble and needed to be cut down to size, but the implication that this necessary unwind had brought the payments system to the verge of collapse was not even remotely accurate.

In fact, after Congress courageously voted down the first TARP bill, the orchestrators of the bailout, Chairman Bernanke and Secretary Paulson, cynically deployed these payments freeze horror stories to spook congressmen and other policymakers into falling in line. As Senator Mel Martinez recalled their pitch, "I just remember thinking, you know, Armageddon . . . if these guys in the middle of it . . . believe this to be as dark as they are painting it, it must be pretty darned dark."

Senator Martinez's recollections reveal the true contagion: it was the contagion of fear which two panic-stricken men, Bernanke and Paulson, spread through the nation's capital like wildfire during the hours after the Lehman failure. Yet nothing like the financial nuclear meltdown alleged by Washington officialdom ever occurred or threatened.

The heart of the false panic was rooted in the money market mutual fund sector. Total short-term deposits at the time of the crisis had reached a big number: $3.8 trillion. So an honest-to-goodness "run" by investors would have been scary indeed. It turns out, however, that the "run" amounted to little more than a circular movement of cash among different money market fund types, with virtually zero impact on the Main Street economy.

As it happened, roughly $1.9 trillion, or half of total money market deposits, were held in a category of fund which invested exclusively in US Treasury and agency debt or tax-exempt muni bonds. During the entire period of the Wall Street crisis, this "governments only" segment of the money market fund industry experienced no losses or investor liquidations whatsoever.

By contrast, the other $1.9 trillion was in "prime" funds. In addition to investing in safe government securities and bank CDs, the prime funds were also permitted to hold commercial paper, thereby slightly enhancing interest rate yields compared to purely government funds.

During the several weeks after the Lehman failure about $430 billion, or slightly less than 25 percent of deposits, fled the "prime" fund half of the industry. This flight was triggered when the largest and oldest of these funds, the Reserve Prime Fund, announced that it "broke the buck" owing to the fact that about $750 million of its $60 billion in assets had been invested in Lehman commercial paper. Yet obscured in the hubbub was the fact that the resulting losses were tiny—just 3 percent of assets. In reality, breaking the buck was a money fund marketing pratfall, not the precursor to Armageddon; it amounted to a modest wake-up call disabusing investors of the industry's phony claim that money market accounts were absolutely safe and immune to loss.

So the unexpected shock from the Reserve Prime Fund's breaking the buck triggered a "run" on the prime funds of significant magnitude during the week or two after September 15. Yet according to the Financial Crisis Inquiry report, most of this so-called flight money did not get very far; that is, 85 percent, or $370 billion, of this outflow simply migrated to what were perceived to be safer "government only" money market funds.

In truth, the "run" was almost entirely within the money market mutual fund sector, with the debit going to the "prime" funds and the credit to the "government" funds. Indeed, this migration frequently involved nothing more than investors hitting the SEND button! They simply moved their deposits between these two types of accounts at the same fund management company.

Bernanke, Paulson, and the other bailsters focused exclusively on the gross outflow from the prime funds and waved this $430 billion bloody shirt incessantly. Needless to say, they did not bother to tell Congress that only a net amount of $60 billion, or 2 percent of total assets, had actually left the money market fund industry during the three weeks before the October 3 TARP vote.

Nor did they mention that most of the $60 billion which did leave the money market sector had gone into CDs and other bank deposits, and that none had ended up in mattresses. Moreover, all of this data was published in real time by the Investment Company Institute, so it should have been evident to policy makers, even in the heat of the crisis, that the circular flow from "prime" funds into "government only" money funds and banks (which got the $60 billion) posed no threat whatsoever to financial system stability.

CHAPTER 3

DAYS OF CRONY CAPITALIST PLUNDER

T HE APPROXIMATE 25 PERCENT SHRINKAGE OF THE PRIME FUNDS did induce a painful corrective adjustment. In this case, the hit was to the commercial paper market, but the ensuing correction was all about losses on Wall Street, not harm to Main Street.

On the eve of the crisis about $650 billion, or one-third of prime fund assets, were invested in commercial paper, making these funds the largest single investor class in the $2 trillion commercial paper market. Consequently, when the wave of money moved from prime funds to government-only funds which could not own commercial paper, open market rates on the A2/P2 grade of thirty-day commercial paper spiked sharply. Loan paper that had yielded only 1 percent prior to the spring of 2008 suddenly soared to over 6 percent during the September crisis.

Any garden variety economist might have suggested that commercial paper had been seriously overvalued. The flight from prime funds was living proof that the market had been artificially buoyed by big chunks of demand from what were inherently risk-intolerant prime fund investors. Now, the commercial paper market was in a violent rebalancing mode, causing borrowers to experience the joys of "price discovery" as interest rates sought a higher, market-clearing level.

THE REAL BAILOUT CATALYST:
JEFF IMMELT'S THREATENED BONUS

At that particular moment, however, General Electric CEO Jeff Immelt was apparently in no mood for a lesson in price discovery. In fact, he was then learning, along with the rest of Wall Street, an even more painful lesson about the folly of lending long and borrowing short. Notwithstanding that General Electric was one of just a handful of AAA-rated American corporations, it was suddenly discovering that its hugely profitable finance company, General Electric Capital, was actually an unstable house of cards.

GE Capital's financial alchemy rested on a simple but turbocharged formula straight out of the Wall Street playbook. At the time of the crisis, GE Capital boasted $650 billion of financial investments from customized deals in real estate, equipment leasing, working capital finance, and private equity. While these highly proprietary investments yielded generous rates of return, they were also highly illiquid and prone to blow up at higher than normal loss rates, thus bearing an asset profile that called for generous amounts of equity capital funding. In fact, however, GE Capital's massive balance sheet was leveraged nearly 10 to 1 and included upward of $100 billion of short-term commercial paper.

Needless to say, this huge load of commercial paper carried midget interest rates (4.7 percent), which helped fuel impressive profit spreads on GE's assets. But this ultra-cheap CP funding also bore short maturities, meaning that GE Capital had to rollover billions of commercial paper debts day in and day out.

When commercial paper rates suddenly spiked during the Lehman crisis, GE was caught with its proverbial pants down. But rather than manning-up for the financial hit that his company deserved, Jeff Immelt jumped on the phone to Treasury Secretary Paulson and yelled "Fire!"

Within days, the sell-off in the commercial paper was stopped cold by Washington's intervention, sparing GE the inconvenience of having to pay market rates to fund its massive pool of assets. The Republican government essentially nationalized the entire commercial paper market.

Even a cursory look at the data, however, shows that Immelt's SOS call was a self-serving crock. His preposterous message had been that the commercial paper market was seizing up and that GE was on the edge of collapse—a risible proposition. Nevertheless, that assertion quickly became gospel among panic-stricken officialdom, and from there it rapidly spread to Wall Street and the financial press.

Not surprisingly, even two years later when the dust had settled and facts were readily available to refute this horary untruth, Secretary Paulson insisted upon repeating the GE legend in his memoirs. Describing round the clock staff activities on Wednesday, September 17, he noted that "our most pressing issue" had been to "help the asset-backed commercial paper market before it pulled down companies like GE."

That was garbled nonsense. GE was not even a significant issuer of "asset-backed commercial paper" (ABCP). Those small amounts it did issue ($5 billion) were non-recourse and self-liquidating, meaning that GE Capital would have already passed ownership of the embedded assets to the ABCP conduit and its investors would have taken a hit, not GE.

By the same token, it was a huge issuer of unsecured commercial paper (100 billion), but even that was not remotely capable of felling the mighty GE. The required rollover funding was less than $5 billion per week, which was petty cash for a $200 billion (sales) global corporation with an AAA credit rating.

Although GE was not heading into a black hole, it was facing the need for a painful bout of liquidity generation which would have required either a fire sale of some of its sticky assets or a highly dilutive issuance of long-term equity or debt capital. Both courses were feasible, but each would have resulted in a sharp blow to earnings and top executive bonuses.

Instead of allowing the free market to resolve the matter, however, the taxpayers were thrown into the breach in still another variation of stopping the alleged "run" on Wall Street's cheap wholesale funding. Again, a necessary and healthy market correction was cancelled while the cronies of capitalism were kept in the clover.

WHY THE ATMS WOULD NOT HAVE GONE DARK: THE SECRET OF "GAIN ON SALE" ACCOUNTING

The commercial paper bailout incited by Jeff Immelt was utterly unnecessary. The facts show that the bailsters conjured up still more economic goblins where none actually existed. What the commercial paper bailout mainly did was prop up the banking industry's "gain on sale" profit scam.

The single most salient fact about the $2 trillion commercial paper market was that upward of $1 trillion was accounted for by the aforementioned ABCP, or asset-backed commercial paper segment. This was just another form of securitization, and it amounted to the financial equivalent of a twice-baked potato.

In this instance, Wall Street had gone to the banks and credit card companies and purchased massive volumes of "receivables" representing payments owed on millions of auto loans, credit cards, student loans, and other installment credit. These receivables were then dumped into a "conduit," which was a legal structure that existed only in cyberspace; the underlying payments on loans and credit cards were processed and collected by their bank and finance company originators.

Nevertheless, the conduits were given a top credit rating by S&P and Moody's because they were over collateralized; that is, they had enough extra assets per dollar of ABCP issued to absorb any likely defaults by the underlying borrowers. Given these AAA ratings, the ABCP conduits were thus enabled to issue billions of commercial paper debt against their "assets," which were actually, of course, debts of the American consumer.

The crucial point about this $1 trillion ABCP market, however, was that it did not originate new loans; it was merely a mechanism for refinancing debts which already existed. Accordingly, no consumer anywhere in America needed the ABCP market in order to swipe their credit card or get a car loan.

Instead, consumer loans of this type were being advanced, day in and day out, to the public by the likes of JPMorgan, American Express, Bank of America, and hundreds of other banks and finance companies. All of the money passing through cash registers from credit cards and into car purchases from auto loans flowed directly from these banks, not the ABCP market.

While the ABCP conduits accomplished nothing for the consumer, they did permit the banks to enjoy the magic of "gain on sale" accounting. Under the latter dispensation of the accounting profession, banks could immediately book the lifetime profits on these consumer loans the minute they were sold to the securitization conduit, even though such loans were months and even years from maturity.

The profits on a five-year car loan, for example, could be booked practically the day it was made. Likewise, credit card companies essentially had their profits fed intravenously; that is, within virtually the same digital nanosecond that a consumer's credit card was swiped, there also transpired a nonrecourse sale of this credit card receivable to the conduit. Right then and there, by means of advanced technology and accounting magic, the bank issuer of the credit card was able to book the estimated "gain on sale" directly to its profit column.

So when Bernanke and Paulson regaled Capitol Hill about the "collapse" of the commercial paper market, what they neglected to mention was that the main thing collapsing was these quickie "gain on sale" profits at JPMorgan, Citibank, Capital One, and the rest of the issuers. No credit card authorization was ever denied nor was any car loan application ever rejected because the ABCP market melted down in the fall of 2008.

That the commercial paper market meltdown had never been a threat to the Main Street economy is now crystal clear: the amount of ABCP paper outstanding today is 75 percent smaller than in September 2008, but the banks have had no problem whatsoever funding credit card and other consumer loans on their own balance sheets out of their own deposits and other funding sources. In fact, the banking system is now actually so flush with cash that it is lending $1.7 trillion of excess reserves back to the Fed at the hardly measureable interest rate of 0.25 percent annually.

Another $400 billion layer of the $2 trillion commercial paper market had been issued by industrial companies and was used to meet working capital needs, including payroll. So it did not take the Washington bailsters long to conjure up frightening scenarios about millions of empty pay envelopes at the giant corporations which were heavy commercial paper users.

Had the bright young Treasury staffers racing around behind Hank Paulson's flaming hair come from the loan department of a Main Street bank rather than the M&A wards of Wall Street, however, they would have known better. At the time of the crisis, there was hardly a single industrial company issuer of commercial paper that did not also have a "standby" bank line behind its program.

Indeed, such back up lines were mandatory features of industrial company commercial paper programs. They were designed to assure investors that if issuers could no longer roll over maturing commercial paper, they would make timely repayment by drawing down their standby lines at their bank.

Moreover, industrial company issuers paid an annual fee of 15 to 20 basis points on these standby credit lines, precisely so that banks would have a contractual obligation to fund if requested. In the event, none of the banks violated their legally enforceable loan contracts to fund these CP standby lines. There was never a chance that corporate payrolls would not be met.

CRONY CAPITALIST SLEAZE: HOW THE NONBANK FINANCE COMPANIES RAIDED THE TREASURY

The final $600 billion segment of the commercial paper market provided funding to the so-called nonbank finance companies, and it is here that crony capitalism reached a zenith of corruption. During the bubble years, three big financially overweight delinquents played in this particular Wall Street sandbox: GE Capital, General Motors Acceptance Corporation (GMAC), and CIT. And all three booked massive accounting profits based on a faulty business model.

When a financial company lends long and illiquid and funds itself with short-term hot money, it needs to regularly charge its income statement with a loss reserve for the inevitable, violent moments of financial crisis when short-term money rates spike or funding dries up completely. At that point, a fire sale of assets at deep losses becomes unavoidable in order to scrounge up cash to redeem their hot-money borrowings as they come due daily.

The big three nonbank finance companies had not provided such rainy-day reserves. Consequently, when the commercial paper market seized up, Mr. Market came knocking, intent on rudely clawing back years' worth of overstated profits. In short order, however, the two largest of these giant finance companies, GE and GMAC, received taxpayer bailouts, proving once again that in the new régime of crony capitalism the kind of muscle which ultimately mattered was political, not financial.

The single most malodorous of the big finance companies was General Motors Acceptance Corporation, which went by the innocent-sounding acronym of GMAC. But it wasn't innocent in the slightest, perhaps hinted at by the fact that its chairman was one Ezra Merkin, whose major line of business had famously been in the operation of multibillion-dollar feeder funds for Bernie Madoff.

GMAC was not only a huge purveyor of some of the worst slime in the subprime auto loan and home mortgage market, but it was also a giant financial train wreck waiting to happen. Leveraged at more than 10 to 1 and funded with massive amounts of short-term commercial paper, it had no ability to absorb even mild losses in its loan book.

GMAC was in the business of accumulating truly rotten loans. Its operating units appear to have scoured subprime America looking for "twofers." Thus, the notorious Ditech online mortgage operation put millions of financially strapped households in homes they couldn't afford. Then it compounded the favor by putting a new car in their garage via a six-year subprime auto loan that was "upside down" (i.e., greater than the value of the car) nearly from day one.

Many of the "twofer" households lured into unsustainable debt by GMAC's subprime predators defaulted on their auto and mortgage loans when housing prices crashed and the economy buckled. As a consequence, GMAC ended up writing down $25 billion of loans, or more than the cumulative profits it had booked during the previous several years.

By every rule of capitalism, an enterprise as foolish, dangerous, predatory, and insolvent as GMAC should have been completely liquidated by a financial meltdown which was functioning to purge exactly that kind of deformation. Instead, it has remained on federal life support owing to $16 billion in TARP funding and an additional $30 billion in guarantees and subventions from FDIC and the Fed.

Yet there is not a shred of evidence that the Main Street economy has benefited from GMAC's artificial life extension program. There has never been a shortage of solvent banks, thrifts, and finance companies to serve the auto and housing finance needs of the nation's diminished pool of creditworthy borrowers. So when the Washington bailsters stopped the commercial paper meltdown on grounds that the likes of GMAC were imperiled, they snatched defeat from the jaws of victory.

Washington's $30 billion lifeline to AAA-rated General Electric was no less gratuitous. At the time of Immelt's SOS call to Secretary Paulson a day after the Lehman bankruptcy filing, the stock and bond markets were in a state of turbulence and panic. Even under those dire conditions, however, the world's capital markets were still valuing GE's common stock at $200 billion and were trading its $400 billion of term debt at a hundred cents on the dollar. Thus, as measured by the fundamental metric of corporate finance known as "enterprise value" (debt plus equity), the markets were capitalizing General Electric at $600 billion during the very midst of the meltdown.

This puts the lie to an urban legend assiduously promoted by the bailsters at the time and repeated endlessly by their apologists ever since. Their preposterous claim was that the $600 billion globe-spanning behemoth known as General Electric could not find replacement financing for the approximate $25 billion of commercial paper scheduled to mature on a fixed schedule (i.e., it was not subject to call on demand) between September 15 and the final months of 2008. The very idea that GE had been incapable of raising even a billion dollars of funding per business day was ludicrous on its face.

That this proposition was seriously embraced by mainstream opinion is undoubtedly a measure of the panic which had been shamelessly induced by the Washington bailsters. The true facts of the case, of course, were more nearly the opposite. GE Capital could have readily generated sufficient cash to meet its CP redemption obligations by selling only 8 percent of its assets, even at fire-sale discounts of up to 50 percent of book value, if that had been necessary.

In the alternative, the GE parent corporation could have raised new debt and equity capital, again at whatever deep discounts might have been demanded by the distressed markets of the moment. For example, a 4 percent increase in its long-term debt would have raised $15 billion, even if it required a coupon double GE's average 5 percent rate. And a mere 10 percent increase in its outstanding common shares would have raised $10 billion, even had they been placed at $10 per share or 50 percent below its $20 stock price at the time.

Thus, the mix of potential asset disposals and stock and bond issuance available to GE was nearly infinite. Any combination chosen would have generated sufficient cash to redeem its expiring commercial paper. Indeed, it is blindingly obvious that the taxpayer-supported bailout of General Electric was simply about earnings per share and the threat to executive bonuses that would have resulted from asset sales or stock and bond offerings.

The fact is, these "self-help" methods of raising cash according to free market rules would have also have whacked GE's earnings by perhaps $2 per share, owing to losses or earnings dilution. Either way, shareholders would have gotten the beating they deserved for having so egregiously overvalued GE's debt-inflated earnings and for putting such reckless managers in charge of the store.

Instead, GE shareholders were spared any permanent damage. Likewise, GE and GMAC had combined long-term debt outstanding of nearly a half trillion dollars, all of which remained worth a hundred cents on the dollar, thanks to Uncle Sam's safety nets.

This means that the bond fund managers who were the "enablers" of these unstable finance company debt pyramids got off without a scratch. So the pattern was repeated over and over. The post-Lehman meltdown in the wholesale money markets, including the various types of commercial paper, was of consequence only in the canyons of Wall Street. The thin slab of permanent debt and equity capital that supported these bubble-era pyramids of inflated assets and toxic derivatives was the only real target of Mr. Market's wrathful attack.

Had this attack been allowed to run its course, hundreds of billions in long-term debt and equity capital that underpinned the Wall Street–based speculation machines would have been wiped out, including huge amounts of stock owned by executives and insiders. Such a result would have been truly constructive from a societal vantage point. It would have implanted an abiding 1930s style generational lesson about the deadly dangers of leveraged speculation.

BERNANKE'S PANICKED DEPRESSION CALL

At the end of the day, the stated purpose of the Wall Street bailouts—to avoid a replay of the 1930s—was drastically misguided. It was based on a phantom threat which arose overwhelmingly from the faulty scholarship of a single official: the former math professor who had come to head the nation's central bank. The analysis was actually not even his own, but was the borrowed theory of Professor Milton Friedman.

Forty years earlier, Friedman had famously claimed that the Fed's failure to run its printing presses full tilt during certain periods of 1930–1932 had caused the Great Depression. Bernanke's sole contribution to this truly wrong-headed proposition was a few essays consisting mainly of dense math equations. They showed the undeniable correlation between the collapse of GDP and the money supply, but proved no causation whatsoever.

In fact, as will be shown in chapters 8 and 9, the great contraction of 1929–1933 was rooted in the bubble of debt and financial speculation that built up in the years before October 1929, not from mistakes made by the Fed after the bubble collapsed. In the fall of 2008, the American economy was facing a different boom-and-bust cycle, but its central bank was now led by an academic zealot who had gotten cause and effect upside-down.

The panic that gripped officialdom in September 2008, therefore, did not arise from a clear-eyed assessment of the facts on the ground. Instead, it was heavily colored and charged by Bernanke's erroneous take on a historical episode that bore almost no relationship to the current reality.

Nevertheless, the bailouts hemorrhaged into a multitrillion-dollar assault on the rules of sound money and free market capitalism. Moreover, once the feeding frenzy was catalyzed by these errors of doctrine, it was thereafter fueled by the overwhelming political muscle of the financial institutions which benefited from it.

These developments gave rise to a great irony. Milton Friedman had been the foremost modern apostle of free market capitalism, but now a misguided disciple of his great monetary error had unleashed statist forces which would devour it. Indeed, by the end of 2008 it could no longer be gainsaid. During a few short weeks in September and October, American political democracy had been fatally corrupted by a resounding display of expediency and raw power in Washington. Every rule of free markets was suspended and any regard for the deliberative requirements of democracy was cast to the winds.

Henceforth, the door would be wide open for the entire legion of Washington's K Street lobbies, reinforced by the campaign libations prodigiously dispensed by their affiliated political action committees (PACs), to relentlessly plunder the public purse. At the same time, the risk of failure had been unambiguously eliminated from the commanding heights of the American economy. Free market capitalism thus shorn of its vital mechanism to purge error and speculation had become dangerously unhinged.

Yet the September 2008 meltdown was a financial cyclone which struck mainly within the vertical canyons of Wall Street, and would have burned out there in short order. This truth exposes the crony capitalist putsch that occurred in Washington during the fall of 2008 and invalidates its self-serving narrative that America was faced with a continent-wide flood which would have wracked devastation across the length and breadth of Main Street America.

There was never any evidence for Bernanke's Great Depression bugaboo, a truth more fully explicated in chapters 28 and 32. So it is also not surprising that bailout apologists cannot explain the origins of the Wall Street meltdown. Indeed, they treat it as *sui generis*, meaning that the "contagion," whatever it was, had suddenly arrived as if on a comet from deep space. And after hardly a ten-week visit, as measured by the return of speculators to the beaten-down bank stocks in early 2009, it had adverted once again to interstellar blackness.

It is not surprising, therefore, that the corporals' guard of Treasury and Federal Reserve officials who carried out this financial coup d'état never once provided any detailed analysis of why this mysterious "contagion" had struck so suddenly; nor did they ever lay out the financial system linkages and pathways by which the contagion was expected to spread; nor did they present any review of the costs, benefits, and alternatives to bailing out the major institutions which were rescued. Hardly a single page of professionally competent analysis and justification for the Wall Street bailouts was presented to the president or any of the leaders of Congress at the time.

Indeed, the Bernanke–Paulson putsch was so imperious and secretive that Sheila Bair, head of the FDIC and the one regulator who thoroughly understood the balance sheet of the American banking system, and also did not buy into knee-jerk fear mongering about "systemic risk," was simply not consulted, and commanded to fall in line. As Bair recounted the events, "We were rarely consulted . . . without giving me any information they would say, 'You have to do this or the system will go down.' If I heard that once, I heard it a thousand times . . . No analysis, no meaningful discussion. It was very frustrating."

Sheila Bair was the single best informed and most tough-minded and courageous financial official in Washington at the time of the crisis. She had a sophisticated grasp of the manner in which deposit insurance had been abused to fund excessive risk taking in the banking system and a resolute conviction that the capital structure enablers—that is, bank bond and equity holders—needed to absorb losses ahead of the insurance fund and taxpayers.

None of this was remotely understood by Paulson's cadre of former Goldman associates led by Neel Kashkari. He was a thirty-four-year-old former space telescope engineer who had done two-bit M&A deals in Goldman's San Francisco office for two years before joining the Treasury Department and being assigned the bailout portfolio.

The fact that the abysmally unqualified Kashkari led the bailout brigade while Bair was systematically excluded from the process speaks volumes as to how completely public policy had fallen into the clutches of Wall Street. Kashkari and his posse had no sense whatsoever about the requisites of sound public finance. So in the fog of Washington's panic, prevention of private losses quickly and completely supplanted any reasoned consideration of the public good.

THE BLACKBERRY PANIC OF 2008

The exclusive diagnostic tool used by the principals during this entire episode was carried in their pockets. This was the BlackBerry Panic of 2008. What was going down hard was not the American economy, just the stock prices of Goldman and the other big banks.

As the "eye witness" accounts contained in the numerous histories written by financial journalists make clear, the driving force behind every action and each decision was the instantaneous oscillation of stock prices and credit spreads, and the openings and closings of financial markets around the globe. Needless to say, the dancing digits on the hundreds of BlackBerries toted about on the field of battle measured nothing of relevance to the public interest, even as they kept instant score on the price of the stocks and bonds of the financial institutions in play.

The journalistic histories also make clear the method of persuasion used by Washington officialdom to deliver the keys to the nation's exchequer to Wall Street and its agents in the Treasury and the Fed. In a word, it was fear—lurid premonitions of cash machines gone dark, payrolls undelivered, air freight grounded, and assembly lines stopped-out.

In the cold light of day, however, it is abundantly clear that none of these catastrophes would have occurred had TARP never been enacted. Trillions of bank deposits were already well protected by the FDIC's existing powers to guarantee deposits and take over insolvent banks, along with the Fed's capacity to make virtually unlimited discount window loans to member institutions on the presentation of standard collateral.

This fear-based stampede to adopt TARP was made all the easier by the White House's virtual abdication from the policy process. Indeed, the contrast between these September 2008 acts of perfidy by the Bush administration and the comparable betrayal of conservative principles by a Republican White House in August 1971 is striking.

Back then, Richard Nixon called his government to Camp David for an entire weekend and personally led the charge for policies—wage and price controls, import protection, and closure of the gold window—which were antithetical to GOP principles. In September 2008, however, George W. Bush simply delegated his raid on the American taxpayers to the Treasury Department and then reverted to his habitual somnolence on matters of economics.

And not surprisingly. During his brief interval of success in scalping a handsome profit from the Texas Rangers franchise, George W. Bush had apparently learned little about business and virtually nothing about the nation's now massively debt-ridden economy. So as president in the white heat of crisis, he was easy prey for the fear-mongering of the cabal lead by Treasury Secretary Paulson and Chairman Bernanke.

At a meeting of the congressional chieftains, the president thus tersely conveyed the entirety of his comprehension of the momentous matter at hand. "This sucker is going down," he told them, and in a comparative flash the nation's petrified legislators wrote out a $700 billion blank check.

And so the TARP bailout was enshrined as a last-resort exercise in breaking the rules to save the system. Ever the master of malapropism, President Bush soon took to proclaiming, "I've abandoned free market principles to save the free market system."

Ironically, however, the truth was more nearly the opposite. The financial meltdown of 2008 was occurring because sound economic principles had already been abandoned—years earlier, in fact. The right solution was to restore these discarded canons, not to eviscerate them further. That meant promptly dismantling the giant gambling halls which had ushered in the crisis.

It also meant returning the Fed to its proper role as guardian of the dollar's value and stern taskmaster of banking system liquidity; that is, to a policy of dispensing discount window loans only at a penalty rate of interest against sound collateral while remanding insolvent institutions to the FDIC for closure. But most importantly, it meant liquidation of the massive pyramids of debt and leveraged speculation that had built up throughout the American economy over more than three decades.

THE ARROGANCE OF WALL STREET: CRONY CAPITALISM, JOHN MACK STYLE

The urgent imperative for the Fed to revert to these canons of sound money can be illustrated by its opposite: the utterly shameful and gratuitous bailout of Morgan Stanley two weeks after the Lehman bankruptcy. On September 29, 2008, Morgan Stanley was insolvent and belonged in the financial morgue on a slab alongside Lehman.

Yet that very day it reported to the public that it had "strong capital and liquidity positions." That statement was utterly misleading, but it never gave rise to an SEC investigation because it could be defended by means of a hair-splitting technicality. A later investigation by the Federal Crisis Inquiry Commission, in fact, showed that Morgan Stanley had $99 billion of liquidity on the date in question. What the investigation also showed, however, was that very same day it had been the recipient of $107 billion in liquidity injections from the Fed's alphabet soup of bailout programs. It was liquid only because it had become a branch office of the New York Fed!

Absent the cash being injected by the Fed's multiple and massive fire hoses, Morgan Stanley would have been deeply illiquid. Its hot-money lenders would have seized tens of billions in collateral, which they would have sold at any loss necessary to retrieve their cash. Lehman's reputed $40 billion loss at the time of its filing would have paled compared to the losses which would have been ripped from Morgan Stanley's tottering $1 trillion balance sheet.

As previously indicated, the survival of Morgan Stanley was of no moment to the American economy. It was a giant leveraged hedge fund being subjected to the mother of all margin calls; that is, its reckless reliance on overnight wholesale money to fund massive amounts of impaired, illiquid, and highly volatile assets was undergoing a flaming crash landing.

The claim that its vestigial capabilities in the mergers and acquisitions arena and in underwriting stocks and bonds needed to be preserved was ludicrous. Neither of these businesses required meaningful amounts of capital, and there were always dozens of pedigreed Wall Street veterans waiting to hang out a boutique investment banking shingle to pick up the slack.

Even though no public purpose was served, the details of the Fed's $107 billion bailout of Morgan Stanley underscore the abject manner in which it had capitulated to the imperatives of crony capitalism. About $61 billion of this amount was obtained from the Fed's Primary Dealer Credit Facility, and the Crisis Commission's data show that Morgan Stanley had put up only $66 billion of collateral against this advance. This meant that the "haircut," or margin of safety, was only 8 percent.

Yet Morgan Stanley's collateral pool was a veritable trash bin of broken and impaired securities. Indeed, about $22 billion, or 32 percent, of the total consisted of common stock, for which the implied 8 percent haircut was a joke since the stock market had been moving by that much in a couple of days.

Likewise, another 10 percent of the collateral pool consisted of junk bonds which at that juncture could not be sold at any price. And another $20 billion, or 30 percent, consisted of assets with an "unknown rating." In short, prior to the crisis of 2008 not one central banker in a thousand would have accepted this Morgan Stanley trash bin as acceptable collateral for an advance of even a fraction of the $61 billion it actually got.

In this episode lies proof of the lasting damage wrought by the bailouts of Wall Street. Morgan Stanley's CEO and chairman, John Mack, was a ruthless gambler and bully who had never hesitated to exploit any available avenue to make a buck, to say nothing of a billion bucks. In the run-up to the crisis, Morgan Stanley had embraced any and all short sale trades that could potentially yield a profit, including a giant short of the housing market which blew up and ended up costing Morgan Stanley a $9 billion write-off.

But after Mr. Market dispatched Lehman Brothers and then Merrill Lynch, the short sellers had turned their sights on Morgan Stanley. It was by then apparent that its wholesale funding was rapidly vanishing, and it would be forced to take massive losses on the junk assets which had accumulated on its balance sheet over years and years of bubble prosperity on Wall Street.

Yet in less than a New York minute, Mack had reversed course and stormed the barricades on Capitol Hill and the White House, demanding an SEC ban on short selling of his stock and that of the other banks and financial institutions. On Tuesday afternoon, September 16, for example, the treasury secretary, according to his memoirs, "got an earful from John Mack . . . the short sellers were after his bank. His cash reserves were evaporating."

Crony capitalism had now reached its apotheosis: one insuperably arrogant prince of Wall Street was commanding his former chief rival, and now occupant of the highest financial policy job of the land, to pull any and all stops to save his firm. From what? The answer was, to save it from its own clients. In fact, prime brokerage customers and trading counterparties were withdrawing their deposits and margin accounts at a furious pace because they knew full well that, like Lehman and Bear Stearns, Morgan Stanley was a house of cards.

The idea that the short sellers were draining Morgan Stanley's cash was a complete canard. Creditors and lenders to Morgan Stanley were fleeing, which would force a fire sale liquidation of impaired assets and thereby render the firm insolvent. Short sellers were furiously attacking the carcass because they knew the firm was finished, brought down by the foolish leverage and hot-money wholesale funding from which it had harvested so much ill-gotten profit in the past.

What the short sellers hadn't reckoned with, however, was the final triumph of crony capitalism. Morgan Stanley was spared because Goldman wanted it rescued. In a phone call to Paulson during the heat of the crisis that day, Goldman's current CEO, Lloyd Blankfein, had left no doubt about the stakes. As the tone-deaf Paulson actually confessed in his own memoirs, he had used the great powers of his office to save Goldman Sachs: "Lloyd was afraid that if something wasn't done, Morgan Stanley would fail . . . And even though Goldman had plenty of liquidity and cash, it could be next."

So within hours of Mack's presumptuous tantrum and with virtually no analysis or due process, the US government met his demands. Chris Cox, the former congressman and purported free market true believer who

George W. Bush had chosen to head the SEC, issued a truly pitiful announcement. In it he explained to American citizens that for the next fifteen days they would be free to buy financial company stocks, but not to sell them.

The short-selling ban was the product of naked Wall Street aggression, and in the case of Morgan Stanley there could be no doubt as to the true purpose. The Morgan Stanley stock had dropped from $80 per share to $40 on the eve of the crisis, had fallen to $20 upon the Lehman filing, and by the end of September was at $7 and sinking fast.

Thus, in the final weeks of September leading to the fateful October 3 approval of TARP, Washington's action was being driven by an overriding Wall Street imperative; namely, saving the stock price of Morgan Stanley—and those of Goldman, JPMorgan, Bank of America, and Citigroup, too—from the fate of Lehman Brothers, and assuring that the personal wealth of John Mack and the remaining Wall Street titans would remain intact.

Within a fortnight, of course, the danger had already passed. Armed with gifts that only the sovereign state can bestow—a ban on short selling of its stock and $100 billion of cash based on junk collateral—Morgan Stanley evaded Mr. Market's wrathful attack and not only remained open for business, but saw its stock price recover smartly. By the end of the year it had tripled, and within twelve months had risen fivefold from the time of its bailouts.

Nor was Morgan Stanley given special rank in the hierarchy of Washington's bailout dispensations. From the same liquidity fire hoses which powered cash into Morgan Stanley, nearly the identical amount went to Citigroup at $100 billion, Bank of America at $91 billion, Goldman Sachs at $80 billion, and nearly equal amounts to the leading banks of Europe. All told, the Fed dispensed nearly $700 billion in emergency loans during the last months of 2008, doubling down on the appropriated money provided by TARP.

At the end of the day, this trillion-dollar infusion of capital and liquidity from the public till had a single overarching effect: it nullified in its entirety the impact of Mr. Market's withdrawal of a similar magnitude of funding from the wholesale money market. So the very monetary distortion—the availability of cheap overnight funding in massive quantities—upon which the Wall Street financial bubble had been built had now been recreated at the lending windows of the Fed, FDIC, and the US Treasury.

The opposite path of liquidating the Wall Street bubble was eschewed, of course, not only because it would have meant massive losses to speculators in the stock and bonds of Goldman Sachs, Morgan Stanley, JPMorgan, and the remaining phalanx of the walking wounded. Crony capitalism also triumphed because in muscling the system during the white heat of crisis, Wall Street had plenty of intellectual cover. The fact is, mainstream economists of both parties were trapped in a Keynesian dead end, proclaiming that the solution to the crushing national debt load which had actually triggered the financial crisis was to pile on more of the same.

Accordingly, banks which were "too big to fail" couldn't be busted up, since they were allegedly needed to shovel more credit onto already debt-saturated household and business balance sheets. Likewise, speculators who should have suffered epochal losses during the meltdown were resuscitated by Fed-engineered zero interest rates in the money market, thereby quickly reviving the same massively leveraged "carry trades" in commodities, currencies, equities, derivatives, and other risk assets which had brought on the crisis in the first place.

THE BONFIRE OF IDEOLOGIES

In a narrow sense, the GOP was responsible for this calamity. Republican administrations had turned the nation's central bank over to money printers and Wall Street coddlers not only by appointing Greenspan and Bernanke, but also by celebrating the phony prosperity they fostered as evidence of triumphant GOP economics.

Worse still, the clique of political hacks around Karl Rove who ran the Bush White House were so unlettered in the requisites of sound money and free market economics that, over and over, they caused the nation's top economic jobs to be filled by statists and Keynesians. Thus, professors Glenn Hubbard, Greg Mankiw, and Ed Lazear had no problem whatsoever advising George Bush that two giant tax cuts and two unfunded wars were entirely copacetic from a fiscal viewpoint. After all, the huge resulting deficits provided a Keynesian pick-me-up to the prosperous classes.

Bernanke had nosily advertised his partiality to unlimited money printing and monetary central planning long before the Rove crowd in the White House okayed his first appointment to the Fed in 2002. The same political clique that vetted and appointed Bernanke also drummed Paul O'Neill out of his job as secretary of the treasury for having the temerity to suggest that the tax cuts and unfinanced wars were a recipe for fiscal catastrophe. Eventually they came up with Hank Paulson, who had spent a lifetime doing M&A deals, but not studying the great questions of economic governance.

Even rank-and-file Republicans on Capitol Hill had remained wary of the financial Frankensteins at Fannie Mae and Freddie Mac, but Paulson did not hesitate to bail out their creditors when he had a perfect opportunity to shut them down in September 2008. Likewise, when the US economy began to falter in the spring of 2008 because the Greenspan-Bernanke bubble was finally bursting, this clueless GOP treasury secretary revived the equivalent of Jimmy Carter's ridiculed $50 per family tax rebate, as if inducing households to buy more Happy Meals and Coach bags on Uncle Sam's credit card had anything to do with sound financial policy.

By the time of the Wall Street meltdown, Republicans had long ago succumbed to the hoary notion that "deficits don't matter," a posture which permitted the floodgates to the treasury to be opened to TARP. In fact, when the House Republican leader had invited his troops to consume a $700 billion "mud sandwich" and vote for a bill that violated every core principle of a free market economy, they did so because their ancient fears of deficit finance had long since evaporated. Now after massive and blatant intervention in every corner of the financial market, and the wider economy too, there were no remaining boundaries to the state at all.

In this context, national economic policy became an ad hoc free-for-all. The GOP could not explain why the calamity had happened. After all, their central bank appointees had promised permanent prosperity, but had fostered instead the now dramatically collapsing financial bubble. Likewise, the American economy was suddenly plunging even though the GOP had supposedly supercharged it with multiple doses of the tax-cut tonic. And Republican governments had resolutely dismantled the last remnants of a fraying structure of financial regulation, but now the nation was being assailed by Wall Street's speculative furies.

So unable to explain or account for the financial and economic conflagration that descended on the nation in the fall of 2008, they adverted to conjuring a mythical past—an alleged golden age of Reaganomics. As detailed in part II, the GOP's escapism into the alleged glories of the Reagan era was pure revisionist history. The Reagan Revolution had actually been a progenitor of the calamity now upon the nation, not an alternative régime that needed to be revived.

At the same time, the Keynesian left channeled FDR and the New Deal to chart a way forward, but it, too, was a lapse into the revisionist past. The New Deal was fundamentally a grab bag of statist experiments which didn't work, and even FDR abandoned much of it along the way. As detailed in part III, it was no golden era of enlightened economic governance, either, and more often than not resembled a political gong show. The New Deal did not end the Great Depression and was irrelevant to the current crisis. What the left was reviving in the fall of 2008 was nothing more than a revisionist illusion.

As will be seen, the causes and roots of the Great Depression were dramatically different than the 2008 collapse of the Wall Street casino and the debt-saturated national economy. The only relevance of the New Deal, ironically, was that it had been the original wellspring of the ills currently at hand; that is, the displacement of sound money and an honest free market economy with statist economics and the crony capitalist régime which inexorably arises from it.

In fact, by the turn of the century New Deal interventionism and welfare state expansion had conjoined with Reaganite fiscal profligacy: Supply-side tax cutting became the Keynesian opiate of the prosperous classes. But what made this unholy union possible was the Great Deformation of central banking, money, and credit which was initiated by FDR but had been crystallized by the Camp David abomination of August 1971.

In an act that cascaded down through the decades, Richard Nixon caused the United States to default on its Bretton Woods obligations to redeem unwanted dollars in gold, and thereby inaugurated an era of global trade imbalance, currency pegging and manipulation, massive debt creation, and financial speculation that had no historic antecedents. It became the era of bubble finance which is chronicled in all its dismal particulars in part IV.

So the triumph of crony capitalism was only confirmed by the bailout spasms of 2008. Its roots were actually buried deep in the decades that had passed between August 1914 and the BlackBerry Panic of 2008. In the intervening decades, a leviathan was arising through a process of economic governance that was halting, piecemeal, and more often than not driven by fleeting emergencies that were of no lasting moment.

But the common thread was the proposition that modern industrial capitalism was unstable and prone to chronic cyclical fluctuations and shortfalls that could be ameliorated by the interventions and corrective actions of the state, and most especially its central banking branch. That was upside down. The far greater imperfections and threat to the people's welfare were embedded in the state itself, and in its vulnerability to capture by special interests—the vast expanse of K Street lobbies and campaign-money-dispensing PACs. Trying to improve capitalism, modern economic policy has thus fatally overloaded the state with missions and mandates far beyond its capacity to fulfill. The result is crony capitalism—a freakish deformation that fatally corrupts free markets and democracy.

PART II

THE REAGAN ERA REVISITED:
FALSE NARRATIVES OF OUR TIMES

CHAPTER 4

THE REAGAN REVOLUTION
Repudiations and Deformations

THE FINANCIAL BREAKDOWN AND CONVULSIVE GOVERNMENT IN-terventions of September 2008 were the very antithesis of the promised land of private prosperity and frugal government that the Reagan Revolution envisioned three decades earlier. In truth, these promises were long faded ideological dreams, but the passage of the Troubled Asset Relief Program (TARP) by a Republican government was the final, jarring end note. It amounted to a stark repudiation of the Reagan Revolution.

It proved that the great tax and spending cut campaigns of 1981 had not bent the contours of history in the slightest. They had been a flash in the pan, which twenty-seven years later illuminated nothing at all.

In fact, there was a Reagan-era fiscal legacy still alive in September 2008, but it was an ironic one which presented itself in twisted, perverse aspect. Ronald Reagan had spent a political lifetime excoriating deficits, but the takeaway from his presidency among Republican politicians was that he had proved the contrary: that deficits don't matter.

Moreover, during the George W. Bush era this insidious idea became operational policy. It was embodied in two costly unfinanced wars and two giant tax cuts which were paid for by massive issuance of treasury bonds.

So when the once-in-a-generation test of the nation's fiscal mettle came in the midst of the Wall Street storm, there was no conservative party left to safeguard the gates to the treasury. In fact, Republican politicians had embraced a dangerous rationalization that weakened any vestigial fiscal resolve; namely, that deficits were the passive result of an underperforming economy, not the deliberate consequence of profligate fiscal policy.

Accordingly, the GOP shifted its deficit-fighting efforts to a more pleasant chore; that is, peddling new tax cut gimmicks to spur "growth." The implication was that without constant ministrations from Washington, the nation's economy would falter. In the heat of crisis, therefore, the GOP became an easy mark for the Bernanke–Paulson canard that Wall Street's long overdue meltdown would pull Main Street America into a vortex of economic collapse.

Republican politicians thus concluded, anomalously, that issuing a $700 billion blank check would result in lower, not higher, federal deficits. It was just another variation of the pro-business Keynesianism that morphed out of the Reaganite tax-cutting religion. Indeed, Republicans became suckers for practically any rendition of the supply-side shibboleth that higher growth means lower deficits, so they quickly rationalized that propping up Wall Street would produce more revenue.

RICHARD NIXON'S FOLLY AND THE
CENTRAL BANK WAREHOUSE FOR TREASURY DEBT

Yet the real culprit behind the fiscal profligacy which descended upon the nation was the final destruction of sound money way back in August 1971. While not evident for decades to come, it was Richard Nixon's default on the nation's Bretton Woods obligation to redeem its foreign debts in gold that actually ushered in the era of "deficits don't matter."

After the gold window was closed in favor of floating fiat currencies, the Fed and the other major central banks of the world, especially those of the Asian mercantilist exporters, went on a rampage of paper money expansion and currency pegging. Financial discipline thus lost its anchor and fiscal rectitude its necessity.

The virtue of fixed exchange rates and continuous settlement of international account imbalances was that chronic budget deficits led to an outflow of reserves and a domestic financial squeeze. The need to counter this threat, in turn, gave politicians cover to enact unpopular spending cuts or tax increases.

When activist fiscal policy gained ascendency after the war, however, Keynesian theorists at first, and statist politicians later, became strongly anti-gold. As the younger Alan Greenspan observed near the end of Bretton Woods: "Opposition to the gold standard . . . was prompted by a much subtler insight: the realization that the gold standard is incompatible with chronic deficit spending."

In the decades after 1971 Nixon's floating-rate currency régime offered a way out. As the flood of unwanted dollars washed around the globe, mercantilist exporters never ceased pegging their currencies to keep the dollar price of their manufactures low.

This currency market intervention resulted in vast accumulations of dollar-denominated assets such as treasury bonds and bills, which were then sequestered in the vaults of these same money-printing central banks.

In fact, by the end of 2012 fully $5 trillion of the nearly $12 trillion in pub-licly held US treasury debt was locked up in central banks and other official institutions, including the Fed.

By this process of debt monetization both at home and abroad, the classic ill effects of fiscal deficits including monetary inflation, higher in-terest rates, and a squeeze on private investment were circumvented. Yet this monetary miscarriage did not eliminate but only deferred the day of reckoning.

Indeed, the counterpart to the flood of dollars abroad was the buildup of towering debts on domestic balance sheets and the associated leveraged speculation in real estate and every class of financial asset. Ironically, then, the fruit of the cheap dollar policy which made fiscal deficits painless had suddenly, in September 2008, turned into a full-fledged financial bust that was to be remedied with even greater budgetary red ink.

By the time of the revote on TARP, after the first vote failed and had un-leashed another fear-inducing stock plunge, the nation was self-evidently fiscally incontinent. There were now two "free lunch" parties operating in a political arena from which all of the ancient taboos and fears about deficit finance had been purged.

In fact, the absorption by central banks of much of the treasury debt is-sued during the three decades after the Reagan deficits first exploded on the scene enabled the rise of an even more pernicious legend; namely, that the Reagan-era fiscal disaster was actually a splendid success because it drew the line on taxes and triggered an extended era of economic growth and capitalist prosperity.

This narrative is demonstrably untrue and amounts to blatant myth making. Moreover, it is these unsupportable Reagan-era fiscal legends that make Washington so vulnerable to the endless financial raids of crony cap-italism.

THE REAGANITE LEGENDS OF FISCAL RESTRAINT AND ECONOMIC REVIVAL

The Reaganite legend begins with the false proposition that the Reagan Ad-ministration stopped the march of "Big Government" and brought a new fiscal restraint to Washington. Yet after the economy had rebounded and recession-bloated spending had subsided during Reagan's second term, federal outlays averaged 21.7 percent of gross domestic product (GDP). That was obviously no improvement at all on the 21.1 percent of GDP av-erage during the alleged "big spending" Carter years, and compared quite miserably to the 19.3 percent of GDP recorded during Lyndon Johnson's fi-nal four years of "guns and butter" extravagance.

Nor had the Reagan Revolution planted any seeds of future fiscal restraint. During the administration of George H. W. Bush, federal spending averaged nearly 22 percent of GDP—still another presidential record and one that came after the end of the Cold War and the resulting 15 percent decline in real defense spending.

But it was the second Bush who took Reaganomics to its logical extreme, demolishing Republican fiscal rectitude once and for all in a fury of "guns and butter," and tax giveaways, too. Federal outlays in the final budget of George W. Bush soared to 25 percent of GDP. That was a post–World War II record by a long shot, but even that figure did not assay the full extent of the Bush fiscal debacle.

Measured in inflation-adjusted dollars (2005$), federal spending increased by 50 percent, rising from $2.1 trillion to $3.2 trillion in only eight years. Accordingly, just the gain on George Bush's watch—$1.1 trillion—dwarfed all prior episodes of profligacy. It was more than the entire $1 trillion federal budget, in the same inflation-adjusted dollars, posted under what Republican orators had long ago pilloried as Lyndon B. Johnson's calamitous "guns and butter" budget of 1968.

Republican apologists have long managed to deny the Reagan fiscal debauch and its (two) Bush progeny, however, by claiming that the Reagan Revolution worked where it counted: in reviving the national economy and then causing it to grow smartly for several decades. The trouble is, that didn't happen either.

Rather than a permanent era of robust free market growth, the Reagan Revolution ushered in two spells of massive statist policy stimulation before it finally ran out of steam at the turn of the century. The first spell of Washington-induced prosperity flowed from the giant Reagan deficits, the second from the money-printing and Wall Street–coddling policies of the Greenspan Fed in the 1990s.

But the proof that these were unsustainable bubbles fostered by the state rather than real growth and prosperity arising from the free market became acutely evident after the turn of the century. Then another round of Greenspan bubble finance and the George W. Bush fiscal profligacy converged in a temporary spree of phony prosperity: the domestic consumption boom and the real estate bubble. Yet now that these have gone resoundingly bust, the data starkly reveal that the nation's economic fundamentals have relentlessly deteriorated for more than a decade.

Long-term investment has grown by less than 1 percent annually since 2000 and the nonfarm payroll count has hardly increased at all for 12 years. Likewise, the real incomes of the middle class have fallen back to 1996 levels—even as the American economy has tumbled into a frightful debt to the rest of the world. In short, the American economy did not falter due to a mysterious "contagion" in September 2008. It had been heading for a crash landing for the better part of three decades.

THE KEYNESIAN BOOM UNDER REAGAN AND BUSH

The first spell of false prosperity was the unacknowledged yet massive exercise in Keynesian deficit finance carried out during the terms of Ronald Reagan and George H. W. Bush. The cumulative federal deficit was an astonishing $2.4 trillion, meaning that the public debt tripled and Federal red ink amounted to nearly 70 percent of GDP growth during those twelve years of Republican rule.

Apologists claim that the Reagan–Bush flood of red ink had nothing to do with the gains embedded in the GDP numbers, but, alas, the nation's GDP accounts were designed by Keynesian economists in the 1930s and 1940s. They most certainly believed that gross borrowings of the public sector are spent in a way that adds to GDP. Government wages and purchases, for example, go straight to GDP, and transfer payments also quickly end-up in the PCE (personal consumption expenditure) component of GDP. Since these three budget items doubled during 1980–1992 it is undeniable that the Reagan deficits gave a mighty boost to GDP.

Moreover, there wasn't much that resembled "supply-side" gains in the makeup of the GDP internals. Real private investment spending—the ultimate measure of supply-side growth—expanded at just 2.5 percent annually during the period. That was far below the 4.7 percent average for 1954–2000. Likewise, private sector productivity, another key supply-side metric, grew at only 1.7 percent per annum and therefore also at a lower rate than the postwar average.

By contrast, the demand side of the GDP accounts, consumption expenditures and government spending, grew nearly 25 percent faster than their long-term average. In combination, therefore, a weaker supply side and stronger demand side added up to nothing special; that is, a 3 percent average GDP growth rate during the twelve-year period which was dead-on the fifty-year average.

Traditional conservative economists, of course, would counter that deficit-fueled GDP growth is illusory because historically some part of deficit spending went into monetary inflation, not real growth, and some private investment spending was crowded out by higher interest rates owing to Uncle Sam's competition for savings.

In the new era of irredeemable floating dollars, however, this was no longer true. Much of the treasury debt issued to finance the deficit went into the vaults of central banks around the globe, and the spending they financed went into fatter GDP accounts at home. There weren't many off-sets.

Nixon famously declared himself to be a conventional Keynesian in 1971. But in striking down the international monetary discipline of the Bretton Woods system, he became much more; namely, the Keynesian god-father of the worldwide boom of the late twentieth century.

In fact, the vast new capacity of global central banks to monetize US treasury debt which inexorably evolved from Nixon's floating-dollar arrangement was laden with a supreme irony. Just one decade later it per-mitted the most conservative president in a generation to launch a deficit-financed Keynesian boom and get away with it.

GLORIOUS TO BE RICH IN CHINA AND TO BORROW MONEY IN AMERICA

The second spell of phony prosperity was also owing to Nixon's 1971 blow to global financial discipline. During Greenspan's first thirteen years at the Fed (1987–2000), the S&P 500 index rose from 300 to nearly 1,500. This hu-mongous fivefold gain has been celebrated by Republican orators as the unfolding of the Reagan prosperity, but it actually measured the arrival of central bank–driven bubble finance: a false prosperity purchased with debt, speculation, and the offshoring of the tradable goods core of the American economy.

In 1994, Deng Xiaoping, the Chinese leader who was the driving force behind his country's radical economic transformation in the late twentieth century, declared it was "glorious to be rich." His government would there-fore ensure that much glory came to the new export factories of China's Guangdong Province. To that end, the People's Printing Press of China flooded the economy with newly minted renminbi (RMB) and lowered its exchange rate against the dollar by 60 percent.

Not surprisingly, millions of Chinese teenagers, trapped in the hopeless poverty created by Mao Zedong's disastrous experiments in farm collec-tivization and backyard industrialization, flocked to Mr. Deng's bright new factories in the east. Whether they came to get rich or just eat, they consti-tuted the greatest migration of quasi-slave labor in human history.

Fueled by virtually cost-free labor, cheap capital and land, nonexistent environmental standards, and a newly trashed currency, the Chinese ex-port machine took off like a rocket. During the decade ending in the year 2000, for example, annual US imports from China rose from $5 billion to $100 billion.

More importantly, China was only the newest entrant in the convoy of East Asian nations which had learned how to peg their currencies to the floating dollar and thereby fuel a powerful new development model of export mercantilism. To spur ever rising exports of manufactures to the United States, they pegged their currencies cheap; and to keep these pegs intact, they bought and hoarded more and more US treasury bonds and bills.

This arrangement defied every tradition of sound international finance, and the harm was soon glaringly evident. During the nine years after 1991, the US trade accounts literally collapsed, with imports growing at 11 percent annually, or nearly double the gain in exports. The trade deficit thus surged from $66 billion in 1991 to $450 billion by the year 2000, thereby reaching nearly 5 percent of GDP. It was an unfathomable figure by the canons of classic finance because it was literally upside down. The reserve currency country was supposed to run a trade surplus and export capital to less developed trading partners, not incur massive deficits and drain capital from them.

By the turn of the century the United States was living far beyond its means, as measured by the cumulative trade deficit of nearly $2 trillion that had been incurred just since the 1991 recession. Under traditional fixed exchange rate discipline, the job of the central bank in these circumstances had always been to tighten money, raise interest rates, and curtail domestic demand sufficiently to eliminate the trade deficit and the associated loss of monetary reserves.

The Greenspan Fed did the just opposite, however, and thereby contradicted every gold standard speech that Alan Greenspan had ever delivered in his earlier incarnation. The result was an artificial domestic borrowing boom unprecedented in peacetime history. Between 1993 and 2001, credit market debt outstanding soared from $16 trillion to $29 trillion, representing an 8 percent annual growth rate.

Even a stable economy cannot sustain debt growth rates of that magnitude. In the 1990s, however, the US economy could not stand even a fraction of that debt growth rate because it was being battered by the greatest deflationary event in history; that is, the pegged currencies that enabled a tsunami of cheap labor and cheap manufactures out of the rice paddies of Asia.

The Fed's failure to respond appropriately to the great Asian deflation is evident in the fact that money GDP growth of $3.6 trillion during this eight-year period paled compared to the $13 trillion growth of credit market debt. In other words, there was $3.60 of debt growth for each dollar of added GDP. And it was getting worse, with credit market debt growth in 2001 alone of $2.2 trillion—6.5 times faster than money GDP.

The great prosperity celebrated in the late 1990s was thus nothing of the kind, and in fact reflected an artificial domestic demand that was bloated by the massive Greenspan debt bubble. Moreover, this artificial domestic demand generated even greater imports and trade deficits, thereby further unbalancing the national economy.

The cure for excess demand and borrowing, of course, is higher interest rates. Yet after the 1991 recession ended, the Greenspan Fed never even returned interest rates to their prerecession levels. It thereby abdicated the historic job of sound central banking—namely, to lean hard against a current account deficit by curtailing domestic demand.

By late 1998, the US economy worked up a massive head of borrowed steam, and the nearly maniacal stock market finally faltered due to the Russian default and the LTCM crisis. Yet rather than letting the bubble wash out, the Fed charged ahead in the wrong direction, pegging short-term interest rates at 4 percent, a level far lower than at the start of the cycle and an inducement for the domestic debt binge to continue. In short, the nation was already living massively beyond its means, but the Greenspan Fed kept hitting the monetary accelerator, not the brakes.

This was really nothing more than Keynesian-style monetary activism—that is, operation of the Fed's printing presses based on whatever whims struck the fancy of its twelve-person open market committee, especially its chairman.

Their fancy, of course, was to purge the business cycle of its natural oscillations and deftly manage the American economy to ever greater heights of performance and prosperity. As the nation's self-appointed central planner, the Fed saw fit to translate its vague legislative mandates to pursue full employment and price stability into an open-ended license to meddle and micromanage.

Any perceived faltering in the growth of employment and output was to be countered by toggling its monetary joystick; that is, the interest rate on federal funds. The central banking branch of the state thereby took custody of the nation's economy.

Ronald Reagan came to Washington to liberate free enterprise. The greatest irony of his presidency, therefore, is the appointment of a Fed chairman who repudiated his essential purpose by institutionalizing a statist régime through the back door of activist monetary policy.

GREENSPAN'S JUNK ECONOMICS: THE CHINA PRICE AND THE FALLACY OF THE TAYLOR RULE

The particular fancy that preoccupied the Fed chairman was that the consumer price index (CPI) trend rate of inflation dropped from around 4 percent before the 1990 recession to about 2.5 percent by the second half of the 1990s. Greenspan concluded that this was the result of a miracle of productivity and the Fed's skill at inflation fighting.

He therefore encouraged the open market committee to embrace a gussied up reincarnation of the Phillips curve trade-off between unemployment and inflation. The new monetarist variation was known as the Taylor rule, but it amounted to the same old demand-side error. It called for lower interest rates and a frothier party on Wall Street on the pretext that reduced inflation and available slack in potential output justified easier money. But this reasoning was upside down. The Taylor rule was mathematical junk posing as monetary science.

The consumer price index was rising at a slower rate not because of a miracle of domestic productivity or because the Fed had scored a roaring success in subduing domestic inflation. And most certainly it was not because the US economy was wallowing in unrealized "potential" output as fantasized by Professor Taylor, who had seen fit to name the rule in his own honor.

The downward pressure on the CPI was actually of exogenous origin. The epochal wage deflation generated by the Chinese export factories was rapidly destroying existing capacity in the American economy. This caused "potential" output to fall, not rise, as the Taylor rule enthusiasts erroneously claimed.

Indeed, the "China price" deflated the cost of both imported goods and import-competitive domestic manufactures so sharply that the average US price level should have actually been declining, not just rising less rapidly. Yet that did not happen. From December 1990 to December 2000 the average annual CPI increase was 2.7 percent, and exceeded 3 percent during the final two years.

Domestic price gains of nearly 3 percent annually were perverse because they thwarted the needed downward adjustment of domestic wages and production costs, an adjustment essential to preserving competitiveness and jobs. Moreover, monetary pass-through of the Asian deflation would have stretched the domestic buying power of nominal wages and bolstered real living standards.

Instead, the Fed showered the American economy with cheap debt, which amounted to a policy of fostering more consumption and less production. It also meant that the CPI index vaulted higher by 30 percent during the decade while employee compensation per hour rose by 35 percent. American workers thus barely kept up with the cost of living, even as they priced themselves out of the world market.

So the Fed's claim of taming inflation during the 1990s was valid arithmetically but was not benign economically. It drastically widened the nominal wage gap with Mr. Deng's new export factories, paving the way for an even higher tide of imported manufactures and even more extensive destruction of the US production and employment base.

In short, Mr. Deng's "glorious to be rich" proclamation signaled the onset of a vast and powerful tide of global deflation in wages and prices. But the Greenspan Fed blew it. Rather than allowing the US economy to harvest the living standard gains of deflation and to adjust to the pains of falling nominal wages and profits, it declared a debt party.

THE FED'S $13 TRILLION DEBT PARTY

The 1990s American economy could ill afford to take on more debt and raise the leverage burden on national income. In fact, its capacity to generate income was declining on a permanent basis in the face of the Asian deluge, meaning that the Fed's policy of fostering massive growth of domestic debt was profoundly mistaken. Indeed, the Fed effectively took itself hostage. It required more and more credit-fueled consumption spending to make up for production and income which was being lost to the Asian export machine. Bubble finance became a substitute for real income and productivity.

The Fed's $13 trillion credit bubble during 1993–2001 also caused a phony boom on Wall Street. The soaring stock averages at the end of the decade in part reflected a near tripling of the valuation multiple (price-to-earnings [PE] ratio) on corporate earnings per share (EPS). This virtually unprecedented expansion of PE ratios implied that the growth potential of the US economy was accelerating.

In fact, it was being badly eroded by soaring debt at home and the explosive growth of manufacturing capacity among the currency-pegging export mercantilists of East Asia. These fundamental forces of economic decay were obscured by the celebration of the tech revolution and the stock market bubble which supposedly reflected it.

What was actually happening, however, was far less benign. Corporate earnings were rising moderately, but mainly on account of consumer spending gains fueled by easy credit and the gathering mortgage debt–driven boom in both commercial and residential real estate.

Likewise, the ready availability of debt financing for corporate takeovers, leveraged buyouts, and share buybacks jigged-up earnings per share as documented more fully in chapters 21 and 22. And as the Fed pushed interest rates ever lower, the so-called cap rate on real estate and other financial assets fell, generating even higher asset prices and feeding speculative appetites still further.

Indeed, the Fed's low interest rate policy caused the price of American labor to become richer relative to Asia while the price of debt became cheaper relative to income. Accordingly, spurred on by Wall Street demands for higher EPS, corporate America soon undertook vast strip-mining operations designed to extract labor costs from the profit and loss accounts during the current quarter, while funding the resulting severance and restructuring costs over many future years out of cheap borrowed funds.

Not surprisingly, business debt soared as companies borrowed money to buy back shares, take over competitors, and buy out workers. Between 1993 and 2001 nonfinancial business debt outstanding increased by nearly 100 percent, rising from $3.5 trillion to $6.8 trillion. Pretax business income only grew by 50 percent, however, meaning that business leverage ratios were steadily rising.

The Fed ignored this evidence of weakening economic fundamentals, too. Instead, it claimed credit for a stock market boom that was in very large part fueled by the giant debt bubble and trade deficits that its own misguided policies had triggered.

At the end of the day, the Fed's Wall Street–coddling monetary policies of the 1990s masked the grave threat to the American economy that was incubating in East Asia. It is ironic in the extreme, therefore, that the credit-based boom in consumption and financial speculation that was engineered by the Greenspan Fed has been touted as evidence of the success of the Reagan Revolution's supply-side policies.

In fact, the Keynesian boom of the 1980s and the money-printing bubble of the 1990s were anti–supply side. Two decades of exporting US treasury debt and fiat dollars was generating damaging economic blowback aimed at the very heart of the economy's actual capacity to produce output and jobs.

On the evidence, it was clear at the dawn of the twenty-first century that the great Asian export machine far outranked every other cost-reducing invention in recorded history. It bested the Internet, Wal-Mart, numerically controlled machine tools, Henry Ford's assembly line, central station electric power, the railroads, steam engine, spinning jenny, and possibly even the wheel.

And the main implication was that American production, jobs, and incomes were at risk. Under the established régime of free trade, domestic jobs and incomes could be maintained only if cost and wage levels were adjusted downward to meet the powerful deflationary challenge of the Asian exporters.

Under these conditions, the very last thing the American economy needed was lower interest rates and rapid household credit expansion.

This invited domestic households to load up with far more debt relative to income than ever before imagined. The household debt-to-GDP ratio, in fact, climbed steadily for three decades, rising from a historic norm of about 45 percent in 1975 to upward of 100 percent after the turn of the century.

At the same time, artificially bloated consumption spending was only partially captured by domestic suppliers of goods and services. On the margin, a rising share of the demand for consumer goods went straight to low-priced foreign suppliers, especially to Mr. Deng's "China price" factories.

The implication was straightforward. In the face of the great Asian export machine, the wage prospects of Main Street households were being impaired and their debt-carrying capacity was being rapidly eroded.

Under these conditions, the Fed should have pushed interest rates far higher to encourage savings and a reduction of household debt, not enabled a spectacular accumulation of even more borrowings. But the Fed was lost in its growth triumphalism and pseudoscientific policy rules.

So at the very worst time possible in the cycle of modern economic history, the nation's central bank enabled households to bury themselves in mortgage and credit card debt. It thereby pushed the production versus consumption imbalance of the national economy to even more perilous extremes.

The 1990s boom, therefore, was not the productivity and technology driven breakout of growth and prosperity that is was cracked up to be. Instead, it was rooted in a massive credit bubble, which masked deep structural challenges to the production, jobs, and income base of the US economy.

THE ANTI-SUPPLY-SIDE PROSPERITY OF 2002–2007

When the dot-com bubble burst and the mild recession of 2001 ensued, the Fed elected to juice the American economy with still another round of rock-bottom interest rates. Washington reciprocated with even more adventures in fiscal profligacy. But this time there was no way to hide the fact that the resulting cyclical rebound, as measured by the modest uptick in the GDP accounts and nonfarm payrolls during 2002–2007, was an unsustainable facade of prosperity.

More than four years after the meltdown on Wall Street, the hard economic data shows that the US economy has actually been stalled out for a decade. During the twelve years ending in December 2012, real investment in business fixed capital grew at only a microscopic 0.8 percent annual rate.

That is not supply-side prosperity by any stretch of the imagination, since failure to invest in productive capacity quashes future growth in GDP and living standards. In fact, real GDP growth has averaged only 1.7 percent during the same twelve-year period, and even that meager growth number would have been zero, or even negative, if inflation were calculated honestly.

Similarly, the September 2012 nonfarm payroll count was 133.5 million jobs, virtually the same number of nationwide jobs reported in late 2000. Of greater concern, the count of full-time breadwinner jobs stands at about 66 million, or nearly 10 percent below its level at the turn of the century. Manufacturing output is not much higher than it was in February 2000.

So the Reagan Revolution did not engender a supply-side miracle, nor cause any improvement in the trend of macroeconomic performance. Its legacy has been obscured by serial policy-induced growth bubbles: the Keynesian deficit boom of 1983–1992, the Greenspan domestic credit and stock market bubble of 1993–2000, and the giant housing and consumption boom spurred by the Fed's absurdly low interest-rate policies after the minor 2001 recession.

All of this came to a thundering collapse in autumn 2008 when the nation's multi-decade debt binge hit its natural limits and the massive imbalances between production and consumption and between exports and imports reached unsustainable extremes. Yet the Reagan Revolution's apologists have never even attempted to explain this dire turn of events, save for blaming the Obama administration for making even worse the economic debacle it found on its doorstep.

Nevertheless, when the false narrative of macroeconomic prosperity is stripped away, what remains is the real story of the Reagan era: how the nation's conservative party fostered the great fiscal breakdown now upon the land, and got away with it by pretending that the money printers it appointed to the Fed were fostering honest prosperity.

The whole narrative was wrong. Reaching back to the time of Reagan, it can be shown that fiscal discipline was destroyed first by the "neocons" who coddled the warfare state in pursuit of national security illusions; and then by the "tax-cons" who dismantled Uncle Sam's revenue base in the name of supply-side doctrine; and finally by the "just-cons," the rank-and-file Republicans who fulminated against Big Government but cowered continuously before the assembled lobbies of the welfare state.

WHY THE RISING TIDE LIFTED VERY FEW BOATS

Nor was fiscal discipline the only casualty of the Reagan Revolution's failures and deformations. The supply-side vision had also foreseen a rising tide lifting all boats, but the last three decades have brought the opposite: economic stagnation to the middle class and a veritable cornucopia of wealth gains and opulence to the top of the economic ladder.

In fact, the current $50,000 median household income has grown by only 0.3 percent annually after adjustment for inflation during the last thirty years, while real hourly wage rates are actually lower. Indeed, the average real wage rate of workers entering the labor force with a high school education has declined 25 percent since 1979, and has remained stagnant even for college-educated entrants.

So the answer after three decades to the fabled question of the 1980 Reagan campaign—Are you better off?—would be quite clear for the broad middle class: not so much.

Indeed, it is in the nature of financial bubbles based on leverage and speculation to deposit a large share of the winnings at the top of the economic ladder. Not surprisingly, the share of net worth held by the top 1 percent of households has risen from 20 percent to 35 percent since 1979 while their share of income has doubled to 25 percent.

When measured by the net worth aggregates reported by the Federal Reserve, the skew toward the top comes into even more dramatic focus. The top 5 percent of households currently hold about $40 trillion in net worth—a $32 trillion gain over the $8 trillion they held in 1985.

By contrast, the net worth of the bottom 95 percent of households at year-end 2011 was just $8 trillion higher than a quarter century back. The top 5 percent have thus gained four times more than the bottom 95 percent.

The rising tide envisioned by the Reagan Revolution was based on the expected societal gain from free market capitalism and the sustainable increases in productivity, output, and real wealth which it generates. In a healthy capitalist economy income distribution reflects the economic justice of the marketplace, not the political engineering of the state, and properly so.

Much of the wealth gain of the last three decades, however, was not the fruit of the free market. As will be seen in part IV, it originated instead in the financial and real estate bubbles which were generated by the profligate borrowing of the state and the money-printing spree of its central banking branch.

The intense political debate surrounding the nation's current palpable misdistribution of wealth—the "class war" issue of the 2012 campaign—is thus deeply ironic. The deformations of sound money brought on by Nixon and Reagan sowed the seeds of these untoward results. Yet it is the very free market that their policies betrayed which now collects the blame.

It goes without saying that the boundaries of the state did not recede, as the Reagan Revolution intended. In both its welfare state and warfare state dimensions, government has become ever more corpulent, even as the tax burden imposed to finance has been repeatedly lightened. Indeed, the Reagan campaign promise that the unstable, stagflationary economy of 1980 would be rebuilt on a foundation of sound money and financial integrity has been roundly repudiated by thirty years of history.

The hallmark of the past several decades has been a debilitating expansion of household and business debt burdens. Indeed, the nation undertook an international borrowing spree that permitted Americans to consume a staggering $8 trillion more than they produced over the past thirty years.

These deformations of the Reagan Revolution were, to some degree, implicit in the errors, contradictions, and confusions of the policy playbook itself. On the surface, its core ideas were a seductive alternative to the failed "tax, spend, regulate, inflate" paradigm that defined national policy from the Johnson administration through those of Nixon, Ford, and Carter.

But once placed on the anvil of governance, the Reagan Revolution fared little better. It eventually proved itself to be a campaign slogan, not a rigorous policy agenda. More importantly, the Republican Party has proven decade after decade since Reagan's time that the small-government principles of his patented speech were intended to be recited often and loudly but honored only in the breach.

CHAPTER 5

TRIUMPH OF
THE WARFARE STATE
How the Budget Battle Was Lost

RIOTOUS EXPANSION OF THE WARFARE STATE WAS FOREMOST among the policy errors of the Reagan Revolution. Within days of Reagan's taking office, the White House made a historically devastating mistake by signing over to the Pentagon a blank check known as the "7 percent real growth top line."

This massive injection of fiscal firepower nearly tripled the annual defense budget from $140 billion to $370 billion within just six years. More importantly, it fueled powerful expansionist impulses throughout the military-industrial complex at exactly the wrong time in history.

THE SOVIET NUCLEAR WAR FIGHTING STRATEGY—
A NEOCON STRAWMAN

The decrepit Soviet economy was descending into terminal decline by the early 1980s. While there were clues and signs everywhere of Soviet industrial decay, the neocon branch of the military-industrial complex trumpeted a new version of the phony missile gap that John Kennedy had promoted during the 1960 campaign.

But the neoconservative version of the alleged "gap" in military capabilities was portrayed as pervasive, ominous, and intensifying. The Soviet Union was hell-bent on acquiring nuclear war–winning capabilities; that is, a first-strike capacity to disable much of the US nuclear deterrent. That was coupled with an alleged massive civil defense system designed to survive any retaliatory strike, even if the Soviets absorbed 25 million casualties or more.

These threatening strategic nuclear capabilities were alleged to include an entirely new fleet of modern heavy bombers and a drastic increase in the scale and accuracy of its MIRVed strategic missiles. Beyond that the

Soviets were purportedly fielding a whole new force of mobile ICBMs and a dramatic expansion of their advanced nuclear attack submarine fleet.

Every facet of this hydra-headed threat elicited demands for new US weapons while the scary neocon narrative about a Kremlin bent on world conquest reignited cold war fears throughout Washington. The consequent drumbeat for rearmament propelled the Reagan defense plan. But, alas, it was all rooted in a monumental confluence of error.

In truth, this Soviet nuclear war–fighting strategy never really existed. Moreover, the huge US military buildup mounted to counter it allocated almost nothing to strategic weapons and countermeasures. Instead, the Pentagon poured hundreds of billions into equipping and training a vast conventional armada: land, sea, and air forces that were utterly irrelevant to the imaginary Soviet nuclear first strike.

Ironically, the Reagan conventional force buildup was still cresting when Boris Yeltsin, vodka flask in hand, mounted a tank and stood down the enfeebled Red Army. Future presidents were thus equipped to launch needless wars of invasion and occupation, mainly because owing to the Reagan armada they could.

THE GREAT DISCONNECT:
THE $1.5 TRILLION PENTAGON WINDFALL

The Reagan defense buildup was fraught with budgetary confusion and disconnects from the very beginning. The quantum jump in five-year defense spending from the 7 percent top-line plan was not based on one scintilla of bottoms-up program detail or even a single hour of professional analysis. It stemmed from a comedy of errors within days of Reagan's inauguration.

It started with candidate Reagan's September 1980 "Chicago speech" which outlined a comprehensive economic and budget program, including a promise of 5 percent annual real growth in defense. However, that figure had not been blessed by the campaign's coterie of neocon advisors led by super-hawk Senator John Tower, who wanted 8–9 percent increases. Instead, the 5 percent growth figure had simply been shoehorned into the plan by Reagan's chief economic advisors—Alan Greenspan and Marty Anderson. It had been designed to show that the numbers weren't impossible—that is, the nation could have a sweeping across-the-board tax cut, a major military build-up, and a balanced budget, too, and all by 1983.

A new administration would normally resolve deep military spending differences through several months of analysis by expert task forces focused on threat assessments and budget resource trade-offs. On the eve of the inauguration, however, two developments conspired to eliminate this rational course of action entirely.

First, the Carter administration had been harshly attacked during the campaign for "gutting" national security, but now its outgoing budget plan proposed to increase real defense spending by 5 percent annually. That eliminated on the spot any willingness by the Reagan White House to adhere to its own Chicago speech growth rate.

Even more importantly, the new administration promised to deliver a comprehensive economic recovery program and five-year fiscal plan by February 18. That meant that it had less than four weeks to essentially redo the entire federal budget.

With no time to develop any bottoms-up defense plan, we resorted to a primitive expedient; namely, a single "placeholder" number for total defense spending for each year of our five-year fiscal plan. The numbers were agreed on during a half-hour meeting at the Pentagon ten days after the inauguration.

From a national security perspective, these five magic numbers were virtually content free. Indeed, the two principals at this four-person meeting, the new secretary of defense and the budget director, knew almost nothing about defense. By the same token, their two neocon deputies, who had already agreed upon the outcome, maintained a discreet conspiracy of silence.

In truth, the very purpose of the meeting, to get a defense top line, was an insult to expertise. There were "no charts, no computer printouts, no color slides, and no colonels with six-foot wooden pointers." The only implements on the table were "a Hewlett Packard pocket calculator and a blank piece of paper."

Defense Secretary Caspar Weinberger, who had not even studied his defense brief, observed that Carter's 5 percent growth plan wouldn't do and that the 8–9 percent demanded by the Tower group was probably too much. Accordingly, he proposed 7 percent. I made a few taps on the Hewlett Packard keypad. The largest five-year defense plan in recorded history was thus agreed upon.

But that wasn't all. The defense budget was in a state of turmoil and rising rapidly owing to continuous add-ons and supplementals. After the hostage rescue fiasco in Iran, sentiment on Capitol Hill intensified in favor of strengthening the military, and the Republicans' hawkish campaign rhetoric about the Soviet threat added further impetus.

In this context, the fiscal 1980 budget of $142 billion had been the piñata attacked by Republicans during the election campaign as evidence of the Carter administration's failed national security policies. Crucially, it had also been used as the starting point for the 5 percent defense growth commitment in the Chicago speech.

In the interim, however, the defense committees first increased Carter's fiscal 1981 budget to $170 billion, and then raised it further to more than $180 billion via mid-year supplemental appropriations. The lame duck Defense Department further ratcheted up the numbers, raising its request for fiscal 1982 to $205 billion.

Even this bloated figure was found to be woefully inadequate by the neocons. So Senator Tower secured a pledge from the White House, even before Reagan took office, for a military pay raise and other operations-type add-ons in what was called a "get well" supplemental. Another $17 billion was thereby added.

When the dust finally settled, the fiscal 1982 defense budget stood at $222 billion—a figure nearly 60 percent larger than the $142 billion piñata that had been so roundly attacked during the campaign. Yet it was from this vastly elevated prospective budget for 1982, not the allegedly deficient actual 1980 spending level, that the annual growth rate calculation was applied.

In the flash of an eye, therefore, the laws of compound arithmetic joined hands with the raw power of the military-industrial complex. The result was a lunatic miscarriage of governance.

Given the inflation assumptions used at the time, the Chicago speech plan of 5 percent real growth would have resulted in a fiscal 1986 defense budget of about $250 billion. But based on 7 percent real growth and the much higher starting point, there was a stunning new number: projected defense spending of nearly $370 billion for fiscal 1986.

In short, before even one dime of domestic spending had been cut, to say nothing of the promised massive tax reductions, the out-year defense budget was 50 percent bigger than had been previously assumed. The fiscal math of the Chicago speech, the only attempt that the Reagan campaign had ever made to reconcile the candidate's warring fiscal objectives, was now on the scrap heap.

I was dumbfounded when I learned about this calamitous result a few days later. The Pentagon's runaway top line amounted to nearly $1.46 trillion over 1982–1986. It was greater than Jimmy Carter's entire federal budget for the previous three years combined, including defense, interest, Social Security, the medical entitlements, the safety net, the national park service, and the tea tasters' board, too.

It all seemed so outlandish. In fact, I was certain the numbers would be scaled back at a later date when a conventional bottoms-up defense plan had been developed. Under the heading of wishful thinking, however, that turned out to be an entry for the ages.

THE DOD SPENDING STAMPEDE

No fresh start or strategically coherent defense plan was ever developed by the Reagan administration. This immense, content-free "top line" was simply backfilled by the greatest stampede of Pentagon log-rolling and budget aggrandizement by the military-industrial complex ever recorded.

In a process that went on week after week for the better part of a year, the huge swaths of empty budget space under the new defense "top line" were converted into more and more of virtually everything that inhabited the Pentagon's vasty deep. Much of it, which had languished for years and decades on the wish lists of the brass and the military contractors, now got funded without much ado.

With defense funds being virtually slopped onto the waiting plates of the four military services, it is not surprising that much of it went to the conventional forces. Notwithstanding all the scary stories about the nascent Soviet nuclear first-strike capabilities, there really weren't many concrete programs to counter it except for a new strategic bomber and an MX missile upgrade.

At the heart of the Reagan defense buildup, therefore, was a great double shuffle. The war drums were sounding a strategic nuclear threat that virtually imperiled American civilization. Yet the money was actually being allocated to tanks, amphibious landing craft, close air support helicopters, and a vast conventional armada of ships and planes.

These weapons were of little use in the existing nuclear standoff, but were well suited to imperialistic missions of invasion and occupation. Ironically, therefore, the Reagan defense buildup was justified by an Evil Empire that was rapidly fading but was eventually used to launch elective wars against an Axis of Evil which didn't even exist.

Among the costly programs which had precious little to do with the alleged strategic nuclear threat was the fabled six-hundred-ship navy. The latter entailed hundreds of billions in new procurement for mostly surface ships and carrier battle groups. These vast iron flotillas had no role whatsoever against a Soviet first strike, save perhaps to burn the last candles for civilization after it was over.

Likewise, hundreds of billions more were absorbed by conventional land and air forces, including 13,000 new main battle tanks and Bradley fighting vehicles. Over the next decade the Reagan buildup also funded about 18,000 new tactical aircraft and helicopters, and hundreds of thousands of cruise missile and guided munitions.

During the first year or two, however, even the Pentagon could not spend money on big-ticket items fast enough to consume all the top-line dollars. So the military services launched a once-in-a-lifetime shopping spree for spare parts, ammo, tools and equipment, electronic components, and every other kind of material on their stock lists. Spending for some items grew by 50 percent annually for several years.

By contrast, only a tiny fraction of this $1.46 trillion defense bonanza actually went into strategic nuclear procurement. For example, about $30 billion—or 2 percent of the total—went to the B-1 bomber, which was based on obsolete pre-stealth technology. Ironically, the last batch of the 100 B-1 bombers was delivered in May 1988—six months before the Velvet Revolution in Prague triggered a swift end to the rickety Soviet empire.

What actually kept the Soviets at bay was the retaliatory desolation that the thousands of submarine based Trident missile warheads would rain down upon its cities, along with an equal number of independently tar-geted warheads launched from land-based minuteman ICBMs. The Soviets had no defense against these land- and sea-based retaliatory forces and had no prospect of developing one.

This deterrent force was what actually kept the nation safe and had been fully in place for years. American nuclear security in 1981 required hardly an incremental dime of expenditure—and certainly not the $20 billion MX "peacekeeper" missile, which was an offensive weapon that undermined deterrence and wasn't actually deployed until the Cold War was nearly over.

Indeed, virtually none of the Reagan defense build-up impacted the strategic nuclear equation. The tried-and-true doctrine of mutual assured destruction (MAD), based on 656 Polaris submarine missiles and 1,054 Minuteman ICBMs already bought and paid for, kept the nuclear peace until the last day of the Soviet Union in 1991.

So the idea that the Reagan defense buildup somehow spent the Soviet Union into collapse is a legend of remarkable untruth. The preexisting nuclear balance of terror never really changed during the 1980s, and the United States spent no serious money to threaten the Evil Empire. The Soviet leadership did end up feeling beleaguered and imperiled, but it was due to the epochal economic failure of an ossified state socialism, not the new US armada of conventional ships, tanks, and planes.

Indeed, the original notion that the Soviet Union was bent on develop-ing global military superiority and nuclear war–winning capability was never plausible. Even at the time, there was no evidence to support it, and it was embraced by no more than a tiny but vocal minority of the national security community.

The now open Soviet archives also prove there never was a Soviet defense-spending offensive. By the early 1980s Soviet military outlays were growing at only 1–2 percent per year, and even that figure was based on the dubious statistics of a command economy which was falling apart.

On the scary weapons front, the Soviets' heavy fixed-silo ICBMs turned out to be far less accurate than claimed, meaning they were never close to being the deadly first-strike weapons the neocons had ballyhooed. The new mobile ICBMs were not accurate enough to function as first-strike weapons, either.

Nor was there any heavy long-range bomber program—only an intermediate range aircraft that could not have actually threatened North American sites. Likewise, there was no massive civil defense program, just a mishmash of disorganized and poorly resourced local boondoggles.

In short, the neocon case against MAD was based mostly on fantasy. The Soviet leadership was not prepared to launch a world-ending first strike because it did not even remotely have the capabilities to do it, even if it had succumbed to suicidal impulses.

The far more relevant truth, which had been evident to free market libertarians all along, was that the Soviet economy was on an inexorable path toward failure. This militated heavily against the prospect that it could have initiated a nuclear war–winning strategy or carried out significant conventional force aggression beyond its own border regions, such as the morass it sunk into in Afghanistan.

Had the United States simply gotten a massive defense buildup that it didn't need, there might have been no lasting impact save for a modest waste of resources; perhaps a few percentage points of GDP. In fact, however, the Reagan defense buildup gave birth to a historical monstrosity: the Bush wars of occupation and imperial pretension that were possible only because of the immense conventional war machine the Gipper left behind.

THE ACTUAL REAGAN BUILDUP:
RISE OF THE AMERICAN IMPERIAL ARMADA

What got built with the $1.46 trillion Reagan budget was a conventional war-making capacity and force projection ability that the only military expert to occupy the White House in the twentieth century, Dwight Eisenhower, had rejected as of marginal value against a nuclear adversary. The fiasco in Vietnam had already proven him correct, demonstrating painfully and tragically that massive conventional forces cannot successfully occupy, pacify, and rebuild third-world nations of the unwilling.

Yet that's exactly what the Reagan top line bought: an occupation force which would have left General Eisenhower rolling in his grave. At the center were fifteen naval carrier battle groups armed to the teeth with attack aircraft, helicopters, cruise missiles, amphibious landing craft, and vast suites of communications and electronic warfare gear. Indeed, the standard aircraft carrier was accompanied by a fleet of eighty aircraft and a dozen escort ships, the equivalent of the entire military establishment of all except a handful of nations.

It is these nuclear carrier battle groups which gave US policy makers their striking imperial arrogance. An example of how these platforms were suited to imperial power projection, not anti-Soviet defense, is the sea-based Tomahawk cruise missile force.

The rise of Tomahawk force began in 1983 during the Reagan buildup, but the demise of the Evil Empire did not slow down its development one bit. By the end of the century the United States had about 150 surface ships and attack submarines that could launch these deadly cruise missiles and an inventory of nearly 5,000 missiles.

Tomahawks have a range of seven hundred miles. This means that from their offshore platforms they can reach three-fourths of the world's population. And during the last two decades they have been used in just this "stand-off" manner against targets in Iraq, Bosnia, Afghanistan, Sudan, Libya, and others—teaching presidents that they could meddle freely without getting bloodied.

The Reagan defense buildup also provided cover for a vast renewal of conventional fixed-wing and helicopter forces, a binge of procurement that had no peacetime precedent. During the eight Reagan years, the Pentagon was authorized to purchase nearly 9,000 planes and helicopters compared to only 3,000 during the previous eight years.

This profoundly wasteful binge was predicated on the specious notion that the Soviets were fixing to launch a suicidal conventional land war in Europe. Yet even then the Red Army was proving every day that it couldn't subdue RPG-toting tribesmen in the barren expanse of the Hindu Kush. Moreover, when the Soviet Union disappeared in 1991 high rates of aircraft procurement continued unabated: Congressmen had no trouble seeing them as "jobs" programs, even if Eastern Europe was now being rapidly occupied by Burger Kings and Pizza Huts.

The Reagan buildup thus bequeathed national security policy makers approximately 13,000 fixed-wing aircraft and helicopters. Except for 20 B-2 stealth bombers this giant inventory was designed for conventional war-making and power projection on distant shores, including 4,000 conventional attack and fighter aircraft and more than 5,000 helicopters whose mission was conventional battlefield support in an attack, transport, or utility role.

The two big land war programs launched during the Reagan build-up—the upgraded Abrams Tank and the Bradley Fighting Vehicle—experienced a similar untoward evolution. At the time of the Reagan top line windfall in 1981, there was ferocious debate among the experts as to whether a new, more expensive generation of the M1 tank should be developed.

Yet issues of cost and efficacy were no longer even debatable after the 7 percent growth top line became operative on January 30, 1981. The empty space in DOD's new $1.46 trillion plan was so vast that both programs were sucked into its budget like air rushing into a vacuum. Over the next decade 7,000 Bradley's and 6,000 M1 Abrams tanks were procured—useless weapons against a Soviet nuclear strike, but ideal for missions of invasion and occupation.

Moreover, once the Bradley and Abrams production lines were open, the odds of closing them down were between slim and none. Armored battle-field vehicles consist of an intensive mix of iron, precision machining, and complex electronic components and circuitry—which is to say, they are a "jobs program" par excellence.

The case in point can be seen in Lima, Ohio, where the M1 tank line re-fuses to shut down—40 years after the 7 percent top line brought it unnec-essarily to life. Since then all of the nation's industrial enemies have either expired, as in the case of the Soviets, or retired to civilian life, as in the case of China.

What passes for a state-based enemy is a nation of 78 million deeply un-happy citizens ruled by twelfth-century mullahs, whose major act of aggres-sion over the past thirty years was to repel an attack by its Iraqi neighbor with twelve-year-old soldiers carrying stick rifles. Still, the military-industrial complex manages to keep retooling, upgrading, and modernizing its fleet of 9,000 Abrams tanks as if the Berlin crisis of 1961 never ended.

When all is said and done, the accidental and unnecessary 7 percent top line of January 1981 gave birth to a vast imperial expeditionary force and conventional war-fighting machine. Yet after the Velvet Revolution of De-cember 1988, it inhabited a world that had no need for imperial expedi-tions or industrial-strength conventional wars.

THE PERSIAN GULF: PROVING GROUND
FOR THE REAGAN ARMADA

The remains of the Soviet empire soon settled into a handful of kleptocra-cies, Europe adverted to welfare-state senescence, and Red China mor-phed into the sneakers and Apple factory of the world. In short, there remained no place for a great expeditionary force to operate, save for the littoral states of the Middle East.

The latter, unhappily, provided the ideal venue. After the fall of the Berlin Wall, the six-hundred-ship navy began to steadily loose girth, but its capacity to rain destruction on the lands ringing the Persian Gulf from a standoff platform in the deep water could not be gainsaid.

Likewise, the helicopter fleets, the close air support and attack aircraft wings, the fighter-bomber forces, and the raft of tactical missiles and smart munitions all proved suited for occupying the Middle Eastern lands of the unwilling and mostly unarmed. Nor could the vast open deserts and the crumbling mud and stone walls of its towns and villages have provided a more conducive proving ground for Abrams tanks and Bradley fighting vehicles.

The only thing missing was any plausible and justifiable reason of state for the deployment of this accidental expeditionary force to the desolate hills and mountains of Afghanistan, the bloody plains of the Tigris-Euphrates, or even the empty, scorpion-ridden dunes of Kuwait. None of this made oil any cheaper, even if that were a valid reason of state, which it is not.

By the Pentagon's own reckoning there were never more than a few hundred Al-Qaeda members in Afghanistan. There should have been no surprise, therefore, when the holy warrior himself was found to have been holed up for six years in a farmhouse with three wives, six children, and a dozen goats. Above all else, Bin Laden's final demise proved that it takes a few bundles of greenbacks, not an expeditionary army, to hunt down such terrorists as actually exist.

There can be little doubt, therefore, that George W. Bush, and his father before him, carried out their imperial adventures in the lands ringing the Persian Gulf because they could. An accident of history had bestowed upon them a massive conventional war-fighting machine, so they went to war without having to prove the case or raise an army by taxing the people and getting a declaration of Congress.

That much is plainly evident from the outcomes. What valid domestic security reason, for instance, can distinguish between the corrupt, violent Afghan warlords still on our payroll ten years later and the equally venal tribal chieftains for whom the bloody terror of the Taliban is a way of life.

Likewise, Iraq now consists of three principalities of corruption and thuggery rather than just one. Yet neither the old régime nor the new régimes did have or will have any bearing on the well-being of the American public.

The same is true of Kuwait next door. From the viewpoint of the true national interest the only difference between the Emir Al-Sabah IV and Saddam Hussein is that the latter is dead, having been on the wrong side of an ancient border dispute that was none of our business in the first place.

George W. Bush was appropriately castigated for landing on the deck of an aircraft carrier and declaring victory after great swaths of the ancient city of Baghdad had been reduced to rubble in only a few weeks. But that was not proof of victory at all, just evidence that wanton destruction could be rained on any city located within a thousand miles of the very aircraft carrier on which the forty-third president stood.

THE WARFARE STATE'S 1981 TIPPING POINT: ALMOST GONE, UNNECESSARILY REVIVED

At the dawn of the 1980s, the Soviet empire was dying under the weight of its statist economic yoke; its militarized "state-within-the-state" was sucking the larger society dry. What the United States needed to do at that juncture was to wait it out—safe behind an ample strategic retaliatory force of Minutemen missiles and Trident submarines. That this more benign course—upon which history had already firmly embarked—was denied at the eleventh hour can be blamed on the neocons primarily.

Yet they prevailed only because they had a powerful assist from the willful obstinacy of two men—Caspar Weinberger and Ronald Reagan. Of the two, Weinberger is by far the more culpable.

During his twenty years holding high positions in Washington, Weinberger gained a reputation as a conservative ideologue, but it wasn't warranted. Weinberger was actually an ersatz statist—a relentless solicitor for whatever branch of the state he was currently heading. His calling card read: "have brief, won't bend."

During his time at the Federal Trade Commission he was an enthusiastic regulator. At Nixon's White House budget office, he became "Cap the Knife." During his stint as Secretary of HEW in 1973–1975, its budget grew by 45 percent—the greatest two-year surge in social spending recorded at any time before or since.

Within ten days of assuming his brief at the Defense Department, the "top line" blanks were filled in and thereafter Weinberger's lawyerly summation never changed: 7 percent defense growth was held to be a first principle, meaning no debate was needed and no deviation was even thinkable.

And so the Secretary of Defense clung to every single dime of the $1.46 trillion—obstinately, dogmatically, indefatigably. A crucial episode in March 1983 illuminates how Weinberger's dogged adherence to the 7 percent top line unnaturally extended the Pentagon's bonanza.

At that point the fiscal equation had hemorrhaged, causing the deficit for the year underway—fiscal 1983—to reach nearly $210 billion or more than 6 percent of GDP. There had never been a deficit remotely that large since the Second World War, so the alarm bells were ringing loudly.

That was especially the case among the Republican mainstream leadership on Capitol Hill, which hadn't been all that enthusiastic about the Reagan Revolution from the beginning. Worse, the President's recently submitted budget for fiscal 1984 was a calamity—calling for $200 billion annual deficits as far as the eye could see, or what amounted to $1 trillion of planned borrowing over the five-year fiscal horizon.

The generation of Republican Congressional leaders then in power still respected the old-time religion of fiscal discipline. They had therefore been horrified by where the President's budget was taking them.

By early that spring, however, the Republican congressional leadership had broken ranks with the White House—at least in the privacy of their cloakroom. The Senate Republicans led by Majority Leader Howard Baker and budget chairman Pete Domenici had hammered out a courageous plan to reduce the out-year deficit by $100 billion annually.

The Baker plan involved real stuff including social security cuts and other entitlement reforms, big reductions in pork barrel spending, and a moderate allowance for further revenue increases beyond the large package of loophole closers that the President had signed into law the previous fall.

But the vital glue which held it together was a 5 percent annual real growth cap on defense spending—that is, just a breather after three years of massive DOD increases. Yet the obstinacy emanating from the big office in the Pentagon knew no bounds. Weinberger portrayed the Senate Republican plan as a grave threat to national security even though real defense spending had already increased by 12 percent each in 1981 and 1982 and by a further 8 percent in 1983—for a total gain of 35 percent. Telling the Republican leadership to take a hike, he then insisted on every dime of the President's budget for 1984, which called for another huge increase of 11 percent after inflation.

Given their fears of the ballooning budget deficits and the political pain implicit in the sweeping domestic cuts they were about to embrace, the idea of permanent double-digit real growth in defense spending was not something that the Senate Republican elders could abide; it made them sputter in disbelief. They saw red, the more Weinberger insisted on it.

Howard Baker thus made one last effort to compromise, proposing real dollar percentage increases of 7.5, 7.0 and 6.0 for the next three years, respectively. Weinberger still refused to yield, and in this intransigence there was irony wrapped in the unconscionable.

Reagan had signed a tax increase bill in August 1982 only on the basis that there would be three dollars of spending cuts for each dollar of taxes.

But included in those spending cuts was $50 billion of defense savings over three years—cuts which had been forgotten by the Pentagon even before the ink on the deal was dry and which had been totally ignored in the President's current budget.

As it happened, Howard Baker's last ditch compromise on the fiscal 1984 budget would have resulted in a $50 billion defense savings over the first three years—that is, the Senate Republicans were willing to settle for "used cuts." Out of a desperate desire to accommodate the White House, the same savings they had extracted in the previous budget cycle would be counted again.

When Weinberger refused to accept even this fig leaf of compromise, the clock finally ran out. The Senate Republicans went their own way, and after that there was no possibility of a comprehensive mid-course correction of the nation's fiscal policy mess, nor any basis for an intelligent and orderly retrenchment of the runaway defense budget.

Yet that wasn't the end of this particular folly. After the economy recovered Reagan took to lamenting the 1982 tax increase deal on the grounds that he had been hoodwinked on the three-for-one spending cut promise. In fact, the primary shortfall from the spending cuts Congress had promised him was the $50 billion in defense savings. So the President had indeed been hoodwinked, and by his own Secretary of Defense.

Nor was this the first time. Weinberger had been misleading the President from Day One—albeit not by means of deliberate untruths with respect to the facts. The larger deception was that Weinberger was not who Reagan thought he was—that is, he was not Cap the Knife.

Clinging to his defense brief with monomaniacal purpose, Weinberger cared not at all about the things a renowned advocate of stinginess in government might have pursued. Running a tight ship was not part of his modus operandi, nor was rooting out waste and duplication, asking hard questions about weapons systems, or looking for ways to accomplish missions at lower cost.

Weinberger thereby denied the President of the United States the honest services expected of any Cabinet officer. Instead, he led the President to believe there were no options, no trade-offs, and no gradations in the immensely complex business of providing for the national security.

Indeed, Weinberger's message over and over was that the DOD top line was a cut-and-dried necessity. The professionals and patriots over at the Pentagon were making scientific choices about its allocation—so no one on the White House side of the Potomac needed interfere or had the competence to do so.

Ronald Reagan's Fatal Mistake:
Blind Reliance on "Cap the Knife"

Ronald Reagan failed miserably as commander in chief. In most other policy areas, even on the matter of raising taxes, Reagan had proven capable of flexibility and compromise when the moment required it.

But he was unbending on the matter of his runaway defense buildup. In a fatal error of judgment, the president had delegated the issue fully and blindly to an advisor, Defense Secretary Casper Weinberger, who was preternaturally obdurate and imperious on everything within his brief.

This exposed the nation's decision-making process to a terrible historical mistake. Ronald Reagan had swallowed hook, line, and sinker the neocon narrative, with its vastly exaggerated notions of the Soviet threat and its spurious theory that the Kremlin was pursuing nuclear war–winning strategies.

Even worse, he possessed an almost childlike confidence in the military. Accordingly, he was oblivious to the fact that interservice rivalries, bureaucratic aggrandizement, and the plain old pork barrel of the military-industrial complex were rampant in the "swampland of waste" known as the Pentagon.

Reagan's startling innocence was especially apparent with respect to the top brass. Whenever the joint chiefs visited the White House, the president seemed awed, as if they had deigned to come down from Mount Olympus.

The truth is, the warfare state never had a more pliable tool in the Oval Office. Ronald Reagan campaigned for three decades as a small-government conservative, but he had come to the creed from the wrong side of the tracks: from the red-baiting precincts of the 1950s. Indeed, after his break with the Hollywood left, Reagan spent his conservative years absorbing the Manichean Cold War gospel of *Human Events* and the *National Review*.

Accordingly, his speeches portrayed an illusory world caught in a titanic struggle between the forces of freedom and the Kremlin's purported quest for world domination. Faced by an apocalyptic threat, Citizen Reagan had found no trouble believing that a massive military establishment kept in a continuous state of readiness was imperative for national security.

In fact, Reagan was an out-an-out statist in the realm of the military and national security. All the well-warranted skepticism he had about Big Government—the empire-building tendency of the bureaucracy, the inherent inefficiency and waste of public sector monopolies, the self-serving propensity of bureaucrats to hide the facts and twist the truth—did not apply on the Pentagon side of the Potomac.

Nor did he have any sense that money spent on defense imposed the same burden on taxpayers and drain on the economy as did all other kinds of government spending. Instead, he would say over and over, "No, when it comes to national security you do not spend based on a budget, you spend based on what you need."

Needless to say, the Pentagon brass and the defense contractors could not have agreed more wholeheartedly. Nor could they have defined "need" more expansively. And so, ironically, the tribune of small government became the great enabler of the 1980s warfare state revival—a project of staggering waste and lamentable historical consequence.

GENERAL EISENHOWER AND THE PATH NOT TAKEN

There is no better way to illuminate the "path not taken" character of the Reagan defense buildup than by comparing its magnitude and spirit to the legacy of President Dwight D. Eisenhower. Ike was the one postwar president who had soberly assessed the dangers of both the Soviet adversary and also the warfare state which had been mobilized to contain it. In so doing, he had established two fundamental national security markers as pertinent to the 1980s as the 1950s.

Firstly, Eisenhower sharply reduced the army and other elements of the conventional forces, believing that the academic concept of limited war favored by the liberal foreign policy establishment was an illusion in the nuclear age. He therefore rebuilt a much smaller and leaner defense budget on the predicate that the Soviet Union could ultimately be contained only by threat of massive nuclear retaliation.

Secondly, he believed that a strong civilian economy and resolute fiscal discipline were as important to national security as military power. In this respect, Ike spent the entire eight years of his tenure in the White House personally engaged in a campaign to not only reduce the conventional force structure, but also to squeeze, scrimp, economize, and retrench wherever possible from programs which were needed.

In so doing, he established what might be termed the "Eisenhower Minimum." Described more fully in chapter 11, it was the level of defense spending that the only war general to occupy the White House in the twentieth century believed was adequate to contain the Soviets. Thus, when he left office the Department of Defense was one-third smaller in real terms than the war-bloated levels he inherited from President Harry Truman.

Expressed in 2005 dollars of purchasing power, Ike's final defense budget was $370 billion compared to $515 billion when he took office. The remarkable fact is that this Eisenhower Minimum reflected Ike's assessment of national security requirements at the very peak of the post-*Sputnik* vigor of the Soviet industrial economy.

By contrast, Reagan's outgoing defense budget was $482 billion, measured in the same dollars of purchasing power. Not only was the Reagan defense spending level 30 percent larger in real terms than Ike's last budget, but it came at a point in history when the Evil Empire was already descending into its final collapse.

Moreover, the fact that the dead hand of the Soviet state had already asphyxiated its industrial economy was by no means a secret: there was plenty of open-source evidence of the looming Soviet breakdown. This historical development brought the possibility of relieving the American taxpayers of the three-decade-long financial burden of the Cold War. Accordingly, defense spending should have declined sharply below the Eisenhower Minimum to perhaps $200 billion by the end of the 1980s.

Instead, it soared recklessly and unnecessarily above it toward the $500 billion mark. One reason for this untoward outcome is surely that in his inordinate deference to all things associated with the military, Ronald Reagan was entirely oblivious to the profound admonition that Eisenhower had issued twenty years earlier.

In his farewell address, Ike famously warned the nation that "we must guard against the acquisition of unwarranted influence, whether sought or unsought, by the military-industrial complex. The potential for the disastrous rise of misplaced power exists and will persist."

Foremost among these potential abuses of political power was the obvious possibility that the military-industrial complex would extract unwarranted and excessive defense spending through the mobilization of fear and the enormous pork barrel dynamics inherent in the warfare state. And here Eisenhower distinguished himself from all of his successors during the Cold War era up to and including Ronald Reagan.

All these presidents could be described as military Keynesians; that is, they believed that defense spending involves a "twofer": the provision of national security and the creation of jobs and technological progress, as well.

By contrast, Eisenhower held the old-fashioned view that military spending is inherently wasteful. It consumes resources that would otherwise be available to meet the needs of the civilian economy.

Indeed, in a stunningly lyrical rife he had once insisted that "every gun that is made, every warship launched, every rocket fired signifies in the final sense, a theft from those who hunger and are not fed, those who are cold and not clothed. This world in arms is not spending money alone. It is spending the sweat of its laborers, the genius of its scientists, the hopes of its children . . . Under the cloud of war, it is humanity hanging from a cross of iron."

Needless to say, none of his successors, including left-wing community organizer Barack Obama, ever came close to such eloquence on the societal cost of military spending. In the Reagan White House, especially, cluelessness was the order of the day as the great defense surge gathered momentum, and the warfare state became its own reason for imperialism abroad and economic burdens at home.

The legends of the Reagan era are legion, but the greatest legend is that the feckless Reagan defense buildup caused the collapse of the Soviet Union. As has been demonstrated, the $3.5 trillion (2005$) spent on defense during the Gipper's term did not cause the Kremlin to raise the white flag of surrender. Virtually none of it was spent on programs which threatened Soviet security or undermined its strategic nuclear deterrent.

In procuring new conventional tanks, planes, helicopters, missiles, and munitions, the United States did not launch an arms race that the Kremlin feared it could not survive. The 1980s race to rearm, in fact, resulted in the creation of a vast expeditionary force for no valid reason of state, and which got used for no redeeming purpose except that presidents could.

If the Reagan defense buildup was not much related to its stated objective of thwarting the Evil Empire, it did fatally undermine any modest prospect for shrinking the domestic welfare state that existed in January 1981. Within a year, in fact, the juxtaposition of domestic versus defense budgetary regimens became so stark and untenable as to thoroughly poison the political well.

The growing fat at the Pentagon generated acrid resentments throughout Washington's civilian branches, even as favored constituencies harvested a bonanza of defense contracts and local economic stimulus. In time, this blowback extinguished even the modest initial quantum of support on Capitol Hill for the White House's prescribed diet of domestic agency austerity.

So when all was said and done, it was not an impecunious public purse, but the rampant fiscal profligacy and flagrant pork barrel excesses issuing from the Defense Department's soaring top line that became the defining fiscal signature of the Reagan era. Indeed, in a supreme irony, Reagan's short-lived challenge to the welfare state in early 1981 was quickly supplanted by its opposite: a rapidly swelling warfare state that was both unnecessary at the time and destined to become an incubator of imperialist calamity in the decades ahead.

CHAPTER 6

———

TRIUMPH OF THE WELFARE STATE
How the GOP Anti-Tax Religion Was Born

THE REAGAN REVOLUTION'S TAX POLICY, TOO, WAS THE PRODUCT of error and confusion. These misfires eventually morphed into a GOP anti-tax doctrine that was stunning in its denial of reality. It literally stood on its head the fiscal orthodoxy that Republicans had uniformly embraced prior to 1980.

Until then, conservatives had generally treated taxes as an element of balancing the expenditure and revenue accounts, not as an explicit tool of economic stimulus. All three postwar Republican presidents—Eisenhower, Nixon, and Ford—had even resorted to tax increases to eliminate red ink, albeit as a matter of last resort after spending-cut options had been exhausted.

These Republican administrations also espoused an economic philosophy of lower taxes to encourage capital formation and private enterprise. But at the end of the day, the tax code stood first and foremost as an instrument of revenue collection, not an all-purpose elixir to promote economic growth.

The story of how this tradition of sound fiscal policy was lost after 1980 is crucial to understanding the economic deformations plaguing the present era. This is especially so because the GOP's extended sojourn in the realm of fiscal know-nothingism has not been so much purposeful and explicit as it has been convoluted and accidental in its origin and institutionalization.

ORIGIN OF THE REAGAN TAX CUTS: KEYNESIAN INFLATION

Although the facts have been obscured by partisan revisionism from both sides, the Reagan tax cuts were initially grounded in this earlier conservative tradition. It was only much later that glib revisionist theories like "starve the beast" emerged. Similarly, the bastardized supply-side notion that tax-rate reductions would not result in revenue loss owing to the Laffer curve had few adherents beyond Laffer himself.

In fact, while the Reagan White House and practical Republican politicians alike believed lower tax rates would stimulate economic growth and some revenue feedback, none believed these cuts would be 100 percent self-financing. The latter became incorporated into GOP catechism only much later—egged on by the rank sophistry of Laffer, Jude Wanniski, and one or two other charlatans who constituted the entirety of the supply-side coterie.

The fact is, when the Reagan administration took office it was confronted by an immense tax roadblock to economic expansion. The pernicious interaction of the 1970's double-digit inflation and the progressive rate structure of the individual income tax code were causing tax rates to rise rapidly due to bracket creep.

Based on the early 1981 outlook for continued high inflation, the existing tax law, owing to bracket creep, would have drastically and automatically raised the federal tax burden on the economy. From a level of about 19 percent of GDP in 1980 the revenue claim on national income would have risen to an unprecedented 24 percent by 1986.

A tax increase equal to 5 percentage points of GDP is no small matter, and would amount to $750 billion annually in today's economy. So what the Reagan administration had inherited was a huge prospective enlargement of the tax burden.

What it also inherited was the legacy of Keynesian fiscal policy activism and the resulting chronic deficits which became institutionalized in the late 1960s and had led to inflationary money printing by the Fed. Paul Volcker was aggressively attacking the latter, but it would take time to subdue.

In these circumstances, it did not require any belief in the finer points of supply-side doctrine to see the need for income tax reductions. If left on automatic pilot, the "bracket creep" then raging would quash the economy's capacity for recovery and growth.

Moreover, this looming, unlegislated escalation of the tax burden was something entirely new under the fiscal sun. To be sure, if the old right had long fulminated against the "abomination of 1913" which saw enactment of both the income tax and the Federal Reserve. But during peacetime, anyway, this potential witches' brew of inflationary money and confiscatory taxation had never really materialized.

During the Roaring Twenties era, for example, consumer prices had averaged a zero rate of change. Thus, there was no bracket creep during the income tax's first peacetime decade, just deep legislated cuts in the high wartime tax rates engineered by the incomparable Andrew Mellon.

Likewise, after plunging by 20 percent during the initial four years of the Great Depression, consumer prices had drifted up only tepidly until the onset of the Second World War. So there had been no bracket creep in the 1930s, just Franklin D. Roosevelt's deliberate legislative enactments aimed at soaking the rich.

When economic normalcy again returned after the Korean War, the consumer inflation rate settled into a peacetime crawl, rising by an average of 1.6 percent annually during 1953–1967. So again, significant bracket creep had still not emerged, while discretionary legislative action had functioned to modestly reduce income tax rates.

As it happened, President Lyndon Johnson's misbegotten "guns and butter" crusade eventually did uncork the evil genie of 1913. During the years subsequent to 1967, a pusillanimous Fed, shorn after 1971 of its last link to the fixed financial anchor of gold, unleashed a runaway inflation for the first time in peacetime history.

This unique outbreak of peacetime inflation is now forgotten, but its importance cannot by overemphasized. Consumer prices rose at an average rate of nearly 7.5 percent annually over the next decade and a half, including four years of double-digit gains. The resulting relentless push of inflation-swollen incomes into higher tax brackets clearly did stifle entrepreneurial energies and erode business investment incentives, thereby contributing to the abrupt slowdown of real GDP growth.

So it was the stagflationary breakdown of the national economy resulting from Nixon's abandonment of sound money in August 1971 which ultimately triggered the Reagan Revolution. Real growth faltered badly for the better part of a decade, averaging just 2.5 percent per annum in the eight inflation-racked years ending in 1981, compared to 3.8 percent during the two decades prior to 1969.

It was these threats to the middle-class living standard which set the stage for the 1980 campaign referendum on the "are you better off" question. Believing that it was worse off and fearing even further decline in the future, the public sent Ronald Reagan to the White House to fix the underlying problem Nixon had bequeathed.

THE REAGAN 10-10-10 TAX CUT WAS DE FACTO INDEXING— NOT LAFFER CURVE MAGIC

The long forgotten truth is that the original Reagan tax cuts essentially amounted to preventative indexing; that is, insulation of the tax code from further bracket creep before the anticipated inflation of incomes actually happened. At the time, Alan Greenspan explicitly argued for the Reagan cuts on this basis. It was also the practical justification embraced by old guard congressional Republicans—few of whom put any stock in the Laffer Napkin and the free lunch theories of its author and purported economist, Arthur Laffer.

De facto tax indexing was in theory fully compatible with the older tradition of Republican fiscal orthodoxy. From the perspective of early 1981, at least, it did not appear to open up an insuperable fiscal gap: moderate tax cuts would simply forestall the bracket creep-driven rise of the tax burden.

In that context, the original Reagan tax plan—the Kemp-Roth rate cuts of 10 percent annually for three years and the business depreciation incentive known as 10-5-3—was not inordinately radical. In fact, while the revenue loss was large and measured out to 4.5 percent of GDP when fully implemented, it merely offset the projected bracket creep over the five-year fiscal horizon at issue.

Thus, the math of the Reagan tax plan brought the projected 1986 tax burden back down to 19.5 percent of GDP, exactly equal to the tax extraction from the American economy that had been embodied in Jimmy Carter's last budget (fiscal year 1981). Contrary to legend, then, the original Reagan tax package did not actually aim to reduce the inherited tax burden at all. Based on projections at the time, it penciled out as merely a reversion to the Carter status quo ante.

THE FISCAL MATH OF HOWARD BAKER'S LIBRARY— IT BARELY WORKED AND SOON CRASHED

The spending side of the final Carter budget had come in at about 22 percent of GDP. After the planned tax rollback there remained a 2.5 percent of GDP deficit, which was viewed in those days as dangerously large. Yet the Reagan Revolution was about shrinking the girth of the state—so a 2–3 percent retrenchment on the spending side seemed entirely appropriate and achievable.

Indeed, balancing the budget at 19.5 percent of GDP did not require especially radical spending cuts relative to recent norms: total federal outlays averaged 20 percent of GDP during the decade of the 1970s, and had been 20.2 percent as late as 1979. What made the Reagan fiscal plan seem radical was the mere fact that domestic spending was to be cut at all, especially after the massive increases of the Nixon-Ford era.

When the Republican leadership gathered in Majority Leader Howard Baker's library to plot fiscal strategy on the eve of the inauguration, the task of balancing Ronald Reagan's conflicting campaign promises was not yet insuperable. With taxes pinned at 19.5 percent of GDP—still high by all prior peacetime history—and the defense build-up still unquantified, rolling back total Federal spending by a few percentage points of GDP was seen by the seasoned Republican leaders gathered there as a daunting but achievable goal.

But not long after the inauguration, the unraveling began. It never stopped. To this day its legacy hangs over the nation's battered financial accounts like a fiscal sword of Damocles.

The defense buildup got far bigger than had been implied by the back-of-the-envelope fiscal math of the Chicago speech. The tax cut also ballooned massively in size during the July 1981 bidding war. At the same time, the national economy and revenue base ended up much smaller than the original "Rosy Scenario" forecasts.

Finally, even the modest domestic spending cuts envisioned in Howard Baker's library proved unachievable. The result was a fiscal hemorrhage that was so abrupt, massive, and unrelenting that its causes were barely understood at the time, and have long since vanished into the fog of partisan disputation.

Still, the rudiments of the budgetary crack-up are reasonably clear and refute the revisionist legends fostered by both sides of the debate. The Democrats are wrong in saying the massive Reagan deficits were deliberate, because they were the opposite; that is, they were the consequence of budgetary innumeracy in the White House and a political gong show among the Republican factions which emerged from the fray.

The Republican legend that the Reagan deficits didn't matter is even faultier: the budget deficits triggered by the original 1981 plan were devastating in magnitude and mitigated only by a series of stiff tax increases during the next several years that amounted to $350 billion annually in today's economy.

Moreover, even after the Reagan tax increases there remained a 3–4 percent of GDP structural deficit. This gap was not cured by the robust economic rebound which did occur when the recession ended in 1982, nor could it have been eliminated by any conceivable amount of higher growth.

The Reagan-era fiscal legacy was, in fact, a permanent policy of massive deficit finance. The destructive consequences of it were not eliminated, but only deferred by the furious central bank buying of Treasury bonds over the next twenty-five years.

ROSY SCENARIO: THE $2 TRILLION ERROR THAT CRUSHED THE REAGAN BUDGET

The major culprit was the five-year economic forecast known from the start as Rosy Scenario. It embodied a mind-boggling $2 trillion error in the form of an overestimate of nominal GDP for the fiscal year 1982–1986 period covered by the original Reagan plan.

In hindsight it might well be asked why anyone was trying to project the economy five years into the hazy future, especially when by early 1981 the economic future was unusually opaque. In the tumultuous environment of the final Carter years, things which had once been considered impossible—13 percent annual inflation, $40 per barrel oil, 20 percent prime rates, and $800 per ounce gold—had become recurring events.

Yet the Reagan Revolution was not about incrementalist tinkering. The change of policy direction it sought would take years to roll out and therefore had to be built on an extended economic forecast, even if it was a stab in the dark.

But where this fateful stab went wrong is not in the area for which it has been so heavily criticized. Rosy Scenario did not necessarily overestimate the economy's potential for a sharp rebound after being liberated from the burden of soaring inflation, bracket creep, and sharply rising marginal tax rates.

In fact, real GDP expanded by 4.5 percent, 7.2 percent, and 4.1 percent, respectively, during the first three years of the Reagan recovery. The resulting 5.4 percent average gain for that period was almost dead-on the growth rates for the initial years assumed in Rosy Scenario. The problem was that it wasn't the same three years!

Like every administration before and since, the 1981 Reagan White House never even considered the possibility that its spanking new supply-side program for economic rejuvenation would initially result in a devastating recession. To the contrary, real economic growth was projected to come galloping out of the gate at a 4 percent annual rate in the 1981 final quarter, rising to a 5.2 percent growth rate in the first quarter of 1982 and for numerous quarters thereafter.

In hindsight this "no recession" assumption might be better described as a willful disregard for reality, given the administration's parallel embrace of a hard-core monetarist attack on inflation. Indeed, the Reagan White House was fully supportive of the harsh monetary contraction that Fed chairman Volcker was then administering, and should have therefore expected the resulting purge of inflationary fevers to be accompanied by a temporary collapse of production and employment.

In the event, that is exactly what happened. On the one hand, inflation plummeted from 9 percent in 1981 to 3.8 percent in 1982, an outcome far better than even Rosy Scenario had contemplated.

At the same time, during the first year of the Reagan tax cuts, real GDP did not surge into the 5.2 percent supply-side growth boom that had been forecast. Instead, 1982 recorded a deep 1.5 percent contraction of output and soaring unemployment which reached nearly 11 percent by year-end.

So the Reagan program worked in sequence, not parallel. The contractionary effects of monetary disinflation came first; the output rebound and supply-side expansion came later. Indeed, by the calendar of Rosy Scenario the output surge came much later, nearly two years behind schedule. And that's where the fiscal numbers were thrown into a cocked hat.

The effects of this sequenced series of economic adjustment were cumulative, which means that the actual path of the US economy diverged more and more from the one that had been projected in Rosy Scenario. Due to lower than forecast inflation and negative real output in 1982, for example, nominal GDP came in nearly $140 billion, or 4 percent, short of the original forecast. This nominal GDP wedge between forecast and actual widened to $370 billion in 1983, representing a 10 percent shortfall to the Rosy Scenario path.

And the wedge kept getting wider in the out-years. By the fifth year of the plan, in 1986, these same forces of tamer inflation and delayed output recovery had widened the nominal GDP gap to $660 billion annually. This meant that the US economy was nearly 15 percent smaller than had been projected by Rosy Scenario when the Reagan Revolution was launched in February 1981.

This vast discrepancy between the forecast and actual path of the American economy during the first half of the 1980s is not simply the detritus of fiscal archeology. It is the key to understanding how subsequently an entire generation of conservative politicians went off the deep end on tax policy.

As a mechanical matter, high growth rates of nominal GDP, whether due to real output or inflation, produce a cornucopia of revenues in a progressive tax system. In the first instance, the tax-paying public is moved en masse into steadily higher tax brackets. At the same time, tax revenues are extracted from a rapidly rising base of nominal income. Taken together, these forces would amount to a confiscatory doomsday machine if allowed to run long enough.

Conversely, in an environment of slowly growing nominal incomes—again, whether due to low inflation or low real growth—the same tax régime will result in lower average tax rates due to less bracket creep. It will also generate measurably reduced aggregate tax revenues because these lower rates will be applied to substantially smaller nominal incomes.

Needless to say, here is precisely where the Reagan Revolution's fiscal math hit the shoals—and it did so before even one sentence of tax-cutting had been enacted into law. Specifically, Rosy Scenario had projected $4.8 trillion of nominal GDP by 1986 on the assumption that inflation would only come down gradually, not abruptly; that there would be no recession; and that real GDP would continuously expand at an average 4.7 percent annual rate over the five-year period.

Under these assumptions, projected 1986 revenue from current tax law, that is, the Carter tax rates, was $1.16 trillion. This reflected a bracket-creep-induced gain in the federal tax take from 19.5 percent of GDP under the last Carter budget to 24 percent of GDP in 1986. And it was from this sky-high "baseline" that the Reagan tax cuts would be subtracted.

In the real world, however, 1986 nominal GDP only came in at $4.15 trillion—a whopping 15 percent lower than the Rosy Scenario projection. And, owing to far less bracket creep, the pre-Reagan tax law would have generated a tax take of only 22 percent of GDP, not 24 percent. This meant that federal revenue under Carter tax law would have amounted to only about $900 billion in 1986—a figure *one-quarter of a trillion dollars smaller than* the Rosy Scenario baseline projections had anticipated.

What this meant as a practical matter was that we were cutting phantom tax revenues in the out-years. Had we been more clairvoyant, or possibly honest, in formulating Rosy Scenario we would have given Volcker his recession first, the monetarists their victory over inflation earlier, and the supply-siders their real growth surge later.

In that event, the administration's February 1981 economic forecast might have tracked quite closely the actual course of the economy described above. But then the huge Reagan tax cuts would have never gotten out the White House door. The revenue baseline would have been so much lower that the Reagan fiscal plan announced on February 18 would have revealed $200–$300 billion annual deficits as far as the eye could see.

That would have stopped Reaganomics cold. Back then, Republican legislators were scared to death of big deficits. I was, too. So possibly was Ronald Reagan.

Admittedly, the lower actual path of inflation also reduced projected baseline spending for indexed entitlement programs like Social Security. By the same token, however, the unplanned deep recession, high unemployment, and huge initial deficits had the opposite effect: ballooning social safety net and debt service expenses far above the Rosy Scenario projections, and thereby washing out of the spending side much of the paper gain from lower inflation.

In short, the Reagan tax-cutting program had started with inherited Carter budget policy. The latter had penciled out to a substantial surplus by the mid-1980s. But this was a mirage. It represented an inflation-swollen economy that was unsustainable but which caused the Office of Management and Budget (OMB) computers to spit out a windfall of phantom revenues from the pernicious process of bracket creep.

The truth of the matter was that Paul Volcker's crushing blow to runaway inflation was unavoidable. It meant that the US economy would be put through the wringer under any fiscal policy variation.

So for all practical purposes, the nation was already mired in deep budget deficits when Ronald Reagan took the oath of office; they were just hidden in a nonsustainable inflation-ridden economy. After the huge Reagan tax cuts were layered on top of this inherited red ink, the fiscal math was prohibitive. It became a generational albatross.

THE 1981 TAX BIDDING WAR:
COALITION OF THE BOUGHT

Within a few months the revenue situation skidded even further into the ditch, owing to the tax bidding war which erupted in conjunction with congressional action on the supply-side tax cuts. But strangely enough, this bidding war originated in legislative sentiment which went in the opposite direction—against any big tax cuts.

As of early 1981, there was not a corporal's guard among congressional Republicans in favor of the original undiluted 30 percent cut in income tax rates. Especially among the old-guard Republicans in the Senate, what had become known as the Kemp-Roth tax cut bill scared the daylights out of them. It was viewed as a huge "riverboat gamble," as Majority Leader Howard Baker put it.

Accordingly, there had been immense pressure on the Republican side of the aisle for dilution and compromise from the very start. Unfortunately, however, in the heat of legislative battle the tax bill careened off in the opposite direction. The tax bill got bigger rather than smaller because the Reagan White House could not remotely obtain the votes based on conviction. So it horse-traded its way to a majority coalition on Capitol Hill.

In the end, the historic 1981 Reagan tax bill was passed not by a team of the convinced, but by a coalition of the bought. Whereas the original White House tax plan had cost 4.5 percent of GDP when fully phased in, the final legislation passed by Congress cost nearly 6.5 percent of GDP in the outyears.

The resulting plunge of the federal revenue base into the fiscal abyss reached stunning dimensions. At the time of the White House tax bill signing ceremony in July 1981, of course, the depth of the recession and the degree to which out-year GDP would fall short of the Rosy Scenario forecast were not yet fully apparent. However, with each new economic forecast update during the balance of 1981 and early 1982, the unfolding fiscal train wreck became ever more evident.

As it finally turned out, the new tax law would have generated less than 16 percent of GDP in tax revenue under the actual disinflationary path of the economy which materialized over the 1980s. Having set out on a multiyear journey to roll back economically destructive bracket creep and end up by mid-decade with the federal tax burden at 19.5 percent of GDP, or within a whisker of Jimmy Carter's outgoing budget, the Reagan Administration's tax-cutting excursion actually landed on a different fiscal planet.

Amid the fog of faulty forecasts and undisciplined legislative battle, therefore, the nation's tax burden had been precipitously rolled back to the level under a much earlier Democratic president, namely, the 1948 budget of Harry Truman.

Alas, that fiscal era was long gone. Truman could pay Uncle Sam's bills on 16 percent of GDP because the Cold War defense buildup had not yet happened, most retirees were not yet eligible to collect Social Security, and LBJ's massive Great Society was not even imagined.

After the dust settled in the summer of 1981, what had been the Republican holy grail of a balanced budget had now been banished to the fiscal hereafter. In its place there was a structural deficit of 5–6 percent of GDP as far as the eye could see. Only in light of subsequent experience—thirty years later—was a permanent deficit of this magnitude not shocking.

Moreover, the internals of this fiscal hemorrhage betrayed an even more foreboding dimension. The tax bidding war of late July 1981 resulted in a compromise plan, Conable-Hance II, a tax Christmas tree of stupendous girth. It was a seminal event in the fiscal deformations of the present era because it revealed the frightening power of crony capitalism to raid the treasury, once released from traditional taboos against deficit finance.

As it had turned out, in order to get one dollar of pure supply-side tax rate cuts for individual taxpayers, the White House had been required to hand out a matching dollar of booty to the coalition of business lobbies and special interest groups it had assembled to secure passage of the bill. Some of this largesse was monumental, such as the virtual exemption of real estate from federal income taxes, owing to ten-year write-offs for commercial buildings designed to last a half century.

Other giveaways, such as tax credits for wood-burning stoves, were merely symbolic but still potent vote gatherers in places like New England. Still other subventions, such as the oil royalty owners' credit and the all-savers certificate, were the price of support demanded by the oil state delegations and the savings and loan industry, respectively.

And some of the revenue giveaways resembled nothing so much as the camel's nose under the tent. The estate tax provisions, for example, had a first-year cost of only a few hundred million dollars but ended up in total repeal by the end of the decade at an annual cost fifty times greater.

In this manner the federal revenue base had been sacked by the marauding army of business lobbyists who had opportunistically enlisted in the supply-side crusade. Moreover, their larcenous raid on the treasury had been heavily "back loaded" into the more distant future in order to obscure the true cost.

Thus, when most of the provisions became fully effective by 1990, the revenue loss was a stunning 6.2 percent of GDP. In today's economy that would compute to an approximate $1 trillion annual loss of tax receipts.

That number can't be emphasized enough—it summarizes the sheer mayhem visited upon the nation's revenue basis in a few short weeks during July 1981. Crucially, more than half of that staggering total had gone toward new tax loopholes and tax subsidies for Washington-sanctioned economic endeavors, not liberating workers and entrepreneurs from the yoke of high marginal tax rates.

The date of July 21, 1981, thus deserves a special notation in the annals of budgetary infamy. While the ideologues of supply-side claimed the victory, it had been the lobbyists of K Street who had delivered the votes. And in their open and notorious campaign of vote buying, they also impregnated the fiscal policy process with the unvarnished cynicism from which crony capitalism was to thrive mightily during the decades to come.

THE STAB-IN-THE-BACK LEGEND: HOW THE
TAX-GRABBERS ACTUALLY SAVED REAGAN'S BACON

The fiscal Rubicon was crossed in July 1981, but the final demise of the old time Republican balanced budget religion took several years more to unfold. Indeed, its death throes left an ironic legacy. Ronald Reagan did sign a half-dozen tax increase measures during the next several years which recovered nearly 45 percent of the revenue base that had been cast into the abyss by the 1981 tax bidding war. These tax bills were pushed under his pen, however, in a manner fraught with stealth and dissimulation.

That process later gave rise to a "stab in the back" legend that Ronald Reagan had been tricked into signing these tax increases, which to some degree he had. Furthermore, the legend grew that these treacherous tax-raising measures had been footnotes at best, with no enduring economic significance. With history thus rewritten, it did not require much of a leap for the next generation of GOP politicians to anchor their new anti-tax orthodoxy in an even greater legend; namely, that the economic boom of the mid-1980s had risen from the original Reagan tax cut bill.

The evidence goes entirely in the opposite direction. In the annals of giant fiscal policy errors the 1981 Reagan tax cut turned out to be an all-time "near miss," but only because the subsequent tax increase bills staunched the flow of red ink to manageable levels. The most important of these was the TEFRA bill of 1982 which alone recovered revenue equal to 1.1 percent of GDP. That would amount to about $150 billion annually in today's economy.

Soon thereafter the so-called Greenspan Social Security rescue plan, which was a thinly disguised payroll tax increase, clawed back another two-thirds percent of GDP. And a similar chunk of revenue was regained by what was labeled "The Deficit Reduction Act of 1984." In all, these "Reagan tax increase bills" would total $400 billion per year if measured in today's economic scale. So the unassailable fact is that the Reagan tax hikes were massive by any reckoning, not a footnote.

The equally unassailable fact, however, was that the president and the White House spin machine never took ownership of these legislative actions. Indeed, the Reagan White House hardly even acknowledged that they occurred.

Consequently, as time passed and the American economy moved into the faux prosperity of the 1990s, a whole generation of Republican politicians grew up without knowing four important truths. The most important was that the 1981 Reagan legislative program had been a fiscal disaster. The huge tax reduction without a matched book of spending cuts caused the structural deficit to literally explode to the then unimaginable level of 6 percent of GDP.

Secondly, the actual deficit during the second Reagan term was brought down to a still exceedingly high 3.5 percent of GDP average only through a series of major tax increases over 1982–1984. These unavoidable measures had actually been grounded in the old-time Republican doctrine that government should pay its bills.

Thirdly, these unavoidable tax measures to pay the government's bills did not block the economic recovery. This was resoundingly affirmed by the 5.4 percent average GDP growth rate during 1983–1985, a three-year expansion rate that was on par with prior recoveries from deep recessions.

Finally, at the time of the "morning in America" celebration, the weighted average cost of the US debt was still in double digits. Had the 6 percent of GDP structural deficit not been corrected by these tax increases, a "debt trap" would have soon erupted as interest payments spiraled out of control. Save for the "tax grabbers" in the White House and GOP congressional leadership, the Reagan economic legacy would have been in ruins before his second term was complete.

THE STARVE THE BEAST MYTH:
NEVER PROCLAIMED BUT INDISPUTEDLY FAILED

The yawning fiscal gap which made these serial revenue recovery measures necessary also provided a real-world experiment in the "starve the beast" theory of tax cuts. It failed the test completely.

At that point in fiscal history, the prospect of a 6 percent of GDP structural deficit during peacetime full employment was truly frightening. So if there was ever a circumstance in which politicians could literally be bludgeoned into large-scale spending cuts, this was it.

Yet notwithstanding the massive outpouring of red ink during the remainder of the Reagan tenure, there was no measureable progress in contracting the welfare state after 1981. This failure to make a dent in the federal spending claim on GDP is evident in the fiscal data for the second Reagan term.

By then the American economy was in a strong recovery, and countercyclical spending for unemployment had largely ceased. Nevertheless, federal outlays still averaged 21.7 percent of GDP—a figure which, as indicated above, is actually higher than the 21.1 percent of GDP average during the four "big spending" Carter years.

The Reagan defense buildup, of course, did add about 1 percentage point of GDP to total spending compared to the Carter average. Yet the real explanation for the fact that Ronald Reagan presided over the highest peacetime spending share of GDP yet recorded is that the US welfare state simply refused to shrink very much during the second Reagan term, even after the huge mandate of the 1984 election and with the tailwind of a strong economy.

Specifically, federal spending excluding defense and foreign security assistance during the second Reagan term averaged 15.5 percent of GDP, representing an exceedingly modest improvement from the 15.9 percent average during the Carter years. The threat of massive structural deficits did not drive a contraction of the welfare state during the post-recession Reagan years because politics, not the exigencies of fiscal policy, had already decided the outcome—way back in the spring of 1981.

THE SCHWEIKER PLAN: REAGAN'S FISCAL WATERLOO

The referendum on domestic spending that Ronald Reagan promised in the 1980 campaign was short-lived, having reached its high-water mark with the passage of the budget resolution in April 1981. After that, nearly every new spending reduction initiative, such as the May 1981 Social Security reform plan, was dead on arrival on Capitol Hill, while many of the initial budget resolution cuts were watered down or circumvented with the passage of time.

The demise of the May 12, 1981, Social Security reform plan within ten days of its unveiling powerfully illuminates this deep political resistance to serious welfare state retrenchment. Needless to say, these powerful headwinds arose from all points on the partisan compass, especially from inside the Reagan White House itself.

There was no real mystery as to why three months after the original Reagan fiscal plan had been launched, and after its apparent triumph in the congressional budget resolution approved in April, that a second sweeping spending cut initiative was being presented to the Congress. The original plan had a big hole in its center; namely, a $44 billion per year spending cut based on additional measures "to be proposed."

This huge due bill had been dubbed the "magic asterisk" by Senate Majority Leader Howard Baker. The Senate GOP leaders had reluctantly gone along with this expedient in the budget resolution, since it was only a nonbinding fiscal blueprint in the first place; in effect, a list of items "to be enacted" in subsequent tax and spending legislation. Still, the GOP fiscal stalwarts who ran the Senate were not happy about balancing the budget with what appeared to be a large quotient of bottled air.

Therefore, they expected additional spending cuts from the White House, meaning that there actually wasn't anything particularly magical about the $44 billion. It most certainly was not some nefarious trick designed to bamboozle the Congress. What Senate GOP leadership had not prepared its rank and file for, however, was that this second installment of spending cuts would inexorably involve a frontal assault on Social Security.

Indeed, the $44 billion had been an obvious "placeholder" for what I had always intended; namely, a direct assault on the misguided "social insurance" foundation of Social Security which dated all the way back to the New Deal. But just as in the case of the DOD top line, the "placeholder" expedient had been resorted to because there had not been time in the short interval between inauguration and February 18 to delve into the program's vast complexity.

Even with the extra time through its May 12 launch, however, the White House Social Security reform plan had been only the opening salvo, not the full measure of retrenchment needed to make the Reagan fiscal plan solvent. Yet the plan did attack an important target; namely, the elimination of some of the more egregious "unearned benefits" which had been added to the program during earlier flush times.

The most important of these was partially eliminating the huge mistake called "double indexing" that the usual suspect, Richard Nixon, had signed into law on the eve of the 1972 election. In addition to the debatable but understandable provision for automatically increasing the benefits of existing retirees by the annual CPI gain, the 1972 legislation had also made an additional huge fiscal mistake. It effectively indexed the wages of the entire active workforce, reaching all the way down to eighteen-year-olds first entering the job market, to each year's gain in consumer prices plus national productivity.

Accordingly, after forty years in the workforce, the benefits of every retiree would now be massively higher than warranted by their own payroll tax contributions, owing to the compounding effect of this wage index kicker. The May 12 White House plan didn't eliminate but did materially dilute these transparently unearned benefits, along with a number of other like and similar reforms.

For instance, the penalty for early retirement at age sixty-two was raised from 20 percent 45 percent. Likewise, the unearned "minimum benefit" was phased out, and extraneous payments to student dependents and certain types of disability recipients were also eliminated.

None of these benefits had been earned and they had not been included in the original scheme. Not only was the principle of reducing unearned benefits eminently sensible, but it also cut about $40 billion from federal spending after a few years of transition, thereby plugging the magic asterisk hole.

Still, these initial reforms amounted to only about 1 percent of GDP. A serious shrinkage of the welfare state would have required a far more extensive and direct attack on social insurance; that is, on the principle of non-means-tested income transfers.

Nevertheless, this modest "unearned" benefit reform plan had actually been one of the few anti-spending measures that President Reagan had firmly grasped and had enthusiastically embraced. At the White House meeting during which the plan was approved, he had summarized the unearned benefits issue succinctly: "I've been warning since 1964 that Social Security was heading for bankruptcy," he had said, "and this is one of the reasons why."

Yet fiscal disaster at some point down the road or not, the White House political staff led by Jim Baker was not about to run the risk of a political disaster in the here and now. It was thus decreed that the plan would not be issued by the White House, but by the secretary of Health and Human Services, Richard Schweiker.

Instantly, the politicians on Capitol Hill smelled blood, and the speed of the plan's demise became one for the record books. The OMB notes from the daily White House staff meeting dramatically map the historical inflection point which was at hand. Three days after the plan's announcement, the staff marching orders were "Social Security—need strong efforts to inform people about the *President's proposal*."

By the seventh day, the daily talking point had become "We're not backing off on this, but the *President will not lead*." And by May 21, ten days of history had been revised with such alacrity as to make a Soviet historian blush: "Social Security—need to get this off the front page. Only submitted to the Hill in response to a request from a Congressional committee for a position. . . . *No Presidential involvement*."

Then and there, it was clear that the welfare state would not give ground, and that it was destined to grow inexorably in the years ahead owing to the embedded demographics of the baby boom, and the relentless indexing of unearned benefits. In fact, the complex of non-means-tested social insurance programs including Social Security, Medicare, and unemployment insurance was 6 percent of GDP in 1981 and is 10 percent today—heading for 15 percent by the end of this decade.

History sometimes kindly provides an exclamation mark to signify the finality or unequivocal nature of an episode. In this case, the political uproar was so deafening that the Senate Republican leadership felt compelled to introduce a resolution condemning the Administration's package of reforms. It passed the same day by a vote of 96 to 0.

Not only did that vote permanently bury any prospect for reforming the dense complex of social insurance programs which comprise the core of the welfare state, but it also implanted a fiscal litmus test for the ages: whenever politicians talk about shrinking the size of government and returning the tax burden to pre-1980 levels, they are either indulging in pure pettifoggery or they mean to embrace the "Schweiker plan" at the very least. The fiscal math simply admits of no other alternative.

Propagators of the myth that Reagan cut domestic spending have attempted to deny this, dismissing the Schweiker plan meltdown as historically insignificant on the grounds that it was flawed and hurried. Yet the historical record proves otherwise.

There may have been a better plan than the ill-fated Schweiker package, but none has been seriously proposed for three decades now. Indeed, the one episode of major legislative action on Social Security—the 1983 Greenspan Commission solvency plan—proves that the door to significant retrenchment of social insurance had now been slammed shut.

The Greenspan Commission plan has been hailed as a bipartisan success, and appropriately so. It did the only thing bipartisan plans can do: it raised taxes substantially—through a higher payroll tax rate, a substantial rise in the taxable wage base, and by forcing state and local government employees into the system.

These measures did keep the mythical "trust funds" solvent in the intermediate term. Additionally, the overall plan attempted to camouflage its front-loaded pile of taxes by means of a well-advertised but modest increase in the retirement age. The latter incepted twenty years from the effective date and did not become fully implemented for forty years, which is to say, not even yet. Thus, in the fiscal here and now the Greenspan plan was a tax increase pure and simple.

Nor did the core tax-raising piece of the plan have only a minor impact. The payroll tax share of GDP was boosted by nearly a full percentage point. Accordingly, middle-class families were permanently shuffled deeper into the regressive zone of the US taxation system.

The average payroll tax burden for middle-income families rose from 9.5 percent of earnings in 1980 to 11.8 percent by 1988. By contrast, the income tax share had fallen and by 1988 was down to 6.6 percent of middle-class earnings, reflecting a burden that was now barely half the payroll tax extraction.

In those days, the bipartisan majority which passed the plan still believed that government had to pay its bills. But in raising taxes on the working class to do so, there was some considerable irony in it.

RONALD W. REAGAN: TAX COLLECTOR
FOR THE WELFARE STATE

At the time the Schweiker plan had been approved by the White House, President Reagan had stoutly insisted that he would not go the easy route of tax increases to paper over the system's insolvency for just a while longer. Indeed, he had a deep disdain for the 1977 Carter legislation which did just that: "They gave us the largest tax increase in history and said it would be sound until the year 2030," the president had remarked. "Now we're here four years later and it's already bankrupt."

Nevertheless, two years later Ronald Reagan fulsomely praised the bipartisan tax-raising plan, using nearly the identical words that Jimmy Carter had employed about achieving long-term solvency. But in assuring the public that Social Security had (again) been made solvent for a generation, the president had crossed a fiscal Rubicon that has been denied by his hagiographers ever since. The truth is, once he abandoned the Schweiker plan in favor of the bipartisan solvency package, Ronald Reagan became the tax collector for the welfare state—no longer its bête noire.

In short, the Schweiker plan and the Greenspan plan were bookends in time which captured a turning point in fiscal history. After that, the true issue was how to finance the welfare state efficiently, fairly, and with minimum damage to the American economy.

To be sure, a minority of junior backbenchers, led by Newt Gingrich, voted against the Greenspan plan in March 1983. For decades thereafter, they denounced any recidivist tendencies within the GOP toward the old-time fiscal religion of balanced budgets as evidence of wanting to do what Ronald Reagan actually did; namely, become tax collectors for the welfare state.

But the questions that subsequent history has proved they could not answer were strikingly evident even then. There was no alternative to higher taxes except to strike at the social insurance core of the welfare state. If not Ronald Reagan, who? If not in May 1981, when?

In any event, history rolled along its chosen course and the American welfare state did not shrink. Outlays for domestic programs in 1986 totaled $516 billion, a figure only 9 percent smaller than the $568 billion that would have been spent under the inherited Carter policies.

The main reason for this tepid reduction is that fully 55 percent of the Welfare State budget even then consisted of social insurance: Medicare, Social Security, unemployment insurance, and other non-means-tested income support programs. Quite evidently, there had been no Reagan Revolution on the social insurance front.

The modest 7 percent reduction that actually had been realized versus the inherited Carter baseline represented minor benefit tinkering and a one-time three months' delay of the Social Security cost of living adjustment (COLA). In the main, however, these savings were achieved by the imposition of un-Reagan-like price controls on Medicare hospitals.

Another sizeable portion of the domestic budget was comprised of spending for veterans and agriculture. These programs were blessed with strong Republican constituencies, and, in turn, were favored with only a token 2 percent reduction.

Even out-and-out "welfare" programs like food stamps, Medicaid, and Aid to Families with Dependent Children (AFDC) had been reduced from the Carter level by just 10 percent. There turned out to be fewer welfare queens and more arguably needy participants in these programs than Republican campaign rhetoric had implied.

At the end of the day, the only deep spending reduction that actually occurred was in a tiny corner of the budget consisting of Great Society employment and community services programs, which were shrunk by 25 percent from the Carter levels. Unfortunately, these savings amounted to just $12 billion annually or hardly 1 percent of the $1 trillion in total federal outlays during 1986.

And so it went. The Reagan Revolution turned out to be nothing of the kind when it came to domestic spending. It did not even constitute an era of meaningful reform. Instead, a few programs were pruned, no new ones were started, and the vast bulk of federal activities carried on as before.

In fiscal terms, the domestic welfare state remained at 15.5 percent of GDP. That was just a hair below where the Carter administration had left it and where it remained through the end of Bill Clinton's second term.

THE GROWTH CURE FOR DEFICITS: SUPPLY-SIDE FANTASY

A bastardized variation of supply-side theory has been embraced by Republican politicians in the years since Reagan. They have not explicitly claimed that deficits are harmless—they have just attempted to define the issue away. The argument has been that deficits are essentially the by-product of a weak economy and that the solution, therefore, is to undertake policy actions directed at growing the GDP, not shrinking the budget columns.

Not surprisingly, the way to get more GDP growth is claimed always and everywhere to be through lower taxes. In due course, fiscal deficits disappear because the economy grows the revenue line back to balance. The trouble with this shibboleth is that it was put to the test and failed a long time ago, during the Reagan-Bush recovery after 1982.

One of the longest sustained GDP expansion cycles on record began after the third quarter of 1982, when the Volcker cure had finally crushed the inflationary fires. During the following thirty-one quarters through mid-1990, real GDP expanded on an uninterrupted basis and for all practical purposes the US economy reached full employment by the end of the period.

In fact, the real GDP growth over this expansion averaged 4.3 percent per annum: the highest rate for any comparable period after the Second World War save for Johnson's artificial "guns and butter" boom ending in 1968. Still, cumulative deficits during this exceptional cyclical recovery cycle—fiscal 1983 through fiscal 1990—totaled $1.5 trillion. That was a previously unimaginable result in a peacetime economy.

Moreover, by the eighth year of the expansion, the federal deficit was still over 4 percent of GDP. In short, it is not reasonable to expect a better macroeconomic backdrop than this eight-year expansion, yet spending remained close to 22 percent of GDP and revenues were at 18 percent of GDP right up to the downturn in the second half of 1990. The deficit gap was plain and simply structural—the result of policy choices, not a weak economy.

Notwithstanding this eight-year string of positive GDP quarters, the federal borrowing requirement had averaged 4.2 percent of GDP. That figure was literally off the charts compared to pre-1980 experience. During the quarter century prior to Reagan's election, the federal deficit had averaged only 1.0 percent of GDP, and that interval included four separate recessions rather than a continuous up-cycle of expansion.

So the "grow your way out" theory had been invalid from the very beginning. Yet by embracing it in the decades since then, congressional Republicans have transformed their real job, managing the finances of the US government, into a sub-branch of statist pretension; that is, centrally managing the growth of the private economy through chronic fiddling with taxes.

THE TRUE REAGAN LEGACY:
FISCAL FREE LUNCHES FOR ALL

These numbers are bad enough, yet they fail to capture the more significant fiscal legacy of the Reagan Revolution. The more profound outcome was that the old-time taboo against chronic deficit finance in peacetime had been jettisoned by the Republican Party. At least since the New Deal, the GOP had been its champion and enforcer in the push and pull of what had been a tolerable two-party equilibrium in budget politics.

By contrast, the nation's fiscal equation would now be drawn and quartered. Even as the liberal spenders continued to push outlay levels higher, the conservative party would become chronically prone to pull the revenue level lower.

The fiscal data for the twelve years of Republican rule under Reagan and Bush show how completely the deficit finance taboo had been routed. There was red ink for twelve straight years, a pattern never before experienced in peacetime. As indicated, cumulative deficits during the period totaled $2.4 trillion, causing the national debt to triple.

A decade earlier, George Shultz and other Republican advocates of business-style Keynesian policies had convinced Nixon to embrace deficit spending in the guise of a "full employment budget." Yet they had at least insisted on a rule of longer-term discipline; that is, any countercyclical deficits incurred during periods of business downturn were to be compensated by surpluses during the expansion phase of the cycle.

Under the new Reagan-Bush dispensation, however, it was all deficits, all the time. In fact, the average federal deficit during this twelve-year period was 4.3 percent of GDP, a level never even imagined by the most aggressive liberal Keynesians before 1980.

Surveying the giant deficits which had already been incurred by 1986 and the prospects for more of the same into the indefinite future, I found these developments alarming. In my White House memoir entitled *The Triumph of Politics,* I complained that the White House "was holding the American economy hostage to the politics of high spending and the doctrine of low taxes."

From the vantage point of early 1986, it seemed certain that "the resulting massive buildup of public debt would eventually generate serious economic troubles . . . the White House claimed a roaring economic success. . . . Yet how can economic growth remain high and inflation low for the long run when the Administration's policy is to consume two-thirds of the nation's net private savings to fund the Federal deficit?"

It had been no exaggeration, therefore, to suggest that the nation had experienced a "lapse into fiscal indiscipline on a scale never experienced in peacetime. There is no basis in economic history or theory for believing from this wobbly foundation a lasting era of prosperity can actually emerge . . . At some point global investors will lose confidence in our easy dollars and debt financed prosperity, and then the chickens will come home to roost."

Except that they didn't. Instead, for two long decades the nation seemed to be blessed with nearly uninterrupted real GDP growth, low and declining inflation, and a sustained bull market in financial and real estate assets with no parallel in prior history. The accompanying boom in mass consumption was startling in its breadth and opulence.

Later we would learn that this was all a simulacrum of prosperity: a house of cards that would collapse with stunning speed and violence. Yet while it lasted, this faux prosperity reinforced the wrong-headed narrative that the Reagan Revolution had been a success; that the 1981 tax cut bill had been the incubator of two decades of prosperity; and that fiscal deficits didn't matter.

As has been indicated, the massive Republican deficits after 1980, which reached their ultimate conclusion in George W. Bush's final trillion-dollar-bailout-nation era, had not been "on the level." Beneath the economic surface, the pernicious force of printing-press money had been gathering volcanic momentum since 1971. And it was this unprecedented monetary deformation which finally accounted for both the debt-fueled illusion of prosperity and for the long, extended deferral of the day of fiscal reckoning.

CHAPTER 7

WHY THE CHICKENS DIDN'T COME HOME TO ROOST

The Nixon Abomination of August 1971

BY THE LATE 1980S, THE COMBINATION OF A STRONG ECONOMY and big deficits presented a conundrum which the old-time fiscal religion could not explain. In violation of all the classical canons of sound fiscal policy, the deluge of Reagan-era red ink was being readily financed, with no apparent boost to inflation or interest rates and no visible harm to economic growth and investment.

This macroeconomic hall pass was a pivotal development in the fiscal unraveling which has now engulfed the nation. It gave birth to the fatuous Cheney theorem—that Ronald Reagan proved deficits don't matter—and gave it credence, too. Republican politicians came to embrace it because the empirical evidence did not refute it. In the epigrammatic phrase of the great French monetary economist Jacques Rueff, the door had been opened to "deficits without tears."

The GOP was thus relieved of the conservative party's true calling in a modern welfare state democracy; that is, hard labor on the oars of fiscal rectitude. Indeed, with the fear of deficits gone, the GOP drifted into what amounted to Keynesianism for the prosperous classes. Tax cutting became its preferred tool for macroeconomic stimulus and for nursing private enterprise to a more vigorous performance path than it might achieve on its own.

There was an irony in this because it made the state and its politicians, rather than the free market economy, the arbitrator of how much growth and prosperity was possible. Any shortfall from the potential growth rate stipulated by the GOP's supply-side oracles became an excuse for further deficit financed tax cuts. Worse still, K Street became the breeding ground for the manifold instruments of this Keynesian-style tax stimulus, thereby placing Washington deep in the business of dispensing "incentives," allocating capital, and superintending the ebb and flow of growth and jobs among industries and regions.

But this was a giant lurch onto the wrong path. It stripped American democracy of healthy two-party competition on the matter of fiscal rectitude versus state largesse. It opened up a destructive dynamic in which the Democrats manned the state's ramparts of spending while the Republicans tunneled through its foundation of income.

As previously suggested, the false narrative about the Reaganite golden age and the nation's current fiscal incontinence are rooted in a common source; namely, the Nixon abomination of August 1971. In jettisoning the monetary anchor of the Bretton Woods gold exchange standard, Nixon paved the way for the eventual deformation of central banking. There emerged in lieu of sound money a makeshift monetary régime that spread around the globe and created a thirty-year interregnum in which trillions of Washington's debt emissions were warehoused in the vaults of the world's central banks. The economic sting of massive treasury borrowing was thereby anesthetized.

This is the reason why post-1980 fiscal deficits did not give rise to the classic economic dislocations. There was no enduring domestic interest rate and investment crunch, for example, because Uncle Sam's deficits were being monetized and exported, not financed out of the nation's savings pool. After the 1980s consumer prices did not surge either because the central banks of the rapidly growing East Asian mercantilists were more than happy to import unwanted inflationary dollars via their currency-pegging operations.

So the irony was large. The Reagan era's wild fiscal misfire on defense, taxes, and domestic spending had been essentially sterilized by another financial deformation; namely, the floating paper dollar monetary arrangement that Nixon and John Connally had forced on the world after August 1971. The story of that travesty powerfully amplifies why the Reagan Revolution was not a golden age of free market capitalism but only a way station on the road to the BlackBerry Panic of 2008.

THE DIRTY SECRET OF FLOATING CURRENCIES

The conservative economists who advised Republicans to jettison Bretton Woods were reflexive free marketers who suffered from monetary amnesia; that is, they ignored the fact that the massive war inflation of 1914–1918 had ended the classic gold standard and changed the fundamental nature of money, making it an artifact of state policy. Failing to note that money would be heavily manipulated by the central banking branches of the world's sovereign states, they erroneously viewed the floating-rate system as a good thing because the free market would purportedly set currency exchange rates.

Yet as wards of the state, the central banks were now indentured to its policy imperatives rather than to the superintendence of sound money. That was proven in spades by the inflationary debacle that exploded during the very first decade of floating. Indeed, by the end of the 1970s it was evident that there wasn't much about the international currency exchanges which resembled the theoretical "free market."

The global currency markets had already become havens of "dirty float" where state manipulation of exchange rates was the modus operandi. Likewise, the only thing "free" about the new arrangement was that the Fed now had a fantastic new license to freely expand its balance sheet at rates never before imagined, and with a result that the conservative economists had not even remotely anticipated. Buying government bills and bonds without the external discipline of redeemability, the Fed injected massive liquidity into the Wall Street banking system—where more and more of it ended up in speculative finance, not the real economy.

So there was nothing "progressive" about the post–Bretton Woods monetary arrangements. In closing the gold window, Tricky Dick brought sound, redeemable money to an unceremonious end, and not because he was a modernizing monetary reformer aiming to rid the system of the "barbarous relic" which even Keynes had been forced to embrace in 1944.

Instead, Nixon was a crass, nationalistic politician who put his own reelection above all other considerations, including the nation's obligation to keep the dollar honest and repay its external debts in a fixed weight of gold. Monetary arrangements must last for the ages if they are to be credible, but according to the cynical Nixonian template, no obligation was admissible which might cause an uptick in the unemployment rate before November 1972.

As will be seen, the Bretton Woods gold exchange standard was fundamentally flawed, so it was only a matter of time before it fell at the hand of a bombastic White House occupant like Johnson or Nixon. Still, when it was finally jettisoned, its indispensable core function of imposing a rough discipline on each nation to live within its means was also lost. What was not even dimly grasped in 1971 was that the demise of Bretton Woods had unshackled the central banks in a manner never previously experienced in modern financial history.

Given the dominant position of the US economy and the dollar at that time, the fatal danger was that the Fed had now been positioned to emit unlimited credit through the US banking system. The only real restraint was the willingness of the rest of the world to accumulate and hold dollar liabilities.

As it turned out, other nations were mighty willing. The flood of dollars into the global economy did not cause its exchange rate to collapse because mercantilist central banks bought dollars hand over fist in order to suppress the exchange rates of their own currencies. This massive, prolonged hoarding of dollar liabilities by foreign central banks had never been foreseen by the conservative economists who championed floating rates.

Indeed, the willingness of statist leaders in East Asia and the Persian Gulf to endlessly swap the resource endowments of their lands and the labor of their people for dollar IOUs, in their pursuit of a flawed mercantilist model of growth and prosperity, knew no historical precedent. It is one of the great deformations on which the modern global economy rests precariously.

After August 1971, this monetary deformation gathered inexorable momentum and girth, one step at a time. Eventually, like a hungry parasite, it would ingest US Treasury and agency debt with gluttonous abandon.

As will be seen, there was no stopping this great monetary deformation because the nation's conservative party failed to comprehend and rectify it at every step along the way. After Nixon and Burns incited the global commodity price explosion of the 1970s, Republicans rationalized the Fed's continued production of excess dollars on the feckless grounds that inflation had to be "financed" and could only be brought down slowly.

In February 1986, a Republican White House essentially fired Paul Volcker—the one Fed chairman who had actually brought down inflation decisively and had restored a semblance of sound money. In the 1990s, an unabashedly Republican Fed chairman compounded the Reagan fiscal mishap by opening the monetary floodgates, enabling a devastating collapse of the nation's current account and tradable goods sector.

After the turn of the century, still another Republican White House populated the nation's central bank with Wall Street–pleasing money printers who confused rank speculation with genuine investment, and a giant debt bubble with sustainable prosperity. When the monetary bubble finally collapsed in September 2008, a Republican treasury secretary closed ranks with a GOP-appointed cabal at the Fed to unleash a wave of free money so immense that it has effectively destroyed the free market in finance. With friends like that, sound money needed no enemies.

THE TURNING POINT: LBJ'S "GUNS AND BUTTER"
ASSAULT ON SOUND MONEY

As will be seen in Part III, the demise of sound money reaches back to the Great War and FDR's embrace of economic nationalism in 1933. But what triggered the final destruction of Bretton Woods was LBJ's "guns and butter" fiscal policies. Beginning in 1966, the US economy began to dramatically overheat, owing to LBJ's unprecedented spree of "borrow and spend." In these circumstances, the Fed's great tribune of sound money and long-serving Fed chairman, William McChesney Martin, urged Johnson to pay for his budget-busting adventures with taxes on the people, not freshly minted credit from the central bank.

LBJ not only stubbornly refused to raise taxes, but also literally manhandled the Fed chairman, forcing him to monetize the rapidly expanding federal deficit. Not surprisingly, the Fed's balance sheet was soon transformed from a model of prudence into a vehicle of pell-mell monetary expansion. In fact, when it succumbed to LBJ's bullying in 1966, the Fed's holdings of government debt stood at just $44 billion. Yet by the time Paul Volcker arrived, fire hose in hand, in August 1979 it had nearly tripled to $120 billion.

These central bank purchases of government bonds, of course, were funded with new Federal Reserve credit to the banking system which was conjured out of thin air. The resulting 8 percent annual growth of new bank reserves for more than a decade was an unfathomable departure from historic monetary discipline. During the previous quarter century of stable, noninflationary economic expansion, for example, the Fed's balance sheet had edged up at just 2.8 percent per year.

NIXON'S MONETARY POLICY:
"GIVE US MORE MONEY, ARTHUR"

Although Martin had reluctantly caved to LBJ's bullying, Nixon took office with a deep grievance against the Fed chairman and availed himself of the first opportunity to get rid of him. Leaving no doubts about his expectations of his replacement, Nixon offered Arthur Burns a "vote of appreciation in advance for low interest rates and more money" at his swearing-in ceremony in January 1970.

On his way out the front door of the Eccles Building, the outgoing Fed chairman minced no words: "We are in deep trouble. We are in the wildest inflation since the Civil War." Martin's words, obviously, could not have been more prophetic.

Professor Arthur F. Burns had not spent a lifetime pandering to power, however, in order to be swayed now, even by the ringing admonition of the greatest central banker the nation had yet known. Nixon wanted more money, and Burns did not disappoint.

In fact, the White House's infamous tape-recording system memorialized Burns' complete surrender of monetary policy to Nixon's reelection imperatives. In a private meeting before the 1972 election, the Fed chairman resorted to what can only be described as abject groveling as he assured Nixon that the Fed would not undo him again—something Tricky Dick fervently believed it had done during the election of 1960.

The chairman of the nation's supposedly independent central bank thus assured Nixon: "I have done everything in my power to help you as President, your reputation and standing in American life and history. . . . No one has tried harder to help you."

That was completely true. During the first two years of his tenure, Burns gunned the money supply like no Fed chairman before him had ever contemplated. Accordingly, the Fed's balance sheet grew by nearly 11 percent two years in a row.

Nor was this an aberration. Under Burns' direction the Fed continued to purchase government debt aggressively in the years ahead, even as inflation soared. By the end of his term in 1978 the Federal Reserve was fast becoming a warehouse for the national debt.

Needless to say, what had been considered a world of stable prices, embodied in the 1.4 percent average rise in the CPI between 1953 and 1966, was left far behind. In its place, this first chapter of printing-press money and unhinged credit growth generated a classic storm of consumer price inflation. At that point, neither floating exchange rates, nor mercantilist central banks, nor masses of cheap rural Asian labor were available to siphon-off excess domestic demand.

Accordingly, the consumer price index had first broken through 3 percent in mid-1967 and then had escalated upward to 4, 5, and 6 percent, respectively, in each of the next twelve-month periods. These were shocking rates of inflation, drastically outside the range of any peacetime experience during the twentieth century.

Through the spring of 1971, the inflationary surge was largely domestic, and there can be little doubt that the soaring growth of bank lending was the catalyst. The US economy was already on the boil owing to massive military spending on top of the booming civilian sector. Capacity utilization levels were at unsustainable all-time highs, but it was the rock-bottom unemployment rate, continuously below 4 percent for more than forty-eight months through early 1970, that best measured the US economy's white heat.

Accordingly, with scarcely any untapped man-hours left in the US economy, let alone unused factory production lines, the Fed's gunning of bank-lending growth, which clocked an 8 percent annual rate of growth, was inexplicable. It self-evidently amounted to pouring kerosene on the already raging fires of excess demand.

In his final months as chairman, Martin finally brushed off the White House pressures, reining in credit growth sufficiently to induce a mild recession in the fourth quarter of 1969. This move was more than warranted, even if the inflationary horse—now galloping at 6 percent—had already left the barn.

The initial hit to growth from Martin's tightening amounted to a pinprick—with real GDP declining by only 0.4 percent during the two winter quarters of 1969–1970. But upon Burns' appointment, Nixon hounded his new Fed chairman relentlessly—so he compliantly engineered a solid recovery during the second and third quarters of 1970. In a real economic sense that was the end of the 1970 recession. What made it appear more imposing at the time was a landmark sixty-seven-day-long strike at General Motors (GM) in the final quarter of 1970. That helped tip the economy back into a slump, but as the data show that was purely statistical—an inventory shuffle between quarters.

Needless to say, Richard Nixon did not like bad economic statistics, and most emphatically so when they coincided with an election. Moreover, back then GM still had serious economic throw-weight, as evidenced by its 50 percent share of the US auto market and its status as the world's largest corporation.

So the strike caused 400,000 GM workers to be idled directly and pushed multiples of that number onto the unemployment rolls across the automotive supplier and dealer infrastructure. All told, the unemployment rate rose from 4 percent at the beginning of the year to nearly 6 percent by Election Day 1970.

The strike ended a few weeks later and much of the output loss proved to be temporary. Yet the strike's blow to the economy in the final quarter of 1970 got Nixon's full and purposeful attention.

NIXON'S POST MID-TERM ELECTION COMMAND: THE US ECONOMY MUST BOOM BY JULY 1972

When the polls closed on the midterm elections, an even worse batch of statistics materialized: the loss of nine GOP seats in the House and negligible gains in the Senate. Ruminating over these unwelcome results, Nixon told his trusty praetorians, Chief of Staff Bob Haldeman and Domestic

Affairs Advisor John Ehrlichman, exactly what he was thinking about economic policy for the coming two years.

Haldeman noted in his diary that "P still concerned about '72. Can't afford to risk a downtrend, no matter how much inflation."

Ehrlichman recorded an even more precise presidential admonition: "The economy must boom beginning July 1972."

Richard Nixon was warming up for his August 1971 demarche: the straitjacket of wage and price controls on the domestic economy and default on the nation's international debts which emerged from Camp David. In one of the greatest paradoxes of modern history, Nixon would be advised on the formulation of that thoroughly statist plan by the largest assemblage of free market economists ever gathered under one presidential roof.

The underlying economic predicate of that weekend's plan—infamously and hilariously christened the New Economic Plan, or NEP, which was the name Lenin had given to his partial relapse to capitalism a half century earlier—was just plain wrong. The Nixon White House was maneuvering to gun the US economy with a fresh wave of credit expansion when it wasn't needed and could on no account be justified.

The pretext had been macroeconomic weakness, but as indicated, the 1970 recession amounted to a head fake. The dip in the winter quarters of 1969–1970 was so mild that it amounted to just $20 billion in today's dollars. Even that momentary pause occurred after thirty-five straight quarters of red-hot GDP growth and in a context in which the economy was operating way beyond its sustainable capacity.

The statistical tables, of course, show a second 4.2 percent annualized GDP plunge in the fourth quarter of 1970. Nearly 85 percent of that decline, however, represented inventory liquidation—a not unsurprising consequence of the sixty-seven-day auto strike which had emptied the nation's car dealer lots and auto supply pipeline.

During the very next quarter, in fact, the rubber band snapped back. Real GDP rebounded by 11 percent in the first quarter of 1971. More than half of that gain represented the scramble to refill the very same automotive pipeline that had just been emptied.

So when the violent, strike-induced inventory swings are set aside, the underlying facts are unmistakable: real GDP on a final sales basis grew at an average rate of 2.5 percent during the four quarters ending in June 1971. There was no downturn for Nixon's aptly named NEP to counteract.

As of mid-year 1971, however, there was ample evidence that the US economy was in the throes of a severe inflationary spiral. Consumer prices were 5 percent above year-earlier levels and wage growth in bedrock sectors of the economy was beginning to soar. Compensation costs in manufacturing were up by 7 percent from the previous year, and construction industry wages were rising by 9 percent, with first-year settlements among unionized firms reaching 18 percent.

As shown below, this intensifying inflationary spiral was bad news for the dollar, since by now large balances of unwanted dollars were accumulating in the major European central banks. But the administration made no effort to placate foreign-dollar holders, and Richard Nixon was outright bombastic on the topic.

When he learned in late 1970 that Burns had resisted too steep a decline in interest rates because of concern about the dollar, Nixon fumed to Ehrlichman that the Fed chairman should "get it right in the chops." Prior to a meeting with him in December 1970, Nixon informed his staff that if Burns brought up the balance of payments constraints on monetary policy again, "I'll unload on him like he's never had."

Punctuating the point that same week, Nixon announced that John B. Connally, who had never met an interest rate he considered low enough, would be appointed secretary of the treasury. From the perspective of history, Nixon was playing with monetary fire. The linchpin of the Bretton Woods system was worldwide trust in US financial discipline. Central banks in Europe and elsewhere held dollars, rather than gold, as foreign exchange reserves because they believed the dollar was as good as gold. Now he was serving them an emasculated Fed chairman and a swashbuckling financial cowboy at the Treasury.

As detailed more fully in chapter 12, foreign confidence in US fidelity to its Bretton Woods commitments had already been badly shaken by Johnson's war deficits and his bullying of the Fed for easier money. In the eyes of traders and foreign central bankers alike, these policies—continued by Nixon—were self-evidently fueling an inflationary domestic boom that was drawing in imports at an accelerating rate, thereby sharply undermining the US balance of payments.

This was alarming to dollar holders everywhere because the United States was already sending massive amounts of greenbacks overseas to finance its Cold War imperium. If it now persisted in streaming even more dollars abroad to live high on the hog on a bloated diet of civilian imports, the stockpile of excess offshore dollars would reach the breaking point.

In fact, a crisis of historic proportion was fast approaching, but by the spring of 1971 Nixon had discarded the two advisors who actually knew something about international monetary affairs. Burns had become an object of contempt despite his furious money printing, and the White House economic advisor, Paul McCracken, was excluded from even attending crucial economic meetings.

So Nixon was listening almost exclusively to Connally, whose ignorance of economic history exceeded even Nixon's meager grasp. And in that development lurked an extreme danger.

The United States was facing a day of reckoning. It urgently needed to restore disciplined fiscal and monetary policies if the rudiments of the crippled but serviceable Bretton Woods monetary system were to be kept intact.

In the alternative, continuing to hurtle down the road of nationalistic financial profligacy was certain to blow the postwar monetary system to smithereens. This was a baleful prospect. Bretton Woods had indisputably fostered worldwide recovery and sustained economic growth while throttling the propensities for inflation and financial speculation inherent in a fiat money system.

Richard Nixon did not recognize the stakes, nor trouble himself with the weighty implications of the decisions at hand. In fact, as revealed in the private papers of his inner circle, Nixon treated these issues with stunning insouciance.

Thus, after about a year in the Oval Office he instructed Haldeman to screen out the topic entirely: "I do not want to be bothered with international monetary matters . . . and will not need to see the reports on international money matters in the future."

It is hard to fathom a more feckless gesture, since almost from the day he entered the Oval Office Nixon was being warned of severe international monetary turmoil ahead. One of the more cogent alarms came from conservative economist Henry Hazlitt, who titled his March 1969 *Newsweek* column "The Coming Monetary Collapse."

Hazlitt publicly warned the White House that "one of these days the United States will be openly forced to refuse to pay out any more of its gold at $35 an ounce." The result, Hazlitt insisted, would be a "run or crisis in the foreign exchange market" that could end convertibility entirely. "If it does . . . the consequence for the United States and the world will be grave."

Hazlitt could not have been more clairvoyant. The postwar monetary order was at a crucial inflection point. It would soon lurch into a forty-year spree of global debt creation, financial speculation, and massive economic imbalance—yet Nixon refused to even read the briefing papers.

So as the crisis came to a head, it was up to Connally to review the reports—and the report on merchandise trade for June 1971 wasn't good.

The US trade balance had still shown a small $3 billion surplus in 1970, even though that did not begin to pay for the $10 billion spent abroad in the military and foreign aid accounts.

But now the trade accounts, too, had turned negative, making it highly probable that the United States would experience its first annual merchandise trade deficits since 1893. The cause of this southward turn after seventy-eight years of surplus was plainly evident. Malevolent foreigners had not suddenly filled their harbors with rocks and turned back ships laden with American exports.

In fact, exports were growing at double-digit rates, but even this was not sufficient to keep up with the flow of imports to domestic factories and retail shelves. The latter had rocketed upward by 65 percent during the previous thirty months, rising from a $30 billion annual rate when Nixon took office to a $50 billion run rate by the summer of 1971.

TREASURY SECRETARY CONNALLY'S MONETARY POLICY— SCREW THEM FIRST

If these facts were known to the treasury secretary, they were not much evident in his take on the mushrooming trade problem. "My basic approach is that the foreigners are out to screw us," Connally told an audience of visitors. "Our job is to screw them first."

In the larger scheme of history, however, Connally had it upside down. Bretton Woods was a gold exchange standard system that depended as much on the political and financial discipline of the reserve currency issuer as it did on the intrinsic value of the yellow metal.

This truth was deeply embedded in the lore of European central banking. A gold exchange standard based on the pound sterling had been tried after the First World War. Exactly fifty years earlier, in fact, the central banks of France, Netherlands, Belgium, Sweden, and others learned a hard lesson about the risks of holding their monetary assets in the reserve currency.

During the late 1920s they had accumulated large amounts of sterling exchange which they could have converted to gold. But they had kept their reserves in pounds sterling in deference to the so-called gold exchange standard that had been promoted by the British Treasury and Bank of England since the early 1920s.

On the morning of September 20, 1931, the great central banks of Europe discovered they had been betrayed, as the value of their reserves had instantly dropped by 35 percent. That occurred when the Bank of England defaulted on its obligation to convert sterling to gold—and did so without warning and notwithstanding its continuous assurances the sterling parity would be defended at all hazards.

So this time the Europeans, especially President de Gaulle of France, were not about to be screwed, either first or again. Gold outflows from the United States intensified in the spring of 1971 and reached alarming levels after the June trade deficit figures became public. Nixon and Connally now faced a run on the bank, but it was a run of their own making.

WHEN A CAMP FULL OF FREE MARKET ECONOMISTS OPTED FOR FREE MONEY

The abomination which emerged from Camp David on the weekend of August 15, 1971, was anchored to a single constant: ensuring the election year economic boom that Nixon wanted by July 1972. Yet an honest boom wasn't possible because the US economy was already in the throes of inflationary fevers.

Under those conditions, the White House desire for an election year burst of economic stimulus measures—business investment tax credits and individual tax relief—plus open-throttle monetary expansion would have turned the heavy gold outflow then under way into a swirling torrent. Yet when the administration's assemblage of free market wise men arrived at Camp David, they promptly checked their intellectual baggage with the marines at the gate and spent the weekend pandering to Nixon's every wish. The heart of the scheme which ensued was a ninety-day freeze on everything—wages, prices, rents, and interest rates.

Presumably, the disciples of Milton Friedman in the room, who had been taught that inflation is "everywhere and always a monetary phenomenon," would have resisted the illusion of bureaucratic controls. Better still, they might have insisted that Fed chairman Arthur Burns, who was also at Camp David, do something meaningful about inflation, such as putting the brakes on credit growth which was then galloping ahead at a 10 percent annual rate.

Professor Friedman's chief disciple on hand that weekend, however, was George Shultz, who had already perfected his patented craft of explaining things to presidents exactly as they preferred to hear them. Referring to the ninety-day freeze, Shultz plied Nixon with a whopper: "In your statement," Shultz advised, "you should show we will use this period to stop inflation in its tracks."

Friedman would have flunked all day long any student who advanced the lame proposition that a roaring monetary inflation could be stopped cold by a president's TV speech. But such hallucinatory economics was apparently contagious that weekend because it afflicted Friedman's long ago doctoral thesis advisor, too, none other than Professor Arthur F. Burns.

In his present capacity as Fed chairman, Burns added to the Camp

David madness with an even more feckless narrative: "I would have a three month freeze, which would have shock value, and give us time to work out the machinery for dealing with stabilization. I would add Congressional leaders to the [wage and price] commission to develop our plan. . . . And there would be the distinct threat that if labor and management can't agree, something would be imposed upon them."

Thus, down in its engine room, the nation's $1 trillion economy was hissing and crackling with inflationary wage and price pressures. Yet Washington was now going to command billions of prices and wages to stand exactly still for thirteen weeks.

Then, during the standstill, an even more implausible scenario would unfold. A tripartite board of politicians would figure out new wage and price edicts, and also how to penalize any citizens who engaged in non-compliant acts of market capitalism.

Never before had there been an act of peacetime economic governance so fatuous. Nor had there been one which had such predictable, calamitous results as did the freeze and the increasingly destructive and ineffectual control "phases" which followed.

Still, had Shultz called it a day after taking a powder on wage and price controls at Camp David, history might have overlooked his perfidy. Nixon and Connally were going to impose them anyway. But his unforgiveable offense was in giving intellectual cover to Connally's assault on Bretton Woods and the administration's cowardly default on the nation's external debts.

GEORGE SHULTZ: GODFATHER OF FLOATING MONEY

Speechwriter Bill Safire, who later in his career became a *New York Times* op-ed page columnist, was a faithful scribe of the proceedings, and his notes leave little doubt about how Nixon came to his decision to close the gold window. Nixon first confessed that on the gold question he had "never seen so many intelligent experts who disagree 180 degrees."

He then went on to pin the tail of the pending US gold default exactly where it belonged: "George [Schulz] and the others like the floating idea."

Now a crack-up boom was only a matter of time. The wage and price freeze couldn't possibly contain the inflationary pressure in the domestic economy, but floating the dollar and then laying a 10 percent import surcharge on top brought a further gale force of rising import prices to American shores.

While the freeze and controls temporarily suppressed consumer level prices, the havoc was quickly evident in energy and raw materials, where prices were largely set in the world market and outside the reach of controls. Within twenty-four months of the Camp David meeting, the price index for crude materials was up a startling 80 percent, and with the final failure of the control apparatus in 1973, the consumer price index quickly followed.

In fact, consumer prices rose by 8.7 percent in 1973 and 12.3 percent in 1974. These were shocking hits to the American cost of living, yet they just kept coming as the decade wore on. During the thirteen years after mid-1966, the cost of living rose by 125 percent.

Nixon's famous Sunday evening televised speech after Camp David, of course, had promised the opposite: to stop inflation in its tracks. Although that was utterly inconsistent with taxing imports and trashing the dollar, Connally had squared that circle, too.

During the fateful deliberations at Camp David, the president wondered how to justify closing the gold window. Even at that late hour, Nixon suffered from an atavistic hesitancy about being the president who "devalued the dollar."

Connally was plagued with no such doubts and was clueless about the vast inflationary consequences of unhinging the dollar. He thus succinctly explained to the nation's chief executive: "Our assets are going out by the bushel basket. You're in the hands of the money changers."

So Nixon, in turn, explained to the nation that he was responding to "an all-out war" against the dollar led by "international money speculators." He was right about a brutal attack on the dollar, but the real truth was that it was being waged by the Nixon administration itself. In fact, even as inflation escalated and world markets dumped the dollar in response to the US default on Bretton Woods, fiscal and monetary discipline was eviscerated even further.

Once again, the executioner of sound policy was George Shultz, former professor of industrial relations at the University of Chicago. Whether Shultz had actually absorbed any "free market" principles while resident at the mecca of free market economics is an open question. Yet there can be no doubt that his affinity for its opposite, "free lunch" nostrums, slackened not one bit as he climbed the rungs of power at the White House.

The most destructive of these free lunch elixirs was the "full-employment budget." This concept had long been embraced by the Keynesian professoriate at Harvard, but now, thanks to Shultz, it was proudly advocated by the Nixon White House, too.

The beauty of the full-employment budget was that you could spend every penny of theoretical revenue that would come into the government's coffers under conditions of "full employment." Never mind if the Treasury's actual cash receipts were far lower and that the budget was bleeding red ink—that kind of borrowing didn't matter.

Better yet, the calculation of these phantom full-employment revenues was based on an even more ethereal construct called "potential GNP." There was a nontrivial possibility, however, that the econometricians tasked with divining this ghostly shadow, wafting above the actual economy, would arrive at a figure exactly suited to balancing the theoretical full-employment "revenue" with the actual spending needs of the White House.

In the event, the full-employment budget cover story served its purpose. Even as Nixon importuned the public to suck in its collective gut and adhere to a wage and price freeze, federal outlays jumped by 10 percent during fiscal 1972, and the actual budget deficit rose from the prior year to a near-record $23.4 billion. And in this outcome the wholly pernicious nature of the full-employment budget revealed itself.

In those days, Washington was still on a June 30 fiscal year, so the path of the economy following the NEP announced in August 1971 maps almost perfectly against fiscal year 1972. Accordingly, during the first two fiscal quarters real GDP expanded at a 2.2 percent annual rate, but then picked up stunning momentum thereafter.

In the next quarter, GDP growth jumped to 7.3 percent and then closed out the June quarter and fiscal year 1972 with a surge to 9.8 percent. In only four quarters out of the 250 quarters since 1950 has the rate of GDP growth come in that high.

Likewise, during the year after Camp David the number of nonfarm payroll jobs soared by nearly 4 percent, one of the largest twelve-month gains ever recorded. In short, Nixon got his booming economy by July 1972 just as he had instructed Haldeman after the midterm elections.

What he also got was a red-hot economic bubble and a mockery of the full-employment budget theory. Fiscal policy was supposed to shift smartly toward restraint in the face of an economy hurtling toward its outer limits. Evidently, the Shultz-Nixon version included a "time-out" for election years.

HOW ARTHUR BURNS GOT OUT OF NIXON'S DOGHOUSE: THE FINAL DESTRUCTION OF SOUND MONEY

On the monetary front, the picture was even worse. Arthur Burns had been yammering for an "incomes policy" for more than a year before Camp David. Needless to say, the essential mission of the Federal Reserve is price stability, so the very fact that the Fed chairman was angling for a tripartite board to meddle with wages and prices was smoking-gun evidence that he was already failing.

Indeed, once he got the official cover of the wage and price freeze, Burns wasted no time hitting the monetary accelerator and thereby getting himself out of Nixon's doghouse. Accordingly, outstanding bank loans grew by $100 billion during 1972, which was a blistering 17 percent rate of growth in an economy already steaming with excess demand and suffering a violent dose of imported inflation from the weak dollar.

Yet Burns was just getting started. Bank loans to businesses and households increased by another 16 percent in 1973. This meant that in the brief span of twenty-four months Burns had presided over a 36 percent expansion of bank credit.

This $200 billion blizzard of new bank lending amounted to 20 percent of GDP, a two-year spree of credit expansion never again duplicated at that rate in the United States. In fact, Burns' record was exceeded only when the People's Printing Press of China, in a desperate bid to keep its red capitalism alive after the collapse of global trade, opened the credit floodgates even wider in the fall of 2008.

In the face of this unprecedented bout of fiscal and monetary profligacy, the newly unshackled dollar did indeed float—and the direction was nearly straight down. During the first twenty-four months after Camp David, the dollar lost almost 20 percent of its value. Not surprisingly, the White House viewed this calamity as vindication of its policies.

This kind of perverse triumphalism was the specialty of George Shultz, who had now been promoted to secretary of the treasury. He then joined hands with the White House's resident Keynesian economist, Herb Stein, in a circle known as the "religious floaters."

A leading historian of the era succinctly captured the surrealism which played out during a lull in the dollar's descent in late May 1973: "At the end of the month, Shultz ventured that floating was 'working nicely.' The next day the Germans raised interest rates, and the dollar began a plunge into the monetary abyss."

So did the American economy. During the period then under way, the second quarter of 1973, real GDP clocked in at $4.9 trillion in today's dollars. From there, real output then fell backward for the next twenty-seven months. It wasn't until the fourth quarter of 1975 that real GDP regained its second quarter of 1973 level. And not before unemployment had soared to 9 percent in May 1975.

During that same month in the spring of 1975, the consumer price index was 21 percent higher than when Shultz had found the floating dollar to be "working nicely" two years earlier. The NEP of the Nixon White House had, in fact, generated the nightmare of stagflation.

THE GLOBAL INFLATION CATASTROPHE
AFTER CAMP DAVID

In the meantime, the global currency markets had plunged into chaos. As will be seen, the free market for exchange rates turned out to be an utter illusion, as government after government jumped into the fray for the purpose of protecting domestic industries and jobs, and to safeguard their citizens against the alleged depredations of speculators and money changers.

Yet this kind of dirty floating was not the ultimate problem. The world economy was now at the mercy of a "reserve currency" that was no longer anchored to anything except the self-restraint of US policy officials, the very missing ingredient that had brought Bretton Woods down.

So what transpired during the early years of floating was a massive worldwide expansion of money and credit fueled by the Fed. This, in turn, generated the greatest bout of commodity price inflation that the world had seen since the postwar fly-up in 1919.

Crude oil led the way. Having been priced on the world market at $1.40 per barrel when Nixon's free marketers gathered at Camp David in August 1971, it rose to an interim peak of $13 per barrel four years later. And that was a way station to its eventual top of $40 per barrel by 1980.

The dramatic post-1971 escalation of worldwide oil prices was blamed by officialdom on political rather than economic forces—and in particular the alleged market rigging of the OPEC cartel. In fact, except for a brief period around the October 1973 Mideast war, there was no systematic withholding of oil from the market.

The problem was not a shortage of oil but a flood of money and inflated demand. During 1972–1974, the global economy reached a red-hot pace of expansion, which in some part was due to the locomotive pull of the Nixon boom. For example, non-oil imports to the United States rose by 15 percent in the first year after Camp David, and then accelerated to 22 percent growth the next year and 28 percent during the twelve months ending in August 1974. These giant gains in imported goods were literally off the charts.

So as blistering US demand ignited production booms around the world, factory operating rates rose and supply chain backlogs surged everywhere on the planet. Moreover, there was another entirely new, even more potent force at work. In response to the Fed's flood of money and credit, other central banks around the world reciprocated with their own fulsome monetary expansion.

They bought dollars and sold their own currencies in foreign exchange markets in order to forestall the upward pressure on exchange rates that was inherent in the brave new world of floating currencies. In other words, the heretofore circumspect central bankers of the world became furious money printers in self-defense as they faced the flood tide of dollars being issued by Arthur F. Burns.

In fact, with exchange rates no longer fixed and visible, a more subtle process of competitive devaluation became the daily modus operandi of the system. In this manner, the Fed propagated its inflationary monetary policies outward to the balance of the world economy.

So it was a storm of money and credit expansion which generated the first commodity bubble after 1971, not the OPEC cartel alone or even primarily. For if the problem had been just the putative rigging of prices by the oil cartel, there is no way to explain the dozens of parallel commodity booms during the same two- to three-year time frame.

Quite obviously, there was no evidence of cartel arrangements in the markets for rice, copper, pork bellies, or industrial tallow, for example. Yet between 1971 and 1974, rice rose from $10 to $30 per hundredweight, while pork bellies climbed from $0.30 per pound to $1.

Likewise, the cost of a ton of scrap steel soared from $40 to $140; tin jumped from $2 to $5 per pound; and the price of coffee rocketed up nearly eightfold, from 42 cents to $3.20 per pound. Even industrial tallow caught a tailwind, rising from $0.06 to $.0.20 per pound, and pretty much the same pattern was reflected in the price of corn, copper, cotton, lead, lumber, and soybeans.

Needless to say, the first inflationary cycle of floating money came as a shock to policy officials, especially the Federal Reserve and its chairman. While Chairman Burns was a pusillanimous accommodator when it came to the game of hardball politics in Washington, as a matter of belief he had remained an anti-inflation hawk.

So when Nixon went into his terminal Watergate descent, Burns got his nerve back and threw on the monetary brakes. Accordingly, double-digit bank credit expansion came to a screeching halt, rising by only 1.2 percent in 1975.

THE 1974 RECESSION: INVENTORY LIQUIDATION AND OUTPUT COLLAPSE CAUSED BY THE CENTRAL BANK

The resulting recession was described at the time as the deepest since the 1930s, but there were really not many parallels. Housing construction did suffer a sharp retrenchment and business investment spending also declined moderately.

Yet on the core component of the US economy—consumer spending, which even then accounted for two-thirds of GDP—there was virtually no reduction. The peak-to-trough decline in real terms was just 0.7 percent. This was hardly the stuff of a near depression and not even in the same ballpark as the 20 percent decline in real household consumption which had occurred during the Great Depression.

Instead, the heart of the 1974–1975 downturn was a sweeping liquidation of industrial and commercial inventories, which accounted for fully two-thirds of the drop in real GDP. Moreover, that generally underappreciated fact followed exactly from the type of inflationary boom that had now been made possible by the destruction of Bretton Woods.

During 1972–1973 the drastic escalation of global commodity prices led to a scramble by businesses to buy forward and accumulate buffer stocks of raw materials, components, and finished goods before prices escalated even higher. This forward buying and accumulation of inventories was at the heart of the post–Camp David boom and bust.

When the monetary expansion was finally halted and pricing pressures subsided, businesses then violently disgorged these same inventories during the subsequent correction phase. Accordingly, what is reported as a deep 3 percent peak-to-trough decline in real GDP during the 1973–1975 recession cycle was only a 1 percent decline based on final sales. All the rest of the deep recession reflected the destocking of what had been excess inventories in the first place.

This rather persuasive evidence that inflationary monetary policy does not enhance long-term growth but only destabilizes the inventory cycle never sunk in among policy makers. In fact, when the downturn did temporarily break the commodity speculation cycle and cause the rate of CPI increase to temporarily dip under 5 percent, Burns and the Ford White House did exactly the wrong thing: they launched a new round of stimulus and soon rekindled an even more virulent inflation.

After assuming the presidency in August 1974, Gerald Ford had started off on the right foot. As a fiscally orthodox Midwestern Republican, he had been frightened by the recent runaway inflation and repulsed by the insanity of the Nixon freeze and the ever-changing wage and price control rules and phases which followed. Ford had also been just plain embarrassed by Nixon's five straight years of large budget deficits.

So for a brief moment in the fall of 1974, he launched a campaign to get back to the basics. Ford proposed to jettison the notion that the budget was an economic policy tool, and demanded that Washington return to the sober business of responsibly managing the spending and revenue accounts of the federal government.

To this end, he called for drastic spending cuts to keep the current-year budget under $300 billion. He also requested a 5 percent surtax on the incomes of corporations and more affluent households to staunch the flow of budget red ink. At that point in history Ford's proposed tax increase was applauded by fiscal conservatives, and there was no supply-side chorus around to denounce it. In fact, Art Laffer had just vacated his position as an underling at OMB.

BILL SIMON'S CRUSADE AGAINST THE
FULL-EMPLOYMENT BUDGET ILLUSION

In attempting to get Washington off the fiscal stimulus drug, Ford was aided immeasurably by the fact that Shultz had vacated the Treasury Department and had been replaced by Bill Simon. The latter was from a wholly different kettle of fish.

In fact, Simon was an inflation-hating bond trader who fervently believed in free markets and smaller government, and had no patience whatever for gussied-up academic theories that justified federal meddling, spending, and borrowing. Thus, when asked at a congressional hearing whether he intended to use the full-employment budget as a fiscal guide, Simon bluntly replied, "No, sir."

Accordingly, Simon wasted no time in summarily discarding the budget for fiscal year 1975 which the Nixon White House had submitted earlier in the year. Shultz had claimed it embodied an $8 billion full-employment "surplus," but it actually amounted to an actual $10 billion deficit.

So from the "day Simon took over the Treasury in May," noted historian Allen Matusow, "his goal was to get rid of this deficit by slashing $10 billion from expenditures."

Peering through Keynesian glasses, Matusow judged Simon's efforts to be "folly," but from the perspective of today's smoldering budgetary ruins, his crusade to cut federal spending looks more like a last, fleeting moment of fiscal sanity. The temporary drop in real GDP during the winter of 1974–1975 was not a valid excuse for higher spending and bigger deficits. It represented the final liquidation of the inflation-swollen inventories that had been accumulated in American factories and warehouse, not the mysterious disappearance of an economic ether called "aggregate demand."

Simon was also criticized for holding the antediluvian view that budget deficits were inflationary. Yet during that era, before mercantilist foreign central banks were heavily in the business of pegging their currencies against the dollar, fiscal deficits did encourage the Fed to accommodate the Treasury's borrowing requirements via rapid expansion of its balance sheet. This injection of reserves into the banking system stimulated lending until a renewed bout of inflation finally forced the Fed to reactively throttle back on runaway credit growth.

In fact, Simon well understood that the pro-business variant of Keynesian macro-management which had become institutionalized in the Nixon White House was a dangerous perpetual motion machine of financial instability. When the Fed fuels inflationary booms, it results in excessive inventory accumulations that will inevitably be liquidated once rapid credit expansion stops.

The so-called "cost" of recession is thus not really an avoidable cost; it is actually only a "giveback" of phony "growth" recorded in the GDP accounts from inventory building a few quarters earlier. The kind of stop-go monetary policy and the resultant business cycle instability unleashed after August 1971 thus generated no lasting expansion, but only what amounted to hopscotch GDP.

Moreover, as shown in chapter 11, the Eisenhower administration had already proven that the essential premise of Keynesian countercyclical stimulus was flawed. By generally refusing to employ discretionary fiscal stimulus during the two 1950s recessions, it had demonstrated that inventory liquidations burn themselves out on their own.

Bill Simon was thus ahead of his time, even if he was dismissed by the enlightened conservative economists of the day as a hidebound Hooverite. He recognized that fiscal stimulus in the face of an inventory liquidation cycle is actually a destructive catalyst for a renewed cycle of boom and bust. In the absence of Volcker-like resolve at the Fed, it initially fosters a recurrence of inflationary monetary expansion, and then a run-up of prices and excess inventory that necessitates a recessionary correction all over again.

HOW THE BUDGET BECAME A JOBS MACHINE

Simon's fiscal fundamentalism embodied another, even more crucial truth. Once the old-time balanced budget rule was discarded and the federal budget was turned into a tool of economic stabilization, the fundamental process of fiscal governance was thrown out of kilter. Every spending program and every feature of the revenue code became a "jobs" program and a tool of countercyclical macro-management.

The current-year budget was thus taken hostage by the alleged performance shortfalls of the national economy. Painful deficit reductions were continuously postponed until the US economy achieved full recovery. Alas, that condition never arrived, but the endless delay of the fiscal reckoning did soon cause a mutation of the budget-making process itself.

The old balanced budget rule provided a policy framework that was focused on the budget's internal details and priorities. Special interest groups had to compete for scarce budget resources and politicians became schooled in the art of making choices and trade-offs.

By contrast, the Keynesian framework transformed the budget into a type of macroeconomic plumbing system under which spending programs and tax expenditures became mere conduits through which to pump dollars into the economy. Such flows would compensate for the alleged shortfall of "aggregate demand," according to the classic Keynesians, or spur underinvested and incentive-deprived sectors of the economy, according to the "business lite" Keynesians.

In either case, politicians became immersed in logrolling among claimants for tax relief or spending increases to spur output and jobs. Meanwhile, their comprehension of the dollars and cents of budgeting was overwhelmed by a cavalcade of spurious economic justifications.

In a process that was subtle, cumulative, and inexorable, the federal budget was thereby captured by the forces of special interest lobbies and crony capitalism. Once the latter occupied the moral high ground and could argue that in raiding the treasury they were actually serving the public good of more jobs and more growth, the frail fiscal defenses of popular democracy were easily demolished.

Bill Simon's militant crusade within the Ford administration for the old-time fiscal religion and unfettered free markets was consequently short-lived. To be sure, his advocacy was not the run-of-the-mill Republican bombast about private enterprise. In speeches and congressional testimony, Simon offered consistent, forceful, and intelligent opposition to all forms of federal market intervention designed to stimulate the general economy or boost particular sectors like housing, agriculture, and energy.

Simon was especially ferocious in his opposition to the bailout of failing industries and enterprises. Indeed, he made no bones about the fact that crony capitalism was as blameworthy as liberalism for the rise of Big Government.

He thus noted later that "the attachment of businessmen to free enterprise has weakened dramatically as they discovered they could demand—and receive—short run advantages from the state . . . I watched with incredulity as businessmen ran to the government in every crisis, whining for handouts or protection."

In famously telling New York City to "drop dead" in its request for federal money, Gerald Ford betrayed a fundamental sympathy with his treasury secretary's approach to fiscal rectitude. Yet the economic wreckage left behind by the Nixon abominations soon overwhelmed Ford's best intentions.

HOW GERRY FORD LOST THE BUDGET BATTLE
AND OPENED THE ERA OF BIG DEFICITS

As the US economy weakened in the winter of 1974–1975, the Ford administration reversed direction at the urging of businessmen like OMB director Roy Ash and big business lobbies like the Committee for Economic Development. In the place of October's tax surcharge to close the budget gap, Ford proposed in his January 1975 budget message that Congress enact a $16 billion tax cut, including a $12 billion rebate to households designed to encourage them to spend.

At length, Congress upped the tax cut ante to $30 billion. It also completely ignored Ford's plea to make compensating spending cuts of about $5 billion.

Then in the fall of that year (1975) the Ford White House escalated the tax stimulus battle further, proposing a tax reduction double the size of its January plan. This led to even more tax-cut largesse on Capitol Hill, a Ford veto, and then a final compromise tax bill on Christmas Eve 1975. Senate finance chairman Russell Long aptly described this final resolution as "putting Santa Claus back in his sleigh."

And so it did, and with permanent untoward results. By the time the ornament-laden tax cut was finally signed into law, it was way too late. The deep inventory liquidation of the previous winter had long since been superseded by a vigorous economic rebound.

In fact, even as the tax relief debate was being heatedly waged on Capitol Hill during the second half of 1975, real GDP had posted a 6.1 percent annualized gain. It then leapt to a 9.4 percent rate of expansion in the first quarter of 1976, a point well before the tax bill impact could be felt in the economy.

Thus, the 1969–1972 cycle repeated itself: by the time the big Ford tax cut was enacted, the inventory liquidation had run its course and a natural rebound was under way. So the 1970s second round of fiscal stimulus was destined to fuel a renewed inflationary expansion, and this time it virtually blew the lid off the budget.

Despite Ford's resolute veto of some appropriations bills, his red pen was no match for the massive Democratic congressional majorities that had come in with the Watergate election of 1974. Their urge to spend would not be denied, as attested by the figures for budget outlays.

Federal spending grew by 23 percent in fiscal 1975 and then by more than 10 percent in each of fiscal 1976 and 1977. All told, federal outlays reached $410 billion in the Ford administration's outgoing budget, a figure nearly double the spending level in place six years earlier when Nixon hustled his advisors off to Camp David.

Federal outlays were now more than 21 percent of GDP. That marker had been breached previously by only one president, Franklin D. Roosevelt, and that was only during the total mobilization of the Second World War.

This was ironic in the extreme. Ford was a stalwart fiscal conservative who went down to defeat in 1976 in a flurry of spending bill vetoes. But the massive increase in entitlement spending enacted during the Nixon years, particularly the 1972 act which indexed Social Security for cost of living increases just as runaway inflation materialized, could not be stopped with the veto pen. In fact, the specious facade of the Nixon-Shultz full-employment budget provided the cover for a historic breakdown of fiscal discipline.

This was strikingly evident in fiscal year 1976, a year in which the budget was falling out of bed, even as the economy bounded upward. During the four quarters ending in June 1976, real GDP grew at 6.1 percent. Yet due to the huge tax cut becoming fully effective during that period, federal receipts dropped to 17.1 percent of GDP, or to pre–Korean War levels.

With spending at a record 21.4 percent, the fiscal deficit soared to 4.2 percent of GDP. Despite the best of intentions, therefore, the Ford administration left LBJ's peak deficit amounting to 2.9 percent of GDP far behind.

Thus, the nation was now on an uncharted fiscal path, one of giant deficits which were entirely gratuitous. The 1974–1975 inventory liquidation had burned out on its own and double-digit inflation had subsided to 5 percent. But with the Treasury's annual borrowing requirement now at a previously unimaginable $75 billion, a shell-shocked Arthur Burns poured monetary reserves into the banking system with almost reckless abandon.

Soon the US banking system was off to the races. Total bank loans grew by 10 percent in 1976 and then surged by a further 15 percent in 1977 and another 15 percent in 1978. In short order inflation was again accelerating.

Exactly twenty-seven months after the CPI had dipped below 5 percent in late 1976, offering some slight hope that the inflationary cycle could be subdued, it had once again exploded to a double-digit gain by March 1979. A renewed commodity price explosion was already under way, with oil prices nearly quadrupling to $40 per barrel within the next twelve months.

HOW THE CARTER ADMINISTRATION TOUCHED OFF THE FINAL INFLATIONARY BLAZE

This addiction to deficit spending and pell-mell expansion of bank lending was bipartisan. The incoming Carter administration attempted to pile on further fiscal stimulus in early 1977 when it proposed a $32 billion package of tax cuts and added spending.

These measures included the infamous $50 per family tax rebate (properly derided as $0.96 per week of pocket change).The Carter package also included public works, make-work jobs, and an increase in countercyclical revenue sharing with local governments.

The very title of this latter program underscores the degree to which fiscal policy had come unhinged. These weren't emergency measures designed to prevent the economy from sliding into the abyss. To the contrary, the CBO forecast at the time projected real GDP growth of around 6 percent in both 1977 and 1978, meaning that the Carter White House was trying to stimulate an economy that its forecast showed was already red hot.

In fact, the real economic challenge was the opposite. The CBO also forecasted a 6 percent increase in consumer prices both years—a rate of gain which would reduce the dollar's purchasing power by 50 percent within the span of a decade. That this baleful prospect was the result of massive deficits and Fed money printing was lost on the reflexive Keynesian, Charles Schultze, who was Carter's top economic advisor: parroting Arthur Burns, he urged the Fed to pour kerosene on the inflationary fires and then jabbered about the need for an "incomes policy."

In short, hopelessly immersed in countercyclical fine-tuning, Washington did not even recognize that it was attempting, unaccountably, to turbocharge an already inflation swollen economy. In the event, real GDP grew by 9.4 percent during the first quarter of 1977 and a solid 5 percent for the full year, even after most of the Carter stimulus plan was abandoned.

On the other hand, inflation was even worse than expected. It rose at a 9 percent rate by the fourth quarter of 1978 and went steadily higher from there.

Moreover, even as its fiscal policy obstinately ignored the resurgent inflationary tidal wave, the Carter White House made absolutely certain that the Fed stood ready to monetize the $50 billion per year in new Treasury debt issuance embedded in its fiscal plans. When Burns' term expired in early 1978, it appointed the clueless William G. Miller, a manufacturer of aircraft parts and golf carts, to succeed him.

Miller didn't even know how to recite the anti-inflation liturgy that Burns had made into a ritual incantation. He just followed orders from the White House Keynesians and injected even more reserves into an already wildly expanding banking system.

So Miller's brief eighteen-month tenure was essentially a final bonus round in the stunning expansion of US bank credit that had begun under Burns. Upon Martin's exit from the Fed chairmanship at the end of 1969, bank loans outstanding were less than $500 billion.

By the time Volcker shocked the financial markets with an unavoidably savage monetary tightening campaign in October 1979, bank loans outstanding had reached nearly $1.5 trillion. In a single decade, bank credit in the United States had tripled, laying the foundation for the monetary régime of bubble finance that made the Reagan-era deficits sustainable.

THE HISTORIC SIGNIFICANCE OF
NIXON'S WRONG ROAD TAKEN

In August 1971, the Nixon administration put the imprimatur of the nation's conservative party on an irredeemable inflationary dollar and an activist, deficit-driven fiscal policy. The first go-round fueled a virulent commodity and wage inflation.

The practice of debt monetization on a massive scale was thereby institutionalized, while its historic bad odor was given political cover by the full employment budget scam. Statists and economic betterment merchants were thus unleashed, free from a resurgent attack by largely silenced proponents of the ancient fiscal verities. When the Asian exporters began to aggressively peg their currencies in the decades ahead, the machinery for US fiscal deficits without tears was already in place.

Yet it didn't have to be. The Nixon abomination at Camp David came only after a long twilight struggle to restore sound money and fiscal rectitude in the aftermath of the New Deal gong show, a witch's brew of primitive statist fiscal experimentation and monetary quackery that did not relieve the Great Depression, and in many respects extended it. As will be seen, the drive by Presidents Truman, Eisenhower, and Kennedy—each in their own way, to reverse the New Deal victories of crony capitalism and populist money—almost succeeded. And in no small measure this was due to the steady hand of William McChesney Martin at the helm of the Fed.

But the course actually taken—Nixon's relapse into Roosevelt-style nationalism, opportunism, and electioneering with the nation's money, public purse, and free enterprise economy—had an ironic consequence. When the Nixon administration's floating-money contraption finally exploded in the financial crisis of September 2008, apologists for even more money printing and fiscal activism revived pro–New Deal narratives and FDR hagiographies that had been written in the 1950s and 1960s.

These works of postwar casuistry were dead wrong about what had given rise to the Great Depression and about what actually transpired during the American economy's long struggle to recover during the 1930s. Most especially, they ascribed recuperative powers to the New Deal's potpourri of false starts, dead ends, and surviving deformations that they never remotely possessed.

That the New Deal revivalists like Professor Paul Krugman of Princeton University are essentially telling fibs and peddling historical legends is not offensive merely because it distorts the distant past. These legends actually compound the deformations of the present by rationalizing policies that cannot succeed and which will only bury the nation deeper in debt. And worse still, they perpetuate the busted monetary system and crony capitalism that arose from the wrong road taken by Richard M. Nixon.

PART III

NEW DEAL LEGENDS AND THE TWILIGHT OF SOUND MONEY

CHAPTER 8

NEW DEAL MYTHS
OF RECOVERY

THE NEW DEAL WAS A POLITICAL GONG SHOW, NOT A GOLDEN ERA of enlightened economic policy. It shattered the foundation of sound money and inaugurated a régime of capricious fiscal and regulatory activism that inexorably fueled the growth of state power and the crony capitalism which thrives on it. But it did not end the Great Depression or save capitalism from the alleged shortcomings which led to the crash.

In fact, the New Deal introduced a severe dose of economic nationalism and autarky at a time when the only hope for speedy recovery was a reopening of world trade and reestablishment of a stable international monetary régime. The singular contribution of Franklin D. Roosevelt, however, was slamming the door on that possibility so decisively, unequivocally, and irreversibly as to guarantee the nation a long slog in a depression economy.

FDR and most of his so-called brain trust failed to comprehend that the United States was in a deep depression because its export markets had collapsed. Consequently, its great industries—capital goods, autos, steel, chemicals, and agriculture—had way too much capacity for the domestic market alone. During the Great War and the Roaring Twenties, these industries exported heavily based on an unsustainable artifice; namely, US vendor-financed loans to worldwide customers who ultimately could not afford to repay.

These vast vendor loans, totaling more than $3 trillion at today's economic scale, came from the US Treasury during the war and from Wall Street during the last five years of the great stock market boom. When the stock market crashed in 1929, however, the giant Wall Street market in foreign bonds cratered even more severely. Yet without fresh funding foreign borrowers soon defaulted in droves. Their purchases of US farm and industrial goods dried up almost instantly, causing output and capacity utilization to plummet during 1930 and the two years thereafter.

The United States needed to take bold action to rejuvenate its foreign customers, but the list of potential actions was short. First and foremost, a sharp reduction in import tariffs and other trade barriers was needed to enable foreign customers to earn enough foreign exchange to buy American goods without further debt extensions.

Washington also needed to cancel the war debts of England and France, so that the French especially would desist in their destructive campaign to extract crushing reparations from the faltering German economy. And the United States needed to take the lead in reestablishing stable foreign exchange markets around fixed currency rates and gold convertibility in order to revive confidence, trade, and capital flows in international commerce.

Roosevelt inherited a weak hand from his predecessor. Herbert Hoover was a stalwart proponent of free enterprise and fiscal rectitude, but unfortunately a McKinley Republican who embraced a fatal contradiction: the gold standard for money but protectionism on trade.

Striking a mortal blow at the recovery of international commerce, Hoover thus signed the infamous Smoot-Hawley tariff bill in June 1930. It caused international commodity prices and trade volumes to take another sharp leg down, further debilitating American agriculture and export-dependent industry. As is well known, it resulted in a destructive spiral of retaliation and beggar-thy-neighbor nationalism, which intensified as the decade unfolded and caused international trade and capital markets to lapse into somnolence.

To his credit, Hoover did implement a one-year moratorium on reparation payments in June 1931, but by then the central European banking system was unraveling and political reaction and economic demoralization were setting deep roots. England's default on its obligation to redeem pounds sterling for gold in September of that year further exacerbated the downward international spiral.

So when FDR took the oath of office on March 4, 1933, he was confronted by a grave crisis. But it was not the domestic banking crisis sensationalized by his liberal hagiographers; the infamous lines at the teller windows happened almost exclusively during the final three weeks of the long interregnum between November and March and were entirely of Roosevelt's own making. They had been triggered by the president-elect's obdurate refusal to cooperate with the Hoover administration on stabilizing the local crisis that struck the Detroit banks in mid-February, and to assure the public that he had no plans to embrace inflationary money schemes.

The banking crisis was over in a matter of weeks. The roughly $2 billion of currency hoarded in mattresses flowed back into the banking system, not because of the New Deal but due to an unremarkable bank reopening plan that Hoover's outgoing Treasury Department had actually designed and stayed on to implement.

By contrast, the real crisis was the de facto shutdown of world trade and the chaos in the monetary system and foreign exchange markets. The last hope for reversing this breakdown was the upcoming London Economic Conference in June, which Hoover had organized but for which FDR had again resolutely refused to cooperate in the planning and preparatory meetings.

NOT YOUR KRUGMAN'S NEW DEAL

FDR personally torpedoed the London Conference in early July 1933. In so doing he struck down the international gold standard, left the reparations issue to fester amid international recriminations, and did not even address the need to open the US market to foreign imports in order to revive international trade. In short, Hoover landed a haymaker on the requisites for recovery of the American export-dependent economy and FDR finished the job—no gold, no trade, no capital flows, and no cancellation of the destructive war debts.

There can be little doubt that these crucial matters did not even register with Franklin D. Roosevelt, because on matters of economics he was a relentless dilettante with an affinity for quixotic schemes and downright quackery. This was especially evident when it came to his simplistic belief that the Great Depression was due to low prices, and that the key to restarting the nation's economic engines was a Washington-initiated "reflation" of cotton, wheat, hog, and steel prices.

What FDR did not have, however, was an affinity for anything that resembled full-strength Keynesian demand stimulus like the $800 billion plan that Larry Summers, the chief economic advisor in the first years of the Obama administration (and secretary of the treasury under Bill Clinton), claimed to have channeled from FDR in February 2009. In fact, Roosevelt met with Professor Keynes once and found the great economist's pitch completely unintelligible, and in that reaction he had considerable company. As outlined below, the only New Deal initiative that even remotely embodied Keynesian demand stimulus was the giant veterans' bonus payment of 1936, and that was a political accident that FDR actually vetoed.

That the New Deal had virtually nothing to do with modern Keynesian theories of countercyclical demand management is crucial to understanding the nation's present economic deformations. Contrary to the claims of unreconstructed Keynesians like Professor Krugman, the giant programs of fiscal stimulus and money printing after the September 2008 crisis had no trial run or validation during the Great Depression. They are based on a false narrative from beginning to end; that is, about why the depression happened and what the New Deal actually did.

In truth, the New Deal was a Chinese menu with little rhyme or reason. It included quasi-fascist schemes to regiment industries and agriculture; public works and regional pork barrel spending to reward the New Deal coalition; price support and production control schemes to levitate farm prices; work relief and social programs to relieve the immense destitution and suffering among the unemployed; and endless special interest legislation sought by unions, the housing industry, and other organized lobbies.

Some of these programs provided humanitarian relief and a safety net. Most either retarded recovery or were abandoned before they could do much harm. And a few—like the industrial union legislation, universal social insurance, Fannie Mae, bank deposit insurance, and farm price supports—lived on to cast a heavy and debilitating shadow over the distant future.

But FDR's opening blow was devastating and long lasting. He outright abolished the basis for sound money at home and personally blocked the revival abroad of stable exchange rates and common international money; that is, currencies redeemable in gold.

FDR accomplished all this during his first year in office. In the process he revealed himself to be a veritable monetary primitive. Indeed, his monetary actions and views made a mockery of the long-settled "sound money" platform of the Democratic Party, and were embarrassingly similar to those of cranks like Father Coughlin and Senator Huey Long.

WHEN FDR GOT THE GOLD

The long-lasting imprint from FDR's famous "Hundred Days" did not stem from the bank holiday, national industrial recovery act, the farm adjustment act, the Tennessee Valley Authority, or the public works administration. Instead, it is lodged in the footnotes of standard histories; namely, FDR's April 1933 order confiscating every ounce of gold held by private citizens and businesses throughout the United States. Shortly thereafter he also embraced the Thomas Amendment, giving him open-ended authority to drastically reduce the gold content of the dollar; that is, to trash the nation's currency.

These actions did not constitute merely a belated burial of the "barbarous relic." In the larger scheme of monetary history, they marked a crucial tipping point. They initiated a process of monetary deformation that led straight to Nixon's abomination at Camp David, Greenspan's panic at the time of the 1998 Long-Term Capital Management crisis, and the final destruction of monetary integrity and financial discipline during the BlackBerry Panic of 2008.

The radical nature of this break with the past is underscored by a singular fact virtually unknown in the present era of inflationary central bank money; namely, that the dollar's gold content had been set at $20.67 per ounce in 1832 and had never been altered. There had been zero net domestic inflation for a century and the dollar's gold value in international commerce had never varied except during war.

The Thomas Amendment nullified this rock-solid monetary foundation and instead permitted the president on his own whim to cut the dollar's gold content by up to 50 percent. So doing, it signaled that money would no longer exist fixed, immutable, and outside the machinations of the state, but would now be an artifact of its whims and expedients.

It was a shocking deviation from FDR's own repeated campaign pledges to preserve "sound money at all hazards" and contradicted the pro–gold standard views of even his own party's mainstream. Likewise, the removal of gold from circulation entirely had never before been seriously proposed, not even by William Jennings Bryan, the populist Democrat presidential candidate best known for his "Cross of Gold" speech.

Self-evidently, bank notes and checkbook money had long been a more convenient means of payment than gold coins, but the function of gold was financial discipline, not hand-to-hand circulation. Redeemability of bank notes and deposits gave the people an ultimate check on the monetary depredations of the state and its central banking branch. Indeed, the public's freedom to dump its everyday money in favor of gold coins and bullion was what kept official currency and bank money honest.

At the time, however, the shell-shocked nation—even the conservative opposition—scarcely understood that the Rubicon had been crossed. The most notable clarion call, in fact, came from Lewis Douglas, FDR's own budget director and key economic advisor. Hearing on April 18, 1933, of the president's intention to endorse the Thomas Amendment, Douglas famously declared, "This is the end of western civilization."

Douglas was at least eighty years premature with respect to timing but his sense of the implication was profoundly correct. In one fell swoop, FDR's capricious actions launched the Democrats down the road to a government-manufactured currency and a purely national form of money.

It thereby repudiated the internationalist hard-money stand of the 1932 Democratic platform, the pro–gold standard candidacies of Al Smith in 1928, John Davis in 1924, and the James Cox–Franklin Roosevelt ticket of

1920. It also nullified the pro-gold principles of Carter Glass and the Democratic majority that had instituted the Federal Reserve Act in 1913 and the Cleveland, Jackson, and Jefferson Democrats who had gone before.

In short, amid the atmosphere of public fear and alarm from his self-inflicted banking crisis, and owing to his willful insouciance in single-handedly scrapping the nation's deep and bipartisan gold standard tradition, FDR essentially parted the waters of monetary history. Until June 1933, virtually everyone believed that gold-redeemable money was the foundation of capitalism, yet within months such convictions had gone stone-cold dormant.

It would, of course, take time for the resulting monetary vacuum to be filled by an aggrandizing central bank and a credit-money-based financial system cut loose from the discipline of gold. In the interim, the Great Depression quashed inflationary expectations and speculative instincts for decades to come, and produced a generation of conservative commercial and central bankers who earnestly attempted to replicate its discipline.

Nevertheless, it was only a matter of circumstances before the policy vacuum was filled by less wholesome propensities. Eventually, Nixonian cynicism and Professor Milton Friedman's alluring but dangerously naive doctrines of floating exchange rates and the quantity theory of money picked up where FDR left off. Notwithstanding Friedman's aura of intellectual respectability, Nixon's crass political maneuvers amounted to a primitive economic nationalism that harkened back to the worst of the disaster that FDR had first sown in the 1930s.

FDR'S LONDON CONFERENCE BOMBSHELL:
THE END OF THE LIBERAL INTERNATIONAL ORDER

After Roosevelt effectively suspended convertibility in the bastion of the world gold standard, money was essentially nationalized. Most of the world's major economies, including the United States', retreated into separate silos of autarky and stagnation, which in turn bred ultra-nationalism, rearmament, and finally world war. But this outcome was not inevitable.

To be sure, the survival of a liberal international economic order had been in doubt throughout the 1920s, as the world struggled to repair the inflationary mayhem of the Great War and resume convertibility of national currencies. Between 1925 and 1928, huge strides toward normalization of exchange rates, capital markets, and trade were accomplished as England, Belgium, Sweden, and even Japan (1930) restored gold standard money.

But all of this tenuous progress had been seriously jeopardized by England's abandonment in September 1931 of the very gold exchange standard it had spent a decade promoting under the auspices of the League of

Nations. So prospects for resumption of the fabulously stable and prosperous pre-1914 liberal international order were hanging by a thread. In this context, historians are agreed that it was FDR who personally delivered the coup de grâce with his famous "bombshell" message to the London Economic Conference in July 1933.

FDR capriciously defied all of his advisors, to the very last man, including the then-chief of his brain trust, Raymond Moley. Flying by the seat of his own pants, he airily dismissed the warnings of his budget director, the brilliant industrialist and financial scholar Lewis Douglas. He also disregarded the firm pro-gold viewpoint of James Warburg, his most senior financial advisor with Wall Street and international finance experience. Moreover, FDR had failed to even solicit the opinion of Senator Carter Glass. Under the circumstances, that was not merely a telling omission; it was damning.

For the better part of three decades, the legendary Virginia senator, also former secretary of the treasury under Woodrow Wilson and principal author of the Federal Reserve Act, had been the Democratic Party's paragon of authority on matters of money and banking. Glass had been an unwavering proponent of the gold standard and had personally written the 1932 Democratic platform in such a manner as to leave no doubt that the Democrats would not resort to easy money and inflationist expedients.

For several weeks before his March 4 inauguration, Roosevelt pleaded with Glass to become his secretary of the treasury. Yet hardly sixty days after Glass finally refused the job, FDR did not even bother to consult him when launching what were epochal monetary policy actions. In essence, FDR's April 1933 gold machinations repudiated the life's work of the very financial statesman he first picked for the single most important job in his government.

Roosevelt's flip-flopping on Glass and gold was a defining moment. It showed that on the raging economic crisis of the hour, Roosevelt's insouciance knew no boundaries; he could believe almost any contradiction that came his way.

It thus happened that after the Hundred Days of emergency actions was completed in late June, FDR headed off to vacation on Vincent Astor's yacht. He sent Moley as his personal emissary to the London conference, which by then had come to be viewed as literally the last hope for retaining an open international trading and monetary order.

The conference had the good fortune that its presiding officer was Secretary of State Cordell Hull. A former Democratic senator from Tennessee and a splendid statesman, Hull had been a staunch advocate of free trade, the gold standard, and an open international economy.

Most of the assembled financial officials, including Hull, recognized that restoration of some semblance of exchange-rate stability was the key to the rest of the conference agenda, especially to rolling back the protectionist trade barriers which were rapidly choking off world trade. The latter had sprung up everywhere after Smoot-Hawley and were being compounded by beggar-thy-neighbor currency manipulation after the sterling-based gold exchange system broke down.

After long and arduous negotiations, the framework for such a monetary stabilization agreement was reached soon after Moley arrived in London. The US delegation, Great Britain, and the French-led gold bloc nations had all managed to find common ground. While Moley had been a strident voice of nationalistic autarky in the Roosevelt inner circle, even he was persuaded by Hull and the British to endorse the tentative internationalist agreement.

The heart of the plan was repegging the dollar to pound exchange rate in a narrow band about 20 percent below the old parity (i.e., at about $4.00 versus $4.86 per pound sterling). From that pivot point, the French franc and other major currencies would be fixed to the dollar.

The significance of this breakthrough cannot be gainsaid. All sides recognized that floating currencies would poison the international trading system, encourage destructive currency speculation, and fuel violent movements of "hot money" among financial centers. The latter would continuously destabilize both national money markets and confidence in the international trading system as a whole.

In one of the great misfortunes of history, however, FDR was literally incommunicado during the hours when a global consensus to reboot the international financial system briefly flickered. Alone on Astor's luxurious yacht, the *Nourmahal*, the president had the advice of only his wealthy dilettante chum Vincent Astor and Louis Howe, his butler and glorified White House "secretary."

When Moley finally found a navy ship to track down the *Nourmahal* and deliver a radio message outlining the nascent London agreement, Roosevelt, Howe, Astor, and perhaps also the yacht's captain, as it were, gathered around a kerosene lamp on the deck. There they scribbled out a handwritten response and turned it over to the navy for radio dispatch back to London.

Roosevelt's message was undoubtedly among the most intemperate, incoherent, and bombastic communiqués ever publicly issued by a US president. It not only stunned the assembled world leaders gathered in London and killed the monetary stabilization agreement on the spot, but it also locked in a destructive worldwide régime of economic nationalism that eventually led to war.

High tariffs and trade subsidies, state-dominated recovery and rearmament programs, and manipulated fiat currencies became universal after the London conference failed. In the months which followed, Sweden, Holland, and France were driven off the gold standard, leaving international financial markets demoralized and chaotic.

At the end of the day, it was only the outbreak of war in 1939–1940 which pulled the world out of the rut of economic nationalism and stagnation to which FDR's quixotic action had condemned it. It also meant that the domestic economy had now been cut off from its vital export markets, condemning the nation to a halting recovery and to continuous and mostly ineffectual New Deal doctoring that succeeded primarily in planting the seeds of welfare state expansion and crony capitalism.

Roosevelt's deplorable action from the deck of the *Nourmahal* tends to be dismissed by historians as a forgivable bad hair day early in the reign of the economic-savior president. In fact, it was the very opposite: FDR's single-handed sabotage of the London conference was one bookend of a thirty-eight-year epoch. The other end was bounded by Richard Nixon's equally impudent destruction of Bretton Woods in August 1971.

In each case the modus operandi was the same. Both Roosevelt and Nixon were aggressive politicians who lacked any enduring convictions about economic policy. Neither had any compunction at all, however, about using the taxing, spending, regulatory, and money-printing powers of the state to achieve their domestic political and electoral objectives. In the great scheme of modern financial history FDR and Tricky Dick were peas in a statist pod.

THE GREAT WAR AND THE ROARING TWENTIES: CRADLE OF THE GREAT DEPRESSION

FDR's mortal blow to international monetary stability and world trade is the pattern through which the New Deal was shaped. Once Roosevelt went for domestic autarky, the New Deal was destined to be a one-armed bandit. It capriciously pushed, pulled, and reshuffled the supply side of the domestic economy, but it could not regenerate the external markets upon which the post-1914 American prosperity had vitally depended.

Herbert Hoover had been correct: the US depression was rooted in the collapse of global trade, not in some flaw of capitalism or any of the other uniquely domestic afflictions on which the New Deal programs were predicated. Indeed, the American economy had been thoroughly internationalized after August 1914 and had grown by leaps and bounds as a great export machine and prodigious banker to the world.

While it lasted, the export boom of 1914–1929 generated strong gains in domestic incomes, which in turn fueled the postwar rise of new durables industries like autos and home appliances. The tremendous expansion of exports and durables output also triggered the greatest capital spending boom in history. Auto production capacity, for example, rose from under 2 million units in 1920 to nearly 6 million by 1929, while whole new industries like radios and washing machines were born almost overnight.

The fact that the American economy had become supersized for continuous expansion of exports and durables, however, was its Achilles heel. In the event of a slowdown in demand for these core manufactures, rapid capacity expansion would stop and the capital goods industries would plummet. Likewise, consumer goods factories would be saddled with vast idle capacity if the bubble-fueled demand of the late 1920s faltered. Then a general spiral of falling incomes, profits, employment, and consumption would ensue.

When the great stock market bubble reached its apex in September 1929, the handwriting was already on the wall. The temporary "wealth effect" of soaring stock prices, along with the huge expansion of consumer installment loans and home mortgage finance, had fostered booming sales of autos, appliances, radios, and other consumer durables. All of this came to an abrupt halt when stock prices came tumbling back to earth.

Yet the financial bubble was not just domestic. It began way back in 1914 when the "guns of August" suddenly transformed the United States into the arsenal and granary of the world and an instant, giant global creditor. This was not a natural or sustainable route to rapid growth but it powered the US economy to a scale and level of prosperity that was palpable.

After the deep but brief post-armistice slump (1920–1921), America resumed its role as a giant creditor and exporter. By contrast, the rest of the world struggled to restart domestic economies and regain financial and monetary normalcy after desperate wartime sprees of government borrowing and currency inflation.

A crucial element of the postwar stabilization process, especially in central Europe and among commodity-producing nations in Latin America, was the $10 billion of foreign bonds underwritten by Wall Street. That was the equivalent of $1.5 trillion in today's economy, and went to borrowers ranging from the Kingdom of Denmark and German industrialists to municipalities from Hamburg to Rio de Janeiro.

On the margin, the 1920s foreign bond market was just the peacetime extension of the US Treasury's vast war loans of 1917–1919. It was these extensive borrowings which allowed many American export customers to finance their purchases, thereby catalyzing the booming domestic economy. Accordingly, during the fifteen years between 1914 and 1929, real GDP growth had averaged nearly 4 percent annually, a rate that has never again been matched over a comparable length of time.

The trouble was that this prosperity was neither organic nor sustainable. In addition to the debt-financed demand for American exports, stock market winnings and the explosion of consumer debt generated exuberant but unsustainable household purchases of big-ticket durables at home. So when the stock market finally broke, this financially fueled chain of economic expansion snapped and violently unwound.

The first victim was the foreign bond market, which was the subprime canary in the coal mine of its day. Within a few months of the crash, new issuance had dropped 95 percent from its peak 1928 levels, causing foreign demand for US exports to collapse. Worse still, the price of the nearly $10 billion of foreign bonds outstanding also soon plunged to less than ten cents on the dollar, meaning that the collapse was of the same magnitude and speed as the subprime mortgage collapse of 2008.

Foreign debtors had been borrowing to pay interest. When the Wall Street music stopped in October 1929, the house of cards underlying the American export bonanza collapsed. By 1933, US exports had dropped by nearly 70 percent.

The Wall Street meltdown also generated ripples of domestic contraction which compounded the export swoon. Stock market lottery winners, for example, had been buying new automobiles hand over fist. But after sales of autos and trucks peaked at 5.3 million units in 1929, they then dropped like a stone to only 1.4 million vehicles in 1932. Needless to say, this 75 percent shrinkage of auto sales cascaded through the auto supply chain, including metal working, steel, glass, rubber, and machine tools—with devastating impact.

The collapse of these "growth" industries also caused a withering cutback in business investment. Plant and equipment spending tumbled by nearly 80 percent between 1929 and 1933, while nearly half of all the production inventories extant in 1929 were liquidated over the next three years. This unprecedented liquidation of working inventories—from $38 billion to $22 billion—amounted to nearly a 20 percent hit to GDP before the cycle reached bottom.

Overall, nominal GDP had been $103 billion in 1929 but by 1933 had shrunk to only $56 billion. Yet the overwhelming portion of this unprecedented contraction was in exports, inventories, fixed plant and equipment, and consumer durables. These components declined by $33 billion during the four years after 1929 and accounted for fully 70 percent of the decline in nominal GDP.

The underlying story in these data refutes the postwar Keynesian narrative about the Great Depression. What happened during 1929–1932 was not a mysterious loss of domestic "demand" that was somehow recoverable through enlightened macroeconomic stimulus policies. Instead, what occurred was an inevitable shrinkage in the unsustainable levels of output that had been reached by exports, durables, and a once-in-a-lifetime capital investment boom, not unlike the massive China investment cycle of 1994–2012.

It was not the depression bottom level of GDP during 1932–1933 that was avoidably too low; it was the debt and speculation bloated GDP peak of 1929 that had been unsustainably too high. Accordingly, the problem could not be solved by macroeconomic pump-priming at home. The Great Depression was therefore never a candidate for the Keynesian cure which was inherently inward looking and nationalistic.

The frenetic activity of the first hundred days of the New Deal, of course, is the stuff of historians' legends. Yet when viewed in the context of this implosion of the nation's vastly inflated export/auto/capital goods sector, it's evident that the real cure for depression did not lie in the dozens of acronym-ridden programs springing up in Washington.

Contrary to the long-standing Keynesian narrative, therefore, the New Deal contributed virtually nothing to the mild recovery which did materialize during the six-year run-up to war in 1939. In fact, the modest seesaw expansion which unfolded during that period had been already set in motion during the summer of 1932, well before FDR's election.

THE HOOVER RECOVERY INTERRUPTED

The New Deal hagiographers never mention that 50 percent of the huge collapse of industrial production, that is, the heart of the Great Depression, had already been recovered under Hoover by September 1932. The catalyst for the Hoover recovery was not Washington-based policy machinations but the natural bottoming of the severe cycle of fixed-asset and inventory liquidation after 1929.

By mid-1932, the liquidation had finally run its course because inventories were virtually gone, and capital goods and durables production could hardly go lower. Accordingly, nearly every statistic of economic activity turned upward in July 1932. From then until the end of September, the Federal Reserve Board index of industrial production rose by 21 percent, while rail freight loadings jumped by 20 percent and construction contract awards rose by 30 percent.

Likewise, the American Federation of Labor's published count of industrial unemployment dropped by nearly three-quarters of a million persons between July 1 and October 1. Retail sales and electrical power output also rose smartly in the months after July, and some core industry which had been nearly prostrate began to spring back to life.

Cotton textile mill manufacturing, for example, surged from 56 percent of capacity in July to 97 percent in October, and mill consumption of wool nearly tripled during the same period. Likewise, the giant US Steel Corporation, which then stood at the center of the nation's industrial economy, recorded its first increase in sixteen months in its order backlog.

Related indicators also confirmed a broad and vigorous recovery. Wholesale prices rose by nearly 20 percent from their early 1932 bottom, marking the first sustained uptick since September 1929. The stock market quickly grasped the picture and rebounded from its depression low on the Dow Jones Index of 41 on July 7, 1932, to 80 in early September, before fears of a Roosevelt victory set it back.

The most important sign of economic rebound, however, was in the beleaguered banking sector. After having experienced nearly three hundred bank closings per month for much of the post-1929 period, bank failures dropped sharply to only seventy to eighty closings a month after June.

Indeed, for the period of July through October 1932, deposits held by banks which were reopened during that interval exceeded those of newly failed banks, a complete break with the month-after-month deposit losses that had occurred until then. In a similar vein, the United States experienced five straight months of gold inflows after July, indicating that the panicked gold flight that had commenced after the British default of September 1931 had decisively reversed.

As one careful journalistic reconstruction of events published during this period noted, "With the defeat of all threatening inflationary legislation in June . . . [and] the complete restoration of foreign confidence in the American gold position—the breath of recovery began to be felt over the land."

No less an authority on the national mood than Walter Lippmann, then at the peak of his game and influence, later summarized, "There is very good statistical evidence . . . that as a purely economic phenomena the world depression reached its low point in mid-summer 1932 and that in all the leading countries a very slow but nevertheless real recovery began."

By election time, however, the rebound had cooled. Subsequently, all the indicators of economic and financial activity weakened sharply during the long interregnum between Election Day and the March 4, 1933, inauguration.

As outlined below, there is powerful evidence that this setback can be attributed to a "Roosevelt panic" in the gold and banking markets that was avoidable and the result of FDR's numerous errors and provocations during the presidential interregnum. The fact is, every other major industrial country in the world also began to recover in July 1932, but none had a relapse back into depression during the winter of 1932–1933.

THE BANKING CRISIS THAT FDR MADE

The Hoover recovery has largely been omitted from the history books, fostering the impression that the American economy had continuously plunged after October 1929 until it reached a desperate bottom on exactly March 4, 1933. That rendition of events was far from accurate, but it did mightily burnish the Roosevelt miracle legend; namely, that FDR decisively reopened the frozen banking system, restarted the wheels of commerce, and restored a heartbeat to capitalism through the swarm of acronyms which flew out of New Deal Washington during the Hundred Days.

But the received version of the March 1933 banking crisis is an invention of Arthur Schlesinger Jr. and other postwar commentators who postulated FDR's "bank holiday" as the dividing line between Hooverian darkness and the Roosevelt miracles. By contrast, the most savvy and erudite financial observers at the time saw it far differently, and for a very good reason: on the Friday evening before Roosevelt's inauguration most of the US banking system was still solvent, including the great money center banks of New York: the Chase National Bank, First National City Bank, the Morgan Bank, and many more.

Indeed, the latter had to be practically coerced into agreeing to the New York State banking holiday signed into effect by Governor Lehman at 4:30 A.M. in the wee hours before FDR's inauguration. As it happened, the governor was a scion of the banking house bearing his name, but the circumstances of 1933 were the opposite of those which accompanied its demise in 2008.

Back then there had been no bank runs in the canyons of Wall Street because the great banks had largely observed time-tested standards; that is, they had been fully and adequately collateralized on their stock loans and were sitting on cash reserves up to 20 percent of deposits. The stock market crash of 1929–1930 had been brutal, of course, but in those purportedly benighted times officialdom had the good sense to allow Mr. Market to make his appointed rounds.

Accordingly, stock market punters by the thousands had been felled quickly and cleanly when upward of $9 billion of margin loans were called after Black Thursday. Indeed, the banks and brokerages liquidated in a matter of months the massive margin loan bubble—$1 trillion in today's economy—that had built up under the stock averages in the final years of the mania.

The fact that none of the great New York money center banks closed their doors during the four years between the crash and FDR's inauguration points to the real story; namely, that the bank insolvency problem had been in the provinces and countryside, not the nation's money center.

In fact, the run of bank failures was largely contained within the borders of the oversized 1914–1929 agricultural and industrial export economy. As the latter collapsed, overloaned banks in industrial boom towns like Chicago, Detroit, Toledo, Youngstown, Cleveland, and Pittsburgh had taken heavy hits.

In the case of the agricultural hinterlands, the Great Depression had started to roll in a decade before the crash, owing to the unique farm country boom and bust which had accompanied the Great War. The unprecedented total industrial-state warfare of 1914–1918 had drastically disrupted European agricultural production and markets, inducing an explosion of export demand, high prices, and soaring output in the American farm belt. There soon followed an orgy of speculation in land and real estate that exceeded in relative terms even the sand-state housing boom of 2002–2007.

Once the agricultural lands of Europe came back into production, however, the great American granary lost much of its artificial war-loan export market, causing farm prices to abruptly plunge in 1920–1921 and then to continue sinking for the next decade. Not surprisingly, thousands of one-horse banks dotting the countryside had been caught up in the wartime frenzy and then suffered massive, unrelenting losses during the long postwar deflation of the farm bubble.

Overall, about 12,000 banks failed during 1920–1933, but 10,000 of these were tiny rural banks located in places of less than 2,500 population. Their failure rate of more than 1,000 per year throughout the 1920s makes for eye-catching historical statistics, but they were largely irrelevant to the nation's overall GDP. Losses at failed US banks during the entire twelve-year period through 1932, in fact, accumulated to only 2–3 percent of deposits.

This extended wave of failures was an indictment of the short-sighted anti-branch banking laws that rural legislators had forced upon the states, as well as a reminder that wartime inflation and disruption had cast a long shadow on the future. The crucial point, however, is that these thousands of failed banks were insolvent and should have been closed. They were not evidence of some fundamental breakdown of the banking system, or failure of the Fed to supply adequate liquidity, or a systemic crisis of capitalism.

Even after the 1929 crash, when the failure rate accelerated to about 2,400 in the twelve months ending in mid-1932, the periodic spurts of bank closures were not national in scope. Instead, they struck with distinct regional incidence in the agricultural and industrial interior. And almost without exception, these regional bank failure breakouts were centered on cities or banking chains which had indulged heavily in speculative real estate lending and other unsound practices.

That was certainly the case with the first significant outbreak of bank runs in November 1930 when the Caldwell banking chain collapsed. A speculative pyramid of holding companies which controlled more than a hundred banks in Tennessee, Arkansas, and North Carolina, it failed when real estate values fell sharply in the upper Cotton Belt. While there was some spillover on local banks, the runs did not spread beyond the region and quickly burned out because deposits were moved to sounder banks, not to mattresses.

The most powerful evidence of the noncontagious nature of the pre–February 1933 bank failures occurred shortly thereafter with the famous collapse of the Bank of the United States in December 1930. An upstart New York City bank, the Bank of the United States, grew by leaps and bounds in the late 1920s through serial mergers, aggressive real estate lending, and pyramiding of holding company capital.

The bank had been a stock market rocket ship, rising from $5 per share in 1925 to a peak of $230 before the crash. But its promoter, one Bernard Marcus, who had been the Sandy Weill of his day, had been more adept at making deals than making sound loans, and thereby soon rendered his hastily assembled banking empire insolvent. Yet there was virtually zero spillover to other New York banks when state banking supervisors shuttered what was then the city's third-largest institution with around seventy branches and deposits on the order of $30 billion on today's scale.

The same pattern occurred the following June in Chicago. There had been a giant real estate bubble in the Chicago suburbs during the 1920s, but owing to Illinois's particularly restrictive anti-branch-banking law the Great Loop banks had been sidelined, leaving the suburban real estate lending spree to poorly capitalized newbies.

Chicago had been an epicenter of the 1914–1929 agricultural/industrial/export boom, so when the party ended abruptly after the stock market crash, the region's economy was hit harder than any other industrial center outside of Detroit. Real estate prices experienced a particularly devastating collapse in the newly developed suburban communities, triggering a wave of defaults in loan portfolios which were heavily laden with commercial and residential mortgages.

Yet with one exception a year later, the Great Loop banks remained solvent and experienced no lines at their teller windows. By contrast, the "runs" on the suburban banks were both swift and warranted because they were deeply insolvent. In short, the Chicago case further illuminates the fact that the wave of bank failures during 1930–1932 was not the result of irrational public sentiment and "contagion," or a fundamental breakdown of bank liquidity, but instead was evidence of a discriminating, rational flight of depositors from unsound banks and markets.

Even when surges of bank failures extended eastward, such as in the Philadelphia runs of October 1931, there was far more rationality to the pattern than the conventional narrative acknowledges. In this case, the overwhelming share of failures was concentrated among newly formed "trust banks" which had been chartered under state law with far less stringent requirements for capital and cash reserves than was the case with national banks.

Again, the late 1931 wave of bank failures in Philadelphia quickly burned out after deposits had moved from the lightly regulated trust banks, which had been on the leading edge of real estate lending and securities speculation, to the far better capitalized national banks. Indeed, the fundamental solvency of the US banking system was dramatically evidenced during this same period when the Fed raised the discount rate in mid-October.

This Fed action is habitually and roundly criticized by contemporary advocates of central bank money printing, but it was actually the proper move under then-extant gold standard rules. Specifically, the initial impact of the British default on September 1931 had been a run on US gold out of fear that the United States would be the next to default. So a discount rate hike was necessary to stop the outflow and, in fact, the rate of gold losses fell sharply in the months ahead and eventually reversed to an inflow by mid-1932.

More importantly, there was no acceleration of bank failures after the discount rate hike, and within weeks the failure rate slackened dramatically while discount borrowings actually increased. This was proof positive that banks were failing not because they were illiquid or could not get emergency funding from the Fed but because they were, alas, bankrupt.

Indeed, Herbert Hoover's unfortunate banking cure at the time—the emergency enactment of the Reconstruction Finance Corporation (RFC) in January 1932—was designed to alleviate insolvency, not provide emergency funding or replace hoarded deposits. Accordingly, the RFC went on to become a paragon of crony capitalism, rescuing dozens of busted railroads and recapitalizing several thousand insolvent banks. Yet the outcome was perverse: the stock and bondholders of bailed-out institutions were rescued, competitors were harmed, and the nation's economy was left to slog it out with far too much railroad capacity and way too many banks.

THE BANKING CRISIS WAS OVER
BEFORE FDR GOT STARTED

Nevertheless, the so-called banking crisis was largely over on the night of FDR's November 8, 1932, election. Nationwide bank failure rates had dropped to less than two dozen per week of mostly tiny country banks, deposit levels were rising, and what remained was a modest cleanup operation for the residue of insolvent banks in the hinterlands.

This adjustment process had now been heavily politicized, meaning that banks sinking into insolvency would receive capital injections from the RFC rather than closure notices from state and federal banking supervisors. But the key point is that there was no significant liquidity problem in the US banking system. The Federal Reserve, bank regulators, and discriminating depositors had already done their jobs and had quietly and systematically moved massive amounts of deposits to sounder banks.

The conventional FDR bank rescue narrative thus cannot explain the fact that during the ninety days between Election Day and February 3, when FDR went aboard Vincent Astor's yacht for a ten-day vacation he had not yet earned, there were no bank runs of any serious import. The proof for this is the daily reports of the comptroller of the currency, which didn't note any material currency hoarding until early February.

In fact, during the three-month post-election period there were only two instances of a citywide banking suspension for even a single day anywhere in the country. Likewise, currency outstanding had fluctuated around $5.5 billion for most of 1932, and even in the week ending February 8, 1933, had only risen by a negligible $8 million per day.

By contrast, partisan historians have created the false impression that there was a rising tide of money panic by cobbling together inconsequential anecdotes from the low-level bank failure noise still in the countryside. Thus, the governor of Nevada declared a bank holiday in November, but it was owing to the insolvency of a single bank chain that had only $17 million of deposits, or less than a few hours' worth of funds-clearance activity at the Chase National Bank or even the big Chicago Loop banks.

Likewise, scattered rural bank failures in Missouri, Tennessee, and Wisconsin and in midsized cities in the interior farm-industrial belt including Chattanooga, Memphis, and Little Rock were simply a continuation of the slow grind that had gone on for years. Some of the noise was even downright clownish, such as Huey Long's instantly declared state holiday in honor of the 1917 suspension of diplomatic relations with Germany, in order to give a major Louisiana bank time to raise extra cash.

The trigger for the pre-election panic, in fact, did not occur until the

morning of February 14, when the governor of Michigan capriciously declared a one-week bank holiday owing to a funding crisis at Detroit's
second-largest banking chain. The Guardian Trust Group consisted of
about forty banks controlled by Edsel Ford and included Goldman Sachs
among its principle stockholders.

It was another of the late-1920s banking pyramids that had been organized with a modest $5 million of capital in 1927 and had grown to a $230
million holding company two years later, through a spree of mergers and
stock swaps. These maneuvers elevated the stock price from $20 per share
to $350 at the 1929 peak.

Unfortunately, the bank's principle assets consisted of loans to insiders
to buy the bank's own stock and loans to both real estate developers and
homeowners in the red-hot Detroit auto belt. Propelled by a population explosion from 300,000 to 1.6 million in the previous three decades, the volcanic price gains in the Detroit real estate market eclipsed the current era's
Sunbelt booms by orders of magnitude.

Consequently, when auto production dropped by 75 percent and triggered mass layoffs, and the Guardian Group's stock price plummeted by 95
percent, the bank's loan book became hopelessly impaired. However, what
might have been embarrassing investment liquidation for Edsel Ford and
his cronies became a national headline when the Guardian Group crisis
turned into a brawl between Henry Ford and his despised erstwhile partner
and then Michigan Democratic senator, James Couzens.

Senator Couzens was the Tyler Winklevoss (he and his twin brother were
involved in the origins of Facebook) of his day and believed that he had
been bilked out of his share of Ford Motor Company by Henry Ford. He
could not abide a move afoot to have the RFC ride to the rescue of Edsel
Ford's mess, so he mustered his considerable weight as US senator and put
the kibosh on the deal.

President Hoover unhelpfully got himself in the thick of the brawl. However, he did quickly recognize that the Detroit headlines were becoming a
catalyst for a financial panic that was already brewing due to a complete
breakdown of transition cooperation and FDR's studied silence on his
prospective financial policies.

Indeed, the increasing flow of hints and leaks from FDR's radical brain
trusters—such as Columbia professor Rexford Tugwell and secretary of
agriculture designate Henry Wallace—that the incoming president would
depreciate the dollar and pursue other inflationary schemes had already
begun to trigger a run on gold and currency. Therefore, on February 18
Hoover penned an eloquent private letter to FDR outlining the peril from
these developments and the urgent need for a reassuring statement from

the president-elect outlining his policies with respect to gold, currency, banking, and the budget.

THE FOURTEEN-DAY ROOSEVELT PANIC

Thereupon began a continuous series of blunders, whereby FDR and his incipient government brought the banking system to a state of paralysis and panic by the time he took the oath of office fourteen days later. During that crucial period, FDR remained completely radio silent, and did not respond to Hoover's letter for ten days—belatedly offering the "dog ate my homework" prevarication that his secretary had neglected to mail his response. On the day of Hoover's letter, the Democratic silver block in the Senate delivered a nationwide radio address entitled "The Enlarged Use of Silver and Inflation." On the following Monday the nation's greatest banking statesman, Melvin Traylor, who was chairman of one of the great Chicago Loop banks and had been a leading candidate for the Democratic presidential nomination in 1932, told the Senate Finance Committee in a private session that "a firm statement from the President-elect against inflation is the only thing which might avert a general national panic."

The next day the Federal Reserve Advisory Committee, consisting of leading bankers from each reserve district, sent FDR a unanimous resolution urging a clarifying public statement. That same day it was announced that Carter Glass had turned down the Treasury Department post and, as the *Baltimore Sun* story made clear, there was no secret as to why: "If satisfactory assurances had been given the Senator that the new Administration under no circumstances would accept inflation as a policy, his answer would have been different."

Instead, Roosevelt announced that an unknown Republican locomotive manufacturer, William Woodin, would become treasury secretary and the basis for his selection was quickly evident. Notwithstanding daily entreaties from Hoover's redoubtable and increasingly desperate treasury secretary, Ogden Mills, the response was a complete stiff-arm: "On each occasion Mr. Woodin insisted the new administration would take no action, accept no responsibility, until March 4."

According to an insider chronicle written at the time, by February 24 FDR and his inner circle had already embraced a purely cynical outlook. By their lights "the national banking situation would undoubtedly collapse in a few days. The responsibility would be entirely with President Hoover."

In fact, that same day Professor Tugwell, who was clueless on monetary matters, leaked the administration's secret plan to place an embargo on gold exports, suspend gold payments to domestic citizens, and implement measures designed to inflate farm and industrial prices to James H. Rand.

The latter was a leading industrialist and outspoken agitator for dollar depreciation through the nationalistic Committee for the Nation which he chaired.

By Monday morning February 27, Tugwell's leak spread far and wide in the financial markets. The panic was on.

As Professors Nadler and Bogen noted in their classic 1933 history of the banking crisis, the "gold room" of the New York Federal Reserve Bank soon became a center of pandemonium: "As the panic week [February 27 to March 3] progressed, long lines formed to exchange ever larger amounts of gold there, until finally the metal was being carried away in large boxes and suitcases loaded on trucks."

During the next five days approximately $800 million, or 20 percent, of the US gold stock was withdrawn by citizens, earmarked by foreign central banks, or implicitly purchased by speculators who took out a massive short position on the dollar. The lessons of the British default of September 1931 were still fresh, and as the smart money took aggressive actions to defend itself, the knock-on effect was almost instantly felt.

As Wall Street historian Barrie A. Wigmore noted in his magisterial history of the Great Depression, owing to the gold hemorrhage "the lender of last resort [i.e., the Fed] for the banking system was in doubt. Frightened depositors lined up for cash, the only working substitute for bank deposits."

Wigmore's point is dispositive. What financially literate citizens knew at the time, and was never grasped by postwar Keynesians, is that Federal Reserve currency notes were then required by statute to be backed by a 40 percent gold cover. The public therefore realized that only a few more days of the panicked gold drain could cause a sharp constriction of both the hand-to-hand currency supply and the banking system overall.

Accordingly, the daily currency figures provide ringing evidence of FDR's culpability for the crisis. By February 23, the daily increase in currency outstanding had risen from the $8 million early February level to about $40 million, and then in the crisis week soared to nearly $200 million on Monday and hit $450 million on Friday, March 3, the day before the inauguration.

All told, the great bank teller window run and currency-hoarding crisis caused currency outstanding to rise from $5.6 billion to a peak of $7.5 billion. Yet $1.5 billion, or nearly 80 percent, of this gain occurred during the last ten days before FDR took office; that is, in the interval between the day Carter Glass said no and the morning FDR took the oath.

Barrie Wigmore's work consists of seven hundred pages of massive documentation and only occasional viewpoints and judgments. But on the question of culpability for the banking crisis he left no doubt: "Roosevelt exacerbated the crisis. If he had handled the 'lame duck' period differently, there would have been no Bank Holiday . . . the banking system was unusually liquid prior to the bank crisis, and [the] recovery from it was unusually rapid . . . [proving] that the peculiar circumstances of Roosevelt's transition were the cause of the crisis."

Four days after FDR officially closed the nation's 17,000 banking institutions, the Senate approved, after seventy-five minutes of debate and no written copy of the bill, the Emergency Banking Act, which empowered the secretary of the treasury "to re-open such banks as have already been ascertained to be in sound condition."

But there was no New Deal magic in the bill at all. It had been drafted by Hoover holdovers and was a content-free enabling act which required no change whatsoever in bank procedures in order to obtain a license to "re-open," and included no standards for review or approval by the Treasury Department.

In fact, the legislation was the first of many FDR ruses. Once Hoover had been implicitly saddled with the blame for what appeared to be a frozen banking system and prostrate economy on March 4, FDR simply moved along to another topic, having had no intention of closing or reforming any banks. Accordingly, with such dispatch as would have made Internet-era number crunchers envious, the White House began opening banks the next Monday (March 13th), and by Wednesday 90 percent of the deposit basis among national banks had been reopened.

Within the following ten days nearly all of the $2 billion in hoarded currency had flowed back into the banking system, and the Fed's gold reserves soon reached pre-crisis levels. By early April, fully 13,000 banks with $31 billion of deposits were open and more than 2,000 more quickly followed after they had been given RFC capital injections.

By contrast, at year-end 1933 only a thousand mostly tiny rural banks with aggregate deposits of less than $1 billion had been closed, thus demonstrating that at the time of FDR's banking crisis only 3 percent of the nation's bank deposits were still in insolvent institutions. In effect, the severe business cycle liquidation of the Great Depression was over even before Roosevelt was elected, and within weeks of his self-instigated banking crisis the US economy had resumed its natural rebound.

By June 1933, economic activity levels attained in the previous September had been regained and a slow upward climb ensued, led by the steady replenishment of fixed assets and working capital. To be sure, recovery was greatly attenuated by the shutdown of international trade, but in a process that was drawn and halting, nominal GDP eventually reached the $90 billion level by 1939. After seven years of New Deal medication, the nation's money income was still straining to reach its 1929 level.

THE EARLY NEW DEAL: GRAB-BAG OF STATIST GIMCRACK

This resumption owed no thanks to the balance of the tumultuous Hundred Days of New Deal legislation, either. Having triggered the demise of the old international order, the Roosevelt program of necessity was a purely domestic grab bag of experiments, gimmicks, and nonstarters. These ad hoc Washington interventions—the Tennessee Valley Authority (TVA), National Recovery Act (NRA), Agricultural Adjustment Act (AAA)—did little to revive the dormant machinery of market capitalism and economic wealth creation and, instead, mainly shuffled income and resources randomly among regions, industries, and even individual business firms.

Some of these New Deal schemes fueled aggregate demand but wasted economic resources, such as in the monumental destruction of the environment and capital that resulted from the TVA boondoggle. Designated by historians as a signature accomplishment of the New Deal, it in truth created at its peak only a few thousand jobs for the purpose of building inefficient dams and power plants that weren't needed—since the region was already drowning in excess utility capacity built during the 1920s boom; and it spent hundreds of millions turning wild rivers into navigable waterways when the region already had more than adequate rail and truck capacity.

Still other classic New Deal measures did immense and long-lasting harm, such as the 1935 Wagner Act. The latter was purportedly enacted to insure collective bargaining rights, but was so badly designed that it left even giant companies legally defenseless in the face of sit-down strikes and other coercive tactics. Eventually the resulting coercive and monopolistic industrial unionism harvested the whirlwind of bankrupt rust-bucket companies in the 1980s and 1990s.

THE BLUE EAGLE CAMPAIGN:
CRONY CAPITALISM RUN AMUCK

The signature legislative action of the Hundred Days was the NRA. By all accounts it actually thwarted economic recovery once implementation got seriously underway in September 1933. The program was essentially a fascist scheme to control supply and replace the alleged "chaos" of the free market by government sanctioned industrial cartels. These were designed to restrict output, inflate wages, and jack-up prices. Operating through 500 separate lines of industry and trade, the NRA cartels would magically inflate business revenues and wages, thereby reflating investment and household consumption. The wheels of the depression-stricken economy would thus be set back in motion.

Adam Smith had wisely admonished, of course, that whenever more than two capitalists confer, a conspiracy in restraint of trade is likely being hatched. In this respect, the NRA left nothing to chance: it actually forced competitors to join industrial syndicates and promulgate precise codes on the manner in which competition would be restricted and prices rigged.

Not surprisingly, a riot of abuse broke out before the ink was even dry on these so-called "Blue Eagle" codes. The mayhem was symbolized famously by the Schechter brothers' non-complying kosher chickens.

Yet, the case of the New Jersey businessman, who was imprisoned for charging less than the prescribed 40 cents to dry clean a suit, was even more to the point. It powerfully crystallized the dangers of converting the American economy—depression or no—into a confederation of crony capitalist cartels.

The Supreme Court's mercy killing of the NRA in May 1935, however, eliminated only part of the blight. The key labor provisions of the NRA cartel arrangements—minimum wages and hours and the right to organize monopoly unions—were resurrected in the 1935 Wagner Act and the 1938 Fair Labor Standards Act. Wrapped in the mantle of social justice, these laws openly allowed the supply and price of labor in the nation's basic industries to be artificially restricted and inflated by monopolistic industrial unions and their captive regulatory agencies. These violations of free market rules occurred with impunity for another three decades, but only due to fortuitous circumstances.

The trade autarky of the 1930s and the supremacy of the American economy and dollar in the immediate postwar decades provided temporary cover for wages to be rigged above market clearing levels. In fact, it was hard for American labor to price itself out of a world market that didn't exist or mattered little.

Yet it was only a temporary reprieve. Ironically, it was the other part of the May 1933 New Deal Foundation—the Thomas Amendment to the AAA—which eventually compelled a reckoning.

FDR'S CRANK MONETARY ECONOMICS:
PROFESSOR GEORGE F. WARREN'S GOLD-BUYING SCHEME

The alphabet soup of agencies were the public face of the early New Deal. At its heart, however, was FDR's crank monetary economics. The latter was a breezy attitude, not a deeply settled conviction because FDR didn't have any. After all, his first legislative enactment of March 14, 1933, was the Economy in Government Act championed by his pro–gold standard budget director. It resulted in a 15 percent cut in federal spending including government salaries and veterans' pensions—an un-Keynesian imitative that historians have airbrushed out of the record.

At the same time, the actual record remains riddled with monuments to FDR's loopy view of money. These episodes reflected his politically driven agenda of building the New Deal coalition but were positively antithetical to revival of world monetary order and trade, the sine quo non for the United States' escape from the Great Depression.

The most egregious and instructive of these was FDR's 1933 infatuation with one George F. Warren, professor of farm economics at Cornell. In that capacity he had written such gems as "Alfalfa" and "An Apple Orchard Survey of Orleans County." But branching off into macroeconomics, he had also written a treatise called "Prices" which essentially argued that the United States should stage a bear raid on its own currency. By driving the gold value of the dollar down it would levitate commodity prices and with them the whole industrial economy.

Roosevelt became aware of Warren's theories about how the magic elixir of higher gold prices could levitate recovery in agriculture and industry from his Duchess County neighbor and gentleman farmer, Henry Morgenthau Jr. The latter had studied horticultural economics under Warren at Cornell and had been brought to Washington by FDR as an aide-de-camp, but soon became secretary of the treasury by a process of default.

After Carter Glass refused the job and rail car manufacturer William Woodin died within months of taking office, the post should logically have gone to the treasury undersecretary, the brilliant and well-experienced Wall Street lawyer, Dean Acheson. Yet with the economy still floundering in the fall of 1933, Roosevelt fired Acheson for openly dissenting from his monetary flimflam.

So apparently determined to have a faithful acolyte in the Treasury post, FDR drafted his young neighbor for the job. Morgenthau's qualification for this crucial role in the midst of the greatest depression in world history was evident to few. But at that stage of the game Morgenthau had FDR's ear and by mid-October 1933 had maneuvered to get a regular hearing for his former professor, too.

In fact, the hearing came every morning in FDR's White House bedroom when the three of them gathered over eggs and toast to plot the price of gold and, therefore, the macroeconomic course of the nation—at least for the day at hand. The focus of discussion was Professor Warren's reams of tissue paper, containing charts and graphs on the prices of agricultural and industrial commodities, gold, and much else reaching back to the California gold rush, the Spanish conquest, and events even earlier.

With the aid of Jesse Jones, who was chairman of the Reconstruction Finance Corporation and had been dragooned into providing the money, the group plucked a number out of the air representing the desired gold price increase for the day. The targeted price gain was promptly sent it off to London to bid with the gold brokers.

Many years later, Morgenthau confessed that the US government's gold bid had not been set very scientifically, to say the least. On one occasion FDR had chosen to raise the price by $0.21 per ounce, explaining, "It's a lucky number, because it's three times seven."

The underlying reason for FDR's infatuation with Warren's crank doctrine was self-evident. The good professor claimed he could raise the price of wheat and other farm commodities and that's exactly what FDR needed to quiet the unrest in his hayseed coalition of agricultural and rural areas of the South and Midwest. The latter had reached a crescendo when farm commodity prices crashed in mid-July. Wheat went down 30 percent in three days, for example, after FDR's London conference bombshell.

At the time, sophisticated financial observers looked on with bemused disbelief. British Prime Minister Ramsay MacDonald, however, was nearly apoplectic, since FDR's breakfast-time gold buying in the London market had the effect of driving up the pound against the dollar. Professor Keynes summed up the episode best when he called it "gold standard on the booze."

Still, scientifically arrived at or not, Roosevelt's gold buying did not levitate the price of wheat, industrial tallow, or anything else. The only discernible gain after several weeks of this routine was in the bank accounts of the London brokers who sold gold to the RFC each morning at a higher price than they had bought it the day before.

In due course, FDR abruptly lost interest in fixing the price of gold and went on to the scheme of another set of monetary cranks in late December 1933. This time he joined the remnants of William Jennings Bryan's free silver campaign, promising to buy unlimited amounts of silver at double the world price.

The Silverites leader, Senator Key Pittman of Nevada, was more modest in his claims for this new commodity levitation effort. Bid up the price of silver, he advised, and the number of Democratic electoral votes in the mining states out west will also rise. On this count he was proven correct.

At the end of the day, Roosevelt had no coherent macroeconomic views or policy, other than the primitive, inflationist notion that the depression had been caused by low prices. In fact, low prices were just a symptom: the consequence of the unavoidable liquidation of the massive worldwide debt and printing-press money created during the Great War and during its aftermath in the Roaring Twenties.

Still, FDR was a pragmatist above all else. He soon discovered that none of the major initiatives of the so-called First New Deal—the NRA, AAA, Professor Warren's gold-buying campaign, and the subsequent January 1934 revaluation of the official gold price from $20 to $35 per ounce—succeeded in raising commodity prices, purchasing power, and industrial production.

So Roosevelt moved on to a new batch of ad hocery. In abandoning the core of the original New Deal completely and unceremoniously, FDR gave proof enough that the solid rebound of nominal GDP recorded through June 1936 occurred despite the New Deal's restrictions on farm and industrial output and its feckless monetary manipulations, not because of them.

THE MYTH OF NEW DEAL KEYNESIAN REFLATION

Foremost among the New Deal myths is the notion that FDR proved deficit spending could lift the American economy out of the depression. It was on that time-worn shibboleth that the massive deficit spending campaigns of the Bush and Obama administrations were predicated to ward off the illusory depression bogeyman in 2008–2011.

In fact, the New Deal enacted only two significant "pump-priming" programs in the classic Keynesian sense. One of these was a sheer accident—the 1936 veterans bonus payment. The other—the Works Progress Administration (WPA)—amounted to a vast patronage machine aimed at an upturn in the election cycle for the Democrats, not at countering the business cycle downturn which plagued the nation.

The accidental stimulus involved American GIs who had survived the pointless carnage in northern France. Upon their return, a grateful nation had promised them a large "bonus" pension to be paid out in the fullness of time or, more precisely, one-quarter century hence in 1942. But motivated by the widespread hardships and deprivations of the Great Depression, the veterans' organizations had launched a determined campaign for early payment.

In early 1936 they finally succeeded in extracting from Congress a whopping bonus payout which amounted to about $300 billion in today's dollars. The resulting fiscal stimulus must be chalked off to accident, however. The Roosevelt administration strongly opposed the payout and FDR actually vetoed the bill, but it was overridden with much Republican help.

According to a careful reconstruction of weekly treasury statements by Professor Lester G. Telser, nearly 60 percent of this massive transfer payment was distributed in a matter of six weeks in June–July of 1936, and nearly all of it went out within a year. Telser found that the three million hard-pressed veterans who received it "most likely spent all of it." Indeed it amounted to a "rebate shock" that would have pleased even Larry Summers. The annualized run rate of treasury cash disbursements during the peak weeks was equivalent to $1.7 trillion in today's economy, meaning that these bonus checks fueled a spectacular spending spree.

As store shelves unexpectedly emptied, orders for replacement goods surged. Soon the entire supply chain of the American economy was pulsating with inventory building, swelling production, and rising payrolls. Even the somnolent precincts of Wall Street woke up on the news that the long-rumored rebound was under way, and the stock index rose by 40 percent in less than nine months.

But then, in the spring of 1937, the US economy went radio silent. Customer traffic in the retail stores fell back to the pre-bonus normal. Consequently, restocking orders dried up, wholesale inventory building came to a screeching halt, production schedules were sharply pared, and soon unemployment was again on the rise.

This huge bonus payment had ripped through the American economy faster than green grass through a hungry goose. This wholly unplanned "stimulus" had nothing to do with New Deal fiscal policy, and instead was a spasm of election-year politics.

Still, Keynesian economists never stop gumming about the "mistake of 1937." They insist that White House policy makers had deliberately tightened the fiscal dials too soon and caused an unnecessary second recession.

The record shows, however, that fiscal policymakers did not elect this huge, concentrated stimulus: the Congressional legislation allowed millions of veterans to cash their bonuses beginning June 15, 1936. Contrary to expectation, most of them did so all at once in a sudden, massive unplanned stampede. Self-evidently, the resulting giant economic bubble was artificial and inherently unsustainable. When it suddenly collapsed after America's veterans finished spending their loot, the cause was not a fiscal policy mistake; it was simply the inevitable result of a poorly planned settlement of these long-standing veterans' claims.

PWA AND WPA: STIMULANTS OF THE ELECTION CYCLE, NOT THE BUSINESS CYCLE

The other claim to Keynesian pump-priming under FDR involved two very different programs whose New Deal style acronyms—PWA and WPA—made use of the same three letters. But on the evidence, neither of these programs did much to lift the American economy out of the depression.

The first of these was the Public Works Administration, or PWA, and it was run by a skinflint lawyer named Harold Ickes. At a glacial pace that spanned FDR's entire 13 years in office, Ickes's PWA did build several thousand airports, courthouses, schools, hospitals, rural power plants, local highways, and bridges—even as it pinched pennies and warded off corruption every step along the way.

Ultimately, it pumped $4 billion into the economy, but the PWA was no anti-depression pile-driver. Its total investment amounted to a negligible three-tenths of 1 percent of GDP over the PWA's long period of operation. Some of the projects which bear its plaques would have been built anyway by local governments, and others were pure white elephants like the massively expensive Grand Coulee Dam. Yet whether resulting in folly or productive public infrastructure, the smooth and glacial flow of PWA funds did not even remotely resemble counter-cyclical fiscal policy.

The Works Progress Administration was actually pro-cyclical, at least based on the even numbered years of the calendar. Very nearly the embodiment of political corruption itself, it mainly functioned as an election-time auxiliary of the Democratic Party.

From a cold start upon its enactment in May 1935, its payroll soared to more than 3.0 million by Election Day 1936. Once the votes had been harvested, however, the WPA payroll swiftly plunged to 1.5 million by late 1937. From there it rocketed back to 3.5 million by November 1938, and then collapsed once again toward the one million levels in 1939. So the cycle in question was evidently not the business cycle.

In fact, the WPA was run as the personal fiefdom of the New Deal's veritable anti-Ickes—one Harry Hopkins. His minimum low regard for the integrity of the public purse was made starkly evident when he once told FDR, "I've got 4 million at work but for god's sake don't ask me what they are doing."

The WPA ended in scandal when it was discovered that Hopkins had run a blatant shakedown in the 1938 campaign and had required employees to contribute their meager salaries to pro–New Deal senators. Moreover, the $11 billion spent over its six year life produced comparatively meager public works—8,000 local parks, 6,000 mobile libraries, 3,000 tennis courts and 800 local landing strips. At bottom, the WPA was a wasteful form of revenue sharing with local communities which delivered a clumsy form of needs tested transfer payments to millions of unemployed farmers, workers, accountants, and musicians, etc.

Under the circumstances, these citizens had a fair claim on the public purse. But the undulations of the WPA's hiring and firing cycle pivoted on

Election Day, not the business cycle. Accordingly, the WPA did not trigger the multiplier effects of Keynesian legend.

THE MODEST 1930S RECOVERY WAS DUE TO THE REGENERATIVE POWERS OF CAPITALISM, NOT THE NEW DEAL

Once the Roosevelt banking panic was over and the Hundred Days emergency session of Congress had been completed without too much damage to the fabric of the American economy, the Hoover recovery resumed. The rebound of business inventories came first, followed by a steady recovery of consumer spending on durable goods and eventually a mild revival of fixed-asset investment.

But the data make clear that the famous spurt of government activity in the first two years of the New Deal did little to revive the private economy. For instance, private nonfarm hours worked in 1934 were flat with the level of 1932. This means the modest rebound within this period was nothing more than the reversal of the post-election slump brought on by the Roosevelt banking panic.

Likewise, nominal GNP reached just $65 billion in 1934, representing only a 6 percent annualized rate of rebound from the 1932 level. Even then, the strongest gains were in consumer durables and fixed investment, the beneficiaries of a natural rebound from their depression lows.

During the middle 1930s, the natural rebound of the nation's capitalist economy continued, but the real truth was that the numbers looked strong on an annual basis only because the export, investment, and durables collapse had been so severe. Still, as of 1939, after which the tides of war preparation took over the economic numbers, the recovery had been slow and halting. Nominal GDP that year totaled $90 billion, a figure that was still 12 percent below its 1929 peak.

Likewise, fixed business investment was still 40 percent below the 1929 level, and private nonfarm hours worked told the same story. The US Bureau of Labor Statistics (BLS) recorded 75 billion man-hours in 1939—an astounding 15 percent below the 90 billion recorded for 1929. Similarly, steel production was still at 55 million tons compared to 62 million tons in 1929, and value added by all manufactures was $24.5 billion, a figure 20 percent below its $31 billion peak prior to the stock market crash.

In short, the New Deal historiography has relied on a trick; namely, the assumption that the US economy would have remained mired in depression without the New Deal, and that the moderate recovery which did occur was entirely attributable to it. That is pure sophistry.

What actually happened is that as the whirling dervish of experimentation that comprised the New Deal stumbled forward, it modestly increased the girth of the state. Government spending amounted to about 5 percent of GDP when FDR took office and was still under 10 percent as of 1939.

For all the Republican arm-waving about Rooseveltian Big Government, that was really the least of the New Deal's evils. Compared to the $33 billion recovery of total GNP between 1932 and 1939, only about $5 billion—just 16 percent—was accounted for by the government-spending component of the national accounts.

In truth, the acronyms which caused this fiscal expansion—NRA, TVA, AAA, WPA, PWA, CCC, etc.—did not constitute a coherent countercyclical fiscal policy and did not cause the US economy to be any larger by 1939 than it would have been had the Hoover recovery continued with Mr. Hoover in the White House.

THE WRONG LEGEND TAKEN

In early spring of 2008, an unschooled treasury secretary and politically craven White House enacted a giant $150 billion proto-Keynesian stimulus in the form of one-time tax rebates to bolster a faltering economy. Hard on the heels of its November 2008 election victory, the Obama administration instantly pushed through a sight-unseen $800 billion stimulus measure that was a true Keynesian dispensation, or so it was certified by the great thinker's current vicar on earth, Professor Larry Summers.

Together these measures, along with the $700 billion TARP and sundry other measures of fiscal largesse, caused $2 trillion in fiscal stimulus to be authorized inside the span of one year to fight an alleged impending economic collapse. The historical significance of this wanton raid on the US Treasury cannot be gainsaid.

For a flickering moment early in the Reagan administration the essential Keynesian predicate had been in headlong retreat; namely, the notion that downturns in the business cycle are avoidable and that the public purse should be aggressively used to counteract them. Now, twenty-seven years later, that predicate was again in full bloom, and with bipartisan enthusiasm.

Ironically, the proximate cause of the economic downdraft that brought the Keynesian project roaring back to life was that the banking monster had escaped its New Deal shackles (see chapter 9) and wreaked havoc on the American economy. In response, desperate politicians began conjuring the ghost of the New Deal, believing that it had been an efficacious shock therapy for a deep economic slump. That was a double irony because the

New Deal had not resuscitated anything. Among its many legacies had been a serviceable banking law (Glass-Steagall) and a feckless assault on sound money. The latter eventually morphed into Greenspan-Bernanke bubble finance. It was the catalyst that caused the unshackled banking system to go over the bend.

Yet outside of banking and money, the New Deal amounted to little more than a politically driven spasm of Washington activism. It did not address the causes of the Great Depression, did not cure or even relieve its pall on the American economy, and amounted to little that was economically coherent or purposeful.

Most especially, the notion that the New Deal had pioneered a road map to recovery by means of countercyclical fiscal policy is mostly a postwar academic legend. It is readily contradicted by the historical record, starting with the fact that, as shown above, the corner had been turned on a natural business cycle recovery before Roosevelt was even elected.

CHAPTER 9

THE NEW DEAL'S TRUE LEGACY
Crony Capitalism and Fiscal Demise

THE NEW DEAL DID NOT ADDRESS THE CAUSES OF THE DEPRESSION, even if its work relief and other humanitarian measures did ameliorate for millions of citizens the terrible costs of its unnecessary prolongation. Still, most of this safety net consisted of ad hoc programs, such as the WPA, which were never institutionalized and did not survive the 1930s.

What did survive is a destructive legacy of fiscal profligacy and crony capitalist abuse of state power. Policy measures like Fannie Mae, deposit insurance, social insurance, the Wagner Act, the farm programs, and monetary activism share a common disability. They fail to recognize that the state bears an inherent flaw that dwarfs the imperfections purported to afflict the free market; namely, that policies undertaken in the name of the public good inexorably become captured by special interests and crony capitalists who appropriate resources from society's commons for their own private ends.

Roosevelt's unprincipled and unbridled activism is a powerful case in point. Orthodox historians have positioned FDR as the scourge of "economic royalists" and the champion of the common man. He was neither. In fact, he was the patron saint of crony capitalism.

As a power-driven politician he recognized no rules or standards for public policy or any particular limits on the role of the state. Indeed, FDR has been nearly defied for being a "pragmatist" who experimented until he found something that "worked." Accordingly, it was only a matter of time before the very capitalists that FDR professed to despise captured for their own ends the programs he legitimized in the name of the public good.

THE NEW DEAL ORIGINS OF FANNIE MAE
AND THE HOUSING COMPLEX

Fannie Mae is a classic crony capitalist progeny of the New Deal that began life in 1938, quite innocently, as still another ad hoc New Deal program to boost the depression-weakened housing market. It grew into something quite different: a monster that deeply deformed and corrupted the nation's entire financial system seventy years later.

The policy aim of Fannie Mae was "forcing water to flow uphill" in the residential mortgage market so that low-rate thirty-year home mortgages became available to wage-earning households of modest means. Such mortgages did not then exist for a good reason: they were not economic. No prudent local bank or thrift would take the underwriting risk.

Fannie Mae would thus override the market's veto by turning local banks and thrifts into government contractors or agents, rather than mortgage debt underwriters. Accordingly, they would be relieved of their aversion to the risk of default loss by means of a Washington-funded "secondary market." The latter would purchase these commercially unappealing mortgage loans for cash, enabling local bankers to reloan this cash again and again in a government-supported rinse and repeat cycle.

Meanwhile, the default losses that the market refused to underwrite would be shifted to taxpayers, since Fannie Mae's funding would implicitly depend on the public credit of the United States. The slowly recovering residential housing sector would thus receive the kind of booster shot much favored by the New Dealers.

What Fannie Mae also did, unfortunately, was to start the home mortgage market down a slippery slope. This included separating the loan origination process from the long-term servicing and ownership of the resulting mortgage, in an alleged financing "innovation" that would give rise to predatory mortgage-broker boiler rooms a few generations down the road.

Likewise, it opened the door to the funding of home loans in the global markets for U. S. sovereign debt, rather than out of the savings deposits of local bank customers. This became possible because Fannie Mae took on quasi-sovereign status, meaning that investors were funding the general credit of the United States, not the specific risk of local mortgage borrowers and separate residential markets.

There were several crucial upgrades in ensuing decades to the original New Deal scheme before it reached its stunning dénouement in Washington's panicky $6 trillion nationalization and bailout in September 2008. Among these milestones were LBJ's maneuver to put Fannie "off-budget" in 1968 in order to hide its exploding use of Uncle Sam's credit card.

LBJ's so-called privatization plan, in turn, paved the way for Fannie to morph into a hybrid entity called a GSE (government-sponsored enterprise) in which ownership was private but its debt issues were implicitly government guaranteed. Politicians and policy makers who inherited

FDR's "anything that works" mantle were pleased to describe the GSEs as creative "public/private partnerships."

They were no such thing. The GSEs were actually dangerous and unstable freaks of economic nature, hiding behind the deceptive good-housekeeping seal afforded by their New Deal–sanctioned mission to support middle-class housing. This was especially the case after Fannie's initial public offering and subsequent ability to tap the public capital markets for virtually limitless funds.

Another crucial step was Wall Street's perfection of the mortgage securitization model. This "innovation" vastly improved Fannie's ability to sweep up mortgages originated by local bankers on a massive wholesale basis, and then guarantee and package them for distribution into increasingly broad and liquid national and international capital markets. When this was combined with high speed computerized underwriting in the 1990s, disasters like Countrywide Financial became inevitable.

As time passed, the evolution of the Fannie Mae monster only got more fantastical. Thus, the rise of the worldwide T-bill standard generated a nearly inexhaustible appetite among mercantilist central banks for US government or quasi-government GSE paper. These vast monetary roach motels were not exactly honest "markets" for mortgage loans from Cleveland or Fort Myers, but GSEs went into overdrive supplying the unquenchable thirst of foreign central banks for dollar liabilities, especially when heavy currency pegging began after 1994.

Not surprisingly, when Treasury Secretary Hank Paulson's fabled bazooka failed and Washington had to nationalize the GSEs, foreign central banks and other state institutions owned more than $2 trillion of American home mortgages, including upward of $1 trillion domiciled at the People's Printing Press of China.

In short, Fannie Mae's journey started in 1938 with a Washington, DC, filing cabinet containing a few thousand mortgage notes which had been gussied up and christened as the nation's "secondary mortgage market." Yet the progeny of this innocent filing cabinet ended up eighty years later scattered around the globe in the trust accounts of Norwegian fishing villages and as a trillion-dollar stash in the central bank vault of Red China.

In the interim, massive social costs and economic losses built up inside the housing marketplace and became ripe to explode. As detailed more fully in chapter 20, the whole GSE scheme functioned to underprice mortgages, undermine lending standards, over qualify home buyers, fuel greedy broker predation, and fund a speculative climate.

In the process, the principal assets of the American middle class, family residences, were turned into an ATM machine and became the object of frenzied buying, selling, and serial refinancing. Unfortunately, this ruinous journey was far more inexorable than it was merely accidental.

At each step along the way, powerful special interest groups—mortgage bankers, real estate developers, home builders, building material suppliers, Wall Street underwriters, law and title firms, appraisers, and brokers— drove policy toward their own benefit. These changes, elaborations, enlargements, and aggrandizements had a common purpose: namely, to enable the Fannie Mae (and Freddie Mac) mortgage-financing machine to harvest ever greater volumes, profits and fees.

Indeed, the Fannie Mae saga demonstrates that once crony capitalism captures an arm of the state, its potential for cancerous growth is truly perilous. More importantly, it underscores that the resulting carnage can be vastly disproportionate to the alleged social ill that justified the original policy intervention.

In this case, the housing market had essentially recovered before Fannie Mae opened its doors. After hitting bottom at 125,000 units per year in 1931–1933, the volume of new starts had nearly tripled by the late 1930s. By then, it was by no means evident that the nation's remaining willing lenders and solvent borrowers were producing the wrong answer with respect to the number of housing starts. So fiddling with an arbitrary goal of higher housing starts, the New Dealers gave birth to what eventually became a crony capitalist monster, and that was all.

SOCIAL SECURITY: THE NEW DEAL'S FISCAL PONZI

The Social Security Act of 1935 had virtually nothing to do with ending the depression, and if anything it had a contractionary impact. Payroll taxes began in 1937 while regular benefit payments did not commence until 1940.

Yet its fiscal legacy threatens disaster in the present era because its core principle of "social insurance" inexorably gives rise to a fiscal doomsday machine. When in the context of modern political democracy the state offers universal transfer payments to its citizens without proof of need, it offers thereby to bankrupt itself—eventually.

By contrast, a minor portion of the 1935 legislation embodied the opposite principle—namely, the means-tested safety net offered through categorical aid for the low-income elderly, blind, disabled and dependent families. These programs were inherently self-contained because beneficiaries of means-tested transfers simply do not have the wherewithal—that is, PACs and organized lobbying machinery—to "capture" policy-making and thereby imperil the public purse.

To the extent that means-tested social welfare is strictly cash-based, as was cogently advocated by Milton Friedman in his negative income tax plan, it is even more fiscally stable. Such purely cash based transfers do not enlist and mobilize the lobbying power of providers and vendors of in-kind assistance, such as housing and medical services.

Social insurance, on the other hand, suffers the twin disability of being regressive as a distributional matter and explosively expansionary as a fiscal matter. The source of both ills is the principle of "income replacement" provided through mandatory socialization of huge population pools.

On the financing side, the heavy taxation needed to fund the scheme has been made politically feasible by the mythology that participants are paying a "premium" for an "earned" annuity, not a tax. Consequently, payroll tax financing is deeply regressive because all participants pay a uniform rate regardless of income.

At the same time, benefits are also regressive because those with the highest life-time wages get the greatest replacement. This regressive outcome is only partially ameliorated by the so-called "bend points" which provide higher replacement on the first dollar of covered wages than on the last.

The New Deal social insurance philosophers thus struck a Faustian bargain. To get government funded pensions and unemployment benefits for the most needy, they eschewed a means test and, instead, agreed to generous wage replacement on a universal basis. To fund the massive cost of these universal benefits they agreed to a regressive payroll tax by disguising it as an insurance premium. Yet the long run results could not have been more perverse.

The payroll tax has become an anti-jobs monster, but under the banner of a universal entitlement organized labor tenaciously defends what should be its nemesis. At the same time, the prosperous classes have gotten a big slice of these transfer payments, and now claim they have earned them—when affluent citizens should have no proper claim on the public purse at all.

Accordingly, social insurance co-opts all potential sources of political opposition, making it inherently a fiscal doomsday machine. It was only a matter of time, for example, before its giant recipient populations would capture control of benefit policy in both parties, and most especially co-opt the conservative fiscal opposition.

Within a few decades, in fact, Republican fiscal scruples had vanished entirely. This was more than evident when Richard Nixon did not veto but, instead, signed a 20 percent Social Security benefit increase on the eve of the 1972 election. Worse still, the bill also contained the infamous "double-indexing" provision which since then has generated massive hidden benefit increases by over-indexing every worker's payroll history.

The fiscal cost of relentless universal benefit expansion has driven an epic increase in the payroll tax. The initial 1937 payroll tax rate was about 2 percent of wages, but after numerous legislated benefit increases, the addition of Medicare in 1965, the Nixon benefit explosion and the Carter and Reagan era payroll tax increases, the combined employer/employee rate is now pushing 16 percent (including the unemployment tax).

Accordingly, Federal and state payroll taxes for social insurance generate $1.2 trillion per year in revenue—four times more than the corporate income tax. So with the highest labor costs in the world, the U.S now imposes punishing levies on payrolls. It thus remains hostage to a political happenstance—that is, the destructive bargain struck eight decades ago when high tariff walls, not containerships loaded with cheap goods made from cheap foreign labor, surrounded it harbors.

Yet there is more and it is worse. The current punishing payroll tax is actually way too low—that is, it drastically underfunds future benefits owing to positively fictional rates of economic growth assumed in the 75-year actuarial projections. As a result, the benefit structure grinds forward on automatic pilot facing no political opposition whatsoever. In the meanwhile, the fast approaching day or reckoning is thinly disguised by trust fund accounting fictions.

In truth the trust funds are both meaningless and broke. Annual benefit payouts already exceed tax receipts by upward of $50 billion annually, while the so-called trust funds reserves—$3 trillion of fictional treasury bonds accumulated in earlier decades—are mere promises to use the general taxing powers of the US government to make good on the rising tide of benefits.

The New Deal social insurance mythology of "earned" annuities on "paid-in" premiums that have been accumulated as trust fund "reserves" is thus an unadulterated fiscal scam. In reality, Social Security is really just an intergenerational transfer payment system.

Moreover, the latter is predicated on the erroneous belief that new workers and wages can be forever drafted into the system faster than the growth of benefits. During the heady days of 1967, for example, Paul Samuelson and his Keynesian acolytes in the Johnson Administration still believed that the American economy was capable of sustained growth at a 5 percent annual rate. The Nobel Prize winner thus assured his *Newsweek* column readers that paying unearned windfalls to current social security beneficiaries was no sweat: "The beauty of social insurance is that it is actuarially unsound. Everyone . . . is given benefit privileges that far exceed anything he has paid in . . ."

Samuelson rhetorically inquired as to how was this possible and succinctly answered his own question: "National product is growing at a compound interest rate and can be expected to do so as far as the eye can see . . . Social security is squarely based on compound interest. . . . the greatest Ponzi game ever invented."

When 5 percent real growth turned out to be a Keynesian illusion and output growth decayed to 1–2 percent annual rate after the turn of the century, the actuarial foundation of Samuelson's Ponzi game came crashing down. It is now evident that Washington cannot shrink, or even brake, the fiscal doomsday machine that lies underneath.

The fiscal catastrophe embedded in the New Deal social insurance scheme was not inevitable. A means-tested retirement program funded with general revenues was explicitly recommended by the analytically proficient experts commissioned by the Roosevelt White House in 1935. But FDR's cabal of social work reformers led by Labor Secretary Frances Perkins thought a means-test was demeaning, having no clue that a means-test is the only real defense available to the public purse in a welfare state democracy.

When the American economy was riding high in 1960, Paul Samuelson's Ponzi was extracting payroll tax revenue amounting to about 2.8 percent of GDP. A half century later, after a devastating flight of jobs to East Asia and other emerging economies, the payroll tax extracts two-and-one half times more, taking in nearly 6.5 percent of GDP. So the remarkable thing is not that wooly-eyed idealists who drafted the 1935 act succumbed to social insurance's Faustian bargain at the time. The puzzling thing is that 75 years later—with all the terrible facts fully known—the doctrinaire conviction abides on the Left that social insurance is the New Deal's crowning achievement. In fact, it is its costliest mistake.

GLASS-STEAGALL:
ANOTHER FAUSTIAN BARGAIN WHICH FAILED

Another untoward legacy of the New Deal is the 1933 enactment of the great banking abomination known as "deposit insurance." The keenest financial minds of the time vehemently opposed deposit insurance because they well understood the inherent dangers of fractional reserve banking, or what really amounts to borrowing short and lending long.

Financial conservatives of that era believed that effective discipline on bankers had to come from the liability side of their balance sheets. Bankers could be prevented from taking reckless credit risk, or foolishly mismatching short-term liquid deposits with too many illiquid long-term loans and investments, it was believed, only if they faced continuous depositor scrutiny and the threat of deposit withdrawals, even a "run" on the bank when all else failed.

Certainly that was the view in 1933 of the intrepid leader of the Senate banking committee, Carter Glass. It was also the position taken by the American Bankers Association, as well as by such distinctively less banker-friendly experts as the original draftsman of the Federal Reserve Act, Professor H. Parker Willis of Columbia University. And not to be overlooked, either, is the fact that deposit insurance was also strongly opposed by Franklin D. Roosevelt himself.

It was only after months of legislative haggling that the Faustian bargain finally materialized. Hailing from the hardscrabble state of Alabama, which had been especially devastated by bank failures, Congressman Henry B. Steagall represented the populist demand for deposit insurance to protect the "little guy." At the same time, the final bill incorporated a regulatory régime for the asset side of the banking system designed by Carter Glass and Professor Willis.

These latter restrictions famously centered on the separation of investment and commercial banking. But they also included restrictions on bank holdings of illiquid real estate and corporate securities, the prohibition of interest on checking accounts, and the remainder of what came to be known as the Glass-Steagall regulatory régime.

The implicit theory of this two-headed compromise, therefore, was that the heavy inducement to risk taking and moral hazard, owing to taxpayer insurance of deposit liabilities, would be offset by strict safety and soundness regulation of banking operations and balance sheet holdings. In effect, traditional marketplace discipline on the deposit and liability side of bank balance sheets would be supplanted by strict regulation of their asset side.

At the time, the "Steagall" and the "Glass" components of the 1933 banking legislation seemed firmly harnessed. The US House of Representatives was a hotbed of anti-banker sentiment during the 1930s, while Senator Carter Glass was a deeply knowledgeable and stern taskmaster.

Even Wall Street grudgingly deferred to him. So the Glass-Steagall legislative fusion seemed immune to banker-sponsored dilution or repeal, and it was on that understanding that Carter Glass, the foremost banking expert of his time, reluctantly embraced deposit insurance.

In the fullness of time, however, it turned out to be just another Faustian bargain which came a cropper. Once the world went on the T-bill standard and inflation soared in the 1970s, Senator Glass's carefully designed harness on the asset and operating side of commercial banking came under relentless pressure for liberalization.

The Great Inflation of the 1970s which followed Nixon's demolition of Bretton Woods, in fact, destroyed the political foundation of Glass-Steagall;

that is, a régime of bad money very quickly spawned a parallel régime of bad banking. The reason is that high inflation flushed the liquid deposits out of banks while crushing the fixed-rate assets that were stranded in them.

A key feature of Glass-Steagall had been interest rate ceilings on bank deposits (Regulation Q). These were designed to discourage banks from aggressively expanding their loan books and then funding them with deposits obtained from their competitors by chasing interest rates higher. This ceiling arrangement was deeply offensive to free marketers, but Senator Glass had well understood that competitive efficiency had to be sacrificed to banking safety, given the moral hazard of deposit insurance and fractional reserve banking.

When Arthur Burns ignited the fires of inflation for Nixon's reelection party, however, Regulation Q caused a perverse outcome that the gold standard Senator from Virginia probably never imagined; namely, a flight of deposits out of the banking system into unregulated money market funds that could offer higher rates. The latter, in turn, were able to invest their inflows in the choicest assets of the banking system, such as high-grade commercial paper and Treasury bills.

At the same time, soaring inflation caused massive mark-to-market losses on the core fixed-rate assets that the commercial banking system did retain, such as long-term Treasury bonds and mortgages. This brutal squeeze not only endangered the solvency and viability of the banking system, but it also generated a more sympathetic reception in Washington for the banking industry than at any time since the 1920s.

It would be no exaggeration to say that Richard Nixon and Arthur Burns were the real executioners of Glass-Steagall—and fully two decades before the Gramm-Leach-Bliley repeal act was even drafted. Ostentatiously displaying their wounds from the Great Inflation, in fact, the banks relentlessly pleaded for flexibility to pursue riskier business while also getting Regulation Q lifted.

The desire on Capitol Hill to help alleviate the squeeze on hometown banks and thrifts is what really fueled the deregulation drive during the Reagan era. For instance, the landmark Garn–St. Germain bill of 1982 conferred vastly expanded asset powers, such as real estate development lending and junk bond investments, on the massively insolvent savings and loan industry.

While the Senate side of this legislative duo had an affinity for free market doctrine, the decisive voice was that of Congressman Freddie St. Germain of Rhode Island. The latter was a practical politician who rarely met a lobbyist he could not accommodate.

St. Germain's case for deregulation was not about the glories of the free market, but simply that it was an unavoidable emergency expedient designed to help thrifts to earn their way out of their current balance sheet disasters. The Great Inflation thus spawned a cure which was worse than the disease. As the thrift industry piled into reckless speculation far afield from home mortgages, it was only a matter of time before virtually the entire industry collapsed into insolvency.

The relentless drive of the commercial banks into new product lines such as securitized mortgages, interest rate swaps and other derivatives, stock and bond underwriting, and eventually market making and proprietary trading had similar roots. All of these ultimately destructive banking charter expansions gained their initial impetus and legislative cover from the unassailable fact that high inflation and double-digit interest rates had busted the balance sheets and business model of traditional deposit banking.

To be sure, the ideology of free markets was inappropriately applied to the banking industry during the Reagan era and ever since. Under modern institutional arrangements, including deposit insurance and the Fed's bailout window, banks are inherently wards of the state and cannot be safely deregulated.

Yet as the Fed fostered a growing speculative climate and financialization of the American economy after 1987 there ensued a step-by-step dismantlement of Glass's regulatory harness, and then its outright repeal in 1999. What was left in the aftermath of repeal was nothing other than the naked moral hazard of Congressman Steagall's deposit insurance scheme.

Once the Fed flooded the banking system with virtually free money after December 2000, the bargain of 1933 became a colossal financial accident waiting to happen. The populist Congressman Steagall would doubtless roll in his grave upon learning that his gift to the "little guy" had enabled the depredations of Citigroup eight decades later. His coauthor and legendary student of banking, Senator Glass, undoubtedly would have retorted, "I told you so."

In all, Glass-Steagall's desultory ending was not atypical of the long-term fate which befell most of what emerged from the devil's workshop that was the New Deal. More often than not, programs born out of desperation or idealism seventy-five years ago have ended up as fiscal time bombs like Social Security, or as captive fiefdoms of one crony capitalist syndicate or another.

THE CRONY CAPITALISM OF FDR'S HAYSEED COALITION

The Agricultural Adjustment Act (AAA) of 1933 was the quintessential product of the New Deal devil's workshop, boasting a record of contemporary economic mayhem and destructive future legacy with few parallels. The giant flaw was that the AAA was an anti-market scheme utterly incapable of alleviating the deep farm depression that sprung from the aberrations of the Great War.

American farms had then functioned as the "granary" to the world after world war broke out in 1914. During that glorious and unrepeatable episode in American agricultural history, farm exports soared from about $1 billion annually to nearly $4 billion at the war-induced peak.

The Great War temporarily transformed the American agricultural heartland into a Persian Gulf equivalent for wheat, wool, cotton, and pork. Wheat prices, for example, climbed from $0.70 per bushel to $2.20. Accordingly, the windfall rents accruing to the suddenly "scarce" supply of American farmlands were enormous. Farm income soared from $3.5 billion in 1913 to $9 billion by 1919.

But even that stunning gain does not capture the full impact: rural economies were transformed into redoubts of never before imagined prosperity, even opulence, almost overnight. This ebullient war prosperity also caused land values to double, spurred robust investment in farm improvements and machinery, and encouraged aggressive credit expansion by country banks.

But in the spring of 1919, the US government abruptly shut down the massive stream of war loans that had been going to the European allies. Within months, the demand for exports from the American granary began to rapidly dwindle, and by the next year (1920) the farmlands of Europe came back into production.

The economic tide in the agricultural hinterlands rapidly reversed during 1920–1921 when farm commodities experienced a violent deflation. Sky-high farm prices were hammered down relentlessly—with wheat, for example, falling from $2.20 per bushel in 1919 to $0.95 per bushel two years later.

The 1920s return to the pre-war equilibrium, however, was exacerbated by an additive factor—the agricultural mechanization revolution—which came cheek-by-jowl with the loss of bloated wartime export markets. In 1914 there were only about 15,000 tractors and 17,000 work trucks on American farms, but by 1930 it was a totally different world. These figures had increased fifty-fold to nearly one million tractors and a like number of farm trucks.

The arrival of this vast armada of farm tractors and trucks tremendously increased farmer productivity at the same that US farm exports were cut in half to $2 billion by 1922 and remained at this level for most of the 1920s. When the foreign bond market crashed after 1928, this last vestige of artificial demand vanished, causing US farm exports to experience another violent down-leg to a mere $750 million by 1932.

During the course of twelve years, therefore, the value of American farm exports plunged by 80 percent. The windfall rents and surging rural prosperity that was the result of the Great War became its nightmarish opposite by the early 1930s.

Not surprisingly, the wartime peak farm income of $9 billion was cut to $5 billion by 1925 and eventually to $2 billion by 1932. Accordingly, farm land prices followed the path of income downward, dropping by 50 percent. By the early 1930s farm land was back to a per-acre value not seen since around 1900.

In the natural economic scheme of things, however, one metric of the farm economy remained elevated to the very day of FDR's inauguration; namely, farm mortgages and other debts. After more than doubling to $12 billion in 1921, farm debts remained grudgingly high at $10 billion through 1933.

Once again, therefore, an old economic truth rudely asserted itself. Debts are contractual and fixed, even as boom-time incomes and asset values plummet back to earth. Indeed, farm income had plummeted by 80 percent whereas farm debt had been reduced by only 15 percent.

Accordingly, the debt service burden on American farmers climbed from 5 percent of income in 1919 to nearly 35 percent by 1933. Not surprisingly, foreclosures reached such epic proportions that nearly all of the rural states enacted moratoriums.

And so, in the fullness of time, the massive farm borrowing spree which had been induced by the windfall rents of the Great War ended in tears. After weighing heavily on the rural countryside in the midst of the nation's temporary urban prosperity of the 1920s, it finished up by crushing the shrunken remnants of the US farm economy when worldwide depression finally materialized in the early 1930s.

THE RISE OF FDR'S HAYSEED COALITION: THE REAL POLITICAL BASE OF THE NEW DEAL

The agricultural corridors of America became the epicenter of the Great Depression. Drained of cash flow by the collapsing prices of its crops and denied credit by its widely insolvent banks, the rural economy by March 1933 had plunged from the pinnacle of wartime prosperity to a deeper depression than ever before experienced in American history.

The inner truth of the New Deal is that FDR's nomination at the 1932 Democratic convention and the electoral votes that put him in the White House were overwhelmingly secured in these same burned-out agricultural districts—the South, the middle border, the Great Plains, and the farm and mining areas of the Southwest and West. Consequently, the essence of Roosevelt's anti-depression policy arose out of the hayseed coalition from these districts, and consisted of the witch's brew of home-made remedies, schemes, reforms, crusades, and monetary quackery that emanated from the stricken farm economy.

The depression theory of the hayseed coalition, a notion which FDR embraced thoroughly, was that the prolonged agricultural depression in the countryside had infected the whole national economy by reducing rural demand for manufactured goods. In turn, this fueled a downward spiral of factory shutdowns and unemployment, resulting in reduced urban incomes and spending.

The whole key to national recovery, therefore, was to levitate farm prices sharply upward. This would cause rural incomes to rebound smartly. Soon, orders for manufactured goods would revive, factories would reopen, workers would have money to spend again, and the great engine of the national economy would gain steam.

Not surprisingly, the farm movement had an elaborate scheme for levitating the price of wheat, corn, cotton, milk, and a host of other commodities. This price-fixing contraption had been known as the McNary–Haugen bill during the 1920s.

At the time, American consumers had escaped being fleeced by its crude levies. The doughty Calvin Coolidge had simply refused to sign a Republican farm bill which enabled self-appointed farm lobbies to form what amounted to a legally binding cartel for every agricultural commodity.

By contrast, FDR embraced agricultural price fixing enthusiastically, planting the seeds of what became another destructive New Deal legacy. The AAA's original seven-crop cartel included corn, wheat, cotton, rice, milk, peanuts, and tobacco, and provided for government controlled acreage and production restrictions and artificial price supports. These schemes were amended repeatedly over the decades such that each became a distinct self-contained domain of rural crony capitalism.

Like in all instances of crony capitalism, economic outcomes are as much as gift of the state as they are the fruits of capitalist virtue. Consequently, the USDA's crop cartels have been vigilantly stationed at the epicenter of American fiscal politics ever since the New Deal, always ready to logroll among themselves, and to trade their votes for virtually anything of interest to urban delegations.

Indeed, the "food stamp" program, which has nothing to do with nutrition and is actually just an income transfer paid in alternative currency, has become an integral part of the USDA budget. It also is also a central element of the periodic authorizing legislation upon which the crop cartels depend, and a potent means of enlisting "urban farmers" in the cause of their perpetuation.

Small-state senators have a hugely disproportionate weight in American governance, and nowhere as much as in the fiscal politics practiced by the crop cartels. Indeed, today's bloated welfare state and corrupted tax code reached their current metastasized condition in large part because at critical inflection points over the decades, farm-state senators—the natural opponents of Big Government—have regularly sold out the public purse in favor of the rural crony capitalists who populate their states.

And in this logrolling, there was nothing for which the farm senators did not swap their votes: housing programs, urban development grants, oil industry tax loopholes, weapons systems, even money for handicapped education were all part of the great legislative trading bazaar.

In fact, the farm programs are anachronistic and economically stupid and could not survive without this raw power politics. Meanwhile, the heavy financial burden resulting from this expression of crony capitalism is paid by the American public in their role as consumers or taxpayers.

The $1 trillion seventy-five-year battle of the rural crony capitalists against the free market's inexorable shrinkage of the nation's agricultural districts has been an exercise in futility. In 1935 there were 35 million people on 7 million farms, who accounted for about 25 percent of national output. Today there are fewer than 2 million Americans on the farm; there are less than 250,000 remaining commercial-scale agricultural enterprises; and farm output represents a mere 4 percent of GDP.

The New Deal's crop cartels, therefore, did not even remotely restore the golden age of World War I farm prosperity. Instead, they ended up institutionalizing vast abuses of state power and conferring undeserved windfall land rents on a privileged segment of rural crony capitalists for generations to come.

Worst of all, they saddled the nation's fiscal politics with a large bloc of swing votes permanently on offer to the highest bidder. Accordingly, the AAA was not just another New Deal program that failed to foster recovery from the Great Depression; it was actually the political axis on which much of the modern welfare state was built.

FDR'S HAYSEED COALITION:
ROOTS OF MODERN MONEY PRINTING

It was not the anti-gold fulminations of J. M. Keynes at the time of the British crisis in 1931 that finally brought down the gold standard and sound money. Instead, its real demise came two years later in the form of the

Thomas Amendment, a powerful expression of the monetary populism which animated FDR's hayseed coalition.

The amendment was hatched at midnight on April 18, 1933, during FDR's famous White House rendezvous with the fiery leader of the hard-scrabble farm belt, and embodied four "discretionary" presidential options to debauch the gold dollar. These measures have been dismissed by historians as a casual sop by FDR to farm state radicals, but they could not be more mistaken.

The Thomas Amendment was a nascent version of today's delusion that economic setbacks, shortfalls, and disappointments are caused by too little money. The true cause, both in the early 1930s and today, was actually an excess of debt. This explanation is never appealing to politicians because there is no real cure for the liquidation of excess debt, except the passage of time and the forfeiture of the ill-gotten gains from the financial bubbles preceding it.

By contrast, the populists of the New Deal era believed that the state could easily and quickly remedy a shortage of money by printing more of it. In this respect they are in a line of descent that extends to the depredations of the Bernanke Fed in the present era.

The line of continuity started with FDR and Senator Thomas and included the latter's guru, Professor Irving Fisher of Yale. It then extended into the present era via Professor Milton Friedman of Chicago, who embraced wholeheartedly Fisher's quirky theory of deflation. The latter, in turn, became the virtual obsession of Friedman's acolyte, Professor Bernanke of Princeton, whose academic work is based on Friedman's erroneous interpretation of the Great Depression.

Upon becoming chairman of the Fed, Bernanke then foisted the Fisher-Thomas-Friedman deflation theory upon the nation's economy in a panicked response to the Wall Street meltdown of September 2008. Yet monetary deflation was no more the cause of the 2008 crisis than it had been the cause of the Great Depression.

The monetary populists of the 1920s and 1930s, including Professor Fisher, had "cause and effect" backward. The sharp reduction after 1929 in the money supply was an inexorable consequence of the liquidation of bad debt, not an avoidable cause of the depression. The measured money supply (M1) even in those times consisted mostly of bank deposit money rather than hand-to-hand currency. And checking account money had declined sharply as an arithmetic consequence of the collapse of what had previously been a fifteen-year buildup of bad loans and speculative credit.

During 1929–1933 commercial bank loans outstanding declined from $36 billion to $16 billion. Not surprisingly, as customer loan balances fell sharply, so did checking accounts or what can be termed "bank deposit money" as opposed to currency in circulation. The latter actually grew by $1.1 billion during the four years after 1929, to about $5.5 billion.

By contrast, it was the loan-driven checking account portion of M1 which dried up, declining from $25 billion to $17 billion over the same period. And the reason was no mystery: the way banks create demand deposits is to first issue loan credits to their customers. Indeed, in the modern world money supply follows credit, and rarely do central bankers inordinately restrict the growth of the latter.

In truth, loan balances and checking account money rose to inordinate heights during the financial bubble preceding the 1929 crash and unavoidably declined thereafter. This had nothing to do with causing the depression. The real reason the American economy was stalled in the early 1930s is that it had lost its foreign customers.

The reduction of M1 owing to the liquidation of bad credit, by contrast, was a sign of returning financial health. Indeed, the major component of bank credit shrinkage had been the virtual evaporation of the $9 billion of margin loans against stock prices that had reached lunatic levels before the crash. In blaming the Fed for the Great Depression, therefore, Professors Friedman and Bernanke implicitly held that the Fed should have underwritten the margin-loan-based speculative mania of 1926–1929 in order to keep M1 from shrinking!

THE THOMAS AMENDMENT'S DEAD-END OPTIONS: FORESHADOWING OF THE BERNANKE FED

The Thomas Amendment thus amounted to a road map for the Bernanke money-printing policies of the present era. While some of its specific mechanisms for injecting money into the economy had a slightly archaic aura, they nevertheless embodied the same destructive theories of monetary central planning that plague policy even today.

The first Thomas Amendment option was an authorization for the Federal Reserve to purchase up to $3 billion of government bonds in the open market. This would have more than doubled the Fed's holdings of government debt (from $2.4 billion to $5.4 billion) in a manner similar to what the Bernanke Fed actually did in 2008–2011. While massive government bond buying, or debt monetization, is supposed to put "money" in the banking system, the contemporary Bernanke escapade proves otherwise.

In the context of systematic private debt liquidation, central bank bond buying mainly results in a huge buildup of excess reserves in member bank accounts stored in the Fed's own vaults. In other words, money grows mainly when commercial bank credit expands, and no amount of Fed bond buying can force member banks to lend into a debt-saturated marketplace.

The second option crafted by FDR and Senator Thomas was based on their recognition that the still sober minded Fed of that day might actually refuse to crank up the printing presses in order to go on a bond-buying spree. Therefore, the amendment also authorized the Treasury Department to activate its own printing press and issue $3 billion of new paper currency, or literally greenbacks.

As a practical matter that option was beside the point. It would have nearly doubled the amount of currency in circulation, yet by late April 1933 the banking panic was over, and $2 billion of hoarded currency was already coming out of mattresses and flowing back into the banking system. Since there was no longer a shortage of currency, any greenbacks issued under the Thomas Amendment would have had no effect on household or business spending.

This seemingly archaic option to print greenbacks, however, actually illuminates the folly of the Fed's modern bond-buying campaigns. Had the White House chosen to exercise the currency-printing option it could have temporarily paid its bills by issuing interest-free greenbacks rather than the 2.5 percent Treasury bonds of the day, but that was a step even Roosevelt shied away from because it amounted to crackpot finance.

Yet eight decades later, Washington finances itself exactly as the Thomas Amendment envisioned. The fact of the matter is that the "greenbacks" of historical ill repute were simply noninterest-bearing debt issued to finance the Civil War. Today the US Treasury issues greenback equivalents. Three-year notes that yield a fractional thirty-five basis points of interest, for example, are only a tiny step removed from printing-press currency.

The US Treasury is able to sell notes at such aberrationally low yields only because the Fed stands ready to absorb any amount of issuance that does not clear the market at its targeted rates. That's currency printing by any other name.

The third option embraced by leaders of the hayseed coalition involved yet another way to artificially inject "money" into the economy. In this instance, the nation's silver miners and speculators were to be the agents of economic uplift. Accordingly, the Treasury was authorized to purchase the entire output of America's silver mines at approximately $1.25 per ounce and then coin these bullion purchases into circulating money.

At the time, the world market price of silver was just $0.35 cents per ounce, so FDR and Senator Thomas were proposing to monetize silver at 3.5X its market value. While this evokes the crank economics of William Jennings Bryan, it involves the same principle as today's money printing by the Bernanke Fed, except the markup on the Fed's coining of digital dollars is nearly infinite.

The resemblance of the Thomas Amendment's silver option to today's Fed policies was evident in another respect, as well. Massive silver purchases at way above world market prices would have obviously delivered a mighty windfall gain to the mining towns and silver speculators.

Yet the New Deal could have created similar ill-gotten windfalls by monetizing tungsten or cow-hides. Indeed, monetization inherently showers speculators with ill-gotten gains. The windfalls harvested today by frontrunning traders who buy classes of Treasury securities and GSE paper targeted for purchase by the Fed would put to shame the modest windfalls harvested by silver speculators when FDR implemented this feature of the Thomas Amendment in 1934.

The final option of the Thomas Amendment was the basis for FDR goldtinkering campaigns, and for his January 1934 decree that gold would hence be worth $35 per ounce versus the $20 per ounce standard that had prevailed since 1832. Obviously, drastically altering the hundred-year-old gold content of the dollar amounted to the same thing as destroying the gold standard. After all, a "standard" which can be changed radically on a whim of the state is not a standard at all.

However, the underlying rationale for changing the dollar's gold content was the truly dangerous feature of the Thomas Amendment. It was the forerunner of today's monetary central planning and embodied the notion that the nation's entire GDP could be managed by simply raising the dollar price of a market basket of commodities. After an initial "reflation" of commodity prices, including gold, the depression would be ended instantly and thereafter the business cycle would be permanently eliminated.

THE HAYSEED COALITION'S EASTERN BRANCH: PROFESSOR IRVING FISHER OF YALE

This provision of the Thomas Amendment embodied the so-called "compensated dollar" plan, the brainchild of Professor Irving Fisher of Yale. It is in the direct lineage of the T-bill monetary standard whose author, Professor Milton Friedman, essentially appropriated Fisher's deflation theory in his own work. Friedman claimed that the Great Depression had been caused by too little money supply, or M1.

Fisher's compensated dollar was based on the proposition that business cycles were the result of mistakes by businessmen in reacting to wide swings in the price level. They would overinvest in production, inventories, and fixed assets when prices rapidly rose. Then when interest rates increased in response to rising commodity prices they would sharply curtail borrowing, liquidate inventories, and reduce production and cutback capital spending, thus triggering the next recessionary cycle or even depression.

Furthermore, these sharply falling prices and customer orders would then induce the opposite mistake, causing businessmen to become too pessimistic about the future. They would then under produce and under-invest in inventories and fixed capital, thereby perpetuating a deflationary cycle like that embodied in the Great Depression.

Fisher's view was that businessmen were forever making mistakes and, therefore, a monetary arrangement was needed to nip these foolish errors in the bud. To that end, Professor Fisher proposed creation of an elite board of government wise men to stabilize the commodity price level by deftly varying its gold content. Once the state insured that commodity prices would never change, businessmen on the free market would never again make mistakes!

Fisher's magical compensated dollar plan, therefore, was the original version of monetary central planning: his "great moderation" would abolish the business cycle and thereby generate permanent prosperity and perpetual full employment. Accordingly, fiddling the gold price was thus an early form of the contemporary Greenspan-Bernanke prosperity management model based on fiddling money market interest rates.

Unlike the incomprehensible J. M. Keynes, Fisher was lucid and made every effort to appeal to politicians, including FDR. During the spring of 1933 Fisher prowled Washington's corridors, and not solely out of the patriotic belief that the depression could be ended by adopting his compensated dollar plan.

His own animal spirits were bludgeoned by the depression. He famously proclaimed ten days before the October 1929 crash that the stock market had reached a "permanently high plateau" and invested accordingly. Unfortunately, though, Fisher lost both the personal fortune he made from inventing the Rolodex and his wife's inherited fortune. In any event, after having advised his greatest Washington disciple, Senator Elmer Thomas, on the amendment which bore his name, Fisher also obtained an audience with FDR in May 1933. He came away elated. "Our fortune is saved!" said the note to his wife, which he scribbled that evening on the stationary of Washington's Carlyle Hotel.

FDR's embrace of the Thomas Amendment and his subsequent bombshell letter to the London Economic Conference were both nearly pure expressions of the Fisher compensated dollar plan as was FDR's subsequent capricious fiddling with gold prices during his escapades with Professor Warren (see chapter 8).

FDR's aim in manipulating the gold content of the dollar had consistently been to raise farm and industrial commodity prices, believing that higher prices would pump purchasing power back into the pockets of both labor and business, and thereby catalyze the engines of economic recovery. So FDR was a firm believer in "pump priming." But it was based on a Fisherite, not a Keynesian framework.

The obstacle to Fisher's reflation scheme, however, was the prostrate condition of world trade where massive excess capacity in worldwide export industries had caused a stunning collapse in the prices of tradable goods. By the spring of 1933, for example, the international wholesale index for industrial raw materials such as cooper and rubber was down by 60 percent, while the index for a standard basket of food prices was down 55 percent. Even the price index for traded manufactures had tumbled by 40 percent from its 1929 peak.

In this context, the US dollar price of gold was a pretty frail lever with which to jack up global commodity prices. Indeed, the only effective route to sustained reflation would have been a sharp rebound in world trade and absorption of this massive export capacity overhang. Yet that was blocked everywhere by trade barriers and competitive currency depreciation.

So FDR's approach to countercyclical management of the domestic economy by means of the Fisher compensated dollar strategy was largely a fizzle. The January 1934 reduction of the dollar's gold content by 40 percent (to $35 per ounce) was supposed to catalyze a further energetic rise in the wholesale prices, but it never happened. The wholesale price index, which had recovered substantially before FDR took office, then stood at 80 and simply flat-lined around that level for years; it was still at just 77 when the US economy was about to shift to a war footing in mid-1939.

In short, the peacetime New Deal did embrace a form of countercyclical policy, but it was Fisher's reflation rather than the deficit finance of Keynes. Nevertheless, at the end of the day the nation's fiscal demise was enabled by the Thomas Amendment's destruction of the gold dollar. Now it was only a matter of time before Professor Friedman would provide Richard Nixon with the rationale to finish the job FDR had started.

GOLD REVALORIZATION AND THE
WHITE HOUSE SLUSH FUND

The one thing that FDR raised with his Fisherite levitations was a White House slush fund called the Exchange Stabilization Fund (ESF). At the stroke of FDR's pen, the price of gold went from $20.67 per ounce to $35, thereby causing the value of the nation's gold stock to rise from $4.2 billion to $7 billion.

Most of this $2.8 billion "revalorization" gain was assigned to the newly created ESF. Under the terms of the Thomas Amendment the fund was available for such purposes as the president directed. During the remainder of the peacetime 1930s, therefore, Secretary of the Treasury Morgenthau became a virtual monetary czar. This dominance was facilitated by the fact that the nation's actual central bank, the Federal Reserve, was near dormant. The reason for the Fed's irrelevance was not hard to fathom. By 1934–1935 the domestic banking system was becoming saturated with idle cash, reflecting negligible demand for loans from the somnolent US economy.

Indeed, the striking evidence that cash was king lies in the buildup of excess bank reserves parked at the Fed. These soared from $2.7 billion in 1933 to $11.7 billion by 1939, and accounted for 75 percent of the Fed's balance sheet growth during the period.

All this money resulted in short-term interest rates which were persistently below 1 percent after 1934. Indeed, there was never any monetary stringency during the 1930s that the Fed failed to alleviate. On the contrary, the record shows conclusively that in the midst of sustained debt liquidation, increases in bank reserves result merely in "pushing on a string," not credit expansion and economic stimulus.

Ironically, the Fed today is generating excess bank reserves in an identical manner to what occurred during the mid-1930s, and with the same lack of effect. Bernanke's reputation as an expert on monetary policy during the Great Depression is thus wholly undeserved: he is pushing on the same string that the great Fed chairman of the day, Marriner Eccles, knew to be incapable of fostering recovery.

To be sure, the massive growth of excess domestic bank reserves during the mid-1930s was due to large-scale inflows of gold from abroad rather than Federal Reserve money printing. Yet that is merely a technical difference. Bank reserves could come from either source. Yet under the prevailing cycle of debt deflation, neither source of bank reserves resulted in a single extra solvent customer for loans.

FDR'S BALEFUL LEGACY: STATE MONEY
WHICH ENABLED PERMANENT FISCAL DEFICITS

As the war clouds gathered in Europe, the United States increasingly became a safe haven. Consequently, the nation's official gold reserves doubled from $10 billion to $20 billion during the second half of the decade and reached two-thirds of total global gold reserves. This gold inflow brought persistent upward pressure on the dollar's exchange value, inducing the Treasury Department to intervene chronically in foreign exchange markets, using its ESF slush fund to do so. Consistent with its Fisherite monetary views, the aim of this White House currency market intervention was mainly to prop up the franc and pound sterling and weaken the dollar.

And so went the string of New Deal monetary policy actions which began with the April 6, 1933, confiscation of private gold. The thread was extended through FDR's embrace of the Thomas Amendment, the London bombshell letter, the breakfast-time gold buying with Professor Warren, the 1934 revalorization of the gold price, and these ESF's foreign exchange market interventions.

When all was said and done, these actions had congealed into a historic policy departure; that is, the nationalization of money. Henceforth, the nation's money would become a subordinated tool of the state's domestic stabilization policies. No longer would money occupy its historic role as a private instrument of commercial exchange and storehouse of value, redeemable for an asset whose price was fixed, intrinsic, and derived wholly apart from the state.

At the end of the day, this was the true New Deal break from the past and from what had earlier been Herbert Hoover's last stand for financial orthodoxy. To his credit, Hoover had never wavered from the gold standard, even as he had succumbed to a variety of dubious expedients such as the RFC bank bailouts, meddling in corporate wage and price setting, and the abomination of the Smoot-Hawley tariff.

The far-reaching implications of the New Deal's radical monetary policies have not been highlighted by contemporary analysts because they did not involve aggressive money printing by the Fed. But they amounted to the same thing. Owing to the weak economy and strong gold inflow, money market conditions were intrinsically easy, at least by the standards of the day. After 1934, commercial paper and T-bill rates were thus stuck under 0.5 percent, long-term government bonds yielded 2.5 percent, blue chip corporate debt yielded 3.5 percent, and cash was superabundant.

Under those conditions the Fed knew better than to "push on a string," and had not yet even dreamed of employing open market operations as a tool of plenary macroeconomic management. Indeed, the Fed's paramount leader after 1934, Chairman Marriner Eccles, was a fiscalist who spent most of his time preaching to the White House about the need for more deficit spending, not easier money.

Still, Irving Fisher's "managed currency" theories, as embodied in the New Deal's monetary tinkering, established the crucial predicate; namely, that monetary manipulation is a legitimate tool of state policy. So doing, it paved the way for latter-day management of the gross domestic product (GDP) by means of Keynesian deficit spending and Greenspan-Bernanke-style monetary central planning.

The truth is, Keynesian policy was a nonstarter under the old régime of gold-convertible money. Fiscal deficits could be body checked at any time by the people themselves, who had the right to dump their paper money for gold whenever they lost confidence in the fiscal discipline of the state.

Thus, Fisher's "compensated dollar" undoubtedly sounds quaint to modern ears. Yet it was the crucial way station to the new world of permanent deficit spending and the T-bill standard money which was eventually to come.

KEYNESIANISM IN ONE COUNTRY: THE GREAT THINKER'S CASE FOR HOMESPUN GOODS AND MONEY

The New Deal also established a supplementary predicate which was equally crucial to an embrace of thorough-going Keynesian macro-management: Namely, the essentially protectionist notion of a closed domestic economy and the subordination of the rules with respect to international movement of goods, capital and money to the dictates of domestic policy. That predicate was the essence of FDR's London bombshell.

It was on the matter of autarky—America first—that the New Deal fell in line with Keynes' true contribution to the depression era policy debate. Indeed, the inspiration for the New Deal was never really the erudite ramblings of the 1936 "General Theory." Instead, it was the rank protectionism of Keynes' 1933 essay entitled "National Self-Sufficiency."

In the latter treatise, the great thinker averred that art, hospitality and travel might properly remain in the sphere of internationalization. But as to the core matter of economics—the movement of merchandise goods and financial capital—the time had come, as Keynes saw it, to roll-back the clock.

The prior 300 years of western progress by nearly every account had been based on international trade and comparative advantage, but Keynes had no compunction about pronouncing Adam Smith wrong. Based on an apparent flash of revelation that had been absent from his writings of even a few years earlier, Keynes now urged for an era of national autarky.

Operating behind moats at the border, the state would thus mobilize and command domestic economic life without interference: "I sympathize, therefore, with those who would minimize...economic entanglements between the nations...let goods be *homespun* whenever it is reasonably and conveniently possible; and, above all, let finance be primarily national."

Keynes fancied himself a dandy, of course, and would never have been caught wearing homespun attire from the equivalent of Gandhi's loom. But when it came to entire nations and their unwashed masses, it is not at all surprising that he thought that nationalistic and autarkic Nazi Germany was the most likely candidate for early adoption of his program. He even took personal care to insure that his works were always available in German.

Perhaps Keynes' newfound distain for international commerce was colored by his experience as a currency speculator during the 1920s when he had repeatedly made bets on the whims of national policy-makers. The topic of Keynes' currency bets was always the same—that is, when and at what parities would various countries—including Great Britain—"resume" convertibility and fixed exchange rates.

Indeed, the trials and tribulations of France, the Belgium, Italy and others during their postwar quest for "resumption" of currency convertibility embodied an unassailable lesson that Keynes had surely grasped. The scope for domestic fiscal policy action and macroeconomic management became sharply constrained when nations embraced honest, gold-redeemable international money.

So during the prolonged debate over British resumption, Keynes became a shrill opponent of the gold standard and the idea of international money as the world had previously known it. The vainglorious professor from Cambridge had thus arrived at the conclusion that "Keynesianism in one country" was the wave of the future and that his nostrums required an essentially closed economy and national fiat money.

In this sense, Roosevelt was the tribune who made Keynesianism possible. By his obdurate rejection of the advice of his internationalist advisors—Lewis, Warburg, Hull, Glass—FDR smothered the last impulse to resurrect a liberal world economic order and valid international money. Roosevelt the Fisherite thus made full strength Keynesianism ultimately possible.

To be sure, having shed the shackles of international monetary discipline, the New Deal didn't really know what to do with its new found freedom of action. As has been seen, many of the New Deal's hallmark legislative enactments—the NRA, AAA, the Wagner Act and the Fair Labor Standards Act—were exercises in economic restriction rather than Keynesian demand expansion.

HENRY MORGENTHAU'S LAST STAND FOR BUDGET ORTHODOXY: WHY US FISCAL BANKRUPTCY TOOK TIME

The irony of the New Deal is thus striking. Even when there was virtually no monetary check on deficit spending, it did not go all-out for Keynesian stimulus owing to a vestigial state of mind; that is, an inculcated belief in balanced budget orthodoxy.

Adherence to the old-time fiscal religion by policy makers was a crucial rearguard force which retarded the adoption of Keynesian policies during the initial four decades after the New Deal. Indeed, in a double dose of irony, it was the abandonment of balanced budget orthodoxy by the GOP after 1980 that led to the nation's rapid fiscal demise thereafter. Yet this eventuality was latent the day FDR embraced the Thomas Amendment and the end of sound money.

As it happened, the principle agent of fiscal orthodoxy in FDR's inner circle was Treasury Secretary Henry Morgenthau. Morgenthau was second only to FDR himself in his ardor for Professor Fisher's radical monetary doctrine of the compensated dollar, but like so many subsequent policy makers of the interwar generation, Morgenthau kept his fiscal and monetary doctrines compartmentalized.

Time and time again Morgenthau fought to restrain New Deal spending and deficits. His famous diary is literally chockablock with expressions of fiscal rectitude, yet the fiat dollar régime he so enthusiastically embraced would have permitted deficits of a scale that would have pleased even Larry Summers.

By the eve of World War II, an exhausted Morgenthau penned an entry expressing a complete lack of faith in deficit spending: "We have tried spending money. We are spending more than we have ever spent before and it does not work . . . I say after eight years of this administration that we have just as much unemployment as when we started. . . . And an enormous debt to boot."

The fiscal trends which alarmed Treasury Secretary Morgenthau, however, turned out to be worrisome only by the chaste standards of the past. During FDR's six peacetime budgets (1934–1939), federal spending never reached even 10 percent of the national economy and the fiscal deficit averaged just 3.9 percent of GDP. And that was during the greatest depression in world history.

American politicians thereafter gradually learned that the ancient discipline of honest money had been lifted, so they steadily pushed out the fiscal boundaries. The fiscal deficit during 1975–1980, for example, averaged 3 percent of GDP and then raced past the New Deal record to an average deficit of 4.3 percent of GDP during the Reagan Administration. And this was during an eight-year span which included six years of "morning in America." Accordingly, the way was paved for the fiscal lunacy of the George W. Bush era and the explosive last gasp of Keynesianism under Obama.

As the curtain closed on the 1930s, Morgenthau's doctrinal contradiction was just the most exaggerated case of the split-screen attitude of the

New Deal's conservative wing. Many of the stalwart southern Democrats who were critical to the Roosevelt coalition—such as Vice-President John Nance Garner, RFC head Jesse Jones, Senator Jimmy Byrnes of South Carolina, and Senator Walter George of Georgia—had generally welcomed soft money and dollar depreciation, even as they remained wary of fiscal deficits.

Eventually, however, the fiscal orthodoxy which had been part and parcel of the gold standard world faded away as its adherents like Morgenthau and the conservative southern Democrats left the scene. Still, even as they went through the motions of their rearguard battle against deficits, the destructive fiscal legacy of the New Deal was just getting started.

The seeds of crony capitalism had been planted in the farm belt and among crippled economic sectors like the railroads and the merchant marine. The ticking fiscal time bomb of social insurance had been institutionalized, even as a régime of industrial union monopoly cast a long shadow on the national economy's ability to shoulder the cost burden.

Likewise, the federal agencies which would fuel the housing mania had been chartered, and only a frail regulatory harness on the banks held the vast moral hazard of deposit insurance temporarily in check. Most important of all, FDR's final destruction of the gold standard had paved the way for open-ended statist intervention and hyperactive management of the domestic economy.

This misguided and fiscally cancerous project would soon be embraced by both parties. It was a development which was bound to end in the triumph of crony capitalism and the fiscal bankruptcy of the nation.

CHAPTER 10

———

WAR FINANCE AND THE
TWILIGHT OF SOUND MONEY

THE NEW DEAL'S AD HOC STATISM WAS EVENTUALLY SUPERSEDED by the real thing: the full-bore warfare state spawned by the Japanese attack on Pearl Harbor. Under the exigencies of total war, all of the tools of modern fiscal expansion and monetary manipulation were discovered, tested, amended, and perfected.

But when the peace came in 1945, the victory of these warfare state–inspired policy tools was neither complete nor immediate. Indeed, over the next quarter century the canons of financial orthodoxy found intermittent, and sometimes poignant, expression under Presidents Harry Truman and Dwight D. Eisenhower, and the long-reigning Fed chairman William McChesney Martin. Even President John F. Kennedy kept orthodoxy alive, at least in the Treasury Department and its international dollar policies.

So the road from Pearl Harbor to Richard Nixon's decision to default on the nation's Bretton Woods obligation to redeem its debts in gold, eventually ushering in printing-press money and giant fiscal deficits, is important to retrace. In the interim there occurred episodes of fiscal and monetary discipline that have long since been purged from mainstream memory. Yet these were signal moments of inspired governance which underscore just how much was lost with the waning of the old-time financial orthodoxy.

One was President Harry Truman's insistence on financing the Korean War the honest way, with higher current taxes. Another was Eisenhower's refusal to adopt tax-cut stimulus during the two recessions on his watch, thereby enabling him to achieve his highest fiscal priority: balancing the federal budget.

Still another shining moment came in August 1958 when Fed chairman William McChesney Martin moved to "take away the punch bowl" in order to discourage stock market speculation only four months after the economic recovery had begun. And rarely noted is that President Kennedy's first economic policy address was a ringing commitment to maintain the nation's Bretton Woods obligations and to defend the gold dollar.

It is entirely accurate and warranted to say that Nixon's embrace of Professor Friedman's floating paper dollar was the fatal turning point which brought a final end to sound money. Yet what the road to August 1971 also demonstrates is that Tricky Dick's abomination was not inevitable. There was, in fact, a twilight of sound money along the way.

WAR FINANCE AND THE RISE OF THE
FED'S OPEN MARKET BOND AND BILL BUYING

Once war was declared, the Roosevelt administration dusted off the techniques discovered during the Great War mobilization of 1917–1918 and soon imposed a complete command-and-control régime that reached into every nook and cranny of the American economy. The steel, auto, metal-working, machinery, and other heavy industries were commandeered to make ships, planes, and tanks. Production of housing, autos, household durables, and other discretionary items was eliminated almost entirely.

In a civilian economy bereft of consumer goods, all prices and wages were put under a straitjacket of bureaucratic controls. Likewise, private incomes were drafted into war service either by means of confiscatory taxation or as quasi-forced savings via the incessant war bond campaigns.

Not surprisingly, the money markets and the capital markets went into deep hibernation in this completely war mobilized economy. Likewise, the Federal Reserve became the financing arm of the warfare state. Making short shrift of any pretense of Fed independence, Treasury Secretary Henry Morgenthau simply decreed that interest rates on the federal debt would be "pegged." Treasury bills would yield three-eighths of 1 percent and long-term bonds would pay a 2.5 percent coupon.

Obviously, the only way to enforce this peg was for the nation's central bank to purchase any and all Treasury paper that did not find a private sector bid at or below the pegged yields. Accordingly, the Fed soon became a huge buyer of Treasury securities, thereby "monetizing" federal debt on a scale never before imagined.

The magnitude of this bond- and bill-buying campaign is dramatically evident in the Fed's balance sheet footings, which showed holdings of $2.3 billion of Treasury debt at the start of the war. By the end of 1945, these holdings had soared to $24.3 billion, a twelvefold expansion during the four years of world war.

The nation's central bank thus became schooled in the art of rigging the government bond market and the Treasury yield curve by persistent massive open-market purchases of Treasury paper. Today this is business as usual, but then it was a radical departure, a theretofore rarely used tool that now became institutionalized owing to the exigencies of wartime finance.

The Fed opened its doors in November 1914. But owing to the exigencies of wartime its purpose and modus operandi were twice turned upside down during its first thirty-one years. It can be fairly said that the Fed became a permanent denizen of the government debt market during its service to the warfare state, forging the T-bill standard, as it were, in the crucible of war. But this massive government bond buying was the very opposite of what its legislative authors had in mind when enacting the Federal Reserve Act of 1913.

A BANKER'S BANK WHEN THERE WAS NO PUBLIC DEBT AND NO RELATIONS WITH WALL STREET

Schooled in the English banking tradition and "real bills" monetary doctrine, the chairman of the House banking committee, Carter Glass, had seen the new Federal Reserve as an agent of the commercial loan market. In fact, he fervently believed that the Fed should not conduct operations in the government bond market, and certainly never envisioned that it would become a massive repository of government debt.

Accordingly, it was intended that the new system would provide liquidity to business and industry through a "rediscounting" process in which the "reserve" banks supplied cash advances to local commercial banks. Such "reserve credit" extensions were to be collateralized by the short-term business loan books of participating banks.

The commercial banking system would thereby be backstopped by a reliable source of cash to meet unexpected depositor withdrawals, while obviating the need for banks to call in business loans and disrupt the flow of commerce. The Federal Reserve System, therefore, was intended to be a "banker's bank," not an agent of national economic management. This founding charter has been literally blotted out of modern day discussions, as has the fact that the original Fed could not have operated through the government bond market in any event because in 1913 there wasn't one.

Total federal debt outstanding at the time of the Fed's creation was $1.2 billion. This amounted to only 3 percent of GDP and $12 per capita in the money of the day, a figure which would still be only $400 per capita in today's massively depreciated dollar. So the Fed was established during an era when policy makers didn't much cotton to running their government on debt.

Dramatic proof is that the $1.2 billion outstanding in 1913 was nearly identical to the national debt level first reached a half century earlier at the time of the Battle of Gettysburg. Fifty years with no growth in government debt, even in nominal dollars, is a mind bender in today's world.

Given the absence of a modern government bond market, it can also be said with certainty that the Fed's designers did not anticipate that it would operate cheek by jowl with Wall Street. Only when the Fed entered the government bond dealer markets and conducted a continuous program of buying and selling Treasury securities did a close liaison with Wall Street become unavoidably necessary.

By contrast, in the mind of Carter Glass and the congressional majority which followed his lead, the very purpose of the decentralized reserve bank system was to wrest control of the nation's money from the long-standing grasp of Wall Street. And this aim was not simply an expression of country-side populism.

Glass's critique of the existing National Banking Act monetary arrangement, which functioned from 1863 until 1914, was cogent and exceedingly relevant to the framers' intent. The studies that Glass's congressional committee conducted showed that the existing system had powerful incentives which caused the nation's liquid banking reserves to drain from the country banks and regional centers into the great city banks of Wall Street.

These reserves were then employed in the lucrative but risky and volatile business of the call loan market. The latter mainly financed speculation, or as Congressman Glass vividly described the old system, "The country banks would bundle off their surplus funds to the money centers . . . to be loaned on call for stock and commodity gambling."

Such speculative enterprise periodically ended in financial panics on Wall Street and ricocheting waves of upheaval throughout the banking system. So Congress created the twelve "reserve banks" in faraway centers like Atlanta, Dallas, Kansas City, and San Francisco.

These locations would provide a safe haven for the liquid reserves of the regional and local banks domiciled in each district. Excess deposits from the country banks would no longer need to make their seasonal road trips to Wall Street.

In attempting to cut off the flow of bank reserves from the hinterlands to Wall Street, Carter Glass exhibited a level of monetary sophistication and learning that has escaped today's Keynesian propagandists entirely. Professor Paul Krugman, for example, constantly cites the panics of 1873, 1884, 1893, and 1907 as evidence that the gold standard was a failure.

At the time of the Federal Reserve Act of 1913, however, nearly every attentive student of the matter, ranging from Professor Oliver Sprague of Harvard to the self-taught chairman of the House banking committee, knew better. The evidence clearly shows that the actual culprit was not the gold standard but the deeply flawed National Banking Act system.

By artificially flushing nationwide banking reserves into the big Wall

Street banks, it fostered an unnatural, over-sized and inherently unstable call loan market for stocks. Punters speculating with margin loans would periodically get carried away, resulting in bubbles that would eventually collapse and cause a violent liquidation of overpriced stocks as call money dried-up. For the most part, these "panics" did not spread to the hinter-lands, nor were they the cause of the long but constructive deflation that unfolded during the last three decades of the nineteenth century.

This well understood truth was readily apparent in the new arrange-ment under the 1913 act. At the time, total deposits in the nation's banking system were about $20 billion. Under the stringent reserve requirements of the new system, about $3 billion or so of cash and other liquid assets were required to be posted against these deposits as ready reserves, rather than being loaned out.

But congressional supporters of the new system were fiercely deter-mined to keep these billions of ready reserves out of the hands of the Wall Street money center banks and functionally divorced from them. The act's principal author later explained this accomplishment in almost lyrical terms. Said Congressman Glass:

"We cured this financial cancer by establishing the regional reserve banks and making them, instead of private [Wall Street] banks . . . custodi-ans of the reserve funds of the nation . . . making them minister to com-merce and industry rather than to the schemes of speculative adventure. The country banks were made free. Business was unshackled. Aspiration and enterprise were loosened. Never again was there to be a money panic."

WAR DEBT AND THE FED'S NEW MISSION

Three decades later, however, the Fed was a caricature of its founders' vi-sion, having become even more immersed in Wall Street than the old na-tional banking system ever had been. As indicated, this development was the result of two wartime borrowing sprees and the resulting wholesale abandonment of the nation's historic balanced-budget discipline. The public debt thereby grew from midget to giant dimension.

Thus, the 1913 national debt of $1.2 billion had exploded to $260 billion by the end of the Second World War, and rather than 3 percent of GDP it was now 125 percent. The epochal nature of the change in the nation's financial structure represented by these public debt figures is dramatically evident in the per capita comparison. In today's purchasing power terms, the $400 per capita number for public debt of 1913 was $30,000 per capita by 1945.

The federal government could never have accumulated debts of this magnitude without a central bank to serve as its fiscal agent and buyer of last resort. The Fed thus became ensconced at the heart of the government debt market, where its operations consisted first and foremost of buying Treasury securities from the Wall Street dealers to prop-up the market for government debt.

While executing this large-scale debt monetization, the Fed also gained invaluable new experience in stage managing the balance sheets of the commercial banking system and in crafting bank earnings. During the war finance period of 1941–1945, commercial bank holdings of US government debt exploded, rising from $20 billion to $84 billion. This gain amounted to 90 percent of total commercial bank balance sheet growth, meaning that as a practical matter the banks functioned primarily as a receptacle for the government's massive outpouring of wartime debt. The Fed's crucial wartime learning experience came from its efforts to make it worthwhile for its wards in the banking system to hold all this government paper. To this end, it capped the discount rate at 1 percent, thereby keeping deposit costs cheap for the duration of the war. At the same time, the banks earned a 2.5 percent coupon from their investments in long-term Treasury bonds.

The Fed thus enabled commercial banks to harvest a generous profit spread over their cost of funds. During the course of the war, in fact, bank earnings on securities held for investment nearly tripled, and net profits doubled. By 1945, the return on capital in the commercial banking system reached peak levels not to be seen again for another quarter century.

Still, something of far greater significance than home front prosperity for the nation's bankers came out of this ad hoc exercise in war finance. What really happened is that the Fed discovered the secret of how to manufacture bank profits by rigging the Treasury yield curve so it sloped in a smartly upward direction—that is, the longer the bond maturity, the higher the yield. Once discovered, this monetary sorcerer's trick remained a staple in the Fed's playbook thereafter.

In its role as fiscal agent of the US Treasury, the Federal Reserve also bade farewell once and for all to the founders' vision that it function passively as a standby provider of liquidity to the banking system. Under its original mission, banks needing cash would bring their eligible loan collateral to the Fed's discount window to obtain a short-term advance.

Accordingly, the commercial banking system was the active agent which drew the Fed's cash into the economy based on the actual pace of local business activity. That is the inverse of today's model in which the Fed proactively injects cash into the system through open market operations, based on where its monetary central planners think the national and world economy ought to be.

Stated differently, under the original vision of the 1913 act, the business economy was in the monetary driver's seat. It generated the ebb and flow of loans, deposits, and reserves in the banking system and the final aggregates of money and credit. Federal Reserve credit arose from commerce that already existed; it did not seek to add even a dime to existing bank loans or GNP.

By contrast, during the period of war finance between 1942 and 1945, the Federal Reserve became a powerful, proactive manager and manipulator of the nation's entire commercial banking system. Its purpose during that interval of national crisis was to manage the nation's ballooning war debt, but these very same tools of banking system management through manipulation of the yield curve were later adapted to management of the GDP itself.

Its apotheosis came six decades later, when the Fed orchestrated a veritable dance of the zombies during the aftermath of the September 2008 meltdown. Reaching back to its school days in war finance, the Fed again engineered a steep Treasury yield curve by driving front-end rates to nearly zero.

In so doing, it gifted legions of insolvent banks with a simulacrum of profits. It thereby reduced depositors to penury, of course, even as it kept zombie institutions alive and their executives in bonuses for a while longer.

THE WARFARE STATE BUDGET: HOW THE FISCAL BOUNDARIES WERE TESTED

Even as the Fed was being domesticated as a branch office of the Treasury Department during the Second World War, the fiscal boundaries of the warfare state were also being dramatically enlarged. And this was something new under the sun. Notwithstanding the "big spending" reputation that several generations of Republican orators have pinned on the New Deal, the peak federal spending claim on the nation's GDP averaged only 9 percent in fiscal 1938–1939.

It was only the arrival of fully mobilized war budgets which actually demonstrated the capacity of the modern state to consume the national income. Accordingly, federal spending reached 44 percent of GDP during 1943–1945.

At the same time, the fiscally conservative Morgenthau was not about to repeat the grave mistake of the First World War. Back then, most of the combatants had refused to finance the massive cost of industrial warfare with taxes, resorting to a destructive level of bond issuance and printing-press money.

Morgenthau instead went for heavy current taxation, and jacked up the 8 percent of GDP federal tax burden recorded during the final years of the peacetime New Deal to nearly double that level by 1943. He then tripled the federal tax burden to 24 percent of GDP by 1945.

The policy measures used to achieve this stunning tax take included confiscatory taxation of the wealthy and merely onerous taxation of everyone else. This tax dragnet included heavy excess profits taxes on corporations and a medley of excise taxes on consumers, along with sky-high income tax rates on all classes of payers.

Morgenthau therefore accomplished what classic nineteenth-century public finance recommended but none of the European powers had achieved the last time; namely, financing at least 50 percent of wartime fiscal costs from current taxation rather than bonds and the printing press.

In fact, during the five war budgets of fiscal 1942–1946 the Treasury accomplished exactly that. It collected $180 billion in cumulative receipts, which amounted to precisely one-half of its $370 billion in federal outlays.

The régime of stiff taxation imposed by the Roosevelt administration during WWII was consistent with an implicit economic model that was classical, not Keynesian. The whole cumbersome bureaucracy of controls and heavy taxes was designed to curtail civilian demand and expand net national savings—the opposite of the Keynesian recipe.

AMERICA SAVED ITS WAY OUT OF DEPRESSION: THE KEYNESIAN MYTH OF MASSIVE WAR DEBT

To a very large degree the model worked. Approximately $100 billion, or 30 percent, of the five war budgets were financed with private sector savings. This outcome partially reflected the success of patriotic war bond campaigns, but mainly resulted from the reality of empty retail shelves. Citizens were forced to save via war bonds because there was nothing else to buy. Indeed, even sugar, butter, meat, tires, shoes, bicycles, and candied yams were strictly rationed.

In summary, then, about 80 percent of the fiscal cost of the massive warfare state that was mobilized to defeat Germany and Japan was paid for with the people's savings in one form or another. About 50 percentage points of this was through the coerced "savings" (i.e., taxes) extracted by the Internal Revenue Service and another 30 points were derived from "voluntary" investments in war bonds and other savings instruments.

The truth is, the American economy did not spend its way out of the Great Depression; it essentially saved its way through the most destructive war in human history.

In the decades since 1945, however, Henry Morgenthau's sternly orthodox scheme of war finance has been twisted beyond recognition by Keynesian revisionists. They have incessantly claimed that the Second World War demonstrated the power of deficit spending and the economy's ability to carry a high ratio of government debt to GDP.

Yet the only thing which is true about this particular Keynesian legend is that for one fleeting moment in 1945 the federal debt outstanding did reach 125 percent of GDP. The far more important data point, however, is the total debt ratio, including both private and public debt. This crucial figure is never discussed or even acknowledged by the Keynesians, and for an understandable reason: total debt outstanding did not rise during the war; it actually declined significantly.

At the end of the wartime fiscal régime in 1945, the total debt-to-GDP ratio was about 190 percent. This figure, which includes business, household, and government debt, was measurably lower than the 210 percent ratio recorded under the peacetime New Deal in 1938.

The actual data thus puts the lie to the endlessly repeated canard that the Second World War was a splendid exercise in debt finance. What actually happened during the war is that the private sector went on a huge savings spree, once the command economy was installed.

For example, the household savings rate averaged about 2.5 percent of GDP during 1938–1939, but then soared to nearly 17 percent during 1942–1945. This was a savings rate not even remotely approached either before or since.

In turn, this explosion of thrift led to a dramatic deleveraging of household and business balance sheets. This clearing of debt accounts was reinforced by the fact that there was virtually no new business or personal borrowing during the war.

As a result of these trends, household debt dropped from about 60 percent of GDP in 1938 to just over 20 percent by 1945, meaning that consumers ended the war virtually debt free. Likewise, corporate business debt also fell sharply during the same seven-year period, dropping from about 90 percent of GDP to 40 percent.

Owing to the forced savings of wartime dirigisme, therefore, private sector leverage (corporations plus households) was rolled back from its prewar ratio of 150 percent of national income to just 60 percent, a level far lower than any recorded since the nineteenth century. Stated differently, the US economy emerged from the war in solid financial shape mainly because the private debt burden had been virtually erased, thereby creating vast "headroom" on the nation's balance sheet for federal debt to be readily absorbed by available national savings.

Furthermore, even this high-water mark was exceedingly temporary. During the immediate postwar period, Washington's vestigial fiscal conservatism played out in one final chapter, resulting in a sharp, speedy reduction in the government's debt ratio. A war-weary nation demanded rapid demobilization of the military machine, so annual federal outlays plummeted from $95 billion in 1945 to only $37 billion in fiscal 1947. At the same time, the heavy régime of wartime taxes was only modestly reduced, permitting the federal budget to swing into surplus during fiscal 1947. It then remained in the black for several more years, until the next war.

The federal government's debt ratio thus completed a sweeping round trip. After having surged from 50 percent of GDP in 1938 to 125 percent at the 1945 peak, the federal debt ratio retraced three-fifths of this wartime gain, falling to under 80 percent of national income by 1950.

Moreover, even with a modest rebound in private borrowing, total credit market debt by 1950 had fallen back to 170 percent of national income, nearly spot-on its historical norm spanning all the way back to the Civil War. In short, what the warfare state of 1941–1945 proved was that wars should be funded with taxes and savings, not that federal deficits are harmless or that they were a cure for the Great Depression.

HARRY TRUMAN'S HONEST WAR

The initial postwar fiscal equilibrium was not destined to be sustainable. It depended upon high wartime tax rates and on a monetary policy régime vested with latent inflationary propensities.

Eventually, the Federal Reserve would capitulate to the bullying of Lyndon Johnson and Richard Nixon by throwing open the switches on its printing press. This unleashed a virulent inflation that would cause consumer prices to nearly triple between 1967 and 1980.

At multiple steps along the way, however, an honor roll of statesmen attempted to resist the tide of fiscal profligacy and monetary debasement which had been set in motion by the New Deal and the warfare state. It began with Harry Truman's resolute stand for fiscal responsibility on the matter of war finance during the Korean action.

From a contemporary vantage point, of course, it is not clear what purpose US intervention on the Korean peninsula ultimately served. Today's prosperous Republic of Korea would have otherwise ended up an equally booming province of China's Red Capitalism, the last great hope according to bullish speculators.

Once the war decision had been made, however, Truman insisted that it be financed the old-fashioned way—with taxes. Accordingly, he promptly pushed through the Congress a hefty tax increase in September 1950, and another one in January 1951 after the war widened at the time Chinese forces poured across the Yalu River.

In the final reckoning, federal spending surged nearly 80 percent during the war period. Yet, amazingly, at least by current standards, the Korean War budgets were financed on a pay-as-you-go basis. Stated in constant dollars (2005), outlays totaled $1.76 trillion during fiscal years 1951–1953, while revenues came in at a nearly identical $1.75 trillion. No elective war has ever been financed with such purposeful discipline.

As it turned out, this episode marked the end of sound war finance, and also the beginning of extended wars of occupation—in Vietnam, Iraq, Afghanistan—that were financed with Treasury bonds. This contrast was not coincidental. Owing to Truman's unwavering insistence on stiff war taxes, GOP conservatives had no stomach for open-ended war in the barren hills of Korea if it meant permanently high taxes, and therefore blessed Eisenhower's decisive move for peace within weeks of his election.

After that, America's imperialistic misadventures in other strategically barren redoubts of the planet faced no such political constraints. Lyndon Johnson set the new tone with his "guns and butter" adventure in Southeast Asia, even when the historical record shows that the Chinese people were now starving in their villages, not fixing to pour across the border of another purported domino.

Yet LBJ couldn't bring himself to ask for war taxes until the very end, a drastic failing that opened the way for equally irresponsible war finance by future GOP administrations. Indeed, four decades later George W. Bush's equally bootless imperial missions were carried out entirely tax free. Indeed, what poured out of China this time was the money to fund them.

THE FED'S 1951 STAND AGAINST THE TREASURY PEG AND THE REPRIEVE OF SOUND MONEY

The next constructive but ultimately unavailing effort to restore sound money occurred in the spring of 1951. At that time, a dramatic Washington political confrontation ended the Fed's wartime servitude to the Treasury Department and eliminated the inflationary "peg" on Treasury interest rates.

The precipitating force was a surge of anticipatory price increases resulting from the threat that Washington would reimpose price controls when the Korean conflict escalated. In short order, the CPI was increasing at double-digit rates well ahead of open market interest rates, which were rising with a lag.

Real interest rates had thus become deeply negative, fueling a "cheap money" burst of bank credit expansion. The growth of new lending, in fact, reached a 20 percent annual rate during the winter of 1950–1951. This was a credit expansion rate that had not been recorded since the Roaring Twenties.

Notwithstanding this frothy surge of inflation and credit, the Fed was still being forced to buy Treasury debt hand over fist in order to keep the long bond at par and prevent yields from rising above the 2.5 percent wartime peg. Not surprisingly, its purchases of government debt shot up by 10 percent during 1950 and were rising at a 20 percent rate in early 1951.

All of this monetization of government debt, of course, was being funded by newly minted reserves which the Fed injected into the banking system. This threatened even more inflationary credit expansion.

The leadership of the Fed, including Chairman Thomas McCabe and the legendary Marriner Eccles, recognized that the Depression-era days of monetary quiescence were over. So as Eccles and McCabe saw it, the Fed had to be consistently disciplined in its provision of reserves to the banking system. In what was now essentially a fiat money régime, the only real barrier to runaway inflation was to keep the banking system firmly in harness. The violent inflationary flare-up in early 1951 was a cogent reminder.

To be sure, the Fed leadership and staff in 1951 were not comprised of scholastic monetarists. Milton Friedman had not yet even revived the quantity theory of money. But Eccles and his fellow board members didn't need academic theories and math models to conduct their business. Having witnessed the runaway credit expansion of the 1920s, especially the explosion in stock market margin lending and the resulting trauma of debt deflation which followed the bubble's collapse, this first postwar generation of Fed leaders possessed an innate, healthy fear of bank credit.

Nor did that generation of Fed leaders harbor the later illusion that cheap debt was the key to economic growth. Consequently, it was evident to the Fed that the Treasury peg had to be ended forthwith, so that it could prudently manage the provision of reserves to the banking system, and thereby permit only a measured expansion of credit to businesses and households.

Testifying before a congressional committee at the time, Marriner Eccles cogently expressed this bank reserve–focused monetary doctrine and the reason for the Fed's insistence on jettisoning the wartime peg: "As long as the Federal Reserve is required to buy government securities at the will of the market for the purpose of defending a fixed pattern of interest rates established by the Treasury, it must stand ready to create new bank reserves in an unlimited amount. This policy makes the entire banking system, through the action of the Federal Reserve System, an engine of inflation."

During the fall and winter of 1950–1951, the Fed leadership repeatedly advised the Truman administration of the rising inflationary danger posed by adherence to the peg. Unfortunately, President Truman was as obtuse on monetary policy as he was courageous on fiscal matters. Worse still, he had appointed a Missouri political crony and small-time banker, John W. Snyder, as secretary of the treasury.

Like many sons of the middle border, Snyder was an adherent of FDR's hayseed coalition when it came to interest rates and monetary matters. Accordingly, he stubbornly demanded that the Fed keep buying bonds at the pegged rates, and eventually lured President Truman into a public showdown with the nation's central bank in February 1951.

Truman had demanded a face-to-face meeting with the Federal Reserve Board. With Snyder's complicity he had afterward made public a letter to the board expressing appreciation for an alleged "renewal" of its commitment to maintain the peg. The Truman letter was a flat-out lie, and it soon triggered one of the great acts of political courage in modern times.

Marriner Eccles probably earned the right to have the Fed's headquarters named after him when he leaked the minutes of the board's White House meeting with Truman to the *New York Times*. The leaked minutes proved beyond a shadow of a doubt that the board had made no such commitment.

The White House soon sought a compromise, and while Secretary Snyder was in the hospital, a clever assistant secretary of the treasury invented a formula that allowed both sides to save face. The Treasury Department was forced to issue nonmarketable long-term bonds with a 2.75 percent coupon, thereby breaking the long-standing 2.5 percent peg. At the same time, the Fed swapped them into another previously issued five-year note at par for a limited number of weeks in order to put a fig leaf on the White House pledge that bondholders would not lose money. In short order, however, the Fed's support operation ended, the five-year Treasury notes slipped to a discount in the secondary market, and the Fed's first era of rigging the government bond market came to a close.

THE RISE OF WILLIAM MCCHESNEY MARTIN: TRIBUNE OF SOUND MONEY

As it happened, the assistant secretary who arranged the White House retreat was William McChesney Martin, who was soon appointed chairman of the Federal Reserve. It did not take long for Martin to establish that he had been on the Fed's side all along, declaring in his speech accepting the appointment that inflation was "an even more serious threat to the vitality of our country" than the aggression in Korea.

Martin then concluded his remarks and began his nineteen-year tenure as Fed chairman, with an expression of support for sound money that, apart from the Volcker interlude of 1979–1987, would rarely be heard again in the halls of the Eccles Building. The statement was plain vanilla financial orthodoxy.

In those sensible times, financial leaders knew that inflation was destructive and unfair, so Martin's words were not rhetorical. He literally meant that inflation should be held close to zero: "I pledge myself to support all reasonable measures to preserve the purchasing power of the dollar."

Martin's stern doctrine of financial discipline and anti-inflation vigilance embodies a stunning contrast to the spurious 2 percent inflation target of today's Fed. The latter is the very antithesis of sound money because it gives the Fed an excuse to fuel credit growth and Wall Street speculation, while silently cutting the purchasing power of the dollar by 50 percent during the working lifetime of every citizen.

By contrast, Martin's sound money views had been formed by his experiences at the epicenter of the financial markets in the 1920s and 1930s. His father had assisted Carter Glass in drafting the 1913 act, and had gone on to play an influential role in the new monetary arrangement as president of the Federal Reserve Bank of St. Louis.

Consequently, Martin had been exposed at an early age to dinnertime monetary discourses by his father's notable colleagues including Benjamin Strong, the powerful chief of the New York Fed, and H. Parker Willis, the era's leading authority on money and banking and the technician who had actually drafted much of the 1913 act.

Professor Willis was also a learned proponent of the classical English banking model, which held that commercial banks should lend only against liquid trade receivables, not real estate, corporate securities, or other illiquid collateral. Indeed, the modern device of an unsecured "cash flow" loan would have struck him as pure heresy.

Willis advocated this stringent approach to permissible bank assets not because he was an anti-market regulator, but because he recognized the inherent danger of fractional reserve deposit banking. The only way to have a stable banking system when the vast majority of deposits are callable on demand, he maintained, was to keep assets equally short term and self-liquidating.

For this reason, the Federal Reserve banks in the framework designed by Willis and his colleagues had a very narrow mandate. The sole function of the "reserve banks" was to help keep the commercial banking system liquid by advancing cash to member banks against their own liquid trade credits whenever they presented them at the discount loan window as collateral.

The central banking system established in 1913 was therefore not in the economic management business and did not need to know whether GDP was rising or falling, or whether housing starts were robust or punk. Most especially, it would not have discounted even a scrap of the illiquid toxic securities that the Bernanke Fed accepted as collateral in September 2008. The $100 billion of advances it provided Morgan Stanley, for example, to cover up the firm's bald-face lie that it was still solvent would have been unthinkable.

The reason that the Willis-designed Fed had been indifferent to Wall Street troubles was that its congressional sponsors, especially Carter Glass, had a profound fear of credit-based speculation. That's why there was no provision in the original act for the Fed to purchase or lend against government debt or to carry out the open market purchase and sale of investment securities.

All of these latter adaptations were designed to inject central bank credit into the financial system for the purpose of stimulating borrowing, spending, and GDP. But Willis believed that central bank credit would be invariably diverted into speculative lending and stock market gambling.

When the New York Fed opened the credit spigots in the summer of 1927, for the laudable purpose of helping the British adhere to their gold standard obligations, he was soon proven correct. The outcome was a giant margin loan bubble which fueled an unprecedented speculative mania on Wall Street during the next two years.

By the time of Martin's reign at the Fed, of course, Professor Willis's doctrines had been steadily diluted and compromised, especially after the Fed became the fiscal agent for the wartime needs of the Treasury. Yet his fundamental admonition about the dangers of unchecked credit inflation and bank-enabled commodity and stock speculation remained central to Martin's monetary philosophy.

In fact, Martin had gotten his Wall Street education firsthand and at an early age. When he was just thirty-one years old he was chosen to become president of the New York Stock Exchange. His job assignment was to sweep clean the Augean stables in the wake of a scandal which in 1938 finally brought down Richard Whitney, the longtime head of the exchange, and his old-guard associates.

Martin accomplished this mission with aplomb, taking away from his six-year tenure a widely praised record of reform in exchange practices and accommodation to the new SEC regulatory régime. But far more important, he also gained a deep appreciation for the degree to which rampant margin lending had turned the stock market into a veritable gambling casino in the run-up to the 1929 crash.

MARGIN LOANS AND THE LESSONS OF 1929

These so called brokers' loans were a volatile form of hot money and were callable on a moment's notice. At the time of the market peak, they had amounted to about 9 percent of GDP, which would amount to the not inconsiderable sum of $1.4 trillion in today's economy.

Moreover, as the speculative wave reached its final peak, broker loans outstanding had ballooned wildly. Outstanding margin credit to stock speculators had increased by 50 percent in the final twelve months of the stock mania.

When viewed through the lens of the carnage which followed the crash, Martin had little trouble seeing that it was this volcanic mountain of margin debt which had lifted the stock averages to insane levels. He thus deeply believed that keeping speculative credit out of Wall Street was essential to the revival of an honest stock market and healthy national economy.

Martin also had little doubt that the Fed's easy-money policies during the later 1920s, particularly the aggressive easing in 1927, had fueled the massive flow of speculative credit into Wall Street. That cardinal fact was lost on postwar historians and monetarists, however, because the margin credit bubble had been hidden between the lines of the commercial banking system loan data. Between 1925 and 1929, for example, bank loans outstanding had increased by a seemingly modest $7.5 billion, or 5 percent, annual rate.

Yet buried in these quotidian aggregates was the fact that bank loans to business and industry, that is, to the real economy, had declined sharply during this four-year period. Consequently the entire reported gain, and then some, was due to the explosion of Wall Street brokers' loans.

The decline of business loans in the real economy was partially the result of improved internal corporate cash flows as the 1920s boom reached its apex. However, the primary driver of this reduced appetite for bank credit was far more perverse, as had been repeatedly pointed out by Benjamin Anderson, the era's most prescient working economist.

According to Anderson, who was chief economist of the Chase National Bank, the boom on Wall Street had permitted corporations to raise far more cash from new stock and bond issues than they needed to meet actual investment needs. Consequently, they not only used this "excess cash" to pay down bank loans, but also recycled much of it straight back to the Wall Street call money market; that is, industrial companies became part-time bankers.

Nearly 60 percent of the total $9 billion of brokers' loans outstanding on the eve of the crash had been advanced not by the banks, but by wealthy investors and corporations recycling cash from earlier stock market winnings. In this manner, the excess liquidity from the Fed's money-printing experiments in the mid-1920s had drained into Wall Street and fueled a self-perpetuating cycle of financial speculation.

Ironically, this same gambit reappeared about sixty years later when the Japanese invented a whole theory called "zaitech" to explain how companies could prosper by moonlighting as financial engineers. In the Japanese version, companies sold stock and convertible debt at the vastly inflated market prices which had been fueled by the Bank of Japan's post-1985 money-printing spree. Japanese corporations then recycled the resulting cash proceeds into stock market speculation, which resulted in even more reported profits and still higher share prices.

Not surprisingly, when the Bank of Japan was forced to puncture the resulting runaway financial bubble in 1989, as the Fed had been required to do in 1928–1929, the zaitech-based house of cards collapsed almost instantly. Japan thus experienced a replay of the very same Wall Street movie which had played six decades before.

In contrast to his present-day Japanese and American counterparts, William McChesney Martin was schooled in the classic doctrines on money and banking, and did not need a rerun of the 1929 crash to know that leveraged speculation in the stock market needed to be avoided at all costs. Consequently, the hallmark of his tenure was his famous quip that the job of the Fed "is to take away the punch bowl just as the party gets going."

WHEN MARTIN TOOK THE PUNCH BOWL AWAY
FROM A FOUR-MONTH-OLD (RECOVERY)

At no time was Martin's resolve to lean hard against a recurrence of speculative excess more evident than in August 1958, when the Fed moved to tighten policy just four months after the start of recovery from the recession of 1957–1958. Not surprisingly, his tool of choice was to raise the margin requirement on stock trading accounts from 50 percent to 70 percent, along with an increase in the Fed's discount rate for emergency borrowings by member banks.

Moreover, three months later the Fed raised its discount rate again. And then to make sure that its message was not misunderstood, it boosted the margin requirement still higher, requiring stock traders to pony up 90 percent cash on each new trade.

By the standards of the day, the Fed had every reason to take this aggressive action. Between 1954 and 1957, bank loans outstanding had soared at a 12 percent annual rate, and CPI inflation had ticked up to 3.6 percent in the year ending March 1958. The Martin Fed found both of these trends deeply troubling and believed that, if left unchecked, they posed dire threats to the Fed's fundamental mission of maintaining the purchasing power of the dollar and financial stability.

Furthermore, today's central bank sophistries, such as levitating the stock market to generate economic growth through the "wealth effect" and discounting reported inflation by excluding items such as food and energy, had not yet been invented. Accordingly, the Fed continued to tighten monetary policy throughout the course of 1959.

Moreover, these moves were decisive. Unlike the ineffectual baby-step hikes of 25 basis points that Alan Greenspan later favored, Martin raised the discount rate by a full percentage point on each of several occasions, and also further tightened stock market margin lending.

In one of its post-meeting statements the Fed zeroed in directly on excessive bank lending. Unlike today's debt-besotted central bankers, the Martin-era Fed worried about too much credit growth, not too little, saying that it was "restraining inflationary credit growth in order to foster sustainable economic growth."

As the year drew to a close, then, Chairman Martin had well and truly demonstrated what "taking away the punch bowl" actually meant. Open market interest rates rose from 1 percent in June 1958 before the tightening started to 5 percent by December 1959, and the Treasury bond yield rose from under 3 percent to nearly 5 percent during the same period.

At the same time, the curative effect of monetary restraint was soon evident in the rapid return of price stability. During 1959, consumer price increases fell back to the 1 percent level, where they remained through 1963.

In a further marker that the inflationary threat had been quelled, the substantial outflow of gold from the United States which had occurred during 1958 owing to inflation fears was staunched by the Fed's resolute stance. US gold stocks remained stable for several years thereafter.

Nor was sound money purchased at the price of a weak economy. Real GDP rebounded at a 6.4 percent annual rate in 1959 and averaged 4.3 percent annually during the five years after the Fed removed the punch bowl.

Indeed, under Martin's leadership the Fed did achieve something of a golden age once the macroeconomic disruptions of the Korean War had passed. Thus, between 1954 and 1963, real GDP growth averaged 3.4 percent while annual CPI inflation remained subdued at 1.4 percent.

There was no subsequent nine-year period that had a better combined performance of these core variables. And none which left the overall economic and financial system so healthy and stable.

CHAPTER 11

EISENHOWER'S DEFENSE
MINIMUM AND THE LAST AGE
OF FISCAL RECTITUDE

CHAIRMAN WILLIAM MCCHESNEY MARTIN'S QUEST TO RESTORE sound money was aided immeasurably during the 1950s by a fiscal policy backdrop that would never again recur. Beginning with Truman's tax financing of the Korean conflict, monetary policy was supported by two successive presidents who were firmly committed to budgetary discipline and who were willing to expend political capital to achieve it.

As it happened, it was Eisenhower who really brought the old-time religion back to the center of peacetime fiscal policy. Ike was a military war hero who hated war. He was also the former supreme commander of the costliest military campaign in history and revered balanced budgets. Accordingly, Eisenhower did not hesitate to wield the budgetary knife, and when he did the blade came down squarely on the Pentagon.

THE FOLLY OF WAR DEFICITS

The essence of Eisenhower's immense fiscal achievement, an actual shrinkage of the federal budget in real terms during his eight-year term, is that he tamed the warfare state. In so doing, he paved the way for Uncle Sam to pay his bills out of current taxation for the better part of a decade.

The enormity of this achievement can only be fully appreciated by contrast with its opposite—that is, three devastating fiscal setbacks during the next half century under Lyndon Johnson, Ronald Reagan, and George W. Bush. In each case, the plunge of the nation's fiscal accounts deep into the red was triggered by a resurgence of the kind of massive warfare state budgets that Ike so resolutely resisted.

In bringing down the fiscal roof, all three post-Eisenhower defense surges were enabled by a vital accomplice: Keynesian theories of prosperity management that manifested themselves in both a leftist "new economics" version and rightist "supply side" variant. The pretension of both ideologies was that the correct policy action by Washington could spur permanent economic growth at extraordinary rates, such as 5 percent annually or even better. Consequently, by embracing this high GDP growth illusion, the White House occupants during these three episodes were led to believe that they could have war budgets without war taxes.

War deficits, of course, are what they actually got. Yet this was a good thing, according to the Keynesian professors, because such deficits inject demand into the economy, thereby lifting output closer to its full-employment potential. The supply-side apostles of Art Laffer's tax-cutting scheme agreed. The incremental GDP growth from incentives to save, invest, and take risk would pay for all the war spending the nation might ever need.

In fact, war deficits are the worst fiscal policy imaginable. They add to civilian demand but generate no marketable output of consumer products or capital goods. Accordingly, war deficits tip the economy toward excess demand, inflationary bottlenecks, rising interest rates, and financial instability. They destroy wealth and lower living standards.

Since time immemorial, therefore, politicians have attempted to alleviate these pressures by financing war bonds with printing-press money. Lyndon Johnson did it and broke the resolve of Chairman Martin and the anti-inflation policy of the Fed.

Likewise, after global money went on the T-bill standard, Reagan and Bush did it, too, by exporting their war bonds to the central banks of Japan and China, and thereby postponing but not eliminating the day of reckoning. Eisenhower's achievement in throttling the warfare state was thus of singular significance, even if it proved to be transient.

IKE'S DISPATCH OF THE BLOATED TRUMAN DEFENSE BUDGET

Eisenhower's campaign for fiscal discipline started with the bloated war budget he inherited from Truman. In a notable episode of hitting the ground running, Ike traveled to Korea immediately after the election in November 1952 and set in motion a negotiations process that made an armistice on the Korean peninsula a foregone conclusion.

Given the expected cutback of war expense, the White House team led by treasury secretary and deficit hawk George Humphrey was shocked by Truman's defense budget for the upcoming fiscal year. It was still 6 percent higher than the current year's. With Eisenhower's blessing, therefore, the inherited Truman budget request was slashed by nearly 30 percent, with more cuts targeted for future years.

Although defense spending never did shrink all the way to Ike's target, the wind-down of Truman's war budget was swift and drastic. When measured in constant 2005 dollars of purchasing power, the defense budget was reduced from a peak of $515 billion in fiscal 1953 to $370 billion by fiscal 1956. It remained at that level through the end of Eisenhower's second term.

Moreover, even though Democrats charged that Eisenhower and Humphrey were "allowing their Neanderthal fiscal views to endanger the national security," the actual record proves the administration's drastic rollback of Pentagon spending was not based merely on penny-pinching. Instead, it flowed from a reasoned retrenchment of the nation's national security strategy called the "New Look."

The new policy doctrine of the Eisenhower administration called for a sharp reduction in land and naval forces, coupled with a significantly increased reliance for nuclear deterrence on the air force bomber fleet and the rapid development of intercontinental ballistic missiles. In addition, the European allies were called upon to play an expanded role in containing Soviet conventional forces on their own borders.

The New Look contrasted sharply with the inherited doctrine known as NSC-68. Written by Truman's coterie of confirmed cold warriors, such as Dean Acheson and Paul Nitze, it stressed maintenance of extensive conventional forces and a US capacity to fight multiple land wars simultaneously.

At the end of the day, the general who had led the greatest land invasion ever undertaken could not be convinced that those scholastic theories of limited war were plausible in the nuclear age. But he did acutely fear that the massive permanent military budgets required by the limited war doctrines of NSC-68 would erode the economic foundation on which true national security finally depended.

The nearly one-third reduction in real defense spending during the Eisenhower period was thus achieved by sharp changes in priorities and force structure. These included shrinking the army by nearly 40 percent, large cuts in naval forces, and an overall reduction in military personnel from about 3.5 million in early 1953 to 2.5 million by December 1960.

Equally important, the military logrolling under which each armed service had been given exactly one-third of the defense budget was decisively abandoned. Instead, under the New Look doctrine of "massive retaliation," the air force was allocated 47 percent of the DOD budget while the army got only 22 percent for its sharply circumscribed missions.

WHY THE LAND-WAR GENERALS QUIT

Needless to say, Ike's drastic change in national security doctrine and downsizing of the conventional force structure sharply curtailed the nation's ability to wage land wars of intervention and occupation. And it also caused an explosion of outrage in the army.

In fact, its two representatives on the joint chiefs of staff, Generals Matthew Ridgeway and Maxwell Taylor, resigned in protest against General Eisenhower's new strategy, the implication being that the army would not be getting another Korea-type assignment anytime soon.

The irony is that Ridgeway and Taylor were later rehabilitated by Robert McNamara, the whiz-kid Ford Motor executive who became defense secretary knowing as little about military and defense matters as Ike did about selling swept-wing sedans. Nevertheless, soon after his appointment by President Kennedy, McNamara rehabilitated NSC-68, along with the extensive conventional forces needed "to prevent the steady erosion of the Free World through limited wars."

Not surprisingly, with Ridgeway and Taylor back in charge "limited war" is exactly what the nation got: to wit, still another misguided land war in Asia which turned out to be even more strategically senseless and fiscally corrosive than the one in Korea.

It also got proof positive that imperial wars too unpopular to be financed with higher taxation were destined to end in bloody failure. On the latter score, the constant-dollar defense budget by fiscal 1968 had rebounded from Ike's $370 billion peacetime minimum all the way back to the $515 billion war budget that Truman left on Eisenhower's doorstep in 1953.

Likewise, the armed forces were expanded by 40 percent from Ike's 1960 level. By the Vietnam peak they had reached the very same 3.5 million that had been attained during the Korean War.

In a few short years, therefore, the national security academics which came to the Kennedy-Johnson administration from the Ivy Leagues took policy on a complete round trip. In essence, they reestablished the dangerous and costly capacity for imperial adventures that the proven warrior from West Point had insisted should not stand.

IKE'S SINGULAR ACHIEVEMENT: CONTAINMENT OF THE WARFARE STATE WHERE HIS SUCCESSORS FAILED

Johnson was not alone in coddling the warfare state. None of Eisenhower's successors replicated his passion for fiscal discipline at the Pentagon. Nor did they share his fear of the enormous logrolling coalitions nurtured on Capitol Hill by the military-industrial complex, and the propensity of its congressional champions to trade guns for butter in an unending rebuke to fiscal discipline.

Indeed, in a few short years after Ike left office, the profound danger of a symbiotic nexus among the warfare state and welfare state became starkly

apparent. Reflecting the imprint of the Hubert Humphrey "guns and butter" liberals, both sides of the budget hit simultaneous peaks in fiscal 1968.
With constant-dollar defense spending back to the $515 billion Korean War
peak, domestic outlays followed suit, reaching an all-time peak of $455 bil-
lion (2005$). The latter was 75 percent higher than Ike's outgoing 1961
budget, meaning that there was no room to finance it within the existing
tax envelope. The Federal deficit thus ballooned to nearly 3 percent of GDP,
another modern peacetime record.

The next phase was even worse. The post-Vietnam demobilization of
the fighting forces and the dismantlement of their massive logistics base
resulted in no restoration of the Eisenhower era fiscal discipline at all—
notwithstanding eight years of Republican rule. Indeed, the Washington
logrolling coalition wasted no time recycling every penny of the $200 bil-
lion "peace dividend" (2005$) back into domestic spending.

Since the federal budget actually gained 20 percent, or $200 billion, in
constant dollars between fiscal 1968 and 1977, domestic spending thus
rose by a stunning $400 billion. The Republican (Nixon-Ford) White House
during this period was presumably equipped with a veto pen, but it rarely
came out of the drawer. In fact, the approximate 80 percent gain in
inflation-adjusted domestic outlays during these eight Republican years
exceeded even the Kennedy-Johnson record spree.

Owing to further modest expansion during the Carter interregnum, the
domestic welfare state stood at $1 trillion (2005$) when Reagan took office,
double its 1968 level. This left no available fiscal space for the second post-
Eisenhower surge in warfare state spending, causing the massive Reagan
build-up to be financed with treasury bonds. As described in chapter 5, the
Reagan defense spending spree also infused the military-industrial complex with unstoppable momentum, fostering a virulent crony capitalism
that eventually drove DOD spending to levels which Eisenhower could
never have imagined.

As indicated, constant-dollar spending in Reagan's fiscal 1989 budget
was 30 percent, more than Eisenhower's last budget, but even the subsequent official end of the Cold War resulted in only a modest rollback. Clinton's final budget was a tad smaller in inflation-adjusted dollars than
Eisenhower's, even though by the year 2000 the United States had no industrial state enemy left on the planet.

Then followed George W. Bush's senseless misadventures in the barren
expanse of the Hindu Kush and on the bloody plains of the Tigris-
Euphrates. These campaigns generated the third great post-Eisenhower
surge in constant-dollar defense spending.

By the time of Bush's final budget, constant-dollar warfare state spending had risen to an all-time high of nearly $600 billion. This was 60 percent more than the $370 billion Eisenhower Minimum, even though by 2008 any semblance of the military threats which existed in Ike's time was long gone.

Finally, on exactly the fiftieth budget anniversary of Eisenhower's farewell warning, evidence of the insuperable power of the military-industrial complex was stunningly evident in Obama's fiscal 2011 budget. The 2008 election, of course, had been even more unequivocally a "peace" election than 1968 had been, because this time the "peace" candidate actually won. Yet election mandate or no, the third great surge in the post-Eisenhower warfare state gave no ground whatsoever.

In fact, inflation-adjusted defense spending in fiscal 2011 of $670 billion was a new record, eclipsing even George W. Bush's final war budget. It was thus abundantly evident that even an out-and-out "peace" president is no match for the modern warfare state and the crony capitalist lobbies which safeguard its budgetary requisites.

Indeed, Barack Obama pushed the frontiers of the warfare state further than ever before. Beating his mandate for plowshares into an even mightier sword, the peace president pushed defense spending to a level 80 percent greater in real terms than General Eisenhower concluded was necessary.

So when all is said and done, the source of Eisenhower's singular success among postwar presidents in actually shrinking the inflation-adjusted federal budget is quite clear: it was due first and foremost to his taming of the warfare state at a time when America still had industrial enemies and the fear of nuclear attacks was palpable throughout a land dotted with radar installations and air-raid shelters. In light of subsequent history, the Eisenhower Minimum was a signal fiscal policy accomplishment, even as it proved to be unsustainable and unrepeatable.

Moreover, in achieving the Eisenhower Minimum, Ike also was able—crucially—to avoid the fiscal logrolling process whereby a temporary peace dividend becomes an excuse to break out the domestic butter. Indeed, it was Eisenhower's resolute fiscal orthodoxy—on both taxes and balanced budgets—that shielded his "peace dividend" from being consumed by the kind of domestic spending sprees that were promoted by politicians of both parties during later cycles of defense retrenchment.

EISENHOWER'S UNMATCHED FISCAL TRIUMPH: SHRINKAGE OF THE STATE

In the final analysis, Eisenhower's fiscal record is one of a kind. Between fiscal 1953 and 1961, total federal spending declined from 20.4 percent of GDP to 18.4 percent. The constant-dollar federal budget was reduced from about $680 billion to $650 billion.

Never again did the nation's inflation-adjusted budget numbers shrink during a presidential term. Not by 4 percent or even by any amount at all.

In contrast to the decline in constant-dollar federal spending during Eisenhower's tenure, real outlays during the three subsequent surges of warfare state spending rose steeply. The Kennedy-Johnson period recorded an increase of 50 percent, while the eight Reagan years saw inflation-adjusted growth in total federal spending of 22 percent.

The all-time record was achieved during the George W. Bush presidency, of course, when constant-dollar federal spending expanded by an even greater 53 percent. During that outbreak of budgetary madness, in fact, it was strikingly evident that domestic spending tends to actually accelerate, owing to fiscal logrolling, when the warfare state is experiencing robust expansion.

Accordingly, during the eight Bush years, constant-dollar welfare state spending grew at 7 percent per annum and there was but one consolation: real domestic spending grew even more rapidly—at 8.5 percent annually— during the Nixon-Ford era. The so-called conservative economic team of that era—George Schulz, Casper Weinberger, and Herb Stein—never managed to encounter, it appears, a significant expansion of the welfare state that they could not rationalize.

Nevertheless, the constant dollar spending growth of $1 trillion (2005$) during the George W. Bush "guns and butter" spree has no peer at all in the record books. It can be fairly said that when it came to defining "Big Government" the Bush era left nothing to the imagination.

And so it came to pass that exactly one-half century after Eisenhower had led the Republican Party back to the promised land of the old-time fiscal religion, his political heirs and assigns had made a mockery of their heritage. This untoward outcome proved that the 1950s twilight of financial discipline rested on the resolve of an aging statesman who had not embraced any of the multiple Keynesian heresies that took charge of policy soon thereafter.

PILLARS OF IKE'S FISCAL SUCCESS

It goes without saying that when Eisenhower left the White House in January 1961, the prospect of today's inexorable fiscal bankruptcy was not even a remote possibility. This benign state of affairs was owing to four additional considerations beyond the thirty-fourth president's seeming pacification of the warfare state.

The first of these was the fact that the nation still had a central bank dedicated to sound money and reluctant to monetize the Federal debt. Secondly, there remained intact a bipartisan consensus in favor of meeting our gold redemption obligations under Bretton Woods. Thirdly, the Republican Party had not yet embraced the specious Keynesian construct of the full-employment budget. Most important of all, the conservative party still viewed taxes as an integral element of budgetary management, not as an all-purpose tool of perpetual macroeconomic stimulation.

President Eisenhower was an exemplar of financial orthodoxy with respect to each of these propositions, but it was on the matter of achieving meaningful spending cutbacks before turning to the popular business of cutting taxes that he left a lasting mark.

THE EISENHOWER-HUMPHREY PREDICATE:
TAX CUTS MUST BE EARNED WITH SPENDING CONTROL

Eisenhower inherited Truman's high war taxes and appointed as his chief economic spokesman and treasury secretary George M. Humphrey, who was a dyed-in-the-wool anti-tax industrialist. According to one leading chronicler of Eisenhower's economic policy, Humphrey "saw high taxes as a greater menace to the US than communism."

Yet notwithstanding his archly anti-tax philosophy, Humphrey was no incipient supply-sider. In fact, he shared Eisenhower's view that tax cuts had to be earned by means of putting spending reductions in place first. Thus, Humphrey minced no words when advising a congressional committee on where he stood: "I will contest a tax cut out of deficits as long as I am able . . ."

Unlike modern GOP treasury secretaries who have eschewed the gore of intra-cabinet spending battles in favor of the glory of running the tax-cutting department, Humphrey served as Ike's leading helpmate in wielding the budget knife. In an early cabinet meeting, for example, Humphrey hectored defense secretary and former GM chief executive, Charles Wilson, on the grounds that his proposed budget trims were woefully inadequate. Thundering in the language of the auto business, Humphrey instructed the defense secretary to throw out his proposed budget and start all over: "Get the best damn streamlined model you ever did in your life. . . . [W]e can't just patch-up the old jalopy."

Still, it was Eisenhower who ultimately resolved the tension between tax cutting and budget balancing in favor of the latter. In the context of 1953, there was a strong policy case for dismantling the wartime régime of high taxes which had been in place for more than a decade.

The latter were most certainly stifling capital formation and economic growth. On top of this, political pressure for tax cuts among Republican business constituencies was overwhelming. After two decades of Democratic rule, Republican businessmen from both Main Street and Big Business were adamant in their demands for relief from the scourge of "tax and spend."

As a philosophical matter, Eisenhower didn't disagree. He readily conceded that under the fiscal position he had inherited from Truman, the nation was fast "approaching the limits of taxation and spending."

Nevertheless, Ike had no doubt that his first priority was to restore a balanced budget as soon as possible. The starting point was a severe reduction in the $12 billion deficit in the inherited Truman budget for the upcoming 1954 fiscal year.

This figure amounted to about 3 percent of GDP, and therefore would be considered a trifling matter by present-day standards. Yet Eisenhower elected to defer the GOP's tax reduction agenda until a balanced budget had been delivered in the here and now, not merely projected for the distant future.

Indeed, in a July 1953 note to a friend, Ike left little doubt as to his fiscal priorities: "Beginning in June 1952 . . . I have always maintained one thing—that the annual Federal deficit must be eliminated before tax reduction can begin. . . . So I spend my life trying to cut expenditures, balance the budget, and then get at the *popular* [Ike's italics] business of lowering taxes."

In fact, notwithstanding a thorough and painful round of surgery on the inherited fiscal 1954 budget, the new president was distressed to discover that after netting out the cuts and re-estimates he would still be recommending a $6.6 billion deficit to Congress. Moreover, it should be noted that this remaining, and as Ike saw it, intolerable level of red ink was measured on the old "administrative budget" basis.

After accounting for an approximate $3 billion Social Security trust fund surplus, the "cash deficit" (later called the "unified budget deficit") was only $3.6 billion, or just 1 percent, of GDP. Yet for Eisenhower the Social Security trust fund was not something to be raided to pay for cotton subsidies and military procurement. Likewise, "close" might count in horseshoes but not in restoring the nation's fiscal discipline.

EISENHOWER'S ESSENTIAL FISCAL STRATEGY: THE ANTI-GINGRICH PARADIGM

Given the absolute priority of achieving budget balance first, Eisenhower declined to seek an early end to Truman's war taxes. Instead, he actually sought the extension of several revenue-raising measures that were scheduled to expire in the upcoming budget year.

As a result of these actions, Eisenhower's place as the anti-Gingrich of modern fiscal history cannot be denied. Unlike the contemporary Republican Party, Ike was willing to be the tax collector for the welfare state (and warfare state, too) once he had exhausted the ability of his administration to cut spending in the budget year at hand.

Nor should the "year at hand" element be overlooked. In those times there was no such thing as a ten-year budget, and Eisenhower wouldn't have put any stock in deferring tough choices into the foggy future, anyway. After all, ten years earlier he had stood on the cusp of the Normandy invasion, not knowing whether civilization itself would survive another decade.

Indeed, Ike's understanding that the budget choices which count are the ones reflected in current-year expenditures and receipts could not have been more jarringly different than what passes for fiscal conservatism today. The much ballyhooed "Ryan Budget" for fiscal 2012 added $7 trillion to the national debt, for instance, before it would achieve a balanced budget twenty-five years later; that is, in 2037. Eisenhower would have thought such a fiscal plan the scribbling of a madman.

Not surprisingly, Eisenhower generated not inconsiderable distress among Republican businessmen when he sought an extension of Truman's excess profits tax in order to further reduce the fiscal 1954 deficit by $1 billion. He also insisted on cancellation of a 5 percent corporate tax reduction scheduled for April 1954 in order to protect the out-year budget.

Moreover, the Eisenhower White House then deployed a full-court press to pry these tax increases out of a reluctant Republican-controlled Ways and Means Committee. In his congressional testimony on the matter, even his anti-tax secretary of the treasury had no trouble making the administration's fiscal priorities crystal clear: "If the Administration has the courage to come in here and ask you gentlemen to extend this tax it is the firmest good-faith showing that we are determined to balance the budget and to accomplish sound [economic recovery]."

Nor did Ike spare rank-and-file Republican voters, either. When Congress passed a bill in mid-1953 to repeal a 20 percent excise tax on motion-picture tickets, Eisenhower vetoed it in order to maintain the revenue level projected for his first-year budget.

It turned out that military spending fell even more rapidly than the administration had projected. Consequently, the brief and mild recession early in the year did not derail the budget, with the fiscal 1954 deficit coming in at only $1 billion. In fact, in the context of a $400 billion economy, the deficit during Ike's first full budget year was essentially a rounding error (0.3% of GDP) even by his own standards.

THE 1953–1954 RECESSION: HOW EISENHOWER ESCHEWED COUNTERCYCLICAL ACTIVISM

During the course of the mild recession of 1954, Eisenhower refused to be panicked into deviating from his course toward a sustainable balanced budget. While he recognized that the deficit would be temporarily enlarged owing to the so-called automatic stabilizers of higher unemployment insurance outlays and reduced income tax collections, he refused to recommend new discretionary initiatives such as tax cuts or spending stimulus.

As it turned out, Eisenhower's resolve was fully justified, since the downturn amounted to hardly even a faux recession. In fact, the historical evidence shows that the 270-day recession, which the National Bureau of Economic Research (NBER) dated from the third quarter of 1953 under its highly mechanical formulae, was simply an economic soft patch: a cooling off from the red-hot economy that had been stoked by the Korean War.

During the 1951–1952 war economy, for example, real GDP growth had averaged 5.5 percent on an annualized basis. Moreover, this strong growth trend had spurted to a 10 percent average during the final quarter of 1952 and the opening period of 1953.

The momentum of the national economy was so strong, in fact, that the unemployment rate as of October 1953—several months after the recession started—was only 1.8 percent (based on BLS definitions used at the time). It was still just 3 percent by year-end. After the war economy momentum was finally broken and a brief dip ensued in late 1953 and early 1954, the US economy was expanding smartly once again by June. By the second quarter of 1954, in fact, real GDP was nearly 7 percent greater than it had been before the final Korean War burst of output. In short, in late 1953 and early 1954 the US economy had not been headed into a deep recessionary hole at all; it had just rebooted itself after the Korean War exertion.

For all his alleged lack of "sophistication" in economic matters, Ike understood that civilian economies always experience a "cooling off" period after a war. Accordingly, he was not about to allow this one to distract from his appointed fiscal course.

Eisenhower's chief economic advisor, Arthur Burns, nevertheless kept a wary eye on the economy during the spring of 1954. He also squinted sourly at Ike's old-fashioned treasury secretary, who consistently advised Ike to keep his powder dry on economic stimulus measures and to stay the course on fiscal discipline.

But in a premonition of far worse things to come during the Nixon era (1969–1973), Burns couldn't let colleagues forget about his renowned expertise on the business cycle and his unique capacity to prescribe just the right policy medicine to help it along. As a result of Burns' pestering, therefore, Eisenhower did not fight congressional Republicans when they passed a reduction in excise taxes.

The people were thus encouraged to spend more on jewelry, movies, and telephones, even though this measure set the budget back by several billions. Burns later boasted that the economy had thereby been stimulated: "We felt the cut might not be a bad idea for countercyclical reasons."

In a similar vein, Ike also permitted Burns to develop a list of "standby" government construction projects which could be speeded up, such as flood control, highways, and merchant marine tankers. At the same time, he made sure that Humphrey kept them on the shelf.

At a press conference in early April 1954, just weeks before the economic upturn began, Eisenhower proved he could tell the difference between an economic soft patch and the onset of another great depression, even if his business cycle expert couldn't. After assurances that the economy was sound, Eisenhower decisively shut down the economic stimulus debate, saying, "Your Government does not intend to go into *any slam-bang emergency program* [my italics] unless it is necessary."

While Eisenhower didn't think it was necessary, Burns continued to pester. So on May 14 Ike gave the go-ahead on the Burns scheme to have each cabinet member get an early start on these "standby" construction projects. Later economic data would reveal, of course, that these tiny speed-up actions amounted to a feckless gesture, since economic recovery was then already under way.

Moreover, the old-time fiscal religion did prevail even in this episode. On Humphrey's advice, Eisenhower refused to allow the construction speed-up program to even be publicly announced on the grounds that it might undermine business confidence! So at the end of the day, the crafty former general pulled off a stealth non-stimulus program in the face of a no-show recession.

COUNTERCYCLICAL FISCAL POLICY AND THE GHOST OF THE GREAT DEPRESSION

Nevertheless, it is evident that at even this early stage in the postwar period the Keynesian ascendancy was well under way and that the days of balanced budgets and sound money were numbered. Indeed, no other assessment is logically possible when the economic results for the boom, dip, and rebound of 1952–1954 are averaged out.

They show a three-year macroeconomic performance trend—3.2 percent annualized real GDP growth and an average unemployment rate of 4.6 percent—which was far superior to the actual sixty-year averages since then for these same indicators. At the end of the day, the minor slump during Ike's first term did not bear even a faint trace of justification for emergency deficit spending and the incurrence of permanent public debt.

So what was really happening under the guise of "enlightened" counter-cyclical fiscal policy is that deficit finance was on the cusp of becoming a permanent way of life. Washington did not yet succumb to Keynesian stimulus in 1953–1954, but only on account of the old-fashioned views of Ike and his doughty treasury secretary.

In fact, Eisenhower's own mind was deeply conflicted on the issue of business cycle stabilization. Possessed with a well-honed sense of history, Eisenhower was keenly aware that as the first Republican president since Hoover it was imperative that a severe economic downturn not occur on his watch. Consequently, he scrutinized the economic data flow intently for any sign of a free-fall and was frequently rattled by Burns' worry-wart proclivities.

Moreover, some of the outside advice coming to the White House on economic matters was as misdirected as that emanating from Arthur Burns. Leading elements of Big Business represented by the Committee for Economic Development (CED) and many business-oriented Republican economists were already embracing a "Keynesian lite" version of counter-cyclical policy.

While eschewing the cruder types of pump priming such as public works, their theory seemed to be that deft adjustments of tax measures and retiming of already approved spending could iron out the kinks in the business cycle. Timely preventative action, as it were, would preclude another downward spiral into depression.

To be sure, these incipient business-friendly central planners did not usually embrace hard-core Keynesian postulates about the structural defects of capitalism which made countercyclical policy necessary in the first place. In fact, the Keynesian lite advocates seemed to have no particular theory of the business cycle at all.

They appeared to simply assume that the Great Depression was proof enough that the US economy was prone to violent self-fueling contractions. The federal government, therefore, needed to stand at the ready with fiscal fire hose and ladder to forestall even a hint of recurrence.

The Great Depression, however, was not the product of a fragile business cycle prone to easy recurrence. As has been seen, it was the result of the unique set of historical developments that had virtually no chance of repetition in the postwar world of the 1950s.

These unique historical antecedents to world depression included the 1920s overhang of heavy war debts and reparations; the massive currency inflation and trade and production dislocations from the Great War; the failed 1920s attempt by the major nations to recreate a workable trade and monetary system under the flawed gold exchange standard; and the Wall Street–financed export boom which brought an artificial global expansion during 1925–1929, followed by a violent collapse of commodity prices and trade volumes after the Wall Street crash.

None of this remotely pertained to the postwar world where the US economy benefited enormously from the revival of global trade and capital flows and from the dramatic repair of domestic balance sheets under the Second World War command economy. There was no monster lurking under the nation's macroeconomic bed. The "fresh start" US economy of the 1950s was not about to relapse into another great depression.

PROFESSOR HELLER'S BAD ADVICE:
THE SPECTER OF THE NEW ECONOMICS

Still, with public memories of the depression hardships still fresh, politicians of both parties were quick to embrace "counter-cyclical" fiscal policy as a convenient hall pass from the discipline of the old-time balanced budget religion. And waiting in the wings to justify that propensity was an even more virulent form of the Keynesian fallacy which became known as the "new economics."

It held that not only was countercyclical fiscal policy needed to forestall another depression, but that it could also actually "fine-tune" the recovery phase of the business cycle. Enlightened economic management would thereby squeeze every last dollar of "potential" GDP out of the American economy.

The leading apostle of the new economics, and the future chairman of the Kennedy administration's Council of Economic Advisors, was Professor Walter Heller. Appearing before the Joint Economic Committee in January 1955, he was not loath to offer some advice on how to goose the recovery that started in mid-1954.

"I feel we are in a period where deficits are constructive," he opined, and then further suggested that "Federal deficits are likely to provoke a higher production response than a higher price response."

The data, however, underscore the ludicrous perfectionism lurking in the new economics. Without any fiscal stimulus at all, real GDP had expanded at a 4.6 percent rate in the third quarter of 1954 and at an 8.3 percent annual rate in the fourth quarter—outcomes which had already occurred before Heller's testimony.

Moreover, even as Heller lectured Congress on how to make things better in early 1955, the US economy was already striding at full gallop. Real GDP expanded at an astonishing 12 percent rate in the first quarter and by about 7 percent and 5 percent in the second and third quarters of 1955, respectively.

In fact, at the time of Heller's testimony on how to improve the nation's growth performance, the US economy was at the midpoint of a five-quarter growth spurt which averaged 7.5 percent per annum. This was the highest five quarter rate in modern American history!

In short, there was no case whatsoever for deficit-financed fiscal stimulus in early 1955. Yet the pretentious professor from the University of Minnesota could not leave well enough alone nor permit the free market economy to generate growth consistent with the private choices and actions of the American people.

Heller also got it completely wrong on inflation. At the time of his testimony, the Korean War inflation had been successfully extinguished by the Fed's 1953–1954 tightening cycle, and the year-over-year CPI was close to zero.

By June 1956, however, consumer prices were 2 percent higher than the prior year and by March 1957 the twelve-month CPI was climbing at nearly a 4 percent rate. So there had indeed been a "higher price response," which Heller said wouldn't happen, and it occurred even without the extra stimulus he did advocate in January 1955.

This worrisome inflationary trend, in turn, reflected the Fed's error in allowing bank credit to expand too rapidly during the recovery, thereby fueling an overheated business expansion and a new outbreak of rising prices and wages. Under these circumstances, obviously, the last thing the central bank needed was Heller's recipe of expanded government borrowing, which would have compounded the overheated credit cycle that it was already having difficulty keeping in check.

THE RISE OF THE FULL-EMPLOYMENT BUDGET; EXECUTIONER OF THE OLD TIME FISCAL RELIGION

Professor Walter Heller was not the first economist to issue a mistaken forecast. Yet at its heart was an insidious economic doctrine that would push fiscal policy into massive systemic error during the 1960s. There had been room to stimulate growth without inflation because by Professor Heller's lights "our rate of production is running some $20 billion short of our potential, maybe more."

In other words, Heller and the new economists had a math model of the economy that told them whether the bathtub of potential GDP was full up to the rim. And if it was not, the model computed the precise quantity of incremental output that could be safely achieved by means of a further shot of "demand stimulus."

At the time Heller testified, the nominal GDP was running at a $400 billion rate, so based on his public statement the implied potential GDP was $420 billion. Yet exactly how did Professor Heller know that the approximate 15 million farms, mines, factories, and service firms then operating in America were collectively capable of 5 percent more output without additional investment, inflationary pressures, or other dislocations?

The answer was both simple and laughably primitive by the lights of subsequent history. Potential output, it seems, was a function of "full employment," which Heller deemed to be achieved when unemployment was pushed down to 4 percent of the labor force.

During the prior year, actual unemployment had been about 5.5 percent, meaning that the 64 million strong US labor force at the time was allegedly capable of generating one and a half percentage points of additional employment. As a computational matter, that amounted to about a million more jobs. And at an average implied output of $20,000 per job, these additional employees would generate $20 billion of extra GDP.

It is hard to say which part of the Heller equation has proved the more specious. During the period since 1950, his 4 percent unemployment target was sustained only during the wars in Korea and Vietnam, when 3.5 million working-age men were under arms. And in both cases the associated red-hot war economy led to a subsequent inflationary blow-off.

So there exists no evidence from peacetime, either before then or since, that an unemployment rate of 4 percent or below is permanently sustainable on a noninflationary basis. Indeed, it was evident from wartime episodes of ultra-low unemployment that serious bottlenecks and disruption invariably occur when key sectors of the national economy become overheated, and that allowance must be made for the frictional unemployment inherent in a dynamic capitalist economy with generally uninhibited labor and capital mobility.

The proof is in the pudding. The US unemployment rate has averaged not 4 percent, but 6 percent during the approximate six hundred months which have elapsed since 1954, exclusive of the four-year Vietnam peak. Average unemployment has thus been about 50 percent greater than the full-employment target postulated by the new economics. In fact, the unemployment rate over this period has reached Professor Heller's 4 percent target only once every thirty months.

That's a pretty decisive trend reflecting the entire range of real-world disturbances which have impacted the American economy. These include external commodity shocks, droughts and floods, housing boom and bust cycles, the rise and fall of major industries, foreign trade disruptions, and much more.

And that was only one of the errors. Average output per employee in 1954 had been only about $7,000. Heller's math model assumed a figure three times that level, meaning that even if filling the macroeconomic bathtub to the rim was an appropriate fiscal policy objective, Heller had vastly exaggerated the scope for additional output, if there was any at all.

At the end of the day, the deeper fault of the new economics was not merely its lack of clairvoyance about the empirical limits of full employment. Its far more onerous sin was encouraging congressional politicians to even entertain the notion that Washington could steer the vast American economy along a path of frictionless perfection, and that this could be accomplished with the blunt instrument of the federal budget.

Indeed, in the fullness of time it became evident that this proposition was upside down: the real structural "imperfection" lay with the state, not the capitalist economy. The inability of capitalism to hew rigidly to the path of full employment was trifling compared to Washington's utter failure to maintain even a semblance of budgetary discipline and honest fiscal reckoning, once the balanced budget rule was jettisoned.

After the new economics was enshrined as official policy in the 1962 "Economic Report of the President," it did not take the newly empowered professoriate long to corrupt the very language of fiscal discourse. Politicians had once rightly feared budget deficits. Plain old budgetary red ink, however, was now rechristened as a "full-employment surplus."

This new formulation was obviously designed to ameliorate recidivist deficit spending fears still held by unenlightened politicians. But its actual import was far more pernicious. By the lights of the new economics, these fanciful full-employment "surpluses" were held to actually harm the macroeconomy because they purportedly restricted aggregate demand. So the cure was to eliminate the full-employment surplus by means of tax cuts or spending increases. Stated differently, the professors invited the politicians to make the actual cash deficit even bigger.

EISENHOWER STAYS THE COURSE
AND DELIVERS FISCAL BALANCE

Fortunately, Eisenhower was having nothing to do with either the Keynesian lite or Professor Heller's full-monty version embraced by such leading lights as Democratic senators Paul Douglas and Hubert Humphrey. By keeping a firm rein on spending, the Eisenhower administration was able to deliver a budget surplus in fiscal 1956 and 1957, and to propose a balanced budget plan for each of the remaining four budgets during Ike's tenure.

The federal budget did swing back to deficits when the automatic stabilizers kicked in during the short but steep recession of 1957–1958. The notable result of this temporary setback, however, was that Eisenhower again refused to embrace countercyclical tax cuts or spending increases to combat the recession, thereby hewing to his long-term fiscal goals.

Furthermore, after the rebound got under way in mid-1958, Ike personally led a full-court press to convert the $13 billion recession deficit into a surplus the very next year. This determined presidential campaign for a balanced budget even included a threat to call a special session of Congress to raise taxes if his spending vetoes were not upheld.

Eisenhower did, in fact, achieve a small surplus in fiscal 1960. Not only was this a testament to his resolute fiscal leadership but, more importantly, it was a stunning repudiation of the Keynesian professoriate. In complete violation of their vaunted math model, Ike's deficit-cutting actions increased the alleged "full-employment surplus" by 2.5 percentage points of GDP between fiscal 1959 and 1960. This swing would have computed to $400 billion in today's economy and was supposed to unleash a bogeyman called "fiscal drag" that would send the economy plummeting back into deep recession.

Yet the bogeyman of "fiscal drag" turned out to be just that: an academic postulate not born out in the real world. During the three-year period from the recession bottom in the second quarter of 1958 through the second quarter of 1961, in fact, real GDP expanded at a 4.2 percent annual rate.

To be sure, during those twelve quarters of solid recovery, the headline rate of annualized GDP change varied widely by quarter, ranging from an 11 percent gain to a 5 percent decline. But those swings were entirely due to inventory fluctuations. With only a few brief exceptions, business investment, consumer spending, and private incomes expanded strongly quarter after quarter throughout the period.

By the time of the 1960 campaign, however, proponents of the new economics were jawing loudly against Ike's "Neanderthal" fiscal policy because reported GDP had temporarily slowed. Within months, of course, the spurious nature of these charges became evident when the US economy reaccelerated, expanding at an 8 percent annual rate by the second quarter of 1961.

And this rebound most assuredly reflected the economy's preexisting natural momentum. There simply wasn't any identifiable economic policy initiative launched by the time the Bay of Pigs invasion of Cuba ensnared the Kennedy administration during its first hundred days in office.

The truth is that the Keynesian professors had been essentially tilting at economic windmills during the 1960 campaign. Their evidence that the economy was lagging turned out to represent mainly short-term fluctuations in the inventory component of GDP.

Reported real GDP growth averaged only 0.8 percent during the four quarters of 1960, but it clocked in at a far more respectable 2.6 percent quarterly average after inventory change is backed out of the headline number. Thus, the Keynesian professoriate's full-throated attack on Eisenhower's circumspect fiscal policy implied that Washington's macroeconomic job description extended all the way to ironing out even the economy's short-run inventory oscillations. The patent absurdity of this proposition would soon be made abundantly clear by the disastrous experiments in "fiscal fine tuning" undertaken in the 1960s and 1970s.

In any event, the turning point which would usher in these calamities had clearly been reached. Kennedy, the winner of the 1960 presidential election, would install Professor Heller and his pretentious gang of Keynesian professors at the seat of power. Worse still, Nixon, who lost the election, would harbor an eternal grudge, blaming the fiscal orthodoxy of Ike and the sound money stand of William McChesney Martin for his defeat.

HOW IKE'S FISCAL RECTITUDE
REINFORCED SOUND MONEY

That Eisenhower's reign of old-fashioned fiscal discipline was crucial to the preservation of sound money cannot be gainsaid. This would become fully evident within the next decade when deficit-wielding politicians on both ends of Pennsylvania Avenue took to demanding that the Fed "accommodate" their fiscal stimulus sprees.

Indeed, when Keynesian fiscal activism became firmly entrenched in Washington, William McChesney Martin's style of resolute monetary discipline was destined to vanish. This development, in turn, doomed the rickety structure of the Bretton Woods gold standard.

Eisenhower's budgetary success, in turn, rested upon what amounts to heresy in the modern Republican Party. Owing to his unwillingness to completely dismantle Truman's war taxes until the budget was balanced first, Ike made only limited progress lowering the tax burden. From a peak level of 19 percent reached under Truman's war taxes, federal receipts were reduced to slightly under 18 percent. At the same time, Ike reduced outlays by two full percentage points of GDP by dint of the defense retrenchment and firm opposition to new or expanded domestic programs.

The nation's fiscal accounts were thus wrestled into reasonable balance at about 18 percent of GDP on both sides of the ledger during Eisenhower's final budgets. This outcome was the embodiment of the old-fashioned notion that taxes must be imposed to pay the government's bills when the avenues for spending control have been exhausted.

Indeed, this testament to fiscal orthodoxy could not have been achieved without purposeful embrace of the inherited Truman tax régime by a Republican White House. And notwithstanding strong pressure from its own rank and file to repeal them.

Given several surplus years and limited "automatic stabilizer" deficits during the recession years, the cumulative deficit in Eisenhower's eight years was minuscule. Total deficits amounted to just $15 billion, or 0.4 percent of GDP. This salutary fiscal outcome has not been even remotely approached by any administration since then.

HOW THE NEW ECONOMICS SABOTAGED IKE'S FISCAL ACHIEVEMENTS

Needless to say, Eisenhower was the last of the fiscal Mohicans. Virtually nothing of the solid fiscal posture he left behind in 1960 survived the new economics' crushing attack on the rule of balanced budgets.

Indeed, once the rank and file of Washington politicians became intoxicated with the sophistries of the full-employment budget and fiscal fine-tuning, they were soon unable to even accurately measure the red ink in the budgetary accounts, let alone feel impelled to relieve it.

At the end of the day, the new economics was a crucial inflection point. In the name of turbocharging the private capitalist economy, it ended up fatally impairing the essential fiscal integrity of the state.

Yet the data prove rather conclusively that after sacrificing the classical fiscal rules, the new economics generated virtually no gain in macroeconomic performance compared to the Eisenhower years. Accordingly, the Keynesian professors should be assessed heavy, everlasting blame for triggering the fiscal and monetary disasters which followed their tenure.

The necessary starting point for that indictment lies in debunking their self-justifying history of the era. The latter holds that the new economics ushered in a quantum leap in economic performance after the alleged somnolence of the Eisenhower years. The latter depiction, however, can be sustained only be measuring Ike's record from an artificial starting point; namely, the red-hot Korean War economy he inherited in January 1953.

Truman's war-fevered economy was not sustainable on a peacetime basis, however, and in any case, the GDP growth figures soon headed south upon the arrival of the Korean armistice a few months later. In fact, comparing what actually happened during and after the Eisenhower era illuminates an even deeper truth detailed below: virtually every period of above-normal real GDP growth since the 1930s has been accompanied by a surge in warfare state outlays.

These defense budget boomlets do not represent a true gain in national wealth, of course, since war spending destroys economic resources and diminishes consumer utility. Indeed, the reported gains in GDP are a statistical illusion, owing to the fact that the GDP accounts only measure spending, not wealth.

THE TRUE EISENHOWER ECONOMIC RECORD:
UNMATCHED ERA OF CIVILIAN ECONOMIC GROWTH

Eisenhower's economic watch, therefore, is more honestly and accurately measured from the point that the Korean War disruption had passed through the national economy; that is, upon completion of the brief "cooling off" recession in the second quarter of 1954. During the seven-year period which followed, a fair part of this illusory defense-spending increment was stripped out of the GDP accounts.

In fact, defense spending actually made a negative contribution to reported GDP growth after mid-1954, given that real DOD spending declined by 22 percent. Consequently, when the defense ramp-down is removed from the figures, real GDP growth averaged 3.5 percent annually during the seven-year post-Korea phase of Eisenhower's tenure. Nonfarm payrolls also grew at a healthy 1.4 percent annual rate during that seven-year period.

At the same time, the war inflation and price control machinery that Eisenhower inherited was eliminated. By the final twelve months of his term, the rate of CPI gain at 0.7 percent annually was about as close to price stability as has been achieved in the postwar world. In other words, the Eisenhower era produced the "Goldilocks economy" of strong growth and low inflation that bullish Wall Street economists only imagined in 2006–2007.

During the decade after Eisenhower, however, three successive presidents aggressively implemented Keynesian fiscal policies. The last two, Johnson and Nixon, browbeat the Fed until it monetized much of the resulting federal debt.

Yet during what might be termed the "Keynesian interlude," which culminated in Nixon's historic gold standard default in August 1971, there was only a modest uptick in the rate of GDP growth and employment gains. On the other hand, the breakout of inflation was so severe and uncontainable that it took the Bretton Woods monetary system down with it.

Unlike during the Eisenhower era, of course, the Kennedy-Johnson doctrine of limited war imperialism soon had the defense growth increment back in the GDP accounts. Real defense spending was 40 percent higher by fiscal 1968. So in order to measure on an apples-to-apples basis it is necessary to remove the national defense expenditure contribution from the GDP accounts.

On that basis, real economic growth during the Keynesian interlude (1961–1971) averaged 4.3 percent annually, or just 80 basis points more than during the Eisenhower era. Likewise, annual nonfarm payroll growth averaged 1.8 percent, or just 40 basis points more than under Ike. Those are truly meager gains when contrasted with the inflationary disorder which descended upon the American economy.

Not only did the CPI rise at a previously unheard of 6.2 percent rate during 1969, but by then the inflationary momentum was so severe that even the modest fiscal and monetary braking actions of late 1968 and 1969 were of little avail. When money market interest rates reached nearly 8 percent—levels never previously seen in the twentieth century—the economy skidded into recession. Even then, the CPI inflation rate only slowed to 5.6 percent by the end of 1970.

So in supplanting the old-time fiscal religion, the professors ushered in a devastating macroeconomic setback for the nation, not the enlightened economic science they claimed to possess. The 1960s Keynesian experiment eventually degenerated into its alter ego after August 1971: Professor Friedman's régime of floating paper dollars. But the latter result did not come out of the blue; it had been gestating for a decade.

Way back when the new economics was first being heralded during the Democrats' "Get America Moving Again" campaign of 1960, the warning signs of big trouble in the monetary system were already flashing. In October 1960, the first serious post–Bretton Woods run on gold flared up in the London market. Speculators were already betting against the new economics. Rightly so.

CHAPTER 12

THE AMERICAN EMPIRE AND THE END OF SOUND MONEY

THE 1960 DEMOCRATIC CAMPAIGN PLATFORM FRONTALLY ATTACKED the "plodding" Eisenhower economy, promising to raise real GDP growth to 5 percent annually. This growth target virtually telegraphed reckless policy experimentation ahead, since it was far larger than had ever previously been imagined, let alone delivered by the modern American economy on a sustained basis. Stated more plainly, 5 percent growth was nuts.

As it became clear in the last weeks of the election that Kennedy could emerge the winner and would bring the new economics professoriate to Washington in pursuit of these aggressive fiscal and monetary policies, the London gold market went into a buying panic. Speculators began to aggressively dump dollars and stock up on gold, betting that the new administration might devalue, that is, raise the dollar price for gold above the existing $35 per ounce parity.

THE LONDON GOLD MARKET PANIC OF OCTOBER 1960: A SHOT ACROSS THE KEYNESIAN BOW

At the time, the London gold market was a genuine free market in which traders, both private parties and official institutions, could buy or sell gold at an auction price. It functioned parallel to the official Bretton Woods system under which transfers of gold among nations in settlement of payments imbalances occurred exclusively between central banks, and only at the official parities centered on $35 gold.

The rub was that this gold settlement process under the official Bretton Woods system was highly discretionary and political, not automatic and market driven as under the pre-1914 gold standard. Consequently, official gold settlements did not necessarily "clear the market" and force immediate monetary tightening and economic adjustments in the deficit countries, as occurred under the classic gold standard mechanism.

Under the dollar-based gold exchange standard, in fact, trading partners with dollar surpluses could be "persuaded" (by Washington) to forego the conversion of these dollars at the US gold window. They were instead forced to accumulate short-term dollar claims which counted as monetary "reserve" assets.

As the hegemonic power during the early Cold War era, the United States self-evidently had the wherewithal to enforce a de facto policy of involuntary reserve accumulation. The overseas hoard of dollars piled up in foreign central banks was thereby steadily enlarged, even as the US balance of payments deficits grew during the 1960s and remained uncured.

The one escape valve was the ability of countries with unwanted dollars to quietly swap them for gold in the London market. Accordingly, in the early days of Bretton Woods, bureaucrats at the International Monetary Fund (IMF) made efforts to get participants to outlaw private gold markets.

They recognized that someday official parities could be threatened if the free market price of gold diverged too far from $35 per ounce. But the presence of makeshift private gold markets in places like Macau, Tangiers, and Hong Kong, along with the steady clandestine sale of gold for desperately needed hard currency by the Soviet Union, finally encouraged the Bank of England to reopen the old London gold market in March 1954.

For the next half decade, the London market operated quietly alongside the official gold window of the US Treasury. This nascent London-based free market in gold provided an outlet for Soviet bullion sales, small transactions by foreign central banks, and a venue for a corporal's guard of private speculators to make small-time bets.

There was little reason to speculate against the gold dollar at $35 per ounce so long as the disciplined fiscal and monetary policies championed by Eisenhower and Martin, respectively, remained intact. But the combination of a modest deterioration in the US balance of payments during 1960 and the prospect that US economic policies would lurch away from orthodoxy quickly ended the quietude.

As Charles A. Coombs, then a key player at the New York Fed's international desk, observed in his memoir of the era, "The market could smell thunder in the air. . . . [S]entiment shifted abruptly during the weekend of October 15, 1960."

After years of somnolent fluctuations around parity, the gold price in the London market thus flared to $40 per ounce in late October 1960, which was an unexpected and shocking development at the time. The free market gold price came off the boil only after candidate Kennedy publicly committed to maintenance of convertibility at the official $35 price. Still, as Coombs further noted, the Fed's earlier worry that "the London gold price would become a barometer of confidence in the dollar was being vindicated with a vengeance."

This pre-election gold panic was the free market's premonition of the lethal threat to Bretton Woods posed by the new economics. Yet the Keynesian professors were largely oblivious to the warning.

Notwithstanding the two full months that Professor J. M. Keynes and comrade Harry Dexter White had spent at Bretton Woods, New Hampshire, perfecting a new world monetary order during the summer of 1944, they had not expurgated the "barbarous relic" of free market gold, after all. In fact, the London gold market was a peephole back into the pre-1914 monetary order.

Under the classical gold standard régime, as previously noted, the propensity of governments and central banks to debauch the official paper money could be swiftly checked by its conversion into gold coins and bullion by private investors and speculators. On the eve of John F. Kennedy's presidency and the arrival of the new economics in Washington, therefore, the ancient discipline of free market gold was energetically reemerging through the London market.

BRETTON WOODS AND GOLD: THE VESTIGIAL LINK
TO THE ANCIENT MONETARY RÉGIME

This development was not exactly anticipated or welcomed by officialdom. In fact, the turmoil in the London gold market was a complete contradiction of the framers' fervid intention that Bretton Woods function essentially as a hybrid form of international money that was ultimately state managed.

Indeed, there was only one reason why gold, rather than Keynes' pure fiat script, called "bancor," had been made the official settlement asset under Bretton Woods, and it had nothing to do with monetary theory. As of July 1944, the United States held 80 percent of the world's stock of gold. Not surprisingly, the US delegation thought the Fort Knox hoard would provide more than enough chips for the international settlements table created by Bretton Woods.

From this signal fact the conference had leapt to the large, although unarticulated, conclusion that the United States could succeed as the reserve currency issuer under a gold exchange standard, notwithstanding the historical precedent of England's miserable failure in the role during the 1920s. And on the surface, of course, that wager was plausible given the vastly different circumstances of the two countries.

The British Empire had emerged from the Great War deeply wounded economically, with its public accounts heavily in debt, the London money market enfeebled, and the Bank of England's gold reserves down to a trifle.

It was only British arrogance that had presumed that a gold exchange standard could be reconstituted on this wobbly foundation.

The Bretton Woods conference appropriately judged that the United States was in a far better position to function as the anchor in this attempted revival of the gold exchange system. With $20 billion of gold reserves behind it, the dollar was a far more plausible candidate to function as a reliable reserve currency; that is, the US dollar of 1944 had every appearance of being the anti-sterling of 1925.

Indeed, in 1944 most of the world's economies outside North America were prostrate. Accordingly, the prospect that the United States would be plagued by chronic balance of payments deficits did not stir the imagination of the conference's leading thinkers.

So the "barbarous relic" had been reinstalled as the "reserve" or "settlement" asset at the heart of the new Bretton Woods system. Yet despite the conferees' genuine desire to revive honest international money after the calamity of 1930s economic autarky and depreciated national currencies, the arrangement ignored the fundamental flaw of the sterling exchange system.

If America's vast gold hoard was ever dissipated, then the danger would arise that the United States, as the issuer of the reserve currency, would find itself in the British position of the 1920s. Like the British, it could be tempted to force its trading partners to accumulate vast unwanted dollar liabilities rather than put its own domestic financial house in order.

THE LESSONS OF THE STERLING EXCHANGE STANDARD UNLEARNED

Owing to the trauma of the 1930s and the totalitarian monsters to which it had given rise, the conferees at Bretton Woods understood perfectly well that a repeat of the British gold exchange standard failure had to be avoided at all hazards. Unlike today, it was then self-evident that in the absence of global financial discipline and settlement of trade and financial accounts on a regular basis, there lurked a monetary terra incognito teeming with financial terrors.

However, in attempting to revive, for the second time, the efficiencies of a single world money and the financial disciplining mechanism of the pre–World War I gold standard, the conference succumbed to the same error as the 1920s go-round; namely, under Keynes's tutelage it focused on accommodating economic growth and the alleged problem of a shortage of gold reserves. The real imperative, however, was resurrecting a mechanism for international financial discipline that did not depend upon the political self-control of the reserve currency issuer.

Indeed, the deeply flawed idea of "economizing" on the world's gold stock by allowing nations to settle their current account imbalances through payments in a designated "reserve currency," as well as gold, had been launched at a 1921 conference in Genoa. It had been convened by the League of Nations to reconstitute the international financial system from the monetary ruins left by the Great War.

The self-serving British theory at the time was that world recovery would be better nurtured by a more ample and elastic system of monetary reserve assets than would have obtained from a return to a pure gold specie system. Since Britain had exhausted all of its gold during the Great War, it amounted to a pauper's monetary standard.

Nevertheless, during the course of the 1920s this "gold plus reserve currency" arrangement became widespread, as more than thirty nations ended wartime fiat money régimes and returned to fixed exchange rates and convertibility of their currencies into either gold or sterling and dollars. As previously indicated, this jerry-built gold exchange standard appeared to be just the ticket, as the entire global economy recovered and grew at a robust pace between 1924 and 1929.

As has also been seen, however, the boom had been fueled by massive Wall Street foreign bond issuance and a temporary surge in US exports and world trade. When that daisy chain of faux prosperity came to a screeching halt, the underlying flaw of the sterling exchange system became apparent; namely, that Britain had neither the resources nor political will to perform its obligations as the reserve currency issuer.

THE BRITISH MONEY-PRINTING SPREE UNDER THE GUISE OF THE GOLD EXCHANGE STANDARD

In fact, the postwar gold exchange standard turned out to be the first great experiment in sovereign debt–based money. In this case, the money in question was the massive accumulation during the 1920s boom of pound sterling monetary reserves by France, Holland, Sweden, Italy, and the central and eastern European nations.

But these "reserves" were just a back-door form of British borrowing which permitted it to live beyond its means. The financial devastation of the Great War had depleted the British industrial economy and left the government and much of industry deeply in debt. But rather than reduce consumption, wages, and living standards in order to rebuild its economy and pay down its war debts, British policy embraced an illusion.

It attempted to return to pre-war exchange rate parity ($4.86 per pound sterling) at postwar wages and prices. Yet since the British price level had risen by 200 percent during the course of its desperate money printing during the Great War, its attempt at "resumption" on the cheap was a disaster. It resulted in an overvalued pound, chronic current account deficits, and an inflationary monetary policy that printed far too much sterling.

In the end, the Bank of England's grand experiment in money printing failed to achieve domestic recovery. The British economy, unlike most of the rest of the world, stagnated for much of the 1920s. But this monetary profligacy did flood the international financial system with more sterling liabilities than were sustainable; that is to say, Great Britain attempted to borrow its way back to prosperity.

This easy way out of the Great War's legacy of debt, devalued sterling, and depleted industries inexorably came a cropper. As has been seen, when the global economy shrank sharply after Wall Street's foreign bond financing machine shut down, world trade plunged even more rapidly. In turn, this downward trade spiral triggered the final unwinding of the worldwide debt bubble that had reached an asymptotic peak in 1928–1929.

The bubble's collapse began in central Europe, where some of the most egregious of Wall Street's "subprime" loans of that era had been made, and most famously resulted in the May 1931 run on Credit Anstalt, Austria's largest bank. Depositors in the Austrian banks, and a month later in German banks, too, correctly perceived that these institutions were insolvent because their hard-hit domestic customers could no longer service their loans—especially their dollar borrowings.

Moreover, their own governments were too financially weak to save their domestic banks, and the taxpayers of the world had not yet bequeathed to the banking fraternity its very own IMF bailout machine. Consequently, there ensued a flight from the imperiled banks and currencies of Austria, Germany, and other central and eastern European nations and a corresponding scramble for gold.

In short order, the flight to gold from the weak paper currencies of continental Europe during the summer of 1931 lapped up on the shores of England, too. As it happened, the British government had the tools in hand to turn back the assault and defend the very gold exchange system it had championed. But like the United States under Johnson and Nixon four decades later, it could not summon the political will to discharge its obligations as the reserve currency issuer.

THE GREAT BETRAYAL OF SEPTEMBER 1931: WHEN THE BANK OF ENGLAND UNNECESSARILY DEFAULTED

In August 1931, only a few weeks before England defaulted, a national unity government had been installed and stern measures to curtail its budget deficit by means of tax increases and reductions in lavish spending for industrial subsidies and social programs had been enacted.

All that was needed was for the Bank of England to deploy its time-tested tool and implement a sharp increase in its discount rate, which was only 2.5 percent at the time, in order to stem the outflow of short-term money from London. Indeed, it was morally obligated to take these painful steps.

For years, the imperious mandarins who ran the Bank of England had urged the French, Swedes, Belgians, and most especially Holland to accumulate outsized reserves of pounds sterling rather than demand gold. But there was no sustainability to it; it was just a kick-the-can ruse to avoid an unwelcome outflow of gold and contraction of England's puffed-up domestic economy.

As it happened, on September 20, 1931, England defaulted in a wave of panic and under withering pressure from its own economic nationalists. Keynes led the charge, declaiming loudly for default in the same words, albeit with better grammar, that Connally would employ four decades later. Like Nixon's government at Camp David, the British wanted to shed the alleged "straitjacket" of fixed exchange rates and convertible money in order to "stimulate" the domestic economy.

Yet in refusing to honor its obligation to convert pounds sterling to gold, Great Britain also crushed what remained of the very gold exchange standard it had so assiduously peddled around the world since 1921. Needless to say, those unlucky nations which had been persuaded to hold their reserves in pounds sterling were left holding the bag, suffering immense losses as the pound exchange rate against the dollar dropped by 35 percent in a matter of weeks.

Holland, in particular, took a beating. On the explicit secret assurances of the Bank of England, the Dutch central bank had refused to reduce its large sterling holdings, despite the gathering market panic, through the very day of default.

Once the dam broke, however, the world experienced a renewed flight from paper currencies and an extended period of gold hoarding and beggar-thy-neighbor protectionism. Then and there, the world plunged into a dark night of economic nationalism, protectionism, fiat currencies, and economic stagnation.

JOHN MAYNARD KEYNES AND THE SECOND ATTEMPT AT MONETARY ORDER: THE IMPERFECT REVIVAL OF GOLD AT BRETTON WOODS

By 1944 the entire world had been bankrupted by war, save for the United States. So when the United States hosted the crucial conference at Bretton

Woods to plan postwar reconstruction of the world financial system and monetary arrangements, it had a unique opportunity to start afresh, applying the lessons learned from both the failed gold exchange standard of the 1920s and the even more disastrous beggar-the-neighbor nationalism of the 1930s.

In one of the cruelest ironies of history, however, Keynes was made chairman of the committee on monetary arrangements. Already approaching his dotage, he nevertheless did not want for domineering pomposity or capacity to dispatch the arguments of the hapless Harry Dexter White (head of the delegation and under-secretary of treasury).

Under Keynes's tutelage, therefore, the conference in due course proceeded to revive the failed British experiment in debt-based money. It is not coincidental that the experiment on which Keynes himself had helped administer the coup de grâce in September 1931 would eventually meet a similar fate.

Modern Keynesian historians now stoutly insist that the Great Depression was caused by the gold exchange standard. In truth, the cause was the hangover from the financial carnage brought on by the Great War, and the subsequent Wall Street foreign bond issuance spree that cantilevered massive debts on top of broken economies and already bankrupt nations.

Yet these revisionists are undoubtedly correct in claiming that the demise of the gold exchange standard after 1929 amplified the decline that was already under way. What they fail to concede, however, is that it was not gold bullion per se, but the "exchange" part of the equation that caused the 1931 breakdown of the international economy.

At the time of the crisis, it was true that the Bank of England had almost no gold and that most of the world's gold reserves were actually domiciled in the United States and France. Still, the fault for this imbalance was not in the yellow metal, but in British policy which for an entire decade avoided financial discipline through the buildup of short-term sterling debt, a pattern which would be replicated under the dollar-based gold exchange system during the 1960s.

In fact, the $3 billion in pounds sterling held by France, Holland, and the remainder of solvent Europe was British debt that had been turned into the world's money. It was also debt which Great Britain voluntarily obligated itself to redeem for a fixed weight of gold under rules it largely formulated.

At the time of the September 1931 crisis, however, Keynes proclaimed that the policy actions needed to defend the pound—higher interest rates and fiscal austerity—were "inconvenient." So international default became the pathway to implementation of his pet nostrums at home, such as cheap money and deficit-financed pump priming via public works and public jobs.

When the conference ended in July 1944, this same disability had been transplanted into the new system. It would only be a matter of time before it came under a new Keynesian assault.

Only this time the nationalist assault would necessarily arise in the United States, and the executioners would be Keynes's disciples. In the first wave, the attack came from liberal economists who acknowledged his tutelage.

But in the end, it was the economic nationalists from the University of Chicago, the closet disciples of Keynes, who found the discipline of the gold exchange system to be as inconvenient in 1971 as he had found it in 1931. So the disciples of Friedman recommended to the president of the United States that the world's richest nation default on its debt obligations, an act so perfidious that even J. M. Keynes himself might have abjured.

THE BRETTON WOODS FLAWS
WHICH TOOK TIME TO EMERGE

Milton Friedman was ultimately able to take down Keynes's Bretton Woods creation, once the great thinker's new economics disciples paved the way. Their successful assault was enabled by two basic chinks in the Bretton Woods scheme to restrict the use of gold to official settlements between the US Treasury and foreign central banks. The first was that the private purchase and possession of monetary gold was outlawed in the United States, but there were no restrictions on American citizens buying and holding gold abroad.

Thus, if a gap developed between the free market price in London and the official $35 parity, it would be quickly arbitraged. It would take little more than a good lawyer and a savvy banking house to get large amounts of American capital into the London gold trade.

And equally consequential was the fact that foreign central banks with unwanted dollars could surreptitiously use them to buy small amounts of gold in the London market, rather than risking Washington's ill will by coming to the official Treasury gold window. During the summer of 1960, in fact, it had been heavy gold buying in London by the Bank of Italy that first catalyzed private speculators.

Thus, the potential existed for the London peephole into the free market for gold to be dramatically enlarged by both private speculators and central banks operating outside the official etiquette. Needless to say, this meant that from day one the new economics was on a collision course with Bretton Woods.

If excessive fiscal expansion and deficit spending forced the Fed into too much monetary accommodation, the nation's current account would deteriorate and its price level relative to the rest of the world would rise. In that event, speculators could effectively short the dollar by piling into the London gold market.

The resulting conversion of unwanted paper dollars—whether held by speculators or central banks—into gold would drive its price rapidly higher. In short, the London gold market was a vestigial organ of the ancient monetary régime. It threatened to chase the Harvard economists right back into the Littauer Library the minute their Keynesian schemes went too far.

To be sure, at the official level the US government might well continue to bully the West Germans or Japanese into foregoing the right to swap unwanted dollars for gold at the US Treasury window, and to refrain from cheating in the London gold market. Yet even heavy Washington diplomatic pressure could not stop private speculators from betting against the sustainability of such monetary imperialism.

The US nuclear umbrella, of course, provided US officials with a powerful lever that the Bank of England did not possess in September 1931. Yet even the American Cold War hegemony had its limits when it came to monetary fundamentals.

Sooner or later the buildup of excess dollars in foreign central banks would reach the breaking point. If they kept buying up dollars at the Bretton Woods exchange rate parities, they would be forced to print excess amounts of their own currency, thereby importing US inflation.

So as the 1960s opened, the new economics amounted to a form of doubling down. There was already a severe dollar outflow owing to the US Cold War imperium and its vast string of military and security operations abroad. On top of that, the new economics was now almost guaranteed to eliminate the US surplus in private trade and services, owing to excess domestic demand and a rising level of merchandise imports. Absent a large surplus in merchandise trade, the vast cost of empire would generate unsustainable deficits in the overall US balance of payments. Speculators therefore had every reason to bet on eventual dollar devaluation and that the price of gold someday would break loose of its Bretton Woods parity.

Stated differently, JFK's Keynesian professors were puffing themselves up to take on the global free market in gold, even if they did not acknowledge it. Yet the battle which played out in the London gold market's daily price auction was one they were destined to lose.

Their theories of intentional deficit spending to goose the GDP were bound to be abused by politicians and would eventually lead to easy money, domestic inflation, trade deficits, and insuperable pressure on the dollar's gold parity. It was only a matter of time before the frail Bretton Woods rendition of the gold exchange standard would fall victim to their math-model economics.

JOHN F. KENNEDY: THE LAST GOLD STANDARD DEMOCRAT

The day of reckoning did not occur until near the very end of the Kennedy-Johnson era, when LBJ shut down the London gold pool in March 1968 (see page 246). Yet, ironically, this long postponement of the inevitable was due to JFK's foresight in staffing the Treasury Department with monetary traditionalists, who managed to find creative expedients to defend the dollar and pay the nation's international debts in gold, even as the flood of unwanted dollars mounted.

In fact, once JFK took the oath of office, it was soon evident that economic policy process had been put on a split screen: an internationalist, hard-dollar policy was consistently enunciated at the Treasury Department, while an aggressively expansionist domestic fiscal policy was loudly proclaimed by the Council of Economic Advisors. The result was continuous conflict.

Keynesian demand management is nationalistic and autarkic, and can only work in a closed economy. So under the actual circumstances it stimulated a growing leakage of dollars abroad, a trend that the Treasury's clever expedients temporarily papered over. Eventually, however, Lyndon Johnson's rampant exercise in "guns and butter" deficits exhausted the capacity of his own Treasury staff to temporize.

Kennedy initially counterbalanced the new economics threat by the appointment of Douglas Dillon as treasury secretary. Dillon was a Republican, a ranking official in the Eisenhower State Department, and the scion of an old-line Wall Street banking house. His appointment was designed to reassure financial markets, and initially it did exactly that.

In fact, Dillon did not allow international financial markets and gold speculators even a brief opportunity to get spooked by the new economics professors who had set up camp across the street in the White House. Just days after the inauguration, he arranged for JFK's first major speech on economics to address international monetary policy and the dollar.

Kennedy's speech pulled no punches. The new president pledged full support of the Bretton Woods system and committed his administration to an "immutable" gold price of $35 per ounce. In those days, presidential words meant something, and there wasn't much not to understand about "immutable."

Secretary Dillon and the Treasury's international staff backed Kennedy's words with a stream of actions designed to ward off pressure on the $35 gold price. These included a central bankers' gold pool, currency swap lines, and even issuance of public debt in foreign currencies ("Roosa bonds").

Secretary Dillon's initiatives to defend Bretton Woods also had an advantage that would never again recur; namely, a Fed chairman who believed in sound money, fixed exchange rates, and meeting the nation's international obligation to keep the dollar good as gold.

Not coincidentally, Chairman Martin began each Fed meeting during the 1960s with a report by the New York Fed on international financial conditions and the foreign exchange markets. In those halcyon days, the New York Fed was a stalwart defender of a sound dollar, not the active debasement agent that it became after the 1990s.

Indeed, it would have been horrified by the weak-dollar doctrine of recent occupants of its top job, such as Tim Geithner and Bill Dudley. Consequently, as the guardian of the dollar's foreign exchange integrity it helped design and operate the London gold pool, which was the Treasury's primary line of defense.

THE LONDON GOLD POOL: PRIMARY LINE OF DEFENSE

The gold pool was formally established in December 1961 by the Federal Reserve and seven European central banks led by Germany, France, and the United Kingdom. The United States provided half of the pool's $270 million stock of gold, with the balance coming from the Europeans. While in theory this central bankers' syndicate could either buy or sell gold in the London free market, the underlying purpose was to sell gold whenever speculators tried to drive its price above $35 per ounce.

The bet of the gold speculators, of course, was that the United States would eventually elect to cheapen its currency, rather than rein in its balance of payments deficits through domestic austerity or retrenchment of its overseas military and foreign aid spending. In that event, the gold price would soar, bringing windfall gains to the speculators.

Initially, however, the central bankers' syndicate kept the speculators at bay, in part because the size of the pool was never made known to the market. In reality, the United States had secretly pledged to its European partners that it would replenish their gold stocks at a later date by the full amount of any sales from the pool. Thus, the United States was still on the hook to defend the $35 parity entirely with its own gold. Yet by warehousing dollars on an interim basis, the European central banks helped minimize the appearance of a drain on US gold stocks.

During the first half of the 1960s, the Treasury's dollar defense was reinforced by the fact that the overall US balance of payments deficit remained moderate. Gold outflows cumulated to just $4 billion during 1961–1965.

Serendipity also gave the Treasury an assist when the Soviet Union had another massive crop failure, forcing it to sell about $1.5 billion of gold during 1963–1964 to feed the starving Russian population. Since these sales had the effect of dousing upward pressure on the free market price of gold in London, speculators shorting the dollar, ironically, got burned by the pratfall of socialist agriculture.

The need for large outflows of US gold to finance the cost of forward defenses against the Soviet menace was thus temporarily averted, as the menace was proving more adept at starving its own people than endangering others. As it worked out, the central bankers' gold pool actually ended 1965 with a billion-dollar surplus.

THE HELLER-TOBIN ASSAULT ON SOUND MONEY

It was all downhill thereafter and mainly because the fundamental terms of the US financing equation steadily deteriorated. On the one hand, the dollar outflow owing to the "cost of empire" intensified, rising from $6–$7 billion per year before Johnson's big 1965 escalation of the Vietnam conflict to $9–$11 billion per year during 1968 and several years afterward.

At the same time, Kennedy's new economics professors had succeeded beyond their wildest dreams. By mid-1962 they had worn down President Kennedy's aversion to deliberate deficit finance, and by year-end had gotten him to deliver a speech on behalf of stimulative tax cuts to the Economics Club of New York City.

Much to Kennedy's surprise, the prospect of a sizeable reduction in personal income tax rates and corporate taxes was widely applauded on Wall Street. The federal budget was still in deficit and a tax cut had not yet been earned under Eisenhower's fiscal rules, but the idea of "stimulative" tax cuts on Uncle Sam's credit card was taking hold.

So Kennedy was emboldened to embrace the new economics game plan and propose a substantial tax cut in his January 1963 budget message. In doing so, he had overridden the concerns of Secretary Dillon that this resort to a deliberate fiscal deficit would undermine the Treasury's dollar defense strategy. History would now record that, apart from the resolute stand taken by Paul O'Neill against the Bush tax-cut mania in 2003, Dillon was one of the last treasury secretaries to defend the nation's revenue base in the name of sound finance.

Moreover, Dillon's dissent had come on top of what by then had become a heated and divisive battle inside the Kennedy administration on the fundamental balance of payments and dollar issue. Only months earlier, in fact, the Keynesian professors led by Walter Heller and James Tobin had proposed an inflationist plan to suspend the gold window, cut domestic interest rates, and negotiate a "long-term borrowing arrangement" with the Europeans.

Already the inherent corruption of language which goes with the Keynesian brief had cropped into the debate. The "borrowing" arrangement proposed by Heller and Tobin was nothing more than a meaningless sleight-of-hand. Rather than pay off the rapidly growing short-term dollar claims held by other central banks, the professors were proposing to relabel them as long-term debt and tell the Europeans to suck it up.

In truth, the Heller-Tobin proposal was a nationalistic, frontal assault on Bretton Woods because it removed the free convertibility linchpin from the system; it told the Europeans who had accumulated dollar exchange reserves in good faith to choke on them.

A much agitated Secretary Dillon, therefore, had to admonish the professors that such a step would "shake the system to its core in the same way as the German standstill announcement of 1931 or the dollar devaluation of 1933 had done."

Secretary Dillon and Fed chairman Martin were able to quash the Heller–Tobin plan after it predictably set off alarm bells in Europe and warnings that it would lead to the early demise of Bretton Woods. Still, justifiably irritated by the constant attacks of the White House professors, Dillon explained in no uncertain terms that sound international policy had to be based on consistent financial discipline, not Tobin's ten-year loan from Europe designed to kick the US balance of payments problem down the road indefinitely.

Dillon thus called out his internal adversaries as follows: "They search for ways to make this very real problem go away without interfering with their own projects—be they extra low interest rates in the US or the maintenance of large US forces in Europe. However, such individuals are asking the impossible. The sine qua non of all international monetary dealings . . . is that no country can run a consistently large balance of payments deficit."

Chairman Martin was equally aghast at the Heller-Tobin prequel, in 1962, to what turned out to be the same flimsy logic as that behind Nixon's actual gold dollar default nine years later. "The proposed plan . . ." he declared, "would hit world financial markets as a declaration of US insolvency and a submission to receivers to salvage the most they could get out of the mess to which past US policies had led. It is incredulous to expect from it any resurgence of confidence."

These were the words of sound-money men at a time when political expediency and debt-based financing schemes could still be called out. Yet it was only a matter of time before their voices would go quiet. The monetary policy battles inside the Kennedy administration did, indeed, demarcate the twilight of sound money.

HIGH TIDE OF THE NEW ECONOMICS

The wisdom of Dillon and Martin did not slow down the White House professors one bit, who instead aggressively pushed the 1963 tax-cut plan to the top of Kennedy's agenda. They insisted it was a watershed breakthrough into enlightened fiscal policy—the international value of the dollar be damned.

Later praising Kennedy and Johnson for doing his bidding, Heller boasted that they had shown a "willingness to use, for the first time, the full range of modern economic tools" and that by "narrowing the intellectual gap between economic advisers and decision-makers . . . the paralyzing grip of economic myth and false fears on policy has been loosened."

Keynesian zealotry was now at high tide. Under the original Heller tax plan there was even an "on/off "switch. Tax rates would be raised and lowered by presidential order depending upon what the White House economists were seeing in the economic weather reports. It was shades of FDR's breakfast with Professor Warren.

In convincing Kennedy to take the first fateful step down the slippery slope of deficit-financed tax cuts, the professors were paving the way for the eventual transformation of the tax code into a tool of national prosperity management. They were also offering it up as a piñata to be battered endlessly by crony capitalist lobbies.

The Keynesian professors had not made much headway on Capitol Hill, however. The bill got bottled up in the Senate Finance Committee, with Republicans declaring the Kennedy tax cut to be "the biggest gamble in history." Only in the wake of the tragic event in Dallas was Lyndon Johnson able to summon a congressional majority willing to abandon the ancient taboo against deliberate deficit finance in peacetime.

For a brief moment thereafter it appeared that the old-time fiscal religion had been benighted after all. Upon enactment of the "Kennedy tax cut," real GDP grew by 5.3 percent in 1964 and 5.9 percent in 1965 while inflation remained subdued, rising at only a 1.5 percent rate during each year.

Yet in a sure fire sign of trouble to come, *Time* magazine put Keynes on its year-end 1965 cover and pronounced that the business cycle had been abolished. According to the editors, policy makers had "discovered the secret of steady, stable, non-inflationary growth."

Needless to say, the same "secret" would be continuously rediscovered in the decades ahead—by the Reagan White House after 1984, by Alan

Greenspan after December 1996, and by Bernanke's specious proclamation of the "Great Moderation" in February 2004.

Time's essay also dispensed copious hokum about the mid-1960s boom being "the most sizeable, prolonged and widely distributed prosperity in history." But it's more cogent, and perhaps unintended, insight had to do with a profound change it detected in the attitude of the business community.

The predicate that economic progress and prosperity would flow from macromanagement by the state, rather than from free market interaction of businesses and consumers, had now been embraced, even by the capitalists: "They believe that whatever happens, the Government will somehow keep the economy strong and rising."

COMEUPPANCE OF THE NEW ECONOMICS

Exactly fifteen months later, in the spring of 1967, the US economy was visibly out of control, with inflation not subdued at all, but running at a 5 percent annual rate and gaining momentum. The White House professors found themselves no longer the toast of the town, but in headlong retreat.

Their putatively "balanced" full-employment budget had morphed into LBJ's huge "guns and butter" deficits. So there emerged in 1967–1968 a white-hot national economy that desperately needed to be throttled back.

Alas, the professors also discovered they had let the "fine-tuning" genie out of the bottle but couldn't get it back in. LBJ and the congressional rank and file were now proving to be far more reluctant to hit the fiscal brakes with tax hikes and spending restraint than they had been to embrace tax cuts and spending stimulus.

This earlier boost to domestic demand resulted in rapid import growth and caused the $7 billion merchandise trade surplus of 1964 to swoon toward zero by 1968, meaning that nothing was coming in to pay for the cost of empire. Even a modest rise in the surplus from income earned on US assets abroad was now being offset by greater private capital outflows.

So on a bottom-line basis, unwanted dollars began to build up in offshore markets once again. This time there was no Soviet famine to douse the London gold market with fresh bullion. Accordingly, the upward pressure on the gold price became intense.

In the interim, the Treasury and Fed had adopted additional support tools—central bank currency swap lines—to bolster their dollar defense. Yet the swap lines were an even weaker reed than the gold pool, and merely bought some modest increment of extra time while upward pressures on the gold market continued to accumulate.

DEFERRING THE DAY OF RECKONING:
SWAP LINES AND ROOSA BONDS

The currency swap lines were in theory a two-way street, depending upon whether the dollar's exchange rate was weak or strong. In practice, however, the swap lines were mainly used by the Fed to mop up unwanted dollars abroad, thereby avoiding their disposal on the London gold market or presentation for official redemption in gold.

The Fed's intentions were initially viewed with suspicion by the European central banks since, as Coombs of the New York Fed noted in his memoir, the swap line initiative looked "like an attempt to devise means of blocking access to the Treasury gold window. This was not far from the mark."

In what would become a familiar kick-the-can syndrome, the swap lines were therefore limited to one-year maturities. This was meant to emphasize that they would be deployed only as a short-term exchange-market-smoothing mechanism, not as a substitute for fundamental financial discipline and correction of the US payments imbalance.

The insuperable challenge faced by the Treasury was that the swap lines became a drug, and the addiction got steadily worse with time. After their 1962 creation they ballooned to multibillion-dollar scale and were used on a routine but haphazard basis to prop up the dollar. The underlying balance of payments issue was never even addressed, let alone ameliorated.

So yet another expedient was invented: the US Treasury's so-called Roosa bonds denominated in European currencies. But the billions of proceeds from these issues were used simply to pay off earlier foreign currency loans, such as D-mark loans from the Bundesbank, as they came due under the one-year rule. They thus amounted to a thinly disguised ruse to violate the very principle—running an indefinite current account deficit—which Secretary Dillon had properly denounced.

At the end of the day, though, the Kennedy-Johnson Treasury was drawn and quartered in financial terms by the war spenders in the Pentagon and the domestic expansionists at the Council of Economic Advisors. Every new gimmick they invented to support the dollar and protect the nation's gold reserves led to a new round of technical complications, but no gain in underlying financial discipline.

Thus, a maneuver called Operation Twist attempted to push long-term interest rates lower to encourage domestic investment and growth while nudging short-term interest rates higher to support the dollar. It actually backfired, however, when foreign issuers raised cheap long-term debt in New York and then promptly swapped the proceeds back into their own currencies, thereby dumping more unwanted dollars on the foreign exchange markets.

So the Treasury came up with a fix to the fix called an "interest equalization tax" to punish such speculators, but that didn't work either and only led to more expedients. A dangerous time bomb was thus being planted just below the surface. Foreign private and official claims on dollar denominated assets—much of it short term—began to build up rapidly after 1965, having been facilitated by the swap lines, the Roosa bonds, and the gamut of additional temporizing measures.

Compared to gains averaging about $2 billion per year in 1962–1965, foreign dollar claims grew by $7 billion, $10 billion, and $13 billion in 1967 through 1969, respectively. The glaring problem was that these off-shore dollar claims were now expanding at an annual rate which was larger than the entire remaining gold stock of the United States.

Any blow to confidence could cause a panic dumping of dollar assets for gold. This would trigger, in turn, an existential challenge to a global monetary system which was now saturated with unwanted dollars.

THE PENULTIMATE BLOW TO BRETTON WOODS: THE BRITISH KEYNESIAN DEFAULT AGAIN

The challenge came decisively in 1967, when the Arab-Israeli Six Day War in June set off a cascade of unsettling forces. The fault line centered on the ragged British economy, which was suffering from the double whammy of a multi-decade decay in its union-crippled industrial sector and the inflationary fevers which had been introduced by the Keynesian policies of its Labour government.

Like the United States, the United Kingdom was living way beyond its means, as reflected in a festering balance of payments crisis. Even though by then it had dismantled most of its empire, it still could not make ends meet, owing to the heavy burdens of its welfare state.

When the Mideast war caused the closure of the Suez Canal, the outlook for the already substantial British trade deficit took a sharp turn for the worse, fueling a powerful new round of exchange market speculation against the pound. British policy had quashed two earlier sterling crises under Labour governments, but the confluence of forces working to undermine the pound now threatened a third and even more virulent drive by speculators to force devaluation.

Faced by this daunting challenge, the Labour government made a far-reaching error which soon triggered a devaluation of the pound, a run on the dollar, and the collapse of the London gold pool. Nixon's final demarche from Camp David would complete the destruction of Bretton Woods a few years later.

The correct solution was embodied in a century and a half of British monetary history. Domestic demand needed to be throttled back by an immediate sharp increase in the Bank of England discount rate, and an emergency budget to staunch the flood of red ink that was financing imports the UK couldn't afford.

These classic measures would attract funds into sterling, curtail imports, and cauterize the payments deficit. They would also signal to speculators that the government was committed to financial discipline and defense of the pound sterling's $2.80 exchange rate.

The British Labour government resorted to the Keynesian playbook, instead, and resolutely refused to permit the Bank of England to raise the discount rate, even though interest rates were deeply negative in real terms. Like today's financially profligate governments, it thus attempted to borrow its way through the crisis, tapping its currency swap lines with the Fed and other European central banks for billions.

The swap lines were no financial bazooka. Despite frantic currency market intervention, the Bank of England could not buy pounds sterling fast enough to absorb the waves of selling by speculators who could see that the Labour government was borrowing its way to financial disaster.

The final match was thrown on this monetary kindling pile on November 14, 1967, when the British government announced that the October trade deficit had been its largest in history. This merely reinforced the obvious truth that the fundamentals of the UK economy were deteriorating rapidly, and that the government's fevered swap-line borrowing and currency support operations were doomed to fail. Four days later the pound was devalued by 14 percent, and the world was well on its way to Nixon's repudiation of Bretton Woods at Camp David.

THE FINAL ASSAULT ON THE LONDON GOLD MARKET: HOW THE NEW ECONOMICS WAS ROUTED

In fact, the pound devaluation was announced on a Saturday, November 17. According to Coombs, by Monday morning "a tidal wave of speculation now swept through the London gold market."

Although the gold pool had been increased to $350 million, this proved to be a trifling sum as the raw power of the free market in gold quickly made itself evident. Indeed, the attack on inflationary economic policies and financial indiscipline now moved swiftly to the dollar. On Monday, November 19th, the pool was forced to sell $27 million of gold to meet free market demand at the $35 parity, which then soared to $106 million on Wednesday and $250 million on Friday.

Altogether, the central bankers' gold pool had been drained of nearly $600 million during the week after the pound devaluation and had to be hastily replenished by its members. In fact, the Treasury had to enlist a military transport to airlift American gold to London!

In the final weeks of 1967, then, the ancient financial discipline inherent in gold-convertible money brought itself to bear on the Johnson White House. LBJ's "guns and butter" fiscal policy and blatant efforts to intimidate the Fed into money printing were being given the Bronx cheer. Private traders and speculators still had the right to demand honest money when they feared the government's paper issue was being debased, and they exercised it lustily.

A new run on gold ensued in December, draining the central bankers' gold pool by another $400 million in just three days. At that point the White House partially capitulated, with Johnson announcing he would seek a 10 percent surtax and take other measures to balance the budget—measures that he had been deferring for months.

Just as under the ancien régime, the gold market was now handing the greatest politician of his generation the needed excuse to ask the legislature for tax increases and spending cuts. The administration also announced a clumsy set of bureaucratic measures to stem the outflow of US dollars, including mandatory controls on direct investment abroad, repatriation of foreign earnings, and, pathetically, an admonition to American citizens to postpone for two years all nonessential foreign travel.

Yet the root problem was excess dollar liabilities. During 1967 alone, the nation's central bank had increased its holdings of Treasury debt by 12 percent, and it had expanded its government debt purchases and bank reserve creation by 21 percent over the preceding twenty-four months. The associated flood of new dollar liabilities had no home, but LBJ refused to do the one thing that mattered most; namely, he did not ask the Fed to stop creating so many unwanted dollars by raising interest rates sharply and reversing the prodigious pace of money creation it had undertaken at the White House's behest.

Within a matter of weeks, therefore, the run on gold resumed, this time with even more ferocious intensity. And it was in the face of the free gold market's clarion call for financial discipline that Johnson's Keynesian economic advisors laid the planking for Tricky Dick's subsequent commission of the actual dirty deed.

After gold began hemorrhaging out of the London pool at $100 million per day on March 8, the Council of Economic Advisors chairman, Gardner

Ackley, urged Johnson to close the gold window—and strand the Europeans high and dry with their vast dollar reserves—if they did not accept his proposal to sell their gold on an uncovered basis to defend America's beleaguered currency. The implication was no less menacing than the British Treasury's treachery of September 1931. Europeans would now be forced to take huge losses on the massive dollar-exchange holdings that they had accumulated over the years on the presumption that the dollar was as good as gold.

To be sure, it took an even ruder Texan than Lyndon Johnson to tell the Europeans that the dollar was our currency, but their problem, as John Connally put it so famously three years later. Yet the remarkable fact remains that none of Johnson's Keynesian advisors betrayed any recognition that it was their inflationary policies which had precipitated the crisis.

As the end of the road neared, the smugly self-assured professoriate had no solution except to put goofy controls on the offshore activities of American citizens. Their position had been reduced to the embarrassingly trivial point that the commission of private acts of capitalism abroad by American tourists and businessmen was the cause of the market's thundering stampede out of paper dollars and into gold.

In the nick of time, a thin majority of the Senate approved an emergency measure repealing the vestigial requirement that Federal Reserve notes be backed with a gold cover of 25 percent. This meant that the Treasury now had access to nearly the full $12 billion of gold stocks reported at the end of 1967 to meet its obligations under Bretton Woods and defend the $35 parity.

Then and there, Washington had one last opportunity to take a stand for sound money. By politically leveraging the nation's humiliating loss of gold in order to drive tax increases and spending cuts through the Congress, and by empowering the Fed to bring the hammer down on inflation, which was then running at a 5 percent annualized rate, the run on gold could have been stopped. The framework of Bretton Woods could have been saved.

Clearly the Europeans, especially the Germans, Swiss, and Dutch, were more than ready to cooperate with any reasonable and decisive effort by the United States to get its financial house in order. But when the gold outflow hit $400 million on March 14, Johnson threw in the towel and shut down the gold pool.

LBJ also proclaimed that the United States would defend the $35 gold price come what may, but that promise was entirely hollow. Henceforth, the only gold which would trade at $35 per ounce was between central banks, when and as Washington pleased.

So-called enlightened economic opinion at the time considered the gold pool closure to be a matter of secondary moment. Already grand plans were under way to create a new form of IMF fiat money called special drawing rights, or SDRs. Yet IMF money, as logic would have suggested then and history would prove later, was inherently even more suspect than the politically compromised greenbacks which were being so unceremoniously dumped in favor of the barbarous relic.

Unfortunately, the Keynesian consensus claimed more science than it actually possessed. The problem at hand was not a shortage of reserve assets in the global monetary system, as the professors argued. To the contrary, it was a shortage of financial discipline in the nation which had insisted that its own currency become the reserve asset in the new monetary system fashioned at Bretton Woods.

Once the link between the dollar and London's free market in gold was severed in March 1968, it was game over. The possibility that US financial discipline would ever again be revived was fatally diminished.

THE CRUSH OF EMPIRE AND THE ROAD TO CAMP DAVID

At the heart of the US financial profligacy was an unwillingness to pay for the huge and largely unacknowledged cost of empire. By the end of 1968, the outflow of funds to support the nation's far-flung military enterprises, the hot war in Southeast Asia, and the growing network of security assistance and foreign aid had accumulated to $70 billion since the start of the 1960s. It would reach nearly $100 billion by the time Nixon closed the gold window at the US Treasury.

By the lights of General Eisenhower, of course, this vast level of expenditure was not necessary to protect the national security, and most especially not that portion of it driven by the occupation of Vietnam. Still, as the free world's hegemonic power and bulwark against those Kremlin factions which harbored aggressive intentions, the United States could have certainly afforded to invest a few percentage points of GDP in the cause of a stable, peaceful, and more prosperous global order.

Yet what it could not do was fund a global empire on borrowed money. To be sure, spending abroad for military bases and economic aid did not automatically cause a balance of payments deficit, any more than did importing anchovies from the Peruvian fisheries or coffee from the Brazilian plantations. What did cause a payments deficit, however, was electing to incur these national security expenditures without earning a sufficient surplus in trade and services to offset the dollar outflow.

As Great Britain had shown in the nineteenth century, an imperial power needed to earn a consistent current account surplus to fund its overseas enterprises, including both investments of private capital and the military projects of the state. That the United States could not operate a financially stable empire in the mid-twentieth century was therefore a tribute to muddled policy, not the inherent economics of venturing beyond its coastlines.

In 1964, the United States had a $9 billion current account surplus excluding defense spending. But this figure declined to $4.5 billion by 1968 and rolled over into nearly a $1 billion deficit by 1972.

At the same time, the drain of dollars to support the nation's imperial footprint, including the land war in Asia and economic aid to vassals and puppets, escalated sharply, rising from just over $6 billion in 1964 to $12 billion eight years later. Due to this rapidly widening gap between diminishing civilian inflows and expanding national security outflows, of course, unwanted dollars piled up abroad at an accelerating rate.

Since Washington was unwilling to implement a sharp retrenchment of the overheated domestic economy in order to pay for the cost of empire, its monetary reserves had steadily ebbed away, notwithstanding the valiant temporizing actions of the Kennedy Treasury. Thus, the nation's gold stock, which had peaked at about $22 billion in 1959, had fallen to below $10 billion by the time of the March 1968 crisis.

Worse still, short-term dollar liabilities held by foreign central banks continued rising and now totaled nearly $20 billion. This meant that the Bretton Woods "reserve currency" issuer had now drastically overdrawn its bank account and, like Great Britain in 1931, it did not have nearly enough gold to support the dollar debts it owed to foreigners.

So in March 1968, having declared himself a lame duck in the face of withering domestic blowback against his Vietnam War adventure, the rudderless Johnson triggered the final run on the dollar by closing the London gold pool. This move predictably fueled rampant speculation against the dollar and caused unwanted private dollar holdings to be cashed in for marks and francs, instead of gold, at the principal foreign central banks. As these dumped dollars rapidly and visibly piled up on the counters at the central banks, the pressure to "short" the dollar only intensified.

THE CORRELATES OF EMPIRE: SOUND FINANCES AT HOME

The necessary correlates of empire abroad, in fact, were budget surpluses and fastidiously sound monetary policy at home. If it wished to quarantine the Soviet tank brigades deep in the interior of Eurasia and furnish the backward peoples of the globe with trousers, ballot boxes, and Coca-Cola, the United States could not afford to inflate its domestic demand and its bill for imported goods with cheap and easy credit.

Yet between 1965 and 1968, when the US expeditionary force in Vietnam rose from 17,000 to 515,000, domestic bank credit grew at a robust 8.1 percent annualized rate. That was the opposite of what sound national finances called for under these circumstances.

When Lyndon Johnson threw in the towel on the gold dollar and on his own political career, it marked a historic juncture in the evolution of crony capitalism. LBJ was the legatee of Roosevelt's hayseed coalition and New Deal statism, having arrived on the scene three decades earlier as a congressman from the south Texas hill country championing the cause of government-supplied rural electric power.

By the end of his presidency LBJ had vastly updated the New Deal, bringing its random form of statism to urban America through programs such as model cities, subsidized housing, the Job Corps, and mass transit aid while completing the loop on social insurance with the enactment of Medicare. Indeed, the Great Society was the "new" New Deal, reconstituted to reflect the migration of the Democratic political base to the north and to the cities.

On its own, this Great Society expansion of the state would not have been fiscally fatal, even if it was wasteful, inequitable, and ineffective. The breakdown came in LBJ's megalomaniacal attempt to extend the Great Society to the Mekong Valley.

In this historically catastrophic venture, he expanded the warfare state by 40 percent from the Eisenhower Minimum, thereby squandering the $150 billion in constant-dollar fiscal headroom that Ike had recaptured. The result was "guns and butter" budgets, deficit-financed elective wars, and the abduction of the nation's central bank into inflationary finance of the state's fiscal excesses.

The riots in the London free market for gold in late 1967 and early 1968 were a cogent warning that financial indiscipline was reaching the breaking point, and that sound money was imperiled. It was also a historic milestone, signifying that the two decades of soldiering in the cause of fiscal and monetary orthodoxy by Harry Truman, President Eisenhower, William McChesney Martin, and even John F. Kennedy's Treasury Department had been for naught.

So the final mile on the road to the Camp David default was embarked upon in March 1968. The so-called two-tier gold market which emerged from the crisis in the London market was destined to be short-lived because the dollar was no longer convertible on the demands of the citizenry, but only at the pleasure and convenience of the state.

As has been seen, Richard Nixon soon found that meeting the nation's obligation to pay its debts in gold and to uphold the Bretton Woods system were distinctly inconvenient to his own reason of state: reelection in 1972.

Moreover, he had found a polyglot of economic advisors who persuaded him to discard the essence of the old-time Republican financial doctrine: the rule of balanced budgets and the gold standard of sound money. Accordingly, both parties would now embrace the prosperity management model, turning fiscal policy into a hapless stepchild of the jobs count and the GDP measurements, and giving a public policy rationalization to endless raids on the Treasury by special interest groups and crony capitalists.

Worse still, severing the link to gold paved the way for the T-bill standard and a vast multi-decade spree of central bank debt monetization and money printing. Since a régime of floating-rate paper money had never been tried before on a global basis, the Keynesian professors and their Friedmanite collaborators can perhaps be excused for not foreseeing its destructive consequence.

The record of the next several decades, however, eliminated all doubt. The combination of free markets and freely printed money gave rise to a toxic financial deformation; namely, the vast financialization of the world economy and the rise of endless carry trades, massive arrangements of speculative hedging, and monumental daisy chains of debts, owned by debts, owned by still more debts.

CHAPTER 13

MILTON FRIEDMAN'S FOLLY
Rise of the T-Bill Standard

T HE STAGE WAS THUS SET FOR THE FINAL "RUN" ON THE DOLLAR and for a spectacular default by the designated "reserve currency" provider under the gold exchange standard's second outing. And as it happened, the American people saw fit to install in the White House in January 1969 just the man to crush what remained of gold-based money and the financial discipline that it enabled.

Richard M. Nixon, as we know, possessed numerous and notable flaws. Foremost was his capacity to carry a grudge against anyone whom he believed had caused him to lose an election, especially any economist, policy maker, or bystander who could be pinned with accountability for the mild 1960 recession that he believed responsible for his loss to John F. Kennedy.

Nixon's vendetta on the matter of the 1960 election literally knew no limits. For example, he insisted that a midlevel career bureaucrat named Jack Goldstein, who headed the Bureau of Labor Statistics (BLS), had deliberately spun the monthly unemployment report issued on the eve of the 1960 election so as to damage his campaign. Eight years later, Nixon informed the White House staff that job one was to determine if Goldstein was still at the BLS, and to get him fired if he was.

It is not surprising, therefore, that Nixon rolled into the Oval Office obsessed with replacing Chairman Martin and bringing the Fed to heel. To be sure, his only real interest in monetary policy consisted of ensuring that the one great threat to Republican success, a rising unemployment rate, did not happen in the vicinity of an election.

Yet it was that very cynicism which made him prey to Milton Friedman's alluring doctrine of floating paper money. As has been seen, Nixon wanted absolute freedom to cause the domestic economy to boom during his 1972 reelection campaign. Friedman's disciples at Camp David served up exactly that gift, and wrapped it in the monetary doctrine of the nation's leading conservative intellectual.

FRIEDMAN'S RULE OF FIXED MONEY SUPPLY GROWTH WAS ACADEMIC POPPYCOCK

Those adhering to traditional monetary doctrine always and properly feared the inflationary threat of state-issued fiat money. So when the CPI reached the unheard of peacetime level of 6.3 percent by January 1969, it was a warning that the tottering structure of Bretton Woods was reaching a dangerous turning point and that the monetary foundation of the postwar world was in peril.

But not according to Professor Milton Friedman. As was typical of the Chicago school conservatives, he simply brushed off the gathering inflationary crisis as the product of dimwits at the Fed. Martin's "mistake" in succumbing to pressure to open up the monetary spigot to fund LBJ's deficits, Friedman insisted, could be easily fixed. Literally, with the flick of a switch.

According to Professor Friedman's vast archive of historic data, inflation would be rapidly extinguished if money supply was harnessed to a fixed and unwavering rate of growth, such as 3 percent per annum. If that discipline was adhered to consistently, nothing more was needed to unleash capitalist prosperity—not gold convertibility, fixed exchange rates, currency swap lines, or any of the other accoutrements of central banking which had grown up around the Bretton Woods system.

Indeed, once the central bank got the money supply growth rate into a fixed and reliable groove, the free market would take care of everything else, including determination of the correct exchange rate between the dollar and every other currency on the planet. Under Friedman's monetary deus ex machina, for example, the unseen hand would silently and efficiently mete out rewards for success and punishments for failure in the banking and securities markets. The need for clumsy and inefficient regulation of financial institutions would be eliminated.

Friedman's "fixed rule" monetary theory was fundamentally flawed, however, for reasons Martin had long ago discovered down in the trenches of the financial markets. The killer was that the Federal Reserve couldn't control Friedman's single variable, which is to say, the "money supply" as measured by the sum of demand deposits and currency (M1).

During nearly two decades at the helm, Martin learned that the only thing the Fed could roughly gauge was the level of bank reserves in the system. Beyond that there simply weren't any fixed arithmetic ratios, starting with the "money multiplier."

The latter measured the ratio between bank reserves, which are potential money, and bank deposits, which are actual money. As previously indicated, however, commercial banks don't create actual money (checking account deposits) directly; they make loans and then credit the proceeds to customer accounts. So the transmission process between bank reserves and money supply wends through bank lending departments and the credit creation process.

Needless to say, the Fed couldn't control the animal spirits of either lenders or borrowers; that was the job of free market interest rates. Accordingly, banks would utilize their reserves aggressively during periods of robust loan demand until borrower exuberance was choked off by high interest rates. By contrast, bank reserves would lie fallow during times of slumping loan demand and low free market rates. The "money multiplier" therefore varied enormously, depending upon economic and financial conditions.

Furthermore, even if the resulting "money supply" could be accurately measured and controlled, which was not the case, it did not have a fixed "velocity" or relationship to economic activity or GDP, either. In fact, during deflationary times of weak credit expansion, velocity tended to fall, meaning less new GDP for each new dollar of M1. On the other hand, during inflationary times of rapid bank credit expansion it would tend to rise, resulting in higher GDP gains per dollar of M1 growth.

So the chain of causation was long and opaque. The linkages from open market operations (adding to bank reserves) to commercial bank credit creation (adding to the money supply) to credit-fueled additional spending (adding to GDP) resembled nothing so much as the loose steering gear on an old jalopy: turning the steering wheel did not necessarily mean the ditch would be avoided.

Most certainly there was no possible reason to believe that M1 could be managed to an unerring 3 percent growth rate, and that, in any event, keeping M1 growth on the straight and narrow would lead to any predictable rate of economic activity or mix of real growth and inflation. In short, Friedman's single variable–fixed money supply growth rule was basically academic poppycock.

The monetarists, of course, had a ready answer to all of these disabilities; namely, that there were "leads and lags" in the transmission of monetary policy, and that given sufficient time the money multipliers and velocity would regress to a standard rate. Yet that "sufficient time" caveat had two insurmountable flaws: it meant that Friedman's fixed rule could not be implemented in the real day-to-day world of fast-moving financial markets; and more importantly, it betrayed the deep, hopeless political naïveté of the monetarists and Professor Friedman especially.

THE MONETARIST CONE:
SILLY PUTTY ON THE WHITE HOUSE GRAPHS

As to practicality, I had a real-time encounter with it during the Reagan years when the Treasury's monetary policy post was held by a religious disciple of Friedman: Beryl Sprinkel. Week after week at White House economic briefings he presented a graph based on the patented "monetarist cone." The graph consisted of two upward-sloping dotted lines from a common starting date which showed where the money supply would be if it had been growing at an upper boundary of, say, 4 percent and a lower boundary of, say, 2 percent.

The implication was that if the Fed were following Professor Friedman's rule, the path of the actual money supply would fall snugly inside the "cone" as it extended out over months and quarters, thereby indicating that all was well on the monetary front, the only thing which mattered. Except the solid line on the graph tracking the actual week-to-week growth of money supply gyrated wildly and was almost always outside the cone, sometimes on the high side and other times on the low.

In other words, the greatest central banker of modern times, Paul Volcker, was flunking the monetarists' test week after week, causing Sprinkel to engage in alternating bouts of table pounding because the Fed was either dangerously too tight or too loose. Fortunately, Sprinkel's graphs didn't lead to much: President Reagan would look puzzled, Jim Baker, the chief of staff, would yawn, and domestic policy advisor Ed Meese would suggest moving on to the next topic.

More importantly, Volcker could easily explain the manifold complexities and anomalies in the short-term movement of the reported money supply numbers, and that on an "adjusted" basis he was actually inside the cone. Besides that, credit growth was slowing sharply, from a rate of 12 percent in 1979 to 7 percent in 1981 and 3 percent in 1982. That caused the economy to temporarily buckle and inflation to plunge from double digits to under 4 percent in less than twenty-four months. Volcker was getting the job done, in compliance with the monetarist cone or not.

In fact, the monetarist cone was just a Silly Putty numbers exercise, representing annualized rates of change from an arbitrary starting date that kept getting reset owing to one alleged anomaly or another. The far more relevant imperative was to slow the perilous expansion of the Fed's balance sheet. It had doubled from $60 billion to $125 billion in the nine years before Volcker's arrival at the Eccles Building, thereby saturating the banking system with newly minted reserves and the wherewithal for inflationary credit growth.

Volcker accomplished this true anti-inflation objective with alacrity. By curtailing the Fed's balance sheet growth rate to less than 5 percent by 1982, Volcker convinced the markets that the Fed would not continue to passively validate inflation, as Burns and Miller had done, and that speculating on rising prices was no longer a one-way bet. Volcker thus cracked the inflation spiral through a display of central bank resolve, not through a single-variable focus on a rubbery monetary statistic called M1.

Volcker also demonstrated that the short-run growth rate of M1 was largely irrelevant and impossible to manage, but that the Fed could nevertheless contain the inflationary furies by tough-minded discipline of its own balance sheet. Yet that very success went straight to an even more fatal flaw in the monetarist fixed money growth rule: Friedman never explained how the Fed, once liberated from the external discipline of the Bretton Woods gold standard, would be continuously populated with iron-willed statesmen like Volcker, and how they would even remain in office when push came to shove like it did during the monetary crunch of 1982.

In fact, Volcker's reappointment the next year was a close call because most of the White House staff and the Senate Republican leadership wanted to take him down, owing to the considerable political inconvenience of the recessionary trauma his policies had induced. Senate leader Howard Baker, for example, angrily demanded that Volcker "get his foot off the neck of American business now."

Volcker survived only because of Ronald Reagan's stubborn (and correct) belief that the Fed's long bout of profligacy had caused inflation and that only a period of painful monetary parsimony could cure it. The next several decades would prove decisively, however, that the process of American governance produces few Reagans and even fewer Volckers.

So Friedman unleashed the demon of floating-rate money based on the naïve view that the inhabitants of the Eccles Building could and would follow his monetary rules. That was a surprising posture because Friedman's splendid scholarship on the free market, going all the way back to his pioneering critique of New York City rent controls in the late 1940s, was infused with an abiding skepticism of politicians and all of their mischievous works.

Yet by unshackling the Fed from the constraints of fixed exchange rates and the redemption of dollar liabilities for gold, Friedman's monetary doctrine actually handed politicians a stupendous new prize. It rendered trivial by comparison the ills owing to garden variety insults to the free market, such as rent control or the regulation of interstate trucking.

IMPLICIT RULE BY MONETARY EUNUCHS

The Friedman monetary theory actually placed the nation's stock of bank reserves, money, and credit under the unfettered sway of what amounted to a twelve-member monetary politburo. Once relieved of the gold standard's external discipline, the central banking branch of the state thus had unlimited scope to extend its mission to plenary management of the nation's entire GDP and for deep, persistent, and ultimately suffocating intervention in the money and capital markets.

It goes without saying, of course, that the libertarian professor was not peddling a statist scheme. So the implication was that the Fed would be run by self-abnegating monetary eunuchs who would never be tempted to deviate from the fixed money growth rule or by any other manifestation of mission creep. Needless to say, Friedman never sought a franchise to train and appoint such governors, nor did he propose any significant reforms with respect to the Fed's selection process or of the manner in which its normal operations were conducted.

This glaring omission, however, is what made Friedman's monetarism all the more dangerous. His monetary opus, *A Monetary History of the United States*, was published only four years before his disciples, led by George Shultz, filled the ranks of the Nixon White House in 1969.

Possessed with the zeal of recent converts, they soon caused a real-world experiment in Friedman's grand theory. In so doing, they were also implicitly betting on an improbable proposition: that monetarism would work because the run-of-the-mill political appointees—bankers, economists, businessmen, and ex-politicians who then sat on the Federal Open Market Committee (FOMC), along with their successors—would be forever smitten with the logic of 3 percent annual money supply growth.

FRIEDMAN'S GREAT GIFT TO WALL STREET

The very idea that the FOMC would function as faithful monetary eunuchs, keeping their eyes on the M1 gauge and deftly adjusting the dial in either direction upon any deviation from the 3 percent target, was sheer fantasy. And not only because of its political naïveté, something Nixon's brutalization of the hapless Arthur Burns aptly conveyed.

Friedman's austere, rule-bound version of discretionary central banking also completely ignored the Fed's susceptibility to capture by the Wall Street bond dealers and the vast network of member banks, large and small, which maintained their cash reserves on deposit there. Yet once the Fed no longer had to worry about protecting the dollar's foreign exchange value and the US gold reserve, it had a much wider scope to pursue financial repression policies, such as low interest rates and a steep yield curve, that inherently fuel Wall Street prosperity.

As it happened, the Fed's drift into these Wall Street–pleasing policies was temporarily stalled by Volcker's epic campaign against the Great Inflation. Dousing inflation the hard way, through brutal tightening of money market conditions, Volcker had produced the singular nightmare that Wall Street and the banking system loathe; namely, a violent and unprecedented inversion of the yield curve.

With short-term interest rates at 20 percent or more and way above long-term bond yields (12–15 percent), it meant that speculators and banks could not make money on the carry trade and that the value of dealer stock and bond inventories got clobbered: high and rising interest rates mean low and falling financial asset values. Accordingly, the Volcker Fed did not even dream of levitating the economy through the "wealth effects" or by coddling Wall Street speculators.

Yet once Volcker scored an initial success and was unceremoniously dumped by the Baker Treasury Department (in 1987), the anti-inflation brief passed on to a more congenial mechanism; that is, Mr. Deng's industrial army and the "China price" deflation that rolled across the US economy in the 1990s and after. With inflation-fighting stringency no longer having such immediate urgency, it did not take long for the Greenspan Fed to adopt a prosperity promotion agenda.

First, however, it had to rid itself of any vestigial restraints owing to the Friedman fixed money growth rule. The latter was dispatched easily by a regulatory change in the early 1990s which allowed banks to offer "sweep" accounts; that is, checking accounts by day which turned into savings accounts overnight. Accordingly, Professor Friedman's M1 could no longer be measured accurately.

Out of sight was apparently out of mind: for the last two decades, the central bank that Friedman caused to be liberated from the alleged tyranny of Bretton Woods so that it could swear an oath of fixed money supply growth has not even bothered to review or mention money supply. Indeed, the Greenspan and Bernanke Fed have been wholly preoccupied with manipulation of the price of money, that is, interest rates, and have relegated Friedman's entire quantity theory of money to the dustbin of history. And Bernanke claims to have been a disciple!

Constrained neither by gold nor a fixed money growth rule, the Fed in due course declared itself to be the open market committee for the management and planning of the nation's entire GDP. In this Brobdingnagian endeavor, of course, the Wall Street bond dealers were the vital transmission belt which brought credit-fueled prosperity to Main Street and delivered the elixir of asset inflation to the speculative classes. Consequently, when it came to Wall Street, the Fed became solicitous at first, and craven in the end.

Apologists might claim that Milton Friedman could not have foreseen that the great experiment in discretionary central banking unleashed by his disciples in the Nixon White House would result in the abject capitulation to Wall Street which emerged during the Greenspan era and became a noxious, unyielding reality under Bernanke. But financial statesmen of an earlier era had embraced the gold standard for good reason: it was the ultimate bulwark against the pretensions and follies of central bankers.

WHEN PROFESSOR FRIEDMAN OPENED PANDORA'S BOX: OPEN MARKET OPERATIONS

At the end of the day, Friedman jettisoned the gold standard for a remarkable statist reason. Just as Keynes had been, he was afflicted with the economist's ambition to prescribe the route to higher national income and prosperity and the intervention tools and recipes that would deliver it. The only difference was that Keynes was originally and primarily a fiscalist, whereas Friedman had seized upon open market operations by the central bank as the route to optimum aggregate demand and national income.

There were massive and multiple ironies in that stance. It put the central bank in the proactive and morally sanctioned business of buying the government's debt in the conduct of its open market operations. Friedman said, of course, that the FOMC should buy bonds and bills at a rate no greater than 3 percent per annum, but that limit was a thin reed.

Indeed, it cannot be gainsaid that it was Professor Friedman, the scourge of Big Government, who showed the way for Republican central bankers to foster that very thing. Under their auspices, the Fed was soon gorging on the Treasury's debt emissions, thereby alleviating the inconvenience of funding more government with more taxes.

Friedman also said democracy would thrive better under a régime of free markets, and he was entirely correct. Yet his preferred tool of prosperity promotion, Fed management of the money supply, was far more anti-democratic than Keynes's methods. Fiscal policy activism was at least subject to the deliberations of the legislature and, in some vague sense, electoral review by the citizenry.

By contrast, the twelve-member FOMC is about as close to an unelected politburo as is obtainable under American governance. When in the fullness of time, the FOMC lined up squarely on the side of debtors, real estate owners, and leveraged financial speculators—and against savers, wage earners, and equity financed businessmen—the latter had no recourse from its policy actions.

The greatest untoward consequence of the closet statism implicit in Friedman's monetary theories, however, is that it put him squarely in opposition to the vision of the Fed's founders. As has been seen, Carter Glass and Professor Willis assigned to the Federal Reserve System the humble mission of passively liquefying the good collateral of commercial banks when they presented it.

Consequently, the difference between a "banker's bank" running a discount window service and a central bank engaged in continuous open market operations was fundamental and monumental, not merely a question of technique. By facilitating a better alignment of liquidity between the asset and liability side of the balance sheets of fractional reserve deposit banks, the original "reserve banks" of the 1913 act would, arguably, improve banking efficiency, stability, and utilization of systemwide reserves.

Yet any impact of these discount window operations on the systemwide banking aggregates of money and credit, especially if the borrowing rate were properly set at a penalty spread above the free market interest rate, would have been purely incidental and derivative, not an object of policy. Obviously, such a discount window–based system could have no pretensions at all as to managing the macroeconomic aggregates such as production, spending, and employment.

In short, under the original discount window model, national employment, production prices, and GDP were a bottoms-up outcome on the free market, not an artifact of state policy. By contrast, open market operations inherently lead to national economic planning and targeting of GDP and other macroeconomic aggregates. The truth is, there is no other reason to control M1 than to steer demand, production, and employment from Washington.

Why did the libertarian professor, who was so hostile to all of the projects and works of government, wish to empower what even he could have recognized as an incipient monetary politburo with such vast powers to plan and manage the national economy, even if by means of the remote and seemingly unobtrusive steering gear of M1? There is but one answer: Friedman thoroughly misunderstood the Great Depression and concluded erroneously that undue regard for the gold standard rules by the Fed during 1929–1933 had resulted in its failure to conduct aggressive open market purchases of government debt, and hence to prevent the deep slide of M1 during the forty-five months after the crash.

Yet the historical evidence is unambiguous; there was no liquidity shortage and no failure by the Fed to do its job as a banker's bank. Indeed, the six thousand member banks of the Federal Reserve System did not make heavy use of the discount window during this period and none who presented good collateral were denied access to borrowed reserves. Consequently, commercial banks were not constrained at all in their ability to make loans or generate demand deposits (M1).

But from the lofty perch of his library at the University of Chicago three decades later, Professor Friedman determined that the banking system should have been flooded with new reserves, anyway. And this post facto academician's edict went straight to the heart of the open market operations issue.

The discount window was the mechanism by which real world bankers voluntarily drew new reserves into the system in order to accommodate an expansion of loans and deposits. By contrast, open market bond purchases were the mechanism by which the incipient central planners at the Fed forced reserves into the banking system, whether sought by member banks or not.

Friedman thus sided with the central planners, contending that the market of the day was wrong and that thousands of banks that already had excess reserves should have been doused with more and still more reserves, until they started lending and creating deposits in accordance with the dictates of the monetarist gospel. Needless to say, the historic data show this proposition to be essentially farcical, and that the real-world exercise in exactly this kind of bank reserve flooding maneuver conducted by the Bernanke Fed forty years later has been a total failure—a monumental case of "pushing on a string."

FRIEDMAN'S ERRONEOUS CRITIQUE OF THE DEPRESSION-ERA FED OPENED THE DOOR TO MONETARY CENTRAL PLANNING

The historical truth is that the Fed's core mission of that era, to rediscount bank loan paper, had been carried out consistently, effectively, and fully by the twelve Federal Reserve banks during the crucial forty-five months between the October 1929 stock market crash and FDR's inauguration in March 1933. And the documented lack of member bank demand for discount window borrowings was not because the Fed had charged a punishingly high interest rate. In fact, the Fed's discount rate had been progressively lowered from 6 percent before the crash to 2.5 percent by early 1933.

More crucially, the "excess reserves" in the banking system grew dramatically during this forty-five-month period, implying just the opposite of monetary stringency. Prior to the stock market crash in September 1929, excess reserves in the banking system stood at $35 million, but then rose to $100 million by January 1931 and ultimately to $525 million by January 1933.

In short, the tenfold expansion of excess (i.e., idle) reserves in the banking system was dramatic proof that the banking system had not been parched for liquidity but was actually awash in it. The only mission the Fed failed to perform is one that Professor Friedman assigned to it thirty years after the fact; that is, to maintain an arbitrary level of M1 by forcing reserves into the banking system by means of open market purchases of Uncle Sam's debt.

As it happened, the money supply (M1) did drop by about 23 percent during the same forty-five-month period in which excess reserves soared tenfold. As a technical matter, this meant that the money multiplier had crashed. As has been seen, however, the big drop in checking account deposits (the bulk of M1) did not represent a squeeze on money. It was merely the arithmetic result of the nearly 50 percent shrinkage of the commercial loan book during that period.

As previously detailed, this extensive liquidation of bad debt was an unavoidable and healthy correction of the previous debt bubble. Bank loans outstanding, in fact, had grown at manic rates during the previous fifteen years, nearly tripling from $14 billion to $42 billion. As in most credit-fueled booms, the vast expansion of lending during the Great War and the Roaring Twenties left banks stuffed with bad loans that could no longer be rolled over when the music stopped in October 1929.

Consequently, during the aftermath of the crash upward of $20 billion of bank loans were liquidated, including billions of write-offs due to business failures and foreclosures. As previously explained, nearly half of the loan contraction was attributable to the $9 billion of stock market margin loans which were called in when the stock market bubble collapsed in 1929.

Likewise, loan balances for working capital borrowings also fell sharply in the face of falling production. Again, this was the passive consequence of the bursting industrial and export sector bubble, not something caused by the Fed's failure to supply sufficient bank reserves. In short, the liquidation of bank loans was almost exclusively the result of bubbles being punctured in the real economy, not stinginess at the central bank.

In fact, there has never been any wide-scale evidence that bank loans outstanding declined during 1930–1933 on account of banks calling performing loans or denying credit to solvent potential borrowers. Yet unless those things happened, there is simply no case that monetary stringency caused the Great Depression.

Friedman and his followers, including Bernanke, came up with an academic canard to explain away these obvious facts. Since the wholesale price level had fallen sharply during the forty-five months after the crash, they claimed that "real" interest rates were inordinately high after adjusting for deflation.

Yet this is academic pettifoggery. Real-world businessmen confronted with plummeting order books would have eschewed new borrowing for the obvious reason that they had no need for funds, not because they deemed the "deflation-adjusted" interest rate too high.

At the end of the day, Friedman's monetary treatise offers no evidence whatsoever and simply asserts false causation; namely, that the passive decline of the money supply was the active cause of the drop in output and spending. The true causation went the other way: the nation's stock of money fell sharply during the post-crash period because bank loans are the mother's milk of bank deposits. So, as bloated loan books were cut down to sustainable size, the stock of deposit money (M1) fell on a parallel basis.

Given this credit collapse and the associated crash of the money multiplier, there was only one way for the Fed to even attempt to reflate the money supply. It would have been required to purchase and monetize nearly every single dime of the $16 billion of US Treasury debt then outstanding.

Today's incorrigible money printers undoubtedly would say, "No problem." Yet there is no doubt whatsoever that, given the universal antipathy to monetary inflation at the time, such a move would have triggered sheer panic and bedlam in what remained of the financial markets. Needless to say, Friedman never explained how the Fed was supposed to reignite the drooping money multiplier or, failing that, explain to the financial markets why it was buying up all of the public debt.

Beyond that, Friedman could not prove at the time of his writing *A Monetary History of the United States* in 1965 that the creation out of thin air of a huge new quantity of bank reserves would have caused the banking system to convert such reserves into an upwelling of new loans and deposits. Indeed, Friedman did not attempt to prove that proposition, either. According to the quantity theory of money, it was an a priori truth.

In actual fact, by the bottom of the depression in 1932, interest rates proved the opposite. Rates on T-bills and commercial paper were one-half percent and 1 percent, respectively, meaning that there was virtually no unsatisfied loan demand from credit-worthy borrowers. The dwindling business at the discount windows of the twelve Federal Reserve banks further proved the point. In September 1929 member banks borrowed nearly $1 billion at the discount windows, but by January 1933 this declined to only $280 million. In sum, banks were not lending because they were short of reserves; they weren't lending because they were short of solvent bor-rowers and real credit demand.

In any event, Friedman's entire theory of the Great Depression was thor-oughly demolished by Ben S. Bernanke, his most famous disciple, in a real-world experiment after September 2008. The Bernanke Fed undertook massive open market operations in response to the financial crisis, pur-chasing and monetizing more than $2 trillion of treasury and agency debt.

As is by now transparently evident, the result was a monumental wheel-spinning exercise. The fact that there is now $1.7 trillion of "excess re-serves" parked at the Fed (compared to a mere $40 billion before the crisis) meant that nearly all of the new bank reserves resulting from the Fed's bond-buying sprees have been stillborn.

By staying on deposit at the central bank, they have fueled no growth at all of Main Street bank loans or money supply. There is no reason whatso-ever, therefore, to believe that the outcome would have been any different in 1930–1932.

MILTON FRIEDMAN: FRESHWATER KEYNESIAN AND THE LIBERTARIAN PROFESSOR WHO FATHERED BIG GOVERNMENT

The great irony, then, is that the nation's most famous modern conserva-tive economist became the father of Big Government, chronic deficits, and national fiscal bankruptcy. It was Friedman who first urged the removal of the Bretton Woods gold standard restraints on central bank money print-ing, and then added insult to injury by giving conservative sanction to per-petual open market purchases of government debt by the Fed. Friedman's monetarism thereby institutionalized a régime which allowed politicians to chronically spend without taxing.

Likewise, it was the free market professor of the Chicago school who also blessed the fundamental Keynesian proposition that Washington must continuously manage and stimulate the national economy. To be sure, Friedman's "freshwater" proposition, in Paul Krugman's famous paradigm, was far more modest than the vast "fine-tuning" pretensions of his "salt-water" rivals. The saltwater Keynesians of the 1960s proposed to stimulate the economy until the last billion dollars of potential GDP was realized; that is, they would achieve prosperity by causing the state to do anything that was needed through a multiplicity of fiscal interventions.

By contrast, the freshwater Keynesian, Milton Friedman, thought that capitalism could take care of itself as long as it had precisely the right quantity of money at all times; that is, Friedman would attain prosperity by causing the state to do the one thing that was needed through the single spigot of M1 growth.

But the common predicate is undeniable. As has been seen, Friedman thought that member banks of the Federal Reserve System could not be trusted to keep the economy adequately stocked with money by voluntarily coming to the discount window when they needed reserves to accommodate business activity. Instead, the central bank had to target and deliver a precise quantity of M1 so that the GDP would reflect what economic wise men thought possible, not merely the natural level resulting from the interaction of consumers, producers, and investors on the free market.

For all practical purposes, then, it was Friedman who shifted the foundation of the nation's money from gold to T-bills. Indeed, in Friedman's scheme of things central bank purchase of Treasury bonds and bills was the monetary manufacturing process by which prosperity could be managed and delivered.

What Friedman failed to see was that one wise man's quantity rule for M1 could be supplanted by another wise man's quantity rule for M2 (a broader measure of money supply that included savings deposits) or still another quantity target for aggregate demand (nominal GDP targeting) or even the quantity of jobs created, such as the target of 200,000 per month recently enunciated by Fed governor Charles Evans. It could even be the quantity of change in the Russell 2000 index of stock prices, as Bernanke has advocated.

Yet it is hard to imagine a world in which any of these alternative "quantities" would not fall short of the "target" level deemed essential to the nation's economic well-being by their proponents. In short, the committee of twelve wise men and women unshackled by Friedman's plan for floating paper dollars would always find reasons to buy government debt, thereby laying the foundation for fiscal deficits without tears.

THE UNSEEN HAND NEVER REPORTED FOR WORK IN THE GLOBAL CURRENCY MARKETS

Open-ended monetization of US Treasury debt by the nation's central bank was only part of the sound money demise triggered by the Camp David events. The decision to destroy Bretton Woods and float the dollar also caused an irreparable breakdown of international financial discipline.

Never again were trade accounts between nations properly settled, and most especially in the case of the United States. As previously indicated, the cumulative current account deficit since 1971 exceeds $8 trillion, meaning that Americans have borrowed one-half "turn" of national income from the rest of the world in order to live permanently beyond their means.

These massive US trade deficits have actually become a way of life since Camp David, yet they were not supposed to even happen. Professor Friedman advised the Nixon White House at the time that market forces would actually eliminate the incipient US trade deficit by "price discovery" of the "correct" market clearing exchange rates.

In this manner, floating exchange rates would continuously rebalance the flows of merchandise trade, direct investment, portfolio capital, and short-term financial instruments according to the changing circumstances of each nation. A global variant of Adam Smith's "unseen hand" would supplant the financial stabilization and trade settlement functions of the old-fashioned gold standard that the discarded Bretton Woods system had been built upon.

In short, international markets would be cleared by the continuous repricing of exchange rates. This meant that deficit countries would suffer currency depreciation and surplus countries the opposite, thereby maintaining international payments equilibrium.

As previously demonstrated, this seemingly enlightened, pragmatic, and market-driven arrangement didn't work in practice. As it turned out, Adam Smith's unseen hand never even reported for work after Professor Friedman's floating-rate contraption was put into global operation.

Instead of floating with market forces, exchange rates have been chronically and heavily manipulated by governments. This is especially the case with respect to the mercantilist nations of Asia in pursuit of an "export your way to prosperity" economic growth model.

In pegging their currencies far below market-clearing levels in monomaniacal pursuit of export advantage, Japan, China, South Korea, and the caravan of imitators along the East Asian rim accumulated more and more dollars. They then parked these excess dollars in Treasury bills and bonds, and sequestered the latter in the vaults of their central banks.

Over the years, these staggering accumulations of dollar liabilities have been labeled as "foreign exchange reserves" in deference to the wholly archaic notion that the dollar is a "reserve currency." But the $7 trillion of dollar liabilities now held by foreign central banks are not classic monetary reserves at all.

The classic system's monetary reserves were designed to function as international petty cash accounts; that is, world money in the form of gold was available to clear temporary imbalances in trade and capital flows between national currency areas. But the current system does not need petty cash reserves to clear international account imbalances because the latter can persist indefinitely so long as mercantilist nations peg their currencies.

Consequently, the more apt characterization of these vast dollar accumulations is that they are vendor-supplied export loans to the American economy. Like any other vendor loan, they are designed to enable American customers to collectively purchase foreign goods and services far in excess of their actual earnings on current production.

This continuous stream of vendor loans was heavily channeled into Treasury bonds and bills, along with the implicitly guaranteed paper of Fannie Mae and Freddie Mac. Thus, the true foundation of the post–Bretton Woods monetary system was US government debt. The latter became the medium of exchange which permitted Americans to consume far more than they produced, while enabling the developing Asian economies to export vastly more goods than their customers could afford.

Indeed, with the passage of time the swap of mercantilist nation exports for US government paper became embedded as the modus operandi of the global economy. Milton Friedman's monetary contraption has thus become a ravenous consumer of Uncle Sam's debt emissions, an outcome that the idealistic professor had apparently never even contemplated.

By the end of 2012, however, the facts were unassailable. After three decades of "deficits don't matter" fiscal policy, the nation's publicly held debt amounted to $11.5 trillion. Yet as indicated, a stunning $5 trillion, or nearly 50 percent, of that total was not held by private investors either at home or overseas. Instead, it had been sequestered in the vaults of central banks, including the Federal Reserve and those of major exporters.

MONETARY ROACH MOTELS:
THE BONDS WENT IN BUT NEVER CAME OUT

This freakish central bank accumulation of dollar liabilities, in turn, was the result of the greatest money-printing spree in world history. In essence, we printed and then they printed, and the cycle never stopped repeating. In this manner, the massive excess of dollar liabilities generated by the Fed were absorbed by its currency-pegging counterparts, and then recycled into swelling domestic money supplies of yuan, yen, won, ringgit, and Hong Kong dollars.

As the US debt-based global monetary system became increasingly more unstable in recent years, central bank absorption of incremental Treasury debt reached stunning proportions. Thus, United States publicly held debt rose by $6 trillion between 2004 and 2012, but upward of $4 trillion, or 70 percent, of this was taken down by central banks.

It could be truly said, therefore, that the world's central banks have morphed into a global chain of monetary roach motels. The bonds went in, but they never came out. And therein lays the secret of "deficits without tears."

American politicians thus found themselves in the great fiscal sweet spot of world history. For several decades to come, they would have the unique privilege to issue bonds, notes, and bills from the US Treasury without limit. Only in the foggy future, when the world finally ran out of mercantilist rulers willing to swap the sweat of their people for Washington's profligate debt emissions, would fiscal limits reemerge.

As it happened, not all American politicians immediately recognized that they had essentially died and gone to fiscal heaven. Hence in the first half of the 1990s, under George H. W. Bush and then President Bill Clinton, old-guard Republicans joined bourbon Democrats in the enactment of comprehensive fiscal plans that did actually reduce spending and raise new tax revenues.

But Bill Clinton's courageously balanced budgets were the last hurrah of the old fiscal orthodoxy. These outcomes rested on a frail reed of personal conviction among politicians who had learned the fiscal rules of an earlier era.

In the emerging world of American crony capitalism, however, fiscal orthodoxy based on mere conviction untethered to real-world economic and financial pressures was not destined to survive. Instead, the assembled lobbies of K Street would soon have their way with the nation's public purse.

In due course, the revenue base would be depleted in the name of spurring the growth of everything from ethanol plants to private aircraft to the gross national product itself. Meanwhile, the spending side of the budget became swollen with new subventions to the sick-care complex, the housing complex, the education behemoth, the farm subsidy harvesters' alliance, and the alphabet soup of energy alternatives.

In the larger scheme of things, the nation's descent into permanent fiscal profligacy during the late twentieth century should not have been surprising. The historical record prior to the T-bill standard quite clearly demonstrates that fiscal discipline had never really depended upon the fortitude of principled statesmen.

GREENSPAN'S BORROWED PROSPERITY

After the Greenspan Fed abruptly abandoned its 1994 effort to impose a mild semblance of monetary discipline, the world's T-bill-based monetary system was off to the races. Frenetic money pumping by the Fed was reciprocated by even more aggressive currency pegging in East Asia, most especially in China, where the exchange rate was devalued by nearly 60 percent at the beginning of Mr. Deng's export campaign in 1994.

Fueled by this reciprocating monetary engine of central bank printing presses, the world economy was soon booming and the US current account deficits swelled to massive proportions. Thus, the current account deficit of $114 billion in 1995 was already an alarming 1.6 percent of GDP, but that was just a warm-up for the coming binge of borrowed prosperity.

Thereafter, the US current account deficit with the rest of the world went parabolic, rising to $416 billion, or 4.2 percent, of GDP by the year 2000. Indeed, for the entire 1990s decade the nation's cumulative deficit with the world was $2.0 trillion—a giant loan from abroad that bought a lot of designer jeans, personal computers, granite-top kitchen counters, gas-chugging SUVs, and luxury cruises that American households had not actually earned.

Yet the borrowing binge fostered by the Greenspan Fed was just getting warmed-up. American overspending financed by exporter nation loans attained nearly riotous proportions after the turn of the century, reaching, a peak current account deficit of $800 billion, or 6.1 percent, of GDP in 2006.

For the decade ending in 2011, cumulative borrowings from the rest of the world tripled from $2 billion in the 1990s to $6 trillion. And so America's garages, pantries, media rooms, and second homes filled up with even more stuff bought on the prodigious flow of credit generated by the world's T-bill-based monetary system.

In the fullness of time, floating-rate money led to fiscal profligacy on a scale never before imagined. Spending without the inconvenience of taxing opened the door to state subventions, bailouts, and endless tax breaks throughout the length and breadth of the American economy.

But the plenary mobilization of the state and all its agencies and organs of intervention, including the prosperity management régime of the central banking branch, is what fueled the rise of crony capitalism. It is a long-standing truism of political science that focused, organized special interests will always trump the diffuse public interest. So once raiding the Treasury and leveraging Wall Street and the banking system were deemed to be the pathway to the greater good, K Street lobbies and political action committees (PACs) captured the instruments of policy and extracted the resources of the public purse like never before.

So the irony was abundant. Friedman the historian was dead wrong on the gold standard and the Fed's responsibility for the Great Depression. Accordingly, the libertarian economist from the University of Chicago, more than any other single intellectual, fostered the Nixonian breakdown of monetary integrity and helped crush the last age of fiscal rectitude so painstakingly restored by Dwight D. Eisenhower.

Proffering what is by the hindsight of history a spurious rule of money supply growth, Friedman gave birth to the T-bill standard and a massively disordered and unbalanced international system in which mercantilist governments swap the labor of their people and natural resources of their lands for "money" which is merely dollar-denominated American debt.

Worse still, the later process became the foundation for the age of bubble finance, a great financial deformation that resulted in a Wall Street crescendo of speculation and rent seeking that had no historical parallel. Neither did Friedman's folly.

PART IV

THE AGE OF BUBBLE FINANCE

CHAPTER 14

PORK BELLIES, FLOATING MONEY, AND THE RISE OF SPECULATIVE FINANCE

N IXON'S ESTIMABLE FREE MARKET ADVISORS WHO GATHERED AT the Camp David weekend were to an astonishing degree clueless as to the consequences of their recommendation to close the gold window and float the dollar. In their wildest imaginations they did not foresee that this would unhinge the monetary and financial nervous system of capitalism. They had no premonition at all that it would pave the way for a forty-year storm of financialization and a debt-besotted symbiosis between central bankers possessed by delusions of grandeur and private gamblers intoxicated with visions of delirious wealth.

In fact, when Nixon announced on August 15, 1971, that the dollar was no longer convertible to gold at $35 per ounce, his advisors had barely a scratch pad's worth of ideas as to what should come next. The nationalists led by Treasury Secretary Connally wanted our trading partners to absorb a sharp devaluation of the dollar. Hence, the illegal 10 percent surtax on imports was to remain in place until they sued for peace.

Others led by Fed chairman Arthur Burns believed that the shocking announcements from Camp David would be merely a catalyst for international negotiations to "reset" the existing Bretton Woods system. The gold parity would be set at a more realistic (higher) level and this would be coupled with more favorable (lower) dollar exchange rates against the other major currencies. Once Bretton Woods was "reset," the Burns traditionalists believed that the advantages of fixed exchange rates and global financial stability and discipline could be preserved.

And the free markets faction led by George Shultz didn't think any follow-up plan was even necessary. Instead, following Nixon's Sunday evening announcement that he was unplugging Bretton Woods, they apparently thought that the "market" would take over the very next morning. No sweat.

THE POST-CAMP DAVID BOLLIX

In fact, the aftermath was thoroughly bollixed. Lacking any semblance of a plausible game plan, the Nixon administration stumbled around for another twenty months seeking to modulate the chaos it had unleashed.

Its first attempted solution was a Burns-Connally hybrid known as the Smithsonian Agreement of December 1971. This originated shortly after Camp David when Secretary Connally pronounced that whatever ailed the American economy, fixing it would be no problem: to wit, the United States needed precisely a $13 billion favorable swing in its balance of trade. This was not to be achieved the honest way—by domestic belt tightening and thereby a reduction of swollen US imports that were being funded by borrowing from foreigners. Instead, America's trading partners were to revalue their currencies upward by about 15 percent against the dollar.

The immediate effect of revaluation would have been a drastic loss on the billions of exchange reserves that major foreign central banks had previously not converted to gold in deference to Washington. This was September 1931 all over again.

Furthermore, along with taking this balance sheet hit, trading partners would also have to tighten their own belts by absorbing more American exports, which would now be cheaper and more competitive in their home markets. At the same time, they would be shipping fewer of their own goods to the American market, because their exports to the United States would now be more expensive and less competitive.

Connally's blatant mercantilist offensive was cut short in late November 1971, however, when the initially jubilant stock market started heading rapidly south on fears that a global trade war was in the offing. Seeing his opening, Paul Volcker, who was undersecretary for monetary affairs, deftly jerked the rug out from under Connally and Nixon. At a finance ministers' meeting in Rome he offered to increase the dollar price of gold by 10–15 percent.

In truth, this was an element of Burns' scheme to reset Bretton Woods at a higher, more defensible gold price. At the moment, however, it was received by the European negotiators as a huge US concession, because until then Nixon and Connally stoutly insisted there would be no change in the gold price. Realignment would consist exclusively of trading partners making their currencies more expensive against the dollar.

As it turned out, a few weeks later Connally's protectionist gauntlet ended in an amicable paint-by-the-numbers exercise in diplomatic pettifoggery. The United States agreed to drop the 10 percent import surtax and raise the price of gold by 9 percent to $38 per ounce. At the same time, the major foreign trading partners who had gathered at the Smithsonian agreed to revalue their currencies against the dollar by an average increase of 8 percent, including a 14 percent upward adjustment by Germany and 17 percent by Japan.

On the surface, these agreements appeared to comprise a comprehensive realignment of the fixed-rate international monetary order, thereby providing the framework for a putative "Bretton Woods II." Indeed, at the closing dinner at the Smithsonian on December 18, Nixon appeared unannounced to herald the agreement as "the most significant monetary agreement in the history of the world."

THE SMITHSONIAN AGREEMENT:
GOLD STANDARD WITHOUT GOLD

In fact, the Smithsonian Agreement was a Texas Special: all hat and no cattle. Quite simply, the United States had made no commitment whatsoever to redeem paper dollars for gold at the new $38 price or to defend the gold parity in any other manner. Yet without an anchor on the dollar, there was absolutely nothing to stop a worldwide process of competitive devaluation in response to excessive dollar creation, an outcome which would doom the newly aligned matrix of fixed exchange rates to chronic turmoil and instability.

In reality, the Smithsonian deal granted the United States a monetary hall pass, allowing the Fed to print dollars at will and the American economy to continue binging on inflationary credit expansion, soaring imports, and an expanding current account debt to the rest of the world. Ironically, the traditionalist Burns had wished the Fed to be actually re-tethered to gold at $38 per ounce; that is, that there be an honest "reset" of Bretton Woods, including a US obligation to redeem dollars for gold when presented by foreign central banks.

But since the new $38 per ounce gold value was only a meaningless reference price, the Smithsonian outcome put him at the end of an altogether different kind of tether; namely, that of heavy-handed demands from the Nixon White House for an election-year spree of easy money. Without the threat of a run on gold, Burns' only defense was a stiff backbone, something he manifestly did not possess.

Paul Volcker had surveyed the scene at the time of Nixon's preposterous pronouncement at the Smithsonian dinner and had delivered a more sober and accurate verdict. "I hope it lasts three months," said the man who years later would be brought into the Fed to stop the monetary mayhem which ensued.

Volcker's cynicism at the moment was absolutely warranted. At bottom, the Smithsonian Agreement attempted the futile task of perpetuating the

Bretton Woods gold exchange standard without any role for gold. It bestowed the responsibility for leadership of this jerry-built arrangement on a White House which quickly went AWOL. Yet without a US commitment to defend the gold parity, the newly minted Smithsonian exchange rates were sitting ducks for speculative attack.

Accordingly, the British pound soon came under heavy fire. By the late spring of 1972 when the pound crisis came to a head, there was no chance that the United States would help defend the system it had foisted on the world just a few months earlier.

By now Shultz had moved to the treasury secretary post, and his automatic refrain on exchange rate issues was to lip-synch Milton Friedman on the virtues of floating. For reasons that were purely political rather than ideological, Nixon was moving his lips on the subject, too. When the British finally gave up on June 22 and allowed the pound to float, Chief of Staff H. R. Haldeman mentioned this development the next morning and offered a briefing. "I don't care about it," retorted Nixon.

When Haldeman persisted with the topic, the White House tape-recording system captured the essence of why chaos was about to descend on the international monetary system. Chairman Burns had informed the White House staff that the British float would encourage further attacks by speculators and that the Italian lira was likely the next currency in the line of fire. "Well," the president of the United States observed, "I don't give a shit about the lira."

During the next eight months, further international negotiations attempted to rescue the Smithsonian Agreement with more baling wire and bubble gum. But the die was already cast and the monetary oxymoron which had prevailed in the interim, a gold standard system without monetary gold, was officially dropped in favor of pure floating currencies in March 1973.

Now, for the first time in modern history, all of the world's major nations would operate their economies on the basis of what old-fashioned economists called "fiduciary money." In practical terms, it amounted to a promise that currencies would retain as much, or as little, purchasing power as central bankers determined to be expedient.

WHEN A SPECULATOR'S PARADISE ARRIVED IN MONETARIST BLINDERS

In stumbling to this outcome, Nixon's advisors were strikingly oblivious to the monetary disorder they were unleashing. Indeed, they were creating a speculators' paradise, but their monetarist blinders did not permit them to see it coming.

In fact, there is no evidence of any awareness among Nixon administration policy makers of the financial pounding that industrial corporations and banking institutions alike would take when exchange rates and interest rates began to gyrate wildly—and over huge amplitudes that had never before been experienced in peacetime. Nor was there any attempt to explore with Wall Street, or other major financial institutions, the development of hedging and risk mitigation arrangements which might now be needed.

Alas, the reason for this glaring neglect was not a rigid White House commitment to laissez-faire. After all, at the time the gold dollar was being flushed, the Nixon White House was busy imposing wage and price controls across the length and breadth of the American economy. In fact, the passivity of the "religious floaters" club in the White House was owing to their reflexive adherence to the profoundly erroneous monetarist doctrines of Milton Friedman.

As detailed in chapter 13, Friedman was a committed anti-statist who had low regard for politicians and much disdain for their attempts at the economic betterment of society. And justifiably so. Yet in pushing the gold standard and fixed exchange rate system onto the scrap heap of history, the modern-day godfather of free markets helped foster the greatest project of statist intervention and subvention ever conceived—that is, monetary central planning of the national and, indeed, world economy by the Federal Reserve.

Milton Friedman never saw this lethal threat to free markets and sound money, however, owing to his blinding disdain for politics and the unaccountable presumption that—somehow—the inner sanctum of the Eccles Building would be populated by monetary eunuchs. Oblivious to short-term economic fluctuations, election cycles, unemployment rates, and sectoral and sectional economic dislocations, as well as the macroeconomic effects of pestilence, drought, and flood, they would operate far removed from the clamor for policy action on both ends of Pennsylvania Avenue.

A Friedmanite Fed would keep the money growth dial set strictly at 3 percent, year in and year out, ever steady as she goes. Like the fabled Maytag repairman of that era, central bankers in the Friedman mold would mostly sit around quietly in the library of the Eccles Building playing Scrabble and reading book reviews.

Not surprisingly, therefore, Friedman's pre-1971 writings nowhere give an account of the massive hedging industry that would flourish under a régime of floating paper money. This omission occurred for good reason: Friedman didn't think there would be much volatility to hedge if his Chicago-trained central bankers stuck to the monetarist rulebook.

Accordingly, Friedman never even entertained the possibility that once the central bank was freed from the stern discipline of protecting its gold reserves, it would fall into the hands of monetary activists and central planners. Most assuredly, he did not realize that once politically driven theories of macroeconomic betterment gained policy dominance, the Fed as an institution would become a fount of rationalizations for incessant tinkering and intervention in financial markets.

And, most certainly, Friedman did not see that an unshackled central bank would eventually transform his beloved free markets into gambling halls and venues of uneconomic speculative finance. Yet that would be the unavoidable outcome of a central bank that contaminated private financial markets with cheap credit, while providing "put" protections for carry trades and accommodation to dirty floats and pegged currencies. All of these deformations tended to fuel violent swings in exchange rates, interest rates, and capital markets.

In fact, Friedman was so blind to the hedging monster that would inexorably arise from his model of fiat central banking that within weeks of the Camp David events the renowned Professor Friedman put a pitifully low price tag on his own ideas for commercial exploitation of floating currencies. The precise number was $7,500, and even in that day it didn't amount to much.

As it happened, Friedman priced his own advice at rock bottom shortly after Nixon closed the gold window. He had been approached to consult on a potential currency-hedging market, but the inquiry did not come from the great currency-dealing international banks of New York, London, or even the big Loop banks in Friedman's hometown of Chicago.

At the time, institutions such as Morgan Guaranty, Citibank, and Continental Illinois were deeply immersed in the financing of world trade and capital and money flows, facilitating billions in currency transactions every week. Yet none of these great financial institutions even anticipated that a new business opportunity of immense magnitude was unfolding with each new monetary stumble in Washington. Even after Camp David very few experienced financiers believed that a purely floating-rate currency régime was likely or workable.

It thus happened that Leo Melamed, a small-time pork-belly (i.e., bacon) trader who kept his modest office near the Chicago Mercantile Exchange trading floor stocked with generous supplies of Tums and Camels, found his opening and hired Professor Friedman. Even as several dozen traders at the Merc labored in obscurity to ping-pong a thousand or so futures contracts per day covering eggs, onions, shrimp, cattle and pork bellies, Melamed was busy plotting the launch of new futures contracts in the major currencies. In so doing, he inadvertently demonstrated how radically unprepared the financial world had been for the Friedmanite coup at Camp David.

THE PORK-BELLY PITS: WHERE THE AGE OF SPECULATIVE FINANCE STARTED

Leo Melamed was the genius founder of the financial futures market and presided over its explosive growth on the Chicago "Merc" during the last three decades of the twentieth century. He understandably ended up exceedingly wealthy for his troubles, but on Friday afternoon of August 13, 1971, it would not have been evident to most observers that either of these outcomes was in the cards.

At the time of the Camp David weekend that changed the world, the Chicago Merc was still a backwater outpost of the farm commodity futures business. It originated as the Butter and Egg Board a century earlier and had recently branched out into livestock. Leo Melamed was its rising star. He had been a sensation at an early age, trading egg, bacon, and onion contracts, and had emerged as a charismatic leader and innovator obsessed with growing the range and volume of contracts traded on the Merc.

The utter unlikelihood that only thirty years hence, tens of billions of trades per hour in worldwide currency, bond, and equity futures contracts would pass through the modern-day CME Group trading platforms (Merc's successor) is underscored by Melamed's singular achievement during the decade before Camp David: he persuaded the exchange's old-timers to relinquish an ancient trading verity which held that futures contracts would only work for storable farm commodities like corn. With this breakthrough, Melamed got them to take a great leap forward; that is, into the trading of cattle on the hoof and uncured bacon on the slab.

The latter became the notable "pork belly" contract, and Melamed perfected the art of day-trading its considerable volume. By 1971, Melamed was managing to scalp several hundred thousand dollars annually from his high-velocity bacon trading and was the biggest hitter among a dozen or so pure speculators who made markets for "hedgers" such as food processors who held seats on the Merc. Still, Melamed's prospects for hitting the big leagues of finance were not evident.

THE ASTONISHING 50,000X GROWTH OF MERC

The next chapters in the tale of Melamed and the Merc are downright astonishing. In 1970, Melamed made an intensive inquiry into currency and other financial markets about which he knew very little, in a desperate search for something to replace the Merc's rapidly dwindling eggs contract. The latter was the core of its legacy business and was then perhaps $50 million per year in annual turnover.

Four decades later, Leo Melamed's study program had mushroomed into a vast menu of futures and options contracts—covering currencies, commodities, fixed-income, and equities, which trade twenty-four hours per day on immense computerized platforms. The entire annual volume of the old eggs contract is now exceeded in literally the blink of an eye.

This stupefying explosion of volume has obviously been enabled by modern information technology. Yet the hundreds of exotic contracts which now continuously career through CME's cyberspace do not exist because Leo Melamed and his colleagues had a superior entrepreneurial facility for inventing new types of futures contracts.

In fact, prior to entry into what became the brave new world of financial futures, Melamed's forays into new contracts on frozen shrimp, frozen broilers, scrap iron, apples, and onions all fell by the wayside. So the reason futures contracts on D-marks and T-bills took off like rocket ships is that the fundamental nature of money and finance was turned upside down at Camp David. In effect, Professor Friedman's floating money contraption created a massive market for hedging that did not have any reason for existence in the gold standard world of Bretton Woods, and most especially under its more robust pre-1914 antecedents.

When currency exchange rates were firmly fixed and some or all of the main ones were redeemable in a defined weight of gold, exporters and importers had no need to hedge future purchases or deliveries denominated in foreign currencies. The spot and forward exchange rates, save for technical differentials, were always the same.

Likewise, interest rates tended to change at a glacial pace, if at all, under the gold standard, especially the pre-1914 variant. During the Bretton Woods quietude of years like 1955 and 1964, for example, the notion of a T-bill hedging contract would have been laughable. There wasn't enough volatility in rates to make it profitable or plausible; in fact, most of the time during those halcyon years, rates did not move at all.

Even more importantly, the newly emergent need of corporations and investors to hedge against currency and interest rate risk caused other fateful developments in financial markets; namely, the accumulation of capital and trading resources by firms which became specialized in the intermediation of financial hedges. Purely an artifact of an unstable monetary régime, this new industry resulted in prodigious and wasteful consumption of capital, technology, and labor resources.

The four decades since Camp David also show that the Friedmanite régime of floating money is dynamically unstable. Each business cycle recovery since 1971 has amplified the ratio of credit to income in the system, causing the daisy chains of debt upon debt to become ever more distended and fragile.

At the same time, the Fed's maneuvers in the financial markets have become increasingly more blatant, massive, incessant, and desperate. The build-up of financial system leverage coupled with intensifying central bank activism, in turn, fueled the headlong growth of pure speculative arbitrage. In fact, the great pools of capital which gravitated to the hedging markets quickly found a more compelling objective than hedging currency risk on container loads of Toyotas.

The infinitely more productive arena for deployment of speculative capital was the Wall Street–centered money and capital markets themselves: economic districts which were once the meeting place of savers and investors. After August 1971, however, they steadily morphed into casinos focused on speculation in the vast array of hedging instruments and markets, not capital raising for the main street economy.

That became evident when in the fullness of time the overwhelming share of activity on the CME and its counterparts around the world boiled down to front-running and arbing the financial currents emanating from the untethered central banks. The provision of hedging services to Main Street businesses and investors impacted by these financial currents, by contrast, amounted to small beer.

Currently, the daily volume of foreign exchange hedging activity in global futures and options markets, for example, is estimated at $4 trillion, compared to daily merchandise trade of only $40 billion. This 100:1 ratio of hedging volume to the underlying activity rate does not exist because the currency managers at exporters like Toyota re-trade their hedges over and over all day; that is, every fourteen minutes.

Due to the dead-weight losses to society from this massive churning, the hedging casinos are a profound deformation of capitalism, not its crowning innovation. They consume vast resources without adding to society's output or wealth, and flush income and net worth to the very top rungs of the economic ladder—rarefied redoubts of opulence which are currently occupied by the most aggressive and adept speculators. The talented Leo Melamed thus did not spend forty years doing God's work, as he believed. He was just an adroit gambler in the devil's financial workshop—the great hedging venues—necessitated by Professor Friedman's contraption of floating, untethered money.

THE LUNCH AT THE WALDORF-ASTORIA
THAT OPENED THE FUTURES

According to Melamed's later telling, by 1970 he had "become a committed and ardent disciple in the army that was forming around Milton Friedman's ideas. He had become our hero, our teacher, our mentor."

On slow days in the pork-belly pits Melamed had snuck into Friedman's classroom lectures: "What I heard made my spirits soar. Here was the voice of supreme economic authority saying that the system of fixed exchange rates was wrong. That it was time for its demise."

Thus inspired, Melamed sought to establish a short position against the pound, but after visiting all of the great Loop banks in Chicago he soon discovered they weren't much interested in pure speculators: "if you didn't have any commercial reasons, the banks weren't likely to be very helpful."

The banking system was not in the business of financing currency speculators, and for good reason. In a fixed exchange rate régime the currency departments of the great international banks were purely service operations which deployed no capital and conducted their operations out of hushed dealing rooms, not noisy cavernous trading floors. The foreign currency business was no different than trusts and estates. Even Melamed had wondered at the time whether "foreign currency instruments could succeed" within the strictures designed for soybeans and eggs, and pretended to answer his own question: "Perhaps there was some fundamental economic reason why no one had before successfully applied financial instruments to futures."

In point of fact, yes, there was a huge reason and it suggests that while Melamed might have audited Milton Friedman's course, he had evidently not actually passed it. There were no currency futures contracts because there was no opportunity for speculative profit in forward exchange transactions as long as the fixed-rate monetary régime remained reasonably stable.

Indeed, this reality was evident in a rebuke from an unnamed New York banker which Melamed recalled having received in response to his entreaties shortly before the Smithsonian Agreement was announced. "It is ludicrous to think that foreign exchange can be entrusted to a bunch of pork belly crapshooters," the banker had allegedly sniffed.

Whether apocryphal or not, this anecdote captures the essence of what happened at Camp David in August 1971. There a motley crew of economic nationalists, Friedman acolytes, and political cynics supinely embraced Richard Nixon's monetary madness. In so doing, they opened the financial system to a forty-year swarm of "crapshooters" who eventually engulfed capitalism itself in endless waves of speculation and fevered gambling, activities which redistributed the income upward but did not expand the economic pie.

So even as a GOP-inspired wage and price freeze descended over the nation in the fall of 1971, Leo Melamed pursued his lonely quest to financialize the impending currency turmoil with no help at all from the established banking system. As he told a reporter a decade later, "Wall Street jeered and Washington yawned. Morgan Guaranty laughed at me and treated me like I had snake bite."

As it happened, Melamed did not waste any time getting an audience with the wizard behind the White House screen. At a luncheon meeting with Professor Friedman at the New York Waldorf-Astoria on November 13, 1971, which Melamed later described as his "moment of truth," he laid out his case.

After asking Friedman "not to laugh," Melamed described his scheme: "I held my breath as I put forth the idea of a futures market in foreign currency. The great man did not hesitate."

"It's a wonderful idea," Friedman told him. "You must do it!"

Melamed then suggested that his colleagues in the pork-belly pits might be more reassured about the venture if Friedman would put his endorsement in writing. At that, Friedman famously replied, "You know I am a capitalist?"

He was apparently a pretty timid capitalist, however. In consideration of the aforementioned $7,500, Melamed got an eleven-page paper that launched the greatest trading casino in world history. It made Melamed extremely wealthy and also millionaires out of countless other recycled eggs and bacon traders that Friedman never even met.

Modestly entitled "The Need for a Futures Market in Currencies," the paper today reads like so much free market eyewash. But back then it played a decisive role in conveying Friedman's imprimatur.

In describing the paper's impact, Melamed did not spare the superlatives: "I held in my hand the Holy Grail for the Chicago Mercantile Exchange. The most influential economic mind of the twentieth century provided the CME with the intellectual foundation upon which to build its financial superstructure."

THE MORNING AFTER THE SMITHSONIAN AGREEMENT: LEO MELAMED'S TIMELY LAUNCH

Friedman's paper arrived just in the nick of time. With his weighty endorsement in hand, Melamed hurriedly announced his new currency futures market the very next business day after the Smithsonian Agreement was announced on December 21, 1971. To be sure, had Melamed and his Merc not invented financial futures, another punter would have come along, because soon thereafter prices of virtually every financial instrument—currencies, commodities, and interest rates—were gyrating wildly as the brave new world of floating exchange rates and printing-press money fully emerged.

Yet the fact that the explosion of hedging products did emerge in the shadows of the University of Chicago is not entirely a historical factoid. As is evident in Melamed's self-described relentless campaign to promote his new products, his born-again pork belly traders also incorporated a significant element of free market evangelism in their pitch.

Referring to Friedman's paper as an "unvanquishable secret weapon," Melamed recounted how his small team of traders had "crisscrossed the nation . . . visited every nation on the planet . . . [and] when we were told that we were crazy, we responded Friedman is one of us! And each and every time, his name made the difference. . . . Presidents, finance ministers, central bankers, businessmen who would not otherwise have given us the time of day . . . allowed us near their door because of his name."

WHEN NIXON'S MONETARY ARSONISTS YAWNED
AND THE D-MARK GYRATED

Much to Melamed's surprise, however, his hurried May 1972 launch of the first currency futures contracts in dollars, lira, pounds, marks, francs, and guilders did not stir much interest or enthusiasm among the very monetary arsonists in Washington who should have understood its significance. "No one really cared," he later recalled. Shultz waved him off and observed that "if it's good enough for Milton, it's good enough for me."

In short, a somewhat rickety but salvageable international monetary system had been rashly and casually jettisoned in a matter of weeks, even though it had embodied the wisdom and best practices of the ages. Yet the White House arsonists didn't care about the currency mayhem just around the corner. So the financial deformation to which the demise of Bretton Woods gave rise—massive, wasteful speculation in financial futures and options—was born largely unnoticed in the humble bacon-trading pits of Chicago, wrapped in the swaddling garb of free market ideology borrowed from the university across town.

In due course, all monetary hell broke loose. Radical fluctuations in exchange rates and interest rates became routine occurrences, charting swings with amplitudes never experienced in peacetime history. The rambunctious journey of the D-mark provides a case in point.

When Melamed opened up his currency futures market in May 1972,

West Germany was the largest trading partner of the United States, and its exchange rate was 3.2 D-marks per dollar. The dollar then fluctuated violently downward in response to the Fed's profligate money printing during the tenure of Arthur Burns and William Miller, respectively. When it reached an interim low of 1.72 D-marks in early 1980, the dollar had lost 45 percent of its buying power.

Under Volcker's relentless campaign to quash domestic inflation and restore the integrity of the US dollar, however, the mark-to-dollar exchange rate abruptly and massively reversed direction in favor of the dollar. By February 1985, the exchange rate was all the way back to 3.05 D-marks per dollar, meaning the greenback had gained 90 percent since early 1980.

Then Jim Baker moved from Reagan's chief of staff job in the White House to the Treasury Building, where he dusted off John Connally's monetary chainsaw and launched another Texas dollar massacre, this one known as the Plaza Accord of September 1985. Bullied into selling dollars with nearly reckless abandon, Japan and Germany joined the United States in flooding the currency exchange markets with an unrelenting "offer" on the dollar.

Consequently, during the next twenty-four months the exchange rate was hammered back down to about 1.6 D-marks per dollar, meaning that by year-end 1987 the greenback had drastically reversed direction yet again, this time losing 50 percent of its value against the D-mark in less than thirty months.

In all, the dollar lost 50 percent of its exchange value against the D-mark during the first fifteen years after the Merc contracts opened, but the violent round trips and fluctuations during the interim amounted to the equivalent of 400 percentage points of gross change. Needless to say, corporations doing business in German marks had no choice except to purchase costly hedging protection against this unprecedented, radical exchange rate volatility.

At the same time, in order to accommodate the massive new demands for currency-hedging protection, Melamed needed gobs of speculative capital to take the other side of his rapidly expanding volume of futures contracts. This turned out to be no problem whatsoever.

The Merc required traders to post an initial margin of only 2 percent on currency contracts. This meant that if the dollar moved by 10 percent, say from 3 marks per dollar to 2.7 marks per dollar, a punter could collect a 500 percent profit. And if this 10 percent move in the underlying currency pair occurred within the span of three months, as happened not infrequently, the annualized rate of return on capital at risk would be 2,000 percent.

WHY CURRENCY FUTURES WERE
NOT EXACTLY GOD'S WORK

In the tradition of the farm commodity exchanges, Melamed considered such outsized returns as evidence that speculators were doing God's work. After all, someone had to take the other side of the trade in order to accommodate the hedging needs of pig farmers and machine tool exporters alike.

But there was a big difference. Speculators in the corn and hog pits do not exactly perform God's work, but they most surely price it. The primary economic function of traditional commodity futures is not to turn corn into casino chips, thereby permitting punters to bet on corn prices over arbitrary time periods.

Instead, these traditional futures markets were essentially seasonal smoothing mechanisms. They were a forum where farmer-sellers could lock in fall harvest prices before they planted in the spring, and buyers at flour mills could stabilize their harvest time grain purchase prices in the same manner.

Since seasonal weather fluctuations are, so far, an act of God, the futures market for farm crops is a marvelous price discovery mechanism. During the corn-growing season, for example, the futures market prices reflect the daily effects of weather—heat, rain, drought, hail, winds, and frost—based on crop condition reports issued continuously by the US Department of Agriculture and private crop services.

Early in the season during June, for example, the reporting services indicate the percentage of the crop which has been "planted" and "emerged" each week, and later in the season they report the percentage of the corn crop which has "silked," "doughed," and "dented," respectively. Expert traders compare this information, and much more, to prior years' data for the same week in the crop cycle and from there extrapolate implications for supply and price, ultimately placing their bets accordingly.

Seasonal weather variation, therefore, was at the heart of traditional farm commodity futures markets: it could cause unpredictable but violent swings in short-term crop prices due to its impact on harvested supply, thereby making the cost of the speculator's capital an efficient investment for buyers and sellers alike.

The same is true of nonfarm commodities like natural gas where weather can radically impact demand, such as summer air-conditioning peaks in gas-fired electric utility use and winter variation in heating degree days. Even in the case of some metals like copper, where demand and inventory levels are highly sensitive to the business cycle, short-term price discovery through futures trading helps buyers and sellers navigate the ex-

treme price fluctuations which can accompany cycles of inventory stock-
ing and reduction.

In short, the speculator's capital provides the liquidity needed to facilitate short-term price discovery in markets for weather-driven crops and
inventory-intensive commodities. The resulting hedges consume modest
real economic resources and allocate sufficient profits away from hedgers
to the speculator community, so as to attract the trading capital needed to
provide these markets with liquidity.

There was, therefore, a perfectly good reason why farm commodity futures markets existed for hundreds of years while there never emerged any
crusading Leo Melamed crisscrossing the globe peddling currency futures.
The truth is that honest money did not require the price discovery services
of speculative capital.

The gold content of the pound sterling, for example, did not change
other than in wartime for 215 years between 1717 and 1931, and the gold
content of the US dollar was set in 1832 and did not change until FDR tin-
kered with it in January 1934.

Indeed, even in August 1971 the dollar did not need price discovery; it
needed the honest defense of a White House that would fulfill its treaty obligations, and an economic policy based on the nation living within its
means. What it got instead was the equivalent of monetary weather fluctuations and, frequently, monetary storms of violent and capricious aspect.

Moreover, in Professor Friedman's brave new world of floating central
bank money, there were no benchmarks—no Fourth of July corn tassel
counts or January heating degree days to tabulate and compare to historic
norms. In fact, the new currency storms were strictly *sui generis*: the random outcome of a continuously shifting batch of central bankers trying to
manipulate interest rates, consumer prices, output, employment, trade,
and eventually sovereign bond prices, and the stock market index, too.

RELAPSE TO THE MONETARY DARK AGES

So a half century after the war disruption of August 1914, the world ironically slipped back into a monetary dark age of economic nationalism and
government-manipulated money. Ironic, because in the half century prior
to 1914 there was nearly continuous monetary progress and enlighten-
ment, toward common world money (gold-linked currencies) and uniform
consumer prices and wages throughout the developed world.

The driver of this convergence had been the automatic movement of
gold and other monetary reserves from countries with balance of payments deficits to those with surpluses. As the enforcer of financial discipline, these gold reserve movements caused domestic banking systems to

expand and contract, thereby inducing the impacted national economy to heat up or cool down.

Accordingly, wholesale and consumer price levels and domestic wages and production costs among countries got constantly leveled and homogenized by this "rule of one price." Countries experiencing a gold drain and monetary stringency tended toward wage and price deflation, while those experiencing a gold gain and easier money markets tended toward inflation.

After the world plunged into the inflationary abyss in the 1970s, however, any remaining knowledge of the pre-1914 world of common international money and price convergence was lost. For example, Keynesians and nationalistic monetarists alike would have been shocked to learn that after adjustment for tariff differences, late-nineteenth-century wage rates in Manchester, Dusseldorf, Lyon, Milan, Barcelona, Pittsburgh, and Chicago were quite closely aligned.

Indeed, when Senator William B. McKinley campaigned for president in 1896 on a "full lunch pail," he recited from memory the wage rates in these cities. Not surprisingly, candidate McKinley was also not loath to explain to voters that it was only the "McKinley tariff" which gave American labor a competitive edge, owing to the margin of the tariff over the world price.

Stated differently, fixed exchange rates harmonized wages and prices among the major developed economies. Working silently through the free market, fixed exchange rates forced a continuous and decentralized process of adjustments in domestic demand, costs, and prices when balance of payments and trade accounts got out of alignment.

By contrast, floating currencies and fiat money caused economic adjustments to shift to external exchange rates rather than internal demand and prices. This led to government manipulation of the adjustment process, and therefore to divergence rather than convergence of industrial world economies, that is, to protectionism, economic inefficiency, and lower real incomes.

In this setting, central banks became a fount of capriciously valued national monies, the very opposite of the pre-1914 régime of a single gold money expressed in numerous paper currencies of constant value. Indeed, Friedman's folly made Melamed and his trader army fabulously rich because it transformed the nation's currency into the residual swing factor in the chain of economic causation.

In effect, the dollar became the Mexican jumping bean of finance. This previously unknown exchange rate volatility sucked speculator capital into the new currency futures markets in a great deluge, where it scalped massive profits from inefficient trading markets still in their pioneering stage.

More importantly, by fueling short-run herd behavior in the trading pits, this restless deluge of speculator capital aggravated the price swings even further among newly unhinged national currencies. In the face of gyrating exchange rates, national economic policy managers attempted to counteract these market forces by implementing polices aimed to push domestic interest rates, prices, demand, and employment in a more congenial direction.

The result was that even greater turbulence was passed down the line in hot-potato fashion to the currency exchanges. Needless to say, this feedback loop was manna from heaven for the newly emboldened currency futures speculators. In the iconic Wall Street vernacular, Leo Melamed and friends were indeed backing up their trucks to the Merc's Jackson Boulevard loading docks.

The truth is, these financial derivative markets do not rationally and efficiently price weather-type forces, nor do today's interest rate and exchange rate fluctuations have an exogenous cause. Most assuredly they are not the work of the financial gods pursuing their own insouciant whims. Rather, they reflect the actions of central bankers engaged in a tug-of-war with the markets themselves: policy action begets market reaction in a continuous loop of adjustment.

For this reason, currency futures markets do not really engage in efficient and useful price discovery. They generate no "public good" because the currency season never ends; it just iterates through an endless loop. Indeed, the modus operandi of central bankers soon became fixed on incessant manipulation of the macroeconomic drivers of the exchange markets, including interest rates, inflation, output, and external trade and capital flows.

Consequently, the currency futures and options markets rapidly became an arena for purely private rent-seeking. Invariably, fleet-footed traders figured out how to exploit and arbitrage the clumsy maneuvers of central bankers.

THE LESSONS OF THE LIRA

During the decade and a half after the Merc began trading currency futures, for example, the Italian lira circumnavigated an even more extreme path than the D-mark, and mostly in the opposite direction. This was due to the fact that Italian fiscal and monetary profligacy far surpassed even that of the United States.

Consequently, the dollar stood at 582 lira in May 1972, but in sharp contrast to its hard fall against the D-mark, the dollar had actually gained nearly 40 percent through early 1980. Then, when Paul Volcker slammed on the monetary brakes, the dollar soared even higher, reaching an exchange rate of 2,040 lira per dollar by the February 1985 peak.

Needless to say, a speculator who had been continuously short the lira on Melamed's futures exchange would have generated a 12,000 percent return over the thirteen-year period. Even had this trader overstayed his hand and been bruised by Baker's dollar defenestration at the Plaza Hotel, he still would have collected 1,300 lira per dollar by the end of 1987, meaning a total return of 6,000 percent.

Yet that was just for starters. Denizens of the Merc currency pits who had been bold enough to skip past the dollar entirely and put on a pair trade of long D-mark and short lira over the initial fifteen years of this new futures market would have reaped a 17,000 percent return. Likewise, any trader who noticed that Japanese statesmen became extremely timid, even sweaty, in the presence of Texas politicians wearing the big hat in Washington would have bet that 360 yen would soon buy a lot more than one dollar.

In fact, after Japanese statesmen had received the Connally "treatment," and professed to enjoy it, they were rewarded thirteen years later by the drastically more bracing Baker "treatment." In the aftermath of the latter, the exchange rate rocketed all the way up to 128 yen to the dollar by December 1987, meaning a 12,000 percent gain on the trade over the fifteen-year period.

In short, the Merc traders had every reason to sing the praises of Professor Friedman, even as they peddled their commercial wares to the hapless exporters and importers caught up in these exchange rate maelstroms. Never before in financial history had such a lucrative casino been established as the one Leo Melamed opened on Jackson Boulevard in the shadows of Milton Friedman's University of Chicago classroom.

"WHOREHOUSE OF THE LOOP" NO MORE

To be sure, few traders were adroit enough to carry these trades to full term and there were maintenance margins to post and big risks of being wrong when trading direction reversed. Yet even after these allowances, the returns on speculator capital were so enormous and so unattainable elsewhere that currency trading became a powerful magnet for financial capital. Indeed, only two decades earlier the Merc had been derisively known as the "Whorehouse of the Loop," owing to the corrupt antics which surrounding its trading in onions and eggs. Now, thanks to currency futures, the inflow of capital to the Merc exceeded during a few brief years the combined capital of all the commodity futures exchanges in the world as of May 1972. Even in purely physical terms, the growth of the Merc was stunning. By 1987, daily contract volume had risen by a factor of thousands and the Merc's trading floor had grown from the size of a modest Chicago neighborhood saloon to encompass a space equal to three football fields.

This tidal wave of resources, transactions, and speculative capital, in fact, was so massive that speculators soon became their own counterparty; that is, bona fide commercial hedgers accounted for a rapidly diminishing share of transactions. By the end of its first decade of currency trading, about 90 percent of transactions on the CME consisted of pure gambling. The exchange's spin doctors, of course, were pleased to describe these gamblers as "liquidity providers," but that claim doesn't even remotely hold up under serious examination.

Melamed himself made no bones about the fact that the Merc aimed to facilitate equal opportunity wagering: "Why shouldn't the individual have the same right as the corporation to trade currency . . . doesn't the individual have a right to protect or enhance his personal estate?"

The answer might have been that the individual home gamer usually didn't have income in D-marks or lira to cover. What was happening, of course, was that the right of consenting adults to gamble on the free market was being confused with the monetary reason why the currency futures market existed in the first place.

The incoming flood of speculative capital also gave rise to a profusion of new financial futures and options products which soon surpassed even the exploding currency markets. Not surprisingly, these new contracts were initially focused in the interest rate arena, and were driven by the same monetary policy activism as the currency futures.

In fact, interest rate movements stemming from the machinations of central banks during the first fifteen years were every bit as volatile as exchange rates. As indicated, this too represented a radical departure from historical experience.

The decade from 1955 through the end of 1964 arguably represents the golden era of Martin-Eisenhower financial discipline. While the Martin Fed had not been loath to nudge money market interest rates at cyclical turning points, its overarching objective had been to keep inflation near zero, the dollar strong, and the financial markets stable on a long-term basis, and to exercise a light touch in its open market operations.

Accordingly, short-term interest rates had moved at only a glacial pace during this golden era. During the 1955–1964 period the interest rate on

Treasury bills, for example, remained in a tight range of 1.5–3.5 percent. In fact, yields traded inside those bounds in 80 percent of monthly observations over the entire decade and rarely moved more than 100 basis points within any twelve-month period.

Needless to say, under these conditions there was no market whatsoever for interest rate futures because businesses using short-term revolving credits or medium-term capital loans were exposed to virtually zero risk of significant interest rate fluctuation. The prime rate for business loans remained at 4.5 percent for a remarkable seventy-five consecutive months between 1960 and late 1965, a span that exceeded the term of 95 percent of bank commercial and industrial loans outstanding at the time. No businessman, rational or otherwise, could have been persuaded to spend good money on hedging interest rates that would not change over the term of his loan.

TALE OF TWO MARKETS

In September 1960 the Merc was down to a single commodity: a dying contract in eggs futures which traded languidly in a small pit surrounded by Ping-Pong tables and card games. Ironically, the egg contract was on death's door because modern poultry farming had brought the hens out of the weather-exposed farmyard and into industrialized egg factories where stable conditions resulted in a constant output of eggs. There was no trading vigorish in eggs which got laid on a regular basis.

Exactly sixteen years later in February 1976, Milton Friedman himself stood on the floor of what were vastly expanded and opulent new digs at the Merc to commence trading in the world's first T-bill futures contract. In contrast to the tranquil performance of the nation's now thoroughly industrialized laying hens, the market for its short-term debt had become tumultuous.

Between January 1972 and mid-1974, for example, the T-bill yield rocketed from 3.2 percent to 9.2 percent. Needless to say, short-term floating rate borrowers had not been prepared for an unprecedented 600 basis points surge in their debt service costs.

Nor were they any more prepared for the sharp slump in rates which followed the initial violent increase. Interest rates plummeted when the Fed brought the US economy to its knees as it attempted to contain the virulent inflation it unleashed. While the experience of a cyclical downturn was not new, the 400 basis point plunge of short-term interest rates during less than fifteen months in 1974–1975 was another unprecedented shock to the commercial loan market.

Overall, the Camp David event spawned interest rate volatility and swings of previously unimaginable magnitude. In a radical departure from its flatlining trend of the early 1960s, the prime rate, which then was still the major benchmark for business loans, became financially hyperkinetic. During the first four years after the Smithsonian meeting, the prime rate changed forty-four times, moving from 5 percent to 12 percent and then back down to 7 percent, thereby traversing 1,200 basis points of change within the lifetime of a typical five-year term loan.

THE BIRTH OF T-BILL FUTURES:
MELAMED TO SPRINKEL TO BURNS

Not surprisingly, when in late 1975 Melamed made the rounds in Washington with his proposed T-bill product, he encountered an amenable audience among the very policy officials who were responsible for the money market turbulence which made interest rate futures plausible. By then he had recruited to the board of the Merc affiliate that conducted currency trading one of Friedman's leading monetarist disciples, Beryl Sprinkel, the chief economist of a major Chicago bank. More crucially, Sprinkel had done his graduate studies under Arthur Burns and would keep Friedman's monetarist candle burning brightly during the Reagan administration as undersecretary of the treasury for monetary affairs.

So Sprinkel did not require a Washington sherpa to pave the way. He simply trotted Melamed into the boardroom of the Eccles Building. There he made his pitch directly to the chairman of the Fed. No other parties were needed.

The timing could not have been more fortuitous. As shown by Burns' own diary published thirty years later, the nation's top central banker by then had become thoroughly flummoxed. He had found he could not explain, predict, or control the sudden violent lurch of the business cycle from boom to bust, and the wild swings in interest rates, commodity prices, exchange rates, and inflation expectations that had accompanied it. Indeed, as a keen student of financial history and prior business cycles, Burns knew full well that the wild financial fluctuations of 1972–1975 had never before occurred in peacetime history.

So Melamed's proposition was a perversely welcome alternative. If the central bank could not deliver stable money to the market, then why not enable the private market to shield itself from the disorders emanating from the Fed. "What a clever idea," Burns is reported to have said, adding, "Such futures contracts would be used by government securities dealers, investment bankers, all sorts of commercial interests, as well as speculators."

The Fed chairman had that partly right. Not only did the big Wall Street bond houses like Salomon Brothers and investment banks like Morgan Stanley and Goldman learn to use financial futures, but within the next decade and a half they had turned their traditional business models inside out.

Historically, they had plied their underwriting and advisory trades on the basis of much trust and sparse capital. Once they piled into the new financial futures markets and the related over-the-counter (OTC) trading venues, however, their balance sheets, leverage ratios, and use of short-term wholesale funding expanded like Topsy. As detailed in chapter 20, asset footing went from the millions to the trillions in less than two decades.

Ironically, the exceedingly lucrative core business of these new Wall Street trading machines involved selling over-the-counter options to their clients and then laying off the risk on the organized futures and options exchanges. Had the pork-belly traders (or other speculators) never been empowered by Friedman's floating money contraption to create the financial futures and options exchanges, the "investment banks"—Bear Stearns, Lehman, Goldman, Merrill, and Morgan Stanley—which thrived on the OTC never would have grown to such massive size.

Yet the most important dimension of Melamed's proposition Burns got plainly wrong. According to Melamed's account of the meeting, Burns had been quick to seize on the "free markets" aspect of the financial futures concept. Turning to Sprinkel he had queried, "This futures contract would become a terrific predictor of the direction of interest rates, isn't that right, Beryl?"

The implication was that the Fed would gain a valuable new tool in the form of free market signals about the price of money and capital that it could use in the conduct of monetary policy. When Sprinkel ventured that such market signals would perhaps be as good as the Fed's own econometric forecasting model, Burns dispatched the economist's musings with proof that he had learned something at Richard Nixon's knee after all.

"That [model]," chuckled the chairman of the Fed, "isn't worth a shit."

Here was the heart of the post–Camp David monetary problem. The Fed had been trying to "manage-to-model," which by Burns' own colorful admission didn't work owing to the deficiencies of the Fed's primitive, even if data and equation riddled, rendering of the massive US economy. Now the suggestion was that the Fed could "manage-to-signal." Since such interest rate signals would putatively emanate from the pure free market—that is, the open outcry trading pits of the Merc—they would be more reliable and monetary policy would therefore be more successful.

That was a misplaced presumption. The new financial futures markets were soon giving out an abundance of signals, but they were not of the wholesome free market character expected. Instead, the futures pits plunged into the business of handicapping and guesstimating the Fed's own future moves. For instance, if traders believed there was an 80 percent chance that the federal funds rate would be increased by 50 basis points in four months, the futures contract for that month would exceed the spot rate by a corresponding amount.

More importantly, beyond handicapping what the Fed "might" do the futures pits also provided Wall Street an avenue to convey what it "should" do. Not surprisingly, the consensus was invariably biased in favor of lower interest rates. Such action by the central bank would elevate the price of dealer-held inventories of stocks and bonds, thereby providing carry gains. It would also ginger the financial environment, enhancing their ability to peddle these securities and other investment products to their customers.

The market-pricing signals that Burns mused about thus eventually became something very different than honest assessment of financial market conditions. In effect, they became Wall Street's marching orders to the Fed. The message was that if Wall Street "expectations" of continuous accommodation by means of low and even lower interest rates were "disappointed," then an economically threatening market sell-off or even panic was likely to ensue.

That is why the Greenspan Fed unilaterally disarmed after the cataclysmic but short-lived stock market meltdown of October 1987. As detailed in chapter 15, the Fed developed a deathly fear of confounding market expectations embedded in the futures markets—so it sheathed the very instruments which could have checked endemic market speculation against its own future policy actions.

All it needed to do in order to curb this bare-faced front-running was to surprise Wall Street with higher margin requirements on stock trading accounts or an unexpected 150 basis point increase in the federal funds rate—or even dust off some bracing rhetoric such as William McChesney Martin's famous admonition that the Fed's job is to "take the punch bowl away just when the party is getting started."

In short, what the Fed needed to do was to openly defy what the market had priced in, thereby pitching the "smart money" surf riders into the drink. Yet, other than its short-lived tightening moves in 1994, the Greenspan Fed allowed the market to dictate monetary policy. In so doing, it transformed the financial futures market into an instrument by which Wall Street captured effective control of the nation's central bank.

The new financial futures trading pits thus were not at all what they seemed. Evangelists like Melamed promoted them as an expression of pure free market innovation. Yet they were actually a free market deformation arising from an anchorless central bank money system that was itself driven by speculators in the pits.

CRONY CAPITALISM, EVEN IN THE
FREE MARKET FUTURES PITS

Since this kind of central bank–enabled financial speculation became fabulously profitable, the participants in these newly opened casinos sought to protect them at all hazards. Ironically, then, financial futures markets soon became a hotbed of crony capitalism as their Friedman-quoting leaders mounted a legislative and regulatory influence-peddling apparatus of immense scale and potency.

As it happened, Melamed's next stop after Burns had been a meeting with the chairman of President Ford's Council of Economic Advisors. And there the improbable transformation of Melamed's eggs and bacon exchange had another serendipitous encounter. Describing this meeting as "a shot in the arm," Melamed recalled that he had been interrupted even before he could explain his proposed T-bill contract. "What a great idea," he reported Alan Greenspan as exclaiming, who then proceeded to "rattle off a dozen uses for such a market."

To be sure, on that particular afternoon in late 1975 Greenspan was merely the Council of Economic Advisors chairman, with not much to do. The Ford White House was still inclined to keep its hands off the US economy. So the future maestro couldn't offer much help except to marvel over the theoretical free market efficiencies which the T-bill contract might bring to finance.

Yet Greenspan's hearty embrace of Melamed's financial futures market that day eventually turned out to be the kind of "shot in the arm" which was literally heard around the world. During his nineteen years' tenure at the Fed, of course, Greenspan tenaciously defended the financial futures market from scrutiny and the occasional challenges of regulators.

There was nothing wrong with that per se, since the free market always needs a defense in the nation's political capital. Yet what Greenspan utterly failed to see was the stunning disconnect between the paean to hard money and the gold standard that he had written as recently as 1966 and the free market romanticism about financial futures which he now so enthusiastically embraced.

Better than anyone else, a lapsed goldbug like Greenspan should have understood that Melamed's currency and interest rate futures market had no rationale for profitability, and therefore existence, unless money was unstable, unreliable, and unanchored in anything more enduring than the ever-changing whims of a board of twelve monetary commissars. Unlike the case of weather-driven corn or natural gas futures, therefore, there was no economic basis for "price discovery" in the Merc financial pits.

The truth was that the market for money futures was being constantly maneuvered, manipulated, and massaged by the central bank. Indeed, had Greenspan given serious reflection to these inescapable truths, he might have realized that fiat money–based futures markets are inherently rent-seeking endeavors; that is, they scalp profits from trading in financial instruments which have no useful or productive economic purpose.

More importantly, he might have also realized that such rent-seeking enterprises could metastasize by leaps and bounds if they were enabled and encouraged by policy actions, such as backstopping speculative asset prices with a central bank put.

In October 1987, in fact, Greenspan rewarded the Merc speculators involved in Melamed's most lethal invention, the S&P futures contract, with just that kind of put, flooding the market with liquidity to rescue speculators even though the main street economy was hale and hearty. From that inflection point forward, Wall Street was off to the races that ended in the meltdown of September 2008.

THE OTHER CHICAGO SCHOOL—OF REGULATORY POLITICS

Leo Melamed had also audited another course in Chicago: the one conducted by Richard M. Daley at city hall. By October 1987, the futures industry had bought and paid for influence in the corridors of Washington in a manner that mirrored the techniques hizzoner had perfected among the aldermen of Chicago. The first was making sure the building inspector knew who he was working for.

At the time Melamed was making his rounds on the T-bill contract, his third stop was with his building inspector, William Bagley, chairman of the newly created Commodity Futures Trading Commission (CFTC). Bagley was a California lawyer and state legislator who knew little about commodities or futures. But he did know Ford's chief of staff, Don Rumsfeld, and the latter had rushed him to Washington in order to open the new CFTC for business by the statutory deadline in April 1975.

Only a few months later Melamed was pressing him to approve the proposed T-bill contract, but Bagley quickly made clear that he knew exactly who he was working for. Although approval of the T-bill contract was technically within the purview of the CFTC, Bagley insisted that a matter of that moment was well above his pay grade. "I love you like a brother and want to do it," he told Melamed, "but I need someone higher up to give me an okay."

That someone was Bill Simon, newly installed secretary of the treasury, but Melamed had not yet made the acquaintance of the legendary bond trader turned policy maker. He was therefore reluctant about making a cold call, reasoning, Chicago style, that "to go without proper protection seemed wrong." To remedy this he began to "call around" and, according to Melamed's account, "Sure enough, I hit pay dirt."

The pay dirt in question was Sanford Weill, the chief of an aggressive trading house known as Shearson and Co. Melamed described Weill as a "shrewd market analyst" who "sensed the great potential of our T-bill contract."

Rarely did Leo Melamed indulge in understatement, but in this instance he surely did. Sandy Weill not only got in on the ground floor, but over the next thirty years proceeded to build a financial trading colossus out of Salomon, Citibank, and dozens of others. In no small measure due to the financial futures markets pioneered by Melamed, Citigroup sported a balance sheet by 2006 which was larger than the entire US banking system had been the day Sandy Weill escorted Melamed into the office of his Wall Street chum.

At least according to Melamed's telling, however, even the formidable Sandy Weill had not actually carried the day alone. As an "additional precaution" he had asked Milton Friedman to call Bill Simon and "again weave his magic." Undoubtedly, it did not require much of Friedman's ample talent for persuasion to convince the free market–loving Simon.

Nor was that outcome either surprising or inappropriate. The problem with Melamed's financial futures was not the free market, but the freely printed money which corrupted it.

When Melamed finally had his audience with Simon "it was a done deal." Yet as in so many other inflection points along the way to September 2008, there was no hearing or issue analysis behind the momentous step of opening up the US Treasury market to the futures pits. According to Melamed's account, Secretary Simon "quickly agreed and signed the prepared approval letter to Bagley."

A TALE OF TWO TRADING HOUSES: SALOMON BROTHERS VS. COUNCIL GROVE NATIONAL BANK

Soon thereafter on January 6, 1976, Milton Friedman rang the opening bell on the Merc's T-bill contract, thereby ushering in the age of interest rate futures. During his usual frenetic campaign to promote interest in the new contract, Melamed had two contrasting encounters which dramatize the true extent of the financial revolution he was triggering.

Salomon Brothers was then the dominant cash market trader of government bonds and accordingly was at the top of Melamed's sales call list. But after giving a polite hearing to Melamed's pitch, the trading house's venerable senior partner, William Salomon, curtly announced that "this is not for Salomon" and thereupon showed the Chicago eggs and bacon trader the door.

Thus, it is perhaps a measure of the radical change in the financial system then in the offing that four and a half years after the events of Camp David, the smartest bond traders in the world had not yet imagined the possibilities of the financial derivatives game. They failed to see that rather than trading cash bonds for thin spreads, they could position themselves on 20 to 1 leverage in T-bill futures, positions that would be driven by and anticipate each and every move of the nation's newly unshackled central bank.

It is perhaps not surprising that even as the House of Salomon took a pass, a Kansas grain farmer with a PhD in financial economics did not have the same reluctance. Wayne Angell operated a 3,300-acre wheat farm and was also a Kansas state legislator, a professor of economics at a local college, and an energetic bank officer at the Council Grove National Bank.

The Kansas bank was a midget and most definitely not on Melamed's call list. So Angell made the call instead, tracking down the Merc's high-profile mover and shaker after reading about the new T-bill futures in the *Wall Street Journal.*

As a veteran user of wheat futures, Angell was fully familiar with calendar "spread trading," which involved a simultaneous short position in one month and long position in another, and also "basis arbitrage" stemming from the difference between the futures price at the exchange and the cash market at any given local delivery point.

Reasoning from these familiar features of wheat futures, Angell told Melamed that he planned to short the T-bill in the cash market and buy the exchange's T-bill futures of the same duration. He would thereby execute an arbitrage that had little risk and would fatten yields on his bank's investment portfolio by a lot more than chump change.

In short order, the Council Grove National Bank was minting money where Salomon Brothers had not yet dared to tread. More importantly, an economically savvy wheat farmer had quickly grasped that financial futures had opened up a vast new arena for leveraged speculation—margin requirements on the new T-bill contract were only 5 percent—and that the "arb" could never really be traded away. Instead, the continuous forays into the Treasury market by the Fed's open market desk would perpetually roil calendar and basis spreads, thereby creating a renewable feast of trading profits.

In any event, there was no special rocket science to Angell's trading math. Within a year Salomon Brothers had been aroused from its slumber, joined the IMM (the Merc financial division), and according to Melamed became "the number one user of our T-bill market and a friend of the IMM for all time."

Indeed, Salomon Brothers soon became the first Wall Street House to go public. It thereby positioned itself to raise the massive amounts of capital that could now be profitably deployed in trades that straddled the cash and futures markets for government debt and a growing range of other securities.

As it turned out, however, Wayne Angell became an even better friend to the Merc than Salomon, and not on account of his small-time trading orders. In 1985, Senator Bob Dole was struck by the idea that the Federal Reserve Board needed nothing so much as the fresh perspective of a small-town banker and farmer who happened to be his constituent. Needless to say, the chairman of the Senate Finance Committee did not need to ask twice the White House chief of staff to approve Angell's appointment, even if Don Regan was a former Wall Street titan not much impressed by country bankers from Kansas.

As vice chairman of the Fed, Wayne Angell saw eye to eye with Greenspan on the merits of financial futures and derivatives. Consequently, when the stock market crash came in October 1987, the message from the leadership suite of the Eccles Building was stereophonic: the S&P futures pit at the Chicago Merc had only been the messenger; unspecified "animal spirits" had been the cause of the crash. In short, in linking up with Greenspan and Angell back in 1976, the clever Leo Melamed had succeeded in erecting some potent defensive perimeters more than a decade before he even knew they would be needed.

CRONY CAPITALISM AT WORK:
HOW THE MERC LINKED UP WITH THE FARM CARTELS

In fact, there was even more. When it came to the art of crony capitalism, Melamed was in a league all by himself. His initial move in the mid-1970s was to secure his base among the good ol' boys who controlled the House Agriculture Committee.

Melamed's experiment with financial rocket fuel should have been of abiding interest to the congressional banking committees, but he helped ensure that the new Commodities Futures Trading Commission, created in late 1974, was in the jurisdiction of the congressional "ag" committees. There it remained secure in the bosom of the wheat-cotton-corn and livestock coalition that ran the US farm cartels.

In enlisting the farm bloc, Melamed hired the chief aide to legendary House Agriculture Committee chairman W. R. Poage as his Washington lobbyist. Not coincidentally, the free market had no more demagogic detractor on Capitol Hill than Poage's fellow Texan Jim Wright, who was majority leader and then House Speaker throughout the 1980s.

Nevertheless, Wright was the first Washington fireman to be offered an "honorarium" to visit the floor of the Merc and had no trouble at all understanding the grand bargain. The free market futures industry would support the anti–free market farm programs and the farm belt Democrats who depended upon them. In turn, the Agriculture Committee kept the free market in the futures pits clear of regulatory interference.

Later, Melamed would note that Wright "understood the Merc and its potential and would become the champion of the industry." Yet what Wright actually understood was that maintenance of the Democratic majority in the House required more and more campaign money, including a fair share of the take from business lobbies.

And in that department Melamed had equipped the futures industry to meet Wright's fondest expectations. In fact, within only a few months of the T-bill contract launch, Melamed had been advised to form a political action committee, which he went about with his usual gusto.

The surprising part, however, was that the prompt had come from "none other than the chairman of the CFTC." Melamed thus invited Bagley to come to Chicago and talk political turkey to five hundred assembled Merc traders. In what was undoubtedly a new advance in the art of crony capitalism, the Washington regulator of Melamed's troops delivered a civics lesson on how they needed to pay to play: "You guys will never have a voice in the process until you have political muscle. For that, you need a political action committee."

The distribution of the largesse from the Merc's PAC was one matter on which Melamed most definitely did not seek the advice of Milton Friedman. In the 1988 presidential campaign, for example, it supplied $20,000 each to the campaigns of Republicans George H. W. Bush and Bob Dole and Democrats Al Gore, Richard Gephardt, and Paul Simon.

Still, the PAC was only the tip of the influencing-peddling iceberg. As Melamed grandly explained, "In the agricultural heyday of the Merc, the visiting dignitary was often a grand champion steer or a prize hog, but after finance came to the Merc, so did politicians."

Accordingly, no fewer than eighty-five senators and two hundred congressmen visited the Merc during the fifteen years after the mid-1970s, where they undoubtedly preened in the same circle on the trading floor where grand champion steers had once stood. The excitement of placing an order for $10 million T-bills or Malaysian ringgit kept the politicians streaming to Chicago, as did the handsome honorarium they were paid upon completion of the trade.

In fact, over the years nearly every politician of national importance was paid to pay a visit to the Merc, including Tip O'Neill, Hubert Humphrey, Ed

Muskie, Walter Mondale, and Ronald Reagan. But there was one habitual visitor who embodied the essence of the new-style crony capitalism which had taken instant root in Milton Friedman's free market in financial futures.

Dan Rostenkowski was the chairman of the House Ways and Means Committee and the leader of the machine Democrats who formed the core of the House majority. At an early 1980s dedication of a still newer and larger Merc facility, Rostenkowski simply noted that "the Merc is to Chicago what oil is to Texas or Oklahoma, what milk is to Wisconsin and what corn is to Iowa."

THE ARRIVAL OF "CASH SETTLEMENT" AND THE EXPLOSION OF LIBOR DERIVATIVES

By 1980, the Merc's currency and T-bill contracts were thriving, and it was also drawing competition in New York, London, and especially from its crosstown rival where the Chicago Board of Trade's thirty-year Treasury bond contract had been a booming success. Yet there remained a more formidable barrier to truly explosive growth than the Merc's exchange rivals; namely, the age-old rejection by traditional agricultural futures exchanges of "cash settlement" upon contract expiration.

In fact, it was the requirement for physical delivery of the product that kept speculation in check. An overly exuberant bidder on the last day of a contract could find himself flooded with carloads of corn or bacon on which he would have to pay storage and ultimately liquidate in the cash market at a loss. Indeed, Melamed himself had once observed that "without delivery, we were not much different than a gambling den."

The Carter-era CFTC chairman, former state insurance commissioner James Stone, thought the same thing, arriving at that conclusion out of an abundance of experience with moral hazard in the insurance business. Accordingly, he would not even entertain the notion of new financial contracts based on cash settlement rather than traditional physical delivery.

As a practical matter, therefore, Stone's stubborn opposition closed the door to what Melamed and his R&D shop could see as the almost limitless next frontier for futures: contracts based on an index or other derivative as opposed to the actual physical unit, such as a carload of bacon or stack of Treasury bill certificates.

And this had become far more than an academic matter. By then the race was on to launch a Eurodollar future in order to tap the market for hedgers and speculators in the vast offshore dollar markets.

That these markets even existed, of course, was a tribute to the post–Camp David breakdown of the international monetary order. Printing dollars with reckless abandon, the Fed had fueled the petroleum and related commodity booms of the 1970s, and these soaring commodity prices, in turn, had generated massive windfall rents which OPEC producers deposited in London-centered dollar deposits.

In the face of the wildly gyrating interest rates that the Fed's maneuvers and manipulations had bestowed on these rapidly expanding offshore dollar markets, the opportunity for profitable speculation was simply mouthwatering. Yet the interest rate in question—the London Interbank Offered Rate, or Libor—was a composite index of short-term deposit rates offered by nearly a dozen leading London banks.

Consequently, the proposed Eurodollar futures could not be settled with physical delivery because there were no actual Eurodollar contracts to dump on some errant trader's lawn. The "commodity" in question was only the paper index published by a banking consortium, an operation which in the fullness of time would be revealed to be crooked to the core.

In the context of this dilemma, the election of Ronald Reagan in 1980 brought an ironic resolution. At the time that Melamed had supported the creation of the CFTC back in 1974, one of his objectives had been most un-Friedman-like. "The thought hit me," Melamed recalled, "that only a federal agency could ordain the legitimacy of cash settlement. If it did, then the Merc could have stock indexes and lord only knows what else."

The crony capitalist cat at the heart of the financial derivatives market was thus let out of the bag. The Merc had been free all along to offer cash settlement contracts because there was no federal law against them. As Herb Stein had put it, they were "voluntary agreements between consenting adults."

What Melamed actually wanted, therefore, was not regulatory permission but federal sanction. The regulatory approval would amount to a good-housekeeping seal for cash settlement contracts. In short, if the Merc was to sally forth from the prosaic world of agricultural market price discovery to an arena of out-and-out gambling, Melamed wanted Uncle Sam's blessing.

He also wanted federal preemption of any exposure to anti-wagering statutes which still cluttered the books of more than a few states, including Illinois. Accordingly, the free market–oriented CFTC commissioners appointed by the Reagan administration soon found themselves immersed in an awkward project.

In the midst of quoting Milton Friedman on the virtues of free market trading pits and the right of traders to agree to settle their contracts with cash, a right they already had, the CFTC ratified the futures industry plan. So doing, they accomplished nothing less than an abridgement of the

Tenth Amendment of the Constitution and the long settled right of states to regulate gambling.

ULTIMATE REGULATORY CAPTURE: WHEN THE CFTC WENT INTO THE FRANCHISED GAMBLING BUSINESS

In the final analysis, of course, state laws against gambling are no more compatible with the requisites of a free society and individual liberty than any other "nanny state" intrusion, whether arising out of mischief on the Potomac River or legislative finagling in the environs of Springfield, Illinois. Yet in gaveling through the 1981 approval of the Merc's Eurodollar contract, the Reagan commissioners did not really strike a blow at the nanny state, as their rhetoric implied.

Instead, they facilitated an act of regulatory capture that literally changed the future course of financial history. Perhaps this outcome was unwitting on the part of some commissioners, but the key CFTC policy maker in this episode, Gary Seevers, fully understood the import. Not long after the ruling he became a Goldman Sachs partner specializing, not surprisingly, in cash-settled financial futures!

So at the end of the day there arose a great irony. According to pure free market theory, the CFTC had no real reason for existence. Yet by virtue of an action which was deceptively portrayed as "deregulation," it had now actually given gratuitous legal and moral sanction to a form of futures contract that would be hazardous even in a stable system of honest money. Under a régime of central bank printing-press money, it was a ticket to catastrophe.

It did not take long for this to become fully evident. The Merc's Eurodollar contract was a smashing success in its own right, but its real "contribution" as viewed by the futures industry was that it validated the concept of cash-settled contracts. This breakthrough then and there opened the door to trading in trillions of new index-based futures and other "derivative" contracts, both on organized exchanges and in over-the-counter trading.

This assessment could not have been more cogently expressed than in Melamed's own words, written in 1993 when the derivatives explosion was just gaining its initial head of steam. "If ever the CFTC needs to prove its value to the marketplace," he opined, "it can, above all else, point with pride at the innovation of cash settlement."

In the event that there was any confusion that Melamed and the incipient financial futures industry viewed the CFTC as their captive enabler rather than independent regulator, Melamed went on to remove all doubt: "I seriously doubt that our industry could have achieved even a fraction of the transaction volume we have already achieved or plan for . . . *without removal of the requirement for physical delivery from futures trade.* That could never have happened *without the CFTC."* [emphasis mine]

THE PERVERSE SEQUENCE:
INFLATION ENDS, GAMBLING STARTS

As it happened, breaking the cash settlement barrier with the Eurodollar contract could not have occurred on a timelier basis. Soon thereafter in April 1982, the Merc launched a truly transformative trading vehicle: the cash settled S&P 500 futures contract.

In less than six months, the wrenching recession which Volcker had triggered to quash the prior decade's virulent inflation reached bottom. Thereupon, a fifty-month run of booming output growth and declining inflation followed, with real GDP growth averaging more than 5 percent annually.

Needless to say, the stock market, which had languished for sixteen years beneath its 1966 peak of 1,000 points on the Dow, now sprung to life and for good reason: corporate earnings began to rebound while the sharp decline in the inflation rate permitted the PE multiple to climb out of the single-digit sub-basement were it had been consigned by the Great Inflation. By early 1983 the Dow zoomed past 1,000 and then reached 2,000 a few years later, finally scaling to 2,700 by August 1987, or more than three times the level it stood at when the S&P futures contract was launched.

While some substantial part of this munificent stock market gain was due to earnings and disinflation, there can be little doubt that the market was now being driven by an artificial turbocharger. Not only did the cash settlement contracts in the S&P futures pits add directly to the speculative froth, but they also facilitated a massive embrace by stock portfolio managers of one of those crackpot trading schemes that invariably bring bull market euphoria to tears.

Mutual fund and other stock portfolio managers had been persuaded that they could ride the bull without trepidation due to a mechanism enabled by the new S&P futures contract called "portfolio insurance." The latter would make them whole for any drop in the S&P index below the set points for which they were insured.

Nor were the mechanics of this swell new financial invention all that mysterious. Whenever the S&P futures price dropped below the trigger points, the portfolio insurer would automatically sell S&P futures, and keep selling until the futures market stopped falling. Thus, if an investor's portfolio declined by 10 percent in the cash market where he was long, this loss would be offset by a 10 percent gain from his position in the S&P futures where he was short.

In reality, however, it was not so simple. As Wayne Angell had intuitively understood from the very beginning, the markets would constantly arbitrage between the cash price and the futures price of the same security or market basket index. That meant that a strong wave of selling or buying in one market would beget a similar pattern in the other. If the wave gathered enough momentum, therefore, this crisscrossing market arbitrage would become a frenzied, self-fueling doomsday machine.

By early 1987, Jim Baker's Texas-style monetary chainsaw had generated a global currency crisis, with the dollar plummeting against virtually every other monetary unit on the planet. So the treasury secretary called another international conference in Paris where he changed the game plan from "student body left" to "student body right."

Now the dollar was to be supported, not trashed. At the center of the so-called Louvre Accord was an interest rate harmonization initiative: the Fed was to snug up interest rates while the Germans did the opposite. New to his post and not cognizant of the financial chaos that lurked beneath the surface of Milton Friedman's floating money contraption, Greenspan did the right thing under the circumstances.

Pursuant to the classic remedy for a weak currency, he began to raise interest rates. In short order it became evident to market veterans that the Fed's efforts to stabilize the dollar could bring the Reagan boom to a halt, which would then widen the already huge federal deficit and thereby drive interest rates even higher.

THE GREENSPAN PANIC OF OCTOBER 1987:
THE ROAD TO THE BLACKBERRY PANIC OF 2008

In response to these darkening financial clouds, the smart money began to sell in September and the first half of October, thereby bringing the stock market's exuberant advance to a grinding halt. Then during the week of October 12, the dumb money began to sell; that is, the portfolio insurance policies which had spread like wildfire began to kick in, causing the S&P futures pits to be swamped in a wave of sell orders that exceeded Melamed's wildest imagination.

On Black Monday, October 19, the doomsday machine which had become implanted in the Merc's S&P pits literally scorched the earth. By the end of the most violent trading day in world history, the S&P futures contract had plummeted by 29 percent, crushing anything which could be arbitraged against it, including the market basket of stocks known as the S&P 500.

Black Monday was the true inflection point in modern financial history. Then and there Greenspan and Angell had a chance to stop the casino by letting the chips fall. Instead, they hit the panic button, ordering the Fed's open market desk to flood Wall Street with cash. Many years later, Greenspan recalled that some of the younger staff at the Fed had counseled, "Maybe we're overreacting. Why not wait a few days and see what happens?"

Ironically, Ronald Reagan's initial response had been identical to these unnamed voices toiling in the Eccles Building. The president had counseled "steady as she goes" and added, "I don't think anyone should panic, because all of the economic indicators are solid."

In fact, they were. The yawning fiscal gap notwithstanding, the nation's economy was not about to plunge into a depressionary spiral. There was a booming 7 percent GDP growth rate in the fourth quarter of 1987 and two more quarters of growth north of 5 percent in 1988.

Perhaps Greenspan knew too much history. Judging that Reagan's statement sounded like Herbert Hoover's infamous "sound and prosperous" pronouncement shortly after the 1929 crash, the new Fed chairman met with Reagan on Tuesday "to suggest he try a different tack." Meanwhile, the Fed plowed ahead in a firefighting mode, ignoring the fact that the economy was in no real danger.

WRONG-WAY CORRIGAN'S LAUNCH OF "TOO BIG TO FAIL"

Worse still, the Fed initiated all the bad habits of seat-of-the-pants meddling by financial officialdom that later became standard operating procedure in subsequent crises. Yet as gratuitous as these 1987 interventions were proven by history to have been, they were not harmless. Garroting the market's effort to clear bad bets and bad behavior, they most surely sowed the seeds of "too big to fail."

As would be the case over and over in the future, this mischief was led by the New York Fed. Its president and future Goldman Sachs partner, Gerald Corrigan, frantically made the rounds on Wall Street, bullying banks and trading firms, demanding that they trade with counterparties they didn't trust. Needless to say, this kind of nanny state operation made a mockery of the very principle that Herb Stein cited in behalf of the cash settled futures ruling: namely, that the state has no business interfering in capitalist acts between consenting adults.

In these instances, of course, one of the adults involved didn't wish to consent. Yet here was the New York Fed issuing marching orders for counterparty trades to be cleared anyway, thereby institutionalizing a kind of paternalistic busybody role which became more blatant with each subsequent financial panic.

It also sowed incalculable moral hazard. Since the Fed manhandled all disputed payments to completion, none failed and no one got fired for unsafe counterparty arrangements. These lax practices were simply allowed to gestate further until the next crisis.

Unaccountably, Alan Greenspan saw no contradiction between his free market philosophy and this kind of capricious meddling. In his memoirs he described Corrigan as "the hero of this effort" and that it was "his job as head of the New York Fed to convince . . . Wall Street to keep lending and trading—to stay in the game."

Stay in the game! Eighteen years later, Chuck Prince, the hapless lawyer put in charge of the Citibank train wreck, said the same thing; that is, that he would keep his traders and bankers dancing until the music stopped.

In the cold light of day, it is evident that Greenspan had already fallen into splitting hairs after less than three months on the job. While acknowledging that "ordering a bank to make a loan . . . would be an abuse of government power," he also approvingly recited Corrigan's standard speech. He purported to instruct hardened Wall Street financiers on the rudiments of customer relations: "We're not telling you to lend . . . just remember people have long memories, and if you shut off credit to a customer . . . he's going to remember that."

You think? Indeed, why this kind of patronizing Business 101 reeducation message should have led Corrigan to "bite off a few earlobes," according to Greenspan's description of Corrigan's technique, is not exactly clear. But the real issue was not whether the New York Fed was "urging" as opposed to "ordering" bankers to accept unwelcome counterparty risks. The question was, why did Wall Street need a governmental nanny to help assess risks and clear trades, even in the heat of a sell-off?

WHEN GREENSPAN WHIFFED: THE END OF FREE MARKET FINANCE

The implication was that free markets don't work when they are most needed, and that the financial system was already broken, dangerously unstable, and not to be trusted in a crisis. And this was at a time in October 1987 before credit default swaps, collateralized debt obligations (CDOs), and many of the other "financial weapons of mass destruction," as Warren Buffet would later call them, had even been invented.

In fact, Greenspan whiffed on his first time at bat, and in so doing he began to eviscerate the market's capacity for self-correction. This breakdown, in turn, ensured that "free money" liquidity–pumping campaigns would be needed repeatedly to offset future panics in the free market. The Fed was already on the slippery slope.

An even more damaging nanny state intervention occurred the day after the crash. On Tuesday, October 20, the market staged an initial dead-cat bounce rally but by midday hit an air pocket as buy orders dried up for even the big-cap names of the day. During a frenzied two-hour interval around midday, the New York Stock Exchange came within minutes of closing, and the Merc actually did halt trading for thirty-five minutes because the markets were bidless and in free-fall.

Then suddenly around 12:30 P.M. the market reignited. It was almost as if the ghost of J. P. Morgan had sent his emissary to the US Steel post and placed a buy order, as he did when he single-handedly stopped the Panic of 1907.

But it was no ghost that placed a flood of buy orders during the post-Tuesday-morning rebound, nor was it even Adam Smith's invisible hand of the market looking for a bargain price. Instead, it was the visible hand of Washington that had begged, browbeaten, and bullied corporate CEOs to rush into the stock market in unison to buy back their own shares.

Apologists might be inclined to excuse this assault on the free market as representing the overwrought emotions of bunkered-down officialdom. Arguably, even the scholarly Greenspan may not have known about Teddy Roosevelt's superb example from the 1907 Wall Street turmoil, when he stayed in the swamps of Louisiana on his bear hunt rather than trouble himself with the commotion at the New York Stock Exchange.

Most assuredly, however, Greenspan and the other officials did not begin to appreciate how booby-trapped the capital markets were with leveraged gambling schemes and speculative computerized trading programs. In fact, by not allowing the market to burn itself out on October 20 and the days that followed, the Fed was actually catalyzing another even more dangerous phase of the speculative bubble.

The market needed an aloof disciplinarian at that historical inflection point. What it got instead was a hand-wringing central bank nanny giving the "all clear" sign when none was warranted.

In truth, the October 1987 crash would have done no lasting damage to the American economy. As in the case of the BlackBerry Panic of 2008, the archives of the Fed and Treasury do not hold even a hastily scribbled analysis of the transmission process by which pricking an immense, artificial bubble in the stock market would have driven the Main Street economy into the drink. As shown in the next chapter, there was no such prospect.

Nor did the Fed even consider the long-run gains foregone due to its market-propping interventions. Portfolio insurance had been an exercise in sheer stupidity, enabled by the cowboys in the S&P pits who were speculating with 5 percent down payments. Mr. Market's vengeful punishment, therefore, was not an irrational outbreak of "animal spirits" as the Fed implicitly held, but simply a necessary and unavoidable purge of the speculative excesses that had been fostered by the central bank itself. The true meaning of Black Monday was that the monetary system was fundamentally broken and that the cronies of capitalism had been steadily booby-trapping the marketplace with dangerous and unstable financial instruments.

THE MOST THUNDEROUS WAKE-UP CALL
IN FINANCIAL HISTORY—IGNORED

The 23 percent stock index drop on Black Monday had been double the 13 percent drop during the worst day of the 1929 crash. The $500 billion in paper losses approximated the GDP of France. Could the nation's central bank have gotten a more urgent warning that the US financial system was already drastically out of kilter?

But the Greenspan Fed misunderstood the most thunderous wake-up call in financial history. Had it not been so attentive to the wails and moans from the trading pits in both New York and Chicago, it might have seen that the post–Camp David régime of printing-press money was also an incubator for speculation and leveraged trading schemes of magnitudes and riskiness that had been theretofore unimaginable.

Greenspan, Angell, and most of the rest of the Fed were perhaps too smitten with the wonders of the free market. Somehow they totally ignored the corrupting influence of the freely printed money they were dispensing.

It's notable that writing about the traumatic events that greeted his first months in office more than twenty years later, Greenspan offered not a single clue as to why the rabid market animal which had bared its teeth on Black Monday had appeared out of the blue. Certainly the Fed had never asked whether the crash had anything to do with its own conduct of monetary policy under the new floating money régime and the now vast marketplace of hedging machinery that had arisen to cope with it.

Instead, the financial futures market was given a clean bill of health, which under the circumstances was preposterous. Leading a whole posse of Wall Street notables gathered to assess the crash, Nick Brady, head of Dillon Read and therefore the managerial heir of the great Douglas Dillon, did not live up to his pedigree. The S&P 500 futures pits had become a raging financial cyclone, dropping by 29 percent in a single day, yet the Dillon Commission did not find much wrong except the need for ameliorative gimmicks like circuit breakers.

So no lessons were learned and seat-of-the-pants monetary policy went on its merry way, functioning increasingly as a central economic planning scheme. For several more years Greenspan remained the incessant data hound, alert to every movement of scrap iron prices, containerboard shipments, and any sign of incipient goods and services inflation. Ironically, however, he largely ignored the growing menace in the financial markets.

So the age of the Greenspan Put began, even if that was the furthest thing from the chairman's intention. Rather than permit the market to purge the first great speculative bubble which had emerged from the Friedmanite régime of floating central bank money, the Fed had charged forward in just the opposite direction.

When the bond market turmoil came in 1994, followed by the peso crisis shortly thereafter and then by the Asian, Russian, and Long-Term Capital Management crisis as the decade unfolded, the patented fire brigade response of October 1987 was repeated with increasing intensity. Eventually the market's capacity for self-correction was eviscerated entirely, setting the stage for the toxic deformation known as "too big to fail."

CHAPTER 15

GREENSPAN 2.0

W ITHIN A FEW YEARS, THE CARNAGE OF BLACK MONDAY WAS merely a historical footnote. It had not left a trace of damage on Main Street, meaning that the Fed had panicked for no good reason. Indeed, it had been a "neutron crash" from which the national economy emerged not only standing but actually expanding. Given that the quarter began with a stock market wipeout of immense violence, the robust 7.1 percent GDP growth rate recorded during the final quarter of 1987 was almost freakish.

Yet it would be a drastic mistake to view Black Monday as merely Wall Street sound and fury signifying nothing. The S&P 500 index had stood at nearly 340 as recently as mid-August before suddenly plunging to 225 on October 19. Other than during the 1930s, there had never been anything close to a one-third drop in the stock market in just sixty days.

BLACK MONDAY: WASTED CRISIS

Black Monday constituted a warning, therefore, but the danger it foretold was actually about the risks and instabilities accumulating within the financial system itself. Already by the late 1980s, Professor Friedman's floating money contraption had resulted in a substantial loosening of the capital and money markets from their historical moorings in the real economy.

Accordingly, what happened on Wall Street would increasingly reflect the machinations of the nation's central bank, not the economic outlook for Main Street. The stock market was no longer a mechanism for discounting corporate earnings; it was becoming a monetary slot machine for placing wagers on the actions of the nation's central bankers.

As seen previously, the Black Monday crash had been fueled and accelerated by the new tools of computerized speculation, and most especially program trading in the S&P futures pits. But the initial catalyst for the selling panic had been a mistaken reaction in the equity markets to the new Fed chairman's tightening moves within weeks of taking office in August 1987. Wall Street appeared to believe that it was dealing with another

Volcker; that is, with a successor who was reputed to be an economic conservative and who had even been tutored on the virtues of the gold standard by Ayn Rand.

Greenspan's weak-kneed response to the stock market plunge readily dispelled that misimpression. It also forfeited a golden opportunity to put financial discipline and sobriety front and center at the nation's central bank. The new Fed chairman only needed to pronounce that the American economy was healthy and to then repair to the sound money posture that Carter Glass had sketched out seventy-five years earlier. In so doing, he would have reminded Wall Street that the Fed had no dog in the equity market hunt and was therefore indifferent to fluctuations in the stock averages. Under free market capitalism, it was the job of investors, traders, and speculators, not the central bank, to determine how the stock market would value prospective corporate earnings.

By putting the stock market on life support following Black Monday, however, the Greenspan Fed crossed another monetary Rubicon. For the first time in its history, the Fed embraced the stock averages as a target of monetary policy and affirmed that the path to economic prosperity wended through the canyons of Wall Street.

This fateful decision set up the unelected branch of the state to be mugged and captured by crony capitalists as it became more deeply ensnared in the machinations of Wall Street speculators. Black Monday, therefore, constitutes another key inflection point in the long cycle of financial deformations that were triggered by the Camp David repudiation of America's external debts and domestic financial discipline.

NO TIN CUP FOR WALL STREET

The transmission mechanism between the central bank and Wall Street is a small circle of authorized, or "primary," bond dealers who execute the Fed's open market purchase and sale of government debt. After the demise of Bretton Woods, the Fed became a chronic and massive purchaser of Treasury securities and only an infrequent seller.

This asymmetry was financially corrosive in its own right, since the Fed buys government bonds by depositing newly created cash in dealer bank accounts. In turn, the heavy flow of new cash into the banking system meant the Fed was fostering far too much cheap credit—funds which fueled speculation in commodities during the 1970s and stocks and bonds in the late 1980s and 1990s.

Yet there was an even more insidious aspect. The Fed's post–Camp David license to perpetually monetize government debt caused a dangerous transformation of its bond dealer network. These banking houses had long been a Wall Street backwater populated by a handful of undercapitalized bond brokers who traded government securities by appointment.

During the Greenspan era, however, it became a phalanx of balance sheet powerhouses aggressively engaged in the Treasury debt moving and storage business. In practical terms, the bond dealers became a potent lobby for easy money, and for obvious reasons: falling interest rates generated windfall gains on the bond inventories carried by the primary dealers and also lowered the cost of carry on their heavily leveraged balance sheets.

Accordingly, the Wall Street pressure to monetize government debt reached toxic dimensions in the years after Black Monday. At length, the first Greenspan stock market bubble was born. Between 1987 and 1998, for example, the Fed doubled its holdings of government debt, thereby pumping freshly minted deposits into the bank accounts of Wall Street primary dealers at a 7.5 percent annual rate. This was a money-printing spree that topped even the record Arthur Burns had set during the inflationary 1970s.

What Wall Street wanted in the years after 1987, however, was the opposite of what the American economy actually needed. Given the great East Asian wage deflation then under way, the US economy needed not easy money and high living, but a regimen of frugality, including steadfastly higher interests rates to slacken household consumption, coax out greater domestic savings and investment, and encourage the sustained deflation of internal prices and costs.

The years after Black Monday thus constituted a splendid opportunity for the Fed to begin disgorging the massive $220 billion hoard of government debt it had imprudently accumulated during the Great Inflation and the Reagan deficit breakout. Selling down its government debt holdings would have forced interest rates higher—probably much higher, but a market clearing price for debt is exactly what the nation's economy required.

By that point in time, however, the primary dealers were not much interested in buying notes and bills from the Fed because that drained cash from Wall Street. Figuratively it amounted to passing a tin cup that functioned to dry-up liquidity, shrink private credit, and heighten the risks faced by speculative traders.

By forcing interest rates higher, demonetization of the public debt and shrinkage of the Fed's balance sheet would also tend to reduce the mark-to-market value of dealer bond inventories, causing lower profits and reduced bonuses. In short, there was nothing about the pathway to financial discipline and sound money that appealed to the Wall Street dealers. As they saw it, the Fed's job was just the opposite; namely, to function as their financial concierge, supplying cash and liquidity to the markets even if it involved monetizing more and more of the federal debt.

THE REPUDIATION OF GREENSPAN 1.0

Unfortunately, the steely resolve needed to drain the Fed's balance sheet of its huge post-1971 build-up of government debt was not in Greenspan's playbook. The sound of accolades for the tech boom proved more compelling. Accordingly, the Fed continued to rapidly accumulate government debt, and thereby provide the monetary fuel for excessive private credit issuance by the banking system, even after the stock bubble moved toward parabolic extremes after May 1997.

That the Greenspan-led central bank elected to pander to Wall Street, rather than suppress the growing speculative momentum, was surprising. This type of Wall Street coddling had been tried before, in the late 1920s, to disastrous effect, and had been famously denounced by none other than Alan Greenspan himself.

In a notable 1966 essay in defense of the gold standard, Greenspan 1.0 had insisted that the source of the 1929 crash and the Great Depression which followed was that the Fed had "pumped excessive paper reserves into American banks" between 1924 and 1928. This mistaken policy had resulted in excessive growth of private credit, which "spilled over into the stock market, triggering a fantastic speculative boom."

If there was any illusion that the late-1920s stock mania had been benign, Greenspan's indictment of the Fed's drastic error and belated attempt to reverse course dispelled all doubt. By 1929, he had noted: "It was too late . . . the speculative imbalances had become so overwhelming that the attempt [to tighten] precipitated a sharp retrenching and a consequent demoralizing of business confidence . . . the American economy collapsed . . . the world economies plunged into the Great Depression of the 1930s."

Needless to say, by the mid-1990s Greenspan had apparently unlearned everything he had previously known about financial bubbles and the terrible consequences of unchecked speculative manias. His previous conviction that by 1929 it had been "too late" and that the boom should never have been fostered in the first place was likewise abandoned, if not explicitly recanted.

So it happened that the revisionist doctrines of Greenspan 2.0 took shape during the maestro's initial decade at the helm of the Fed. Not only did he shed his long-standing philosophical opposition to monetizing the federal debt, but also Greenspan 2.0 readily succumbed to pressure to feed the Wall Street dealers with a continuous flow of fresh cash.

WALL STREET'S NEW CONCIERGE:
HOW BUBBLE FINANCE WAS BORN

The Fed's capitulation to Wall Street in an economic environment which was strongly deflationary had incendiary effects in the capital and money markets. The continuous minting of fresh cash stimulated rampant credit growth by means of the shadow banking system's rehypothecation multipliers and through fractional reserve lending by conventional banks.

This outpouring of new credit was overwhelmingly used for speculation in real estate and financial assets, rather than finished goods. On the margin, the latter were increasingly priced by deflationary East Asian labor. This meant that businesses, expecting the price of goods and components to fall, did not build anticipatory stocks as they had during the 1970s. Excessive credit growth was thereby channeled to asset markets, not the goods and services in the CPI.

At the same time, there was growing realization among traders that the Fed stood ready to inject massive dollops of cash into the primary dealer market in the event of an unexpected market setback; that is, undergird the stock market with the Greenspan Put. This encouraged bolder and even more leveraged carry trades, a catalyst which accelerated asset price appreciation still further and generated even more collateralized debt creation.

The Fed's embrace after 1994 of speculation-friendly monetary policy also generated effects that reached far beyond the stock exchanges. As indicated, it enabled Wall Street to extend the tentacles of financialization deep into the nation's home finance market through thousands of mortgage boiler rooms operated out of rented Main Street storefronts. These shoestring brokers were wholly dependent upon the generous warehouse credit lines extended by Wall Street, but with no skin in the game they became dangerous dispensers of bad housing credit.

These egregious mortgage-funding arrangements were by no stretch of the imagination an invention of the free market. No banker in his right mind would have funded financial warehouses stuffed with billions of illiquid mortgages of dubious credit quality, unless he was confident that the Fed would keep interest rates pegged to its stated policy targets. Only when the Fed functioned as Wall Street's reliable concierge would dealers have sufficient time to securitize and unload these vast accumulations of raw assets to the unsuspecting. Indeed, under a Volcker-type monetary régime wherein the markets were always at risk for unexpected changes in central bank policy, it is virtually certain that the mortgage boiler rooms, and legions of like and similar vehicles of credit-based speculation, would never have gotten off the ground.

Likewise, strip malls, office buildings, and McMansion subdivisions sprang up across the nation in great profusion based on acquisition, development, and construction (ADC) loans that violated every canon of sound lending. These so-called ADC facilities were habitually underwritten at more than 100 percent of costs, allowed developers to extract huge up-front fees and profits, and depended for repayment entirely on "takeout" financing at property prices which far exceeded the present value of available cash flows.

Again, this kind of dodgy financing was rooted in the Fed's monetary largesse. Even the small community banks which originated these cheap construction-period credit lines were confident that upon project completion, borrowers could access low-cost takeout financing from the Wall Street securitization machine.

In hindsight, these egregious financial excesses beg a great unanswered question: Why did Chairman Greenspan permit this vast financial sector deformation to metastasize during the years leading to the dot-com crash and later the housing crash? After all, these bubbles were a virtual replay of the 1920s financial mania he had so accurately diagnosed.

THE 1990S BORROWED PROSPERITY AND THE MYTH OF CHINESE SAVERS

The maestro had taken tea at Ayn Rand's gold standard salon after working hours, but made his living during the day as an industrial economist. During two decades of practicing this craft he learned to read the entrails of orders, inventories, shipments, and unit costs more expertly than virtually all of his peers—a practice that continued during his tenure at the Fed.

With each passing year, however, the price of scrap iron and the level of containerboard inventories were less relevant: the steel industry was turning into a rust bucket and the demand for industrial packaging migrated from the upper Midwest to Guangdong Province.

So the somewhat benign readings issuing from the old economy's entrails provided false comfort. They showed moderately expanding output, subdued inflation, and falling unit labor costs. More than 30 million new jobs were added between 1987 and 2000, for example, while business plant and equipment spending more than doubled in real terms, and consumption spending grew at a real rate of 3.5 percent annually. Adding frosting to the cake, the exploding technology boom emanating from Silicon Valley implied an unprecedented outbreak of technological innovation and entrepreneurial vigor.

At the end of the day, however, the 1990s technology boom left a dazzling trail in the financial firmament, but it provided only a tiny boost to output and jobs down at ground level. Moreover, away from the flashy precincts of high tech the national economy was deeply bifurcated: sectors subject to international trade experienced external competitive shocks like never before in American history. At the same time, most of the gains in the domestic service sector were fueled by debt, capital gains, and government spending.

In the former instance, there were about 22 million jobs in the nation's agricultural, manufacturing, forestry, mining, and energy industries on the eve of Black Monday. After a decade-long macroeconomic boom during the 1990s, however, the job count in these tradable goods sectors had actually declined by 7 percent, and that was just a warm-up for the crushing blows experienced by the tradable goods sector when the China export machine reached full power in the decade which followed. During the first twelve years of the twenty-first century, employment shrank drastically to only 14 million jobs and the tradable gross share of output dropped to preindustrial–era levels.

The apparent jobs boom during the thirteen years ending in June 2000 skewed almost entirely to secondary and tertiary activities, not primary production. The big jobs growth categories included gains of 20 percent in real estate and finance, 24 percent in retail, 33 percent in construction, 41 percent in leisure and hospitality, and nearly 60 percent in health and education services. In essence, the nation was consuming, borrowing, and financing its way to prosperity.

More crucially, the principal manifestations of this financial deformation according to Greenspan 2.0 were attributable to the verdict of the free market. That which was going terribly wrong, such as the explosion in the national leverage ratio or the collapse of the trade accounts, could therefore be ignored or at least dismissed as the superior wisdom of the unseen hand.

As will be seen, Greenspan carried this to a ludicrous extreme. Even after leaving the Fed, he continued to dismiss the collapse of the nation's trade accounts and the consequent offshoring of huge chunks of the middle-class economy as clinically explainable market outcomes. There was nothing untoward or even unnatural about this devastation, Greenspan 2.0 argued. Instead, the market of global savers had somehow voluntarily decided to invest in massive hoards of US investment securities.

Greenspan even invented a specious concept called the "home bias" to explain the soaring current account deficits which resulted from his own cheap dollar policies. Explicating this thesis in his memoirs, the maestro explained that a "decline in home bias is reflected in savers increasingly reaching across national borders to invest in foreign assets. Such a shift causes a rise in the current account surpluses of some countries and an offsetting rise in the deficit of others."

The part he didn't explain was why most of these newly mobilized cross-border "surpluses" were coming from poor people who had just emerged from the rice paddies of East Asia. Nor was it evident why the US assets purchased with these "savings" were heavily concentrated in central banks that unabashedly pegged their currencies to promote exports. The fact that the ultimate users of these "savings" were increasingly indebted US house-holds wasn't explained, either.

In short, Greenspan's "home bias" theory boiled down to a convoluted rationalization for the explosion of household debt, which had risen from a historical trend of 45 percent of GDP prior to 1980 to more than 80 per-cent by the turn of the century, and ultimately to 100 percent of GDP before the final housing bubble burst in 2008. But that lamentable development, Chairman Greenspan insisted, was due to the intrepid multitudes of "savers" who populated the export economies of East Asia, not low interest rates and easy money at home.

Having just emerged from the poverty of the villages and rice paddies, these skinflints, according to the maestro, had virtually forced the United States to run large current account deficits. The profligate overconsumption of imports by American consumers was thereby explained. American households ended up deep in debt because the unseen hand of the free market had ordered it.

Undoubtedly, Greenspan 1.0 would have rejected the home bias theory as rank nonsense. The American economy was not being pleasured by one billion rampaging Chinese savers. Indeed, the well-known patterns of true global capital mobility that had obtained under the pre-1914 gold standard pointed in exactly the opposite direction.

This relevant stretch of financial history demonstrated that the so-called home bias had been abandoned not in the 1990s, as Greenspan pro-pounded, but in the 1870s. And it had been abandoned not by the poorest nations, but by the richest.

For the better part of a half century before the First World War, English capitalists had flooded the far-flung lands of the British Empire as well as the United States, Argentina, China, and Latin America with their excess savings. There was nothing new about capital exports.

Yet, as a true expression of capital mobility under a régime of sound money, the British, and to a lesser extent the French, savings outflow of this period had a distinguishing hallmark which put the lie to Greenspan's im-plausible revisionism. English capitalists had sent their savings abroad to invest in productive assets like railroads, mines, and factories which could be expected to produce a return. That was a far cry from the present era, where capital was being exported by mercantilist central bankers and their domestic wage slaves, not genuine capitalists.

More importantly, these purported "savings" ended up stuffing the kitchens, closets, and living rooms of American households. Needless to say, the US Treasury bonds taken back by the mercantilist central bankers were the obligations of unborn American taxpayers, not income-producing assets.

While it lasted, this borrowed prosperity gave enough buoyancy to the traditional economic indicators such that their weakening "internals" could be glossed over. The Bureau of Labor Statistics archives show, for example, that 22 million jobs were added to nonfarm payrolls between the mid-1990 and the mid-2000 cyclical peaks. The startling reality was that only 3 percent of these 22 million jobs were generated by the technology industries, even when inclusively measured.

There were about 800,000 new jobs in the computer design and engineering sector, for example, but that was only part of the story. These gains were substantially offset by 20 percent employment shrinkage in the actual manufacture of computers, peripherals, and electronic components. When all was said and done, the tech boom produced more financial fireworks than domestic economic growth; it was not the next great mass-production industry like textiles or automobiles.

The Greenspan mantra of growth, technology, and free markets was thus fatally incomplete. Technology was generating miracles of invention, but only a modest addition to economic output and a pittance of new jobs. As will be later shown, the vaunted jobs growth of the 1990s was based mainly on old-style service sector jobs in retail, bars, restaurants, beauty parlors, municipal agencies, and real estate brokerages, to name a few. Underlying surging demand for these services was the bubble finance of stock market gains and household and business debt.

BLINDED BY THE EXUBERANCE:
WHEN STOCK PRICES GREW TO THE SKY

The 1990s ballyhoo about the resurgence of free market prosperity was a case of mistaken identity. What was actually happening was an unsustainable boom fueled by the massive rise of household and business debt and capital gains windfalls of unprecedented magnitude.

Front and center was a bull market eruption of the stock markets that dwarfed the legendary mania of the 1920s and defied any semblance of rationality relative to the actual economics of the 1990s. As it happened, it required about twenty-four months after Black Monday for the equity markets to regain their composure and the stock index to retrace its August 1987 high.

But even upon restabilization in 1989, the stock market was not cheap by any historical benchmark. With the S&P 500 at about 350, the broad market index was trading nearly spot-on its historic average at 14.5X earnings.

A decade later, the stock index was in an altogether different financial universe. It had quadrupled to 1,470 and represented an unprecedented 28.5X the actual 1999 earnings of the 500 companies in the S&P index. This valuation multiple was sheer lunacy. The earnings growth trend during the prior decade had been solid but not spectacular, rising at an annual rate of just under 8 percent. So the raging bull market of 1999–2000 was valuing the stock market at nearly four times its earnings growth rate.

While the Fed leadership could not bring itself to even utter the bubble word, any junior securities analyst not caught up in the mania could have explained it. Even high-growth companies with a sustainable product, cost, or technology advantage were not ordinarily valued at more than twice their earnings growth rate, or at a so-called PEG (price-earnings to growth) ratio of two times.

Self-evidently, therefore, the PEG ratio of four for the entire S&P was beyond the pale. This was especially so because even the S&P's modest earnings growth rate during the 1990s had been achieved largely through profit margin expansion—something that could not occur indefinitely because by the end of the decade, corporate profit margins were at their highest point in forty years.

If any further proof was needed that the stock market was in a nosebleed section of financial history, it only had to be recalled that this bountiful valuation multiple had been applied not just to the fleet-footed companies comprising the so-called "new economy," but to the earnings of the entire range of bread and butter firms which made up the S&P 500, including smokestacks, airlines, grocery chains, and utilities. In fact, only 20 percent of the S&P 500 could be even vaguely described as technology growth companies.

The true mania, of course, raged in the technology sector itself. When it reached its frenzied peak in March 2000, the NASDAQ index stood at 100X earnings, causing Mr. Market to finally throw in the towel. Even then, the Fed maintained its vow of silence, although it no longer mattered.

By early 2003 the bull market was a smoldering carcass, with the S&P down 45 percent and the NASDAQ off by 80 percent. This collapse was testimony enough that the Fed had fostered a stock market bubble of historic proportion. The final punctuation point, if one is needed, lies in the fact that more than a decade later the NASDAQ index remained 40 percent below its dot-com bubble high, and the S&P finished 2011 at a level it first crossed way back in March 1999.

WALL STREET'S IRRATIONAL EXUBERANCE ATTACK: HOW GREENSPAN THREW IN THE TOWEL

The Fed's willful disregard of the financial bubbles its policy engendered is glaringly evident in Greenspan's treatment of the whole "irrational exuberance" episode in his memoirs. The gist of his narrative, written with the hindsight of a half decade and yet another bubble in the housing sector, was that the bullish madness of the 1990s was an outcome driven by the free market and that the Fed had been powerless to stop it.

As to the latter point, William McChesney Martin would have been spinning in his grave at the implication that the Fed no longer controlled even its own punch bowl. As a student of the 1929 crash, Martin would have recognized easy money–fueled speculation when he saw it, just as Greenspan 1.0 had done in his 1966 essay.

Martin would have also rejected as patently absurd the notion that the 1990s stock market mania was simply the work of the market's unseen hand. Yet, whether out of memory lapse or guile, Greenspan 2.0 never questioned that assumption. He preferred to believe that thousands of buyers and sellers engaged in price discovery on the free market had bid equity market prices to a madcap four times the growth rate of earnings all on their own.

Ensnared in this false premise, Greenspan's explanations for the mania are so threadbare as to be actually illuminating. Better than almost anything else, they reveal how it happened that the nation's central bank, dominated by a lapsed devotee of sound money, fostered a debilitating financialization of the American economy.

Greenspan's famous irrational exuberance speech of December 5, 1996, had not slowed the rampaging bull one bit, and for obvious reasons. His warning constituted just a single paragraph fragment which suggested that the Fed really didn't care about bubbles—if output, jobs, and inflation were not adversely impacted. Furthermore, the clear implication was that no adverse impact was likely since, as the chairman pointedly noted, even the brutal "stock market break of 1987 had few negative consequences for the economy."

At the next board meeting on February 4, 1997, Greenspan led a discussion on the possible need for a "preemptive move," but his tone indicated that the Fed had already developed a paralyzing fear that the market might have a hissy fit if it tightened, and that this would spill over into the political arena: "If we raised rates and gave as the reason that we wanted to rein in the stock market, it would have provoked a political firestorm. We'd have been accused of hurting the little investor, sabotaging people's retirement. I could imagine the grilling I would get in the next congressional oversight hearing."

Paul Volcker might have noted that getting grilled good and hard on Capitol Hill was near the top of the Fed chairman's job description. Instead, Greenspan finished off the discussion with a pussy-footing game plan right out of the Arthur Burns' playbook. With the FOMC's consent, he would first publicly hint at a tightening move, deferring an actual increase in the Fed funds rate until the next meeting. As he explained to the committee, "What we are trying to avoid is bubbles that break."

Accordingly, at its next meeting on March 25 the FOMC approved a pinprick. It voted to raise the funds rate by just 25 basis points to 5.5 percent, thereby insuring that, indeed, no bubble would be broken. Greenspan leaves no doubt about his authorship of this half-hearted whiff. "I wrote the FOMC's statement announcing the decision myself," he noted, emphasizing that he had spoken purely in terms of "underlying economic forces that threatened to create inflation, and did not say a word about asset values or stocks."

This was now the bubble whose name could not be spoken. Yet, perhaps wondering momentarily whether the Fed was their friend after all, the punters on Wall Street caused the market to sell off by about 7 percent in response to the rate increase. After a few weeks, however, traders appeared to realize that the bubble word had not been spoken aloud because the Fed had no stomach for defusing the gambling frenzy under way on Wall Street.

Accordingly, the bull came roaring back later in the spring, recouping the loss and pushing the market up by another 10 percent by mid-June 1997. And with that, Greenspan's quixotic campaign against irrational exuberance came to an abrupt and permanent end.

His parting thoughts on this matter, as outlined in his memoirs, are a stunning admission that in the pursuit of its foggy prosperity management agenda, the Fed had lost all sense of its core mission to maintain sound money and financial discipline. So doing, it had now become a wholly owned vassal of Wall Street. "In effect," Greenspan concluded, "investors were teaching the Fed a lesson."

Yet a strange lesson it was. If there was any mantra among Wall Street traders at the time it was "Don't fight the Fed." So even as late as the spring of 1997, a stout move against the market's bullish sentiment would have been a potent weapon, had the Fed really wished to quash speculative excesses.

Unfortunately, Bob Rubin, the Goldman Sachs emissary on the third floor of the Treasury Building, had by now convinced Greenspan to unilaterally disarm. In the name of the free market, the nation's central bank was to become the speculator's best friend. Greenspan made this perfectly clear in his reprise of these events: "Bob Rubin was right: you can't tell when a market is overvalued, and you can't fight market forces."

Rubin had been a famous arbitrage trader, and getting the Greenspan Fed to roll over was his greatest arb job of all. By its silence the Fed would signal an intention to accommodate an unlimited run-up of the stock averages, giving Wall Street a wide birth to front run a rising market. Then, after the stock indices surged even higher, the Fed would turn a blind eye to the financial mania it was feeding, on the grounds that it couldn't fight the very market it had bulled up.

Greenspan 1.0 would have rejected such sophistry out of hand. Even recent history proved that a Fed committed to sound money should not hesitate to rebuke short-run market manias. Indeed, faced with a similar case of runaway speculation in the market for commodities and oil in October 1979, Volcker did not ask speculators if they would please to stand down in return for only a 25 basis point increase in their cost of carry. Instead, he raised the cost of speculation by 800 basis points and never looked back.

Needless to say, the Greenspan Fed elected the very opposite course of action: "We looked for other ways to deal with the risk of a bubble," Greenspan recalled, but after May 1997, "we did not raise rates any further and we never tried to rein in stock prices again."

THE LTCM CRISIS OF SEPTEMBER 1998:
WHEN FED PANDERING WENT ALL IN

In fact, about eighteen months after the Fed abandoned its effort to prick the equity bubble, the market made its own sharp correction in response to the Russian and LTCM shocks. But even then, the Greenspan Fed could not see its way clear to stand aside and allow the market to do the dirty work. Instead, the Fed moved aggressively in the final quarter of 1998 to actually nullify the market's own corrective adjustment.

Thus, the policy of letting "market forces work their will" was now revealed to be operative only on the upside, not when flagging animal spirits took the stock averages for a tumble. The post-LTCM easing campaign confirmed that the Greenspan Put was now fully in place, thereby igniting the final, nearly hysterical blow-off phase of the stock market bubble.

Indeed, the track record of the Fed's policy actions during this interval is one of outright pandering to Wall Street speculators. After its abortive effort to prick the bubble in March 1997, the FOMC had kept the Fed funds rate constant at 5.5 percent through July 1998. Seeing that it had been given the "all clear" signal, the market took stock prices on a parabolic romp, with the S&P index rising from around 750 to nearly 1,200 in just fifteen months. By any conventional reckoning, this 60 percent gain on top of the prior huge market advance elevated the market to a perilous extreme.

Not surprisingly, therefore, the market retreated swiftly after the Russian default and the LTCM fiasco became public in late August 1998. By the end of September, the S&P index was down by 12 percent, a modest pullback under the circumstances.

Nevertheless, that was enough to spur the Fed into a full panic mode. It hurriedly cut the federal funds rate three times within fifty days, thereby stopping the market correction in its tracks. The wonder in hindsight, however, is why the Fed went into headlong bailout mode when the stock market index was still 40 percent higher than it had been in March 1997, the point at which the FOMC had first detected a bubble and had half-heartedly tried to prick it.

Greenspan's answer requires full citation because it is too damning to be fairly summarized. Staff studies at the time of the Russian default concluded that the Russian default would have negligible impact on the American economy. In Greenspan's telling, "It was highly likely that the US economy would continue expanding at a healthy pace."

So why give financial speculators, who had become increasingly brazen, an unmistakable assurance that the Fed would send the pumper brigade to flood Wall Street with cash in response to the slightest economic hiccup? Greenspan's answer was no more compelling than the case for buying crash insurance from an airport vending machine.

Notwithstanding the solid outlook for the real economy, the Fed had opted to ease interest rates due to "a small but real risk that the default might disrupt global financial markets . . . we judged this unlikely but potentially greatly destabilizing event to be a greater threat to economic prosperity than the higher inflation that easier money might cause."

Obviously, the threat of higher inflation wasn't the real issue and was, in fact, a red herring in a world in which the red factories of East China were expanding at breakneck speed. Likewise, during the fall of 1998 the considerable short-run momentum of the national economy was transparently evident in the Fed's key high-frequency indicators on orders, shipments, consumption, and investment.

Thus, during the fourth quarter real consumption increased at a 6.3 percent annual rate, fixed investment spending rose by 13 percent annually, and exports climbed at a rate of 16 percent in real terms. That data is stunning proof that there was no economic emergency.

The Main Street economy had not faltered one bit in the aftermath of the Russian and LTCM crises, and for good reason. Those events, like comparable financial panics in the decade ahead, were not economically "contagious" and largely played out in the gambling halls of New York, London, and Moscow.

Indeed, the national economy's bottom-line measure, real GDP, actually surged at a 7.1 percent rate during the final quarter of 1998. So while the macroeconomy plainly needed no help from the Fed, the clear and present danger actually facing the nation's central bank was the risk of reigniting the raging stock market mania which the LTCM crisis had temporarily cooled.

GREENSPAN'S CONTENT-FREE RATIONALIZATION
FOR THE POST-LTCM EASING PANIC

When the Fed cut interest rates on September 28th, the stock market was still at a breathtaking high and could have fallen another 25 percent before it retraced even its March 1997 level. Greenspan's reasoning as to why the stock index could not be allowed to fall to at least a level which only months earlier he had viewed as manifesting "irrational exuberance" was content free. As during the BlackBerry Panic of 2008, a lurid metaphor was held to be dispositive: "Panic in a market is like liquid nitrogen—it can quickly cause a devastating freeze."

It can be well and truly said that with such lame arguments from friends, the free market needed no enemies. The S&P 500 index was mildly correcting at a level which was triple where it had been a decade earlier. So the Fed's easing action under that circumstance was unaccountable; it boiled down to the implicit proposition that the stock market had become a doomsday machine and that if left on its own it would plunge straight into the abyss.

If this was Greenspan's reason for easing, then Wall Street had already passed the point of "too big to fail." A financial system that couldn't absorb the collapse of the Moscow stock market—a backwater den where thieves gathered to fence their stolen property—or the liquidation of a modest-sized betting pool like LTCM, in fact, was implicitly too dangerous to exist.

Greenspan's proposition was not remotely true, however. There was no economic calamity in letting the stock market come to its senses the hard way, as was evident two years later after the S&P 500 had plunged by 50 percent from its mid-2000 peak. Notwithstanding this purported destabilizing shock, the truth was that the Main Street economy barely faltered and the 2001–2002 downturn proved to be so shallow as to barely qualify as recession.

So the truth was that the Fed had turned its monetary fire hose on the stock market in September and October 1998 for no good reason. These misguided "emergency rate cuts" had caused the S&P 500 index to soar from 1,000 to nearly 1,500 by June 2000. This amounted to a 50 percent flare-up in less than twenty months, and one which was destined to come plunging back to earth.

During this final flameout, the maestro's blindness to the speculative mania that the Fed itself was fostering became palpable. In the middle of the final parabolic run of the market in 1999, Greenspan told a congressional committee that the Fed would not "second guess hundreds of thousands of informed investors."

Yes, Wall Street investors were "informed," but what they were informed about was the eagerness of the nation's central bank to put an absolute floor under the stock market and thereby make even rank speculation a "can't lose" proposition. In his congressional testimony, the chairman of the Federal Reserve actually put speculators on public notice that the Fed would continue to eschew any and all efforts to impose financial discipline.

Henceforth, if a financial bubble should break, the Fed would clean up the mess after the fact. Needless to say, that utterance guaranteed that the stock bubble would keep on inflating because now there was no fear whatsoever that the Fed would rediscover Martin's punch bowl and take it away. Even when the Fed did begin raising interest rates in mid-1999, it was in baby step increments of 25 basis points and well telegraphed to the market.

Through it all, Greenspan was apparently operating on a truly misbegotten assumption; namely, that financial bubbles are an ordinary-course market upwelling that need not trouble policy makers overly much. "While bubbles that burst are scarcely benign," Greenspan opined, "the consequences need not be catastrophic for the economy."

Thus reassured, the financial markets partied on. Yet here was the essence of the giant error that would lead to irreversible financial deformations in the years ahead. The Fed chairman was disingenuously attributing the rampant financial mania all around him to the verdict of the free market rather than the monetary jet fuel the Fed was pouring into it.

FREE MARKET CATECHISM AND
THE ELEPHANT IN THE ROOM

So free market catechism, ironically, became an ideological cover for what amounted to reckless negligence by the central bank. Even long after the fact, when it was evident that capital markets had been turned into dangerous casinos, Greenspan did not hesitate to exonerate the Fed's failure to rein in the very stock market bubble it had fostered: "I'd come to realize we'd never be able to identify irrational exuberance with certainty, much less act on it, until after the fact. The politicians to whom I explained this did not mind; on the contrary, they were relieved that the Fed was disinclined to try to end the party."

It goes without saying that the occupational calling of politicians is enabling the party, not ending it. Yet by 1999, even Washington didn't need a central banker to explain the science of bubble detection—it was plainly evident that the Wall Street party had now succumbed to the madness of the crowd. The parabolic path of the NASDAQ index during that final period left nothing to the imagination.

In January 1997, when the Fed had been in the middle of its cogitation about irrational exuberance, the NASDAQ index had stood at 1,200. After it completed its post-LTCM panic-easing cycle in late 1998, the index had doubled to 2,400. And then it doubled again, reaching 5,000 just over a year later in early March of 2000.

In all, the punters on the NASDAQ had bid up the index by an insane magnitude: to wit, by 320 percent in just thirty-nine months. The legendary story of Japanese herd behavior on the eve of its own spectacular crash had now become operative on this side of the Pacific. "If we all cross the street together when the light is red," the saying went, "how can we meet any harm?"

The catastrophic aftermath of the Japanese equity bubble was plainly evident by the final years of the 1990s, and the harm wasn't merely semibenign, as the Fed's "wait till it crashes" stance implied. Instead, it was deeply injurious and debilitating, as demonstrated by Japan's post-crash economic stupor.

Japan had been viewed as the world's unstoppable engine of growth at the time Greenspan became chairman in August 1987, but when the Nikkei index plunged from a peak of 50,000 in 1989 to below 10,000 a few years later, the Japanese economy fractured. It recorded virtually zero GDP gain for the entire decade of the 1990s and its financial system collapsed into a smoldering heap of busted assets and unrepayable debts.

This lamentable breakdown did not happen because Japan's fabled "salary men" got tired of working, or because Japanese factories suddenly lost their competitive edge, or because Japan's total dependence on imported raw materials and energy became too burdensome. These were long-standing structural realities and nothing about them changed after 1989.

The Nikkei crash simply did not arise from the real economy. Rather, the Japanese fiasco was the handiwork of Japan's central bank and its reckless attempt to engineer prosperity by flooding the economy with bank credit, especially after the 1985 Plaza Accord.

So, with the Japanese example squarely on its viewing screen, it was nothing short of astounding that the Greenspan Fed fostered a retracement of nearly the exact bubble path trod by the Bank of Japan. And it did so with about a ten-year lag, meaning it already knew how the movie was going to end.

Indeed, in what amounted to a replay of the Japanese banking bubble, the US banks and the various shadow banking institutions grew by leaps and bounds during the Fed's long money-printing campaign through the eve of the dot-com crash. When this campaign began at the time of the black Monday crash in October 1987, total bank loans and investments along with assets held by money market funds, GSE securities, commercial paper, and repo amounted to about $4.5 trillion.

By the time the NASDAQ began its violent descent in March 2000, however, this total had grown to $17 trillion. And the responsibility for this breakneck rate of expansion in financial assets, almost 11 percent annually over nearly a decade and a half, belonged squarely on the doorstep of the Fed.

In fact, it was self-evident that the $17 trillion in liabilities needed to fund these swollen asset footings had not been generated by a sudden surge in the propensity of households and businesses to save out of current income. The national savings rate had actually plummeted from about 10 percent to 4 percent during this thirteen-year period, meaning that households were putting less into savings accounts, not more.

Instead, the Fed's constant injection of high-powered reserves into the banking system, coupled with the ever increasing visibility and credibility of the Greenspan Put, had fostered a financial chain reaction: newly minted central bank money stimulated rapid private debt extensions, which was used to bid-up asset prices, which elicited more collateralized credit, which drove asset prices still higher.

HONEST SAVINGS VS. CONJURED CREDIT

The Austrian economist Ludwig von Mises had explained this type of credit boom cycle way back in 1911, but by the 1990s the hubris of monetary central planners superseded the plaintive monetary wisdom of an earlier age. In those benighted times, economists and legislators alike knew the difference between the honest savings of the people and bank credit made out of thin air.

To be sure, this staggering explosion of credit money in the banking system had not been a deliberate objective of policy. It happened by default because by the mid-1990s the Fed had become totally preoccupied with fomenting prosperity by fiddling the funds rate. It had ceased to really care about the growth rate of money and credit.

Indeed, Greenspan had by then put a Nixonian kibosh on Friedman's fixed-rate rule of money supply growth; that is, he had declared it "non-operative," and for good reason. As indicated, once the Fed permitted overnight "sweep" accounts, whereby demand deposits are turned into savings accounts while we are sleeping, the Fed could no longer measure "money supply" accurately.

Thus, as the now published minutes of its deliberations show, the Fed staff assiduously tracked hundreds of economic variables, including obscure indicators like rail car loadings of crushed stone and gravel. But as the records of its proceedings also show, the FOMC gave short shrift to tracking and assessing the actual mother of all economic variables, which, of course, was credit in all its traditional and shadow banking permutations.

So as the Greenspan era settled in at the Fed, all the historic rule-based approaches to central bank policy, including even Milton Friedman's fixed M1 growth rate, were abandoned. The fusty notions of sound money and financial discipline embodied in the Greenspan 1.0 doctrine had no resonance whatsoever.

Instead, the Fed had declared itself to be in the immodest business of macroeconomic growth and prosperity management. This was the Greenspan 2.0 agenda, and it was to be pursued purely from the ad hoc wisdom and judgment of the twelve members of the FOMC as they parsed and cogitated on the "incoming data."

Needless to say, there was no small irony in the fact that Ayn Rand's disciple had turned the Fed into a monetary politburo. With a self-assigned mandate to rule the US economy in a manner which was at once plenary and ultimately based on a capricious stab at the unknowable future, the Greenspan Fed insouciantly ambled forward, permitting a huge, boisterous party to rage on Wall Street when every signal light was flashing red with the same warnings that had accompanied the final years of the Japanese bubble.

HOW THE FED TOOK ITSELF HOSTAGE TO WALL STREET

This stance, heedless of history, was rooted in a fatal illusion, widely shared in the Eccles Building, about the Fed's powers to control the American economy. The nation's monetary politburo had come to believe it could deftly maneuver the course of a then-$10 trillion economy through a combination of open market and open mouth operations. Main Street could then be steered, stimulated, boosted, and braked along whatever glide path of growth, jobs, and inflation the Fed deemed appropriate.

All of this grandiose central planning assumed, of course, that the FOMC had a reliable and efficacious transmission mechanism through which it could implement its intentions. But that is something it did not possess, not by any stretch of the imagination. All of its commands and signals had to be processed by Wall Street, which is to say, the money and capital markets. However, in reacting to the Fed's buying and selling of securities and its targets for the federal funds rate or verbal cues and smoke signals with respect to future policy moves, Wall Street was not positioned as an honest broker.

In fact, it functioned as an aggressive counterparty engaged in trading, arbing, and front running everything the Fed did or said. Moreover, as the Fed pumped more and more reserves into the banking system and displayed an increasing disinclination to lean hard against the resulting bubble in credit and equity prices, its policy target drifted. Stabilization of its Wall Street transmission mechanism, rather than management of the macroeconomy, progressively took control of monetary policy.

As Greenspan candidly admitted in his memoirs, the Fed eventually took itself hostage because it could not rein in its agents on Wall Street. He thus noted that when the Fed's first tightening episode came to an end in February 1995, stock prices had swiftly reverted to their upward path and that "when we tightened again in 1997 . . . prices again resume[d] their rise after the rate move."

As the maestro saw it, the Fed was caught in a "puzzle palace" where tightening would have the same effect as easing: "We seemed in effect to be ratcheting up the price move. . . . If Fed tightening could not knock down stock prices . . . owning stocks became an ever less risky activity."

The giant defect in this ratchet theory, however, is that it was based on the Fed's tepid quarter-point federal funds rate moves and its well-telegraphed warnings ahead of time. By contrast, a Volcker-style surprise in which money market rates were dropkicked skyward would not have been so impotent. Greenspan acknowledged as much: "A giant rate hike would be a different story . . . [With that] we could explode any bubble overnight."

Not surprisingly, Greenspan rejected that option out of hand because it was in direct conflict with the Fed's prosperity management agenda. Any stringent moves to discipline the financial system and curtail the rampant asset inflation then under way would have been "devastating [to] the economy, wiping out the very growth we sought to protect. We'd be killing the patient to cure the disease."

Disease was an excellent, if inadvertent, choice of metaphor. By 1998 the US financial system had, in fact, become disease ridden, exhibiting a metastasizing growth of leverage and speculation which the Fed's own printing-press policies had caused. But in Richard Nixon's memorable phrase, the Fed now found itself to be a "pitiful helpless giant," fearful of confronting the very bubble it had spawned.

THE HOUSING BUBBLE WAS WAITING
IN THE FED'S DRAWER

As conceded by the maestro in slightly more delicate terms, "The idea of addressing the stock market boom directly and preemptively seemed out of reach. . . . Instead, the Fed would position itself to protect the economy in the event of a crash."

As will be seen below, the Fed's election to wait it out ignored all of the collateral damage that was being engendered by the 1990s stock market bubble while it was still inflating. Worse still, there had already developed a "consensus within the FOMC" to implement an aggressive money-printing campaign on a post-crash basis.

Greenspan later recalled that having put such a plan in the drawer, the Fed essentially stood around waiting for the stock market to crash; then after the bubble broke "our policy would be to move aggressively, lowering interest rates and flooding the system with liquidity to mitigate the economic fallout."

Needless to say, what the Fed actually had in the drawer was the next bubble—the housing and real estate mania that would spread the speculative fevers across the length and breadth of Main Street America. Self-evidently, the Fed learned nothing about the danger of keeping interest rates too low and policy too friendly to Wall Street during the stock market boom.

The Fed's panicked reaction to the dot-com crash and the subsequent collapse of telecoms and other high-flying sectors in its aftermath make this abundantly clear. The federal funds rate stood at 6.5 percent on Christmas Eve of December 2000. During the following year rates came tumbling down the monetary chimney, as it were, with a clatter.

THE GREENSPAN RATE-CUTTING CAMPAIGN OF 2001:
CENTRAL BANK PANIC WITHOUT REASON

The Fed cut its policy target rate on eleven separate occasions, so that by Christmas Eve 2001 it had plunged to 1.75 percent. If Wall Street ever had any doubt about the Fed's capacity for panic, this inglorious retreat removed it.

Never in the history of the Federal Reserve had there been anything close to a 75 percent reduction in the policy rate in such a brief time. Yet there was absolutely no emergency on Main Street. Real personal consumption expenditures during the fourth quarter of 2001 were actually 2.8 percent higher than a year earlier when the rate-cutting panic was initiated. Likewise, real GDP was still at its highest level in history, notwithstanding a heavy liquidation of business inventories during the final four months of 2001 in response to the 9/11 shock.

Thus, the Fed's furious money printing was about braking the fall of the stock averages, not keeping the national economy afloat. And this unnecessary money-printing campaign was indeed furious. By the time the S&P finally hit bottom in February 2003, the Fed's hand-over-fist buying of Treasury debt totaled $120 billion. This represented a 24 percent expansion of its holdings in just twenty-four months.

To be sure, in the new vocabulary of prosperity management, as dispensed in the Fed's post-meeting communiqués, all this bond buying was explained in highly antiseptic terms. Conjuring vast amounts of new cash out of thin air in order to pay Wall Street for its bond purchases, the nation's central bank maintained it was merely effectuating an "accommodative policy stance" and "easing financial conditions."

Yet these words had no inherent economic meaning; they were just a smoke screen obscuring the plain fact that during the 2001–2002 stock market slump, the Fed pumped $120 billion into primary dealer accounts for no good reason. The purpose all along was to salve Wall Street's self-inflicted financial wounds resulting from the speculative excesses of the equity bubble.

Moreover, the floor under the stock averages resulting from the Fed's flood of cash could not be justified as a desperate last-ditch bulwark to forestall calamity. In fact, the February 2003 market bottom at 840 on the S&P 500 represented nearly a 9 percent compound annual rate of gain for the period stretching all the way back to Black Monday in October 1987.

Was that not enough? In fact, this 9 percent annual rise was the highest consecutive sixteen-year rate of stock price gain in recorded history! Accordingly, there was no reason at all for the Fed to worry about the stock averages or to flood Wall Street with so much cash that a new bubble was inevitable. Indeed, there are fewer things more striking about the deformation of the nation's financial system after August 1971 than this episode.

There was no valid economic emergency. Notwithstanding the 2000–2002 equity market bust, Main Street had only been modestly set back and could have recovered in a healthy, sustainable manner, even if halting, on its own steam. By contrast, there was every reason to purge the borrow, spend, gamble, and get-rich-quick regimen that the Fed had implanted in the American economy. The painful losses from the stock market bust could have served as a powerful catalyst, had gamblers and speculators been left to lick their wounds without hope of more juice from the central bank.

In short, the dot-com bust was the last chance for the Fed to pivot and liberate the American economy from the corrosive financialization it had fostered. A determined policy of higher interest rates and renunciation of the Greenspan Put would have paved the way for a return to current account balance, sharply increased domestic savings, the elevation of investment over consumption, and a restoration of financial discipline in both public and private life.

Needless to say, the Fed never even considered this historic opportunity. Instead, it chose to double-down on the colossal failure it had already produced, driving interest rates into the sub-basement of historic experience. This inexorably triggered the next and most destructive bubble ever.

CHAPTER 16

BULL MARKET CULTURE AND THE DELUSION OF QUICK RICHES

W HEN THE FED FINISHED ITS EASING CYCLE IN JUNE 2003, short-term money rates were at 1 percent and had been slashed by more than 85 percent in just thirty months' time. Needless to say, this kind of unprecedented, madcap policy action cries out for an explanation.

The short answer is that by the turn of the century the nation's central bank had come in complete thrall to Wall Street. In part this was due to the Fed's embrace of a faulty monetary theory; that is, the notion that it could micromanage the vast US economy to prosperity by rigging interest rates and periodically flooding the primary dealers with freshly minted cash. Unfortunately, this had almost nothing to do with the real challenges then confronting the American economy.

These growing structural headwinds included massive trade deficits, rapid offshoring of jobs and output from the tradable goods sector, swiftly rising levels of household debt, a collapsing domestic savings rate, and a buildup of vast overcapacity in some of the bubble sectors like telecoms. None of these genuine challenges, however, could be ameliorated by 1 percent interest rates; they all required less consumption and higher savings, not a cheap money–fueled buildup of even more debt.

Yet the Fed's insensible slashing of interest rates in the wake of the dot-com bust to levels not seen since the Great Depression cannot be entirely explained by the ideological conceits of the nation's new monetary politburo. By 2001–2003, a more insidious force had captured control of monetary policy.

During the thirty years after Camp David, a powerful bull market culture had arisen on Wall Street and spread across the land, based on the proposition that stock prices grow to the sky and that vast riches are obtainable through parabolic gains in the value of financial assets and real estate. Now, as the twenty-first century dawned, the Fed literally was afraid to unsettle the raging bull.

So, as prosperity management through ultralow interest rates became settled Fed policy, not only was it exactly the wrong cure for the real problems of overconsumption and too much borrowing, but it also rewarded what had become an addiction in the markets. Indeed, the Fed's aggressive money-printing campaigns over the prior three decades had finally contaminated the very warp and woof of the financial system. It had spawned a speculative bull-market culture like the world had never before seen.

FABULOUS RICHES AND EFFORTLESS GAINS: HOW SAVING BECAME OBSOLETE

The idea took root, first in the trading precincts of Wall Street and then across the land, that quick riches were there for the taking. The spectacular gains being routinely garnered in the stock market seemed to imply that the traditional rules of capitalist wealth creation—inspiration, perspiration, and patience—had been superseded. Now there was a shortcut to fabulous riches based on effortless gains from leveraged financial speculation.

Get-rich-quick schemes always abound along the margins of capitalist economies, even financially healthy ones. But the Fed's new prosperity management model resulted in an aberrational period of massive and unsustainable financial asset appreciation, owing largely to a drastic rise in valuation multiples. Not surprisingly, there is not even a hint that the self-assured mandarins who ran the FOMC ever once stopped to consider whether the scorching stock price gains its policies were fueling could be damaging to the nation's financial culture.

This phenomenon of multiple expansion—the proposition that an asset which had been worth five times its cash flow yesterday was now worth fifteen times that very same cash flow—was hardly a novel development. It had been at the heart of the late 1920s stock market boom, and had been repeatedly warned about by sound money commentators of the era such as the venerable Benjamin Anderson, chief economist of Chase Bank.

There is no evidence, however, that Greenspan 2.0 ever revisited any aspect of the 1920s stock market bubble, let alone the drastic inflation of valuation multiples which had eventually brought it to ruin. Indeed, among all the ruminations about stock market bubbles contained in nearly a decade's worth of published FOMC minutes there is not even a grade-school discussion of the 1929 crash, by Greenspan or anyone else.

It was as if the 1966 insights of Greenspan 1.0 had been flushed down the memory hole in the basement of the Eccles Building. Consequently, when the Fed succumbed to its easing panic after the LTCM crisis, it did not even remotely recognize that the subsequent run-up in PE multiples followed the identical parabolic rise which had occurred during the final months before October 1929.

In fact, a cursory review of pre-Keynesian commentary from the 1920s would have put the Greenspan Fed into a cold sweat, even if these voices did belong to long defunct economists of an earlier era. Keynes had once used this expression to ridicule any and all wisdom predating his own, but in this instance Benjamin Anderson, Professor Willis, and many of their sound money contemporaries had quite plainly seen the disaster of 1929 coming.

In their view, the 1920s Federal Reserve System fostered way too much private credit. As previously documented, much of this excess had flowed into the call loan market on Wall Street. It grew fourfold after 1922 and had nearly doubled in size, from 4 percent to 9 percent of GDP, in the final fifteen months before the crash. Even Herbert Hoover had fretted about the stock mania fueled by call money speculators.

In his scintillating but long-ignored history of the boom and bust of that era, Benjamin Anderson noted that once the Fed triggered the speculative credit bubble and the broker loan boom went unchecked, the stock market collapse was only a matter of time: "With the renewal of the Federal Reserve cheap money policy late in the summer of 1927, a sharp acceleration of the upward movement of stock prices began . . . a great collapse was certain the moment that doubt and reflection broke the spell of mob contagion . . ."

The 1998–2000 replay was not much different, except this time hot money had taken more sophisticated forms. Speculators did not need to pile up margin loans, because now they could obtain more extensive and even cheaper leverage in the form of stock options and futures and an inexhaustible supply of OTC-based wagers crafted by their Wall Street prime brokers.

Needless to say, by the time the stock market bubble reached its fevered top, the Fed and its staff were so pleased with their own prowess in managing the nation's economy that they had scant use for musty historical narratives. So when the initial Greenspan bull market finally reached its traumatic end, the Fed became focused on reviving Wall Street as rapidly as possible. It never even considered the possibility that the dot-com crash had been a blessing, and that the more urgent need in its aftermath was to thoroughly purge this bull market culture and its now engrained tendency toward speculative excess.

So the way was paved for an even more virulent new round of bubble finance. An equity market boom which lasted almost continuously for the better part of two decades had inculcated vast popular delusions about financial returns. Indeed, the final NASDAQ blow-off generated such immense, almost freakish, capital gains that even the thundering stock market collapse of 2000–2002 could not extinguish the gambling impulses these windfalls had fostered on Wall Street and Main Street alike.

At the end of the day, the first Greenspan stock market bubble had exhibited a greater amplitude and duration that any pervious mania in financial history. Consequently, during the interval between 1983 and 2000, the get-rich-quick paradigm migrated from the margins to the very center stage of the national economy.

ORIGINS OF THE GREENSPAN BUBBLE:
THE CURSE OF UNSOUND MONEY

The nation's get-rich-quick culture reached a fevered pitch during Greenspan's dot-com mania and housing bubble, but it was rooted in the monetary deformations which arose from Camp David. Slowly, but progressively and ineluctably, the Friedmanite floating money contraption poisoned, deformed, and destabilized the capital markets. The resulting radical oscillations of the equity cycle eventually fostered the illusion that stock prices grow to the sky.

In fact, the sequence of goods inflation in the 1970s, and then asset inflation in the late 1980s and thereafter, compounded the illusion. Owing to the first phase, equity markets were depressed. During the next phase of printing-press money, they became manic. Eventually they crashed. As these permutations played out during the four decades after 1971, the free market's price discovery mechanism became the servant of rent-seeking speculation rather than an agent of capital efficiency and economic growth.

The first phase occurred during the decade between mid-1972 and August 1982. It was the era of the Great Inflation and was therefore a terrible time for equities. The period's soaring CPI and double-digit interest rates crushed the PE multiple, and appropriately so. Nominal earnings were being eroded by runaway inflation, meaning that they should be capitalized at a less generous rate.

Accordingly, the PE multiple on the S&P 500 was cut in half, dropping from 20X in 1972 to a modern low of 10X a decade later. Not surprisingly, even substantial growth in nominal EPS during the 1970s was not enough to offset this huge contraction of valuation multiples. Thus, when the US economy finally hit bottom in August 1982 after the Volcker monetary crunch finally tamed the Great Inflation, the S&P 500 index stood at 110.

This was the very same level it had registered in August 1972. Needless to say, zero nominal stock price gain during a decade of soaring inflation resulted in a 50 percent decline in the real value of investor holdings.

It was not by coincidence, therefore, that *Business Week* ran its famous cover story declaring the death of equities near the end of this lost decade. By then investors had been demoralized for so long that they viewed the stock market with loathing. Yet this was merely the beginning of the disorder in the equity market arising from the August 1971 demise of sound money.

When Volcker's determined campaign to crush inflation succeeded, it had the coincident effect of generating a second round of equity market distortion. This time it was in the form of rebound euphoria. As the rate of inflation fell, investors reduced their discount on future earnings. Accordingly, the stock market's PE multiple snapped back toward more traditional levels, causing the stock averages to soar.

This sudden, sharp reawakening of equities after their decade-long malaise was duly incorporated into the "morning in America" theme by the 1984 Reagan reelection campaign. But the stock market liftoff from its 1982 bottom was not a testament to supply-side tax cuts; it was essentially attributable to the Volcker disinflation and the robust expansion of PE multiples which it catalyzed.

By late 1986, for example, the S&P 500 had surged by nearly 90 percent from its trough level, yet earnings per share for the index composite had gone nowhere. After having bottomed at about $14 per share in 1982, S&P profits were still only $15 per share by 1986. So what caused the stock market to pop was not the pace of earnings growth, but the valuation multiple. During this period it rose from a deeply subpar reading of ten times earnings to a very healthy seventeen times.

In financial terms, the market was removing the inflation penalty that had been priced into stock valuations during the Great Inflation, thereby normalizing the capitalization rate for corporate earnings. That completely rational adjustment, however, generated enormous windfall gains for investors who were prescient enough to get back into the stock market upon the initial success of Volcker's campaign to restore some semblance of sound money.

To be sure, the free market does not preclude windfall profits: inventions, discoveries, and entrepreneurial breakthroughs can generate staggering first-mover profits. But what was unfolding in the equity markets now were capricious windfall gains and losses owing to the machinations of the central bank, not bursts of creativity and destruction emanating from Schumpeterian entrepreneurs. The mid-1980s rebound of the stock market PE multiple was thus merely the first of many bullish eruptions rooted in monetary distortions, not sustainable free market prosperity.

Contrary to White House propaganda at the time, therefore, the Reagan Revolution had not unleashed a new era of booming growth and profits. The stock market euphoria had arisen from a one-time valuation adjustment in response to disinflation. For the time being, equities were back because sound money had been partially restored.

To his great credit, President Reagan had rejected the advice of his political advisors to waffle on Volcker's brutal round of monetary restraint. As previously explained, however, it was a victory that did not last long and for a reason that the president did not even remotely recognize. When the famous Don Regan–Jim Baker swap (Baker from White House chief-of-staff to treasury secretary; Regan from treasury secretary to chief-of-staff) occurred in early 1985, it meant that Texas-style economics took over the Treasury and, with it, administration economic policy.

JOHN CONNALLY'S REVENGE: THE PLAZA ACCORD OF 1985 AND THE RETURN OF TEXAS DOLLAR TRASHING

Jim Baker, who hailed from Houston, Texas, had no particular convictions about inflation and money, but he did skew heavily toward the Connally-style insistence that the job of the Fed, above all else, was to stimulate the economy with low interest rates. During his four years as chief of staff he also became expert at maneuvering around Ronald Reagan's core policy instincts.

It was only a matter of time, therefore, before the new treasury secretary would end the president's principled commitment to sound money. By the same token, Paul Volcker, the architect of the singular monetary triumph of modern times, found himself out of a job. In fact, Texas economics grabbed control of monetary policy within months of Baker's appointment, culminating in the ill-fated Plaza Accord of September 1985. Not by coincidence, the days of the initial, healthy equity market recovery were soon numbered as well.

Sound money had been on the road to recovery with the CPI hitting a two-decade low of 1.5 percent in the year ended May 1986. But the dollar's sharp plunge after the Plaza Accord caused import prices to steadily rise, and soon Volcker's hard-won victory over inflation was in jeopardy. One year later in May 1987 the CPI was already 4 percent higher, forcing Greenspan's hand within weeks of arriving at the Fed and triggering the monetary tightening moves which led to Black Monday.

GREENSPAN'S FORTY-FOUR-MONTH EASING CAMPAIGN: RE-BIRTH OF THE BULL, 1987–1992

The next phase of the stock market deformation was the raging bull market of the second half of the 1990s. The planking for this speculative explosion, however, was laid between 1987 and 1992 when Greenspan eschewed the Volcker playbook in favor of coddling Wall Street and massively monetizing the Republican deficits in the face of resurgent inflation.

Greenspan's prolonged easing campaign was not only utterly unjustified, but it also gave birth to the false narrative underpinning the bull market; namely, that the nation's central bank could deftly smooth out the business cycle, elicit an improved trade-off between inflation and employment and propel higher trend growth in productivity and real GDP, thereby establishing the basis for a sharp upward re-rating of stock market valuation multiples.

In pursuit of this false narrative, Greenspan shed his sound money views once and for all in favor of a hybrid of Keynesian macroeconomics and ad hoc interest rate pegging. Needless to say, this was exactly the wrong way forward: resurgent inflation and the burdensome Reagan deficits actually called for a bracing round of monetary austerity and unrestricted headroom for free market interest rates to purge the nascent bubble of debt and speculation.

As it happened, the dollar-bashing policies of the Baker Treasury generated a renewed inflationary cycle, while the massive Reagan deficits were putting heavy upward pressures on interest rates. So 1988 was the perfect time for another episode of Volcker-like resolve: the Fed had all the policy reasons it needed to get out of the government debt market and force a steep, market-clearing rise in interest rates.

Instead, the Greenspan Fed opted to temporize, delay, and adjust interest rate policy in tepid baby steps, and the reason for this drastic error is not hard to divine: Alan Greenspan was not about to bite the hand that had anointed him. Behind all of his econ-speak was an embrace of Republican triumphalism that was utterly unwarranted and which contracted all the sound money principles that he had once held. It is no exaggeration to say, therefore, that the Greenspan apostasy was the crucial turning point on the road to the BlackBerry Panic of 2008.

The abandonment of sound money was already evident during the Fed's half-hearted campaign, begun in the spring of 1988, to reverse the surging gains in consumer prices. During the next year the Fed raised interest rates numerous times, but always in bit-sized increments of 25 basis points that did not surprise or disturb Wall Street. Unlike Volcker, however, the

Greenspan Fed lost its nerve in May 1989 on the first hint that macroeconomic conditions were weakening.

At that point in time, the CPI was still rising at a 6 percent annualized rate, but the Fed threw in the towel anyway and began an easing campaign that would last for the another forty-four months, through February 1993. In this manner, it eschewed the double-digit interest rates that would have been required to decisively quash inflation. Yet it did so not because the US economy was too weak to bear the needed financial discipline.

In fact, the unemployment rate was then just 5 percent and real GDP growth averaged nearly 3 percent during the four quarters after the Fed began its 1989 easing campaign. The real reason for capitulation, therefore, was not that the economy was falling out of bed but that after Black Monday Greenspan had come to reflexively dread another stock market meltdown, and was determined to prevent it at all hazards.

The Greenspan Fed's fear of disturbing Wall Street also allowed the Reagan deficits to go unaddressed during the final year of the Gipper's reign. This cemented the legend that deficits don't matter and enabled the GOP to abandon its job as the agent of fiscal rectitude in American democracy. In fact, had the Fed pursued even a vague semblance of honest monetary policy it would have forced a financial crisis in 1988, crushing both the incipient bull market and the Reagan economic legacy.

Under the circumstances, a sound money policy would have also forced the US Treasury to crowd hard into the nation's modest savings pool to finance the still swollen Reagan deficits. That would have pushed interest rates sharply higher, generating carnage in the government bond market and bringing the so-called bond vigilantes out in full strength. Rather than becoming impaled upon his foolish campaign statement to "read my lips," George H. W. Bush would have been required to take ownership of a sweeping emergency deficit reduction plan during 1988 that most assuredly would have included major tax increases as well as painful cutbacks in defense and entitlements.

The road not taken would have quashed the subsequent legend that Reaganomics was a roaring success because the Fed's refusal to finance the deficit would have precipitated a severe recession, leaving the Main Street economy as bad off in 1989 as it had been in 1981. Likewise, had Reagan been forced to sign an emergency deficit cutting plan on his way out the White House door, the Gingrich wing of the GOP would have had no stab-in-the-back case on which to ride to power. Crucially, the roaring bull market of the 1990s could not have happened without the Greenspan Put that was sealed by a long easing campaign during 1989–1992.

As it happened, of course, the Greenspan Fed elected to stuff more government bonds into the vaults of the nation's central bank. During its forty-four-month-long easing campaign, the Fed expanded its holdings of government debt by $70 billion, or more than 30 percent. In hindsight, this turned out to be a crucial fiscal bridge: in short order the People's Printing Press of China and the remaining convoy of mercantilist currency-pegging central banks joined the treasury bond–buying binge, paving the way for two decades more of deficits without tears.

Meanwhile, the Greenspan Fed's 44-month bond buying campaign gave birth to a quasi-Keynesian policy rationale that could not have been better suited to bolstering the Wall Street machinery of speculation and the bull market culture on Main Street. Thus, when Greenspan's easing campaign began in May 1989 the CPI was up by 5.4 percent over the prior year and fairly cried out for a hard slam on the monetary brakes. But Greenspan cranked up the printing presses anyway because the former industrial economist and forecaster had become smitten with the Fed's giant macroeconomic model of the US economy.

As seen in chapter 14, even the hapless Arthur Burns had concluded the model was worthless, but now it was being embraced by his former student for a stunningly anti-capitalist reason; namely, to permit the Fed to go into the monetary central planning business, guiding the US economy based on the Keynesian worldview embedded in the Fed model.

In the spring of 1989 the Fed's model forecast that the galloping rate of CPI gains would begin slowing in the years ahead. So when the Fed began easing right into the jaws of 5 percent inflation, the rationale for violating every known rule of sound money was purely Keynesian: based on the *prospective* easing of inflation the Fed now had more leeway to "accommodate a higher level of employment and output."

This new stance was expressed in the matter-of-fact prose of Fedspeak, but it embodied a shocker: while quietly financing the giant Reagan deficits, the Fed was embracing a gussied-up version of the Phillips curve—that is, averring that with inflation receding in the future, it had more room to stimulate job growth in the present. The rout of Greenspan 1.0 was now complete. The Fed would henceforth monetize more and more of the public debt in order to stimulate aggregate demand and therefore more GDP growth and jobs as long as inflation was within acceptable bounds.

Self-evidently, it was no longer the case that a large volume of government debt "can be sold to the public only at progressively higher interest rates," as the Maestro had once insisted in his 1966 essay. Back then he had also observed that "government deficit spending under a gold standard is severely limited" but that "the abandonment of the gold standard made it possible for . . . [governments] to use the banking system as a means to an unlimited expansion of credit . . ."

Needless to say, Greenspan's about-face during the 44-month easing campaign won accolades from the Keynesian professoriate and the Wall Street speculators alike. Yet he had also observed in his now "non-operative" essay that "the law of supply and demand is not to be conned. As the supply of money increases . . . prices must eventually rise."

As it happened, the American public was not conned. Greenspan incurred the worst inflation record of any previous Fed chairman during his first four-year term, save for the hapless Arthur Burns. The CPI increased by an annual average of 4.6 percent during this period, a rate of inflationary erosion that would have cut the value of the dollar in half every fifteen years.

The period from August 1987 through mid-1991 provides a true test of Greenspan's monetary policy, because it predated the tidal wave of wage deflation which rolled in from China and East Asia in the final years of the twentieth century. The results show that Greenspan 2.0 had become a closet inflationist and that the credit he was accorded for subduing inflation later in his tenure was undeserved.

The assertion in Greenspan 1.0 that "prices must eventually rise" had resonance far beyond the miserable performance of the CPI during this period. The pre-Keynesian sound money tradition had recognized that inflation of asset prices was an equally untoward result of printing press money and that the resulting collapse of financial bubbles would do immense and unnecessary economic harm.

Yet that's exactly where the new Greenspan monetary doctrines would now lead—that is, to the most virulent and sustained financial asset inflation in recorded history. Indeed, in the hindsight of history it is evident that his post–Black Monday panic and subsequent refusal to crush the renewed inflationary spiral were telling, and powerfully so. These actions reassured Wall Street speculators that they were not likely to face a Volcker-style crunch, and that the Fed was now more focused on supporting the stock market than on enforcing monetary discipline.

This conclusion was reinforced by the Fed's incremental dithering on interest rates between May 1989 and the end of 1992. During this forty-four-month-long easing campaign, the Fed cut interest rates by tiny increments (25 basis points) on no less than two dozen separate occasions.

In this manner, the federal funds rate was walked down an exceedingly steep slope—from a starting point of 9.75 percent all the way down to 3 percent in December 1992. Needless to say, Wall Street got excited: the S&P 500 rose from 300 to 450 during that period, or by nearly 50 percent. At the same time, there had never been an easing campaign that resulted in such a prolonged and deep cut in interest rates with so little justification in the entire history of the Federal Reserve. Not surprisingly, a deeply symbiotic relationship between the central bank and the stock market became firmly implanted during the Fed's 675-basis-point march toward money market rates which were so low as to leave interest rates at negative readings after inflation.

THE FED'S PHONY VICTORY OVER INFLATION
AND THE ARRIVAL OF THE "CHINA PRICE"

When CPI inflation soared above 6 percent in late 1990, the Fed claimed nothing was amiss except an oil spike owing to the Kuwait crisis, yet that was only partially true and wholly misleading. For the next several years the Greenspan Fed claimed that a one-time inflation bulge from the Gulf War was being squeezed out of the reported CPI numbers and its money-printing campaign was therefore fully compatible with its disinflation goals.

Yet this was a double shuffle: what was really happening was that the "China price" was driving tradable goods inflation out of the CPI entirely, permitting the headline number to be backfilled with domestically generated inflation from the Fed money printing campaign. Accordingly, Wall Street got its juice while the monetary central planners in the Eccles Building claimed a great victory over inflation.

During the next dozen years, the headline CPI did rise at only a 2.6 percent annual rate compared to the 4.6 percent rate of Greenspan's initial four-year term. Yet true domestic inflation barely slowed down at all, remaining hidden in the bifurcated basket of prices which make up the CPI.

Between 1991 and 2003, for example, there was no net rise in the price of durable goods and the index for some entirely imported categories, such as shoes and apparel, actually declined. By contrast, the index for services, which represented purely domestic production, rose at nearly a 3.5 percent rate during the twelve years after 1991.

Quite evidently, the appearance of benign inflation was not owing to the Fed's success, but was due to the "China price." Imported consumer goods reflecting the great wage deflation coming out of Asia were dragging down the overall CPI. In reality, Fed policy was causing the tradable goods sector to be offshored, while accommodating excess inflation in domestic services.

In the face of the great deflationary rise of East Asia, sound monetary policy would have generated a far different result. It would have resulted in falling domestic prices and wages in order to keep the American economy competitive and to curtail the massive deficit in the trade accounts.

The actual policy of the Greenspan Fed simply hollowed out the American economy and shifted monetary inflation from the reported CPI to the S&P 500 index; it led to vast impairment of the Main Street economy even as it fueled a destructive eruption of bull market mania on Wall Street.

STUDIES IN BUBBLE BLINDNESS: WHY THE DOZEN HIGHFLYERS HAD TO CRASH

It was in this context that the next phase of the equity cycle gathered momentum after the 1991 recession and never looked back. By the time the bruising stock market crash of 2000 finally materialized, the get-rich-quick culture had sunk deep roots in both Wall Street and Main Street. All told, *the S&P 500 index accomplished in eighteen years what should actually take a half century.*

The index rose from 110 in August 1982 to a level of 1,485 before it finally stopped rising in August 2000. That amounted to a 13.5X gain and a 15.5 percent rate of compound growth for nearly two decades. There had never been anything like that anywhere, at any time, in modern financial history. It did seem to prove that financial trees grow to the sky. That illusion was especially evident in the maniacal excesses that occurred underneath the overall stock averages. Indeed, the true extent of the Greenspan mania can only be seen in the case studies which taught a generation of investors that stocks can grow to the sky.

Perhaps the poster boy is Dell Inc., the iconic manufacturer and make-to-order business model pioneer of the PC era. Between 1990 and March 2000, its stock price rose from the pre-split equivalent of $0.05 per share to $54—an increase of 1,100 times in ten years.

Dell generated immense growth in output, profits, and customer utility in the course of its spectacular ascent, but it hadn't invented a perpetual motion machine. Twelve years later in 2012, the PC was already becoming obsolete, and Dell's stock price languished 85 percent lower at $10 per share. After tipping the scales at $130 billion at its 2000 peak, Dell's market cap has shrunk to a current value of only $18 billion, notwithstanding that its sales have nearly tripled in the interim.

The damage from Greenspan's runaway bull market was not only that its inevitable crash left investors financially wounded and, in some cases, destitute. In drastically overvaluing the current earnings of Dell and thousands of other companies, it had also effectively stripped the stock exchange of its fundamental economic function, which is to rationally discount future corporate profits.

In the case of Dell's towering stock price at the bubble peak, its share price implied a future of endless, sizzling earnings growth. Yet Dell had no meaningful patents, no unique products, and was not surrounded by technology moats of any kind; its success had been based on an innovative business model—global supply chain management and assemble-to-order product delivery—which could be copied and was.

Dell's exuberant growth rate thus did slow sharply after the turn of the century, with net income rising at a prosaic 5.6 percent annual rate during the eleven years ending in fiscal year 2011. Needless to say, its 70X PE multiple at the 2000 tech bubble peak—13X its actual future growth rate—was not even remotely warranted and was a reflection of Greenspan's financial bubble, not sustainable economics.

When the dot-com crash finally came in the spring of 2000, Dell's share price fell hard, causing more than $100 billion to rush out of its market capitalization, as if it had been bottled air. Yet this was not evidence of free market exuberance being brought to ground, nor merely the correction of a mistake emanating from the market's endless process of price discovery.

Instead, it was proof that printing-press money had touched off a speculative mania of historic proportion. It had afflicted millions of retail investors who had ridden the Dell stock up its spectacular 1,100-fold ramp with the delusion that instant riches are only a matter of good stock market timing. Even when this particular ride ended in tears, newly enabled punters viewed their losses as a matter of poor exit timing, not the fact that Dell's moon shot had been the result of a mania-driven stampede.

The tech bubble was not historically unique. Dell was just one of a multitude of new-age companies of the 1990s whose spectacular rise and then flaming descent was reminiscent of the trail blazed by new-era highflyers of the 1920s. In that age, radio had been the booming new industry, and Radio Corporation of America (RCA) the archetype for stock prices which grow to the sky.

During the five years ending in October 1929, RCA had soared from $5 per share to $400. Thereupon it proved that companies valued at 200X earnings, no matter how brilliant their invention or breathtaking their growth, are the result of bull market manias, not entrepreneurial genius. Back at $10 per share after the 1929 crash, this lesson was powerfully taught and remained embedded in Wall Street's institutional memory for the better part of six decades.

So another ill-effect of the 1990s Greenspan stock bubble was the erasure of what remained of Wall Street's hard-learned lessons. Cisco Systems was a dramatic case. Its stock price had started at the equivalent of $0.10 per share in 1990 before reaching a peak of $77 in early 2000. That amounted to an 880-fold gain, causing Cisco to become a "must own" stock in millions of 401(k) portfolios.

At its momentary peak in March 2000, it became one of the first companies to reach $500 billion in market cap, and in that figure the frenzied extent of the mania was plainly evident. It represented nearly 26X Cisco's sales during fiscal year 2000, and nearly 200X its net income. Not surprisingly, $400 billion, or 80 percent, of Cisco's half-trillion-dollar capitalization at the NASDAQ peak consisted of the same bottled air as Dell's exaggerated worth. Today, Cisco's market cap is just $100 billion, notwithstanding the fact that it has continued to soldier along inventing new products and steadily growing its sales.

Cisco's moon shot valuation was evidence of a far more malignant force than stock market exuberance, irrational or otherwise. What it actually illuminated was the stunning financial aberration that had been fostered by the Greenspan Fed. Cisco had plenty of company in the shooting-star trade. Yahoo!'s market cap, for example, skyrocketed from $5 billion to $120 billion in only twenty-four months and then collapsed to only $4 billion shortly thereafter. And the mania extended far and wide. During the final stages of the stock market's two-decade-long ramp, nearly every sector was levitated, whether new economy racers or old economy warhorses.

The five big telecoms—Lucent Technologies, Juniper Networks, Nortel, WorldCom, and Global Crossing—went from being valued at about $90 billion before the LTCM bailout to nearly $1 trillion at the peak. Then they crashed, plummeting to hardly $10 billion. And in that violent deflation, the fundamental deformation of the financial system was plainly evident. The free market does not make pricing errors of this colossal size unaided; speculative bubbles of this magnitude are always and everywhere a product of central bank money printing.

The PE multiple of AIG, which consisted mainly of a prosaic insurance company subjected to pervasive regulatory constraints on profitability, reached nearly 40X. AIG's stock price quadrupled in the four years ending in October 2000, lifting its market cap from $125 billion to $500 billion. But General Electric, with its stock rising from $12 to $60 per share during the same four-year period, was the real canary in the coal mine. Its old-line industrial businesses plus its far-flung finance company operations most definitely did not warrant the 30X new economy multiple that lifted its stock price skyward. Indeed, prior to the Greenspan Bubble it had traded at 10X, or a steep discount to the broad market owing to its lumbering portfolio of low-growth legacy businesses like locomotives, light bulbs, and washing machines and its heavy reliance for upward of 40 percent of its profits on the "low quality" earnings generated by its finance company.

In truth, GE did nothing to warrant the spectacular expansion of its earnings multiple during the 1990s. Jack Welch made a cult of managing quarterly earnings to the penny and the ferocious extraction of costs from its prosaic businesses. Yet the artificial smoothing of short-term earnings is irrelevant to the long-term capitalization rate of global-scale corporations, and cost cutting is inherently a dead-end street that does not merit a high terminal value.

At the end of the day, therefore, it was not Neutron Jack alone who brought good things to GE's shareholders. In fact, it was Alan Greenspan who turned the legendary leader of America's largest conglomerate into Magic Jack, causing GE's market cap to soar from $125 billion to $600 billion in the four years ending in October 2000. In truth, this massive windfall to shareholders was made in the Eccles Building on the Potomac, not at GE's Six Sigma school at Croton-on-Hudson.

Ironically, the most spectacular case of bull market mania was Microsoft. Undoubtedly one of the greatest capitalist enterprises of all time, it dominated the ecosystem of an entire industry—the personal computer— like never before in history and had the financial results to prove it. During the last twenty years its sales have risen from $2 billion to $70 billion, and its current net income of $25 billion per year represents a 17 percent compound rate of annual growth since the mid-1990s.

But the Greenspan bull market carried Microsoft's market cap into the realm of sheer lunacy. Valued at about thirty times its very promising earnings in 1990, its market cap of $6 billion then traced a parabolic upward curve, rising a hundredfold to $600 billion by January 2000.

Yet this represented a wholly untenable and unsustainable windfall. Microsoft's $600 billion market cap represented 64X its current year (FY 2000) net income, and under the circumstances was nothing less than delusional. By that point in time, Microsoft had grown to $24 billion in annual sales and recorded nearly $10 billion of net income.

Even at an implicit PEG ration of 2.0X, its market multiple at the bubble peak implied that within a decade, that is, by fiscal 2010, Microsoft's net income would have grown at 30 percent annually and reached $150 billion. The implied figure, alas, was larger than the global sales of the entire personal computer industry at the time.

Needless to say, Microsoft's income grew by 6 percent per year, not 30 percent, over the next decade to $18.5 billion; that is, its net income grew by about 2X rather than by the 15X gain that had been implicit in its valuation at the tech bubble peak. Today Microsoft is still valued at only about $200 billion, meaning that at the peak of the mania in 2000 there had been about $400 billion of bottled air in its share price.

Nor was the Microsoft mispricing an isolated error. None of the great free market creations of the 1990s technology revolution escaped the mania. Intel's dominance of advanced semiconductors and microprocessors stood shoulder to shoulder with Microsoft's accomplishment in software. Intel's powerful technology edge was reflected in the massive growth of sales and profits it recorded during the span between 1990 and 2000: annual revenues grew from $4 billion to $34 billion, and its net income climbed at a 32 percent annual rate to $10.5 billion.

Yet the Greenspan bull market capitalized these sterling business results as if they were the financial equivalent of the second coming. Intel's stock price rose seventy-five-fold during the course of the decade, and in no small part because its PE multiple reached 48X earnings by the time of the 2000 peak. Consequently, its market cap soared to $500 billion, compared to only $10 billion in 1990, once again showering punters with previously unimaginable windfall gains.

Needless to say, this half-trillion-dollar gain on the stock of an already large and maturing company was unimaginable by the lights of prior history. Its 48X valuation implied that its net income would reach $100 billion by fiscal year 2010. In point of fact, Intel's net income in fiscal year 2010 was only $11.5 billion, meaning that during the decade after 2000 its earnings grew at only a 1 percent annual rate.

Two recessions, the rise of competition from Korea, Japan, and Taiwan, and the law of large numbers all played a role in bending Intel's financial performance toward the flat line after the turn of the century. In the process of economic reality setting in, Intel's $75 stock price cratered to $17 per share by the fall of 2000, thereby shrinking its market cap by about $400 billion.

THE $2.7 TRILLION BUBBLE THE MAESTRO COULDN'T SEE

At the time the thundering dot-com collapse was gathering momentum in April 2000, Chairman Greenspan would have none of it. Asked during a meeting of the Senate Finance Committee that month whether an interest rate increase would prick the stock market bubble, he responded: "That presupposes I know that there is a bubble . . . I don't think we can know there has been a bubble until after the fact. To assume we know it currently presupposes that we have the capacity to forecast an imminent decline in [stock] prices."

Rarely have the words of a high official been so thoroughly mocked by the unfolding of real-world events. During the next eighteen months, the dozen highflyers of the stock market, mentioned above, experienced nearly a 75 percent average decline in shareholder value. This meant that $2.7 trillion of market cap vaporized just among these highly visible corporate majors. That staggering loss constituted the core of more than $7 trillion in market cap decline for the stock market as a whole.

Contrary to the maestro's Senate Finance Committee testimony, Greenspan and his monetary politburo did not need a crystal ball to spot the impending flameout. The mounting danger of a market crash was palpable, but the Fed obstinately refused to even assess the evidence that was plainly displayed in its rearview mirror.

The explosion in the market value of the highflyers had no historic precedent, not even during the stock mania of 1929. In fact, the parabolic rise in the market value of these big companies was just plain preposterous, and meant that a meltdown of historic proportions was waiting to happen.

Only forty months elapsed between the worried message of Greenspan's "irrational exuberance" speech and the unaccountable bubble blindness conveyed in his April 2000 testimony. During that period, the market cap of the dozen highflyers reviewed above grew from $600 billion to $3.8 trillion. In that ascent, the known laws of economic value creation were grossly violated.

There is simply no plausible circumstance on the free market in which the true value of giant companies like these can increase sixfold in such a brief interval. This outbreak of irrationality, therefore, was not merely a curiosity on the margin, nor was it a flash in the pan signifying nothing of lasting import. In fact, it was decisive evidence that the financial markets had been fundamentally unhinged by the Fed's continuous money printing and pandering.

The maestro might have reviewed the fate of these dozen highflyers before plunging into the lunacy of 1 percent interest rates and the housing bubble which followed. Needless to say, there was no reason to believe that $2.7 trillion of equity value could have just gotten "lost" on the free market.

The evidence as to its ultimate fate soon arrived and it was unequivocal: the big-cap highflyers at the very center of the first Greenspan stock market boom never experienced even a dead-cat bounce. Instead, they remained at their lows throughout the 2002–2006 period when the Greenspan Fed was busy transplanting bubble finance to neighborhood real estate markets throughout Main Street America.

In fact, as of twelve years later in 2012, four of these companies have disappeared and those which remain have a combined market cap of $850 billion. In the final reckoning their share prices did not grow to the sky; the market value accruing to shareholders of this legendary dozen highflyers has actually grown at only a 2.5 percent rate over the last sixteen years.

Neither the Greenspan Fed nor the mad money printers of the Bernanke era which followed ever leveled with the American public about the sobering truth evident in the saga of these highflyers; namely, that there is no such thing as effortless, instant riches on the free market.

THE PERVERSE UNTRUTH OF BUBBLE FINANCE: HONEST SAVINGS ARE NOT NECESSARY

The Fed might have been better advised to dissect the bubble's deflation, not promote a new one. It would have found that the Greenspan stock market mania had led millions of investors to embrace the instant riches of stock market gambling, when the very paragons of that mania—the dozen highflyers—have produced only a 2.5 percent compound price appreciation over the last sixteen years.

Yet, instead of coming clean and embracing sound money policies which would have induced the American middle class to revert to frugal living and saving for retirement, the thrust of Fed policy since the dot-com crash has been to perpetuate the lie. Accordingly, the massive baby boom generation that desperately needed to save has remained enthralled to the financial delusions that the Greenspan Fed foisted on the public.

Unfortunately, this wrong-headed policy has not only made the Federal Reserve a hostage of Wall Street, but it also has warped and deformed the very foundation of the nation's economy. Having fostered a bull market culture of stock gamblers during the 1990s, the Fed simply broadened the casino's offerings after 2001 to include housing, real estate, and derivatives.

By so doing, it kept the party going for a spell, but in the process implanted the most pernicious possible error in the workings of the American economy; namely, the belief that savings out of current income is unnecessary and even counterproductive because higher savings would allegedly reduce consumption expenditures and the rate of GDP growth.

Under the Fed's new prosperity management régime, by contrast, the buildup of wealth did not require sacrifice or deferred consumption. Instead, it would be obtained from a perpetual windfall of capital gains arising from the financial casinos. In this manner, the historic laws of sound finance were mocked by the nation's central bank: households would grow steadily richer, even as they enjoyed the luxury of borrowing and consuming at rates far higher than the sustainable capacity of their incomes. The bull market culture had now totally deformed the free market.

CHAPTER 17

SERIAL BUBBLES

THE PERIOD BETWEEN GREENSPAN'S ARRIVAL AT THE FED IN 1987 and the dot-com crash in early 2000 brought a remarkable change in the finances of American households. Bubble finance supplanted the old-fashioned habits of savings and frugality. At the center of this transformation was the soaring value of household investments in stocks and mutual funds, which grew from just under $2 trillion to nearly $13 trillion during this time period.

There had never been a wealth gain anywhere close to this magnitude, even during the Roaring Twenties. And there was good reason for this: such massive leaps in wealth defy sustainable economics.

During the twelve years of the Greenspan stock market mania, for example, the value of stocks and mutual funds held by households grew at a 17.5 percent compound rate compared to an average nominal GDP growth rate of only 5.7 percent. Obviously, the implication that stock market wealth can grow permanently at three times the rate of national output growth is not plausible.

Common sense is enough basis to reject that proposition on its face. But a simple exercise in compound math surely underscores its absurdity. Household investments in stocks and mutual funds had amounted to about 40 percent of GDP in 1987, but had climbed to a record 130 percent by the bubble peak in 2000. Had stock valuations continued to rise at three times the growth of GDP for another twelve years, household stock and mutual fund investments would have reached nearly 500 percent of GDP.

Such extremes were never even remotely approached during the Japanese stock mania of 1989 or the Chinese moon shots of 2007. The Greenspan Fed was thus heading down a blind alley, dragging Main Street straight into harm's way.

THE COST OF THE GREENSPAN STOCK BUBBLE:
DESTRUCTION OF MAIN STREET THRIFT

By the turn of the century, household finances were clearly on an unsustainable path. The Greenspan Fed's bubble finance deluded Main Street America into believing it was far wealthier than was actually the case, inducing households to radically reduce their savings out of current income. Indeed, the change in savings and spending behavior was so extreme that it is a key hallmark of the financial deformation emanating from the Greenspan Fed.

Between 1955 and 1980, the household savings rate fluctuated narrowly in a band between 7.5 percent and 10 percent of disposable personal income. On average, it posted a benchmark of about 8.5 percent over these two and a half decades. Even as late as 1986, the year before Greenspan took over the Fed, the savings rate had clocked in at the bottom of its historic range at 7.6 percent.

From the time that the Greenspan Fed embraced its régime of easy money and Wall Street pandering after Black Monday, however, the savings rate of American households dropped below its historic range and headed steadily downhill. By 1993 it slipped to 5.8 percent, followed by an even lower 4.6 percent rate in 1997. It then plunged to a never-before-recorded low of 2.5 percent during the six quarters ending in December 2001.

This headlong retreat from the historical norm for household savings could not have occurred at a worse time. By 2001, the first cohort of the giant baby boom generation was just a decade from retirement, and 75 million more boomers were queued up right behind it.

The clear and present danger, therefore, was that the bubble wealth stored in 401(k) and mutual fund accounts would prove to be illusory or could not be extended for another decade. In that event, the Greenspan Fed's drastic error of supplanting the thrift habit of the American people with central bank–manufactured bubble wealth would have grave implications for the long-term future of the American economy.

As it happened, the post-2000 collapse of the stock market bubble did not awaken Main Street America to the fact that it had been stranded high and dry by the Fed's bubble economics. The nation's monetary central planners refused to let financial reality break through, no matter how deep the hole resulting from the dot-com crash. And, in fact, the hole in household balance sheets was deep. By the end of 2002, the value of household investments in stocks and mutual funds had declined by 42 percent from the $13 trillion dot-com peak, and now stood at only $7.4 trillion.

This massive cratering of household wealth should have been a clarion call for drastic revival of thrift, since fully 50 percent of the 1987–2000

Greenspan bubble gain in stock and mutual fund holdings had been vaporized by the market correction. Yet after only a brief, anemic rebound to the 3–4 percent range, the savings rate cratered again, falling to virtually zero by the time of the 2008 financial crisis.

The reason was not mysterious. After the dot-com crash the Fed conducted what amounted to an extended Charlie Brown and Lucy gambit with the American public. Time after time, the public was tricked into believing that the Fed's latest and greatest new financial bubble obviated the need to curtail consumption and begin to save for a fast approaching era of baby boom retirement.

Consequently, the fundamental ailment of the American economy as it entered a new century—too much consumption and not enough savings—went unaddressed by the very central bank responsible for this condition. Moreover, the Fed's indifference with respect to the extended collapse of household savings was a signal to Wall Street that the low-interest-rate party could be extended indefinitely.

DO NOT BE TROUBLED: THE SAVINGS FUNCTION HAS BEEN OUTSOURCED TO CHINA

The American savings deficit was transparent after the turn of the century, but the Fed flat-out didn't care. As detailed in chapter 15, Greenspan and his monetary central planners had a glib answer: do not be troubled, they admonished, the Chinese have volunteered to handle America's savings function on an outsourced basis.

So instead of addressing the growing deformations of the American economy after the dot-com crash, the Fed choose to repeat the same failed trick; that is, it once again cranked up the printing presses with the intent of driving down interest rates and thereby reviving speculative carry trades in stocks and other risk assets.

Needless to say, it succeeded wildly in this wrong-headed game plan: by pushing interest rates down to the lunatic 1 percent level during 2003–2004, the Fed sent a powerful message to Wall Street that the Greenspan Put was alive and well, and that the carry trades now offered the plumpest spreads in modern history. Under the Fed's renewed exercise in bubble finance, asset prices could be expected to rumble upward, whereas overnight funding costs would remain at rock bottom.

That is exactly what happened and the equity bubble was quickly reborn. After hitting bottom at about 840 in February 2003, the S&P 500 took off like a rocket in response to virtually free (1 percent) money available to fund leveraged speculation. One year later the index was up 36 percent, and from there it continued to steadily rise in response to reported GDP and profit growth, albeit "growth" that would eventually be revealed as largely an artifact of the housing and consumer credit boom which flowed from the very same money-printing policies which were reflating the equity markets.

In the event, the S&P 500 crossed its old tech bubble high of 1,485 in May 2007 and finally peaked for a second time at 1,560 in October of that year. Accordingly, in one fell swoop the Fed cancelled the painful lessons that had been absorbed by stock market punters in 2000–2002, juicing the markets sufficiently to cause the S&P 500 to rise by 85 percent during just fifty months. By late 2007, the belief in instant riches from stock market gains was again alive and well on both Wall Street and Main Street.

Utilizing the institutionalized channels of stock market levitation outlined in chapter 21, the Fed thus enabled households to recover all of their $5.6 trillion loss on stock and mutual fund holdings from the dot-com crash. Indeed, this benchmark was achieved by late 2006. As even greater unsustainable gains were clocked by the stock averages thereafter, the paper wealth of American households continued to rise to new record levels. By early 2008, the value of household stock and mutual fund holdings reached $14.2 trillion. So, once again, the old-fashioned virtue of thrift was mocked by the prosperity managers at the Fed. The message repeated over and over in the minutes of monthly Fed meetings was that the economy was strong because Americans were again spending everything they earned and all they could borrow.

Meanwhile, the Fed would levitate financial markets so that household asset values would keep rising parallel to the growth of household debt. Society's savings function would be handled by the swelling army of Chinese industrial serfs, whose wardens at the People's Printing Press of China could not seem to get enough Treasury bonds and Fannie Maes.

WHEN ALAN SHRUGGED:
150 MONTHS OF IRRATIONAL EXUBERANCE

Needless to say, Lucy moved the football again during the Wall Street financial crisis. By year-end 2008, the household ledgers showed equity and mutual fund holdings had plunged from more than $14 trillion to only $9 trillion. This meant that $5 trillion of stock market wealth had disappeared—for the second time. Moreover, the reflated equity bubble of 2003–2008 had been built on an even shakier foundation of speculation and hopium than had been the dot-com bubble.

The S&P 500 went through a violent correction in 2008–2009, breaking through the old Greenspan bottom by early 2009 and eventually plunging to 675 on March 9. The sheer mayhem of central bank manipulation of the stock market was starkly evident at this panic bottom. During the dark hours of early March 2009, the S&P 500 was an incredible 10 percent lower than it had been twelve years earlier at the time of Greenspan's irrational exuberance speech of December 1996.

In hindsight, that famous speech might have better been designated as *Alan Shrugged*. The Fed was on a destructive path, but refused to even acknowledge it. Consequently, irrational exuberance was the order of the day during the 150 months following the Greenspan speech.

Never before in history had the nation's financial system been pummeled by two gigantic bubbles and two devastating crashes in such a brief interval. That Greenspan's heir apparent managed to detect the Great Moderation at the midpoint of this cycle of financial violence was only added testimony to the degree to which monetary policy had become unhinged.

It was no longer plausible, therefore, to describe the New York Stock Exchange, NASDAQ, and the various venues for equity derivatives as a free market for raising and trading equity capital issues. Instead, they were violently unstable casinos, ineptly stage-managed by a central bank that had now become addicted to the printing press and a timorous vassal to the raw forces of Wall Street speculation.

WHEN BERNANKE WENT BERSERK: THIRTEEN WEEKS OF MONEY-PRINTING MADNESS

Still, the hapless monetary central planners were not done with their bubble making. Indeed, the Bernanke Fed had not only forgotten the wisdom of Greenspan 1.0, but positively scorned it. Running the printing presses like never before in all of historical time, the Fed did succeed in spotting the football one more time, inflating its third equity bubble in fifteen years.

By now the routine was familiar. In a state of feverish panic which made the Greenspan Fed after Black Monday seem like a model of deliberation, the Bernanke Fed expanded its balance sheet at a pace which sober historians someday will describe as simply berserk. As of the week ending September 3, 2008, the Fed's balance sheet stood at $906 billion, a level it had taken ninety-four years to build up to after it opened its doors for business in October 1914.

Now, driven by the panicked demands for relief from Wall Street speculators and their agents in the US Treasury department, the Fed added another $900 billion to its balance sheet in just seven weeks. Ninety-four years of reasonably deliberative history was thus replicated in three fortnights of panic inside the Eccles Building.

And still the madness continued. By the week of December 10, just thirteen weeks after the Lehman failure, the Fed's balance sheet stood at $2.25 trillion. The nation's central bank had thus expanded its footings by 2.5X in what amounted to the blink of a historical eye.

The root of Bernanke's staggering monetary deformation is that in the years since October 1987 the nation's central bank has effectively destroyed the free market in interest rates. Once the Fed embraced easy money and prosperity management through the Wall Street–based wealth effects, the character of interest rates changed fundamentally—rates became a bureaucratically administered value emanating from the FOMC, not a market-clearing price representing the true supply and demand for money and debt capital.

Owing to the destruction of free market interest rates, a modern Wall Street panic and its aftermath unfolded in a manner which is the very opposite of the principles of sound finance manifested during the great panic that erupted on Wall Street precisely 101 years earlier in October of 1907. The Fed was not then run by a math professor from Princeton, nor did the nation even have a central bank.

J. P. MORGAN AND THE PANIC OF 1907: HOW FREE MARKET INTEREST RATES FELLED THE SPECULATORS

Wall Street was managed during those tumultuous weeks by the great financier J. P. Morgan. Presiding over the markets from his library in midtown Manhattan, Morgan did not have a printing press, but he did possess the extraordinary financial wisdom garnered during a lifetime of high finance in an era when money was a fixed weight of gold, and interest rates were the price which cleared the free market.

In a word, Morgan knew that Wall Street was rotten with speculative excesses which had built up during the previous decade, and that market-clearing interest rates were needed to cleanse the system. Accordingly, during the most heated weeks of the Panic of 1907 the benchmark interest rate of the day—the call money rate—soared by 3 to 5 percentage points on some days, and reached a level of nearly 25 percent at the crisis peak.

In this setting, J. P. Morgan presided over a financial triage that saved only the truly solvent, not an indiscriminate Bernanke-style bailout which propped up all the speculative excesses which had triggered the crisis in the first place. Accordingly, as the call money rate soared, margin loans were systematically called, and the punters of the day were felled without mercy.

Among the financially departed were copper barons, several highly leveraged railroads, legions of real estate speculators, and numerous poorly funded trust banks. The toll also included thousands of stock market operators who had built fortunes on margin loans.

Needless to say, after the smoke cleared from the battleground, the financial follies of the day had been burned out of the system and bullish enthusiasm went into an extended dormancy. The stock market did not regain its September 1906–1907 peaks for another five years, and by then the US economy had grown by nearly 30 percent.

BEN BERNANKE AND THE PANIC OF 2008: HOW SOCIALIST INTEREST RATES REWARDED THE SPECULATORS

By contrast, the distinguishing hallmark of the September 2008 panic is that the Bernanke Fed shut down the money market instantly, thereby preventing free market interest rates from making their appointed cleansing rounds. Thus, on the Friday before Lehman failed, the overnight Libor rate—the closest thing to a true money market interest rate—stood at 2.1 percent and was in the range that had prevailed for most of the previous summer. The Lehman news caused it to spike to 6.2 percent on Tuesday, a mere flicker by the standards of J. P. Morgan's day.

Nevertheless, this modest upwelling of open market interest rates set off alarm bells on Wall Street, and soon the cronies of capitalism were demanding a huge dose of socialist intervention to flatten interest rates. Mr. Market's initial attempt to ignite the cleansing flame of rising rates was doused on the spot by the Fed's emergency lending fire hoses. Interest rates quickly fell back.

Rates then spiked a second time to 6.5 percent on September 30 when the first TARP vote failed, but thereafter they were literally flattened by the Fed's flood of liquidity. Overnight Libor thus subsided to 2 percent by October 10, then to under 1 percent by the end of the month, and finally to 15 basis points—a comic simulacrum of a price for money—by the end of December 2008.

Nearly four years later, Libor still remained at that exact level, a lifeless victim of the Fed's foolish tidal wave of fiat money. It goes without saying that speculators in J. P. Morgan's time did not come out of hiding for several years after the grim reaper of free market interest rates had passed through the canyons of Wall Street. By contrast, it took only about a hundred stock market trading sessions under the free money régime of the Bernanke Fed until speculators concluded that the "all clear" had been sounded.

Indeed, observing the abject way the Fed bowed to the demands of Wall Street in the days after Lehman, speculators concluded that the nation's twelve-person monetary politburo, holed up night and day in the Eccles Building, feared another hissy fit on Wall Street more than anything else. And for good reason. Never before had overnight wholesale money been literally free, nor had a central bank ever promised that it would remain free for the indefinite future.

CHARLIE BROWN LUNGES AGAIN:
THE FED'S THIRD STOCK MARKET BUBBLE

With the free market interest rate mechanism deeply impaired if not de- stroyed, and downside risk virtually eliminated from the price of equities and other risk assets, the stock market bounded upward by 50 percent from its post-crisis bottom by March 2010. It didn't matter that the Main Street economy was still underwater. At that point, real GDP was still 3 per- cent below its 2007 cyclical peak, while payroll employment was off by 7 million jobs and industrial production was lower by 10 percent.

So it was evident that Wall Street was not pricing a conventional eco- nomic recovery. Instead, Wall Street was pricing in a brimming confidence that it could compel the Fed to continue supplying monetary juice for the indefinite future.

The punters were not mistaken. By early 2012 the S&P index reached 1,300 and was therefore up by nearly 100 percent from its March 9, 2009, reaction low. Once again, stock prices seemed to be growing to the sky. But also, once again, not really. The S&P 500 index had first crossed the 1,300 level thirteen years earlier in March 1999. Charlie Brown was now lunging at the football for the third time.

The Fed's data for household balance sheets nailed the story. By year- end 2011, when the Fed was well along inflating its third equity bubble, the figure for household stock and mutual fund holdings stood at $12.7 trillion. That was uncannily identical to the $12.7 trillion level posted in December 1999.

So three equity bubbles notwithstanding, Main Street America had spent a decade going nowhere, even as it was violently whipsawed along the way. Still, the idea of instant riches was kept alive by the Fed's continu- ous attempts to levitate the stock market. Moreover, the Fed's press releases and other smoke signals now added an especially nasty twist to its bubble syndrome; namely, that Charlie Brown would be forced to lunge at the Fed's third equity bubble, whether he wanted to or not, because the na- tion's central bank made it perfectly clear that it intended to eliminate all the alternatives.

In fact, by promising to keep nominal interest rates on low-risk money market funds at zero for six years, from December 2008 until mid-2015,

Bubbles Ben Bernanke threatened to confiscate the real wealth of Main Street America unless it cooperated and chased after high-risk asset classes. Nor would this confiscation be trivial. The CPI will have averaged 2.5 percent per year during the Fed's "era of ZIRP (zero-interest-rate policy)" while no-risk and liquid money market funds will have yielded essentially zero after taxes.

The math implies a 15 percent reduction in real wealth during Bernanke's six-year experiment in savings destruction. It is not surprising at all, therefore, that the bubble-vision financial news networks are able to find an endless string of money managers who expect the stock market to go up because "the Fed is forcing you to buy equities." They will be proven right—until the third bust materializes from the Fed-sponsored speculations now under way.

Whatever the longevity of the Fed's third equity bubble, it cannot be gainsaid that the historical thrift habits of the American middle class have been kept dormant for another decade. Even after a devastating housing crash and another equity market meltdown, the household savings rate rebounded only tepidly, and stood at just 3.5 percent near year-end 2012.

Consequently, after a decade in which American households saved out of current income in a niggardly manner, and chased the illusion of instant riches from financial speculation instead, they are deeper in the hole than ever before. The violent inflation and crash of the Greenspan stock market bubble in 2000–2002 proved to be not a warning bell, but just the catalyst for another dose of monetary heroin, which under the Bernanke Fed became an addiction.

HOW THE $11 TRILLION HOUSING BUBBLE BLOATED MAIN STREET CONSUMPTION

The greatest housing bubble in history obscured this underlying impoverishment for a time. Indeed, when the Fed slashed interest rates down to 1 percent by June 2003, thereby igniting a ferocious housing price escalation, Greenspan, Bernanke, and the rest of the monetary politburo professed not to notice the bubble. Nor did they acknowledge that it was compounding the problem of low savings.

Someday historians will surely wonder how it was that the Fed herded the nation's aging population to nearly a zero savings rate by 2007, when it was evident that the soaring gains on household real estate were artificial and unsustainable. According to the national balance sheet data that the Fed itself publishes every quarter in the "Flow of Funds" report, the market value of household real estate actually surged from $11.8 trillion at the end of 1999 to $20.2 trillion at the end of 2004.

Only a willfully oblivious central bank could have viewed a 75 percent increase in the value of real estate holdings in just five years as anything except a dangerous deformation. After all, these soaring home prices did not represent a snap back from a deep housing depression. The value of household real estate had been rising for decades and, in the more recent past, had already clocked in at a robust 5.3 percent annually during the long 1987–1999 span of the first Greenspan stock market bubble.

In the end, the national balance sheet entry for household real estate experienced the same Lucy and Charlie Brown syndrome as did equities. Housing asset values kept climbing until they peaked at $23.2 trillion in 2006. The bubble makers at the Fed duly published that number in early 2007, but could they possibly have believed that the value of household real estate in the United States had risen by $11.4 trillion in just seven years? Or that this represented anything other than a vast accident waiting to happen?

In the event, the accident did happen and it was a doozy—the largest financial catastrophe in American history in terms of the breadth and depth of losses on Main Street. Household real estate values plunged for five consecutive years to just $18.0 trillion at the end 2011. So another $5 trillion bubble had vanished.

In all, the Fed's serial bubble making during the years after the dot-com peak kept Main Street distracted by hype and hopium, even as overall net worth stagnated. After the flashy bubbles in equities and real estate were liquidated, the gain in total household assets barely kept up with inflation, while the household debt burden doubled over the twelve-year period.

Accordingly, the net worth of American households rose by just 2.5 percent in constant dollars during the entire first decade of the 21st century, yet even that miserly figure obscured the reality that the median household net worth actually declined by 27 percent in real terms, from $106,000 to $77,000. Since the after-inflation net worth of the top 10 percent of households actually rose by 17 percent, all other households experienced steep declines.

This perverse skew can be laid directly on the doorstep of the Fed. The net worth of the bottom 90 percent of households is heavily concentrated in residential property. In its wisdom, the nation's central bank encouraged households to massively increase their mortgage debt, but then proved incapable of preventing the collapse of the resulting housing asset bubble. In the crunch resulting from a 35 percent housing price decline versus mortgage debt obligations which remained contractually fixed, the net worth of Main Street households was hammered like never before.

LIVING HIGH ON THE HOG: $1.3 TRILLION PER YEAR IN BORROWED CONSUMPTION

If a decade of real wealth setback was the only adverse effect of the Fed's incessant juicing of Wall Street speculators, it might be argued that only limited harm has been done and baby boomers would be destined for a far more frugal retirement than they now imagine. In fact, however, irremediable damage has been done to the very foundation of the American economy because a two-decade-long holiday from a normal savings rate has come at a steep price.

Specifically, the excess consumption enabled by subnormal household savings resulted in year after year of recorded GDP growth that amounted to little more than theft from future generations. Compared to the historic benchmark savings rate of 8.5 percent, the actual rate of 3 percent registered over much of the last decade means that nearly 6 percent of the nation's disposable personal income, or about $600 billion per year, has been released for extra consumption expenditures.

Unfortunately, Professor Friedman's floating money contraption blocked the negative offsets that would normally boomerang back to an economy living too high on the hog. The classic effect of a savings drought under a régime of honest money is that interest rates soar. In the first instance, investment in productive assets is sharply suppressed, but eventually consumption falls and the savings rate rises in response to an increased reward for deferred gratification. Thus, free lunch economics tended to have a short-dated shelf life, at least until Camp David.

But under the dollar's "exorbitant privilege" conferred by the post-1971 T-bill standard, most of this excess consumption has been funded by means of borrowing from abroad, mainly from mercantilist central banks and their domestic financial wards and servitors. To date, the nation's cumulative domestic savings shortfall has been covered by $8 trillion of such foreign borrowings, thereby obviating the ill effects that would otherwise impact domestic interest rates and investment.

Those rising debts to the rest of the world will weigh heavily on American households when one day the Fed's con job on the price of government debt comes to an end. Its financial repression policies have crushed yields, but only because speculators believe that the Fed and other central banks will keep buying enough treasuries on the margin to keep the price propped-up far above market-clearing levels. When that confidence breaks, speculators and foreign central banks too will begin to sell and then to desperately stampede toward the exit as bond prices plummet and dollar interest rates soar.

In turn, the excess consumption of heavily indebted American households will drop with a thud in response to a surging interest due bill. The magnitude of the collapse will not only be startling, but will dramatically expose the phony GDP growth of the Greenspan-Bernanke era.

During the Eisenhower-Martin golden age of 1954–1965, for example, personal consumption expenditures averaged about 62.5 percent of GDP. This trend level was indicative of what might be expected in a reasonably healthy, steadily growing, noninflationary economy.

After traditional financial discipline was abandoned by Richard Nixon in August 1971, the consumption share rose steadily and reached about 65 percent of GDP by 1986. When the Greenspan money-printing era commenced in earnest, however, the personal consumption share of GDP headed resolutely upward and never looked back. By 1993, it stood at 67.3 percent and then rose above 69 percent after the turn of the century, finally hitting 71 percent of GDP at the peak of the credit bubble in 2007.

Moreover, during the subsequent fiscal "stimulus" régime, under which household spending has been heavily medicated by massive deficit-financed transfer payments and tax cuts, the consumption share of national income has risen even further. In fact, it reached an all-time high of 71.5 percent in 2010, a figure which far exceeds that for every other major nation on the planet.

The nation's bloated consumption ratio is among the principle deformations which now afflict the American economy. Its sheer magnitude is stunning. At the current level of 71.5 percent, the consumption share of GDP is 9 percentage points higher than the 62.5 percent ratio which prevailed during the 1954–1965 golden era.

At the GDP level recorded in 2010, this upward shift amounts to $1.3 trillion of extra annual consumption. Self-evidently, when this unsustainable ratio unwinds, the drag on GDP growth will be a harsh echo of the munificent boost which was realized on the way up.

Yet the actual story is even worse. While private residential construction is recorded in the GDP accounts as "investment" rather than consumption, the housing services actually provided by owner-occupied units amount to consumption no less than do purchases of sneakers or pizza; the GDP accounts just pretend that households "invest" in shelter and then "rent" it back to themselves.

So during the great housing boom new home square footage rose from an average of 1400 to 2400, spending on interior appointments soared, and McMansions sprang up on suburban tracts across the land. "Residential fixed investment" thus became more opulent, but it should never be confused with investment in productive business assets.

The true extent of the deformation brought on by the Greenspan bubble, therefore, can be more accurately measured by the sum of personal consumption expenditure (PCE) plus owner-occupied housing investment. The figures for peak-to-peak growth between the Greenspan bubble peaks of 1999 and 2007 leave no doubt that the US economy was being warped by a consumption spree of epic proportions.

During that eight-year period, the nation's nominal GDP expanded by 50 percent, or $4.7 trillion. Yet $3.9 trillion, or fully 82 percent, of the entire gain in reported GDP was attributable to the increase in personal consumption plus residential investment. By contrast, the benchmark standard for these two sources of consumption spending during the golden era of 1954–1965 averaged just 67 percent of national income.

Household consumption spending during the Greenspan bubble era was thus extended so far out on the limb that it defied all historical experience. And this deformation was enabled by a parabolic rise of debt.

Not surprisingly, the Fed exhibited no cognizance whatsoever of the role of debt in fueling the nation's consumption spree. Indeed, during the same 1999–2007 period total credit market debt outstanding doubled, rising from $25 trillion to $50 trillion, but the minutes of FOMC meetings during that era have almost nothing to say about this stunning eruption of borrowing by households, business, and governments alike.

This was the elephant in the room and it was also growing at an elephantine pace. During this same seven-year interval, nominal GDP grew by only $4.5 trillion, meaning that total debt on the nation's balance sheet had grown five times faster than national income. While the FOMC apparently never noticed this freakish development, there is no doubt that it was this debt explosion which fueled the Greenspan consumption bubble.

THE FED'S THIRD MONEY-PRINTING PANIC AND THE $25 TRILLION DEBT ERUPTION

So during the span between the end of 1999 and the final quarter of 2007, the deformations and contradictions of Greenspan bubble finance reached their apogee. Above all else, this meant that the central events of the period were not what they were cracked up to be.

The Fed claimed to be engineering a fulsome cyclical recovery and rising national prosperity, and the stock market and real estate sector pretended to be pricing it in. In fact, these trends were really all about the $25 trillion in new debt the Fed pumped into the American economy after launching its third money printing panic in December 2000.

Its hand-over–fist buying of government debt was unconscionable, especially given the fact that there was no crisis whatsoever in the Main

Street economy. Yet in the four years ending in December 2004 the Fed bought $200 billion of the public debt, causing its balance sheet to expand at a blistering 8 percent annual rate.

Needless to say, the data make a mockery of the Fed's claim that all of this wild money printing was necessary because the economy needed a supersized jolt of monetary stimulus, including an aberrationally low 1 percent interest rate, to avoid tumbling into the drink. In fact, the "recession" of 2001 was so faint that in later versions of the data it was essentially "revised" out of the government's own statistical record.

The official data now show that real GDP dipped by only microscopic amounts. Real output fell by just 0.3 percent in the first quarter of 2001, rebounded to a positive 0.6 percent during the second quarter, slipped again by 0.3 percent in the third quarter, and then expanded every quarter thereafter through the end of 2007. Even more to the point, real consumption spending never faltered, growing at nearly a 3 percent rate during the alleged "recession" year ending in December 2001, and by higher rates thereafter.

As the data now make clear, the entirety of the 2001–2002 downturn consisted of temporary inventory liquidation in response to 9/11. While there was also a mild slowdown from the red-hot pace of fixed business investment that accompanied the tech stock bubble, this was actually the smoking-gun proof that it was not a weak economy which motivated the Fed's third round of aggressive money printing: business capital spending never fell below the boom-time level it had reached at the top of the tech frenzy in 1999.

The Fed's panicked reaction to conditions during 2000–2001 was from the same playbook that Greenspan had used in October 1987 and September 1998. Once again the driving force was Wall Street's demands for monetary juice and Greenspan's misguided embrace of the "wealth effect" as a tool of central bank policy. This time the Fed generated the aforementioned $25 trillion debt bubble, which ignited leveraged speculation on both Wall Street and Main Street as never before. The resulting rapidly inflating housing and equity bubbles, in turn, stimulated temporary and artificial increases in output and employment, which then induced speculators to bid asset prices even higher.

Meanwhile, the FOMC kept the printing presses running at full tilt, insisting that rapidly rising housing and stock prices merely reflected the healthy economic expansion that its own policies were fostering. Answering a question on CNBC in July 2005, Bernanke blindly and willfully gave the housing bubble talk short shrift: "Well, unquestionably housing prices are going up quite a bit, but I would note that the fundamentals are very strong—a growing economy, jobs, incomes . . . much of what has happened [with home prices] was supported by the strength of the economy."

What was heralded as a brilliant exercise in business-cycle management by the Greenspan Fed was actually a whirl of monetary delusion. The American economy was not experiencing a linear business cycle expansion, as the charts of Wall Street stock touts proclaimed; it was actually gestating twin $5 trillion housing and equity bubbles which were warping and deforming the very foundation of the Main Street economy.

THE GREENSPAN PUT AND THE
UNHINGING OF CREDIT GROWTH

The combination of the Greenspan Put and 1 percent interest rates unleashed frightful forces of speculation—economic impulses that in a healthy monetary system are held in check by market-clearing interest rates and the fear of loss posed by the inherent risk in pyramids of financial leverage. Indeed, in the now lost world of sound money, debt financing was mainly available for long-lived capital projects with high enough risk-adjusted returns to attract the community's savings.

By contrast, with virtually no cost of carry and the perception that the Fed had put a one-way escalator under asset prices, the free market became a veritable devil's workshop—credit for speculative endeavors came pouring out of both conventional fractional reserve banks, as well as from every nook and cranny of the vast shadow banking system. Soon this explosion of speculative credit would prove that the monetarists' preoccupation with the key historic ingredient of money supply—bank reserves—had been made obsolete by Camp David, too.

Under the T-bill standard the only real limit on credit creation was financial capital, not the cash reserves of chartered banks. Moreover, the amount of capital needed per dollar of new credit was a function of what speculative markets would tolerate.

Banks and Wall Street broker-dealers were under regulatory capital minimums, of course, but these were so loophole ridden as to be meaningless. So, if capital was not a limiting factor in the vast unregulated shadow banking world, then new extensions of collateralized debt could soar as the value of collateral, ranging from residential real estate to copper futures contracts, raced upward.

The reason lenders funded rising asset prices at commensurately higher loan advance levels (i.e., did not set aside more capital to cover potential credit losses) was that they believed the central bank had their back. In effect, the market monetized the Greenspan Put, thereby erasing the need for genuine lender capital. Obviously, the more heated the various financial bubbles became, the more the financial markets monetized the Greenspan Put. In effect, the market substituted the central bank's promises to prop up asset prices for real balance sheet capital.

The daisy chains of rehypothecation—that is, pledging an asset that was already pledged—gathered momentum. Homeowners, for example, pledged their houses to mortgage lenders; the mortgages held by lenders were pledged to securitized trusts; the bonds issued by securitized trusts were pledged to CDO conduits; the CDO obligations were pledged to CDO-squared conduits; and so on.

The pyramids of credit grew rapidly. In effect, the Greenspan Put supplanted the scarcity of capital that would otherwise have put a brake on speculative lending in the free market. Accordingly, the liabilities (debt) of the shadow banking system, including repo, asset-backed securities, money market funds, commercial paper, and GSE mortgage pools exploded during the Greenspan bubble era, rising from $2 trillion in 1987 to a peak of $21 trillion by September 2008. In short, the unregulated, unreserved shadow banking system generated credit growth at an astounding 12 percent compound annual rate for 21 years running.

This was the real evil of the Greenspan/Bernanke Put because it permitted the multiplication of debt without growth of savings and the dramatic bidding-up of asset prices without growth of income. When asset prices finally broke during the BlackBerry panic, however, confidence in the Greenspan/Bernanke Put quickly evaporated in the face of the ensuing selling panic. And with vastly insufficient capital under the nation's pyramid of debt, collateral was called in and bubble-era credit was violently liquidated.

Yet, while speculator confidence in the Greenspan Put lasted, there had been virtually no constraints on the growth of credit market debt throughout the Main Street economy. Thus, in the second year of the Fed's post-dot-com money-printing panic, credit market debt outstanding grew by $2.5 trillion. This was an 8.6 percent increase and more than six times the growth of national income in the year ending December 2002. From there, the nation's balance sheet entry for total debt outstanding just kept expanding by larger amounts and by a greater percentage each and every year through the final peak in 2007.

During 2004, for example, as the housing bubble heated up and the stock averages continued to climb, annual debt growth reached $3.2 trillion, thereby clocking in at a 9.2 percent annual rate. Indeed, by the end of the cycle, the debt bubble literally turned parabolic: credit market debt outstanding surged by $4.7 trillion in 2007, or at a 10.3 percent annual rate.

Evidence that an explosive financial deformation had now reached a breaking point lies in the fact that nominal income grew by only $670 billion in the year ending December 2007. Debt was now expanding at seven times the rate of income growth in the American economy. Still, in the minutes of its last meeting of the year on December 7, the Fed mustered only the absurdly anodyne observation that "debt in the domestic nonfinancial sector was estimated to be increasing somewhat more slowly in the fourth quarter than in the third quarter."

THE POSSE OF DEBT-BUBBLE DENIERS
WHO INHABITED THE ECCLES BUILDING

By that point in time, the nation's leverage ratio had reached a "Defcon 1" status. At 3.6 times national income, the leverage ratio was so far above its historical chart lines that it threatened to vault off the top of the page. Yet the Fed did not take the slightest notice because it had no fear of debt. Indeed, the inhabitants of the Eccles Building espied prosperity across the land when they were only seeing the feedback loop from their own ceaseless money printing.

As will be seen in chapter 29, Bernanke was an outright Keynesian who believed that debt is the eternal elixir of economic life. At the same time, Greenspan had held the profoundly mistaken view that rapidly rising debt was evidence of an outpouring of financial innovation, not the rank speculation that it had signaled throughout financial history.

Likewise, most of the business economists who served on the Fed during the Greenspan bubble years followed the maestro's lead and simply toted up what the nation's billowing debt had bought during the most recent reporting period; that is, so many housing starts, coal shipments, retail sales, job gains, and the like. They never asked whether the underlying trend was sustainable, clinging instead to an illusion of prosperity derived from the positive numbers being chucked out of the government's statistical mills.

These reports were heralded as evidence that the Fed had engineered a perfectly balanced "Goldilocks economy" of low inflation and steady real growth. In fact, the government data mills measured only economic gossamer floating on the profoundly unstable and destructive debt bubble which was building down below.

The preposterous Fred Mishkin headed the posse of debt-bubble deniers who dominated the Fed's supporting cast. Prior to joining the Fed in 2006, he had conducted a major study for the government of Iceland which concluded that its banking system was sound and that the only bubbles in Iceland were those welling up from its famous hot geysers.

Yes, the balance sheet footings of Iceland's banking system were ten times larger than its GDP. Somehow Mishkin found this to be a source of competitive advantage, not a freakish economic accident waiting to happen.

So Mishkin had already demonstrated perfect 20/20 bubble blindness before he was appointed to the Fed and, as vice chairman, did not allow his talents to lie fallow. From that perch of authority he could be seen continuously on the financial news networks assuring viewers that the American economy was stronger than ever before. Indeed, when the housing bubble was already showing large cracks, he assured his FOMC colleagues during its December 2006 meeting that there would be "no big spillovers" from a downturn in housing.

Moreover, just twelve months before the onset of the worst recession since the 1930s, Mishkin revealed himself (December 2006) to be as blind to the fundamentals of the American economy as he had been to those of Iceland. "There is a slight concern about a little weakness," he averred, "but the right word is I guess a 'smidgeon,' not a whole lot."

This stunning misperception was not about the difficulties of forecasting the foggy future. Instead, it reflected the fact that the monetary central planners on the Fed were mesmerized by their own doctrine. For obvious reasons, they could not even begin to acknowledge that their chosen instruments of prosperity management—low interest rates, stuffing the primary bond dealers with fresh cash via constant Treasury bond purchases, and the Greenspan Put—would inherently unleash a Wall Street–driven tidal wave of credit expansion and leveraged speculation.

Accordingly, as the debt-bloated and speculation-driven American economy approached its inexorable crash landing, most of the FOMC supporting cast echoed Mishkin's insensible denial that trouble was at hand. Thus, in July 2007 and a few weeks before Wall Street's first mini-crash in August, Governor Kevin Warsh uncorked an observation that ranks among the most foolish blather ever uttered by a high financial official: "We don't see any immediate systemic risk issues. . . . *The most important providers of market discipline are the large, global commercial and investment banks.*" [Emphasis mine]

Even before the September 2008 Wall Street meltdown, it took a confirmed Kool-Aid drinker to believe that the "investment banks" were a source of "market discipline," and Warsh had deeply imbibed. Before joining the monetary politburo at age thirty-five, he had spent seven years as a junior Morgan Stanley associate, presumably helping to fuel the financial bubbles. Thereupon, he soldiered four years in the Bush White House writing memos that celebrated the resulting simulacrum of prosperity.

The conspiracy minded could thus find support for their theories in the case of Governor Kevin Warsh. The evidence was unassailable that he had been sent to Washington straight from the Wall Street boot camp.

Yet three months later, Warsh's investment banker talking points were given scholarly sanction by Governor Randall Kroszner, erstwhile professor of economics at the University of Chicago Business School. During his ten years in that bastion of free market theory, he might have learned something about sound money, and perhaps have spread the word during his tenure at the Council of Economic Advisors between 2001 and 2003.

But it didn't happen that way. Instead, after fully embracing the economic triumphalism of the "deficits don't matter" Bush White House, Kroszner was rewarded with an appointment to the Fed, perhaps to help ensure that the Bush deficits would be financed with central bank bond buying, as needed. To this end, Kroszner left no doubt that the Fed's six-year-long money-printing spree had not put even a scratch on the purportedly solid foundation of the nation's banking system.

Thus, in September 2007—after Countrywide Financial had cratered, 125 mortgage companies had already imploded, and a crucial money market indicator called the Libor-OIS spread had soared during the August mini-panic—Professor Kroszner opined that all was well: "Effective banking supervision has helped foster a banking system . . . *that today is safe, sound and well-capitalized* . . . US commercial banks are strongly capitalized, reflecting years of robust profits." [Emphasis mine]

During the year which followed this unaccountable utterance, the US banking system recorded more than $100 billion in losses. Kroszner's "years of robust profits" were effectively wiped out, owing to the fact that Wall Street had been booking phantom gains from underwriting and from trading loans, securities, and derivatives which were the progeny of the Fed's bubble finance. So, if the monetary planners in the Eccles Building did not have a clue that the financial system was built on a house of cards even at the eleventh hour in the fall of 2007, it is not surprising that they had no clue as the bubbles evolved each step along the way.

THE GREAT MODERATION: A DELUSION FOR THE AGES

The monetary politburo was blind to the vast deformations it was unleashing on the American economy. In the aftermath of the dot-com crash the Fed was just plain petrified of another stock market hissy fit. As indicated, it therefore launched an orgy of interest rate reductions that had no parallel in monetary history, and was profoundly irrational in light of the massive bubbles it was bound to produce.

Thus, in November 2000 the Federal fund rate had stood at 6.5 percent. That was not unreasonable—given the prevailing 2–3 percent inflation and the desperate need to revive the faltering domestic savings rate. As has been seen, however, the FOMC frantically hacked away with non-stop interest rate cuts of 25 and 50 basis points over the next 30 months until after 17 separate cuts the funds rate reached a rock bottom 1.0 percent in June 2003.

In a flight of desperate interest rate cutting, the Fed had thus gone all-in with its "wealth effects" theory of prosperity management. In due course the stock market did have a rebound back into the bubble zone but the route to this dubious, short-lived success wreaked mayhem upon Main Street all along the way.

It caused a fixed asset investment boom, but only for domestic real estate—since the grim reaper of the "China price" warded investors away from anything related to the production of tradable goods. It caused a Main Street consumption boom, but mainly from mortgage equity withdrawal, or MEW—not income honestly earned.

It also spurred a huge increase in retail sales of durable goods, but on the margin the source of increased supply was almost entirely East Asia. It generated a surging demand for consumer services ranging from real estate brokerage to yoga classes and personal shoppers, but the demand for these services was mainly financed from transient sources like home ATM borrowings and stock market gains, rather than a permanent increase in real incomes and capacity to spend.

Needless to say, as the effects of the Fed's poisonously low interest rates twisted and turned through the Main Street economy, they did cause the standard measures of economic activity to tick upward, thereby perpetuating the illusion of economic recovery and growth. Meeting after meeting, year upon year, the FOMC minutes noted the improved indicators while congratulating itself for the policy astuteness that had purportedly fostered these pleasing macroeconomic results.

The extent of its blind hubris was starkly evident when the leader of these prosperity howlers famously delivered a speech in February 2004 modestly titled "The Great Moderation." In this statement the future Fed chairman, who would preside over the most brutal drop in employment and output since the 1930s, noted the "remarkable decline in the variability of both output and inflation" over the prior two decades. Not surprisingly, Bernanke insisted that "improved performance of macroeconomic policies, particularly monetary policy," should be given the credit for this purported golden age of steady, unending growth.

In fact, goods inflation had been pinned down to the global economy's floorboard by the currency-pegging central banks of East Asia and the tens of millions of rural serfs who flooded out of the rice paddies and into the export factories of East China after 1990. By contrast, asset-price inflation had gotten more cyclically violent than at any time since 1929. That seminal fact of life would have been obvious to Bernanke, had he bothered to think about the implications of the two bruising stock market crashes (1987 and 2000) which had occurred precisely during the period of the Great Moderation.

Keynesian models recognize debt only when it shows up as current-period spending rather than as a permanent entry on the balance sheet, perhaps owing to the fact that Keynesian models do not even have a balance sheet. Peering through these Keynesian blinders, therefore, Bernanke blotted out a huge chunk of worrisome macroeconomic reality in divining his Great Moderation.

Even more importantly, the "moderation" in the business cycle alleged by Bernanke was an utter illusion. It resulted from the arithmetic of GDP computation under conditions of massive credit growth. Specifically, the $25 trillion credit bubble that the Fed was busy inflating flowed right into GDP. It showed up as incremental aggregate demand, mainly in the form of personal consumption expenditures, but also in the investment accounts for residential and commercial real estate.

But this was credit-money growth, not honest organic expansion. Had the GDP reports been constructed by double-entry bookkeepers, they would have offset some or all of these debt-fueled spending gains with a debit for future credit losses and busted investments. At the end of the day, the Great Moderation, like the Roman Empire, depended upon the spending power of exogenously obtained loot. In this case, it came from the freshly minted credit arising from the Wall Street machinery of leverage and speculation that the Fed so assiduously attended and enabled.

CHAPTER 18

———

THE GREAT DEFORMATION
OF CAPITAL MARKETS
How Wall Street Got Huge

THE COLLAPSE OF THREE SEPARATE $5 TRILLION FINANCIAL BUBBLES in less than a decade attested to the deeply impaired condition of the nation's capital markets. Yet the spectacular round-trips of the S&P 500 and Case–Shiller housing price index were not the only progeny of the Fed's bubble finance. There was actually an even greater deformation lurking beneath these wild rides; namely, the aberrant journey of the giant government bond market which forms the foundation of Wall Street and drives the financial rhythms by which it operates.

During the 1970s the financial system, in the aftermath of Camp David, endured the near-destruction of the government bond market. But then for the following thirty years it was favored with continuously rising bond prices constituting not only the greatest uninterrupted market rally in financial history, but also the greatest deformation.

It instilled in Wall Street the utterly false lesson that fortunes can be made in the carry trade, an illusion that is possible only when the Treasury bond price keeps rising, rising, and rising. Yet under a régime of sound money it is not possible for public debt to appreciate for long stretches of time, and most certainly not for thirty years.

THE GLORIOUS REIGN OF THE BRITISH CONSOL:
GOVERNMENT BONDS IN THE ERA OF SOUND MONEY

This truth is illustrated by the glorious reign of the 3 percent British consol, a perpetual bond of the British government. First issued in 1757, it remained in circulation until 1888. Other than temporary wartime fluctuations, the price of the 3 percent consol did not change for 131 years. Accordingly, no punter got rich riding the consol on leverage, yet no saver lost his shirt by owning it for its yield. The consol was a sound public bond denominated and payable in sound money.

After August 1971, by contrast, the US Treasury bond became the "anti-consol"; that is, the poker chip of speculators, not the solid redoubt of savers. The thing to do was to short it during the 1970s when the Great Inflation crushed its value; own it during the 1980s and 1990s when disinflation lifted its price; and rent it after December 2000 when well-telegraphed bond-buying campaigns by the central bank made holding the bond a front runner's dream.

The crucial difference between the stable era of the consol and the volatile era of the anti-consol, of course, is the monetary standard. The gold content of the pound sterling did not change for 131 years; in fact, not for 212 years. By contrast, for the last forty years the dollar has had no content at all, aside from the whim of the FOMC. Needless to say, what is implicated here is far more than "fun facts" about the classical gold standard.

The era of the anti-consol demonstrates that capital markets eventually lose their capacity to honestly price securities under a régime of unsound money; they end up dancing to the tune of the central bank; that is, pricing the trading value of financial assets based on expected central bank interventions, not the intrinsic value of their cash flows, rights, and risks.

This profound deformation of capital markets during the last forty years shaped the evolution of present-day Wall Street. These financial institutions had a near-death experience during the Great Inflation, when the value of stock and bond inventories was pummeled and activity rates in brokerage, underwriting, and mergers and acquisitions (M&A) advisory withered. But Wall Street was born again when Paul Volcker broke the back of wage and commodity inflation, thereby triggering the thirty-year ascent of the Treasury bond.

During this long upward march, Wall Street progressively learned that the Fed was operating much more than a disinflation cycle that would run its course. Instead, it had set in motion an asset inflation scheme that it would nurture and backstop at all hazards. The thing to do, therefore, was to accumulate financial assets, fund them with short-term debt, and harvest the positive spread.

More or less continuously over thirty years, bond prices rose and the cost of carry in the wholesale money markets fell. At length, this fundamental yield curve arbitrage, along with a plethora of variations on that trade, generated stupendous profits.

Some profits filtered down to the bottom line of Wall Street profit and loss statements (P&Ls), but much of the windfall was corseted in the salary and bonus accounts of the major Wall Street houses. In either case, the signal was unmistakable: the Fed's deformation of the financial markets was turning Wall Street balance sheets into money machines: the bigger the balance sheet, the better the money.

WHEN WALL STREET TRADING DESKS AWOKE IN SPECULATORS' HEAVEN

The crucial first step in fostering the carry trade bonanza was bringing money market interest rates down to ground level after they had erupted into double digits during the Great Inflation. At the peak of the Volcker monetary crunch in mid-1981, open market commercial paper rates reached 16 percent before receding to a 6–8 percent range during the following decade and a half. In this period the Fed steadily reduced the trend levels of short-term rates, but usually with a decent regard for the state of the business cycle and the rate of progress on disinflation.

An inflection point was reached at the time of the dot-com bust, however, and this cautionary approach was abruptly jettisoned. Indeed, soon after the Fed commenced its manic interest rate–cutting campaign in December 2000, Wall Street trading desks thought they had died and gone to speculator's heaven.

The interest rate on AA-rated financial commercial paper, the benchmark for Wall Street wholesale funding, then stood at 6.5 percent. By the end of the following year, unsecured financial paper rates had dropped to 4 percent and then to 2 percent by the end of 2002 and eventually to 1 percent by the spring of 2003. Moreover, repo financing, which was secured by collateral, dropped even more sharply.

In the face of an 85 percent plunge in Wall Street's cost of production—that is, the cost of funding its assets—there was hardly an asset class imaginable that did not generate gushers of positive cash flow. When financed with this 1 percent wholesale money, the much bigger yields of Treasuries, corporates, GSEs, real estate loans, junk bonds, and junk mortgages all produced fat profit spreads. Indeed, given standard leverage in excess of 90 percent on most of these asset classes, the huge "spread" gifted to Wall Street by the Fed was equivalent to handing dealers their very own printing press.

HOW FIVE WALL STREET "INVESTMENT BANKS" GREW 200X

It thus happened that the Keynesian prosperity managers at the Fed took aim at levitating the GDP, but instead unleashed the assembled genius of Wall Street in hot pursuit of balance sheet growth at all hazards. The most spectacular case was the five so-called investment banking houses—

Goldman, Morgan Stanley, Merrill Lynch, Lehman, and Bear Stearns. On the eve of the 2008 crisis, these five Wall Street houses had combined balance sheet footings of $5 trillion, meaning that their girth exceeded the GDP of Japan at the time.

As recently as 1998, however, the combined balance sheet of these firms or their predecessors was only $1 trillion. And back in 1980, before these "investment banking" houses were reborn as hedge funds, their footings had totaled only a few ten billions. The five behemoths thus started their thirty-year ride on the rising bond market when they were less than 1 percent of the size where they ended.

As previously indicated, there was a good reason for this historic modesty. The old-time Wall Street businesses of securities underwriting, merger advisory, and stock brokerage didn't require much capital; they made money providing value-added financial services, not by scalping the yield curve and trading swaps.

Furthermore, the devastation of financial markets by the Great Inflation so sharply diminished demand for investment banking services that Wall Street had been virtually drawn and quartered. Two-thirds of all firms doing business in August 1971 had been carried off the field or merged by the time Chairman Volcker had finished his bleeding cure. So, when the market hit its July 1982 bottom, Wall Street didn't have much of a balance sheet or much of a business.

What remained was born again during the next thirty years, but in an entirely new financial body. Salomon Brothers was the prototype, and by 1985 it was the undisputed king of Wall Street, enjoying a prosperity not seen among financial houses since 1929. Perhaps that's why there was a berth for me when I arrived there in early 1986, a fugitive from the government budget business and clueless about corporate balance sheets.

I soon learned while hanging around the partners' dining room, however, that a singular fact explained what the born-again Wall Street firms were really all about; namely, on days that interest rates went down (and bond prices therefore rose), Salomon's P&L was in the black. Conversely, when bond prices fell, its P&L was in the red. It rarely happened otherwise.

The moguls behind the screen, of course, could not acknowledge that the way to make big money was to stand around catching falling interest rates in a Wall Street rain barrel. So Salomon's unrivaled profitability was attributed to wizardry, specifically to the mathematical trading alchemy of John Meriwether and his team of quants who themselves would one day be reborn as Long-Term Capital Management.

It was true that Meriwether had discovered that tiny pricing discrepancies in the government bond market could be profitably arbitraged by means of computerized trading technology. But in building up a huge proprietary trading book, at least by the standards of the day, he had also discovered an even more important truth; namely, that being "leveraged and long" was even better. In fact, it was almost guaranteed to yield a perennial winning hand. In a fixed-income world rebounding from double-digit inflation, bond prices were almost always going up.

The roots of that aberration, however, went way back to the generation of bond investors who had been destroyed in the monetary hell of double-digit bond yields during the 1970s. The Great Inflation scourge was not quite the wheelbarrow inflation of Weimar Germany, but it still left investors deeply traumatized.

So, when they finally stopped dumping their bonds and cursing the very idea of fixed-coupon debt in the early 1980s, they had actually overdone it. At its 15 percent peak in July 1981, the long-term Treasury bond yield reflected not merely compensation for CPI inflation, which had averaged about 9 percent during the prior four years, but also a deep distrust of the reckless post–Camp David monetary policies which had brought so much carnage to the fixed-income markets.

In short, there was a fiat money penalty in the government bond rate which would take three decades to dissolve. Yet dissolve it did—slowly, steadily, ineluctably. Except for brief cyclic gyrations, the ten-year treasury yield never strayed from its long march downhill, breaking back under the double-digit line in 1985, tracking into the 6–7 percent range during the mid-1990s, crossing through 5 percent by the turn of the century, and eventually finding a bottom at 1.5 percent thirty-one years later.

This meant that had a modestly leveraged Rip Van Winkle put on the long-bond trade in 1982, he could have quadrupled his money while sleeping peacefully for three decades, and made many times more than that with the heavy leverage employed by the big trading houses. At the end of the day, there is no secular trend in modern financial history that is even remotely comparable in protean power and transcendent significance.

Surfing the long descent of the bond yield became the pathway to money making in the born-again Wall Street. In due course, traders learned that the odds were strikingly large that bond prices would be higher (reflecting the falling yield) month after month. This also meant that the risk of owning the bond on high leverage was small, and that the amplification of returns on the reduced amount of capital deployed in a leveraged trade was huge.

After the Fed settled into the Greenspan Put and Bernanke's Great Moderation, traders were not only confirmed in their directional bet, but now they had an official safety net, too. Owing to the central bank's incrementalism with respect to changes in its pegged federal funds rate and its continuous emission of smoke signals and verbal cues about future policy, traders who stayed even partially sober during market hours had no reason to fear owning the Treasury bond on 95 percent short-term borrowings.

If their cost of carry was going to rise, they would get plenty of warning from the Fed. Meanwhile, harvesting the spread on larger and larger positions that required only tiny amounts of permanent capital, they proved that money could be legally coined, even outside of the US mints.

INSIDE THE BOND ARB AT SALOMON BROTHERS

It wasn't so automatic in the initial years, however. In the summer of 1987 Salomon began to wobble badly, so John Gutfreund, the firm's legendary CEO, appointed a high-level task force to come up with a plan to fix the firm's faltering profit machine.

Part of the problem was the usual Wall Street warfare between investment bankers and traders. Qualified as neither, I was apparently added to the task force in order to occupy the fire field between the warring factions. There were three memorable facets to the circumstances at hand.

First, the ten-year Treasury bond had reached a low of 7 percent in early 1987 and then had been steadily backing up for most of the year; it eventually flared up to 9.5 percent during the initial Greenspan tightening scare of late August and September 1987. So, if you were standing around with a financial rain barrel trying to catch falling interest rates, it wasn't working out at the moment: the market value of the long bond suffered an abrupt 30 percent loss in nine months.

Secondly, duly noting that Salomon's giant government and municipal bond trading operation had incurred deep losses during the recent several quarters, the investment bankers on the task force pronounced it a "bad business." Their "restructuring" plan therefore proposed to get out of "flow" trading for customer accounts and refocus the firm's giant bond operation on the immensely profitable "prop" trading business run by Meriwether.

But even though his proprietary trading unit had its own P&L, staff, computers, and fame, John Meriwether wanted nothing to do with dumping the government bond operation. How would his traders get "market intelligence" about client portfolios?

Thereupon, the Salomon investment bankers were made to understand that "flow" trading—that is, front-running clients—was essential to the firm's "prop" trading riches, and so the government bond operation lived for another day. Likewise, after Greenspan flinched on Black Monday, bond yields resumed their fall and Salomon's P&L began to rebound smartly.

Soon the task force was disbanded, nothing at the firm was "restructured," and the thirty-year run of bond price appreciation resumed its course.

Thereafter, Salomon Brothers grew fulsomely in the "leveraged and long" modality of born-again Wall Street, and was eventually swallowed up by Sandy Weil's serial acquisition machine. The highly leveraged trading model Salomon had pioneered in the 1980s thus metastasized in the underbelly of Travelers Smith Barney at first, and then ultimately in the behemoth known as "Citi."

Given an ever more reliable and compliant central bank policy, the route to elephantine profits at the Citigroup trading colossus was pretty much a no-brainer. The formula was to accumulate financial assets aggressively, fund them largely in the low-cost commercial paper and repo markets, and then book the profit spread in a manner that proclaimed the streets of Golconda were once again paved with gold. Moreover, after enough profit had been booked to satisfy a 20 percent return on equity objective, the vast remainder of trading gains flowed into bonuses and employee profit sharing.

As the years and mergers rolled on, the true financial dimensions of this corpulent son of Salomon faded into in the fog of Citigroup's undecipherable financial reporting. But success invariably has its imitators on Wall Street and before the 1990s ended, the five former investment banks had all been reborn, reshaped, and remodeled on the Salomon template.

HEDGE FUNDS IN INVESTMENT BANKER DRAG

The $1 trillion, or thirty-five-fold, growth in combined balance sheet footings of the five investment banking houses between 1980 and 2000 had nothing whatsoever to do with "investment banking" or regulated securities "underwriting." M&A bankers and corporate advisory services still didn't need a dime of capital.

They got paid on account of the "regulatory brand equity" of the major houses; that is, the safe harbor value at the SEC and plaintiff's bar that Morgan Stanley's blessing, for example, conferred on the typical economically dubious M&A deals undertaken by CEOs and their boards. Likewise, standard equity and bond underwritings were essentially a "best efforts" placement of securities in the public market by dealer cartels.

They almost never underpriced these distributions, meaning that the risk of loss was small. Their investment banking departments thus were operated on a "capital lite" basis. The huge underwriting spreads, as high as 7 percent on equity deals, reflected returns to regulatory brand equity, not capital risk-taking.

By contrast, what had grown by leaps and bounds were the sales and trading operations of the five "investment banking" houses and especially the units they were pleased to label as their "prime broker" divisions. Obviously, these units were not anything like what the name implied; they did not resemble in the slightest an institutional market version of Merrill Lynch's doctors' and dentists' stock brokerage. The latter, at least in theory, were in the customer service business.

The truth was that the five broker-dealers had become hedge funds. While they still dressed up like investment banks, their old white-shoe businesses had actually become a sideline. Instead, they were now deep into the balance sheet businesses, positioning large-scale inventories of securities for active counterparty trading against their external hedge fund "customers."

Likewise, the "underwriting" that was really of interest to them, outside of the SEC-chaperoned IPO bubble, was OTC underwriting. That, too, was a form of trading which involved slicing and dicing existing securities so that the pieces and parts could be swapped into custom-tailored (bespoke) trades.

This financial alchemy took place through a private-dealer venue where whole loans, securitized loan pools, and derivatives of these pools could be traded on a bilateral basis outside of the regulated exchanges. In most instances, the "hedges" they sold on an underlying security or index basket were not against positions actually owned by their so-called customer. In fact, both parties to these trades were usually just gambling during working hours.

All of these new-style trading and OTC product activities were balance sheet intensive. This breakneck growth, therefore, should have encountered a formidable barrier on the free market; namely, the requirement for large dollops of equity and other risk capital to fund these mushrooming (and risky) balance sheets.

In point of fact, however, the five born-again investment houses didn't have much equity capital. Even by 1998, they had posted a combined net worth of only $40 billion, meaning they were levered 28 to 1. There is not a chance that the free market would have tolerated such radical leverage ratios; that is, absent the assurance that the central bank stood behind the distended balance sheets of these firms no one would have done business with them.

Indeed, that assurance was the very essence of the Fed's reprehensible bailout of Long-Term Capital Management in September 1998. By then the Wall Street house of cards was plainly evident. Notwithstanding all of the post-crisis finger-wagging by the financial establishment against LTCM's "massively leveraged" trading book, the true facts were damning: LTCM had obtained these massive borrowings from its "prime brokers" whose "investment bank" parent firms were nearly as levered as their now infamous hedge-fund customer.

Contrary to the cover story, therefore, LTCM was not some kind of rogue outlier; it was actually one of "da boyz." John Meriwether, the firm's chief, was not doing anything under his own shingle in Greenwich that he had not done at Salomon, and that had not been copied, replicated, and enhanced by the rest of Wall Street.

What the Fed's LTCM bailout really did was give a green light to the approximate 30 to 1 leverage ratio that already existed all around Wall Street. Indeed, in its misguided belief that the bloated stock averages of September 1998 were the linchpin to national prosperity, the Fed had authorized a cartel of dangerously leveraged gamblers—the rest of Wall Street—to bail out one of their own.

WHEN FIFTEEN GAMBLERS GOT 30X LEVERAGE BLESSED AT THE NEW YORK FED

At the end of the day, the Fed's craven sponsorship of the LTCM bailout might have been even more lethal than the panic rate cuts of 2001. The former action, in fact, amounted to a vastly upgraded Greenspan Put. As such, it surely paved the way for the final, massive growth of Wall Street balance sheets during the next decade.

As it happened, the head gambler for each of the fifteen major Wall Street banking houses had attended the crucial LTCM bailout meeting convened at the headquarters of the New York Fed. There they had duly noted the fearful perspiration and wobbly knees of officialdom and had concluded, accurately, that the Fed would prop up the casino at all hazards.

After that learning experience, it is not surprising that the five "investment banks" put their balance sheets on financial steroids. In fact, their footings quadrupled between the LTCM warning shot and the thundering meltdown of September 2008. The "financial crisis" thus arose from the vast deformations of the financial system to which the Fed's interest rate repression and "put" pandering had given rise.

Fed apologists have attempted to deflect culpability by means of a false narrative with respect to the increased leverage limit for broker-dealers. But these SEC rule changes occurred much later and were largely meaningless. When they became effective in 2004, it was long after 30 to 1 leverage was deeply implanted on Wall Street. The five investment houses already had dangerously high leverage ratios in place by 1998 at the "holding company" level where it counted. By contrast, the SEC rule changes applied to the infinitely malleable but irrelevant balance sheets of their "regulated" broker-dealer subsidiaries.

These "broker-dealer" subsidiaries, however, were not observable, operational businesses. They were essentially pro forma accounting boxes whose financial statements could be shoe-horned into compliance with virtually any regulatory standard. Consequently, the 2004 increase in the SEC-permitted leverage ratio was mainly an accounting annoyance and was noticed only by green eyeshades at the time.

What happened to the holding company balance sheets of the five investment houses during the nine years after 1998 is the real story. It amounts to a searing indictment of Fed policy. When the mortgage and credit bubble reached its fevered peak in 2007, the five "investment banks" were posting $140 billion of net worth, meaning they had generated about $100 billion of additional equity since the LTCM crisis. This gain was almost entirely from "retained" earnings, much of which later proved to be dubious accounting gains.

During the same nine-year period, their asset footings grew, too, by the astounding sum of $3.4 trillion, or by thirty-four times more. Needless to say, the distended balance sheets of these five former white-shoe advisory and retail brokerage firms, which now stood at $4.5 trillion, were a screaming affront to the free market. In the absence of the Greenspan and Bernanke Puts and the Fed's fully telegraphed interest rate pegging policy, it is not possible that such colossal accumulations of assets and leverage could have been assembled.

Had capital and money markets been fully at risk, investors would have lowered the boom on the Salomon "leveraged and long" model well before 1998. Consequently, the $4.5 trillion balance sheet of the "investment banking" houses never could have been assembled. No rational investor, if fully at risk, would have been part of a $4.35 trillion debt pool supported by only the $140 billion pittance of common equity being posted by the Wall Street houses.

In truth, the real equity underpinning the swollen balance sheets of the five investment houses was the Greenspan Put. After the LTCM bailout, the financial markets had been monetizing the maestro's fear of truly free markets all along.

In the meantime, of course, these bloated balance sheets became a virulent breeding ground for endless varieties of toxic mortgage securitizations and gambling hall derivatives. The reason was straightforward: wholesale money markets had become fearless.

Accordingly, almost anything that trading desks could acquire or concoct could be funded. With short-term repo financing available on almost any class of asset—including junk bonds, equities, and illiquid private loans, as well as mortgages and mortgage-backed securities of nearly any quality—there was virtually no limit on either the size or quality of Wall Street balance sheets.

GARBAGE IN THE BELLY OF THE BEAR

The evidence for this lies in autopsy data from Bear Stearns, among others. From 2000 to 2008, Bear's balance sheet grew from $90 billion to $400 billion. Yet its funding profile shortly before it collapsed bespoke a financial powder keg. Its fiscal 2007 financial statements showed only $12 billion of shareholder equity and just $55 billion of long-term debt.

This meant that the remainder of its $400 billion of liabilities was comprised primarily of "hot money" loans, including $100 billion of short-term repo, $30 billion of unsecured finance paper, and $75 billion of customer payables. What happened when its balance sheet quality was called into question after big unexpected losses in the second half of 2007 was obviously a run on these hot-money funding sources. Accordingly, repo counterparties refused to roll their paper, unsecured borrowing lines were curtailed or cancelled, and customers demanded payment of their outstanding trade balances.

The evidence of the precariousness of Bear Stearns's balance sheet lies in its having to roll approximately $60 billion of repo each morning; that is, 15 percent of its balance sheet had a one-day shelf life. As the crisis had intensified, the firm's secured lenders had continuously choked up on the bat, cutting thirty-day repo to fifteen days, and then five days, and finally just one day.

Worse still, about one-third of this massive daily repo roll was based on mortgage-based collateral that Bear Stearns's accountants had found necessary to classify as "level III" assets. This meant these securities were so toxic that there was absolutely no outside market for the paper, and also that there was no basis on which to value it other than by make-believe or what was euphemistically called "mark to model."

So there is no mystery as to why Bearn Stearns's liquidity literally vanished in its final days. When these overnight lenders began refusing to roll for even one day, what had been $20 billion of available cash on Thursday, March 3, drained down to $12 billion by the next Tuesday and had disappeared entirely two days later.

Accordingly, the firm's hapless interim CEO, Alan Schwartz, had not really misled anyone during his appearance on financial TV the day before Bear's demise. His predecessors, especially the insufferably swinish Jimmy Cayne, had been pettifogging about the viability of their preposterously leveraged gambling hall for years.

Needless to say, Bear Stearns did not represent a one-off outlier. The events at Lehman and the other Wall Street houses six months later simply replicated the run on these same classes of hot-money funding. Indeed, the sudden collapse at Bear Stearns in March 2008, should have been proof positive to the Fed that its stock market coddling and the implicit "put" under the price of risk assets had led to a vast deformation of Wall Street's finances.

But this "Defcon 1" warning provoked no reconsideration whatsoever, only a panicked scramble to protect Bear's lenders and counterparties through what amounted to a sweetheart deal with JPMorgan. In light of the sheer perfidy of Bear Stearns's financial stewardship, it is evident that officialdom at the Fed and Treasury were willfully blind. The splattered remains of Bear Stearns told anyone who bothered to investigate that there were ticking time bombs all around.

THE MERGER MANIA OF THE MEGA-BANKS

The Greenspan Fed unaccountably believed that the aberrations festering on Wall Street were the fruit of financial innovation and that it was levitating prosperity via the wealth effect of rising asset prices. So it was oblivious to this Wall Street balance sheet explosion, and the fact that the mushrooming footings of the five "investment banking" houses were only a small piece of the threat.

During this same 1998–2007 time frame, the five largest US bank holding companies underwent a similar balance sheet multiplication. In addition to standard deposit banking, all of these holding companies developed significant trading and underwriting operations, and a growing dependence on wholesale funding. Moreover, each was a product of the M&A frenzy unleashed by the Fed's prosperity management model.

Already by 1998, the predecessors of what would become the five mega-banks—JPMorgan, Citigroup, Bank of America, Wells Fargo, and Wachovia—did not bear much resemblance to the staid institutions of the post–New Deal commercial banking market. Each of these giants had been assembled from a breakneck pace of M&A during the first Greenspan decade, a development which was totally alien to the prior fifty-year history of the banking industry.

During that earlier half-century, there had been virtually no mergers of big money center banks or of broadly based retail banking chains. So the abrupt 1990s break from this sedate history might have raised questions about where all the noisily trumpeted "synergies" and consolidation "efficiencies" were suddenly coming from. Entrepreneurs in the regulated deposit banking industry had evidently not discovered any during the prior fifty years. Nor were there any current studies which documented significant economies of scale in commercial banking. There still have been none.

As it happened, empire-building CEOs did not need studies. Operating in the government franchised, supervised, and insured banking industry, they were largely immune from normal free market pressures which always militate toward efficient-scale enterprises rather than sheer size for its own sake.

By contrast, what empire builders like Citigroup's Sandy Weill and Hugh McColl of Nations Bank actually had going for them was the Greenspan Fed. As it drove PE multiples ever higher during the stock market bubble of the 1990s, it was almost impossible for serial acquirers to dream up a deal that wasn't "accretive" and therefore a good thing for shareholders.

In still another variation of the M&A racket, the financial consolidators had gotten themselves awarded a high PE multiple based on their alleged potential for strong growth. Such turbocharged stock valuations, in turn, functioned as an "acquisition" currency: a variety of money produced by speculators, not producers and investors.

In a typical bank merger, for example, the acquirer's 15X multiple made the earnings of an 8X acquisition target accretive to its earnings-per-share. So the acquirer's market cap rose at the get-go, even after allowance for a significant takeover premium. These post-merger stock price gains, in turn, validated the growth-by-acquisition model of the financial empire builders, thereby encouraging them to repeat the exercise over and over.

Needless to say, serial bank M&A also produced massive "diseconomies of scale" that remained submerged inside these financial behemoths as they steadily became too big to understand or to manage. The sheer chaos that erupted inside these institutions after September 2008 was stunning proof that merger mania had destroyed efficiency, discipline, and value. Yet over the long years of the financial bubble and the bank merger spree it did not seem to matter.

Momentum-chasing fund managers like Bill Miller of Legg Mason kept accumulating the stock of the mega-banks and didn't need to bother with questions about how all this financial magic was working. Steadily rising stock prices were explanation enough; that is, the "market action" proved that these financial empire builders could do no wrong.

THE BANK SYNERGY SCAM: QUADRUPLE DIPPING

These banking behemoths were built on threadbare theories impervious to evidence. Thus, the financial "supermarkets" notion had been Citigroup's mantra, yet there was no validation that it had actually generated sustainable "cross-selling" or other incremental revenue gains. Likewise, the mega-banks' formulaic claims for cost savings from each acquisition were completely implausible, and amounted to double, triple, and quadruple dipping.

The sequential strings of merger upon merger were so long that the serial cost reduction synergies claimed for them were logically impossible. Bank of America, for example, claimed it would squeeze large savings out of FleetBoston following its acquisition in 2004. Yet the predecessor entities had made the same claim when BankBoston merged with Fleet Financial Group in 1999. The latter, in turn, had been a serial acquirer which presumably squeezed out all redundant head counts and operating costs when it merged with Shawmut National bank in 1995.

Even by that point, the potential for synergies was questionable, since Fleet Financial Group had earlier claimed it had picked redundant costs clean when it merged with Bank of New England in 1991; and this large redundancy savings, if it happened at all, had come on top of cost takeouts that Fleet Bank had claimed from its merger with Norstar Bancorp of Albany in 1988. In short, the endless chain of synergies was a delusional racket.

The Bank of America merger chain was only one strand of the M&A "roll-up" wave that hit the banking system between 1992 and 2007. All told, tens of billions in cost synergies were claimed during this tidal wave of M&A, and most of it was in head count and payroll.

Yet there was no proof in the pudding. In fact, Bureau of Labor Statistics monthly payroll data showed that there were 1.76 million jobs in depository banks in 1992 and slightly more—1.82 million—in 2007. The massive head-count reductions claimed in the industrywide merger wave, in fact, were just so much press release eyewash.

Based on the financial agitprop of the bank empire builders, of course, the impression was also easily garnered that these M&A deals were driving a ripping wave of productivity and efficiency throughout the banking system, and that redundant and obsolete bricks-and-mortar branches were being aggressively shuttered. In fact, the nation had been blessed with 115,000 bank branches and offices in 1992 and was nearly doubly blessed with 165,000 of them in 2007.

WHY THE CLAIMS FOR BANK M&A WEREN'T ON THE LEVEL

Gary Cooper would have doubtless found the claims of the banking empire builders in 2005 to be no more "on the level" than he had found the claims of Communism in the 1950s. The actual fact was that giant strides in information technology and inventions like the ATM were sharply reducing the cost of plain old deposit banking during this period.

Yet there was no evidence that these actual productivity breakthroughs depended upon the roll-up of trillion-dollar financial supermarkets, or that the bank merger mania added any independent benefit to these underlying technology-driven gains. In fact, some of the most efficient banks in the United States have asset footings of under $50 billion (i.e., 2 percent of Citigroup), yet have not been denied economies of scale with respect to any aspect of the information technology revolution in banking.

The former Hudson City Bancorp, for example, had the lowest operating cost-to-revenue ratio of any publicly traded bank in the United States, but had only $45 billion of assets and 135 branches. In fact, its operating cost ratio was less than half that of its mega-bank competitors such as Chase Bank and Citibank, with which it went head-to-head on its New Jersey turf.

Not surprisingly, Hudson City Bancorp had no trading operations or prop desk, and was strictly in the residential mortgage and community banking business. Unlike the banking behemoths, it did not suffer from "dis-economies of scale" and thereby maintained a pristine loan book. It never wrote a single subprime loan or any other risky "innovative" mortgage, and boasted a mortgage portfolio where the loan-to-value ratio averaged a rock-bottom 60 percent; that is, virtually none of its borrowers were "underwater."

Accordingly, Hudson City Bancorp was the poster boy for prudent and proficient underwriting: it had only 500 bad loans out of 80,000 in its mortgage book. It also put the lie to the entire "size matters" propaganda that arose from the merger mania. Hudson City Bancorp not only suffered no scale disadvantages but also avoided the underwriting chaos of its Too Big to Manage competitors.

In truth, there are no significant economies of scale in retail banking above $50 billion in assets, period. Consequently, the massive "roll-ups" of retail banking should never have been tolerated by bank supervisors.

Nor was the case any more compelling with respect to corporate lending and securities underwriting. The relevant marketplace for these operations is global, yet that's exactly why almost every corporate financing of size is widely syndicated. The latter process—often involving dozens of financial institutions presenting widely differing geographies, customer bases, and scales of operations—represents the opposite of the mega-bank principle; the very purpose of syndication is to disaggregate scale, not concentrate it.

The constant claim by the likes of JPMorgan that it got huge because its global customers "demanded" it is mocked by the facts. JPMorgan is actually the top corporate loan syndicator on the planet. In that capacity it does not throw its multitrillion balance sheet at customers but, instead, "arranges" new loans by spreading the credit exposure far and wide.

The remaining operations of the mega-banks basically consist of massive internal hedge funds and related trading and prime brokerage operations. Whether there are economies of scale in these internal hedge funds or not is irrelevant. As the great Carter Glass might have declaimed, those activities should not have been allowed within a country mile of deposit banking in the first place.

None of these considerations bestirred the Fed, the one agency that could have shut down the empire builders cold. In fact, the Fed actually encouraged the traditional money center and leading regional commercial banks to merge. Furthermore, by embracing the Glass-Steagall repeal it gave the green light for these commercial bank "roll-ups" to then branch out into all the trading markets, thereby transforming themselves into the very Wall Street behemoths that came crashing down on the Fed's own doorstep just a few years later.

Needless to say, the monetary central planners were so blindly focused on levitating the nation's economy through higher stock prices that they failed to read the warning signs in their own domain. The rip-roaring share prices of the mega-banks were evidence not of national prosperity but of massive speculation on Wall Street and in the credit markets. The disaster of "Too Big to Fail" was being erected right under its nose, and yet the Fed did not stop a single M&A deal of significance.

Indeed, the combined market cap of the five mega-banks grew from a few billion dollars posted by their predecessors in 1987 to $800 billion by 2008, but these munificent gains were serial gifts from the Fed. What caused the valuations of these insensible agglomerations to soar was swollen PE multiples, cheap wholesale funding, and a regulatory blind eye to the insanity of the banking merger mania.

It goes without saying that with all boats being lifted by a rising tide of stock prices—even transparently unseaworthy vessels like Citigroup—the free market could not do its job of capital allocation and assessment of the earnings quality being reported. So the market caps of these burgeoning financial mishaps kept rising, as mutual fund managers and newly emboldened Main Street punters alike piled into another momentum chase.

In the fullness of time, of course, it became evident that these behemoths were "too big to comprehend," "too big to manage," and "too big to be profitable" on a sustainable basis. Still, soaring stock prices gave CEOs, boards, and M&A bankers all the reason needed for ever larger mergers and consolidations.

BANK MERGER MANIA:
EXECUTIONER OF GLASS–STEAGALL

The lamentable thing about the eventual crack up of the mega-banks is they were erected one step at a time in full view of Washington officialdom. By the end of 1998, the five great mega-banks had accumulated combined balance sheets of $2.5 trillion: a thirty-five-fold gain from the modest girth of their 1987 predecessors. Yet, rather than giving pause, these elephantine numbers seemed to only accelerate the chase.

By that point, for example, Chemical Bank had already merged with Manufacturers Hanover which, in turn, combined with Chase Manhattan. While each had thrived nicely as an independent money center bank since the 1930s, the threesome proved to be not up to the task of bubble finance. Accordingly, the huge firm then known as Chase Bank next merged with JPMorgan, thereby rewriting in one fell swoop the map of post-depression-era finance.

In short order, of course, the rewriting resumed when BankOne was brought into the Morgan fold in 2004. That merger brought along with it First Chicago and a whole landscape of midwestern community banks that the combo's namesake had accumulated over several decades. Accordingly, JPMorgan had now crossed the $1 trillion mark in total assets and was rapidly on the way to $2 trillion four years later.

The final flurry of bank merger mania also brought the ill-starred 1999 union of one of the nation's premier money center banks, Citicorp, with a discombobulated collection of financial services companies that Sandy Weill had assembled under the Travelers Group. The pieces and parts of the latter were a veritable history of Weill's 1990s M&A adventures including Salomon Brothers, Smith Barney, Travelers, parts of Aetna, the retail brokerage of Shearson, the insurance and consumer credit operations of Primerica, and countless more.

The result was a $2 trillion monster that the M&A king himself couldn't manage and that the world-class banker who came with the deal, John Reed, was never allowed to run. At length, the whole train wreck was seconded to what amounted to a trustee lawyer, Chuck Prince. The latter had no clue about what to do, but famously assured the gamblers who day-traded his stock that he would "keep dancing until the music stops." In the event, he did, and it did.

The incongruous manner in which Citigroup spent the last few years of its pre-bailout life drifting toward the iceberg speaks volumes about the financial deformations that had settled on Wall Street. It goes without saying that no one saw any danger at its creation. It was literally voted through by officialdom, since Chairman Greenspan, Treasury Secretary Rubin, his deputy Larry Summers, and the banking committees of both houses had all supported the Glass-Steagall repeal which enabled the Citibank-Travelers merger.

Then when troubles were already mounting down below, regulators allowed Citigroup to consume $100 billion in cash through stock buybacks and dividend payouts during 2004 through September 2008. This was turning a blind eye with a vengeance, but also perhaps explains why Ben Bernanke, Hank Paulson, and the rest of the bailout crew had no explanation for the thundering financial crisis of September 2008.

By their lights, it was all due to a mysterious "contagion" which had arrived unexpectedly, perhaps on a comet from deep space. The possibility that totally misguided public policies—including interest rate repression, the Greenspan Put, and the green light for bank merger mania—had brought down Citigroup and the other mega-banks did not cross their minds.

The other mega-banks arose and fell along the same timeline. The serial acquisition machine called Nations Bank combined with Bank of America in 1998, and the combo then scoured the land, absorbing regional banking chains like so many dominoes. The identical playbook was used by Wachovia Bank, which merged with First Union Bank in 2001.

Each of these latter two banks had previously "rolled-up" numerous regional banking chains and, once combined, actually accelerated their feeding frenzy, culminating in the disastrous acquisition of Golden West Financial in 2006. That bank was a giant financial turkey so stuffed with liar's loans and "negative amortization" mortgages that Charles Ponzi would have doubtless invented it, if he'd only had sufficient imagination.

Accordingly, during the five years after the LTCM bailout, the balance sheet footings of these five mega-banks had grown to $3.8 trillion, or by 50 percent. Moreover, after 2003 growth actually accelerated as these newly consolidated depositories tapped heavily into the same wholesale funding market which had fueled the explosive growth of the investment banking houses. The footings of the five mega-banks thus nearly doubled again to nearly $7 trillion by 2007.

The 1999 repeal of Glass-Steagall had been a mere formality: the real point was that the whole prudential banking régime that had been established by Glass-Steagall was gone, too. What had actually swept it away was a decade of merger mania that the Fed had blessed every step along the way, and which the maestro had actually heralded as another triumph of capitalist innovation and energy.

DEPOSIT BANKS ARE WARDS OF THE STATE
AND NEED STRICT SUPERVISION

Yet there was more, and it was worse. As wards of the state, chartered deposit banks needed to be strictly regulated in order to prevent abuse of their fractional reserve banking privileges, to say nothing of the moral hazard implicit in taxpayer-supported deposit insurance and in their right to access the Fed's discount window for emergency loans.

Once again, however, the same misguided application of free market theory, which had led to a feckless posture of "hands off" with respect to bank mergers, came into play. Accordingly, these new behemoths were permitted to wander into every type of gambling activity known to Wall Street.

Thus, all five mega-banks were soon knee-deep in equity trading and underwriting, prime brokering, options and futures trading, commodities, swaps and derivatives, private equity, internal hedge funds, and much more. They had, in substance, become European-style "universal banks" and had a massive presence in all the traditional Wall Street dealer and investment banking markets.

Not surprisingly, therefore, by 2008 the five mega-banks, which had emerged from a decade and a half of merger mania, banking deregulation, and relentless penetration into nondepository markets, had reached colossal size by every historic standard. In fact, their balance sheet footings were now *a hundred times larger* than that of their predecessors in August 1987 when Greenspan arrived at the Fed.

It is also remarkable that only a modest share of the massive balance sheet expansion of these five institutions after 1998 was funded by depositors, notwithstanding their status as FDIC-insured banks. The preponderant share of funding growth was obtained from the wholesale money markets.

What happened was that new assets were being snagged and then piled on these mushrooming balance sheets in a hand-over-fist manner. These newly acquired assets were then hocked in the repo market as fast as they arrived. Like their investment banking cousins, therefore, the five mega-banks were also becoming financially unstable and vulnerable to a wholesale money market run.

As these aberrations gathered force the Fed took no notice whatsoever. It had no clue that the $7 trillion of combined balance sheets assembled by these five mega-banks in barely a decade were essentially helter-skelter agglomerations, not managed banking portfolios in any traditional sense. Nor did it recognize that in due course these far-flung financial institutions would inevitably lose track of what was in their own turbulent balance sheets, to say nothing of those of their far-flung counterparties.

WHEN THE MONETARY CENTRAL PLANNERS
MISSED THE $11 TRILLION TRAIN WRECK

The FOMC minutes show the Fed's leadership circle ignored these mega-bank threats because it falsely assumed the US economy was strong. The vulnerability of these jerry-built balance sheets to the adverse macroeconomic trends actually under way, such as the massive increase of household debt, declining real wages, and the giant trade deficit and resulting offshoring of the tradable goods economy, escaped notice entirely.

Even as severe financial strains broke out in the subprime market and on Wall Street dealer balance sheets in the second half of 2007, the Fed's take on the nation's economic pulse was feckless. It consisted mostly of spurious patter about the monthly economic weather patterns and short-term fluctuations in financial ratios and spreads. Indeed, the tone of the Fed minutes in the run-up to the crisis was ostrichlike.

With their heads in the sand, the monetary central planners in the Eccles Building thus kibitzed about the trivial blips in regional purchasing manager surveys, construction jobs, and retail sales. Meanwhile, they blithely ignored the inescapable fact that in less than two decades Wall Street had been radically transformed and was now comprised of ten teetering financial behemoths.

By the end of 2007, the five investment banking houses plus five mega-banks posted a combined balance sheet of $11.4 trillion. They were now 300 percent of the size they had been in 1998, notwithstanding that the real economy had grown by only 29 percent during the decade.

So once again bubble finance generated a vast deformation. During the course of just eight years, these monuments to runaway M&A and the wholesale-market money shuffle expanded their balance sheets by the staggering sum of $8 trillion. Needless to say, this kind of insensible growth could only occur in a wholly financialized economy driven by a central bank that had rigged interest rates at absurdly low levels.

On the free market, by contrast, the endless hypothecation and rehypothecation of collateral which underpinned the massive balance sheets of these giant banks would have been stopped dead in its tracks. The reason stems from nothing more mysterious than the law of supply and demand.

In a wholesale money market with a freely functioning pricing mechanism—that is, one not contaminated by central bank interest rate repression—the explosion of Wall Street demand for repo and other short-term funding would have caused interest rates to rocket skyward. The effect would have been similar to what occurred in the pre-1914 call money market when the supply and demand for excess savings got out of whack; namely, money market rates would have soared into double digits.

Double-digit money market rates, in turn, would have quashed the demand for wholesale funding because the carry trades, which are the fundamental source of repo demand, would have been deeply negative. Stated differently, carry trades don't work when the interest cost on borrowings is higher than the yield on the pledged mortgages, corporates, governments, or even junk bonds.

Furthermore, the elimination or even shrinkage of repo credit, which was mostly manufactured out of thin air by lenders who sold the collateral short, would have forced the mega-banks to seek plain old deposit funding. Needless to say, a scramble for deposits on the free market would have been a further potent antidote to expansion of Wall Street balance sheets.

Genuine Main Street savers would have demanded far higher interest rates to forego additional amounts of their now beloved consumption. Indeed, to get consumers to throttle back on consumption would have required drastically higher inducements than those which prevailed under the Fed's price-controlled money markets. The magic profits of balance sheet arbitrage would have thus been largely eliminated on the free market.

Absent the money market carry trades enabled by the Fed, therefore, the $8 trillion expansion of Wall Street balance sheets would never have happened. And this means, in turn, that Wall Street's financial meth labs, which manufactured trillions of subprime mortgages, CDOs, and other toxic securities, could not have opened for business. Without repo and other wholesale money markets, there would have been no place to fund the garbage.

By the time the final Greenspan-Bernanke housing and stock market bubble reached its peak in late 2007, however, any institutional memory of free markets in money—that is, the pre-Fed call money market—had long since vanished. Wall Street and policy makers alike had come to embrace as the "new normal" a rigged money market that was pinned down by midget-sized, Fed-administered interest rates.

Not surprisingly, therefore, policy makers did not recognize these bloated balance sheets as the freakish financial aberrations they actually were. Nor did they apprehend that these balance sheets were loaded with impaired and illiquid assets that had been recklessly accumulated by bonus-driven trading desks. In short, the Fed did not see the train wreck that was thundering toward it at full speed.

WHEN $1 TRILLION OF MARKET CAP VANISHED IN THE CANYONS OF WALL STREET

At the end of the day, the vast financial deformation embodied in these ten Wall Street mega-banks had been fueled by the lunatic overvaluation of bank stocks engineered by the Fed. The incentive for empire builders to assemble train wrecks like Citibank and Bank of America, and for bankers to invent financial tommyrot like CDOs-squared, is evident in the parabolic rise of bank market caps after 1987. The vast riches it bestowed on bank managements through stock options and stock-based cash bonuses had never before been seen in the financial system.

Thus, the implicit market cap of the ancestors of these ten mega-banks had been perhaps $40 billion prior to Black Monday in October 1987. By the end of the first Greenspan stock market bubble in late 2000, their combined market cap had reached $500 billion. Then, after the Fed launched its 2001–2003 rate-cutting spree, the market cap of the ten Wall Street banks literally shot the moon, reaching $1.25 trillion by mid-2007.

In short, ten sprawling financial behemoths which provided almost no value added to the Main Street economy had experienced a thirtyfold gain in market cap in less than two decades. Yet not long after bank executives garnered hundreds of billions in cash bonuses and stock option cash-outs based on these preposterous valuations, the full extent of the bank stock bubble became evident.

By March 2009, after the Wall Street meltdown had taken its toll, four of the ten mega-banks were gone and the market cap of the survivors had shrunk to $250 billion. And so it happened that $1 trillion of market cap disappeared from the canyons of Wall Street in a financial market minute.

The monetary central planners did not give a moment's thought to the implications of this violent collapse of what was a trillion-dollar bubble. And it wasn't just another bubble of the type that had become standard fare under the Greenspan Fed; that is, the home builder, telecom, dot-com, and high-tech stock bubbles which had gone before. In this instance, the very financial transmission system, the primary dealer network that the Fed relied on to implement its policies, had lost 80 percent of its market cap.

These ten institutions constituted the overwhelming bulk of the primary dealer market through which all of the Fed's interest rate pegging, debt monetization, and risk asset pumping operations were conducted. In any reasonable world, the shocking revelation that this crucial policy transmission mechanism had been run by reckless gamblers, and that their balance sheets consisted of a heaving mass of financial assets rented by the day, would have been conclusive.

By the time of the September 2008 financial crisis, the ten mega-banks posed an existential threat to the entire prosperity management model on which the Fed operated. Not surprisingly, the nation's panic-stricken monetary politburo chose to bail out the misbegotten behemoths rather than reconsider its own ill-conceived model.

CHAPTER 19

FROM WASHINGTON TO WALL STREET
Roots of the Great Housing Deformation

T HE LONG CYCLE OF MONETARY DEFORMATION TRIGGERED BY THE events of August 1971 stood at the heart of the home mortgage crash in 2007–2008. Needless to say, it took time and numerous twists and turns to get there.

First came the brutal margin squeeze on traditional bank and thrift mortgage lenders during the Great Inflation of the 1970s. In Old Testament fashion, that breakdown begat the misguided deregulation and crash landing of the savings and loan industry in the 1980s. The demise of these traditional bricks-and-mortar Main Street lenders, in turn, begat the explosive growth of broker-based mortgage finance by Freddie and Fannie in the 1990s.

In due course, the spread of mortgage boiler rooms from coast to coast enabled the rise of Wall Street–based subprime finance after the turn of the century. All the while, the Fed's interest repression policies fostered massive overinvestment in mortgage finance and housing, thereby aggravating these deformations still further.

THE GREAT INFLATION'S LEGACY: BUSTED MORTGAGE LENDERS THE FREE MARKET COULDN'T FIX

The repudiation of sound money at Camp David and the subsequent monetary depredations of Arthur Burns led to the Great Inflation and its assault on the balance sheets of traditional mortgage lenders. Yet, even after double-digit inflation was crushed by Paul Volcker in 1980–1982, its long shadow weighed heavily on the future of home finance.

In fact, Volcker's signal success came too late. By then the traditional home mortgage finance industry had been essentially bankrupted by the negative spread between soaring interest rates on deposit liabilities and the low fixed rates embedded in legacy mortgage portfolios. Self-evidently, the resulting hemorrhage of losses among bank and thrift mortgage lenders was an artifact of failed monetary policy, not a product of the free market.

The free market could not be expected, therefore, to solve a problem it hadn't created, meaning that deregulation of the savings and loans (S&Ls) was a profoundly misguided cure for the ill effects of bad money. The only real solution was wholesale liquidation of thousands of insolvent banks and thrifts.

Needless to say, not even the Reagan administration had the political stomach for the correct free market answer. So its well-intended alternative, liberalization of S&L lending charters, actually made matters worse.

Deregulation, as we will see below, encouraged traditional bricks-and-mortar bankers, who knew everything about home mortgage lending, to flee into commercial real estate and junk bond investment, about which they knew nothing. In this wholly discombobulated setting, the housing finance industry clung for dear life to the only lifeline available; namely, the government-sponsored mortgage guarantee programs at Freddie Mac and Fannie Mae.

CRUSHED BY THE GSES

Not surprisingly, high on the Reagan administration's free market agenda was the elimination of the GSEs and their taxpayer-subsidized channel of housing finance. As director of the Office of Management and Budget, I championed a plan to eliminate the GSEs through a slow financial euthanasia.

The mechanism was a federal "guarantee fee" designed to raise the cost of Freddie and Fannie financing to private market–clearing levels. It would have permitted the taxpayers to capture the spread between the private market rate and the Treasury's lower cost of financing.

Needless to say, if the GSEs had been required to pay market rates for their capital and funding, there is no reason to believe they would have survived competition from the traditional "originate and hold" model of depository institutions. For that reason, the guarantee fee catalyzed the forces of crony capitalism like rarely before in the history of federal housing programs. Home builders and suppliers of lumber, hardware, HVAC, and electrical products joined real estate agents, mortgage bankers and brokers, title lawyers, and dozens more in a mighty coalition to keep private enterprise humming on cheap, socialized credit.

As Ralph Nadar observed years later, "Fannie Mae and Freddie Mac are fast learners . . . [they] have swiftly and skillfully managed to pick up the roughshod tactics of the private corporate world . . . [and] cling tightly to one of the Federal government's deepest and most lucrative welfare troughs."

The danger of government subsidization and control of housing finance would eventually be painfully evident. But in 1981, when the GSEs were still in their relative infancy and there was an honest chance to smother them in the cradle, Republicans on Capitol Hill led the charge to kill the OMB-proposed guarantee fee. The American housing industry, they averred, was too important to be left to the whims of the free market.

Four decades after its accidental birth in New Deal–era filing cabinets, therefore, Fannie Mae was adopted by Republican foster parents. Now it would morph into a destructive monster with no legislative check on its growth. Thus, during the first Reagan term, the combined guarantees and direct mortgage holdings of the GSEs doubled from $200 billion to $400 billion and then doubled again by 1988.

When George H. W. Bush left office in 1992, the footings of the GSEs totaled $1.5 trillion. During twelve years of Republican rule, the balance sheets of Freddie and Fannie (and Ginnie Mae) had not simply grown rapidly; they had, in fact, metastasized, reaching a size that was seven times greater than when they had been furtively challenged by the Reagan Revolution.

VOODOO ECONOMICS STRIKES BACK

So the era of Republican rule did not roll back Big Government in the nation's largest industry; that is, housing construction and finance. Even worse, in one of his final acts as president, George H. W. Bush signed the calamitous Housing and Community Development Act of 1992.

This abomination gave new meaning to the term "voodoo economics," the very epithet Bush had thrown at Ronald Reagan in the 1980 primary campaign. Yet in his final act as president it was Bush who turned out to be the greater practitioner of economic folly.

One major title of the bill, for example, made a mockery of its own bold-print heading. Under the rubric "financial safety and soundness," Freddie and Fannie were permitted to leverage their balance sheets 200 to 1 in the case of guaranteed mortgage pools, and by more than 100 to 1 overall.

The Bush White House's woolly-minded rationalizations for this madness surely delighted the crony capitalists who crowded the signing ceremony. Embracing the bill as the second coming of motherhood, Bush averred that it would "target assistance where it is needed most, expand homeownership opportunities, ensure fiscal integrity and empower recipients of Federal housing assistance."

What the bill actually did was set in motion a pervasive, relentless degradation of underwriting standards that was pure financial poison. The so-called affordable housing goals initially required that 30 percent of GSE volume consist of low- and moderate-income borrowers (later raised administratively in steps to 56 percent). It further provided that underwriting standards could be drastically weakened to achieve these targets, including authorization for the GSEs to virtually scuttle the historic requirement that borrowers have "skin in the game" in the form of a meaningful cash down payment.

It goes without saying that nonrecourse mortgage loans with token down payments, in the context of what turned out to be a decade-long bubble in housing prices, were a recipe for disaster. While it took the GSEs time to chip away at their traditional underwriting disciplines, one signal breakdown occurred several years later when Fannie Mae introduced its "Flex 97" product. That bit of affordable housing lunacy permitted borrowers to post a mere 3 percent down payment, and it didn't even have to be their own cash.

This initiative was symptomatic of Washington's truly foolish obsession with promoting home ownership, especially in the face of housing prices which were rising preternaturally. In those circumstances, the GSEs should have significantly boosted, not eviscerated, their required down payment ratio in order to provide a cushion against subsequent market reversals in the value of housing collateral.

The true evil, however, did not lie in the affordable housing mandate per se. Conservative critics were wont to complain loudly that the GSEs were being saddled with inappropriate "social policy" missions, but that was an oxymoron; the GSEs themselves were social policy undertakings and they had always been inappropriate, owing to the inherent danger of crony capitalist capture.

Accordingly, what the ill-defined and elastic "affordable housing" mandate actually did was unleash full-bore crony capitalism in home finance. Indeed, in only a few years' time stock-option-crazed executives turned Freddie and Fannie into housing bubble machines funded by Uncle Sam's credit card.

HOW THE STOCK OF FREDDIE AND FANNIE SHOT THE MOON

For a moment in time, the stock prices of Freddie and Fannie took on the trajectory of a moon shot. Yet these billowing Wall Street valuations were always preposterous, a truth eventually punctuated by the hapless Hank Paulson. Standing knee-deep in the carnage of the GSEs in July 2008, he vainly attempted to prop up what remained of their stock prices by claiming that he had a bazooka in his pants pocket.

Still, this failed moon shot had taken a quarter century to run its course. When the House Republicans rescued the GSEs from the threat of free market economics in 1981, the market cap of Fannie Mae was less than $1 billion, and Freddie Mac was not yet even publicly traded. By the time George H. W. Bush signed the misbegotten housing bill eight days before the 1992 election, their combined market cap amounted to only a few billion.

Soon thereafter, however, the stock prices of Fannie and Freddie went parabolic. As it happened, the 1992 statute was virtually a blank check of authority to promote home ownership, and thereby perfectly suited to the agenda of the genuine liberals Clinton installed in the Department of Housing and Urban Development (HUD) and the GSEs. HUD Secretary Henry Cisneros soon devised the "National Homeownership Strategy" and launched it with much hoopla at a conference in August 1994 attended by crony capitalists and community organizers in equal numbers.

Since Uncle Sam was picking up the tab, the two sides found themselves in remarkable unanimity. In a strategy document that was embraced by both ACORN (Association of Communities for Reform Now) and the mortgage bankers, it was agreed that huge gains in home ownership could be achieved if only the inconvenience of down payments and monthly mortgage payments could be overcome! In a fit of blinding insight, the document thus noted that "the lack of cash to accumulate the required down payment and closing costs is the major impediment to purchasing a home" and that many households "do not have sufficient income available to make monthly payments."

The answer to this roadblock was "financing strategies, fueled by the creativity and resources of the private and public sectors." The obvious "resource" in question was the balance sheet of the GSEs, which expanded by one-half trillion dollars during the next four years.

Yet the thing which really grew was the market cap of Freddie and Fannie. By 1997 they had a combined market cap of $80 billion, and by early 2000 Wall Street was valuing the stock of the GSE twins at an astonishing $140 billion. Here was the jet fuel that ignited the final housing craze.

While the miraculous ride of the GSE stocks stirred the speculative juices on Wall Street, the real mania broke out right inside the C-suite of Freddie and Fannie. Stock options exploded in value, causing top GSE managers to become as obsessed with their stock price as the most myopic dot-com executives; and that, in turn, meant feeding Wall Street increasingly higher earnings and ever more spectacular feats of growth.

FREDDIE AND FANNIE:
PURE ECONOMIC PARASITES, ALL THE TIME

Unfortunately, the GSEs had only one route to achieve growth, and that was reaching deeper into the sludge at the bottom of the nation's potential mortgage credit pool. This dubious route to higher financial postings was, in turn, a function of the dark truth of the GSEs; namely, that they were not real businesses, nor did they contribute any value added to the US economy. Accordingly, they had no honest way to grow and couldn't possibly have been worth $140 billion, or even $14 billion, or really anything at all.

Despite their massive balance sheets and towering Wall Street valuations, the GSEs were essentially economic parasites which harvested rents by deploying the public credit of the United States at no charge from the Treasury. The smoking-gun evidence that they produced no economic value added was hidden in plain sight on their income statements: the GSEs had virtually no cost of production beyond the trivial head counts which were needed to man and maintain their data processing systems.

During fiscal 2000, for example, Fannie Mae booked $7.0 billion of interest income and guarantee fees but had only $900 million of operating expenses, resulting in 87 percent gross profit. In truth, there was nothing behind the imposing brick exterior of Fannie Mae's headquarters except a toll booth where fees were collected in return for stamping "guaranteed" (implicitly by Uncle Sam) on pools of conforming mortgages.

Based on pure accounting theory, of course, the GSEs' true cost of production was future losses, similar to any other insurance company. Every time they stamped "guaranteed" on another pool of mortgages, therefore, the GSEs should have incurred an expense for loan loss reserves. Yet during fiscal 2000 it set aside only $100 million for future losses, a trivial 1.7 percent of revenues.

It was on this obvious point that the era of bubble finance made a shambles of GSE financial reporting. Virtually from the day of the Clinton administration's August 1994 housing conference, housing prices started rising and never looked back. At the same time, the newly launched national crusade to increase home ownership pushed GSE credit quality into its relentless cycle of deterioration.

This confluence carved a toxic path into the future. On the one hand, the GSEs' historical credit loss experience became increasingly irrelevant to each year's new book of lower-quality business. At the same time, briskly rising housing prices were masking growing losses owing to continuous refinancing of delinquent mortgages.

THE MOTHER OF ALL CREDIT BUBBLES:
130 STRAIGHT MONTHS OF HOUSING PRICE GAINS

Beginning in July 1995, national housing prices rose every single month for nearly eleven years. By the midway point at the end of 2001, the Case-Shiller index was up by 60 percent, and at the final peak in May 2006 it had gained 195 percent. In short, under what was an utterly freakish financial deformation, even if it was one that the nation's monetary politburo insisted, ludicrously, could not be detected, housing prices rose at a compound rate of 11 percent for eleven consecutive years.

As a result, the true credit losses owing to the home ownership crusade were nowhere to be found in the GSE performance data. When borrowers got behind, their mortgages were simply refinanced, usually with a big enough increase in principal to re-pay the arrearage. Serial refinancings and the constant churn of the existing housing stock temporarily buried the growing GSE losses in Alan Greenspan's monetary bubble.

The tailwind of rising housing prices and negligible actual default losses enabled the GSE management teams to book exceedingly minimal reserves for future losses. Accordingly, they continued to book nearly 90 percent profit margins on a soaring volume of business. These sterling results caused their stock prices to rise by further leaps and bounds, providing powerful incentives for management to drive GSE underwriting standards still lower and mortgage volume ever higher.

Thus, in 1998 alone, the combined GSE balance sheet grew by $200 billion, or by the amount of total footings that had existed at the time of the Reagan challenge. Three years later, the GSE balance sheets expanded by nearly $400 billion, bringing their total outstanding mortgage credit exposure to $3.1 trillion. In the face of soaring volumes and virtually no charges for future losses, Freddie and Fannie were literally minting profits.

This pell-mell volume and earnings growth did wonders for the stock price of Freddie and Fannie, which in turn generated fabulous management bonuses and stock option gains: several billion dollars over the span of 1990–2002. In a financial folly that had no precedent, a housing-crazed government had thus turned over the public credit of the United States to a small cadre of GSE executives and Wall Street punters who then gorged themselves on ill-gotten windfalls.

Needless to say, when the housing price bubble peaked and reversed direction in 2006, the hidden losses buried in the GSE mortgage portfolios began to emerge—slowly at first and then with an explosive rush after mid-2008. Accordingly, the nearly $200 billion of losses recorded by Freddie and Fannie since then have wiped out all of the profits they ever booked historically, and then some.

CRONY CAPITALISM AND THE FOUNDATION OF SUBPRIME

Apart from the unearned windfalls that were bestowed on Wall Street punters, the preposterous $140 billion market cap of the GSEs had another untoward impact. It gave Freddie and Fannie so much walking-around money that there was literally no one they couldn't buy in Washington and throughout the byways of the housing-industrial-finance complex. The creation of the Fannie Mae foundation from the sale proceeds of a tiny fraction of its red-hot stock became a $350 million slush fund. It flat-out bought policy support from housing sector participants ranging from academic researchers to city councils and community organizers.

ACORN, the controversial poor people's housing advocacy organization, was virtually a wholly owned subsidiary of the Fannie Mae foundation. The foundation even nakedly invaded Capitol Hill, providing direct funding to the nonprofit arms (so-called) of the congressional black caucus and the congressional Hispanic caucus.

By the end of the 1990s the fatal nexus was in place. Through its foundation, Fannie Mae was actually funding a vast mobilization of housing advocates and cronies to bring lobbying pressure on exactly itself. The gambit was to claim it had been "forced" by political pressures to reduce its own underwriting standards and to virtually eliminate down payments.

SECRETARY CUOMO'S EXCELLENT
ADVENTURES ON K STREET

At the same time, the Clinton administration's home ownership strategy had been turned into a sweeping crusade, especially after it was taken over in 1997 by HUD Secretary Andrew Cuomo. A cynical political power broker, Cuomo saw home ownership as a vehicle for liberal Democrats to lock up business support throughout the housing finance complex. More than fifty separate "national partnerships" with K Street lobby organizations were thus established to promote easier credit standards and higher home ownership rates.

These so-called public-private partnerships amounted to crony capitalism on parade. There were separate partnerships with the Appraisal Institute, the Mortgage Bankers Association, the National Association of Home Builders, the National Association of Real Estate Brokers, and many more. All of these capitalist lobbies had their oars in the water and were rowing in the direction of a statist coxswain, Secretary Andrew Cuomo, in nearly perfect rhythm.

The K Street lobbies had more in mind than the civic satisfaction of getting poor people into their own homes. What they were actually seeking was more brokerage commissions, housing starts, mortgage originations, property appraisals, title insurance policies, etc. The route to a higher volume of business in the housing complex, however, always led back to the same place: reduced down payments and weakened underwriting standards.

Indeed, the Clinton administration's charter for this crusade was laid out in a HUD document aptly entitled *The National Homeownership Strategy: Partners in the American Dream*. The "dream" part of it was baldly evident in the hundred distinct policy actions which this document embraced. Among these were such gems as "Subsidies to Reduce Downpayment and Mortgage Costs."

It goes without saying that a "subsidy" to reduce a "downpayment" is an oxymoron: it defeats the very purpose of home owner "skin in the game." In fact, all of these policy actions amounted to financial dreaming because they ran smack-dab counter to the powerful underlying macroeconomic current previously identified; namely, the harsh wage deflation flowing from the "China price."

Its corrosive impact on middle- and lower-class incomes and contribution to rising job insecurity undermined the ability of these households to shoulder the financial cost of home ownership. More broadly, these wrong-headed measures provide another poignant illustration of why crony capitalism wreaks havoc with both the free market and rational public policy.

The HUD ownership strategy identified housing "down payment" as some kind of arbitrary and unjust social barrier, like racial discrimination, that purportedly could be mitigated by government intervention. But that was profoundly wrong: down payments were actually a fundamental impulse of the free market arising from the fact that, under American law and custom, the traditional fixed-rate nonrecourse mortgage loan amounts to a one-way call option.

If interest rates go up, borrowers are protected and enjoy the savings; if they go down, borrowers can refinance without penalty; and if the borrower's income fails he can mail the keys back to the lender without fear of a stint in debtor's prison or its equivalent civil punishment. Owing to these features, meaningful borrower skin in the game in the form of large cash down payments is fundamentally necessary to deter abuse and generate a market return to mortgage investors.

AT THE CENTER OF THE HOME OWNERSHIP CRUSADE: CRONY CAPITALIST FOLLY

The preponderant reality of contemporary governance is money-based interest group politics. Accordingly, if a class of citizens merits income transfers from the state under some imaginable public policy standard, the worst possible answer is to shower a random subset of that class with in-kind subsidies through the private market.

These in-kind subsidies almost always get captured by vendors and providers; they become the sustenance for yet another syndicate of crony capitalist rent-seekers. The better answer is to impose a means test and mail cash to eligible citizens. In the case at hand, such cash transfers would allow beneficiaries to choose between applying the cash to rent, a mortgage, or something else.

When viewed in this framework, it is evident that pursuit of social uplift through home finance subsidies was a huge policy error. Indeed, the crude quantitative goal of the Clinton administration's crony capitalist coalition—raising the home ownership rate to 67.5 percent by the year 2000—was especially pernicious. The graph of long-term home ownership trends proves why and with startling clarity.

From the first quarter of 1987 through early 1995, the graph line was flat at 64 percent, oscillating tightly around that level, and for good reason: the real incomes of the lower half of US households declined by about 15 percent during this period. Owing to this weakened capacity to service a home mortgage, including the contribution of an economically meaningful down payment, an increase in the home ownership rate was simply not warranted.

Furthermore, 1994 was the fulcrum year when China radically devalued its currency and triggered the rise of a mercantilist export machine that was bound to further erode American working-class incomes. In a word, if the free market had its way, the curve on the home ownership graph after early 1995 would have headed down, perhaps eventually into the 50–60 percent range as nationwide capacity for home ownership fell steadily.

Instead, public policy drove the curve sharply upward. When shortly after the turn of the century the home ownership rate broke above 69 percent, the implied variance between that policy-induced outcome and a plausible free market "contrafactual" case was huge. Perhaps 10–20 million households were artificially induced to take on a home mortgage, or to refinance one they already had in order to extract MEW.

THE $6 TRILLION GSE BALANCE SHEET EXPLOSION

Not surprisingly, Washington's crusade to artificially raise the home ownership rate via relaxation of mortgage standards soon gathered formidable momentum. Consequently, the balance sheet footings of the GSEs exploded in a manner never before seen in the accounts of an American state agency. When the national home ownership strategy was launched in 1994, the GSE's total balance sheet exposure was $1.7 trillion. During the remaining six years of the Clinton term these obligations grew by 70 percent, to $2.9 trillion.

By then, the crony capitalist coalition was so deeply entrenched in both parties that the feeble efforts of the George W. Bush White House staff to slow down the freight train were utterly unavailing. By 2004, the GSE balance sheets had ballooned to $4 trillion and, when Hank Paulson finally nationalized this rogue lending machine, footings had reached nearly $6 trillion.

Needless to say, a $5 trillion gain in government-backed housing finance in 14 years was a profound deformation of finance. Owing to the money-printing policies of the Greenspan Fed and the currency-pegging mercantilism of the Asian central banks, there were virtually unlimited buyers for US government debt paper, including the GSE variant. There was nothing to stop the parabolic rise of GSE housing guarantees and investment except the self-discipline and underwriting standards of Freddie and Fannie themselves.

But, alas, all of the economic and political forces were moving in the opposite direction at dizzying speed: the Greenspan stock market bubble was transforming Freddie and Fannie executives into stock option speculators; the crony capitalist coalition endlessly hammered GSE underwriting standards lower; and Washington officials heralded every increment of its success in raising the home ownership rate from 64 to 69 percent.

At the same time, it failed to see that the GSE balance sheets had gotten freakishly large as they leapt upward by the trillions; that loan-to-value ratios were increasing rapidly; that credit scores of new borrowers were steadily falling; and that housing prices were rising so fast that fundamental credit risk was being thoroughly papered over.

By the turn of the century, it could be well and truly said that the GSE-based mortgage finance system had become a doomsday machine with no braking mechanism and no sentient pilot. In fact, however, this was just the warm-up phase. The more virulent subprime stage of the housing mania was yet to come, but the launching pad for it was a direct by-product of the GSE explosion fueled by Washington's wholly misguided home owner-ship strategy.

MORTGAGE BROKERS GONE WILD

This massive expansion of what amounted to a socialized credit pool for housing changed everything about the home finance market, but the most crucial aspect was the vast expansion of "takeout" financing available to mortgage brokers and other nonbank originators. Since, unlike depository banks, the latter were largely unregulated, the rise of mortgage broker finance was heralded as another triumph of the free market. It wasn't, not by a long shot.

As has been seen, most of this purported "capital markets funding" for home mortgages was actually coming from the Freddie and Fannie branch of the US Treasury, so there was nothing "free market" about it. The reason this cardinal reality got continuously overlooked, even by honest free market advocates, was the illusion that the GSEs ran a "secondary market" for home mortgages.

As demonstrated above, however, it actually amounted to a fee-scalping operation, a digital version of the same New Deal filing cabinets where it had started. While its PR flacks claimed it was a "deep" and reliable source of mortgage finance "liquidity" that lowered mortgage financing costs, the GSE market was liquid only because it was a sub-branch of the Treasury bond market. GSE mortgage costs were low because they were written against Uncle Sam's credit.

The rest of the GSE story was just a marketing smoke screen that took the focus off what was really happening to the structure of home finance; namely, that bricks-and-mortar banks and thrifts were being driven out of the mortgage-lending business by the very "secondary market" that was allegedly the savior of housing.

Banks and thrifts were being replaced by pure mortgage brokers; that is, by what were effectively fee-for-service mortgage origination contractors to the US government (i.e., Fannie and Freddie). And, as at the Pentagon, it was essentially a "cost-plus" business: the greater the volume of services, the larger the harvest of fees.

So here was another profound deformation of the free market. The K Street lobbies for the mortgage bankers and brokers portrayed their clients as capitalist entrepreneurs who plied their trade in the unregulated markets. But mortgage brokers really had no reason for existence, because the separation of underwriting from long-term investment in the resulting mortgages did not create any value added. As shown in chapter 20, what this artificial divorce did create, as history would soon prove, was ample opportunity to destroy value, owing to underwriting error, information disconnects, and fraud and abuse along the daisy chain of securitization.

HOW WASHINGTON DESTROYED THE
REAL HOME MORTGAGE BANKERS

Prior to August 1971, home mortgage finance had remained largely in the province of local savings and loan banks because their "originate and hold" model was a source of deep competitive advantage. The economics of home mortgage lending, after all, turn entirely on the default loss rate over the long contract period of fixed-rate mortgages, not on trimming nickels and dimes from application processing costs. Profitability in home finance was always and everywhere a function of borrower selection.

Accordingly, traditional thrifts and banks accumulated a huge intangible asset in the form of their knowledge of neighborhood economic and social trends, along with their files on borrower histories and character, and the information obtained from rigorous loan applicant assessment procedures. These intangible assets, along with direct and immediate accountability for soured loans and strong incentives to cure delinquencies, were the source of their underwriting proficiency.

The long-forgotten truth is that the traditional mortgage industry was based on the skill of seasoned "bankers." Now, owing to the triumph of the GSE securitization model, bankers were obsolete: what counted was the sales patter and typing speeds of the glorified document clerks who populated the mortgage broker offices.

As indicated above, this inferior mortgage banker and broker model triumphed because the traditional thrift-based mortgage industry was among the foremost casualties of the raging inflation and double-digit interest rates which resulted from Arthur Burns' monetary mayhem. By 1980, for example, the federally regulated S&Ls held about $425 billion of home mortgages bearing an average interest rate of 4 percent in an environment in which open market interest rates had soared to 15 percent. On a mark-to-market basis, therefore, the industry was deeply insolvent.

As indicated above, a recurrent pattern now set in where one deformation from the breakdown of sound money only begat another. In this case it was a witches' brew of accounting make-believe and deregulation served up by the Reagan White House. The heart of the problem was that the S&L industry was heavily concentrated in Republican congressional districts, thereby militating in favor of some kind of reprieve from the harsh medicine of the free market.

VOODOO ECONOMICS: THE ORIGINAL PLAN
TO EXTEND AND PRETEND

Yet the thrift industry was so deeply insolvent that it would have required a $25 billion bailout, a figure nearly as big as Reagan's entire spending cut package. As budget director, I feverishly opposed giving back one dime of those hard-won spending cuts in order to transfer cash to the insolvent thrifts. At the same time, the White House politicos led by Ed Meese waved their Adam Smith banners furiously, insisting that the thrift industry deserved Uncle Sam's help because the S&Ls had not caused the crisis, which was more or less true.

Not a problem, came the answer from the Treasury Department. The S&Ls would be enabled to raise billions in "regulatory" equity by selling net-worth certificates to the government insurance fund which, in turn, would pay for this new stock, not with cash, but with IOUs. Self-evidently, an arrangement in which bankrupt S&Ls loaned money to the federal government so that it could buy their own worthless equity would have made Charles Ponzi proud.

Treasury officials rationalized this scam as a bridge to buy time so that, as it turned out, an even more misguided cure could take hold; namely, deregulation of the S&Ls' asset powers. Their seat-of-the-pants theory was that home mortgage lending was a "bad business" and that S&Ls could survive only if they were permitted to escape from their alleged balance sheet prison, where traditionally 80 percent or more of assets consisted of home mortgages. Diversification into commercial real estate, business loans, and capital securities including junk bonds, on the other hand, was heralded as an especially good idea because these were purportedly "higher return" investments.

It is hard to find a more discombobulated confluence of confused ideas and bad policies. Home mortgage lending was actually a good business in which the S&Ls had built long-term core competence, but it had been turned into a nightmare by the inflationary monetary policies of the Fed. Now, in an effort to mitigate the damage, the S&Ls were being turned loose to enter the commercial real estate lending business—about which they knew nothing, and at the worst possible time.

As described in chapter 6, the "coalition of the bought," which had pushed through the giant 1981 tax cuts, had included full representation from the commercial real estate development industry, and they had come away from the trough with a stupendous prize; namely, the privilege of ultra-rapid (ten-year) tax depreciation on office, hotel, and other buildings which ordinarily had useful lives of thirty to fifty years. Accordingly, as soon as the economy emerged from the Volcker recession, commercial building was off to the tax-incentivized races, and the newly liberated thrifts were in the thick of the lending.

ROGUE'S ARMY OF BORN-AGAIN THRIFTS

The Reagan-era "fix" of accounting gimmicks and deregulation thus resulted in a rogue's army of born-again thrifts. They were permitted to grow like Topsy based on phony "regulatory capital," and to load their balance sheets with commercial real estate and junk bond risks they did not understand.

Furthermore, they often funded themselves by raising taxpayer-insured liabilities in the deregulated market for brokered deposits. Needless to say, this jerry-built calamity was an offense to every principle of sound banking. It is not surprising, therefore, that it hit the wall and splattered into the $150 billion S&L disaster by the end of the 1980s.

In the long run, however, the huge cost of the Washington-conducted S&L cleanup was only a small part of the price tag. During the years before these mutant thrift institutions met their final demise, they retrenched dramatically from home mortgage lending, the very area where their core competence had historically resided. Between 1980 and 1986, for example, home mortgages dropped from 80 percent of S&L assets to 55 percent, and continued to fall for the balance of the decade.

In short, the Fed's Great Inflation and the Reagan administration's misdirected treatment of banking institutions as agents of the free market, when they are inherently wards of the state, resulted in the demise of the nation's competent base of mortgage-lending institutions. In 1970, home mortgage lending had been a healthy, vibrant industry financing the rise of the American middle class. Twenty years after Camp David, the home lending business was fatally impaired, just as Washington launched its misbegotten crusade for increased home ownership.

WHEN JACK KEMP GOT ROLLED BY THE ORANGE MAN

The double whammy of a busted savings and loan industry and a booming GSE takeout channel for mortgage loans catalyzed the parabolic rise of an entirely new (and distinctly inferior) channel of home finance: the mortgage broker industry. Thus, in 1987 there were 7,000 mortgage brokers nationwide, but this figure grew to 16,000 by 1992 and then surged to 36,000 by 1998 and more than 53,000 as of 2004.

In terms of dollar volume, mortgage brokers accounted for only $110 billion of housing loans in 1987 but this figure had soared to $1 trillion by 1998. And that was just the beginning. During the epic refinancing boom in 2003, mortgage brokers originated more than $2.6 trillion of home loans, meaning that mortgage broker volume grew by a factor of twenty-six times in only a decade and a half.

Broker operations which inhabited the backwaters of home finance in 1981 thus became the monster of the Main Street midway. These fee-for-service mortgage contractors were now omnipresent in the neighborhoods of America, and had nearly eliminated old-fashioned at-risk "banking" from the home loan market. Not only did borrowers have progressively less skin in the game, but now the preponderant share of home loans was being originated by brokers who had no skin in the game at all.

Moreover, the business evolved far beyond its mom-and-pop roots, such that by the end of the 1990s the nation's largest single mortgage originator, with nearly $200 billion annually in new home loans, was a broker: Countrywide Financial. Most of its thousands of branches had no teller windows or vaults. Rather than intermediating bank deposits, it was a giant sales agency that kept new loan paper flowing to Freddie and Fannie in prodigious volume.

Befitting its Southern California homeland, Countrywide's irrepressible leader, Angelo Mozilo, had a perpetually deep tan which gave off an orange glow during his endless appearances on financial TV. His incessant message was that Countrywide could put every American family in their own home. Accordingly, he didn't cotton much to any Washington official who had the temerity to interfere with the ceaseless flow of mortgages between his boiler rooms and the GSE balance sheets.

During his stint as HUD secretary in the George H. W. Bush administration, for example, Jack Kemp had tried to revive the gospel of free markets by again proposing to curtail the GSEs. The Mozilo-dominated Mortgage Bankers Association floridly touted itself as a triumph of the free market, but when one of the true champions of free market economics actually proposed to apply those principles to the GSE financing machine, it was another matter.

Since Countrywide's entire business model depended upon its ability to rent Uncle Sam's credit card for a razor thin spread, Mozilo quickly leapt to the offensive. Jack Kemp was "the worst person who could possibly have been put in that position," fumed the kingpin of boiler-room home loans.

Kemp's jousting on behalf of free market capitalism proved to be futile, and disappeared without a trace into the curb drains of K Street, but two lessons from his failed challenge did endure. Most importantly, Countrywide Financial and its ilk were now the true face of home finance; for all practical purposes "at risk" bankers were obsolete.

Secondly, once the Clinton home ownership strategy worked up a full head of steam, the idea that housing finance was too important to be left to the free market became inviolable. Now the only capitalism that counted was the crony kind, and at the heart of it stood the profoundly uneconomic business of home mortgage securitization.

THE PHONY ECONOMICS OF MORTGAGE SECURITIZATION

As has been shown, the Freddie and Fannie variety of mortgage securitization did not create societal value; it just extracted rents from the public credit. These windfalls, in turn, were largely captured by GSE executives and stock market speculators, including some large mutual fund managers.

Bill Miller of Legg Mason, for example, even got himself nominated for the "next Warren Buffet" prize by loading up his mutual fund with Freddie and Fannie stock early, and then riding it all the way to the top (and eventually over the cliff). In this manner, the GSE scalpings from the nation's 150 million taxpayers were capitalized and transferred to a few ten thousands of investors in Miller's mutual fund and to those of his many momentum-stock imitators.

The Wall Street–based private-label mortgage securitization business was also uneconomic. However, unlike GSEs, which were AAA-rated wards of the US Treasury and could therefore raise virtually unlimited amounts of funding with hardly a modicum of scrutiny by investors, the private-label underwriters faced a more significant challenge finding investors.

Large institutional fixed-income investors such as corporate pension funds and life insurance companies were always looking for enhanced yield, but in those early days the Fed had not yet repressed interest rates low enough to kindle much interest in the intricacies and novelties of private-label mortgage-backed securities (MBSs). Indeed, since Wall Street could not compete with the GSEs for prime-quality mortgages, underwriters had to sell investors on a dual proposition.

First, the highest-rated tranches of private-label MBSs achieved AAA ratings as a result of structured finance, meaning that investors had to get comfortable with a whole new breed of bond indentures which sliced and diced the mortgage pool cash flows in favor of the more senior tranches. Second, investors could not help noting that the underlying mortgage pools, however they might be wacked up, consisted of high-risk loans with above-average default profiles from lower-end markets ranging from the exurbs of Orange County to inner-city Cleveland.

Accordingly, only $11 billion of private-label subprime MBSs was issued by Wall Street in 1994, a mere 1.4 percent of the mortgage market during the year the Clinton home ownership crusade was launched. Two years later, private MBS issuance rose to $35 billion and by 1998, volume hit $85 billion. Yet that was still less than 6 percent of national mortgage originations, reflecting the fact that Wall Street had not yet thrown its balance sheet into the breach.

The fact that Wall Street was still largely on the sidelines as of the late 1990s was the crucial restraining factor in delaying the arrival of the subprime plague. Most certainly, the mortgage broker industry was ready. By the mid-1990s, it was swarming with hucksters who would write loans to any applicant with a heartbeat.

What was lacking, however, was sufficient warehouse credit lines and a deep private-label MBS market to package and distribute junk mortgages. For this reason, Countrywide hadn't even bothered with subprime before 1997; its GSE business was booming and the private-label MBS market was not yet robust enough to move the needle on its massive scale of operations.

AMERIQUEST: ROLAND ARNALL'S PREDATORY SALES MACHINE

Nevertheless, the subprime industry was a financial cancer waiting to metastasize. The GSEs had now spawned a massive mortgage banker and broker industry. What was needed was for Greenspan to light the match, enabling Wall Street to get into the business of providing warehousing financing and a securitization takeout market for junk mortgages.

In this environment, a crony capitalist operator named Roland Arnall had already spawned a far-flung web of operations. It included a holding company he controlled called Ameriquest Capital Corporation (ACC) and also a plethora of imitators such as New Century and Option One, which were run by former subordinates who had ventured out on their own. Together, these operations perfected the high-pressure selling machinery and the range of high-risk mortgage products which exploded onto the scene after the Fed's panicked rate cutting in 2001–2003.

Ameriquest Mortgage eventually grew to more than three hundred boiler rooms scattered around the nation and generated $80 billion annually in subprime mortgages. It was an ultra-high-pressure sales machine that was happy to hire ex–car salesmen when possible, but also enlisted ex–car wash employees if necessary. The point of Ameriquest's recruiting policy was maximum possible ignorance about mortgage lending, so that brokers would be focused solely on moving product at daily quota rates which were equivalent to those of factory production lines.

To keep the boiler rooms humming, Ameriquest invented many of the classic subprime products, including the stated income or "liar's loan" and the 2/28 mortgage. The latter had a low teaser rate for two years and then converted to a much higher adjustable-rate mortgage for the next twenty-eight years, a trap that often caused hapless borrowers to "refinance" and end up in the same place two years later.

What made these boiler-room operations so successful is also precisely what should have made the Arnall-style subprime mortgages extremely unappetizing to investors; namely, huge upfront points and fees. Indeed, the financial results for Arnall's holding company over the period 2002–2004 are prima facie evidence that nothing about the nation's leading subprime mortgage broker was on the level.

During this three-year period, Ameriquest originated about $150 billion of subprime loans which it temporarily funded on warehouse lines and then sold en bloc to Wall Street underwriters. From this flow of new mortgages, which revolved through its warehouse borrowing line approximately every twenty days, it scalped almost $7.5 billion of revenue.

This was a stunning haul for a pure brokerage operation and implied that the yield from fees and upfront points amounted to 5 percent of loan originations. Accordingly, Ameriquest's boiler rooms were raking in margins at about six times the normal rate for prime-quality GSE loans.

Not surprisingly, Arnall's holding company extracted $2.7 billion of profits over the period from these generous revenue flows, meaning that its return on the pittance of capital it had invested in Ameriquest was so high as to be immeasurable. But the more damning aspect had to do with what was left from its revenue take after profits had been carted away.

Ameriquest's financial results implied that it had incurred $5 billion of expenses in generating these loans. Yet it had no permanent capital to service and operated from low-cost rented offices with virtually no overheads except data processing. Even after allowing for several billions to pay interest on warehouse credit lines and provide wholesale discounts to Wall Street underwriters, the surplus available for salesman compensation was extraordinary. Literally billions of dollars were paid in commissions, bonuses, and perks to a few thousand salesmen who carried the title of "loan officer."

Needless to say, the incentive for predatory selling and outright fraud was overwhelming, a proposition well amplified by the legends which swirled around the company's run-amok sales culture. As one former manager later wrote: "My managers and handlers taught me the ins and outs of mortgage fraud, drugs, sex, and money, money and more money . . . At any given moment inside the restrooms, cocaine and meth were being snorted by . . . more than a third of the staff, and more than half of the staff was manipulating documents to get loans to fund, and more than 75 percent just made completely false statements . . . a typical welcome aboard gift [to new employees] was a pair of scissors, tape and whiteout."

CHURN AND BURN, SUBPRIME STYLE

Meanwhile, the signs were blindingly evident that Ameriquest and its subprime brethren were not on the level financially. The most egregious of these was towering levels of profitability that defied economic common sense. Arnall thus showed up on the *Forbes* list in 2004 as being worth $2 billion, a figure which grew to $3 billion shortly after he completed his public service stint as co-chair of the January 2005 Bush inauguration.

Given the thin margins normally available for simply brokering loans, it was impossible that Ameriquest was worth even a fraction of the *Forbes* figure. Any diligent buyer of product from Ameriquest's mortgage origination machine, therefore, might have smelled a rat.

In fact, the huge revenue margins, massive compensation pools, and outsized profits obtained by Ameriquest were not possible on the free market. No rational investor would have paid anything close to par for mortgages that were so recklessly underwritten, serially refinanced, ill documented, and dependent upon such onerous reset mechanisms as the Ameriquest mortgages.

Stated differently, based on Ameriquest's observable modus operandi, diligent investors would have demanded a deep discount on these hair-ridden loans. Yet had Ameriquest been forced to sell its loans at even 95 percent of par to compensate investors for the virtually unknowable risk inherent in its business model, its revenues would have been wiped out entirely, thereby vaporizing its fabulous profits and lunatic compensation pools.

At the end of the day, Ameriquest and its subprime imitators operated an incredibly destructive feedback loop. Based on stupidly high Wall Street prices for their junk mortgages, they paid salesmen wholly uneconomic levels of compensation, which fueled their predatory sales machines; the huge volumes flowing through this machinery, in turn, generated even larger compensation pools which catalyzed even greater volumes of junk mortgages.

So the whole subprime industry depended upon an egregiously overpriced market for junk mortgages, and there is no secret as to why it existed, especially after 2001. Wall Street created it and grew it to stupendous size. As detailed in chapter 20, the $100 billion market in high-risk mortgages that had built up by the year 2000 suddenly morphed into a trillion-dollar monster within just six years.

THE FED'S PERFECT STORM: HOW 1 PERCENT INTEREST RATES FUELED THE BONFIRES OF SUBPRIME

The truly insidious aspect of the subprime assault on America's neighborhoods was not that operators like Roland Arnall and a handful of imitators got preposterously rich running a few thousand boiler rooms populated with predatory salesmen. America is riddled with dial-for-dollars operations, some of them just as seedy.

The difference is that Arnall wasn't selling aluminum siding or cosmetics, but $500,000 mortgages that could never have been funded in the absence of the Fed's prosperity management model. As has been seen, the latter was based on the primitive notion that any amount of money printing was permissible, so long as it did not put undue upward pressure on commodity and product prices.

Yet that was no constraint at all. In a world of massive US current account deficits and the "China price," the American economy was, in effect, importing gale-force wage and product deflation. And it would continue to do so until China's rice paddies were drained of excess labor and the People's Printing Press stopped pegging its exchange rate.

So the Fed's panicked money-printing campaign after December 2000 was a pact with the devil in economic terms: it permitted the US economy to live high on the hog in the short run, while it offshored the nation's traceable goods industries and buried its balance sheet in external debt in the longer run. One of these obligations, ironically, was mortgage debt in the form of GSE paper.

Foreign central banks led by the People's Printing Press of China owned less than $100 billion of GSE paper before the Fed ignited the mortgage boom in 2001. Through continuous absorption of excess dollars remitted by their exporters, however, they had accumulated upward of $1 trillion of Freddie and Fannie paper by July 2008. Sequestering unwanted dollar claims, the mercantilist central banks of Asia thereby ensured there would be no flare-up of CPI inflation and no sell-off in the bond market.

With the bond vigilantes incarcerated in a red vault in Beijing, as it were, 1 percent money market rates revived Wall Street's speculative juices and ignited the carry trade like never before. Indeed, it is difficult to imagine a better setup to induce Wall Street to feed the marauding bands of subprime mortgage bankers with warehouse credit, and to carry hundreds of billions of junk mortgage inventory until it could be sliced and diced into private-label MBSs.

As the great housing carry trade gathered momentum on Wall Street in 2002–2003, however, the folly of the Fed's bubble finance was palpable. In a credit-saturated economy, the price that matters above all else is the price of credit; that is, the interest rate on short-term borrowings and the yield curve across the spectrum of longer-dated debt securities.

Yet the Fed's prosperity management model completely ignored the need for honest and accurate pricing of liquid credits and debt capital. In fact, by completely disabling free market interest rates, it fueled both the final binge of household mortgage borrowing and also fostered Wall Street's capacity to fund and securitize the junk mortgage loans being generated by the brokers' boiler rooms.

At the end of the day, the great housing fiasco did not represent a failure of the free market. It happened because the free market had been supplanted by two great financial deformations of the state: the GSEs which gave birth to the predatory mortgage boiler rooms and the central bank which favored them with a rogue funding machine parked at each and every notable Wall Street address.

CHAPTER 20

HOW THE FED BROUGHT THE GAMBLING MANIA TO AMERICA'S NEIGHBORHOODS

T HE EFFECT OF THE FED'S 2001 MONEY-PRINTING PANIC WAS THAT "cap rates" on long-lived assets like real estate were driven sharply lower, thereby causing prices to soar. Soon the increased collateral value of properties, both homes and shopping malls, begat even more lending and even higher prices.

Furthermore, Main Street was now populated by a small army of former dot-com speculators who were bitterly disappointed, but also eagerly looking for the next asset class that could generate instant riches. Accordingly, they quickly caught on to the homeowners' leveraged buyout (LBO) gambit: repeatedly refinancing and flipping properties as valuations rocketed.

The figures for mortgages crystallize the massive debt loop which emerged in the domestic real estate markets. In the case of the residential sector, home mortgages outstanding rose by $750 billion, or 13.2 percent, in 2002. This was a robust figure under any circumstances, but extraordinary in light of the fact that the US economy was just emerging from its post-dot-com slump.

During the course of 2002, there had been zero net job creation and wage and salary incomes had grown by less than 1 percent. From day one of the home mortgage boom, therefore, the driving force was rising housing asset prices, not burgeoning household incomes and capacity to borrow.

As the housing bubble inflated, the level of outstanding home mortgages just kept growing at faster and faster rates. During 2003 mortgage debt outstanding increased by 15 percent and then grew by another 15 percent in 2004. The latter gain represented an annual increase of $1 trillion and was no aberration: annual home mortgage debt growth remained in the trillion-dollar-per-annum league until the housing bubble finally started cooling off in the second half of 2007.

By any historic standard, these were outlandish gains. Annual home mortgage growth, for example, had averaged only $170 billion per year during the five years after the 1990 recession and had peaked at just $425 billion in 1999.

Yet the parabolic climb of home mortgage debt outstanding, which rose from just over $5 trillion to $11 trillion between 2000 and 2007, is actually the subdued part of the home mortgage story; it does not begin to capture the explosive churning which was going on underneath in the form of a refinancing boom.

THE EPIC CHURN OF HOME FINANCE: HOW $20 TRILLION OF MORTGAGES FUELED THE HOUSING PRICE BUBBLE

The refinancing boom meant that massive amounts of existing mortgages were being replaced by new ones. As a result, the figure for "gross originations" was many times larger than the net gain in mortgage debt outstanding cited above. In fact, it was literally off the charts by the standard of any prior experience.

During 2002, gross home mortgage originations totaled $3.1 trillion, or 4.1X actual new home purchases. The Fed's interest rate repression policy and the rapid spread of floating rate and teaser mortgages which were priced off short-term money rates thus conferred on homeowners a massive windfall of mortgage savings.

As the Fed manically pursued what amounted to an interest rate destruction campaign and brought short-term interest rates down to 1 percent in June 2003, the mortgage financing system literally came off the rails. Gross home mortgage originations for the full year totaled $4.4 trillion. This meant that in a single year, the red-hot machinery of home finance generated gross proceeds amounting to nearly 40 percent of GDP. By contrast, prior to 2001 gross home mortgage financing had never exceeded 17 percent of GDP and normally averaged about 12 percent.

During the second quarter of 2003, mortgage financings literally shot the moon: gross origins clocked in at a stupendous $5.4 trillion annualized rate. Yet during the same period, the Fed poured kerosene on the fire, cutting interest rates yet again. The minutes of the June meeting at which it ratcheted the federal funds rate to the near free money level of 1 percent made no mention whatsoever of the raging mortgage boom. Instead, the Fed's statement justified the rate cut as necessary to "provide additional insurance that a stronger economy would in fact materialize."

Nor did the frenzy abate after 2003. Gross originations remained above

$3 trillion annually and totaled nearly $20 trillion over the housing boom period of 2002–2007.

The cascade of negative repercussions on the Main Street economy from this deluge of cheap mortgage money started with the unprecedented and manic surge of housing prices, as detailed in chapter 19. These kinds of gigantic price increases in short time intervals can occur for nonmonetary reasons in commodity markets owing to big supply disruptions; for example, a drought in the corn belt or a major copper mine strike. But in a decentralized asset market with low turnover and high transaction costs like residential housing, such huge, sudden price gains were possible only due to the aberrationally cheap mortgage financing enabled by the Fed. The housing price spiral most certainly did not reflect the opposite; namely, organic demand owing to meaningful gains in the earned income of the American households. In fact, while housing prices were soaring by 50 percent during 2000–2003, wage and salary incomes rose by only 6 percent in nominal terms during that three-year period, and actually declined after adjusting for inflation.

Needless to say, this initial price spiral accelerated when house flipping became a national pastime, accounting for up to 35 percent of activity in many overheated markets. Flippers were willing to pay higher and higher prices, believing that they could quickly capture the gains and then reload for another go-round. Whether intended or not, the Fed's money-printing spree effectively transplanted the gambling mania from dot-coms to residential housing.

THE MEW MADNESS: LINCHPIN OF
THE FED'S PHONY PROSPERITY

Not everyone wanted to sell the family castle, of course, so refinancing became the alternative of choice. In an environment of rapidly escalating prices, this gave rise to the infamous MEW trade; that is, mortgage equity withdrawal from owner-occupied properties. MEW represented the excess proceeds from a new mortgage at current housing prices after paying off an older mortgage which had been financed at lower property values and, frequently, at a much lower loan-to-value ratio.

The amount of cash that could be extracted from ordinary homes in this manner amounted to a stupendous windfall. Nothing like it had ever before been seen on Main Street.

For instance, when a $100,000 home which carried a partially paid-down mortgage of $60,000 was refinanced at a doubled appraisal of $200,000 and a 92 percent loan-to-value ratio, the cash takeout after closing costs would have been $120,000. Accordingly, during the peak of the

MEW boom in 2003–2007, thousands of Main Street households walked away from mortgage settlement conferences every day with $50,000, $100,000, and even $200,000 of found money.

MEW thus generated a powerful sense of instant riches along the length and breadth of Main Street because it brought unexpected and undreamed of dollops of hard cash, not just the paper gains of the dot-com stocks. Needless to say, it also resulted in massive increases in contractually fixed household debts, propped up for the moment by wildly inflated asset prices which were bound eventually to come back to earth.

MEW was one of the worst economic poisons ever fostered by a central bank, but the Greenspan Fed actually embraced it as an important tool of prosperity management. The minutes of the same June 2003 meeting in which the FOMC voted to goose the economy with a 1 percent federal funds rate also claimed a double-barreled wealth effect.

In the first instance, improved economic growth would result from "the effects of rising stock market wealth on consumer balance sheets." Not done with the wealth effect elixir, the Fed minutes also anticipated an economic lift from "continued opportunities for many consumers to extract equity from the appreciated value of their homes."

Widespread home equity extraction through borrowing would have horrified sound money men only a few decades earlier. But the Fed's debt-pusher-in-chief urged that there was no cause for alarm about the massive raid on home ATMs being triggered by rising housing prices and easy mortgage credit. Indeed, by issuing a "do not be troubled" advisory, the future Fed chairman proved he didn't know the difference between honest GDP growth earned by labor and productivity and a "higher print" reflecting speculative borrowing.

"Higher home prices have encouraged households to increase their consumption," Bernanke noted in March 2005, and that was "a good thing." Bernanke further allowed that living high on the hog was well justified because it reflected "the expansion of US housing wealth, much of it easily accessible to households through cash-out refinancing and home-equity lines of credit."

What the monetary central planners didn't explain, however, was why there should be so much "appreciated value" to be harvested from owner-occupied residences in the first place. That fact is, there is no reason for residential real estate to appreciate under conditions of sound money where inflation is minimal. In fact, the pioneering work of Professor Robert Shiller of Yale showed that there had been no increase in the inflation-adjusted value of the typical American home for the entire century ending in the early 1980s.

The reason is straightforward economics. There is no scarcity of land in the United States, so there is no reason for real prices to rise over time. Indeed, public policy tends to heavily subsidize housing development on the urban periphery, thereby enhancing the free market's built-in price flattener: namely, the process by which land prices in urban centers are capped as residential construction invariably moves to cheaper land on the urban periphery.

Soaring housing prices were thus a monetary phenomenon owing to an artificial bid from the explosion of cheap mortgage money. Indeed, during the peak of the Greenspan mortgage party, the true economic interest rate on subprime and Alt-A mortgages—which were the marginal sources of housing demand—was often negative after adjusting for probable default losses and inflation.

THE $5 TRILLION TIDAL WAVE OF MEW

It is not surprising, therefore, that low and even negative effective mortgage rates, coupled with the long-standing tax subsidy for mortgage interest payments, unleashed a tidal wave of MEW. When this wave crested during the second quarter of 2005, households were extracting equity from their homes through mortgage financings at a $1 trillion annualized rate. This amounted to an astounding 10 percent of disposable personal income and represents a telltale measure of the financial deformation that had emerged from the Fed-sponsored mortgage bonanza.

In all, the cumulative MEW over 2001 thorough 2007 was nearly $5 trillion. The government statistical mills duly reported the fruits of this giant deformation as evidence of rising prosperity. Thus, the spend-out of MEW materialized throughout the nooks and crannies of the American economy as personal consumption expenditures for wide-screen TVs, vacations, restaurants, maids, and landscaping services, among countless others.

But MEW was also heavily channeled into home improvement and remodeling expenditures, which gets recorded as (housing) investment spending. According to the Fed's own data, MEW-based spending on granite countertops, new bathrooms, outdoor decks, and the like amounted to 100 percent of reported "residential improvements" in the GDP accounts during much of the housing boom period.

Not coincidentally, the powerhouse home improvement retailers which arose to meet this fulsome demand—Home Depot and Lowe's—had spectacular gains in financial results. Between 2000 and 2007 their combined sales doubled from about $65 billion to $130 billion, thereby providing a perfect tracker beam on the borrowed prosperity emanating from the Fed's financial repression.

A half decade later, by contrast, the combined sales of Lowe's and Home Depot are nearly 8 percent below the 2007 peak. What the striking shrinkage of powerful free market enterprises like these two firms dramatizes is not the loss of business acumen or market share, but the evaporation of artificial demand from both contractors and do-it-yourself customers who depended upon MEW.

At the end of the day, the post-2001 recovery generated by the Fed's prosperity management stratagem was a hothouse concoction fueled by waves of credit expansion over its six-year run. The foundation was $20 trillion of gross mortgage financings and $5 trillion of MEW.

The credit money spending which resulted from these borrowings produced one-time sales which flattered the reported GDP, but did not generate permanent economic growth or higher sustainable wealth. In fact, what it actually generated was a permanent overhang of vastly expanded household mortgage debt that would subtract from economic growth in the more distant future.

WHEN THE FED'S "INVISIBLE" HOUSING BUBBLE CRASHED: FINANCIAL CLIFF DIVING

The residential investment component of the GDP accounts illustrates in spades the manner in which reported economic growth funded by the mortgage boom amounted to little more than stealing from the future. During the prosperity of the 1990s, housing had gotten its fair share, but it had not experienced an outright boom.

New housing construction starts drifted up from about 1 million units annually after the 1990 recession to about 1.5 million by the end of the decade. Likewise, the residential investment component of GDP rose at a circumspect 4–5 percent annual gain after inflation.

Once the Fed got interest rates down to 1 percent and kept them there for an extended period, however, the fur began to fly. Residential housing investment grew by 7 percent in 2001 and then by 10 percent the next year, followed by 17 percent in 2003 and then another 15 percent each year in 2004 and 2005.

Altogether, the annual rate of residential housing investment, which includes both new construction and renovation, surged from $450 billion at the end of 2000 to $810 billion by the fourth quarter of 2005. Reported housing starts attained liftoff as well, rising from a 1.5 million annual rate to a peak rate of 2.3 million annualized units in January 2006.

The significance of these figures lies not merely in the steepness and speed of their climb, but in the proof implicit in their subsequent total collapse that the reported prosperity during 2002–2007 was largely an artifact of Greenspan's bubble finance. The sad facts of the housing crash are well known, of course, but it is the sheer vertical drop which is the smoking gun.

From the January 2006 peak, new housing starts dropped by 80 percent before hitting bottom forty months later in May 2009. Even more pointedly, when total residential investment rolled over at its $800 billion top in late 2005, it seemingly never stopped plunging—until it finally found a bottom at $330 billion annualized rate at the end of 2010.

Activity rates which deflate by magnitudes of 60–80 percent in a major sector of the national economy do not represent free market capitalism succumbing to a bout of cyclical instability. Instead, this kind of economic violence—100 percent up and 70 percent down—attests to the visible hand of the central bank attempting to administer prosperity through the blunt instrument of interest rate pegging and the avaricious machinery of the Wall Street dealer markets.

In this respect, it is not coincidental that at the very moment the Fed-induced housing mayhem reached its 2004–2005 apex and was on the cusp of a violent plunge, Bernanke was issuing his paean to the Great Moderation. The arrogant foolishness of it needs no elaboration.

In truth, the central planners in the Eccles Building never troubled themselves with the actual health or the real wealth of the Main Street economy. They were strictly paint-by-the-numbers monetary plumbers. Their focus was not on the sustainability of fundamental trends, but simply on keeping the GDP game going one quarter at a time, and on enabling Wall Street to keep pumping up the price of equities and other risk assets based on the flavor of the month.

A central bank focused on the fundamentals would not have been celebrating the strength of the housing sector. Instead, it would have been deeply alarmed by a mortgage financing bubble which was visibly out of control, and the fact that household income growth was not remotely sufficient to support the boom-time rate of housing expenditures.

Between 2000 and 2005, for example, nominal wages and salaries grew at only a 3.3 percent average rate, meaning that purchasing power gains were tepid, even before adjusting for inflation. By contrast, during the same five-year period, new housing starts rose at a 7.5 percent annual rate, home improvement spending was up at a 10 percent rate, and total residential investment spending soared at a 12.5 percent annual rate.

The huge gap between modest household income gains and the soaring growth metrics of the housing sector was obviously bridged by the explosion in mortgage lending and MEW extraction. These trends were not remotely sustainable, yet in embracing the housing boom and promising to keep interest rates low and the Greenspan Put reliably in place, the Fed gave the all-clear signal to new speculative deformations.

MORE TREES WHICH GREW TO THE SKY: THE PREPOSTEROUS RISE AND COLLAPSE OF THE HOME BUILDERS

This time the home builders became the flavor-of-the-month in yet another Wall Street chase for easy riches. The publicly traded home builder stocks soon became red hot, particularly the six big nationwide companies which produced standard-plan suburban homes in new tracts called "communities." As the stocks of these companies rocketed skyward between 2000 and 2005, they became a popular landing pad for speculators jumping out of the still-burning windows of the dot-com edifice.

The stock of the largest of these, D.R. Horton, soared from $4 to $40 per share during this period while the shares of its rival, Hovnanian Enterprises, climbed a vertical wall from $3 to $70 per share. The stock prices of the other four—Pulte Homes, Lennar, Toll Brothers, and KBH Homes—followed almost the identical trajectory, rising tenfold during the five-year period. Not surprisingly, the combined market cap of the six national home builders experienced an impressive advance, rising from a mere $6.5 billion in 2000 to $65 billion by their 2005 peak.

These high-flying home builders powerfully illuminate of the "wealth effect" folly perpetrated by the Greenspan Fed. A stock market that was still in the business of discounting the earnings capacity and prospects of individual companies, rather than trading the monetary dispensations of the central bank would never have carried these six economically hollow home builders to the stratospheric levels they obtained during 2004 and 2005.

The massive overvaluation of these home builders was especially grotesque because in truth they were essentially "made for financial TV" storefronts. They generated almost no value added and reported temporarily munificent profits, which mainly represented winnings from gambling on vacant land.

Indeed, the payrolls of these purported home builders included virtually no carpenters, plumbers, or electricians. Likewise, they did not own any power saws, cement mixers, or tape measures. Nor did they have any long-term supply arrangements with lumber vendors, paint companies, or roofing manufacturers.

What they did have was a modest contingent of accountants, salesmen and land buyers—and also a CEO telegenic enough to appear regularly on CNBC to tout the sector. As the housing bubble unfolded, viewers could hear a nonstop parade of the executives explaining the latest uptick in orders, deliveries, new communities, and customer traffic.

Yet the one thing they didn't explain was crucial; namely, that none of these red-hot home builders made any money at all building homes! Instead, they were land speculators who assembled, developed, and marketed subdivisions, but contracted out everything having to do with the building and selling of homes.

Consequently, the Greenspan Fed was the patron saint of the national home builders. Driving interest rates to the sub-basement, it escalated the value of home builder "land banks" to the rooftops. Then, as housing prices spiraled upward, the home builders hired contractors to turn their inventory of low-cost land into high-priced new homes, booking profits the moment that a local real estate broker delivered a signed purchase contract.

Needless to say, the stock market was capitalizing one-time windfall profits from overvalued land holdings, not a sustainable stream of earnings from building homes. Still, the home-builder stock bubble wasn't just a ramp job in the trading pits. In fact, the absurd overvaluation of the home builders was merely the next link in the vast chain of deformations and malinvestments which flowed from the Fed's money-printing spree after December 2000.

In this instance, deflation of the home-builder bubble came fast and furious. Even the $3 trillion flow of annual mortgage financing could not drive housing prices higher indefinitely, so by the second half of 2005 housing prices and new home sales began to stall out. A year later, new home sales were down 30 percent, and had fallen 50 percent by October 2007. At the same time, unsold builder inventories were piling up rapidly, from three to four months' supply during the boom phase, to six months of supply by October 2005, and eleven months' supply by the final quarter of 2007.

It was still a year before the September 2008 financial crisis, but already the highest flyer among the home builders, Hovnanian Enterprises, had been stripped of a zero. Its stock price by mid-2007 was $7 per share, not $70.

Within a few months all of the home-builder stock prices were back to the December 2000 starting gate. Their combined market cap stood, once again, at $6 billion rather than $65 billion. Charlie Brown and Lucy had had another go.

THE SUBPRIME BLOW-OFF TOP:
HOW THE FED UNLEASHED THE PREDATORS

It goes without saying that the fiasco in housing and the smoldering collapse of the home builders signaled immense harm to the Main Street economy, most notably in the sudden disappearance after the housing peak of more than 3 million bubble-era jobs attached to home construction and its infrastructure of suppliers and vendors. Yet the Fed continued to assure Wall Street that prosperity was on track and that under no circumstances would it yank the punch bowl while the party still roared.

Instead, beginning in June 2004 it began raising the absurdly low 1 percent Federal funds rate in baby steps—25 basis points at a time, month after month, for the next two years. Dithering with the Wall Street gambling halls in this manner, however, merely enabled them to push bubble finance into new crevices of the national economy.

As detailed in chapter 19, the most consequential of these hot spots was the final flourishing of the subprime and other high-risk mortgages. Even a cursory analysis demonstrates the Fed's direct culpability for the fiasco which eventually materialized and that its plodding pace of short-term rate increases resulted in the worst of both worlds.

On the one hand, firming monetary conditions did steadily curtail the growth of adjustable rate mortgages, or ARMS, which had been the driving force of the refinancing boom. Thus, when the one-year ARM rate rose from 3.5 percent in April 2004 to 5.5 percent two years later, the issuance of ARMs to creditworthy (prime) households fell sharply, falling from a peak rate of $2.5 trillion to only $1 trillion by 2006.

At the same time, the Fed's continuous assurance that rates would rise at only a snail's pace gave the Wall Street mortgage warehousing and securitization machine sufficient time and cheap funding to dramatically crank up subprime lending volumes. In this manner, the hole left by prime-quality ARMS and other conforming mortgages (which could be sold to Fannie Mae) was backfilled with a huge rise in high-risk mortgage issuance funded on Wall Street.

The Fed's temporizing was exactly the wrong prescription. What was needed now was a Volcker-style policy pivot that would have shut down the nation's vastly oversized mortgage lending machinery before it could wreak any more damage. Instead, the Fed effectively turned the dogs of Wall Street loose on the lower middle class.

The reason for this destructive venture was obvious: by that point the ranks of willing, credit-worthy borrowers were getting increasingly thin. A dramatic sign of that was the soaring inventory of existing homes for sale, which rose from a normal level of 2 million units in January 2005 to 4 million just twenty-four months later. The ranks of available purchase mortgage buyers had materially dwindled, perhaps because after housing prices flattened out the prospects for instant gains were no longer so compelling to flippers.

At the end of the day, however, it was the final surge of the home owner-ship rate which provided the telltale sign that the mortgage lending ma-chine was morphing into a financial predator. By June 2003, the home ownership rate had already reached an all-time high at 68.2 percent. As previously shown, it had been climbing steadily for nearly a decade from an apparent equilibrium level of 64–65 percent that had prevailed from 1980 through 1994.

Had the Fed not chosen to designate itself as Wall Street's juicing vendor of first resort, it surely would have recognized that the bottom distribution of American households was becoming decidedly less capable of home ownership. Household income in the lower brackets was then falling rap-idly in real terms, owing to the withering pressure that had been visited upon American wage scales by the export factories of East Asia. Yet the home ownership rate was pushed still higher in the final flurry of "no doc" and "neg am" subprime lending, and hovered above 69 percent during most of 2004 through early 2007.

In the egregiously cynical nomenclature of the subprime world, the first of these newly invented mortgage finance terms meant a borrower could lie about his income, and the second meant that it didn't matter anyway. If a household came up short on cash, it could elect to add some, or possibly even all, of its monthly payment to the outstanding balance of its mortgage.

Not surprisingly, the boiler-room mortgage brokers had no trouble dis-pensing massive dollops of cash from Wall Street's warehouse lines to fi-nance borrowers who didn't have the ability or need to pay their monthly mortgage. So doing, they touched off an economic flash flood. The result-ing sudden surge and then abrupt end of subprime mortgage originations is among the greatest financial deformations ever fostered by the prosper-ity managers in the Eccles Building.

HOW WALL STREET BROUGHT SUBPRIME OUT OF THE PAWNSHOPS

While the subprime business fully emerged from its historic pawnshop-style venue during the 1990s, it had remained a modest segment of the mortgage market, accounting for only 9 percent of total home mortgage originations during the eight years ending in 2002. By 2004, however, sub-prime originations had spiked from about $125 billion per year to $530 bil-lion and thereafter climbed above $600 billion each year during 2005–2006. At that point, subprime loans accounted for nearly 25 percent of total mortgage lending.

Moreover, these totals do not include the only slightly less dodgy "Alt-A" segment which sported somewhat higher credit scores, but consisted overwhelmingly of "no doc" and "neg am" mortgages. These "liar loans" grew like Topsy, rising from $60 billion in 2001 to $400 billion by 2006.

But that's not all. During this same interval, the "second lien" mortgage business of the big money center banks like JPMorgan and Bank of America also went into high gear. Second mortgages are inherently lower quality because they get the scraps in a foreclosure, and only after the primary mortgage is paid off in full. Still, in the sizzling mortgage markets of 2001–2006, originations of second mortgages and home equity lines of credit grew from $130 billion annually to $430 billion per year.

Needless to say, this explosion of second liens put millions more Main Street households in harm's way because the financings frequently brought total loan-to-value ratios (including the first mortgage) close to 100 percent. These borrowers simply had no margin for error in terms of either an unexpected housing price drop or the loss of employment and income.

On an overall basis, therefore, the three classes of higher-risk credit accounted for almost 50 percent of new mortgages during 2006 and totaled nearly $1.5 trillion that year alone. The degree to which the mortgage market came unhinged is hard to overstate: more "high risk" mortgage money was dispensed in 2006 than the annual total for all mortgage lending during any year prior to 2001.

The Fed's baby-step (25 basis points) interest rate increases during 2004–2006 therefore did not shut down the housing boom; it just drove it into the highest risk neighborhoods in America and piled debt on households which were least capable of coping with it. The prosperity managers at the Fed should have been scared out of their wits by this development but the record shows that, actually, they didn't give a wit.

Throughout the entire period of 2004–2006, the meeting minutes celebrate the strength of housing and the manner in which financial "innovation" such as mortgage securitization was spreading the blessings of home finance. Not a single meeting focused on the drastic and unprecedented deterioration of mortgage credit quality that was under way.

Nor was there any mystery about the data. A private industry-based publication called *Inside Mortgage Finance* faithfully reported, week in and week out, all of these trends and the drastic shift after 2003 to high-risk mortgages. So the nation's monetary politburo should have known during the final housing surge of 2004–2006 that an economic time bomb was being planted at the very center of the Main Street economy: cumulative originations of subprime, Alt-A, and second-lien mortgages totaled a staggering $4 trillion over that final period.

No thanks to the Fed, the high risk mortgage party did eventually have its Wile E. Coyote moment. In response to rapidly surging default rates, new originations of these loans dropped right off the cliff, plunging to a negligible $100 billion in 2008.

As in so many other instances, however, the extreme violence of the sub-prime/Alt-A/second-lien cycle was not an honest manifestation of business activity on the free market. The eight year round trip from annual issuance of $150 billion to $1.5 trillion and then back to $100 billion was still another deformation fostered by the age of bubble finance.

JOHN MAYNARD GREENSPAN AND THE CULT OF THE "PRINT"

It goes without saying that the explosion and then crash of the high risk mortgage market amounts to an everlasting black mark against the Fed. Its culpability lies not merely in the grotesque amount of predatory lending that unfolded, but even more acutely in the fact that it turned a blind eye in pursuit of its prosperity management model. The only thing which mattered in the Eccles Building was the quarterly and annual pace of mortgage originations. In purely Keynesian fashion it embraced the mortgage explosion because the proceeds from these loans goosed consumer and investment spending in a manner that was indistinguishable from spending out of current income.

In turn, higher spending meant more GDP, rising asset prices, and a higher stock market. At bottom, the prosperity model of the Greenspan Fed was a revival in modern guise of the old illusion that a nation can borrow its way to prosperity.

There was a large irony in this. Greenspan 1.0 had been anti-Keynesian to the core and had rightly debunked the asset bubble of the late 1920s as an artificial by-product of too much speculative credit. By contrast, Greenspan 2.0 embraced what was surely a proto-Keynesian viewpoint by turning his old equation upside down.

In the new version, rising asset prices came first. Whether this asset inflation was caused by sunspots or the machinations of the Fed itself, the maestro did not say. But, mirabile dictu, the mountains of debt piling up on the nation's balance sheet were not worrisome because the value of housing assets had risen even more. The debt-to-asset ratio had actually fallen!

So the $4 trillion explosion of high-risk mortgage debt during 2004–2006 went unremarked by the monetary central planners because this mighty flow into current spending boosted the "print." The latter consisted of a dozen or so regular economic "stats"—including nonfarm payrolls, retail sales, disposable personal income, housing starts, existing home sales, capital spending, corporate profits, and GDP—that purportedly summarized the macroeconomic picture. These indicators provided Wall Street speculators with leads on the likely direction of the Fed's prosperity management policy and, therefore, the most attractive trades to front-run.

By the time the mortgage market deformation reached its apex in 2004–2006, the Fed was totally in the tank for Wall Street. It did not even dare talk publicly about the unhealthy trends and deteriorating structural conditions which threatened the nation's surface prosperity, for fear of spooking the speculators who were keeping stock prices and risk asset values rising. The mortgage bubble was contributing to an improved current period "print," and that's all that counted. The profound deterioration of credit and the economic deformations which were brewing down below were simply ignored.

THE LEGEND OF FINANCIAL "INNOVATION": WHY MORTGAGE SECURITIZATION REALLY HAPPENED

In truth, the vast outpouring of subprime and other high-risk mortgages were not underwritten by the descendants of George Bailey's savings and loan. Community-based banks and thrifts universally eschewed subprime loans if they had to fund them out of their own deposits and assume the permanent balance sheet risk.

The experienced underwriters working in their mortgage departments could readily see that there was not enough margin, even at the elevated subprime interest rates, to cover probable default losses. Accordingly, fully 82 percent of the subprime loans written during 2004–2006 were bundled, securitized, and laid off on the capital markets; that is, not retained on the balance sheets of the original lenders.

It is now evident, of course, that separation in this manner of mortgage underwriting from long-term balance sheet retention had been a fatal mistake. Yet, at the time, the official propaganda from both the Fed and Wall Street described this division of economic functions as one of the great "innovations" of modern finance because it permitted risk to be sliced, diced, and reallocated to allegedly better suited investors.

Even when dressed up in all its academic finery, however, this shiny new theory of "risk shifting" actually boiled down to a clever rationalization for money printing. There really wasn't any economic merit to it. The major attribute of structured mortgage finance was that it generated endless opportunities for rent seekers to extract fees, scalp trading spreads, and misprice the original risk as it wended its way through the chain of securitization.

The truth of the matter is that "risk" in a mortgage is created on the spot where it is approved and funded. From that point forward, every time a mortgage is handed off—from the loan production office, to the mortgage wholesaler, to the mortgage bond underwriter, to the rating agency, to the CDO packager, to the Wall Street sales and trading desk, to the Norwegian fishing village's investment fund—the original risk gets pooled, averaged, structured, and obfuscated.

Yet the original underwriting risk does not get reduced or mitigated. Therefore, the stated rationale for all of these dead-weight transaction and information costs along the way, to say nothing of the exposure to fraud, was "portfolio diversification" and investor risk selection.

As it happened, real-world outcomes have made a laughingstock of these diversification theories. The alleged gains to investors from a wider mix of geographies, mortgage structures, and borrower profiles were swamped by the disinformation that accumulated along the chain of securitization. Likewise, the tranching of securities issued by mortgage-backed conduits misled investors seeking to calibrate their exposure to losses because the risks embedded in the underlying pools were drastically underestimated.

Accordingly, losses to date on the $3 trillion of non-GSE mortgages that have been securitized total an estimated $1 trillion. This means that had these mortgage derivatives been accurately priced (i.e., to cover losses) in the first place, the true economic cost to investors of achieving portfolio diversification—through this crude form of model-driven, multibillion mortgage pools—would have been prohibitive.

Stated differently, the entire mortgage-backed security (MBS) and collateralized debt obligation (CDO) industry would never have gotten off the ground on the free market. Since giant mortgage pools do not make underwriting risk go away, the only real justification for securitization was lower processing and servicing cost. Yet there was never any empirical evidence of meaningful economies of scale in pooling mortgages after they are written. Indeed, a few years later the evidence against it is unequivocal: the world's lowest cost mortgage processing programs can now be accessed anywhere on the planet from an iPad.

The preponderant form of mortgage securitization was the $6 trillion of government-guaranteed securities written by Fannie Mae and Freddie Mac. But as shown in chapter 19 these are just gussied up Treasury bonds that shouldn't even exist. Likewise, the $2.5 trillion of "private label" mortgage-backed securities packaged by Wall Street from subprime and Alt-A loans thrived for a brief interval owing solely to the bubble finance policies of the Greenspan Fed.

As explained in chapter 1, these money-printing policies showered Wall Street with artificially cheap wholesale funding which enabled it to float massive, high-risk mortgage pools. These mortgages were first gathered by predatory brokers who scoured Main Street neighborhoods looking for junk mortgage borrowers and then funded the resulting loans on Wall Street–provided "warehouse" lines. When these lines were periodically flushed onto Wall Street balance sheets, the loan paper was held only long enough to scalp a generous slice of profits as it passed through the securitization machinery and out into the world of unsuspecting and, often, clueless institutional money managers.

At the back end, Wall Street's sales and trading operations foraged the planet for institutional investors who were foolhardy enough to "lift" its offers of essentially incomprehensible math-model securities. But in unloading this toxic waste, Wall Street was not functioning as an agent of the free market bringing consenting adults together for a trade; there simply wasn't any free market in subprime mortgages.

NO SUBPRIME ON THE FREE MARKET—
JUST FED-ENABLED RE-FI

As indicated, sub-prime lending emerged from the shadowy world of pawnshops, but there was no resemblance in business models at all. The pioneers of this new model, such as the notorious Guardian Savings and Loan and Long Beach Savings, operated on a fundamentally different principle—that is, bad loans were refinanced, not re-possessed.

Whereas old fashioned hard-money lenders like Household Finance and Beneficial had made financial ends actually meet by seizing collateral upon borrower default, the new subprime brokers only made ends appear to meet by refinancing loans as soon as they got in trouble. This maneuver made for better default statistics and drastically reduced collection costs but, alas, it was fatally dependent upon a continuously rising housing market.

The broker-based subprime model was thus an offspring of the Fed's bull market in housing and, in fact, was guaranteed to fail the minute the housing price spiral stopped. The founder of Guardian Savings, for example, famously insisted that borrower ability to make the monthly payment had nothing to do with his new-style subprime lending. "If they have a house, if the owner has a pulse," quipped Russell Jedinak, "we'll give them a loan."

Sometime later, one of Jedinak's disillusioned collaborators completed the picture with respect to Guardian's business model: "They were banking on a model of an ever rising housing market."

Needless to say, rising housing prices and serial refinancings did wonders for reported default rates. Before failing loans could hit the default statistics, subprime lenders kicked the can down the road, converting imminent or actual defaults into new originations. Bearish evidence of stress and underwriting failure was thereby transformed into bullish signs of growth in lending volumes.

Not surprisingly, nearly 85 percent of these early vintage subprime mortgages were refinancings. Often these were of the "cash-out" variety, meaning that borrowers were given enough extra cash to meet the monthly payments until the next refinancing. In this manner, such borrowers remained "current."

This kind of "churn" was an old trick of scam artists in traditional securities markets. But prior to the 1990s there had never been a strong, chronic inflation of residential housing prices in the context of deregulated financial institutions. Accordingly, even one of the astute founders of the government mortgage-backed securities business, Larry Fink, could not imagine a market for privately securitized subprime loans.

Asked by a congressional committee in the late 1980s whether Wall Street might try to securitize risky mortgages, Fink dispatched the notion cleanly: "I can't even fathom what kind of mortgage that is . . . but if there is such an animal, the marketplace . . . may just price that security out [of existence]."

In short, the subprime mortgage industry was not a natural product of the free market. Instead, it was a deformed by-product of the financial asset inflation the Fed persistently fostered after its October 1987 Black Monday panic. Larry Fink failed to imagine that highly risky mortgages could be economically securitized because he had not yet realized that cheap mortgage debt and rising housing prices would converge in a hidden default cycle of rinse and repeat.

CHURN AND BURN: HOW THE HOUSING PRICE SPIRAL FOSTERED THE MORTGAGE BROKER PLAGUE

The financial innovation labs of Wall Street did, in fact, invent the estimable mechanisms of credit enhancement such as overcollateralization and senior-subordinated tranching of subprime mortgage pools. But all the razzmatazz of structured finance did not make subprime lending safer or more financially viable.

Securitization just shuffled around among the various investor classes the drastically underestimated default loss projections cranked out by subprime underwriters. Not only did these projections suffer from the inherent refinancing bias of a bull market in housing, but this contamination of the performance data actually became more severe as the housing price spiral accelerated.

This pernicious feedback loop was crucial to the final explosion of the subprime mortgage market in 2004–2006. It was not coincidental that the single most nefarious operator among the rogue's gallery of subprime entrepreneurs, Roland Arnall of Long Beach Savings and Ameriquest fame, ceremoniously ditched his thrift charter in 1994. This was a smoking gun. Just as the subprime party was getting started, its most important figure elected to go the pure mortgage banker and broker route—funding his originations with warehouse credit lines and wholesaling the resulting mortgages to the incipient Wall Street securitization machine.

Here, then, was one of the great financial deformations which emerged from the age of bubble finance. A multi-trillion business in dodgy housing loans was eventually built by mortgage brokers who could not actually raise capital or funding on the free market and, indeed, not even in the state-supported market for insured deposits. At the end of the day, it was only when the Fed flooded Wall Street with liquidity after December 2000 that Larry Fink's "impossible" market achieved liftoff.

Indeed, absent the rise of the mortgage banker and broker industry and the GSE and Wall Street financing channels on which they were wholly dependent, the next decade's disastrous breakdown of mortgage credit quality might never have happened. The data show that the stiff-necked loan officers who populated the Main Street banks and thrifts which survived the savings and loan meltdown gave subprime mortgages a wide birth, putting up less than 1 percent of their balance sheets for these risky assets.

The nation's epic housing disaster was thus not inevitable, but was spawned by Washington policy makers who adopted serial measures that put housing and mortgage finance squarely in harm's way. So doing, they brought the gambling mania to America's neighborhoods, and, in the end, to the most economically vulnerable among them.

CHAPTER 21

THE GREAT FINANCIAL ENGINEERING BINGE

THE MENACE POSED BY THE TOTTERING MEGA-BANKS, THE MASSIVE housing bubble, and the household consumption binge, among others, was definitely not noticed in the Eccles Building. Instead, the Fed went all-in on the Great Moderation, and after January 2006 was led by the theory's own self-deluded proponent. Wall Street had christened this alleged combination of low inflation and moderate growth as the "Goldilocks economy" and, believing Bernanke could perpetuate it indefinitely, drove the stock averages back to their dot-com bubble highs and beyond.

There was no Goldilocks economy, however, and the stock indices were being artificially levitated by a spree of destructive financial engineering fostered by the Fed. The real numbers showed that the American economy was failing: inflation was being temporarily repressed by the export factories of China, not by the deft maneuvers of the Fed. And real GDP was actually just limping along at its worst rate since the 1930s, notwithstanding the wholly unsustainable growth of household debt.

So the nation's monetary politburo should have been focused on quashing the debt-fueled outbreak of corporate financial engineering, that is, leveraged buyouts, M&A takeovers, and stock buybacks. That these true dangers were completely ignored was in large measure attributable to the fact that the Fed was now in the hands of a timorous academic who didn't have a trace of Volcker in him—who wouldn't even dream of facing down the Wall Street gamblers, looters, and empire builders who were taking the financial system over the edge.

BERNANKE'S DEFLATION HOBGOBLIN
AND MORGAN STANLEY BAILOUT II

The reason that Bernanke could not do his job and bring Wall Street's speculative furies to heel was not merely personal weakness. He was obsessed by theoretical hobgoblins of deflation and depression. As detailed in chapter 8 and explicated further in chapter 29, these were not remotely relevant to the actual circumstances of the American economy. So when the destructive Greenspan bubble began to deflate, the Fed did not permit the markets to liquidate what remained of the Wall Street train wreck it had fostered.

Instead it retreated into headlong panic, pulling out every imaginable stop to reflate these dying financial behemoths. The Bernanke worldview thus engendered a level of desperation in the Eccles Building that knew no bounds. Falsely believing that the US economy was heading for a Great Depression 2.0, the Fed not only expanded its balance sheet by $1.3 trillion in thirteen weeks—that is, by $600 million per hour—but did so in a manner that was utterly indiscriminate and without principle or plan.

As detailed in part 1, the Fed's alphabet soup of cash-pumping programs effectively nationalized the entire $2 trillion commercial paper market, guaranteed the checking accounts of everyone including Exxon, Microsoft, and Warren Buffet, and wantonly handed AAA-rated General Electric $30 billion of loan guarantees. It even artificially propped up the ABCP market so that the likes of Citigroup could continuing booking profits the very nanosecond customers swiped their credit cards.

These cash-pumping actions were so reckless that even the outrageous anecdotes to which they gave rise can scarcely capture the lunacy rampant in the Eccles Building. In one ludicrous case, therefore, the nation's central bank actually guaranteed upward of $200 million that had been borrowed by two New York housewives to start a new business. Amazingly, the purpose was to enable this intrepid duo to purchase large volumes of securitized auto loans about which they knew nothing.

Even in November 2008, the American economy did not need two amateurs to make car loans. The Main Street banks were flush with cash and willing to make such loans to any creditworthy buyer. Likewise, these two housewives most especially did not need a bailout from the Fed: their husbands were the top executives of Morgan Stanley, a firm that by then had already received its own bailout.

Foolish episodes like this one underscore the pathetic consequence of Bernanke's doctrinal error. He was so desperate to prop up Wall Street that he approved a $200 million car loan to Christy Mack, the wife of John Mack of Morgan Stanley, and her social pal, Susan Karches.

In truth, the real problem facing the Fed was not another externally based industrial collapse like the Great Depression, but a long twilight of internal debt deflation. The tip-off was evident in two key economic variables with sharply divergent peak-to-peak growth rates during the alleged economic boom of this century's first decade.

The first of these was nominal GDP, which grew at a modest annual rate of 5.1 percent over the seven-year business cycle ending in late 2007. The second measure was total credit market debt outstanding, which bounded upward at nearly double that rate, rising by 9.2 percent annually. It wasn't a sensible or sustainable equation, a truth that is self-evident in the whole numbers.

Total debt outstanding surged by $23 trillion, rising from $27 to $50 trillion between 2000 and 2007. The nation's nominal GDP, however, grew by only $4 trillion (from $10 to $14 trillion). During the second Greenspan bubble it thus took nearly $6 of new borrowings to generate another $1 of national income.

The Fed's radical interest rate repression campaign, which fostered this unprecedented debt explosion, was thus an utterly misbegotten enterprise. The very notion that the central bank would deliberately peg the money market rate at 1 percent was just plain off the deep end; it defied all historical canons of sound finance.

The end result was a vicious financial bubble that exploded from its inner tensions and instabilities in September 2008. Yet the Fed couldn't explain why the Wall Street meltdown happened owing to a singular reality: the stock market had been propped up all along by a financial engineering binge that had been enabled by the Fed's own policies.

WHEN HELICOPTER BEN CRIED WOLF ABOUT DEFLATION

The unwinding of the massive Greenspan debt bubble implicated an extended deleveraging cycle in which the phony growth of the bubble years would be given back and there would be persistent downward pressure on consumer prices. But a modest reprieve from the relentless forty-year rise in the cost of living, which meant that a dollar saved in 1971 was now worth just twenty-five cents, would have been beneficial to much of society. Wage workers and retirees whose incomes had not even kept up with the understated CPI-U (consumer price index for all urban consumers) would have especially benefited.

This kind of slow, constructive deflation owing to the end of the American debt binge, however, would not have been even remotely comparable to the 30 percent drop in consumer prices after the 1929 crash, nor would it have triggered a depressionary collapse of output and employment (see chapter 29).

In truth, Professor Bernanke was exploiting his reputation as a Depression scholar to peddle the Keynesian canard that price stability—that is, zero inflation plus or minus—is a bad thing. Indeed, Bernanke had gone fully Orwellian: what "deflation" meant to the money printers at the Fed was the absence of 2 percent "inflation." Through some economic alchemy that has never been proven, they insisted that the way to get more jobs and output growth was to debauch the money by 2 percent each year; that is, reduce the dollar's purchasing power by 50 percent over a standard working lifetime.

This was the second time that Bernanke had played the "deflation" card. Back in 2002–2003, he had provided exactly the same rationale for the Fed's first round of panicked interest rate cutting. Freshly appointed to the Fed, he had hinted darkly about a 1930s-style deflation. But the actual data soon proved that to be balderdash.

Goods and services inflation was still very much alive and kicking and remained so right through the last days of the Greenspan bubble. The aforementioned $4 trillion debt-swollen gain in nominal GDP during 2000–2007, for example, was rife with inflation. More than half of this figure, $2.2 trillion, did not represent real output gains; it simply quantified the impact of the very rising prices that Professor Bernanke had claimed would soon be smothered in a vortex of deflation.

Bernanke's howling at the specter of deflation, in fact, proved to be loony: the CPI actually increased at a 2.7 percent annual rate during the five years through 2007, and that rate wasn't benign. It meant that inflation would steal nearly 60 percent of the dollar's purchasing power every thirty years. So there was a menace in the price trend: with the cost-of-living rising stoutly, it put "paid" to Bernanke's "deflation" warnings.

That should have also roundly discredited the Fed's radical interest rate cutting campaign, which was predicated almost exclusively on Bernanke's phony deflation scare. Instead, Professor Bernanke got promoted in 2005 to the top economic job in what was ostensibly a "sound money" Republican White House.

To their everlasting discredit, Karl Rove and the Bush apparatchiks around him could administer a litmus test on abortion to any schedule-C job seeker who came along. Yet they did not know they had brought a Keynesian money printer into their midst, an unabashed believer in Big Government who had publicly described exactly how to drop money out of a helicopter.

THE GREENSPAN-BERNANKE MONEY-PRINTING SPREE WAS A DUD: WEAKEST GROWTH IN HALF A CENTURY

All of the Fed's money printing and interest rate repression during this period did not do much for the economy of Main Street, either. During the seven-year period through the 2007 peak, national output adjusted for inflation expanded at just 2.3 percent per year. That was the lowest seven-year rate of GDP growth since the 1930s, meaning that the Fed's wild money printing produced a dud.

What it actually generated, instead, was a lot of spending from borrowed money and very little growth in real investment and earned incomes. In fact, the three consuming sectors of the American economy—personal consumption (PCE), residential housing, and government expenditures—accounted for virtually all of the growth. These sectors expanded by $4.1 trillion between 2000 and 2007, thereby accounting for a remarkable 98 percent of the entire gain in nominal GDP.

Debt growth in all three of these sectors was exceedingly robust. On the margin, therefore, much of the gain in the GDP "print" during the Greenspan boom was simply a feedback loop: the higher GDP "prints" embodied in roundabout fashion the debt being injected into the spending side of the economy by the central bank.

In contrast to the debt-funded spending side, growth on the investment and income side was punk. Real spending for fixed plant and equipment, for example, rose at only a 1.7 percent annual rate during these seven years and actually by less than 1 percent when the Great Recession period "payback" is averaged in. Likewise, real private wage and salary incomes grew at just 1.6 percent annually—a plodding rate which obviously begs the question of how real personal consumption spending managed to grow at nearly twice that rate, or by about 2.8 percent, during the same period.

There was really no mystery. The US economy was now getting deeply entangled in an accounting illusion. Part of the extra margin of household spending compared to private wages and salaries reflected cash that was being dispensed from home ATM machines and recorded in the drawdown of the savings rate. But there was also a huge supplement to household consumption which came through the debt economy's back door; that is, from the spend out of transfer payments and government payroll disbursements.

As detailed in chapter 29, most of the growth in these latter categories was not owing to the honest "repurposing" of national income that occurs when transfer payments are funded with taxes. Instead, it was derived from public sector borrowings; that is, new money supplied by foreigners and their central banks or from the printing-press-funded purchases of Treasury debt by the Fed.

Notwithstanding Republican White House cheerleading, therefore, it was transfer payments—which grew at double the rate of private wages—and government payrolls that comprised the fastest growing slice of the income pie. During the seven-year Greenspan bubble these disbursements rose from $1.8 trillion to $2.8 trillion, and accounted for nearly half of the nation's entire pre-tax income gain. That was hardly an indicator of booming capitalist prosperity.

When government borrowing of this magnitude occurs on the free market, of course, there is an offset. Interest rates are forced up and interest-sensitive spending on capital goods and consumer durables soon buckles, thereby short-circuiting any tendency of legislators to imbibe in free lunch economics. As previously detailed, the trick that made the faux prosperity of the Greenspan era possible was the nation's giant current account deficit with the rest of the world. The latter reached a peak of $750 billion and 6 percent of GDP in 2006, underscoring that the prosperity of the Greenspan bubble years was being imported on container ships from East Asia and funded by soaring indebtedness to the rest of the world.

By the end of the Greenspan bubble, therefore, the United States was getting poorer by about $2 billion each and every day, owing to its hemorrhaging current account and the orgy of consumption which it enabled. Yet the financial system had become so divorced from the Main Street economy that even as the latter grew poorer, the value of financial assets and especially the stock market averages clambered to new highs on the back of corporate financial engineering gone wild.

$13 TRILLION OF FINANCIAL ENGINEERING GAMES AND THE SIMULACRUM OF PROSPERITY

The stock market's daily narrative, especially as conveyed by financial TV, only appeared to embody the traditional focus on corporate profits and the business outlook. In reality, the proximate drivers of the stock averages were Wall Street financial engineering games: mergers, stock buybacks, and LBOs. These transactions generated the arithmetic of EPS growth by shrinking the share count, thereby giving Wall Street traders financial rabbits to chase.

The massive capital markets churning attendant to financial engineering maneuvers, however, was rooted in state policy, not the free market. The common catalyst was cheap and ample debt, the Greenspan-Bernanke Put, and the tax-favored status of leveraged balance sheets. After the Fed's easing panic began in 2001, these catalysts caused the pace of financial engineering transactions to accelerate and never look back.

Altogether, the value of M&A transactions in the United States over the years 2001 through 2008 totaled about $8 trillion, along with $2.5 trillion of stock buybacks and another $2.5 trillion of LBOs. During the course of the

Greenspan bubble, therefore, these financial engineering deals cumulated to $13 trillion.

Moreover, all three types were designed to drive up the price of existing common stock by shrinking the pool of available shares. Wall Street thus cycled a sum equivalent to the nation's entire GDP into these stock market transactions. Yet none of this raised a dime of new equity capital for productive investment.

This point goes to the heart of the bubble finance fostered by the Greenspan-Bernanke Fed. The purpose of secondary share trading on the free market is to create sufficient liquidity for savers and investors so that there is a dynamic capital market that companies can tap when they need funds for growth. By contrast, aside from the temporary insanity of the dot-com IPOs, there were only trivial amounts of primary equity raised during the entire run of the two Greenspan stock market booms.

The trading frenzy which peaked in 1999–2000 and then again in 2006–2007 consisted almost entirely of secondary market speculation where the driving force was the opposite of capital raising; which is to say, stock prices were being lifted by the liquidation of shares through buybacks, buyouts, and M&A takeovers. Even in the latter case, the overwhelming majority of M&A deals were for cash, not shares of the acquiring company, as had been the case historically.

In fact, the "Flow of Funds" data published by the Federal Reserve reveals that the maestro presided over a two-decade trend of corporate equity decapitalization. During the entire span between 1988 and 2008, there were only three years in which nonfinancial businesses actually raised net equity, and those were during the recession of the early 1990s. After that, the rate of net equity withdrawal from the business sector soared as the Fed's prosperity management model became increasingly more aggressive.

Thus, nonfinancial corporations extinguished $300 billion of net equity during 1988–1994, owing to the excess of buybacks and cash M&A takeovers compared to new equity issuance. This was followed by nearly $700 billion of net equity liquidation during the next seven years. So, while this latter period coincided with the tech boom, corporate equity was actually being drastically shrunk, the mantra of growth notwithstanding.

But it was after the Fed slashed interest rates in 2001, causing business debt issuance to explode, that the cash-out of corporate equity went parabolic. Buyout and buyback transactions drained nearly $2.3 trillion of corporate equity out of the system over the period 2002–2008. In 2007 alone, the "Flow of Funds" reports show that "net new equity issues" amounted to negative $800 billion. Hurtling this much buyback cash at a rapidly diminishing supply of common stock levitated the stock market to the wholly artificial and unsustainable peaks of 2007–2008.

Needless to say, the Bernanke Fed was sleepwalking, furtively looking-out for deflationary goblins as it went along. Accordingly, it did not notice that the balance sheets of corporate America were being strip-mined in a manner similar to the mortgage-driven assault on household balance sheets. In fact, owing to these financial engineering transactions there had been nearly $3.5 trillion of corporate equity withdrawal, or CEW, during the two decades ending in 2008. Thus did the avalanche of credit enabled by the Fed warp and weaken the financial foundations of the nation's private economy.

STRIP-MINING CORPORATE CASH:
THE FREE MARKET DIDN'T DO IT

The rise in equity prices which resulted from these financial engineering maneuvers did not increase the national wealth. Nor did these transactions promote economic efficiency, job growth, or improved corporate management. Beyond that, there was a still more insidious aspect; namely, the false impression promoted by Wall Street and often echoed by the maestro himself that financial engineering and equity liquidation on this massive scale was a good thing because it was the work of the free market.

The idea at work here was that takeovers and buyouts arise from the so-called market for corporate control and represent the verdict of the marketplace just as in the case of a successful product or invention. Consequently, it is claimed that shareholder interests are served when poorly run companies are taken over by more competent managements. Likewise, society is said to benefit from economic efficiency gains when equity-incentivized LBO executives squeeze out waste and sloth from "under-performing" companies.

In fact, corporate control transactions on the free market can generate these salutary effects. But the crucial caveat is that debt capital needs to be priced at market rates and the tax régime must be reasonably neutral. The underlying reality during the Greenspan bubble era, however, was more nearly the opposite, suggesting that the $13 trillion explosion of financial engineering transactions during 2001–2008 was inherently suspect.

The tip-off is the extremely high failure rate of M&A transactions and the fact that stock buyback programs often resembled giant financial laundering schemes (see chapter 22), wherein corporations purchased their shares from the public in order to issue new stock options to top executives. Likewise, as detailed in chapters 24 and 25, LBOs have been mainly cash strip-mining operations, not a unique arrangement for conducting business more efficiently. These financial engineering transactions, therefore, did not really reflect a market-driven quest for tangible economic gains, as claimed by Wall Street salesmen and free market triumphalists alike.

Instead, the boom in financial engineering transactions points to another motivating force; namely, the taxation and monetary policies of the state. It goes without saying that after the turn of the century debt became pitifully cheap. That was even more true on an after-tax basis, reflecting the long-standing deductibility of corporate interest payments but not dividends. Yet the most powerful force unbalancing the playing field was a radical reduction in the capital gains tax.

THE K STREET STORM FROM GUCCI GULCH

Alongside the Fed's cheap credit régime, there arose a noxious distortion of the tax code best summarized as "leveraged inside buildup." The linchpin was successive legislative reductions of the tax rate on capital gains that resulted in a wide gap between high rates on ordinary income and negligible taxes on capital gains. This huge tax wedge became a powerful incentive to rearrange capital structures so that ordinary income could be converted into capital gains.

To his everlasting credit, Ronald Reagan faced down the lobbies of Gucci Gulch and had gotten income taxes on a level capitalist playing field in the Tax Reform Act of 1986. The top income tax rate had been lowered to 28 percent, but this was done under a policy framework in which the tax base was also greatly broadened. Consequently, all forms of personal income—wages, salaries, dividends, and capital gains—were taxed at the same 28 percent maximum rate.

When the technology mania got going in the 1990s, however, the K Street lobbies for venture capital, private equity, hedge funds, real estate developers, and assorted other special interest groups formed a mighty coalition in the name of entrepreneurs and "job creators." By the mid-1990s, it had lined up both the Rubin Democrats and the Gingrich Republicans behind the proposition that technological progress and business invention were crucially dependent upon low rates of taxation on the winnings from successful acts of capitalism.

By then, of course, some of the most stupendous acts of capitalism in all recorded history had already happened. The great companies of the technology revolution—Microsoft, Intel, Cisco, Apple, Dell, and legions more—had been born and grown to giant size. Yet the tax rate on capital gains during their several decades' gestations had never been lower than the 28 percent rate achieved in the 1986 Reagan tax reform and mostly had been far higher.

Nevertheless, Washington cut the capital gains rate to 20 percent in 1997, ostensibly to further liberate entrepreneurs from the alleged yoke of taxes. In so doing, however, it also left in place the top rate on ordinary income, which it had raised to 39 percent a few years earlier to help balance the budget. The tax code was now back to its historic wide gap, with top-bracket "ordinary" income taxed almost twice as heavily as capital gains.

Although the playing field was thus decidedly unlevel when the Bush Republicans took over Washington in 2001, it did not take long for it to go full tilt. Presently, K Street lobbyists came storming out of Gucci Gulch clamoring for a further reduction to 15 percent. At that moment, of course, the smoldering ruins of the dot-com bust proved that wild risk-taking by investors could be readily accomplished at the existing 20 percent rates. Betting billions on the ability of Silicon Valley start-ups to monetize eyeballs, for example, had required no extra incentives from the IRS.

Nevertheless, when the dust settled there was a huge gap between the top rate of taxation on ordinary income at 35 percent and the new rock-bottom rate of 15 percent on capital gains. Cynics were wont to refer to this as the tax accountants' full-employment act, but it was actually far worse.

It not only enabled tax planners to find ingenious new ways to convert ordinary income to capital gains, but also biased the entire warp and woof of the financial system toward the leveraged "inside buildup" of corporate value. The idea was to load companies with debt so that current income would be absorbed by tax-deductible interest payments and cash flow would be allocated to paying down debt. During a holding period of three, five, or even ten years current taxes would thus be minimized.

Then when the company was eventually sold, the equity value gain would be captured on a one-time basis and taxed at only a 15 percent rate. In this manner, high-tax current income would be systematically converted into low-tax capital gains, a potent incentive for highly leveraged capital structures.

Indeed, tax policy and monetary policy now conjoined to generate a potent financial deformation. The leveraged inside buildup had long been the financial modus operandi of real estate developers. Now it became a universal template that caused leverage to swell throughout the business economy.

The folly of the ultra-low capital gains rate was thus not the low rate per se, but its combination with the tax preference for debt versus equity capital. Moreover, the heavy tax bias in favor of "leveraged inside buildup" was a gift to LBO speculators, not to backyard inventors.

It thus happened that Robert Noyce and Gordon Moore, the genius founders of Intel and the semiconductor industry, made all their breakthroughs when the capital gains rate was 35 percent. Even more to the point, the actual rate was much higher because the calculation of the gain was not even indexed during that era of high inflation.

Likewise, Bill Gates and Michael Dell each created multibillion giants which dominated the personal computer space at a time when the tax rates on capital gains and ordinary income were the same. In the most pointed case of all, Steve Jobs created Apple, got fired by the board, and then returned to launch a final blaze of glory, all before the capital gains rate was lowered to the Bush levels.

Needless to say, as long as governments are paying their bills, lower tax rates on income are better than higher rates. Yet a huge differential between capital gains and ordinary income is always a source of economic mischief, and this was especially so under the circumstances of the Greenspan bubble. Indeed, it actually became an immense obstacle to economic growth and long-run financial health because it contributed heavily to Wall Street's massive pursuit of CEW in the final years of the bubble.

THE $12 TRILLION TOWER OF BUSINESS DEBT
AND THE MYTH OF PLENTIFUL CORPORATE CASH

This debt-fueled financial engineering spree took a deep toll on the balance sheets of American business, especially after the Greenspan Fed went all-in with cheap credit beginning in December 2000. At that point in time, total debt on American nonfinancial businesses stood at $6.6 trillion, and it amounted to just over 50 percent of the replacement value of operating assets; that is, structures, equipment, and inventories.

During the next eight years business debt soared and operating assets didn't. Consequently, the numbers map out to the equivalent of a collective LBO on American business. By the time of the financial panic in September 2008, business debt had grown to $11.4 trillion. This nearly $5 trillion gain represented a 7.5 percent annual growth rate. By contrast, business operating assets had grown at only a 2.8 percent rate during the Greenspan bubble.

Accordingly, the huge wave of business borrowing had not funded a commensurate expansion of productive assets; it had simply increased the level of business leverage. Business sector debt thus rose to 60 percent of the replacement value of operating assets.

Contrary to the urban legend assiduously promoted by Wall Street, however, American business is not now sitting on a sea of cash, basking in the pink of financial health. Cash holdings have increased by about $650 billion since the business cycle peak in late 2007, but business debt is now $850 billion higher. In effect, the much ballyhooed surge of business cash holdings represents nothing more than borrowed money that has been parked on the other side of company balance sheets.

The business debt burden today actually stands at an all-time high of $11.6 trillion. This tower of borrowings self-evidently dwarfs the $3.3 trillion of cash balances currently held by the business sector as a prudential reserve against the vast uncertainty arising from the nation's broken economy. The real truth is that American business buried itself in debt during the financial engineering games of the Greenspan bubble. After three and a half years of alleged recovery, it still has not even begun to dig itself out.

One thing is certain, however. The American economy had never experienced a Great Moderation, only a phony, debt-driven boom fostered by the Fed's 1 percent money. Likewise, the stock market ramp of 2003–2007 had never been real. It resulted from a state-enabled financial engineering raid on corporate balance sheets which left American business saddled with nearly $12 trillion of debt.

CHAPTER 22

THE GREAT RAID ON
CORPORATE CASH

THE SECOND GREENSPAN BUBBLE WAS THUS INFLATED BY A VAST financial strip-mining machine that rumbled across corporate America. In the process of goosing the stock market, it ripped cash and equity out of business balance sheets to the tune of $13 trillion during the eight years ending in 2008. So doing, it drastically weakened the nation's financial foundation, even as it enabled CEOs and boards to raid their own treasuries for the purpose of boosting share prices and the value of executive options.

It goes without saying that the $2.5 trillion of LBOs during this period pleasured shareholders with cash that wasn't earned, but was simply stumped-up by hocking corporate assets. But the blistering pace of stock buybacks and M&A takeovers were driven by the same bias toward debt and capital gains. As a mild form of leveraged buyout, they too effectively distributed corporate cash to the marauding bands of "fix" hungry speculators who came to dominate the stock market during the era of bubble finance.

BACKDOOR LBOS: SHARE BUYBACKS AND TAKEOVERS

Like other forms of corporate equity withdrawal (CEW), stock buybacks and cash financed M&A deals channel cash into shrinking the share count and thereby boosting stock prices. They result in capital gains to outside shareholders and the inside buildup of debt on business balance sheets.

In this scheme of things, stock buybacks are a particularly insidious progeny of the Greenspan bubble. Under the seemingly wholesome banner of "returning cash to shareholders," they enable top management to subtly disguise the appropriation of corporate resources; that is, stock buybacks help managements obfuscate the heavy, shareholder-unfriendly dilution which results from massive stock option programs.

This stock recycling syndrome is baldly evident in the case of many of the big-cap blue chip corporations. Buyback programs undertaken in recent years have been truly massive, yet share counts have typically been reduced only modestly. The reason is that a substantial portion of shares bought from public stockholders were handed right back to inside executives as new option awards.

Stock buybacks and M&A deals are also triggering events, or what are known as "catalysts" among the momentum ("momo") traders. Both rumors and announcements of these financial engineering actions typically trigger sharp inflows of speculative buying and thereby push stock prices upward, quite apart from any change in the underlying earnings fundamentals.

Accordingly, top managements can be easily seduced into financial engineering maneuvers. They produce a pop in the stock and opportunities to haul down stock option compensation in that special envelope marked "tax once over lightly" (at 15 percent). Self-evidently, these stock pops become addictive, encouraging CEOs and boards to bang the deal lever over and over.

CISCO SYSTEMS: THE GREATEST STOCK-LAUNDERING MACHINE EVER INVENTED

The poster boy for the extreme rinse-and-repeat form of stock buybacks has undoubtedly been Cisco Systems, one of the original bright stars in the technology firmament which has since grown long in the tooth. Until very recently, it never paid a dime of dividends and its stock price had languished for years at just under $20 per share, a level first reached in November 1998.

At first blush, the fact of zero returns to shareholders over an entire fifteen-year period seems wildly inconsistent with Cisco's well-known posture as a heavy buyer of its own stock. In fact, cash spent on buybacks totaled $37 billion during fiscal 2007–2011, enabling it to repurchase approximately 28 percent of its shares.

This massive buyback amounted to 102 percent of the company's net income and towered over the mere $6 billion Cisco spent on capital expenditures (CapEx) during that period. This flinty CapEx figure not only represented just half of its depreciation and amortization charges, but was also only 3 percent of its $200 billion in revenue over those five years, a level drastically below the 5–10 percent of sales devoted to capital spending by most of its global technology peers.

The implication was that boosting its stock price, even at the cost of drastically underinvesting in its productive assets, had now become the preponderant purpose of the technology industry's former growth dynamo. It is virtually inconceivable, however, that this drastic allocation of cash to the repurchase of its own shares would have occurred in an environment where taxes were on a level playing field and financial markets had not been converted into speculative casinos.

The worst part of the Cisco story is that despite the repurchase of 1.8 billion shares, the implied drastic shrinkage of its float didn't happen. The company's fully diluted share count during this five-year period dropped by only 700 million shares, or by less than 40 percent of its gross buyback.

The balance of these repurchased shares was recycled back into the company's various employee stock option plans, which currently have 1.2 billion share equivalents outstanding. Not surprisingly, Cisco's CEO, John Chambers, has long been an evangelist in behalf of low taxes on capital gains.

The truth of the matter, however, is that Cisco was running a shareholder-subsidized scheme for transforming the pay of Chambers and his top executives into IRS-proof winnings. Accordingly, during this period Cisco executives, employees, and insiders harvested capital gains from stock options in excess of $15 billion. Self-evidently, these winnings were touched only lightly by the tax man.

Nor was Cisco Systems an outlier in the buyback game. Between the end of 2004 and the first quarter of 2011, the S&P 500 companies alone completed $2.3 trillion of stock buybacks. This meant that a continuous wave of corporate cash flow was being flushed back into the stock market, thereby placing a potent bid under stock prices while providing generous headroom for the continuous award of new stock options. The top twenty blue chip giants that dominate the S&P 500 were especially voracious purchasers of their own stock, buying back nearly $800 billion during this period.

The leader was ExxonMobil, which repurchased $160 billion of its own shares during 2004–2011. It was followed by Microsoft at $100 billion, IBM at $75 billion, and Hewlett-Packard, Proctor & Gamble, and Cisco with $50 billion each. Even the floundering shipwreck of merger mania known as Time Warner Inc. bought back $25 billion.

The standard defense of stock repurchase is that it represents the highest and best use of corporate cash as determined by executives and boards; that is, it is an efficient outcome on the free market. If that's true, of course, then the massive scale and pervasive extent of stock buybacks during recent times imply that American corporations have run out of plausible growth opportunities. Presumably, they have determined that investments on the floor of the New York Stock Exchange offer higher returns than CapEx on the factory floor or a drill bit on the ocean floor.

In fact, buybacks are driven by policies of the state far more than by acts of pure capitalism on the free market. Feeding the speculative mob while pocketing low-tax capital gains is what drives CEOs to act. Cheap debt and a stock market badly deformed by the Greenspan-Bernanke Put are what enable the game.

EXXONMOBIL'S $125 BILLION DRILLING CAMPAIGN ON THE FLOOR OF THE NEW YORK STOCK EXCHANGE

The case of ExxonMobil, among many others, raises considerable doubt on the proposition that stock buybacks reflect a free market choice. It would be just plain implausible to contend that the world's largest private energy producer, operating in the context of $100 per barrel of oil, is faced with a paucity of opportunities to reinvest its prodigious cash flow.

Yet that is exactly what ExxonMobil's cash deployment patterns imply. Stock buybacks, not capital investment, absorbed the preponderant share of the $175 billion in net income that ExxonMobil generated during 2007–2011.

The company spent $125 billion on share repurchases over this period, which enabled it to buy in nearly 1.7 billion, or 30 percent, of its outstanding shares. By contrast, capital spending net of depreciation and depletion amounted to less than $50 billion over the same period. This means that, notwithstanding the evident windfall profits that are available from bringing incremental hydrocarbon production on stream, ExxonMobil elected to allocate 70 percent of its net income to drilling for returns on Wall Street.

This lopsided allocation, however, was not exactly proof that buybacks were ExxonMobil's highest and best use of cash. This is evident in the fact that the company's share count shrank only modestly despite this $125 billion tsunami of stock buybacks. Outstanding shares fell by just 17 percent during the entire five-year period, or by a little more than one-half of the gross stock buybacks.

Given the company's fulsome trend in executive compensation via stock options, this gap is not all that mysterious: shares were being recycled to insiders, not retired to the company's treasury. For example, the company's long-reigning CEO, Rex Tillerson, was paid $150 million over the period, most of it in stock awards.

The truth of the matter is that the management and board of ExxonMobil, like those of most public companies, are addicted to share buybacks. Buybacks are the giant prop which keeps share prices elevated, existing stock options in the money and the dilutive impact of new awards obfuscated. They are also the corporate laundry where Federal income taxes are rinsed out of top executive compensation through the magic of capital gains.

IF THE FED HAD NO DOG IN THE STOCK MARKET HUNT

Several decades of money printing and stock market coddling by the Fed, therefore, has turned the nation's top corporate executives into stock option hounds. The primary job of CEOs has now become chasing their share prices ever higher by allocating huge amounts of available cash, including the proceeds of borrowings, to financial engineering maneuvers like buy-backs. Were the Fed ever to declare it has no dog in the Wall Street hunt and that it is indifferent to the stock averages, the truth of that proposition would become readily apparent.

Left to their own devices on the free market and on a level tax field, cor-porate executives would pay cash dividends to provide a return to share-holders. They would reinvest their remaining cash flows to become more competitive, whether through paying off existing debt or acquiring addi-tional productive assets.

Or in the event they were in a sunset industry, as implied by the buyback addiction of most large US companies, they would use excess cash flows to pay down debt in order to survive. Whatever their external situation, how-ever, corporate executives would not issue huge amounts of debt to chase their share prices higher in order to gorge themselves on stock options; an honest stock market and level tax system wouldn't let them.

An honest stock market would also see through the financial engineer-ing game, recognizing that, in the main, stock buybacks have been a cam-ouflage for the lack of true earnings growth. ExxonMobil's operating results, for example, have been flat as a pancake over the cycle. It earned $41 billion in net income and $70 billion in EBITDA (earnings before inter-est, taxes, depreciation, and amortization) during 2007 and posted identi-cal amounts on both measures of income in 2011. So the fact that the company's EPS rose from $7.26 to $8.42 per share during this four-year pe-riod is exclusively due to the share buybacks.

The cynic might wonder why ExxonMobil paid CEO Rex Tillerson $150 million during a period in which its share price rose by just 3.5 percent an-nually amidst the greatest bull market in energy industry history. Indeed, owing to policy distortions emanating from the central banking and taxing branches of the state, there is a far more insistent issue: Namely, why is ExxonMobil being operated as a (slowly) liquidating trust? During the past five years it has distributed $165 billion to shareholders in buybacks and dividends, an amount equal to 93 percent of its $175 billion in cumulative net income.

Perhaps it is a "sunset" company despite the widespread belief that the value of hydrocarbon reserves has nowhere to go except up. Yet under a level tax playing field it is highly unlikely that stock buybacks and stock price pumping would be the preferred strategy for a sunset company. Tax-indifferent shareholders, in particular, might strongly prefer to collect their returns in dividends they could control rather than stock buybacks which elevate stock prices temporarily, but also leave the resulting "paper" gains exposed to open-ended market price risk.

Under the Greenspan-Bernanke Put, however, true free market risk is heavily discounted, and logically so. Wall Street expects the Fed to keep stock prices propped up at all hazards. So with stock market risk minimized and the tax code heavily biased toward inside buildup and capital gains, ExxonMobil chooses to pay only a modest 2.5 percent dividend and retains the rest of its 10 percent net income yield to fund its massive stock price–pumping operation.

As the largest and most profitable corporation on planet earth, its strategy fully embodies and promotes the deformations of finance that result from current policy. And if the misguided policies of the state warp and shape the financial model of even mighty ExxonMobil, it cannot be gainsaid that they drive the entire corporate economy. Most of the other great blue chip corporations, in fact, have demonstrated the same pattern.

PROCTOR AND GAMBLE CO.:
"DUMP AND PUMP," CORPORATE STYLE

The paragon for "dump and pump" corporate finance is the venerable Proctor & Gamble (P&G). During the last five years it has dumped $35 billion of buyback funds into the stock market, and has thereby pumped its stock price modestly; indeed, very modestly. Its share price of $67 at the end of 2011 was up just 4 percent from the $64 level where it stood at the beginning of 2007.

Even as the share price inched upward, P&G's income statement went nowhere. During this five-year period its pre-tax income was flat at $15 billion annually, and EBITDA actually declined from $20 billion in 2007 to $17 billion in 2011. The only thing that kept its EPS rising was a drop in its tax rate and a 12 percent shrinkage of its share count.

Roughly speaking, a liquidating trust is distinguished by the fact that it can pay out more than it earns. In pursuing its "dump and pump" corporate finance strategy, P&G functioned in exactly that manner during the past half decade. Its combined stock buybacks and dividend payments totaled $60 billion, a figure well more than 100 percent of its net income of $55 billion. So, notwithstanding its vaunted brands, the company had implicitly thrown in the towel and was slowly liquidating itself in a strained effort to keep its stock price rising and management stock options above water.

When a company like P&G implicitly embraces a sunset strategy and chooses not to reinvest in its operating businesses, an infinitely better use for cash would be to pay down debt, since a no-growth enterprise is inherently risky. The Fed's ultra-low interest rate régime, however, closed that door completely. During the last five years, P&G did not use its massive free cash flow to pay down even a dime of its $30 billion in debt.

With a market cap of nearly $200 billion, Proctor & Gamble stands at the center of the US corporate sector. Its adoption of a corporate finance model based on dumping cash into buybacks and pumping its stock price, therefore, has broad ramifications. Since this model does not reflect the natural inclinations of the free market but, instead, arises out of bad tax and monetary policies, it is evident that unsustainable bubble finance has penetrated deep into the corporate economy.

FINANCIAL ENGINEERING RUN AMOK: THE LOOTING OF HEWLETT-PACKARD

Unfortunately, Proctor & Gamble is only a mild case of the financial deformations attendant to these misguided policies of cheap debt and unbalanced taxation. A far more virulent template is found in the tattered financial carcass of Hewlett-Packard, the former powerhouse in the information technology and personal computer industry.

It has been run for more than a decade now by a succession of CEOs who excelled mainly at appearing on CNBC to tout their stock. Their consistent theme was that the company's massive share buybacks and serial M&A deals were a sure-fire formula for robust EPS growth and a fabulous upside for shareholders.

Yet, since the spring of 2010, Hewlett-Packard's stock price has been savaged because it finally became evident that financial engineering had felled the business operations and balance sheet of one of the nation's storied technology companies. Indeed, the spectacular collapse of its market cap, which since then has dropped from $120 billion to $30 billion, is a striking rebuke to several generations of Hewlett-Packard CEOs.

It is also much more. It crystallizes the manner in which the Fed's fixation on levitating the stock market has lured a whole swath of corporate executives into playing destructive financial engineering games—maneuvers that are further reinforced by the Washington policy bias toward debt and capital gains.

When Hewlett-Packard's stock price rolled over at $53 per share in the spring of 2010 and began its unrelenting plunge toward $15, it meant that the company's share price had retreated all the way back to its June 1997 level. And that was in spite of a massive campaign of financial engineering maneuvers in recent years that had few peers among big-cap technology names.

During the five years ending in fiscal 2011, Hewlett-Packard repurchased $48 billion of its own stock, even though its net income during the same period was only $39 billion. Furthermore, total shareholder distributions, counting its modest dividends, came to 133 percent of net income. The company's financial strategy amounted to eating its own tail.

Distributions to shareholders greatly in excess of net income are rarely a formula for long-term financial health, but in this case were especially counterproductive because Hewlett-Packard was also drastically underfunding its fixed-asset base. It recorded $22 billion of depreciation and amortization charges during this five-year period, compared to only $18 billion of capital expenditure, notwithstanding that it was the largest high-tech equipment manufacturer in the world and faced brutal East Asian competitors who did not usually play by capitalist rules.

Investors on the free market would have given a thumbs-down to such self-destructive policies long before its stock price rolled over in the spring of 2010. But that had not happened because liquidity-juiced Wall Street speculators had ramped the stock over and over, initiating a new run-up each time another M&A deal was announced or rumored, and whenever the board renewed or extended its massive stock buyback program.

The promise of huge synergies from acquisitions was a particularly potent catalyst for periodic stock ramps because Wall Street is replete with rumors and inside information about M&A deals. As shown in chapter 23, takeover speculation is one of the crucial inner mechanisms of profit capture in the hedge fund–driven casino which now operates on the stock exchanges.

In the fullness of time, however, it became evident that the $37 billion that Hewlett-Packard spent on M&A deals during this five-year period did not have the flattering impact on earnings its deal-making CEOs had so loudly advertised. In fact, this M&A spree brought a vast expansion of its corporate footprint and complete disorder to its business operations and strategy.

Consequently, even as annual sales surged from $100 billion to nearly $130 billion, nothing at all fell to the bottom line, with net income of $7.3 billion in 2007 remaining flat at $7 billion four years later. Needless to say, when the M&A trick finally failed to satisfy the market's Pavlovian expectations for growth, the speculators moved on to more promising targets.

The abysmal failure of Hewlett-Packard's serial M&A deals became starkly evident when it was recently forced to write-off nearly $20 billion of goodwill and assets for just two acquisitions, Electronic Data Systems and a British company called Autonomy. What was also evident is that in massively overpaying for bad deals, the company had wrecked its balance sheet. During this five-year spree of financial engineering, Hewlett Packard had spent $90 billion on shareholder distributions and M&A deals, but had generated only $45 billion in operating cash flow after capital expenses.

In short, the stock market–obsessed CEOs of Hewlett Packard had spent twice as much on financial engineering projects as they had available in cash flow. The company's net debt thus inexorably mushroomed, rising by $25 billion over the period and leaving one of the nation's technology giants hobbled by the excrescences of bubble finance.

Here was powerful testimony against the Fed's "wealth effects" policy and the consequent propping and juicing of the stock averages attendant to it. Owing to these machinations, the stock market was crawling with speculators capable of powerful hit-and-run forays that encouraged CEOs and boards to do their bidding; that is, feed the speculative mob with another stock buyback or M&A deal. Great companies like Hewlett-Packard were now being run not by adult professionals but day-trading punters.

Boards and CEOs who strap on their helmets and resist the pressure to mete out another "fix" face the real risk of getting swept out by the clamoring herd. Certainly the prospect of harvesting capital gains from stock option winnings, if financial engineering works, and keeping share prices rising is the more appealing scenario.

But there is another reason why CEOs capitulate and feed the beast. They are not operating on a level playing field, whether they know it or not, due to the Greenspan-Bernanke Put. It provides the speculative marauders who dominate the stock market cheap downside insurance against a big drop in the broad market averages, such as the S&P 500.

On the free market, of course, there would be no Greenspan-Bernanke Put, meaning that the cost of an honest to goodness put on the S&P 500 index would be far higher than prevails in the Fed-sponsored casino today. Since most speculators—whether big-name hedge funds, trend-following mutual fund managers, or home gamers who are prudent enough to stay solvent—must continuously buy downside protection to remain in the game, the problem is obvious: the cost of market-priced downside insurance would consume much if not all of their winnings from piling on the momentum raids.

At the end of the day, the Greenspan-Bernanke Put is a profound distortion of the free market. In this case, it induced one of the great progenies of American capitalism to essentially commit financial hara-kiri. Still, the looting of Hewlett-Packard was all in a day's work in the Wall Street casino.

BIG BLUE: STOCK BUYBACK CONTRAPTION ON STEROIDS

IBM's huge share buyback program, by contrast, shows that financial engineering does not always produce such immediate untoward results. Yet it is nonetheless a dramatic illustration of how the Fed's bubble finance régime enables companies to literally "buy" themselves a higher stock price, at least temporarily, by plowing massive amounts of cash into share repurchases, thereby creating the false impression of robust earnings growth.

Big Blue's reported earnings thus surged 16 percent annually from $7 per share in 2007 to $13 in 2011, but those results were not apples to apples by any stretch of the imagination. The company's stock buyback program reduced its net share count by 22 percent, and profits on its massive overseas operations had been artificially boosted by a double-digit decline in the dollar. IBM's reported results also reflected a 12 percent reduction in its tax rate and $16 billion of acquisitions, all highly accretive mainly because they were financed with ultra-cheap long-term debt.

In the absence of these one-timers and financial engineering maneuvers, however, the picture was not so buoyant. Based on organic revenues, constant exchange rates, and no reduction in tax rates and share counts, earnings per share grew by about 5 percent annually, not 16 percent, over the past five years. It is far from evident, therefore, that IBM's true mid-single-digit growth rate justified the doubling of its share price during the period.

Upon closer examination, in fact, IBM was not the born-again growth machine trumpeted by the mob of Wall Street momo traders. It was actually a stock buyback contraption on steroids. During the five years ending in fiscal 2011, the company spent a staggering $67 billion repurchasing its own shares, a figure that was equal to 100 percent of its net income.

This massive and continuous stock-buying program brought approximately 550 million, or 36 percent, of the company's 1.5 billion of outstanding shares into its treasury, but needless to say, they did not all stay there. Nearly two-fifths of these shares reentered the float, mainly to refresh the management stock option kitty.

It goes without saying that in this instance the interests of stock traders and top management were aligned—perversely. The steady, deep shrinkage of the IBM float kept a bid under the stock and thereby delivered a "perfect" price chart, rising almost continuously from $100 to $200 per share over the past five years. It was a carry trader's dream.

Likewise, top executives got big-time pay packages they may or may not have deserved, but in any event they were dispensed in envelopes marked "tax once over lightly." Former CEO Sam Palmisano, for example, cashed out $110 million worth of stock options a few weeks after his retirement party.

This rinse-and-repeat shuffle of stock buybacks and options grants is undoubtedly a significant source of left-wing jeremiads about executive pay having gone to three hundred times the average worker's compensation when, once upon a time, allegedly, the ratio was more like 30 to 1. But the issue is not simply whether this kind of financial engineering has contributed to the sharp tilt of income flows to the top 1 percent in recent years. There can be little doubt, on the math alone, that it has.

The more crucial question, in this instance, is whether the massive CEW evident in IBM's numbers is setting up another of the great iconic American companies for a fall sometime down the road, similar to Hewlett-Packard. The data on this score are not encouraging. Total shareholder distributions, including dividends, amounted to $82 billion, or 122 percent, of net income over this five-year period. Likewise, during the last five years IBM spent less on capital investment than its depreciation and amortization charges, and also shrank its constant dollar spending for research and development by nearly 2 percent annually. Neither of these trends is compatible with staying on top in the fiercely competitive global technology industry.

Most especially, however, IBM's earnings—like nearly all the big cap global companies—could not be flattered permanently by the Fed's bubble finance. Already, the plunge of the euro has taken a toll on the company's reported results, causing the artificial translation gains it booked on its huge European businesses during the weak dollar cycle through 2011 to now unwind. Indeed, with nearly two-thirds of its sales outside the United States, the company's sales are now actually falling in dollar terms, and will likely continue to do so for the indefinite future.

THE WORST $225 BILLION DEAL EVER

In many cases, financial engineering did not work out so well for either management insiders or Wall Street speculators. One such example is Time Warner Inc.'s ill-starred merger with AOL, which was announced just in the nick of time to perfectly top-tick the dot-com mania in January 2000.

Needless to say, the path from there had been an extended sojourn on the downside, with the company's post-AOL market cap dropping from a peak of $225 billion to only $20 billion. Soon after the merger, AOL Time Warner set a corporate record that still astounds; namely, the $100 billion net loss it recorded in the single year of 2002.

This financial bone-crusher triggered a continuous corporate exercise in "demerging" the discordant parts and pieces that had been accumulated by the Time Warner acquisition machine during the two decades prior to AOL. These spin-offs included books, music, magazines, cable, the Atlanta Braves, and much else. AOL itself was ultimately cast out of the fold.

By early 2006, the stock price had dropped from a peak of $228 to $65 per share, but Wall Street financial engineers had not yet completed their work on the corpse. At that point a group of raiders led by Carl Icahn forced the company into a further restructuring plan under which it divested still more of its historic M&A spree, absorbing deep write-downs from the destruction of value it had accomplished during the holding period. Accordingly, Time Warner recorded cumulative net income of just $5 billion on sales of $200 billion during the six-year period through fiscal year 2011. Even as the net income line came up punk, however, the company did undertake $26 billion of stock buybacks pursuant to the financial engineering deal with Icahn.

Having essentially no cumulative earnings during this period, Time Warner therefore funded the buybacks by continuously shrinking. Annual revenues of $46 billion in 2007 fell to $29 billion by 2011, and EBITDA was reduced from $14 billion to $7 billion. This drastic downsizing was a rational antidote to the thirty years of feckless M&A, but despite all of the de-merging and $26 billion of stock buybacks, value could not be created were none had really existed. By the end of 2011, Time Warner's stock price was $35 per share—down by 85 percent from the Greenspan Bubble high of January 2000.

THE DECAPITALIZATION OF THE FORTUNE TOP 25

This drastic decline is often cited in condemnation of the AOL merger as the worst M&A deal of all time. Most surely it is that, but the prolonged unwinding of the whole edifice of AOL Time Warner Inc. also exposes the shaky financial engineering foundation which underpinned the faux prosperity of the Greenspan bubble era.

As the bubble reached its final peak in 2007, financial TV reported what sounded like healthy corporate earnings and stock prices at all-time highs. But the underlying data told another story. As shown below, what was being reported as "earnings ex-items" vastly exaggerated true profitability. At the same time, the American economy was being decapitalized by rampant financial engineering. Cash was not flowing toward productive investment and growth—not in the slightest.

This was starkly evident in the manner in which the largest twenty-five companies on the Fortune 500 list disposed of their fulsome earnings. Their net income aggregated to $242 billion during 2007, but only 15 percent ($35 billion) of that hefty total was reinvested in their own businesses; that is, allocated to additional capital expenditures and other working capital after funding depreciation and amortization of existing assets.

By contrast, these same twenty-five companies—which included a medley of giants from Wal-Mart to ExxonMobil, AIG, Home Depot, JPMorgan, Philip Morris, and AT&T—invested nearly $345 billion in financial engineering and shareholder distributions. This stupendous total represented 140 percent of the aggregate net income of these leading companies.

These sharply contrasting numbers spoke volumes about the financial priorities in corporate America. These giant companies effectively elected to send ten times more cash outside of their corporate walls for acquisitions, stock buybacks, and dividends than they invested in growth of fixed and working capital inside their current operations.

To be sure, stockholders are entitled to a share of profits, and the Fortune Top 25 did distribute $90 billion in dividends, or nearly 40 percent of net income. The distortion lies in the fact that they also spent an additional $250 billion on stock buybacks and M&A deals—or more than 165 percent of net income after dividends. So they had to borrow $100 billion to fund their massive stock buybacks and M&A deals, and that was the rub. While there is no reason to believe that dubious financial engineering projects of this scale would have passed muster on the free market, it is virtually certain that rational executives and boards would not have borrowed $100 billion to try.

Unbalanced taxation plus the Fed-enabled stock market casino and cheap debt had thus taken a profound toll. The stock averages implied that an era of unparalleled prosperity had descended on the nation, but everywhere stood signs suggesting that what had actually descended was a riot of reckless speculation on Wall Street.

GE'S ROUND TRIP TO NOWHERE ON THE WALL STREET MOMO TRAIN

One sign that the Fed's "wealth effects" levitation strategy has delivered the stock market over to marauding bands of speculators is the violent "ramp jobs" that they have done on General Electric's stock price over the last fifteen years. This roller-coaster history is totally out of character with GE's stolid corporate persona.

General Electric remains a tightly run conglomerate that spans a vast cross-section of both the domestic and global economy. Its vast earnings power together with its AAA credit rating makes it the epitome of a blue chip corporate giant, synonymous with gravity, reliability, and constancy. Yet owning GE's stock over the last two decades has been more hazardous for the average investor than dabbling in the pink sheets.

Contrary to the periodic bouts of Wall Street storytelling about GE's credentials as a "growth stock," the astonishing reality is that it has been just the opposite: a veritable "no growth" stock. When the maestro experienced his irrational exuberance moment in December 1996, GE traded at $17 per share. At the end of 2011, it also clocked in at $17 per share.

Still, the fact of zero appreciation over fifteen years is not actually the hazardous part of the story. During its long round trip to nowhere, GE's stock resided on the Wall Street "momo train," enduring such violent thrills and spills as would have induced vertigo in the average investor.

The first four-year ramp during the Greenspan tech bubble elevated GE's $17 stock to $60 per share by mid-2000. Traders and speculators were gifted with a "four-bagger" over four years. During the following twenty-four months, however, the stock came crashing back to earth, settling at $23 per share in early 2003. A 60 percent stock price meltdown is supposed to happen to high-flying newcomers, not hundred-year-old, well-run diversified blue chips.

The next ramp job, which coincided with the second Greenspan bubble, also took four years to unfold, and its peak $42 share price in September 2007 amounted to roughly a two-bagger. The subsequent cliff-diving phase was quicker and more violent, however. When GE's stock price reached bottom in March 2009, it was a smoldering ruin at $10 per share, meaning that it lost 75 percent of its value during the second plunge of the momo train.

Presently, the third ramp job got under way as the Fed ignited the Bernanke bubble and propped up GE's teetering finance company with a $30 billion bailout loan. This time the ramp job was even more flaccid: by the end of 2011 GE's stock price was still struggling to get back to the $17 per share threshold it had first crossed in December 1996.

This roller-coaster ride on the Wall Street momo train happened, of course, precisely because there is no honest free market in the financial system. In fact, a giant company with the underlying earnings consistency of GE would not suffer consecutive 60 percent and 75 percent stock price plunges within the span of a decade on the free market. The reason for these aberrations is that the ramp jobs preceding each plunge were artifacts of the stock market deformations fostered by the Fed.

The Greenspan-Bernanke Put has made downside insurance too cheap for the marauding gangs of professional (and some day-trading) speculators. It does not take even an amateur chart specialist to see that during the nearly uninterrupted four-year ascent of each ramp job, it would have been possible for traders using options and leverage to garner prodigious returns, even after collaring market risk with "cheap" S&P puts.

Each time the market-wide Greenspan bubble finally collapsed under its own weight, it was the well-insured Wall Street speculators who lived for another day. The naked and the naïve, of course, got carried out on a stretcher, more often than not by way of Main Street.

Arguably, GE's first moon shot was owing in part to the solid profit performance of the Jack Welch years; but in the main it was attributable to the wild and unsustainable expansion of market-wide PE multiples, including GE's 40X multiple, which occurred during the Greenspan stock mania of the late 1990s.

After GE's valuation multiple had been brought down to earth in 2001–2003, however, the next ramp job would never have happened on the free market. This new ramp was due to the company's unabashed and reckless financial engineering games, maneuvers which lured more and more speculators onto the momo train—some with protection, others not.

Again, the issue is not just about how much upside the 1 percenters scalped and how much downside the home gamers endured, although undoubtedly the computations would not be pretty. The problem is that, as detailed below, GE's financial engineering gambits have been so extreme and extensive during recent years that they will badly impair the company's future prospects.

The potential for significant future impairment is suggested by the magnitude of GE's financial engineering spree in 2007, a catalyst which helped goose its stock price to that year's $42 peak, which was 20X the company's trailing EPS as filed with the SEC. Even if that earnings number had been sustainable, which it wasn't, 20X was a decidedly sporty multiple for a conglomerate consisting overwhelmingly of old-line industrials like white goods, jet engines, plastics, light bulbs, generators, and locomotives, as well as the huge but potentially volatile finance business.

GE's finances, however, were not on the level. During fiscal 2007 it posted net income of $22 billion, but it actually spent the rather stupendous sum of $48 billion attempting to pump its stock price and expand its asset base. This included $25 billion for buybacks and dividends, $17 billion on M&A, and $8 billion on fixed-asset acquisition on top of recycling its depreciation charge back into capital spending.

It did not require great financial acumen to see that even an AAA company could not spend two times its net income for long. In fact, eighteen months later GE's net income had fallen by 50 percent, its stock price was below $10 per share, and its CEO had begged for and received a massive government bailout of GE Capital's wobbly finances.

GE's financial filings, in fact, screamed with warnings that its highly engineered EPS was not remotely worth $42 per share. It was easy to see in its disclosures, for example, that the huge profits of its finance company were not true earnings, but the product of a lopsided tower of financial arbitrage wherein $600 billion of risky, illiquid assets were being propped up with massive debt and cheap hot-money funding.

As it happened, GE's sustainable earnings have been barely half of the hopped-up number it reported at the Greenspan bubble peak. During the two-year period through March 2011, for example, its EPS averaged only $1 per share, compared to the $2.20 per share in 2007.

Based on the forward-year earnings that it actually delivered, therefore, its stock price at the 2007 bubble peak was being valued at 40X. Not coincidently, at the peak of the 2000 dot-com bubble it had also traded at 40X, a valuation multiple as loony then as it was in 2007.

FINANCIAL ENGINEERING GONE WILD

As the roller-coaster ride of GE suggests, the monetary central planners were determined to get the stock averages back to year-2000 levels and to resuscitate $5 trillion of household net worth which had been vaporized by the dot-com crash. Therefore, a stock market continuously juiced by 50 percent "takeover premiums" and nonstop share repurchase campaigns suited the Fed's purpose.

As with the explosion of household mortgage debt, the Fed had no trouble remaining oblivious to the soaring business debt which underpinned these financial engineering ploys, maneuvers, and outright scams. As the latter mushroomed throughout the corporate world, the stock averages rose mightily, and that was the main thing. After all, the purpose of stock market levitation was to induce households to spend because they felt richer, whether they actually were or not.

Not surprisingly, financial TV happily parroted the Wall Street shibboleth that massive corporate spending for buybacks and M&A on the floor of the New York Stock Exchange proved American business leaders were bullish on the future. What it actually proved, however, was that runaway financial engineering was generating unheard of levels of Wall Street profitability from speculative trading and transaction fees and finance. In 2007, for example, global M&A fees alone reached $50 billion, compared to an average of $20 billion per year during 2002–2004. And this was a tiny tip of the iceberg.

Not surprisingly, the Fed's meeting minutes from 2007 do not evince even a hint of worry that the surging stock market averages were being "bought" by means of massive cash and equity extraction from the balance sheets of American business. Nor was there any recognition that the deluge of financial engineering transactions was reaching a truly freakish extreme.

For example, as recently as 2005, M&A deals in the United States had totaled about $1 trillion and at that point represented an all-time record. Yet during the second quarter of 2007, the annualized run rate of M&A deals hit nearly $3 trillion. At the same time, prices paid for new deals were soaring.

Takeover premiums thus reached an all-time high of 60 percent compared to a traditional norm of 25–30 percent, while purchase multiples literally flew off the charts. Compared to a traditional ratio of total enterprise value to EBITDA of five to six times, the average purchase multiple during the mid-2007 deal frenzy exceeded eleven times EBITDA.

During the same quarter, new LBOs clocked in at an $800 billion run rate, four times higher than a few years earlier. And in the third quarter of 2007, stock buybacks shot the moon, hitting a run rate of $1 trillion annualized. That compared to $300 billion per year as recently as 2004, which at the time was considered robust.

These trends in the aggregate volume of financial engineering transactions were truly an aberration. Yet they did not trouble the nation's monetary central planners because all three variations were rationalized as representing the free will of the free market.

This proposition had been stoutly embraced by the supreme voice of monetary authority, Chairman Greenspan, and had become catechism in the Eccles Building. Indeed, over the years the maestro had continuously lent his imprimatur to this deal mania, praising it as evidence of a robust market for corporate control.

Buyouts, buybacks, and takeovers, Greenspan explained, all embodied the free market at work, recycling capital and other business resources to higher and better uses. In so doing, he claimed, this energetic market for corporate control endowed the US economy with unparalleled flexibility and capacity for self-renewal, a dynamism largely unavailable to its competitors elsewhere in the developed world.

As in so much else, Greenspan was right in theory but failed to recognize that free markets go haywire when inundated with unsound money and central bank manipulation of key financial prices, like interest rates and stock indices. Accordingly, the idealized financial market which Greenspan envisioned may have existed once upon a time, but had long since disappeared. Its demise was owing to the post-1971 rise of printing-press money and, especially, the Wall Street–coddling version of monetary central planning that, ironically, the maestro had himself fashioned during his long tenure as chairman of the Fed.

PROOF OF DEFORMATION:
GENERAL ELECTRIC'S AAA TOWER OF DEBT

The evidence that Greenspan's idealized markets were actually vast financial deformations was in plain sight in the case of General Electric, whose CEO sat on the prestigious advisory board of the New York Fed in good crony capitalist fashion. Had CEO Jeff Immelt only been asked to describe GE's financial engineering binge, it might have given pause even to the money printers.

For much of his nineteen years at the helm, Jack Welch had conned Wall Street into embracing the financially impossible; namely, that GE's mammoth, highly cyclical, globe-spanning businesses could generate clocklike growth of "operating profit," hitting the company's guidance to the penny.

These monotonously (and comically) reliable gains came straight from the accounting cookie jar, but at least under Welch they were profits that GE had earned the old-fashioned way: out of fanatical cost discipline, product innovation, and aggressive marketing. The cookie jar didn't invent profits, it just shuffled and smoothed them among the quarters, as needed.

But after Welch's retirement, General Electric had gone all-in for financial engineering of a less innocent type. Between early 2000 and early 2008, its total debt doubled from $400 billion to $800 billion, and most of this had gone into stock buybacks, M&A deals, and purchase of both operating and financial assets at rates which were self-evidently unsustainable.

Its fevered borrowings were not hidden from either investors or the authorities, or the ratings agencies. According to its SEC filings, GE's balance sheet grew by $100 billion just in fiscal 2007, or by 19 percent. And the smoking gun was plain to see. Only $4 billion of this sizzling growth had been funded by equity; $81 billion was attributable to new debt and the balance to sundry other fixed liabilities.

Something was rotten in Denmark when the nation's top blue chip AAA-rated credit was expanding aggressively on 96 percent leverage, and resorting to balance sheet contortions to feed the stock market with a rising quotient of engineered EPS. Yet the Fed blithely persevered in its prosperity management gig, coaxing the stock averages higher through mid-2007 in an attempt to perk up GDP growth with more of its wealth-effect elixir.

THE "EARNINGS EX-ITEMS" SMOKE SCREEN

One of the reasons that the monetary politburo was unconcerned about the blatant buying of earnings through financial engineering is that it fully subscribed to the gussied-up version of EPS peddled by Wall Street. The latter was known as "operating earnings" or "earning ex-items," and it was derived by removing from the GAAP (generally accepted accounting principles)-based financial statements filed with the SEC any and all items which could be characterized as "one-time" or "nonrecurring."

These adjustments included asset write-downs, goodwill write-offs, and most especially "restructuring" charges to cover the cost of head-count reductions, including severance payments. Needless to say, in an environment in which labor was expensive and debt was cheap, successive waves of corporate downsizings could be undertaken without the inconvenience of a pox on earnings due to severance costs; these charges were "one time" and to be ignored by investors.

Likewise, there was no problem with the high failure rate of M&A deals. In due course, dumb investments could be written off and the resulting losses wouldn't "count" in earnings ex-items.

In short, Wall Street's institutionalized fiddle of GAAP earnings made PE multiples appear far lower than they actually were, and thereby helped perpetuate the myth that the market was "cheap" during the second Greenspan stock market bubble. Thus, as the S&P 500 index reached its nosebleed peaks around 1,500 in mid-2007, Wall Street urged investors not to worry because the PE multiple was within its historic range.

In fact, the 500 S&P companies recorded net income ex-items of $730 billion in 2007 relative to an average market cap during the year of $13 trillion. The implied PE multiple of 18X was not over the top, but then it wasn't on the level, either. The S&P 500 actually reported GAAP net income that year of only $587 billion, a figure that was 20 percent lower owing to the exclusion of $144 billion of charges and expenses that were deemed "non-recurring." The actual PE multiple on GAAP net income was 22X, however, and that was expensive by any historic standard, and especially at the very top of the business cycle.

During 2008 came the real proof of the pudding. Corporations took a staggering $304 billion in write-downs for assets which were drastically overvalued and business operations which were hopelessly unprofitable. Accordingly, reported GAAP net income for the S&P 500 plunged to just $132 billion, meaning that during the course of the year the average market cap of $10 trillion represented 77X net income.

To be sure, after the financial crisis cooled off the span narrowed considerably between GAAP legal earnings and the Wall Street "ex-items" rendition of profits, and not surprisingly in light of how much was thrown into the kitchen sink in the fourth quarter of 2008. Even after this alleged house cleaning, however, more than $100 billion of charges and expenses were excluded from Wall Street's reckoning of the presumptively "clean" S&P earnings reported for both 2009 and 2010.

So, if the four years are taken as a whole, the scam is readily evident. During this period, Wall Street claimed that the S&P 500 posted cumulative net income of $2.42 trillion. In fact, CEOs and CFOs required to sign the Sarbanes-Oxley statements didn't see it that way. They reported net income of $1.87 trillion. The difference was accounted for by an astounding $550 billion in corporate losses that the nation's accounting profession insisted were real, and that had been reported because the nation's securities cops would have sent out the paddy wagons had they not been.

During the four-year round trip from peak-to-bust-to-recovery, the S&P 500 had thus traded at an average market cap of $10.6 trillion, representing nearly twenty-three times the average GAAP earnings reported during that period. Not only was that not "cheap" by any reasonable standard, but it was also indicative of the delusions and deformations that the Fed's bubble finance had injected into the stock market.

In fact, every dollar of the $550 billion of charges during 2007–2010 that Wall Street chose not to count represented destruction of shareholder value. When companies chronically overpaid for M&A deals, and then four years later wrote off the goodwill, that was an "ex-item" in the Wall Street version of earnings, but still cold corporate cash that had gone down the drain. The same was true with equipment and machinery write-off when plants were shut down or leases written off when stores were closed. Most certainly, there was destruction of value when tens of billions were paid out for severance, health care, and pensions during the waves of head-count reductions.

To be sure, some of these charges represented economically efficient actions under any circumstances; that is, when the Schumpeterian mechanism of creative destruction was at work. The giant disconnect, however, is that these actions and the resulting charges to GAAP income statements were not in the least "one time." Instead, they were part of the recurring cost of doing business in the hot-house economy of interest rate repression, central bank puts, rampant financial speculation, and mercantilist global trade that arose from the events of August 1971.

The economic cost of business mistakes, restructurings, and balance sheet house cleaning can be readily averaged and smoothed, an appropriate accounting treatment because these costs are real and recurring. Accordingly, the four-year average experience for the 2007–2010 market cycle is illuminating.

The Wall Street "ex-item" number for S&P 500 net income during that period overstated honest accounting profits by an astonishing 30 percent. Stated differently, the time-weighted PE multiple on an ex-items basis was already at an exuberant 17.6X. In truth, however, the market was actually valuing true GAAP earnings at nearly 23X.

This was a truly absurd capitalization rate for the earnings of a basket of giant companies domiciled in a domestic economy where economic growth was grinding to a halt. It was also a wildly excessive valuation for earnings that had been inflated by $5 trillion of business debt growth owing to buybacks, buyouts, and takeovers.

CHAPTER 23

THE RANT THAT SHOOK THE ECCLES BUILDING

How the Fed Got Cramer'd

FTER CLIMBING STEADILY FOR FOUR AND A HALF YEARS, THE stock market weakened during August 2007 under the growing weight of the housing and mortgage debacle. Yet in response to what was an exceedingly mild initial sell-off, the Fed folded faster than a lawn chair in a desperate attempt to prop up the stock averages. The "Bernanke Put" was thus born with a bang.

The frenetic rate cutting cycle which ensued in the fall of 2007 was a virtual reenactment of the Fed's easing panics of 2001, 1998, and 1987. As in those episodes, the stock market had again become drastically overvalued relative to the economic and profit fundamentals. But rather than permit a long overdue market correction, the monetary central planners began once more to use all the firepower at their disposal to block it.

The degree to which the Bernanke Fed had been taken hostage by Wall Street was evident in its response to Jim Cramer's famous rant on CNBC on August 3, 2007, when he denounced the Fed as a den of fools: "They are nuts. They know nothing . . . the Fed is asleep. . . . My people have been in the game for 25 years . . . these firms are going out of business . . . open the darn [discount] window."

In going postal, Cramer was not simply performing as a CNBC commentator, but functioning as the public avatar for legions of petulant day traders who had taken control of the stock market during the long years Greenspan coddled Wall Street. What the Fed utterly failed to realize was that these now-dominant Cramerites had nothing to do with free markets or price discovery among traded equities.

AUGUST 2007: WHEN THE FED CAPITULATED
TO FINANCIAL HOODLUMS

The idea of price discovery in the stock market was now an ideological illusion. The market had been taken over by white-collar financial hoodlums who needed a trading fix every day. Through Cramer's megaphone, these punters and speculators were asserting an entitlement to any and all government policy actions which might be needed to keep the casino running at full tilt.

If that had not been clear before August 2007, the truth emerged on live TV. The nation's central bank was in thrall to a hissy fit by day traders. In a post the next day, the astute fund manager Barry Ritholtz summarized the new reality perfectly: "I have two words for Jim: Moral Hazard. Contrary to everything we learned under Easy Alan Greenspan, it is not the Fed's role to backstop speculators and guarantee a one way market."

Yet that is exactly what it did. Within days of the rant which shook the Eccles Building, the Fed slashed its discount rate, abruptly ending its tepid campaign to normalize the money markets. By early November the funds rate had been reduced by 75 basis points, and by the end of January it was down another 150 basis points. As of early May 2008 a timorous central bank had redelivered the money market to the Wall Street Cramerites. Although the US economy was saturated with speculative excess, the Fed was once again shoveling out 2 percent money to put a floor under the stock market.

This stock-propping campaign was not only futile, but also an exercise in monetary cowardice; it only intensified Wall Street's petulant bailout demands when the real crisis hit a few months later. Indeed, on the day of Cramer's rant in early August 2007, the S&P 500 closed at 1,433. The broad market index thus stood only 7 percent below the all-time record high of 1,553, which had been reached just ten days earlier in late July.

Ten days of modest slippage from the tippy-top of the charts was hardly evidence of Wall Street distress. Even after it drifted slightly lower during the next two weeks, closing at 1,406 on August 15, the stock market was still comfortably above the trading levels which prevailed as recently as January 2007.

Still, the Fed threw in the towel the next day with a dramatic 50 basis point cut in the discount rate. Although no demonstration was really needed, the nation's central bank had now confirmed, and abjectly so, that it was ready and willing to be bullied by Cramerite day traders and hedge fund speculators. The latter had suffered a "disappointing" four weeks at the casino; they wanted their juice and wanted it now.

Needless to say, the stock market cheered the Fed's capitulation, with the Dow rising by 300 points at the open on August 17. The chief economist for Standard & Poor's harbored no doubt that the Fed's action was a decisive signal to Wall Street to resume the party: "It's not just a symbolic action. The Fed is telling banks that the discount window is open. Take what you need."

The banks did exactly that and so the party resumed for another few months. By the second week of October the market was up 10 percent, enabling the S&P 500 to reach its historic peak of 1,565, a level which has not been approached since then.

Pouring on the monetary juice and signaling to speculators that it once again had their backs, the Fed thus wasted its resources and authority for a silly and fleeting prize: it was able to pin the stock market index to the top rung of its historic charts for the grand duration of about six weeks in the fall of 2007. There was no more to it, and no possible excuse for its panic rate cutting.

HOW THE FED GOT CRAMER'D

The Fed's abject surrender to the Cramerite tantrums in the fall of 2007 was rooted in ten years of Wall Street coddling. Mesmerized by its new "wealth effects" doctrine, the Fed viewed the stock market like the famous Las Vegas ad: it didn't want to know what went on there, and was therefore oblivious to the deeply rooted deformations which had become institutionalized in the financial markets. The sections below are but a selective history of how the nation's central bank finally reached the ignominy of being Cramer'd by financial TV's number one clown.

The monetary central planners only cared that the broad stock averages kept rising so that the people, feeling wealthier, would borrow and spend more. It falsely assumed that what was going on inside the basket of 8,000 publicly traded stocks was just the comings and goings of the free market—and that this was a matter of tertiary concern, if any at all, to a mighty central bank in the business of managing prosperity and guiding the daily to-and-fro of a $14 trillion economy.

But what was actually going on in the interior of the stock market was nightmarish. All of the checks and balances which ordinarily discipline the free market in money instruments and capital securities were being eviscerated by the Fed's actions; that is, the Greenspan Put, the severe repression of interest rates, and the recurrent dousing of the primary dealers with large dollops of fresh cash owing to its huge government bond purchases.

This kind of central bank action has pernicious consequences, however. By pegging money market rates, it fosters carry trades that are a significant contributor to unbalanced markets. Carry trades create an artificially enlarged bid for risk assets. So prices trend asymmetrically upward.

The Greenspan Put also compounded the one-way bias. For hedge fund speculators, it amounted to ultra-cheap insurance against downside risk in the broad market. This, too, attracted money flows and an inordinate rise in speculative long positions.

The Fed's constant telegraphing of intentions regarding its administered money market rates also exacerbated the stock market imbalance. By pegging the federal funds rate, it eliminated the risk of surprise on the front end of the yield curve. Consequently, massive amounts of new credit were created in the wholesale money markets as traders hypothecated and rehypothecated existing securities; that is, pledged the same collateral for multiple loans.

The Fed's peg on short-term rates thus fostered robust expansion of the shadow banking system, which as indicated previously, had exploded from $2 trillion to $21 trillion during Greenspan's years at the helm. This vast multiplication of non-bank credit further fueled the "bid" for stocks and other risk assets.

Fear of capital loss, fear of surprise, fear of insufficient liquidity—these are the natural "shorts" on the free market. The paternalistic Dr. Greenspan, trying to help the cause of prosperity, thus took away the market's natural short. In so doing, he brought central banking full circle. William McChesney Martin said the opposite; that is, he counseled taking away the punch bowl, thereby adding to the short. Now the punch bowl was overflowing and the short was gone.

Speculators were emboldened to bid, leverage their bid, and then to bid again for assets in what were increasingly one-way markets. As time passed, more and more speculations and manipulations emerged to capitalize on these imbalances.

"Growth stocks" were always a favored venue because they could be bid-up on short-term company news, quarterly performance, and rumors of performance (i.e., "channel checks"). During these ramp jobs, which ordinarily spanned only weeks, months, or quarters, traders could be highly confident that the Fed had interest rates pegged and the broad market propped.

Financial engineering plays such as M&A and buybacks came to be especially favored venues because these trades tended to be event triggered. Upon rumors and announcements, these trades could generate rapid replication and money flows. Again, speculators were confident that the Fed had their back, while leveraged punters were pleased that it had seconded to them its wallet in the form of cheap wholesale funding.

At length, the stock market was transformed into a place to gamble and chase, not an institution in which to save and invest. Since this gambling hall had been fostered by the central bank rather than the free market, it was not on the level. That means that most of the time most of the players won and, as shown below, the big hedge funds which traded on Wall Street's inside track with its inside information won especially big and unusually often.

Needless to say, frequent wins and hefty windfalls created expectations for more and more, and still more winning hands. As the Greenspan bubbles steadily inflated—both in 1997–2000 and 2003–2007—these expectations morphed into virtual Wall Street demands that the Fed keep the party going. Wall Street demands for a permanent party, at length, congealed into the presumption of an entitlement to an ever rising market, or at least one the Fed would never let falter or slump.

Finally, this entitlement-minded stock market became a blooming, buzzing madhouse of petulance, impatience, and greed. Cramer embodied it and spoke for it. By the time of his rant, the Fed had become captive of the monster it had created. Now, fearing to say no, it became indentured to juicing the beast. After August 17, 2007, there was no longer even the pretense of reasoning or deliberation about policy options in the Eccles Building. The only options were the ones that had gotten it there: print, peg, and prop.

DEAL MANIA I: THE RISE OF "CHASE AND CRASH"

One of the great ironies of the Greenspan bubbles was that the free market convictions of the maestro enabled the Fed to drift steadily and irreversibly into its eventual submission to the Cramerite intimidation. It did so by turning a blind eye to lunatic speculations in the stock market, dismissing them, apparently, as the exuberances of capitalist boys and girls playing too hard.

By the final years of the first Greenspan bubble, however, there were plenty of warning signals that there was more than exuberance going on. Hit-and-run momentum trading and vast money flows into the stocks of serial M&A operations were signs that normal market disciplines were not working. Indeed, the M&A mania was a powerful indictment of the Fed's prosperity management model.

These hyperactive deal companies with booming share prices were being afflicted ever more frequently with sudden stock price implosions that couldn't have been merely random failures on the free market. Yet, as in the case of the subprime mania, the central planners undoubtedly read the headlines about these recurring corporate blowups and never bothered to connect the dots.

The WorldCom train wreck of 2001, for example, was as much a consequence of Bernie Ebbers' penchant for serial M&A as it was the result of his desperate efforts to cook the books when his deal making failed. Years of overpaying for acquisitions and the incurrence of massive debts finally came home to roost when WorldCom announced a shocking $20 billion goodwill write-off in the spring of 2001. Celebrated for years by the financial press for its prowess in deal making and as a pioneer in the deregulated long-distance phone market, the stock imploded on the spot. It had been a debt-ridden house of cards all along.

The two telecom equipment flameouts of that era, Nortel and Lucent, had also been hotbeds of serial M&A. In the short span between April 1998 and late 2000, for example, Nortel had completed nearly two dozen deals valued at more than $30 billion. Not to be outdone, Lucent had executed a new deal almost every month during the same period, racking up $44 billion in total M&A transactions in less than three years.

Yet after the 2001 crash landing of these two telecom equipment giants, any residual value from this barrage of acquisitions was hard to find. By September 2002, for example, Lucent's market cap had plunged to just $4 billion, meaning that its three-year spree of M&A deals were being valued at essentially zero after giving even minimum value to its massive base of assets, customers, and technology inherited from its prior one-hundred-year history as Western Electric.

Likewise, Nortel's market cap peaked at $400 billion. Twenty-four months later it crashed and burned, its market cap reduced to a $5 billion rounding error. Again, Lucent and Nortel had not been shooting stars off the pink sheets or highflyers inhabiting the margins of the economy. They were the giant former equipment divisions of the Bell Telephone monopolies in the United States and Canada, and had $60 billion of sales and 200,000 employees between them.

As monsters of the deal maker's midway, they had dominated financial TV and were omnipresent in the investment banking and trading precincts of Wall Street. So when they imploded in a sudden, fiery crash, it was a sign that something was haywire in the stock market.

Still, the ultimate monument to the merger mania which became pandemic by the end of the first Greenspan bubble was the JDS Uniphase acquisition of SDL. The deal had been announced on July 10, 2000, a date which was virtually the high noon of the tech frenzy. At that moment the market cap of JDS Uniphase was $90 billion and it paid $40 billion for SDL.

Soon thereafter, however, the market value of the combined firms deflated so rapidly and violently as to evoke Ross Perot's famous "sucking sound to the south." By early 2002, the post-merger company traded at just $2 billion, meaning that 98 percent of its high-noon market cap had been wiped out. What had been advertised at the time as the largest M&A

deal in tech industry history had, in fact, been a merger of bottled air all along.

THE GREENSPAN PUT AND THE DEFORMATION OF M&A

The first Greenspan bubble provided fair warning about the dangers of rampant financial engineering. This unprecedented wave of M&A had not only supplied rocket fuel for the final stock market blow-off, but also had frequently generated the flaming mishaps mentioned above; that is, failures too ludicrous to be chalked up as ordinary business mistakes on the free market.

In fact, the Wall Street coddling monetary régime which became institutionalized during the Greenspan era had deeply transformed M&A. What had traditionally been a limited tool of corporate business strategy became an all-encompassing mechanism for speculative finance. It generated a steady diet of windfalls for takeover speculators and generous exit stipends for the top executives of target companies. On the other side of the table, top executives at acquiring companies obtained a mechanism to build empires, stock options, and an interval of apparent, if unsustainable, earnings growth.

Another attribute of this new-style financialized M&A was also critical; namely, that it put paid to the idea that there existed an honest "market for corporate control." Irrationally high takeover premiums, giant golden parachutes for target company executives, blatant abuse of merger accounting reserves, and spectacular crash landings of M&A empires like WorldCom and Lucent were evidence of an excess supply of takeover finance, not an abundance of undervalued corporate assets.

By the late 1990s, M&A had more often than not become an instrument of corporate value destruction. Companies were routinely paying such huge takeover premiums as to preclude any reasonable probability that they could be earned back through synergy. Yet the free market failed to arrest this spree of value destruction because its natural checks and balances were disabled.

As in so many other venues, monetary distortion was the culprit. During the final forty-month interval leading up to the April 2000 stock market peak, the Fed fostered a speculative environment on Wall Street that rivaled the late 1920s. The S&P 500 index doubled and NASDAQ quadrupled. At the same time, the Fed's panicked response to the LTCM crisis in September 1998 left no doubt that downside risk had been sharply neutered by the Greenspan Put.

Given this febrile environment, it is not surprising that deal making quickly became nonsensical and reckless. Empire-building CEOs in the tech, telecom, finance, and diversified sectors, among others, had little reason to fear that their stock prices would be punished owing to dilution from overpaying for acquisitions. Potential hits to earnings per share were being obfuscated by short-term "accounting benefits" from merger reserve kitties and wildly expanding PE multiples.

Owing to Wall Street expectations that the Fed wouldn't allow the market to falter, the damage from rampant financial engineering remained hidden below the surface. The normal disciplinary forces of the free market were thus disabled, even as the runaway M&A spree was heralded as an expression of free market vigor.

In the late 1990s professor Mark Sower of Columbia University published a startling finding from an extensive study of M&A deals; namely, that 65 percent of large mergers destroyed shareholder value: "Clearly this negative evidence raises serious doubt over the value of the takeover market as a mechanism for disciplining poor-performing or self-dealing managers as proposed by the market for corporate control hypothesis."

That was a heavy-duty proposition because it stripped corporate takeovers of their beneficent aura. The dislocations visited upon takeover targets were supposed to generate efficiency gains, improved asset utilization, and other economic synergies which would yield higher profits. Yet if shareholders of acquiring companies in the main do not benefit from M&A deals, then takeovers are just a random generator of unearned rents.

This goes to the very heart of bubble finance: it took M&A out of the toolbox of corporate asset management and transformed it into a thundering stampede of Wall Street rent seeking. In fact, the huge "announcement" gains in takeover stock prices are exactly the type of capricious windfalls generated by casinos, not honest capital markets. On the evidence, therefore, Wall Street became a veritable geyser of unearned M&A rents during the bull market top of 1998–2000, a pattern which would repeat itself in 2005–2007.

That most M&A deals fail was taken as a given by the Wall Street cynics who practiced the merger trade. But as that truism became evident in the 1990s M&A takeover spree, it posed an acute challenge to Greenspan's own doctrine, under which it was axiomatic that the free markets could not be wrong two-thirds of the time.

The monetary central planners in the Eccles Building did not resolve this contradiction, or even acknowledge that the eruption of M&A was destroying value, not expressing free market impulses. Instead, they embraced the merger wave because their prosperity management model required that stock prices be levitated at all hazards.

DENNIS KOZLOWSKI: BUBBLE FINANCE PERSONIFIED

The Fed should have been embarrassed by the M&A frenzy, and Dennis Kozlowski was striking evidence of why. He had been Wall Street's favorite 1990s deal maker and master builder of Tyco International Ltd., a confection of serial M&A deals which put AOL Time Warner, WorldCom, and the rest of the corporate deal junkies to shame.

On their face, Tyco's facts were absurd. Between 1992 and 2002, for example, it completed upward of one thousand M&A deals worth a stunning $70 billion. The result was a motley hybrid: part deal machine, part closed-end mutual fund, and mainly a hodgepodge of cast-offs and orphans from throughout corporate America.

When this pell-mell acquisition spree caused Tyco's reported sales to soar from $7 billion in 1997 to $34 billion by 2001, the 50 percent per annum rate of sales growth did not signify that underperforming business assets were being recycled to better and more efficient uses. Instead, it showed that Tyco was a whirling dervish of financial engineering that had no plausible business justification.

In fact, its real purpose was providing a vehicle for absorbing the powerful waves of Wall Street speculation unleashed by the Greenspan Fed. The hapless Dennis Kozlowski didn't create Tyco International; Wall Street did, stampeded by speculators who had come to believe that the Fed would never let the party fail.

Indeed, the veritable explosion of Tyco's stock price after the mid-1990s was proof positive that the Greenspan stock market bubble was rooted in a monetary deformation. Tyco was the very embodiment of an anti-dot-com enterprise: a prosaic assemblage of old-economy businesses which on an organic basis grew at less than 3 percent per year by the company's own reckoning. Yet its stock price soared from $25 per share in early 1994 to a peak of $250 per share in January 2001.

This tech-style 10X gain in its share price was not due to a commensurate explosion of profits. What did explode was the company's valuation multiple. The latter rose from 17X EPS in 1994, which was already too generous for an industrial conglomerate, to a peak of 67X in late 1999, which was pure madness.

At that point, the stock market was obviously turning a blind eye to the warning signs emanating from virtually every pore of the company's balance sheet. Between 1994 and 2001, for example, the company's $500 million of debt soared to $43 billion, meaning that its debt burden grew ninety-fold in seven years. Not surprisingly, its goodwill zoomed from $1 billion to $40 billion, reflecting the company's chronic overpayment for acquisitions, while its tangible shareholder equity went straight south, reaching negative $20 billion by the end of 2001.

Kozlowski ended up the chump whose visage in the pantheon of America's greatest CEOs was removed at a speed rivaling that of politburo portraits in Stalinist Russia. After a hurried do over by the financial press, Kozlowski was rechristened as the rogue CEO who stuck his shareholders with $6,000 shower curtains and a $2 million birthday party on Sardinia featuring an ice sculpture of Michelangelo's *David* urinating Stolichnaya vodka.

The true sin in the matter, however, was a financial environment that carried Tyco's market cap to $125 billion by 2001, when it was plainly a disheveled trunk of pots and pans from America's industrial pawnshop, led by a crude schemer who couldn't resist the bait. The bait, of course, was the kind of bull market hagiography which put him on the cover of *Business Week* in 2001 as America's most aggressive CEO.

Needless to say, the deflation of Tyco's wildly bloated stock value came fast and furious. By the time Kozlowski was forced out in June 2002, the company's market cap stood at only $25 billion. More than $100 billion of market cap had vaporized in less than six months.

That kind of violent repricing does not occur on the free market, and wasn't owing to the discovery that some of Kozlowski's pay and perks had not been diligently vetted by the board. Rather, Tyco was the poster boy for Greenspan's first stock market bubble and its sudden, violent demise was a wake-up call that was wholly ignored.

WHEN MOMENTUM TRADERS STRIPPED CEW FROM THE LAND

The Fed's frenetic interest rate cutting and renewed commitment to the Greenspan Put after December 2000 generated another spree of financial engineering. In all three variations, buybacks, buyouts, and M&A takeovers, the common effect was equity extraction from the business sector. However, unlike the case of mortgage equity withdrawal by households, where the cash windfall was distributed widely across the middle class, corporate equity withdrawal resulted mainly in cash distributions to the very top of the economic ladder. In generating a cornucopia of CEW, therefore, financial engineering functioned as the ATM of the prosperous classes.

That CEW went overwhelmingly to the bank accounts of the wealthy is a balance sheet given. By the end of the first Greenspan bubble, about 80 percent of financial assets were owned by the top 10 percent of households, which therefore got at least 80 percent of the cash from buyouts and buybacks. In fact, far more than a proportionate share went to the top, and even then the windfall was not so egalitarian in the manner in which it was whacked up among the affluent classes. Among the 10 percent at the top, it was the 1 percent at the very top who got the lion's share of the CEW.

The reason for this ultra-skew to the very top lies in the subtle and convoluted manner in which monetary inflation deforms the financial markets. What happens is that cheap credit and market-pegging actions by the central bank foster an irregular and syncopated path of financial asset inflation. This bumpy rise is punctuated by sudden windfall gains in stocks and other risk assets which occur with increasing scale and frequency.

These windfalls are heavily "event" driven, as in the case of 75 percent M&A takeover premiums, corporate announcements of giant stock buyback programs, and the huge short-term price ramps that periodically occur among so-called growth stocks. By providing opportunities for outsized rewards to agile traders, as distinguished from fundamental investors, such event driven windfalls recruit more and more speculators to the craps tables.

During the first Greenspan bubble, these storied windfall events and episodes arose initially from the tech sector, such as when Cisco's stock hit its red-hot stage and witnessed a $350 billion market cap gain in just eight months. In like manner, Intel once gained $250 billion in only four months; the stock price of JDS Uniphase tripled in three months; and, of course, tech IPOs were even more spectacular. Beginning with Netscape's $14 to $78 per share ramp on August 9, 1995, these tech IPOs often produced massive gains in a single day.

Moreover, while the 10X stock price gains in deal companies like Time Warner, Lucent, and Enron required a slightly greater time frame to unfold, they, too, embodied the principle of rocket-ship gains. So the turbulent financial asset markets which were endemic to the Fed's money-printing campaigns fostered a growing posse of financial storm riders.

In the fullness of time, this posse became an enormous swarm. The Greenspan Fed thus fostered the mother of all malinvestments; namely, the massive array of hedge funds, private equity firms, highly leveraged real estate partnerships and like venues that flourished around and about Wall Street and came to constitute the fast money trading complex.

These financial vehicles were pleased to call themselves "investment" partnerships, but their game was speculative trading, frequently with leverage in all its forms. They pursued numerous strategies and techniques, but the common denominator was foraging in a financial arena that offered outsized returns based on inside information.

To be clear, the implication is not that the fast money trading complex was involved in something illegal, such as trading based on the foggy concept of corporate inside information of the type proscribed by the SEC. Rather, the "inside information" at issue here was mainly legal; it was inside knowledge of what the Wall Street wise guys were chasing as the flavor of the week, or day, or sometimes even the hour.

Stated differently, lightning fast triple-digit stock price gains or sudden $100 billion market cap demolitions do not happen much on the free market in response to fundamental investment research. In fact, genuine value-changing information capable of causing violent price movements can only rarely be kept secret and sprung on the market without warning; it is the vast exception, not the rule.

By contrast, the stock market "rips" and "wrecks" that became chronic during the Greenspan era were signs that the financial system had been corrupted and deformed by a régime of credit inflation and easy money. After all, what causes asset prices to rise like greased lightning or plunge like a hot knife through butter is the whispered tips of speculators. And easy credit and an accommodative central bank are the mother's milk of speculation.

HEDGE FUNDS AND THE REGIME OF INSIDER TRADING

Accordingly, as the Fed transformed Wall Street into a casino, the mechanisms and arrangements for insider speculation took on massive size. In 1990, hedge fund footings amounted to about $150 billion; by the turn of the century, they had reached $1 trillion; and by the 2007–2008 peak, they had soared to $3.0 trillion.

The scale of hedge fund operations thus grew by twenty times in as many years. At the same time, the trading books of the Wall Street banks grew even more explosively, expanding by thirty times during this period to approximately $3 trillion. Together that formed the inner arena of speculative finance, the fast money complex.

Moreover, the highest-value information inside this mushrooming fast money complex was not about the corporate issuers of the securities being traded; it was about the bets being made by other traders. Likewise, the most valuable corporate information was about tradable news events: quarterly financial results and financial engineering moves, not fundamental business trends and strategies which actually drive long-term value.

Needless to say, the last thing hedge funds do is hedge, an economic service that might actually contribute some value added in a capitalist economy. What hedge funds actually do is churn, chase, pump, and dump. They play wagering games which extract economic rents but contribute little if any value added to the Main Street economy.

Wall Street is the link between financial engineering in the corporate sector and the wagering games of the hedge fund complex. Wall Street originates financial engineering transactions in its investment banking departments; it then lubricates the hedge fund complex with information and trading services out of its prime brokerage operations. What washes from one side of the Street to the other is the high-powered trading tips and gossip out of which momentum surges arise.

Thus Wall Street investment bankers advise corporate boards about the size and timing of stock buybacks. Educated guesses leak out. Significant corporate M&A transactions are only undertaken with the good-housekeeping seal of a Wall Street "league table" advisor. More hints leak out.

Leveraged buyouts are even more Wall Street centered because they encompass multiple sets of M&A advisors and also activate the vast machinery needed to underwrite and syndicate junk bonds and leveraged loan facilities. The deal process for LBOs leaks like a sieve, even before the required SEC filings are made.

Needless to say, the market-moving information which pours in from all of these sources excites small waves of buying or selling, as the case may be, among insiders in the fast money trading complex. These wavelets periodically attract reinforcements, thereby imparting momentum and more replication of the original trades.

At length, full-powered momentum trades become energized, and money piles on from the four corners of the hedge fund universe, along with that of momentum-chasing mutual fund managers, retail punters, and computerized trading algorithms. In this manner, new rips are continuously mounted and sudden wrecks are quickly abandoned.

THE MOMOS AT WORK:
THE CHASE AND CRASH AT CROCS AND GARMIN

While many of the rips are so silly as to pass for financial humor, they do dramatize the extent to which the capital markets have been deformed. Left to its own devices, the free market would never deliver up the endless series of fad stocks and sectors which have flourished under the Fed's prosperity management régime. During 2006–2007, for example, one of the more preposterous shooting stars was Crocs, a maker of brightly colored blow-molded plastic shoes that were a cross between ugly and impractical.

Nevertheless, in response to an initial fad-driven sales boom, Crocs' stock price soared from $14 to $70 per share in only twelve months. At its peak, the stock sported a PE multiple of 40X, implying that the nation's closets would soon be jam-packed with polypropylene.

As it happened, however, Crocs' stock deflated back to $2 per share when the accounting illusion behind its spectacular growth became too evident to ignore. The culprit was its ballooning figures for accounts receivable and inventory, which rapidly became uglier than its shoes.

These ballooning balance sheet ratios had been reported every quarter. But only belatedly did the momentum chasers recognize their obvious meaning; namely, that Crocs had continued to produce and to ship massive volumes of inventory long after its podiatric clunkers went cold with the kids.

Since it couldn't dispose of its towering two hundred days of inventory or collect cash from the trade "stuffed" with all this unwanted product, it was only a matter of time before the jig was up. By the same token, there was never a time when Crocs was prosecuted for fraud, and for the good reason that there wasn't any.

In fact, the evidence that Crocs was a flash in the pan was contained in the company's SEC reports all along, but was resolutely ignored by the stock market punters. The data they cared about could not be found in 10Ks and 10Qs anyway; it consisted exclusively of stock price momentum indicators such as twenty-, fifty- or hundred-day moving averages, and numerous like and similar charting benchmarks embedded in the stock market's entrails.

Needless to say, Crocs was no outlier. There were hundreds of crocks just like it. During the two years prior to its October 2007 peak, for example, Garmin had been even more of a rocket ship. Its stock price had risen from $20 to $120 per share, only to crash back down to $20 a few months later. While its innovative portable GPS device for autos was actually a viable product, Garmin's peak EPS multiple of 40X was no more plausible than that for Crocs.

Even as the momentum traders heralded its 100 percent sales growth in the year ending December 2007, it was plainly evident that the auto companies were scrambling to install navigation systems as original equipment and that demand for Garmin's portable "aftermarket" product would dry up rapidly. In the event, its sales growth rate fell to 20 percent by June 2008 and turned negative by year end.

The fact that Garmin's sales today are actually 40 percent lower than their 2007 peak level was predictable at the time, since the new model cars carrying their own navigation systems were already in the well-advertised automotive pipeline. As the second Greenspan bubble approached its peak, therefore, it is evident that the stock market was not discounting future corporate sales, earnings, or much of anything else except the expectation of more juice from the Eccles Building.

By the time of the 2008 bubble peak, the great financial deformation reduced the stock market to a momentum-driven gambling hall. Indeed, the senseless overvaluation that punters affixed to the likes of Crocs and Garmin was cut from the same cloth as the implausibly high valuations which had been assigned to the home builders, the mortgage brokers, Fannie and Freddie, and the Wall Street investment banks themselves.

Yet as hundreds of other highflyers like the solar energy stocks, the teen retailers, and the casino stocks took their turn in this malignant pattern of chase and crash, apologists for the status quo always had the same answer. On the occasion of these crashes they advised onlookers to move along, insisting there was nothing to see except some minor breakage attendant to animal spirits that occasionally get too rambunctious.

HEDGE FUNDS AND THE RULE OF RIPS AND WRECKS

The Wall Street–hedge fund casino is all the more volatile because it deploys massive leverage in many forms. The tamest form of this leverage, funding obtained in the wholesale money and repo markets, is potent enough. As has been seen, most of the time the resulting carry trade produces handsome spreads and funds a steady bid leading to higher asset prices.

But at junctures of extreme financial stress, the high level of carry trade funding, which builds up during the bubble expansion, results in violent market reversals. In these circumstances, wholesale funding evaporates and involuntary asset sales cascade into a bidless abyss. The devastating broad market collapse of 2000–2003 (45 percent) and 2008–2009 (55 percent) was dramatic proof.

The most potent amplifier of volatility in the hedge fund arena, however, is the embedded leverage of options and OTC derivative concoctions. Exchange traded options require regulatory margin, of course, but in the case of momentum trades the margin factor actually turbocharges volatility.

Options are an accelerator on the way up, since no extra margin deposit is required as the underlying asset price rises, while on the way down, they become a widow maker: any price drop requires the posting of additional margin on a dollar-for-dollar basis. Needless to say, when momentum trades start cratering, the margin clerks become purveyors of pole grease.

Compared to exchange traded options, the OTC derivatives fashioned by Wall Street dealers are even more combustible. In these unregulated bilateral trades, margin requirements are not standard, regulated, or continuous, meaning that margin calls are often lumpy and precipitate; they tend to exacerbate losing positions as the dramatic, margin call–driven demise of Lehman, AIG, and MF Global demonstrated. Such OTC positions are also festooned with fillips like knock-out and knock-in triggers which produce drastic value changes when these defined trigger points are hit. In effect, these "weapons of financial mass destruction," as Warren Buffett once called them, can simulate leverage ratios so extreme and opaque that they cannot even be meaningfully quantified.

THE MYTH THAT SPECULATORS ARE LIQUIDITY PROVIDERS

The Wall Street fast money casino is thus land-mined with potent agents of volatility. Yet these huge and financially metastasized secondary markets are, paradoxically, portrayed by apologists as agents of economic advance. Hedge funds and Wall Street trading desks are held to be doing God's work; that is, providing trading liquidity in return for a tiny slice of the turnover.

What looks like churn and hit-and-run speculation, they contend, is actually a sideshow. The real function of these rollicking secondary markets is enabling corporate issuers to sell new securities efficiently and permitting savings suppliers such as pension funds, insurance companies, and 401(k) investors to smoothly enter and exit investment positions.

Like the case of Bernanke's Great Moderation, however, the truth is more nearly the opposite. The Fed's prosperity management régime has actually fostered a vast increase in capital market volatility, not a gain in liquidity. The proof is in the pudding. If these vast trading venues were meaningfully enhancing liquidity, then volatility would be abating over time, not reaching increasingly violent amplitudes and frequencies. In fact, the highly leveraged carry trades, the financial elixir of the Greenspan era, actually evaporate abruptly under stress and therefore amount to anti-liquidity.

True market makers, by contrast, minimize leverage in order to maximize their market-making capacity during periods of stress. By thus keeping their powder dry, they can take advantage of that part of the cycle where the bid-ask spread is the widest and dealers can earn above-average returns on their working inventory.

For these reasons, the liquidity function conducted by genuine dealers on the free market bears no resemblance to the leveraged, momentum-chasing prop traders. Beyond that, the free market seeks out efficient solutions to resource allocation, but having trillions of hedge fund capital absorbed in the "dealer" function does not meet that test by a long shot.

It can be correctly assumed, therefore, that the $6 trillion of hedge funds domiciled in Greenwich partnerships and Wall Street banks do not toil in the service of the Financial Almighty. They exist not to bring liquidity to asset markets, but to extract rents from them.

Needless to say, today's hedge funds do not operate on the free market, and they are neither dealers nor investors. Their business of hit-and-run speculation generates no economic value added but nonetheless attracts trillions of capital because the state and its central banking branch make it profitable.

Cheap cost of carry and the Greenspan-Bernanke Put are the foundation of this hothouse profitability. They mitigate what would otherwise be the substantial costs of funding portfolios at normalized interest rates and of reserving for asset price risk on the free market. Without these artificial economic boosts, the high-churn style of hedge fund speculation would be far less rewarding, if profitable at all.

THE "KEYNESIAN" FOUNDATION OF HEDGE FUNDS

What really makes hit-and-run speculation remunerative, however, is financial engineering in the corporate sector. It catalyzes momentum trades, a venue where the peculiar type of inside information which percolates through the Wall Street–hedge fund complex is concentrated. Indeed, financial engineering is what puts the "Keynesian beauty contest" principle of investment, as once described by John Maynard Keynes, at the front and center of the hedge fund trade.

In his famous 1936 treatise on macroeconomics, the learned professor prescribed how to compete in a theoretical newspaper contest to pick from among six pictures the girl the public would judge to be the prettiest. Keynes, who had been an inveterate speculator of some renown, advised not to pick the girl who appears to be the prettiest, or even the one that average opinion might select.

Parse the matter still further, he urged: "We have reached the third degree where we devote our intelligence to anticipating what average opinion expects the average opinion to be. And there are some, I believe, who practice the fourth, fifth and higher degrees."

Needless to say, there is much more snake oil of this tenor in the general theory of employment, interest, and money. But what Keynes wrote about the art of speculation in 1936 could not have been more apropos to the behavior of hedge funds in the deformed financial markets that his theories brought to full flower seventy-five years later.

Mr. Market has seen fit to deliver to the hedge fund complex $6 trillion of capital, which is to say, a wholly insensible amount. This anomaly is explainable, however, by the fact that hedge funds operate in a financial setting ideally suited to the great thinker's methodology.

Thanks to the Fed, momentum trading is cheap and reasonably safe from unforeseen general market declines. Yet individual stocks are volatile enough to enable traders to profitably practice the "Keynesian" method; that is, to trade what they judge other traders will be buying based on whatever pictures of the corporate contestants come their way from legal sources, or perhaps not.

Furthermore, the hedge fund industry ensures that only the astute judges in the Keynesian beauty contest thrive, or even survive. Capital is continuously reallocated and concentrated in hedge funds that get the momentum trades right; that is, hedge funds which buy stocks that others decide to buy.

At the same time, funds which are persistently wrong shrink rapidly or are completely liquidated. Quarterly withdrawal rights for investors are the key tool of this winnowing process, but the quite improbable mechanism of the "fund of funds" also plays a major role.

It is not immediately evident how much value-added fund of funds provide in return for their 5 percent share of investment profits plus fixed management fees, but it consists of advice to punters on where to punt based on the latest punting results from the universe of hedge fund punters. Stated differently, they perform a dispatching function, continuously reallocating capital based on short-term results—sometimes even daily and weekly—to the best-performing beauty contest judges.

This constant reallocation is vitally important owing to the heavy fee burden; that is, 20 percent to the hedge fund, 5 percent on top to the fund of funds, and the 2 percent management fee spread all around. It goes without saying that momentum trading has to be unusually successful in order to absorb such heavy fees, meaning that investors must quickly exit funds that are failing or treading water and scramble into partnerships that at the moment are surfing on winning waves.

So the fund of funds is essentially momentum traders of momentum traders. They function as financial concierges, scheduling and slotting their high-net-worth customers and other large investors into the right mix of hedge fund styles and short-term performance metrics.

Taken together, these allocation mechanisms are a potent financial laxative; they unclog immobile money and cause it to flow to the winning trades with a vengeance. The resulting uplift to any particular flavor-of-the-moment trade, in turn, begets more momentum chasing and further replication by new players who pile onto the rising tide.

PRIME BROKERS AND THE WHIRLIGIG OF WALL STREET FINANCE

Until winning trades finally finish their run and reverse direction, copycat replication is low risk because it is facilitated by the prime brokerage desks of the Wall Street banks. These desks keep their hedge fund clients posted on "what's working" for the hottest funds and, mirabile dictu, the flavor-of-the-moment bandwagon rapidly gains riders.

To be sure, Wall Street prime brokerage operations perform valid services such as margin lending, consolidated reporting, trade execution, and clearing and settlement. Indeed, it is the independent clearing functions of the prime brokers which safeguard against the Bernie Madoff style of self-cleared "trades" that were actually not all that.

In this independent trading and clearing function, however, Wall Street banking houses take in each other's laundry, unlike Madoff's in-house method. This means that the hedge funds embedded in each of the big banks—operations which are otherwise pleased to characterize themselves with meaningless distinctions such as "prop," "flow," and "hedge" traders—use one of the other banks as their prime broker.

JPMorgan's now infamous "London Whale" trading operation, for example, used Goldman Sachs as its prime broker. It would require a heavy dose of naïveté to believe that the invisible Chinese walls maintained by these two banking behemoths actually stop any useful trading and position information from circulating throughout the hedge fund complex.

Besides a steady diet of tips about hot trades, the hedge fund complex also needs incremental cash, preferably from low cost loans, in order to pile into rising trades. This, too, the prime brokers provide in abundance through what amounts to a variation of fractional reserve banking. The mechanism here is "rehypothecation," and it amounts to a miracle of modern finance.

Prime brokers are essentially in the business of selling used cars twice, or even multiple times. When they execute trades for a hot hand among their hedge fund customers, for example, they retain custody of the securities purchased on behalf of the customer. But under typical arrangements, the prime broker promptly posts these securities as collateral for its own borrowings; that is, it hocks its customer's property and uses the cash proceeds for its own benefit.

The precise benefit is that the prime broker relends the proceeds to another client who is advised to jump on the same trade with the new money. The resulting purchase of securities by the second customer begets even more collateral, which triggers another round of rehypothecation. Needless to say, this enables the prime broker to lend and whisper yet a third time, imparting even more momentum into the original trade. In this manner, financial rocket ships are born.

It is not surprising, therefore, that the hedge fund industry remains arrayed tightly around the brand name prime brokers: Goldman, Morgan

Stanley, JPMorgan, Merrill Lynch, and Barclays (nee Lehman). Indeed, the whole nexus of the Wall Street–hedge fund arena is cut from a single cloth.

The Wall Street investment banking departments supply financial engineering catalysts for the momentum trades, while their prime brokerages supply back-office services, cash, and inside tips to hedge fund customers, including prop traders and "hedging" desks within the Wall Street banks. The hallmark of this vast momentum trading arrangement, therefore, is that it is both incestuous and so highly fluid as to resemble a giant, undulating financial amoeba rather than a classic atomized marketplace of independent firms.

To this end, hedge funds come in and out of existence at dizzying rates, reflecting fluidity not even remotely matched in any other industry. In 2010, for example, 935 new hedge funds came into existence, while in 2009 more than 1,000 hedge funds were liquidated. Using common back-office infrastructure maintained by the prime brokers, the hedge fund complex is not so much a conventional industry as it is a giant moveable trade: Wall Street trading desks frequently morph into independent hedge fund partnerships, and senior hedge funds often sire "cubs" and then sons of cubs. The protean ability of this arrangement to spawn, fund, and replicate successful momentum trades cannot be overstated, and has generated trillions of permanent momentum-chasing capital.

The hedge funds run by John Paulson, the celebrated trader who massively broke the sub-prime mortgage market, demonstrates the manner in which momentum-chasing hot money had come to dominate the Wall Street casino. The one constant illustrated by the Paulson saga is that the pool of hedge fund money lives by the law of relentless reallocation.

THE HOT HANDS WENT STONE COLD

For most of his career Paulson was a steady and astute journeyman who managed a modest-sized hedge fund specializing in merger arbitrage. But in 2005–2006 he chanced upon the "greatest trade ever"—the monumental subprime short—and during the next several years generated astounding investment returns. His fund profits measured out at more than a 300 percent annual rate.

The inflow of new money to the several Paulson hedge funds was astonishing and instantaneous, even by the standards of contemporary Wall Street. Paulson's AUM (assets under management) went from $4 billion to $40 billion in a financial heartbeat. The inflow of capital was so great, and the timing of his momentum trades so effective, that during 2006–2010 Paulson's personal share of profits was reputed to be nearly $15 billion, a figure that exceeded the entire AUM of the largest hedge fund as recently as 2001.

Still, these heaving pools of hedge fund capital care only about what managers have done for them lately. The violent unwind of the Paulson funds is dramatic proof. By early 2012 his funds had shrunk to $20 billion and investors had fled in droves.

This breathtaking rise and fall is not about capitalist freedom to succeed and fail, or even a morality play about an investor becoming overconfident in his own genius. Instead, it is evidence that the great financial deformation has spiked the system with opportunities for huge, misshapen speculations that could never arise on the free market.

On the free market uncorrupted by the state—and especially the money-printing and Wall Street coddling policies of its central banking branch—there would have been no reckless boom in mortgage lending nor the resulting rampant inflation of housing prices. In turn, there would also have been no "big short" against bad real estate prices and bad housing debt.

As it happened, however, this wager amounted to the chance of a lifetime to extract billions of windfall profits and attract billions more of momentum-chasing hedge fund capital. Furthermore, these enormous windfalls from busted mortgages enabled the suddenly giant hedge funds run by Paulson to pivot on a dime and place tens of billions of new bets behind highly speculative theories which soon proved to be disastrously wrong.

After early 2009, for example, Paulson wagered that the United States would experience an inflationary boom and therefore bet heavily on gold, banks, home builders, and other sectors that would benefit. John Paulson had no special macroeconomic expertise, but he had chanced upon a dog-eared copy of Milton Friedman's quantity theory of money. When Bernanke flooded the economy with a humongous quantity of money in the fall and winter of 2008–2009, Paulson placed his bets accordingly.

Unsung economic forecasters have been making erroneous bets for decades based on Professor Friedman's faulty theories about money, but this time upward of $30 billion had been placed on Friedman's money supply growth equation. So when the inflationary boom didn't happen, Paulson's funds experienced shocking losses which amounted to 45 percent by the end of 2011.

Still, apologists for the Fed's evisceration of the capital markets could not see that the tens of billions flowing first toward the Paulson bets and then in headlong flight from them were evidence of profound financial disorder. Indeed, the apparent view from the Eccles Building was that John Paulson was just some kind of hedge fund Casey—a mighty trader who aimed for the fences and had struck out at the plate.

Yet the truth was more nearly the opposite. The Fed had unleashed the financial furies in the violent momentum trading modus operandi of the hedge fund casino. Paulson was only the most visible practitioner.

HEDGE FUNDS: HAVEN OF HIT-AND-RUN CAPITAL FOR THE 1 PERCENT

The operative word with respect to these giant hedge fund pools is "capricious." Savers traditionally functioned on the free market as agents of financial discipline, allocating funds to asset managers who had established a well-seasoned record of diligence, rigor, and consistency. By definition, old-fashioned savers on the free market deliberately chose to defer immediate consumption and gratification; they were looking for stable, reliable returns over the longer haul, not overnight riches.

Needless to say, the Fed's prosperity management model has led to the extinction of the traditional saver class. During the fourteen-year period since the Greenspan Fed panicked at the time of the LTCM crisis, its interest rate repression policies have resulted in an inflation-adjusted return on six-month bank CDs of exactly zero percent. In so many words, the policy message of the nation's central bank was "don't save through any instrument which is liquid."

This unconscionable blow to traditional savers was especially perverse because it harmed the middle class far more than the wealthy. Much of the middle class was discouraged from saving entirely, as the dismal data on the household savings rate clearly documents. Worse still, out of desperation, greed, or both many others were induced to speculate in the serial stock market and housing bubbles generated by the Fed after September 1998, a course of action which led to serious loss of capital.

At the same time, the Fed's destructive interest rate repression policies literally revolutionized the saving and investment habits of the top tier of wealthy households. Unlike hapless savers among the middle class, the rich had an escape route. In their wisdom, regulatory policy makers had decreed that the legal drinking age for financial risk taking is $5 million of liquid net worth. Accordingly, hedge funds were exempted from SEC regulation as long as they didn't solicit undersized speculators.

For several decades after the SEC was established, this financial carding threshold didn't matter too much because the wealthy had no reason to get frisky with their savings. Between 1953 and 1971, annual inflation-adjusted returns on bank deposits averaged 2 percent; corporate bonds yielded 3 percent after inflation; and equities including dividends returned 5 percent in inflation-adjusted dollars.

By contrast, the incidence of rocket-ship gains was very low. As has been seen, the likes of Marriner Eccles and William McChesney Martin didn't see great merit in the speculative urges.

When the Greenspan Fed inaugurated the era of bubble finance, however, the picture changed dramatically. The wealthy did not arrive at their august financial stature out of conviction that the meek shall inherit the earth. So when flushed out of their traditional fixed-income safe havens, they proactively formed "family offices" and hired professionals to pursue alternatives to negative real returns.

At the same time, the rise of financial market leverage and momentum trading dramatically increased the probability of hitting the jackpot in risk asset markets. It became rational to speculate and especially to "buy the dips" because it was the deliberate policy of the nation's central bank to inflate risk assets.

For fleet-footed traders who could stay ahead of the Fed's money market maneuvers and smoke signals, the odds were particularly rewarding. They could chase the continuously revolving cast of highflyers in the speculative precincts of the market, while relying on the Greenspan-Bernanke Put to insure their trading book against an unexpected plunge in the broad market averages.

It is ironic that the Fed has never comprehended the awful damage the Greenspan Put wreaked upon the financial markets, because the proof was right there in its Long-Term Capital Management birth event. The proximate cause of the great LTCM crisis, in fact, was the failure of the downside insurance mechanism that John Meriwether perfected to protect his speculative book. In that case, LTCM's "long" speculations were embedded in a massive portfolio of exotic fixed-income and currency positions, so the downside risk was the threat of significant rise in "benchmark" interest rates as embodied in the yield of US Treasuries.

An increase in benchmark rates would result in sharp losses to LTCM's entire book of yield-sensitive speculations. The insurance mechanism, therefore, was shorting the Treasury market so that if worldwide interest rates rose, possibly due to a tightening by the Fed, LTCM would profit from falling Treasury bond prices. In this manner, gains on the Treasury short position would offset the losses on LTCM's book of speculative longs.

This downside insurance worked like a charm for Meriwether over the better part of twenty years, until the Russian default of August 1998. That triggered a violent flight to safety in US Treasury paper that was unprecedented in speed and scale, and could be found nowhere in the data histories that drove LTCM's Nobel Prize–winning trading models. Indeed, it was the first great "risk off" panic of the Greenspan era. It turned LTCM's portfolio of advanced financial alchemy into the equivalent of a bug on the world's financial windshield.

The fund's longs got clobbered due to the flight from risk assets. At the same time, its short position in Treasury debt turned out to be not a rainy-day insurance policy but a protracted nightmare. Treasury bond prices did not fall like they were supposed to but, instead, rose relentlessly. A global tidal wave of panicked treasury buying thereby caused gargantuan losses on LTCM's long-standing short. In only a matter of days, therefore, LTCM's insurance plan devoured the fund's assets and the end came hard upon.

What this celebrated episode actually revealed was that Meriwether had been wrong all along about the true cost of his portfolio insurance: it was much higher than he had been booking during years and years of prodigious profits.

The true high cost of the short Treasury hedge lay hidden in the financial market weeds, as it were, until it showed up as the sudden, violent inflation of a "fat tail." Accordingly, Meriwether's access to underpriced portfolio insurance led the team of gifted traders he assembled over two decades to run a book that did not have a sufficient loss reserve for the fat tail cost that someday would come all of a sudden. Indeed, had the all-knowing accountant in the sky been charging Meriwether's accounting statements each and every quarter with a pro rata share of the coming fat tail loss, the curve of his spectacular earnings history would have been crushed back toward the mean.

The spectacular blow up of LTCM was therefore a godsend. It warned that the maestro's fretting about "irrational exuberance" in December 1996 had been spot-on and that risk taking and leverage had already reached dangerous extremes by August 1998. But even more crucially, it highlighted the incendiary effects of underpricing downside insurance against an unexpected plunge of the broad market.

LTCM's demise came because its downside insurance had been under-reserved. But now the Fed's solution to the modest market turmoil its demise caused was to extend downside insurance to the entire machinery of Wall Street speculation at essentially zero charge. What had been a de facto Greenspan Put now became explicit commitment, and thereby was taken by speculators as a near-solemn pledge that the central bank henceforth had their back.

Then and there, the deformation of the stock market went into a far more virulent and ultimately destructive phase. Now the surging pools of speculative capital being assembled by the hedge funds would become ever more reckless in their trading behavior and ever more insistent that the Greenspan Put be honored at all hazards.

WHEN KEYNES WAS RIGHT

By the end of the century, therefore, the financial asset inflation fostered by the Fed was having exactly the consequence that Professor Keynes had in mind in his famous 1919 essay warning about the Treaty of Versailles. The consequence of debauching the currency then was no different than the present policy of the Fed. In his parting shot from the British Treasury, the younger and more sensible J. M. Keynes nailed the danger: "As the inflation process proceeds . . . the process of wealth getting degenerates into a gamble and a lottery."

Accordingly, as the Greenspan Fed pursued a course of extreme monetary inflation, it became exceedingly rational for the wealthy to push their assets through the SEC regulatory loophole and into the hedge fund arena of momentum-chasing gunslingers and punters. Steadily at first, and then with a rush after the Fed's September 1998 capitulation and its December 2000 interest rate cutting panic, wealthy investors abdicated their historical gating and disciplining function. Instead, they channeled trillions of capital in hot pursuit of the most recent jackpot winners.

It is a law of economics that when both the supply and price of something rise parabolically there also exists an equal upwelling of demand. Accordingly, once the Greenspan Put was explicitly in place wealthy investors were literally chasing after new hedge funds with fists full of money.

Thus, there were 1,000 hedge funds with a mere $150 billion under management in 1990. After two decades of bubble economics, the sector exploded to 10,000 funds and better than $6 trillion of AUM (when the embedded hedge funds of the Wall Street banks are added to the total).

It thus happened that financial markets became warped and destabilized by whirling dervishes that inhabited the fast money complex. Unlike any financial force up till then, they were capable of launching a multibillion-dollar dash straight over the proverbial financial cliff. Indeed, the power of hedge fund wolf packs to obliterate the signaling and disciplining mechanisms of the free market has now become plainly evident.

So the Greenspan Put had unleashed the Furies on Wall Street. The hedge funds became marauding gangs of hit-and-run speculation, propelled by the $13 trillion outbreak of financial engineering in takeovers, buybacks, and LBOs.

Like the dot-com version, this second Greenspan bubble was so immense, the rising debt so crushing, and the speculative trading games so reckless that sooner or later it had to collapse under its own weight. By the time it did go bust, of course, the maestro had vacated the Eccles Building. But his acolytes and accomplices were still there, momentarily frozen in place when the house of cards began to falter in August 2007.

Then came the rant that shook the Eccles Building. Soon it was evident that the central bank of the United States had been taken hostage by the petulant Cramerite hordes. The deformation of finance would now take on an even more virulent and destructive aspect. The Bernanke Put had been born.

CHAPTER 24

WHEN GIANT LBOS STRIP-MINED THE LAND

F INANCIAL ENGINEERING IS THE MOTHER'S MILK OF SPECULATIVE capital. Big hedge funds which can move money with massive throw weight and lightning speed thrive on it. It is a prolific generator of the exact kind of market moving events—rumors and announcements of buyouts, takeovers, and buybacks—that generate windfall gains largely unrelated to company fundamentals.

The hedge fund flash mobs which swarm around these financial engineering deals must be consistently paid off or the speculation games would quickly die. Accordingly, during the Greenspan bubbles the vital financial lucre which kept the stock market casino going was CEW (corporate equity withdrawal).

The business sector, however, did not generate nearly enough free cash flow to fund the trillions of CEW payouts. So companies borrowed from the credit markets prodigiously in order to fund buyouts, buybacks, and takeovers. In the process, the accumulated equity of American business was strip-mined and transferred mainly to the top 1 percent; that is, to the preponderant owners of hedge fund capital.

HEDGE FUNDS AND THE GREAT CEW SHUFFLE

The consequence was a deterioration of the collective balance sheet of US businesses. In December 1996, at the time of Greenspan's warning about "irrational exuberance," business debt outstanding was $4.4 trillion. By the time the financial system buckled at the end of 2008, total business sector debt had nearly tripled and stood at $11.4 trillion.

From a macroeconomic perspective, this $7 trillion rise in the business debt burden could not have come at a worse time. Faced with a massive flood of cheap goods and services from mercantilist exporters, American business needed to minimize debt service costs and direct its free cash flows to heavy investment in productivity.

This was obviously impossible given the due bill for financial engineering deals. So needing to fund $13 trillion of deals completed through 2008, companies borrowed hand over fist. This forced the collective leverage ratio for the business sector upward by more than one-third, from 44 percent of fixed and working assets in 1996 to more than 60 percent by 2008.

Moreover, contrary to the urban legends about the post-crisis improvement of corporate financial health so assiduously promoted by Wall Street, this leverage ratio remained at 60 percent through the end of 2011. The great CEW raid of the decade ending in September 2008 thus left a permanent, heavy millstone on the collective balance sheet of American business.

This grave impairment would not have happened on the free market. To the contrary, the severe shortage of domestic savings would have caused interest rates to rise sharply in order to clear the market. In response to a steep and rising price for debt, business borrowing would have declined, not lurched into an all-out binge as it did after the turn of the century.

So it was the Fed which fostered the multitrillion-dollar spree of financial engineering and CEW that commenced in the years after the dot-com bust. By means of its panicked easing campaign, it generated a bow wave of borrowing and speculation. This, in turn, caused untold trillions to be transferred from the business sector of the American economy to the Wall Street financial casino, causing hedge fund AUMs to climb by nearly $400 billion each and every year between 2002 and 2007.

The underlying cash-stripping raids on the business sector during this five-year period dwarfed all prior benchmarks. Annual stock buybacks grew sixfold, from $100 billion to $600 billion. Total M&A takeover volume quadrupled, rising from $400 billion to $1.6 trillion per year. At the heart of this surge in financial engineering deals, however, were leveraged buyout transactions which rocketed from $60 billion in 2002 to $600 billion annually at the 2006–2007 peak.

TIDDIE BIDDIES: HOW HEDGE FUNDS GET THE CASH

Except for a small 15 percent share of M&A deals paid in stock, all of these financial engineering transactions were funded with cash. As money poured into the accounts of stockholders, a disproportionate share was captured by fast-moving hedge funds based on their inside knowledge of the deal market. The fast money traders got to the deal stocks early, before the price had run, and it was no mystery as to how.

The infamous Raj Rajaratnam, former proprietor of the Galleon hedge fund and current guest of the US government, did it the illegal way. Each day before Rajaratnam's "morning meeting" at his fund, a Goldman Sachs managing director sent him an e-mail containing "tiddie biddies." Needless to say, the latter seem to have immeasurably aided Rajaratnam's un-canny sense of timing and the superlative returns which issued from it.

Yet it doesn't take illegal e-mails to circulate hunches, educated guesses, reliable sources, sage opinion, reasonable probabilities, potential scenar-ios, and "gut feelings" through the interconnected networks of traders, bankers, and hedge fund managers. It's what Wall Street does all day and, in an honest market, would amount to the noble work of "price discovery."

But it's not an honest market owing to the deformations of bubble fi-nance. The latter puts an overpowering premium on information about deals and announcements as opposed to business fundamentals. Accord-ingly, price discovery has turned into a high-stakes scramble for "tiddie biddies" about price-moving rumors, events, and announcements.

Needless to say, on the free market stock prices mostly rise slowly, re-flecting the organic process of productivity growth and the usually meas-ured but continuous harvest of returns on capital, technology, and ideas. Watching the grass grow in this manner, Wall Street bankers and traders would needs be in the business of heavy-duty fundamental research, not the collection of "tiddie biddies."

THE DERANGEMENT OF LEVERAGED FINANCE: $100 BILLION IN LBO DIVIDEND RECAPS

The wherewithal for financial engineering came from the leveraged loan market that had been on death's door after "risk" went into hiding during the dot-com bust. But when the Fed caused interest rates to tumble to lows not seen for generations, the market for leveraged finance literally exploded.

Issuance of highly leveraged bank loans plus junk bonds leapt higher by $1 trillion annually, rising from $350 billion in 2002 to $1.35 trillion by 2007. Funding available for LBOs and leveraged recaps thus quadrupled. Alto-gether, a total of $4.5 trillion of so-called high-yielding debt was issued dur-ing this six-year interval. This astounding number exceeded all of the high-yield debt ever issued in all previous history.

Moreover, the surging quantity of available high-risk debt was only part of the story. The deterioration in quality was even more spectacular. The riskiness of leveraged loans is usually measured by the interest rate spread over LIBOR; the more risk the larger the spread. This LIBOR spread on leveraged bank loans, for example, dropped from 375 basis points to 175 basis points, meaning that compensation to lenders for the risk of loss posed by highly leveraged borrowers virtually disappeared.

Likewise, under a euphemism called "covenant lite" traditional borrower restrictions were essentially eliminated from junk bonds, transforming them into financial mutants. Under standard bond covenants, company cash could not be paid out to common equity holders who stood at the bottom of the capital structure unless bonds were well covered. But under "covenant lite," private equity sponsors could suck huge self-dealing cash dividends out of a company, bondholders be damned.

Implied default risk also increased sharply as measured by average deal multiples, which rose from 7X cash flow to nearly 11X. Moreover, near the end of this leveraged lending spree an increasing share of junk bonds were of the "toggle" variety. This meant that if the borrower came up short of cash it could just send the lender some more IOUs (bonds); that is, it could borrow to pay interest just like under "neg am" home mortgages.

The ultimate indicator of the drastic deterioration of loan quality during this period, however, was the eruption of leveraged "dividend recaps." LBO companies were able to issue new debt on top of the prodigious amounts they already owed, yet not one penny of these new borrowings went to fund company operations or capital expenditures.

Instead, the newly borrowed cash drained right out of the bottom of the capital structure and was paid as a dividend to the LBO's private equity sponsors. This sometimes permitted sponsors to recoup all of their initial capital or even book a profit within a few months of the initial buyout transaction, and long before any of the initial debt was paid down.

Leveraged dividend recaps during the second Greenspan bubble (2003–2007) were off the charts relative to all prior experience. Thus, more than $100 billion was paid out during this period, compared to generally less than $1 billion annually in the late 1990s. Since private equity sponsors normally are entitled to a 20 percent share of profits, a couple of dozen buyout kings and their lesser principals pocketed $20 billion from these payouts.

The real trouble, however, was not so much the greed of it as it was the sheer recklessness of it. Most of these dividend recap deals were done by freshly minted LBOs, some of them so fresh, in fact, that they had hardly gotten to their first semiannual coupon payment.

So the feverishly overheated leveraged loan market was the real culprit. Investors were indiscriminately devouring any high-yield paper offered, and for the worst possible reason. As the 2003–2007 Greenspan bubble steadily inflated, fund managers became convinced that the monetary central planners at the Fed had truly achieved the Great Moderation; that is, recessions had more or less been banished.

While implausible it nevertheless caused a drastic mispricing of junk bonds. They carry a high yield owing to their embedded equity-type risks, the most important of which historically had been the sharp impairment of cash flows and rise of default rates triggered by business cycle downturns.

Now that the risk was attenuated or even eliminated entirely, high-yield bond managers started acting as though they owned a Treasury bond with a big fat bonus yield and commenced buying junk bonds hand over fist. The demand for new paper became so frenetic that Wall Street underwriters virtually begged private equity sponsors to undertake "dividend recaps" so they would have product to sell to their customers.

This was another sign of the reckless speculation induced by the Fed's bubble finance. During seventeen years in the private equity business, I never observed these firms reluctant to scalp a profit when, where, and as they could. But most firms believed the prudent strategy was to get a new LBO out of harm's way as soon as possible by paying off debt and ratcheting down the initial leverage ratio. Rarely did sponsors think about piling on more debt in the initial stages, and certainly not to pay themselves a dividend. Even during the final red-hot years of the first Greenspan bubble (1997–2000), dividend recaps were rare, with volume averaging only $1.7 billion per year.

During the second Greenspan bubble, by contrast, annual volume soared to $25 billion. Junk bonds and leveraged loans were so cheap and plentiful and the overall financial euphoria so intense that even the great LBO houses succumbed to violating their own investing rules. In fact, $100 billion of dividend recaps on the backs of dozens of companies already groaning under huge debt loads was not just a violation of time-tested rules—it bordered on a derangement and madness of the crowds.

This eruption of leveraged dividend payouts dramatically exposed one channel by which cash from CEW was recycled to the top 1 percent. More importantly, however, it also laid bare the whole self-feeding web of bubble finance that the Fed's monetary central planners unleashed while attempting to levitate asset prices.

In this instance, the stock market bust of 2000–2001 and the modest economic slump which followed brought the excesses of leveraged finance to a screeching halt. Accordingly, the secondary market for high-yield debt cratered, new loan issuance slumped badly, and LBO activity stalled out at low ebb.

The financial market was attempting to heal itself for good reason. Default rates on leveraged loans soared from an average of 2 percent of outstandings during 1997–1999 to 10 percent during 2001–2002. These high default rates, in turn, sharply curtailed the investor appetites for junk bonds, causing new issues to drop by two-thirds between 1998 and 2000.

In effect, the free market was attempting to close down the LBO business as it had been practiced during the late 1990s boom years when the cash flows of buyout companies had been drastically overleveraged.

Not for the last time, however, the Fed refused to permit the financial markets to complete their therapeutic work. When the federal funds rate was slashed to 1 percent by June 2003, the collateral effects on the junk bond market were electrifying, precisely the opposite of what the doctor ordered.

During the twenty-four-month period between mid-2002 and mid-2004, junk bond interest rates plunged from 10 percent to under 6 percent. Since bond prices move opposite to yield, the value of junk bonds soared and speculators made a killing on what had been deeply "distressed" debt. Indeed, in a matter of months, a class of securities that had been a default-plagued pariah became a red-hot performance leader.

This massive windfall to speculators was not the result of prescient insights about the future course of the US economy. Nor was it owing to any evident "bond picking" skill with respect to the performance prospects of the several hundred midsized companies which constituted the junk bond issuer universe at the time. Instead, junk bond speculators made billions during the miraculous recovery of leveraged debt markets during 2003–2004 simply by placing a bet on the maestro's plainly evident fear of disappointing Wall Street.

Wall Street underwriters, in turn, had no trouble peddling new issues of an asset class that was knocking the lights out. These gains were not all they were cracked up to be, of course, because junk bonds had not become one bit less risky (or more valuable) on an over-the-cycle basis. But the Fed's interest rate repression campaign made these gains appear to be the real thing, demonstrating once again the terrible cost of disabling free market price signals.

Moreover, when the rebounding demand for risky credits enabled the issuance of nearly $3 trillion of highly leveraged bank loans and bonds during the three years ending in 2007, the result was a "dilution illusion." The junk debt default ratio fell mainly due to arithmetic; that is, the swelling of the denominator (bonds) rather than shrinkage of the numerator (defaults).

Thus, by the end of the second Greenspan-Bernanke bubble the total volume of leveraged debt outstanding was nearly three times higher than in 2001–2002. At the same time, the temporary credit-fueled expansion of the US economy caused new junk bond issues to perform reasonably well. Due to this happy arithmetic combination, the measured default rate plummeted sharply, dropping all the way down to 0.6 percent by 2007.

Yet this was a preposterously misleading and unsustainable measure of junk bond risk, since it implied that the Fed could prop up the stock market and extend debt-fueled GDP growth in perpetuity. Nevertheless, having quashed the free market's attempt to cleanse the junk bond sector in 2001–2002, the Fed had now enabled the leveraged financing cycle to come full circle.

HOW THE GREAT MODERATION SPURRED A DAISY CHAIN OF DEBT

During the final stretch of the bubble in 2006–2007, the junk bond yield stood at about 7 percent and was juxtaposed against what appeared to be negligible default rates. Not surprisingly, this generated a vast inflow of yield-hungry money into the junk bond market, and a blistering expansion of the market for securitized bank loans.

The latter were called CLOs, for collateralized loan obligations, and were another wonder of bubble finance emanating from the same financial meth labs that produced mortgage-based CDOs. In this instance, however, Wall Street dealers sold debt to yield-hungry Main Street investors that had been issued by what amounts to financial "storefronts." These shell companies were stuffed with LBO junk loans rather than subprime mortgages.

The daisy chain of financial engineering was thus extended one more notch: leveraged buyouts were now financed from the proceeds of bank debt which, in turn, was funded with the proceeds of CLO debt. Nor was that the end of the leverage chain. Not infrequently, these CLO "storefronts" also employed leverage to enhance their own returns. Thus did the true equity in the system retreat ever deeper into the financial shadows.

By the top of the cycle in 2006–2007, the CLO market of debt upon debt upon debt was expanding at a $100 billion annual rate, compared to less than $5 billion at the prior peak seven years earlier. In its headlong pursuit of asset inflation, therefore, the Fed was spring-loading the financial system with a fantastic coil of debt.

As it happened, however, the miniscule 2007 default rate for junk loans was no more sustainable than had been the initially low default rates for subprime mortgages. By 2009 defaults were actually back above 10 percent, signaling the third junk market crash since 1990.

Accordingly, investors and traders fled the leveraged loan markets even faster than they had stormed into them. Junk debt issuance plunged by 85 percent from peak levels. The CLO market disappeared entirely.

This cliff-diving denouement should have come as no surprise. Near the end of the boom, many issuers were simply borrowing to pay debt service and few had sufficient excess cash flow to withstand a sharp economic downturn. The massive coil of LBO debt fostered by the Fed's financial repression policies had thus been an accident waiting to happen.

Yet the leveraged finance boom went on right until the eve of the 2008 Wall Street meltdown because risk asset markets had been sedated by the myth of the Great Moderation. If the Fed had indeed abolished the risk of steep and unexpected business cycle downturns, as Bernanke claimed, the corollary was that deal makers were free to push leverage ratios to new extremes. This was a matter of spreadsheet math: the banishment of recessions obviously meant that the cash flows of leveraged business wouldn't plunge in a downturn.

It also meant that the junk bond interest rate spread over risk-free treasuries would stay narrow, owing to reduced expectation of recession-induced defaults. So the junk market's read on the Great Moderation was that it meant a floor under cash flow and a cap on default risk. Better still, since many junk bonds now had the "toggle" feature, they couldn't default; they could just add the coupon to what they owed.

If defaults were thus minimized or eliminated, the hefty yield on junk bonds would be pure gravy. Not surprisingly, the leveraged loan market became fearless, happily assuming that the Fed had infinite capacity to prop up the economy and peg the price of risk. Nearly two-thirds of all the junk bonds issued in 2007 were of the so-called covenant lite variety, and that was another canary in the coal mine.

The purpose of covenants is to trap an LBO's cash flows inside a company's balance sheet for the benefit of the bondholders. So when these protections were permitted to fall away, it meant that high-yield investors were no longer looking to the borrower's cash to keep themselves whole. Instead, they assumed that borrowers who didn't have the cash to redeem their debts at maturity would simply refinance; that is, investors would get their money back not from original issuers but from the next punter in the Ponzi.

Likewise, purchase prices for larger LBOs soared to more than 10X cash flow, compared to 6.5X when Mr. Market was endeavoring to heal the excesses of the previous leveraged finance bubble back in 2001–2002. Indeed, the light was flashing green for issuance of every manner of risky credit. These included second-lien loans, which effectively meant hocking an LBO company's receivables and inventory twice.

THE CORNUCOPIA OF PRIVATE EQUITY: EXIT AND RELOAD

Owing to this outpouring of leveraged finance, all of the deal markets were on fire during 2005–2007, thereby instigating a fantastic feedback loop. Owing to the debt-fueled explosion of buyouts, buybacks, and M&A takeovers, the S&P 500 was levitated to an all-time high north of 1,500. In turn, the booming stock market facilitated a surge in so-called "exit" transactions by sponsors of existing private equity deals through IPOs or M&A auction sales. In turn, these "exit" transactions, along with dividend recaps, permitted sponsors to return huge amounts of cash to their institutional investors such as pension funds and insurance companies.

Not surprisingly, these large distributions to investors helped reignite the cycle all over again. Whereas only $30 billion of new private equity commitments were made by institutional investors in 2003, this number went on a tear, rising to $160 billion in 2005, followed by $200 billion in 2006 and nearly $300 billion in 2007. The latter single-year total was so astonishingly large that it exceeded all of the private equity ever raised from the time of the first famous private equity deal, the Gibson Greetings home run in 1983 through the end of 1999.

It is well-nigh impossible to exaggerate the speculative firepower implicit in this tenfold escalation of annual new commitments. The $1 trillion of new private equity money during 2004–2008 was off the charts by orders of magnitude, but it was just the high-powered apex of the leveraged-deal pyramid. At the going rate, LBO balance sheets required a 20–30 percent equity contribution, meaning that the $1 trillion of new private equity could fund $3–$5 trillion of leveraged buyouts and recapitalizations. No more powerful stimulant to the speculative mania already rampant in the deal markets could have been imagined.

It would have been virtually impossible to put this much money to work in the $200–$400 million sized "middle market" deals prevalent during the first two decades of LBO history. Consequently, the era of the mega-LBO was born, but the resulting $10–$50 billion scale deals had faint resemblance to the entrepreneurial management model which had been the original rationale for leveraged buyouts.

THE $300 BILLION CARRIED INTEREST JACKPOT
AND THE RISE OF MONSTER LBOS

These mega-LBOs were simply opportunistic exercises in leveraged speculation. They arose because private equity sponsors were not about to allow their immense new inventory of committed capital to sit idle. The economics of private equity investing were too compelling.

Over a five-year holding period, for example, this $1 trillion of new capital implied private equity fund profits of $1.5 trillion, assuming an industry minimum 20 percent annual rate of return. In turn, the 20 percent "carried interest" share of profits allocable to general partners who ran private equity firms would have been worth $300 billion. It goes without saying that a jackpot of that magnitude, even if only theoretical, presented what were truly stupefying incentives for deal making.

The fact of the matter was that 80 percent of these massive new private equity commitments were attributable to a few dozen major LBO firms. The implicit $300 billion carried interest jackpot, therefore, would have been realized by a few dozen senior partners and a few hundred principals overall. Never before in history had a central bank deformation of financial markets delivered such massive opportunities for speculative gain to so few.

Rather than a dot-com bubble, the deformation this time was a runaway string of supersized leveraged buyouts. Even a cursory review of the facts establishes that these massive transactions had no rational purpose except to strip-mine cash from the business sector and recycle it to the hedge funds and private equity firms which had come to occupy the center of the nation's financialized economy.

STRIPPING THE YELLOW PAGES: HOW CEW HAPPENED

The order-of-magnitude increase in deal size that materialized in the leveraged buyout market was kicked off in 2003 by the $7.5 billion Dex Media transaction. Since the company had only $1.6 billion of revenue and its yellow pages were a dying business in the Internet age, the deal price of nearly 5X revenues was truly astonishing.

It was also a forewarning of the speculative mania to come. Within just a few months of the deal, its private equity sponsors led by the Carlyle Group took out a $1 billion dividend by piling more debt on the $6 billion from the initial transaction. Yet, in a world the Fed favored with 1 percent interest rates and a renewed policy of stock market levitation, this growing mound of debt made no waves at all.

In fact, during mid-2004 Dex Media was taken public at a value of about $3 billion for the equity on top of the LBO debt which remained at its original level. So on an apples-to-apples basis, the IPO was valued at approximately twice the $1.5 billion equity investment that its private equity owners had made only fifteen months earlier.

This saga of quick riches only got better, rapidly. As the Greenspan bubble gathered momentum in 2005, the Washington insiders who ran the Carlyle Group might have sent the maestro a case of champagne. In October of that year, they sold Dex Media to another yellow pages publisher, the venerable R.H. Donnelley & Sons, for $4.3 billion plus the assumption of all the LBO and dividend debt.

So the whole investment life cycle consumed only about forty months, but the rounds of debt upon debt were stunning. There was a huge $6 billion debt issuance at the time of the LBO; another large debt issuance to fund the quickie dividend; and then an M&A takeout by a heavily leveraged company that for all practical purposes was a publicly traded LBO. The post-merger company, in fact, had about $11 billion of debt.

A cascade of debt thus built up inside the company and its successor. In the meantime, the private equity sponsors were favored with a CEW extraction of startling magnitude. During their brief interval in the yellow pages business they pocketed more than $5 billion from the dividend and the sale of their Donnelley shares shortly after the merger.

That amounted to 3.3X their original investment for adding no detectable value. On an organic basis, the sales and EBITDA of these scattered yellow pages operations continued to decline, meaning there is little evidence that the Carlyle Group and its other private equity sponsors did much (or could have) to put Dex Media's three-hundred-odd local phone directories on a life extension program.

What is indisputable, however, is that Washington reduced the tax on capital gains and dividends to a historic low of 15 percent at the beginning of their holding period. Carlyle and its other investors were thereby enabled to harvest their multibillion-dollar windfall essentially tax free.

This private equity windfall bore another distinctive hallmark of the speculative tide then cresting; namely, that the deal amounted to a fraudulent conveyance in economic terms, if not as a legal matter. Indeed, the underlying business reality was that the deal from which Carlyle extracted the preponderant share of its cash winnings, the ultra-leveraged merger with R.H. Donnelley, had been destined for a crash landing from the start.

On a post-merger basis, Dex Media and Donnelley combined had $2.8 billion of revenue and $1.1 billion of operating income compared to a debt load in excess of $11 billion. Even the proverbial "cash cow" type business on which LBOs had originally been predicated would have been hard pressed to sustain an 11 to 1 leverage ratio across an entire business cycle.

In fact, by January 2006 when the merger was completed, the yellow pages already had the aspect of a milk cow heading for the great pasture beyond. Their revenues and cash flow were being inexorably Googled away.

Worse still, there wasn't much magical merger "synergy" to exploit because Dex Media was twice the size of Donnelley, and its LBO sponsors had already picked its cost structure to the bone. Accordingly, pro forma operating margins were already at 40 percent and there was little evidence elsewhere in the industry that they could be pushed much higher.

At length, nearly every single yellow pages publisher has stumbled into bankruptcy after years of bravely insisting it could make the transition from cellulose to silicon. R.H. Donnelley suffered the same fate, but it was symptomatic of the 2005–2008 financial mania that lenders had ever believed otherwise.

This thoroughgoing suspension of disbelief contrasted sharply with the LBO business only a decade earlier, when annual LBO volume for the entire industry had been less than R.H. Donnelley's debt. In these more sober times, my colleagues at Blackstone had considered any traditional business being stalked by the Internet as strictly off limits. These businesses were not only seen as the equivalent of a dead man walking, but they had also been avoided for another reason: Alan Greenspan had not yet thrown in the towel on irrational exuberance and mainstream investors did not yet assume that the Fed had abolished the business cycle.

In short, a sunset industry was no place to become trapped with a boatload of debt. Yet that is exactly where the yellow pages business stood after the turn of the century. That it was a dying industry was no state secret, but investors now assumed that the risk of any business cycle downside was in the nature of a rounding error. Owing to the Great Moderation, therefore, five- and ten-year loans would get repaid before the yellow pages ran out of cash.

Accordingly, R.H. Donnelley's $11 billion of debt traded at par, and its stock price climbed by 25 percent within a year or so of the merger. Since it had pioneered the directory business more than a hundred years earlier, speculators in both its debt and equity apparently assumed that Donnelley possessed a secret sauce. But it had none—only the dubious franchise right to sell ads in a shrinking phone book.

What it also had was a book of sales which depended upon the continued willingness and ability of car dealers, bowling alleys, and about 600,000 other mostly small businesses to buy advertising. On those facts alone, R.H. Donnelley's days were numbered.

The roaring bull market paid no note. It priced the company's pro forma earnings of $2.25 per share at $78, meaning that a far-flung set of three hundred local phone books which experienced no organic revenue growth for five years were being valued at 35X net income. This was the "audacity of hope" before the term was invented and before the Fed's bubble economy finally buckled.

In the event, the severe slump in yellow pages advertising by Main Street businesses during the recession caused the company's cash flow to plummet. The resulting balance sheet kill was quick and clean: when Donnelly filed a prepackaged bankruptcy plan in June 2009, its market cap of $5 billion had vaporized and it was forced to write off $6 billion of its debt.

In the course of four years of leveraged deal making, therefore, Dex Media–Donnelley had mounted $11 billion of enterprise value which proved to be entirely phantom-like when the equity vanished and the bonds were cut in half. In the interim, private equity operators and those stock market punters who got out before Donnelley's share price plunged extracted more than $6 billion in windfall gains. Here was the mark of CEW. These dying yellow pages never would have been leveraged at all on the free market.

THEN CAME THE DELUGE: THIRTY GIANT LBOS

The Dex Media–R.H. Donnelley saga was not an outlier, but a prototype for the string of giant LBOs and the fantastically leveraged deal making at the heart of the second Greenspan bubble. In fact, it was these huge debt-financed deals which drove the stock market and other risk assets skyward during the final phases of the mania.

The mountains of the debt piled upon target companies during the mega-LBO mania could never be sustained in the fragile, credit-addicted economy that the Fed spawned. So the entire mega-LBO boom was the equivalent of a state-assisted fraudulent conveyance. Hundreds of billions of CEW was extracted from the balance sheets of the target businesses and transferred to speculators on the top rungs of the economic ladder. But it was financed with so much debt that most of these deals were candidates for eventual insolvency under any realistic long-term economic scenario.

For that reason, virtually none of these mega-LBO deals, as detailed more fully in chapter 25, would have passed muster on the free market. They were the spoils from the central bank's drastic repression of honest market-clearing prices for debt and risk.

The sheer magnitude and speed of this supersized buyout wave is difficult to exaggerate. But we can see its importance through a string of thirty giant LBOs occurring from early 2005 through the spring of 2008. Each was seemingly larger than the previous one but most shared a common fate: they ended up teetering on bankruptcy, undergoing voluntary restructuring, or limping along as financial zombies which labor to this very day under an unshakeable load of debt.

The largest was nearly $50 billion and the average size was $17 billion. This average size for two and one-half dozen LBOs was remarkable because with the exception of the 1989 RJR-Nabisco deal there had never been a single leverage buyout that large. Furthermore, the aggregate value of these deals was a staggering $500 billion, meaning that nearly half of the $1.1 trillion of LBOs completed during this period was accounted for by just these thirty giant deals.

Two data points vivify the enormous financial shuffle embodied in these mega-LBOs. First, approximately $115 billion in new money was invested by the private equity sponsors, representing about a 25 percent equity ratio in the deals. At the same time, existing shareholders were paid out the staggering sum of $375 billion in cash at the deal closings. That was CEW on steroids. Most of the cash circulated back through the Wall Street–hedge fund complex looking for the next upside speculation.

Secondly, to finance this enormous CEW extraction the balance sheets of these thirty mega-LBOs were freighted down *with $375 billion in debt, an amount nearly four times the debt they carried prior to the buyouts.* As shown below, however, most of these companies were decidedly not good LBO candidates, and almost all the deals drastically overvalued future cash flows.

As a consequence, after five to seven years virtually none of this debt has been paid down in the manner of the classic LBO model. Nearly half of the thirty companies have entered bankruptcy or voluntary restructuring. Most of the remainder are financial zombies which have managed to use the Fed's third financial bubble during 2009–2012 to delay their debt maturities through "extend and pretend" refinancings.

What remains, therefore, is a $400 billion wall of debt that will eventually tumble over during the next recession, or when the corporate pachyderms which are lugging it finally buckle under the weight.

THE FIRST WAVE OF MEGA-LBOS:
$40 BILLION OF CEW AND NINE TIMES MORE DEBT

The first out of the box in March 2005 was Toys R Us Inc. at $7 billion, and the scale-up was steep from there. Next came Realogy Corporation at $9 billion, Univision Communications Inc. at $12 billion, Hertz at $15 billion, and Freescale Semiconductor Inc. at $18 billion. All five of these deals were completed before the end of 2006; none were logically viable candidates for a leveraged buyout; and all have hit the wall or have been consigned to financial zombie land ever since.

The combined value of these five buyouts was $62 billion, and $45 billion of this was funded with new junk bonds and leveraged bank loans. Their dubious suitability as LBO candidates is pointedly suggested by the fact that these companies had only $5 billion of debt among them prior to the transactions. They were the type of enterprise which had historically eschewed leverage, but now they had nine times more debt.

For example, Toys R US was locked in a viciously competitive struggle for market share with Wal-Mart and could ill afford to be weighed down with a millstone of heavy debt service claims on its cash flow. Likewise, Freescale was a pure commodity play in the violently cyclical semiconductor industry that had always been off limits to LBOs.

These deals also aptly demonstrate how mega-LBOs cycled massive amounts of CEW out of business sector equity accounts and into the financial markets. Private equity sponsors invested $17 billion of their new capital hoard in these mega-deals, but at the closings of these five transactions $57 billion of cash flowed the other way, back into the financial markets as proceeds to the selling shareholders. The great CEW raid was on.

STEPPING INTO HARM'S WAY: THE TOYS R US BUYOUT

That these deals were insensible at the time is evident from their struggles for survival ever since. Toys R Us was emblematic. In early 2005 it was a shadow of its former glory with its same-store sales in perilous decline. They had dropped by nearly 4 percent during 2004 and by nearly 10 percent from levels attained in 2001, reflecting Wal-Mart's powerful drive to dominate the toys category and eject Toys R Us from its twenty-five-year reign on top.

It largely succeeded. By the time of the buyout deal, Wal-Mart's 25 percent market share was well ahead of the 16 percent still held by Toys R Us. Indeed, Wal-Mart had already demonstrated that trying to compete against it as an LBO could be hazardous. The second-largest big-box toy retailer, KB Toys, had been put on the LBO bus by Bain Capital a few years earlier and had landed squarely in Chapter 11 by early 2004.

It was a sign of the mania, however, that not only were these competitive realities ignored, but the deal price was so high as to add insult to injury. When Bain Capital and KKR won the auction they got no bargain, paying an astounding 22X operating income (earnings before interest and taxes). The apparent justification was that if you didn't count depreciation as an expense, then the multiple of EBITDA was only 10X.

This way of reckoning purchase multiples was standard fare in the LBO business. In some cases, however, companies needed to spend every dime of their depreciation on capital expenditure to stay competitive and viable, and a death struggle with Wal-Mart to get fickle consumers in the front door was surely one of those cases.

Worse still, Toys R Us earned 100 percent of its fiscal-year 2004 EBITDA of $660 million in the fourth quarter. So even by this preferred measure of earnings, Toys R Us would be starting its LBO life just one bad Christmas season away from disaster.

When the deal closed, the company had $5.4 billion of debt, or eight times its EBITDA. A decade earlier, even aggressive LBO houses would not have marched an LBO straight into the jaws of Wal-Mart with even half that leverage ratio, in part because the high-yield debt market would not have financed it.

As it turned out, neither the passage of time nor the "magic" of private equity management could cure the profound disabilities that resulted from the company's crippling level of debt. At the end of fiscal 2011, Toys R Us still had $5.2 billion worth of debt; its leverage ratio was still more than five times EBITDA; and it was still just one bad holiday season from hitting the wall.

In fact, the saga of Toys R Us perfectly resembles that of most of the financial zombies which came out of the mega-LBOs of 2005–2008. The LBO deal boosted the retailer's debt from $500 million to nearly $5.5 billion, thereby permitting $5 billion of CEW to be extracted and recycled to Wall Street.

In the aftermath, however, the company now struggles with tired stores and a tired strategy and is locked in a straitjacket of LBO debt that it cannot reduce. And the debt itself has been refinanced and kicked down the road repeatedly. The company thus stands only a new recession or another frontal attack by Amazon or Wal-Mart away from eventual demise.

FREESCALE SEMICONDUCTOR: ACCIDENT SCENE OF BROKEN RULES

The Freescale Semiconductor story is worse. This $17.6 billion deal was led by Blackstone, but on the numbers it wasn't the cautious, investment rule–based Blackstone I had known during twelve years there as a partner through 1999. In those earlier times we had avoided cyclical businesses, especially those with a heavy technology and an R&D component because sales could experience sudden displacement by new technology. LBO candidates which competed with East Asian cheap labor, government subsidies, and pegged currencies got short shrift, too.

By 2006, Blackstone apparently succumbed to the mania of the hour and abandoned most of those old-time disciplines. Semiconductors were the very embodiment of cyclicality and especially so with Freescale, due to its sales mix. Nearly 45 percent were in the purely cyclical automotive market; another one-third of sales went to its former parent, Motorola, which had already fallen drastically behind the competition in the cell phone market. So the company's sales base was unusually vulnerable, but even these sales were not all they seemed.

Freescale also required a massive $1.2 billion annual R&D investment, 20 percent of sales, to stay up with the competition and changing technology. This meant that these costs were largely fixed even if short-term revenues plummeted. On top of all that, Freescale operated in the crosshairs of fierce competition from Japan and the Korean semiconductor powerhouses led by Samsung.

The great LBO houses formed tag teams and conducted a bidding war in the fall of 2006 as the bubble neared its fevered peak. Blackstone and its top-drawer partners, TBG Group and Carlyle Group, won over KKR and its equally pedigreed partners, but at a price which was ludicrous by any rational reckoning. Despite all of Freescale's unsuitability for a leveraged buyout, the $17.6 billion winning bid amounted to nineteen times the company's 2006 operating income of $950 million.

The sponsors rationalized that the multiple of EBITDA, as opposed to operating income, was "only" in the low double digits, but that was a non sequitur. No company up against the likes of Siemens, Samsung, Toshiba, or Qualcomm would have proposed to skimp on capital expense, meaning that every penny of the depreciation charge was already spoken for. So the deal was done at a lunatic multiple against performance numbers that could well have represented a cyclical peak.

In fact, they represented high watermarks that would never be seen again—not by a long shot. The $6.4 billion of sales inherited in 2006 actually dropped by 10 percent the next year, even before the recession began, and then plunged steadily until they hit bottom at $3.5 billion in 2009. This calamitous 45 percent reduction in top-line sales is exactly the kind of horror story scenario we had spent the 1990s fastidiously avoiding in Blackstone investment committee meetings.

The fear had always been that costs at big industrial operations were "sticky" in the near term and that operating income and EBITDA would therefore take a beating in the event of a cyclical collapse in sales. In this respect, Freescale turned out to be a case that revalidated the textbook.

By the 2009 cycle bottom operating income had vanished and posted at negative $150 million. The company's EBITDA also collapsed to $300 million, meaning that its debt of $7.5 billion stood at twenty-five times EBITDA. Even that deathly leverage ratio was achieved only after the sponsors injected about $2 billion of additional equity to retire debt in a desperate effort to keep the company alive.

While Freescale has slowly limped back from its near-death experience of 2009, it remains a financial zombie. Sales at $4.5 billion are still 30 percent below the level at the time of the buyout, while operating income and EBITDA are still down 20 percent and 33 percent, respectively. Debt remains at $6.6 billion, meaning that aside from the partner's equity injection the debt burden remains about where it started.

Accordingly, Freescale has been reduced to a rounding error in the global semiconductor industry and will never survive the next cyclical downturn. It remains a monument to the irrational exuberance of the second Greenspan bubble, and a complete perversion of whatever justification LBOs originally had. The only purpose of this one had been to extract about $10 billion of CEW and recycle it back into the Wall Street casino.

None of the other three deals in this group have made much progress in lessening their debt burden, either. Univision's $9.3 billion of debt, for example, has not been diminished at all and still represented fourteen times its operating income in fiscal 2011. The largest Spanish-language TV network thus hangs on by a financial thread, having recorded net losses every year since the 2006 LBO and cumulating to more than $6 billion.

Overall, these five mega-LBOs started with $45 billion of debt, and save for modest equity injections by sponsors have not paid down a single dime. The four which remain private and financially precarious desperately pursued an IPO in 2010–2012, hoping that the Fed could keep its third bubble going long enough to unload stock onto the next round of punters. It didn't happen, and so they remain financial zombies, lugging a massive load of debt they cannot escape and which will eventually cripple the business enterprises which labor underneath.

THE SEVEN BIGGEST LBO MONSTERS OF ALL

As the binge gathered momentum, the deals grew skyward like some kind of financial beanstalk. The nation's largest radio broadcasting operation, Clear Channel Communications, was taken private in a $23 billion deal. Alltel Corporation, a large cellular utility, and Hilton Hotels each underwent $27 billion LBOs. First Data Corporation, the nation's leading financial services processing vendor, came in at $28 billion, followed by Harrah's, a huge casino operation, at $29 billion, and the nation's largest hospital chain, HCA Inc., at $32 billion.

Finally, TXU Corporation, a giant Texas utility, became the largest LBO of all time at $47 billion. All of these mega-LBOs occurred in a twenty-month interval between late 2006 and early 2008, and on a combined basis amounted to $210 billion of transaction value. Still, they absorbed only a modest $40 billion increment of the massive private equity hoard then foraging for deals.

Accordingly, these seven deals were the true leverage monsters of the second Greenspan bubble. The preponderant share of their funding came from $175 billion of bank loans and junk bonds, resulting in an 80 percent debt-to-capitalization ratio. Yet with the possible exception of HCA, which had already gone private once before, none of them would have been considered plausible LBO candidates by past standards, and most especially not with debt ratios at the outer edge.

Nearly all of these final giant deals were the outcome of heated bidding wars between ad hoc coalitions, or "clubs," of the private equity houses.

The result was outlandish deal prices that virtually guaranteed failure but were made possible by the state of near delirium in the high-yield debt markets. The latter enabled the private equity "clubs" to keep bidding higher until they tapped out the last dime of available debt funding.

When the smoke cleared on these seven mega-LBOs, their combined capitalization of $210 billion amounted to sixteen times operating income and eleven times EBITDA. Under the facts at hand, such valuation multiples had no discernible relationship to sanity. They were computed against earnings near the top of the business cycle, and which mostly arose from mature businesses with trend growth rates tethered to GDP, meaning that these multiples were double what would have made sense in ordinary times on the free market.

Most of these giant companies also had substantial recurring capital investment needs. Drastic overvaluation at the setup, therefore, was not amenable to the classic LBO remedy; namely, to strip virtually 100 percent of operating cash flows so that the initial crush of debt could be steadily alleviated.

The proof that these deals were a derangement of classic proportion is in the pudding. More than a half decade later, hardly a dime of their original $175 billion debt capitalization has been paid down. In fact, on an apples-to-apples basis, the current debt of the seven companies is $165 billion, and most of this minor difference is accounted for by sponsor swaps of fresh equity for the distressed junk bonds of their own companies.

This failure to pay down debt is fatal because it is fundamentally inconsistent with the true economic function of an LBO, which is massive debt issuance in order to prepay selling shareholders for future excess cash flows. Accordingly, when this initial LBO debt doesn't get paid down, it means there was no excess cash flow in the first place.

That is precisely what occurred with these seven mega-LBOs. A huge amount of putative future excess cash flow was monetized by these deals. Accordingly, more than $160 billion was paid out to existing shareholders in the most concentrated episode of CEW extraction during the entire second Greenspan bubble, but, alas, the implied huge magnitudes of excess cash flow were not really there.

These seven companies have been able to generate only enough cash flow to pay the interest and meet the minimum reinvestment needs of their businesses. Accordingly, they have become permanent beasts of financial burden, lugging a massive debt that cannot be repaid and that has left them on the ragged each of insolvency and continuous resort to "extend and pretend" refinancings. They will go down for the count in the next recession.

CHAPTER 25

DEALS GONE WILD

Rise of the Debt Zombies

THE WILDEST SPECULATORS IN LEO MELAMED'S PORK-BELLY RINGS at the Chicago Merc could never have dreamed up a commodity trade as fantastical as that underlying the $47 billion LBO of TXU Corporation. It was basically a bet on a truly aberrational price gap between cheap coal and expensive natural gas—a "fuels arb"—that couldn't possibly last. So the largest LBO in history was the ultimate folly of bubble finance.

THE TEXAS GAS BUBBLE MASSACRE

Electric power utilities are normally stable generators of cash flow, plodding along a tepid path of growth. But TXU's financial results in the year before its February 2007 buyout deal had been mercurial, making its initially benign leverage ratios an illusion. Thus, TXU had posted about $11 billion of revenue and $4.5 billion of operating income prior to the buyout, but by fiscal 2011 the company's sales were down by 35 percent, to $7 billion, and operating income was just $960 million. Its bottom line had plummeted by nearly 80 percent from the pre-LBO level.

Accordingly, the company's leverage ratio has become a horror show. Its fiscal 2011 debt stood at $36 billion and thereby amounted to nearly thirty-eight times its reported operating income. In LBO land that ratio is beyond the pale—it's a veritable financial freak.

How the largest LBO in history ended up this far off the deep end is a crucial question because it goes right to the heart of the great deformation of finance. The TXU deal is the financial "Vietnam" of the Greenspan bubble era, not some dismissible aberration from the main events. It was sponsored by the "best and brightest" in the private equity world including KKR, the founding fathers of LBOs, and David Bonderman's TPG, which was also a successful LBO pioneer of legendary rank.

Since the equity portion of the financing at $8 billion was only 17 percent of the total capitalization, TXU's existing $12 billion of conventional utility debt had to be tripled, to $38 billion, in order to close the deal. Accordingly, Wall Street had a money orgy coming and going. Fees on the new deal exceeded $1 billion, and at the LBO closing there was an epic $32 billion payday for selling shareholders, including the hedge funds which had front-run the deal.

At the time, the reckless wager embodied in the TXU buyout was rationalized as nothing special. The purchase price at 8.5 times EBITDA was purportedly in line with the 7.9X average for publicly traded utilities. Yet when the onion was peeled back by a year or two it became clear that the buyout was being set up at a lunatic multiple: an astonishing 18X the company's EBITDA in 2004.

This jarring difference reflected the fact that TXU's income was temporarily and drastically inflated by a utility deregulation bubble floating on top of a natural gas bubble. Under the Texas deregulation scheme, wholesale electric power prices were set by the marginal cost of supply, which was natural gas fired power plants. But TXU generated most of its power from lignite coal and uranium, so when natural gas prices soared its own fuel costs remained at rock bottom. The company's revenue margin over the cost of fuel, therefore, also soared, rising from 38 percent in 2004 to nearly 60 percent in 2006. The gain was pure profit.

If deregulation meant a permanent increase in TXU's profit margins, of course, the heady February 2007 LBO valuation of its current cash flow might have made sense. The underlying reality, however, was that the price of wholesale electric power in Texas at the moment had been inflated by a humongous natural gas price bubble which flared-up in the wake of Hurricane Katrina's August 2005 disruption of offshore gas production.

Natural gas prices had soared to the unheard of range of $10 and $15 per thousand cubic feet (Mcf), compared to a band of $2–$5 per Mcf that had prevailed for years. So TXU's fulsome cash flow was running on the afterburners, as it were, of one of the greatest commodity bubbles of recent times.

At the same time that TXU was booking revenues of 13.7 cents per Kwh based on natural gas prices, the fuels cost at its base-load nuke plants was 0.4 cents per kWh and just 1.2 cents in its lignite coal plants. Thus, at the coincident peaks of the Greenspan credit bubble and the natural gas price bubble in February 2007, TXU was selling electric power at 12X and 36X the cost of its lignite- and uranium-based power, respectively.

These markups were off-the-charts crazy. Even after absorption of modest fixed operating costs (labor and maintenance) at its power plants and corporate overhead, the profits were staggering. It was only a matter of time, therefore, until the natural gas bubble ruptured and TXU's power margins came crashing back to earth.

HOW THE FED HELPED BUSHWHACK TXU

As it happened, the Fed's rock-bottom interest rates were contagious and fueled a boom in debt-financed gas drilling that soon caused supplies to soar and natural gas prices to plummet. In this manner, the power plant "fuels arb" was flattened and with it the company's financial results. The Fed thus unintentionally bushwhacked the largest LBO in history. So doing, it demonstrated just how badly the nation's central bank had mangled the free market.

When Bernanke slashed interest rates to nearly zero, it triggered a Wall Street scramble for "yield" products to peddle to desperate investors—at the very time that the natural gas patch was swarming with drillers willing to issue just such high yielding securities. The natural gas price bubble had encouraged a drilling boom based on horizontal wells and chemical flooding of gas reservoirs. This "fracking" process can liberate prodigious amounts of natural gas that otherwise would remain trapped in low-porosity shale reservoirs, but it also slurps capital in vast amounts: fracked wells generate bountiful gas output during their first few months of production but then peter out rapidly. Thus, the whole secret of the so-called fracking revolution was to drill, drill, and keep drilling.

The tens of billions of fresh cash required for the shale-fracking play was not a problem for the fast-money dealers of Wall Street, who had just the answer: namely, high-yielding natural gas investments called VPPs (volume production payments). These were another form of opaque off-balance sheet debt. In this case investors provided up-front funding for gas wells in return for a fat yield and a collateral claim on the gas.

Accordingly, a flood of Wall Street money found its way to red-hot shale gas drillers like XTO, which was soon swallowed whole by ExxonMobil, and to the kingpin of the shale-fracking play, Chesapeake Energy. Its balance sheet grew explosively between 2003 and 2011, with proven reserves rising from 2 trillion cubic feet to 20 trillion and total assets climbing from $4 billion to $40 billion.

It was virtually limitless Wall Street drilling money that accounted for this pell-mell expansion. During this same eight-year period, Chesapeake's outstanding level of "high yield" borrowings—bonds, preferreds, and VPPs—soared from $2 billion to $21 billion. In this respect, Chesapeake was only the most visible practitioner of what was an industry-wide stampede to "borrow and drill."

This debt-driven explosion of reserves, production, and injected storage eventually left giant drillers like Chesapeake gasping for solvency; massive new gas supplies caused prices to steadily weaken and then crash. By the spring of 2012, natural gas was trading at a price so devastatingly low ($2.50 per Mcf) that even the monster of the gas patch, ExxonMobil, cried uncle. "We are losing our shirts" complained its CEO, Rex Tillerson.

With little prospect that natural gas will revive anytime soon, TXU's revenues and operating income will remain in the sub-basement. The $36 billion of LBO debt raised at the top of the Greenspan bubble is therefore almost certain to default owing, ironically, to the aftershocks of the even larger debt bubble which fueled the fracking binge.

The larger point is that artificially cheap debt causes profound distortions, dislocations, and malinvestments as it wends its way through the real economy. In this case underpriced debt fostered a giant, uneconomic LBO and also massive overinvestment in natural gas fracking. When the collision of the two finally brings about the thundering collapse of the largest LBO in history, there should be no doubt that it was fostered by the foolish money printers in the Eccles Building and the LBO funds who took the bait.

WHY DEBT ZOMBIES REMAIN:
GOLDMAN AND TPG'S THIRTY-WEEK RAID ON ALLTEL

The massive debt created by the giant LBOs of 2006–2008 has stuck to the ribs of the US economy ever since. This is true even in the $28 billion Alltel buyout, where the private equity sponsors of the deal, Goldman Sachs and TPG, were able to harvest a $1.3 billion profit without breaking a sweat during their thirty-week stint as at-risk owners. But the $24 billion of debt used to fund the LBO didn't go away when the sponsors collected their quickie winnings. It was just shuffled along to the buyer, Verizon, where it was added to its existing debt of $42 billion.

The Alltel LBO thus functioned as a financial laundry. The company's debt was raised from $2 billion to $24 billion and an equal amount of cash was paid out to its public shareholders and speculators. Then, after only a few months in the garb of an LBO, its heavily mortgaged assets were passed on to a new corporate owner.

The Alltel LBO was thus recorded as a roaring success because its sponsors made a 50 percent annualized return. Yet that was possible only because the next owner—a lumbering quasi-public utility that has been destroying shareholder value for a decade—kissed the buyout shops with a modest premium on their small equity investment, and then carried the whole mountain of LBO debt forward on its own balance sheet.

This preposterous debt shuffle could not have occurred on the free market because Verizon's purchase price at 19X operating income was ludicrous. This was especially so since the Alltel wireless business was overwhelmingly a "contiguous" rather than an "in-market" acquisition, meaning that there were virtually no cost savings.

The real synergy, in fact, was purely financial. Verizon's after-tax cost of debt was only 3.7 percent, meaning that its debt financing cost on the $28 billion purchase price was just $1.0 billion annually. Since Alltel's $1.5 billion of operating income substantially exceeded this figure, the acquisition computed out to be "accretive."

Plain and simple, the deal was driven by state policy—the tax deductibility of debt capital and the radical financial repression policies of the Fed. Undoubtedly, the monetary politburo had visions that its ultra-low interest rate régime would spur investment in plant and equipment or IT system upgrades. In fact, it was supplying high octane fuel for financial engineering—a signal to corporate executives to grow their asset base the easy way—that is, on the floor of the New York Stock Exchange.

The proud new owner of Alltel's $24 billion of LBO debt, however, was actually a poster boy for failed financial engineering. For more than a decade Verizon's serial M&A had caused the scope of its operations to continuously swell, even as its earnings had gone steadily south, falling from $2.70 per share in 2004 to less than $0.90 in recent years. Despite the capital intensive nature of telecom, Verizon had skimped on CapEx, causing the inflation-adjusted value of its plant and equipment to shrink by about 25 percent over 2002–2011. Yet the decade-long M&A spree of executives obsessed by merger mania and pumping their stock price caused its nominal asset base to grow by $60 billion, or 35 percent.

So the smoking gun wasn't hard to find: nearly 90 percent of that asset gain was due to a doubling of its goodwill—that is, M&A deal premiums. Indeed, Verizon's goodwill now totals more than $100 billion and represents nearly 45 percent of its asset base.

Such massive goodwill, alas, is a telltale sign of a debt-ridden deal machine of the type fostered by the Fed's bubble finance. The startling fact, therefore, is that the nation's largest telecom services vendor has a tangible net worth of negative $17 billion. Its deal-making executives have been destroying value for more than a decade, aided and abetted by central bank money printers.

HOW KKR STRIPPED THE BEDS IN AMERICA'S LARGEST HOSPITAL CHAIN WITH SOME HELP FROM BUBBLES BEN

The November 2006 HCA buyout was notable for its then-record breaking

$33 billion size and its exceedingly thrifty approach to the equity account. KKR and its partners put up only $3.9 billion of fresh equity, or about 12 percent, of the capitalization of this monster deal. Funding the $28 billion debt balance required a veritable Noah's ark of every kind of debt known to Wall Street, including revolvers, term loans, junk bonds, foreign loans, and even a far-out instrument called "second-lien toggle notes."

At first glance, HCA's 160-unit hospital system might appear to be exactly the wrong candidate for massive permanent leverage. After all, the HCA system obtained 45 percent of its revenues from Medicare and Medicaid, government programs which have long been on the fiscal ragged edge and which are increasingly subject to indeterminate and unpredictable regulatory and reimbursement risk.

Yet the stunningly aggressive manner in which KKR and Bain have literally plundered cash from HCA since the mega-buyout implies just the opposite. After loading HCA with $28 billion of debt to fund the original buyout, KKR and Bain have since extracted dividends and stock buybacks amounting to another $7 billion. These massive payouts to the sponsors have absorbed every dime of available cash and borrowing capacity at HCA. In fact, during the four years ending in fiscal 2011 the company generated just $5 billion of income from operations net of capital spending and investing activities, meaning that the dividends and buybacks amounted to an incredible 140 percent of HCA's free cash flow.

By every traditional rule of leveraged buyouts, all of that free cash flow should have been allocated to paying down debt, so that the company could have edged out of harm's way. In fact, HCA's debt mountain had not been reduced by a net dime after four years, and it was a preposterously overleveraged deal in the first place.

Perhaps the most telling evidence of the latter point came from the company's own CEO, Jack Bovender. When asked what had been the biggest shock which came out of the LBO, he replied, "Honestly, the fact that you could borrow $28 billion."

KKR had been able to borrow $28 billion because the second junk loan bubble was red hot at the time of the original deal, but after collapsing into the depths in 2009 it had made a roaring comeback just in time to fund the HCA dividends in 2010. Indeed, Bernanke's maniacal money printing after the Lehman event had catalyzed a virtual stampede back into the very same risk-asset classes which had been reduced to smoldering ruins during the financial crisis.

In fact, junk bonds had undergone their third miraculous rebirth since the age of bubble finance began in 1987. Once again, it was speculator driven money flows into the junk bond asset class that levitated prices, not the credit facts on the ground. Most leveraged issuers were still limping operationally and had neither paid down significant debts nor had any prospects of doing so.

Nevertheless, the Fed so juiced the carry trade with free "funding currency" that astute speculators now anticipated a rising junk bond market. This trend, in turn, would permit troubled LBO borrowers to refinance or otherwise "extend and pretend," and thereby sharply reduce the realized rate of defaults and make existing junk bonds far more attractive. Accordingly, by November 2010 junk bond prices were up a stunning 85 percent from their post-Lehman lows.

Hedge fund speculators were now essentially operating in the third degree of Keynes' beauty contest (see chapter 23). Punters were buying ugly credits hand over fist because they anticipated that other punters would find these credits considerably more attractive, once their struggling borrowers had kicked their current balloon of maturing obligations down the Fed-sponsored road of perpetual refinance.

Not surprisingly, 2010 and 2011 became record years for junk bond issuance, notwithstanding an economy that was still furtively laboring to "recover" and, according to the leading Keynesian shaman, Larry Summers, had not yet obtained "escape velocity." Nonetheless, $500 billion of junk bonds were issued in those two years—65 percent more than during the previous peak of 2006–2007 when the mega-LBOs had been spawned.

In the context of the 2010–2011 junk bond boom, the leveraged dividend recap made a reappearance like clockwork. Thus, in November 2010 KKR and Bain announced they would pay themselves a $2 billion dividend and that it would be financed with a new issue of junk bonds to be piled on top of HCA's $28 billion of debt.

Moreover, this was actually their third dividend payday of the year. The first two payouts had been even more egregious: the private equity sponsors borrowed $1.75 billion in February 2010 from HCA's bank revolver to pay themselves a dividend and then, unbelievably, banged the revolver again in May for another $500 million dividend.

Lender permission to strip dividends out of a revolver would have been scarcely imaginable only a few years back. By 2010, however, the Fed's embrace of "too big to fail" had induced the great LBO banks of Wall Street to permit borrowers to raid their own vital liquidity lines (i.e., credit revolvers) like a piggy bank. In previous times the Wall Street banks had at least insisted that unsecured or subordinated lenders be tapped for the honor of fronting the dividend money. Now, in its desperate post-Lehman efforts to encourage "risk on," even that had gone by the wayside. The Fed had thus unleashed the financial Furies.

At the end of the day, the multiple HCA dividend recaps underscored that the world of junk debt and LBOs had taken on a whole new modus operandi. The great Wall Street banks no longer even worried about repayment risk because the Fed was now vividly confirming that redemption of debt wasn't necessary.

Instead, under the Bernanke dispensation corporate debt was meant to be perpetually refinanced. Not coincidentally, these "evergreen" pools of debt, like HCA's $28 billion, would also favor Wall Street with a constant stream of underwritings and refinancing fees.

Furthermore, the job of the Fed under this perpetual refinancing régime was to stand ready with a liquidity hose, prepared to fund any amount of faltering debt that Wall Street banks might be choking on during periods of "financial crisis." Such bad debts historically had caused banks to suffer painful losses and accountable executives to get fired. Now such failing credits had been redefined as evidence of a new financial disease called "contagion" and "systemic risk" which needed to be combated at all hazards, even if it rewarded the perilous breach of sound underwriting standards so blatantly evident in the HCA dividend episode.

At it happened, by the spring of 2011 things got even better for KKR and Bain. The Bernanke bubble now had the risk asset market so cranked up that HCA was able to launch an IPO, with most of the proceeds again going into the sponsor's bank accounts rather than into the company's coffers to pay down debt. Based on the previous dividends, the IPO stock sales, and the value of their remaining stock at the $30 per share IPO price, KKR and Bain stood to harvest a windfall profit of $3 billion each on their original $1.2 billion equity contributions to the deal.

THE HCA PRIVATE EQUITY PLUNDER:
STATE POLICY RUN AMOK

At the end of the day, the circumstances of the $33 billion HCA buyout are a screaming indictment of current policies of the state. HCA is the nation's largest hospital chain, but it thrives only by dint of the $15 billion it collects each year from Medicaid and Medicare. These revenues are vastly inflated compared to what HCA would obtain if it had to compete for patient dollars in an honest consumer-driven market.

Worse still, the KKR-Bain deal had thrived only because an effort by the Bush administration to reform the rickety machinery of hospital reimbursement under Medicare had been shut down by a mighty crony capitalist coalition of hospitals and other medical vendors at the time of the HCA buyout in 2006. The Bush reform effort would have reduced the payment rates for DRGs (diagnostic review groups) by upward of 33 percent for certain high-cost hospital services such as Cardiac, Neurosurgical, and Orthopedic.

The Medicare DRG rates for these services became drastically inflated over the years and now accounted for upward of 70 percent of hospital profits in institutions like HCA. These bloated profits were also gifts that had originated way back in the Reagan administration, when in desperation we had resorted to a disguised system of hospital price controls to curb the explosively growing Medicare budgets.

We had been warned at the time that the DRG system was not the great reform it was cracked up to be. Yet we embraced it because it was a significant improvement on the prior system which paid hospitals a per diem rate based on their actual costs—a system which obviously rewarded unnecessarily long stays and padded cost structures. By contrast, the DRG scheme established a lump-sum payment per case, regardless of the length of stay, for about 450 distinct diagnostic groups such as heart surgery, and was based mainly on systemwide cost factors rather than the hospital's own costs.

This arrangement did reduce the worst incentives of the old daily rate approach, but the problem was that hospitals would soon learn to game the system. In a phenomenon called "DRG creep" sophisticated procedures were developed by hospitals to "code" each admission to the DRG with the highest payment rate.

Accordingly, within a few years an annual allowance typically of 2 percent in DRG rates to compensate for general inflation would end up producing an actual 6 percent gain after allowing for the "DRG creep" of the caseload into high-paying categories. The only real solution, therefore, was regulatory vigilance and a periodic downward reset of DRG rates for the most abused procedures.

Needless to say, these DRG rates were bureaucratic prices, not market prices. Consequently, the rate-setting process (i.e., price controls) was tailor-made for manipulation by crony capitalists and their hired K Street lobbies. Every species of impacted vendor—from manufacturers of artificial hips to general hospital chain operators—was fully engaged in this bureaucratic price fixing.

Moreover, in this instance crony capitalism was actually a family affair. Fully $1 billion of the equity capital for the HCA buyout was supplied by the estimable Thomas Frist, the original founder of HCA and energetic foe of the very Big Government on which his fortune was based. In waging this campaign the Frist family left no stone unturned, placing Bill Frist in the US Senate and seeing to it that he eventually became majority leader.

Needless to say, the Senate majority leader required no schooling as to why Federal bureaucrats needed to be prevented from reducing payments for stent surgery by 33 percent, or cutting the Medicare payment for a defibrillator implant from $30,000 to $22,000. In fact, the entire proposed DRG reset was designed to drive these kinds of expensive specialty treatments away from high-cost general hospital chains like HCA and toward a medical version of low-cost, high-volume "focused factories."

The estimate at the time was that this sweeping change in the Medicare reimbursement régime could have reduced its hospital payments by 30 percent and would have struck a mortal blow at high-cost general hospital chains like HCA. Stated differently, much of the inflated EBITDA which was absorbing HCA's $2.0 billion annual interest bill would have been clawed back to the benefit of taxpayers.

As it happened, Bill Frist retired from the Senate at the end of 2006 in a blaze of glory for numerous deeds which had allegedly taken a nick out of Big Government. Among these was a congressional kibosh on the proposed Medicare reimbursement reforms, an action that actually made Big Government fatter by tens of billions per year; a favor it bestowed upon the Frist family fortune as well.

With the Medicare reimbursement spigot locked in the "wide-open" position by congressional mandate, HCA has generated a healthy 5 percent growth in revenues since 2005 and a 5.5 percent annual gain in EBITDA. This has permitted it to service its $2.0 billion per year interest tab and still make the huge dividend payments described above.

Still, the fact that $28 billion in debt can be serviced in this manner is only possible owing to the interest rate repression policies of the Fed and the tax deductibility of interest payments. This case makes self-evident that together these policies have fostered an insanely leveraged capital structure that would never see the light of day in a genuine free market with neutral rules of taxation. Moreover, the régime of "too big to fail" now adds insult to injury by encouraging banks to fund reckless self-dealing dividends which would have been shocking even to the LBO industry one decade earlier.

In short, the KKR and Bain buyout of HCA makes for a fitting tombstone on free market capitalism. In a world in which the financial maneuvers described above can happen, the discipline of the free market has long since disappeared.

THE DEBT ZOMBIES KEPT ON COMING

All the founders of the LBO industry—KKR, Blackstone, Apollo, TPG, and Bain Capital—have been stuck in giant deals that have turned into debt zombies. Accordingly, the outbreak of mega-LBO mania during 2006–2007 was not simply the result of one or two firms becoming overly exuberant.

Instead, it reflected a financial market deformation that sowed mania and recklessness across the entire private equity space.

The eventual result might best be described as turnkey bidding wars. Syndicates of the big Wall Street banks offered turnkey financing packages consisting of multitudinous layers of secured, unsecured, and exotic "toggle" and "second-lien" debt to competing private equity bidding groups. The latter only needed to "slot-in" a 20–30 percent equity commitment at the bottom of these turn-key debt structures in order to reach a total bid price for giant companies put up for auction by other groups of Wall Street investment bankers.

The heated bidding wars among the top tier private equity houses thus resulted in a "topping-up" of transaction prices which were being set in the yield-crazed debt markets. In this frenzy even the most disciplined private equity houses lost their heads because by now a second fatal assumption had planted deep roots on Wall Street—namely, that the Fed's Great Moderation guaranteed that GDP would not falter and that financing markets would remain buoyant.

The $28 billion buyout of First Data Corporation, the nation's largest processor of credit and debit card data for banks and merchants, dramatically illustrates the sheer insanity of these LBO bidding wars. In theory, First Data might have escaped the zombie debt trap since—for better or worse—credit cards have been a growth industry and, in fact, the company's revenues have risen at a 7 percent rate since 2007, notwithstanding the Great Recession.

But First Data has actually made no progress at all in reducing the $22 billion LBO debt it took on in September 2007 for a single overpowering reason: the speculative climate fostered by the Fed was so frenzied that even the gray eminence of the industry, KKR, was induced to acquire a good company at a preposterous price. The $28 billion price tag thus represented an astounding 51X the pro forma operating income of the company during 2007 and nearly 16X EBITDA.

It goes without saying that the company's modestly growing sales and cash flow have been no match for $2 billion of annual interest expense. Accordingly, during the eighteen quarters since the buyout, First Data has recorded nearly $7 billion in net losses. After netting capital spending and minority partner payments against income from operations, the company generated less than $450 million of free cash flow during the entire period. Needless to say, at that rate ($25 million per quarter) it would take First Data 220 years to pay off its debt!

In truth, a crash landing has been prevented so far only because billions of LBO debt has been subjected to "extend and pretend." During the first quarter of 2012, for example, the company refinanced $3 billion of bank debt at higher interest rates, thereby deferring these maturities from 2014 until 2017. At free market interest rates, by contrast, First Data could never refinance its $23 billion of loans as they come due. Keeping the debt zombies alive, therefore, is just one more deformation that flows from the Fed's financial repression policies.

CLEAR CHANNEL COMMUNICATIONS: DEBT ZOMBIE ON A "STICK"

In May 2008 Bain Capital and Thomas Lee saw fit to pay fourteen times operating income for a company that was the communications industry equivalent of the proverbial buggy-whip maker. Clear Channel Communications, in fact, had been a speculator par excellence in the humble business of owning what were called radio "sticks," or FCC licenses, to operate AM and FM radio stations.

By the time of its $23 billion LBO, it owned 850 radio stations, and it could not be gainsaid that radio stations were profitable. During 2007 Clear Channel had generated about $1.6 billion of operating income, a figure which amounted to a healthy 24.1 percent of its $6.8 billion in net revenues.

Thus, the deal sponsors did not hesitate to pile on the debt, pushing the company's borrowings from $5 billion to $20 billion in order to fund an $18 billion payday for the current stockholders. This massive debt load was readily raised, however, because radio "sticks" were a favored offspring of the Greenspan bubble era.

Due to abundant and increasingly cheaper debt financing, LBO operators large and small had driven the value of radio sticks steadily higher, from less than $8 per pop (population served) to nearly $20 per pop at the peak in 2007–2008. At that point deals were being valued not on their operating income, but on their resale value; that is, based on stick flipping.

Accordingly, Clear Channel's $23 billion LBO reflected the trading value of its massive collection of sticks and billboards, not the company's operating income which had increased at only a prosaic 4.5 percent rate during the four years ending in 2007, and even much of that was due to acquisitions. The magic value gains of radio sticks, however, rested on a double helping of bubble finance; that is, consumer advertising growth and cheap debt.

Radio advertising revenue grew moderately during the bubble era because the heaviest advertisers—auto dealers, home builders, restaurants, and bars—were the beneficiaries of the housing boom and consumer spending obtained from their home ATM machines. In effect, valuations rose because consumers were spending borrowed money which fueled radio station advertising and cash flow. And then, cheap financing for leveraged radio deals caused stick valuation multiples to be bid up even further.

Needless to say, the music stopped in September 2008. Radio advertising has not recovered from the sharp decline triggered by the violent collapse of the auto and housing industries. And now radio operators are also confronted with gale-force headwinds owing to the migration of advertising dollars from broadcast to the Internet, and to competition from alternate technologies such as Internet radio (e.g., Pandora).

Not surprisingly, Clear Channel's financial results have headed irrevocably southward. During fiscal 2011 its revenues were still 10 percent below 2007 levels, but, more importantly, the fat profit margins which once reflected the state-bestowed gift of scarce radio spectrum are now beginning to rapidly erode in the face of genuine free enterprise competition.

Thus, by 2011 Clear Channel's historic 24 percent operating margin had diminished to just 16 percent. Consequently, the double whammy of lower revenues and rapidly weakening margins has taken a huge bite out of operating income. In fact, its 2011 figure of just $1 billion was down nearly 40 percent from the pre-LBO total of $1.65 billion reported in 2007.

So its $2 billion annual interest bill is now double its operating income, meaning that the game of "extend and pretend" is getting increasingly dicey. The company is now leveraged at twenty times its operating income, yet faces a huge debt maturity cliff in the immediate future: $4 billion is due in 2014 and another $12 billion of debt must be repaid in 2016. Yet by then advertising revenues will be in deep secular decline due to competitive venues, and the value of its "sticks" will be vaporizing. The digital technology revolution is, in fact, turning the company's portfolio of FCC licenses into the world's largest collection of buggy whips.

BERNANKE'S (UNTOUGH) LOVE CHILD: THE $27 BILLION AFFAIR AT THE HILTON

The very idea that LBOs can carry massive debt loads that never have to be paid down defies the historical first principles of leveraged buyouts. It was once taken as axiomatic that any buyout deal lacking a realistic five-year plan to materially ramp down its initial LBO debt was destined to fail.

The reason is simply time and risk. Few businesses can remain financial zombies on the ragged edge of insolvency for a decade or longer because cash flows invariably hit a rut in the road, whether owing to faltering demand, product or technology obsolescence, the rise of an aggressive new competitor, or simply a downturn in the macroeconomic cycle. Accordingly, LBO deals would not get done on the free market if they carried so much debt relative to current and prospective cash flow that they were virtually guaranteed to become capital-destroying debt zombies.

Blackstone's $27 billion LBO of Hilton Hotels completed in late 2007 is exactly one of these free market defying zombies. Without the deep tax subsidy for debt and the Wall Street–coddling policies of the Fed this mega-LBO deal, which five years later still remains one global business slump away from bankruptcy, would never have seen the light of day. The Hilton Hotels deal thus illuminates the entire syndrome of bubble finance and the financial engineering deformations which afflict the American economy.

At any time prior to the 2006–2007 mega-LBO frenzy, the Blackstone offer would have been an unfinanceable bad joke; at 21X Hilton's actual operating income of $1.3 billion for 2006, the deal price broke all the rules. It meant that from day one, the deal would be going in the hole because it didn't even earn its annual interest tab of about $1.5 billion.

During those heady moments, of course, the LBO crowd preferred to focus on EBITDA rather than operating income, because the exclusion of charges for depreciation and amortization (D&A) made profits look bigger and the leverage ratio smaller. In this case, the purchase price also amounted to fifteen times EBITDA, but that should have been cold comfort. Hilton Hotels was then a heavy user of capital; that is, the D&A charges had to be reinvested and were not available to service its massive LBO debt.

The company's actual business plan for 2007, for example, was to spend about $1 billion on CapEx and generate $1.8 billion in EBITDA, or just 4.5 percent more than the prior year. The recklessness of the deal price is therefore evident in these numbers, which were not secret, but constituted the company's own financial "guidance" to public investors at the time. They implied that Blackstone's purchase multiple would amount to a mind-boggling 32X its projected $830 million of free cash flow.

In short, the deal amounted to an ultra-high price for exceedingly slow earnings growth at the very top of a business cycle. Indeed, the Hilton deal was so pricey that its sponsors were struggling to close the bank financing until the day of Cramer's famous rant (chapter 23). When Bernanke buckled in response to the minor stock correction then under way and went into a full panic mode with the emergency discount rate cut on August 17, the true nature of the "emergency" became apparent.

Ground zero of the crisis was on Wall Street and its bulging pipeline of financial engineering deals like Hilton. At the time, American businesses did not need cheap loans for capital equipment or new technology; they were drowning in excess production capacity already. The part of the economy that needed the stock and debt markets propped up, in fact, was the private equity houses and leveraged financial engineering players.

It was they who were stuck in uncompleted CEW maneuvers and needed to issue tens of billions of new high-yield debt without delay. At that moment in August–September 2007, in fact, there were nearly $100 billion of unfunded deals in the Wall Street pipeline, and therein lay the true secret of central bank bailouts and the continuous resort to "shock and awe" financial intervention which commenced only a few months later.

Thus, when Bernanke threw caution to the wind, the Hilton deal was miraculously revived, thereby bringing another happy CEW day to Wall Street in early October. The Hilton deal was thus an offspring of the Fed's patented style of untough love.

The deal's morning-after windfall to existing shareholders amounted to a payout of $21 billion. It goes without saying that recipients were soon thanking their lucky stars. Within twelve months the stock price of Hilton's twin sister, Starwood Hotels and Resorts, plunged from $60 per share to $10 owing to the collapse of hotel occupancy and pricing, and also to the abrupt disappearance of third-party financing for room-count expansion on which these go-go hotel stocks had been valued.

THE WALL STREET BRIDGE TO BAILOUTS

As it happened, Blackstone's underwriters were not able to sell a planned $12 billion commercial mortgage-backed securities (CMBSs) deal or syndicate an $8 billion mezzanine debt loan, either. Instead, the deal was funded entirely with three-year "bridge loans" taken down by seven Wall Street underwriters who were a who's who of the financial meltdown which materialized exactly twelve months later.

When the Wall Street banking houses funded an unprecedented $20.5 billion bridge loan it was one of the most reckless syndications ever undertaken. Fittingly, it closed on the very day of the all-time S&P 500 index peak, itself merely a dead-cat bounce from Bernanke's initial round of panicked stock market coddling.

Not surprisingly, the lead underwriter of nearly one-quarter of this preposterous bridge loan was none other than Bear Stearns, which piled onto its own already wobbly balance sheet $4.7 billion in short-term credits to what was essentially a hotel management and franchising company. Prior to the buyout, in fact, Hilton had already pawned most of its hard assets to third-party real estate investors in order to scrap up cash to pump its stock price via dividends and share buybacks.

Accordingly, it owned only 54 of its 2,500 hotels at the time of the deal. This meant that it had no real estate to pledge and that the bridge loan was secured only by flimsy claims on income flows from its long-term franchise agreements. Only in the late hours of a speculative mania would such intangible assets be confused with legitimate loan collateral.

When Bear Stearns hit the wall a few months later, one of the largest "toxic" assets on its balance sheet was the dodgy bridge loan backed by Hilton's bottled air. Accordingly, JPMorgan insisted the taxpayers underwrite any loss on the $4.7 billion Hilton bridge loan before it swallowed up Bear's good assets.

Not far behind on the swaying Hilton bridge were Bank of America, Goldman, and Deutsche Bank with nearly $4 billion each. Like the corpse of Bear Stearns, all three of these "too big to fail" institutions would soon be gorging on funds from TARP and the Fed's bailout lines. Finally, the $5 billion balance of the deal went to the hindmost of the Wall Street pack: Merrill Lynch, Morgan Stanley, and Lehman.

All three went down for the count within twelve months, owing to balance sheets that cratered under the weight of deeply impaired and illiquid assets like the Hilton bridge loan. Perhaps indicative of the financial madness then under way, Lehman was still carrying the Hilton bridge at 93 percent of par by June 2008, when it was already evident that the commercial real estate financing market was dead and the US economy was heading south.

The Hilton Hotels bridge loan is thus a testament to the destruction of financial discipline and rationality fostered by the Greenspan-Bernanke era of Wall Street coddling. As it happened, the Main Street economy plunged into the Great Recession and the "takeout" financing markets which the bridge lenders were banking on—junk bonds and commercial real estate securitization—were stone cold by early 2009. Also by then Hilton's EBITDA had dropped by 30 percent, so there was not a remote chance of refinancing the deal on commercial terms.

Needless to say, in an honest capital market the Hilton tower of debt would have been foreclosed upon. Once again, however, the free market's therapeutic discipline was negated by the Fed's panicked slashing of short-term rates to almost zero. While this foolish policy crushed middle-class savers, it did achieve its intended effect: it provided a huge interest subsidy (that is, virtually free overnight money) to carry-trade speculators so they would put a bid back into the market for risk assets.

Accordingly, beginning in the second half of 2009 this Wall Street–friendly form of monetary "stimulus" flowed into the busted markets for securitized commercial mortgages and hotel real estate investment trusts (REITs). In short order, leveraged speculators drove the price of these beaten-down asset classes upward by 50 to 90 percent. Soaring prices for what had been deeply distressed loan paper only months earlier, in turn, enabled banks to revert to a full-bodied "extend and pretend" mode, pushing out maturities, waiving covenant violations, and deferring scheduled repayments.

This miraculous "recovery" in the hotel debt market was both a stupendous gift from the Eccles Building to speculators and a complete distortion of market signals. Yet it did the trick. In April 2010 the banks agreed to extend the Hilton loan maturities until the end of 2015, reduced outstanding debt by $1.8 billion in return for an $800 million cash payment from Blackstone, and swapped another $2 billion of junior debt for preferred stock.

Still, the company remains saddled with $16 billion of debt, which represented about sixteen times Hilton's free cash flow after CapEx during 2011. Accordingly, this so-called restructuring deal is evidence that the financial markets are being medicated by the Fed to support debt zombies, not that the company's fundamental prospects have measurably brightened.

In fact, Hilton's 2011 EBITDA of about $1.9 billion represented a tepid growth rate of only 1.6 percent annually from the pre-LBO outcome in 2006. Self-evidently, a company with such anemic long-term trends can't grow out of its debts.

So the Hilton Hotels mega-LBO remains a ward of the state's central banking branch. The company's $16 billion debt maturity cliff in 2015 would result in Hilton's demise were the Fed to normalize interest rates and thereby send the carry-trade speculators who own its debt scrambling for cover.

But that won't happen. The nation's central bank has already promised to keep middle-class savers pinned to the floorboards through 2015 in order to sustain an artificial bid for risk assets. Indeed, the Princeton math professor that Karl Rove brought to the Eccles Building has implemented the precise monetary strategy which that self-avowed Keynesian, Paul Krugman, urged on Greenspan back in 2002 in the wake of the dot-com bust.

Rather than allowing the free market to dispatch speculators to the ruin they deserved, Krugman urged a massive stimulus campaign to put them back in business. "To fight this recession the Fed needs more than a snapback," the learned professor intoned, "Alan Greenspan needs to create a housing bubble to replace the NASDAQ bubble."

Greenspan followed that fatuous advice and millions of Main Street families are in ruins for it. Now Bernanke adds insult to injury through maniacal adherence to money-printing policies which inflate the middle class's cost of living and demolish its rewards for thrift in order to keep leveraged speculators in business and the debt zombies solvent.

CHAPTER 26

BONFIRES OF DEBT AND THE ROAD NOT TAKEN

W HEN THE MAIN STREET BANKS AND THRIFTS WERE DRIVEN out of the home mortgage business by brokers pumping loans into the securitization machinery, these traditional lenders scrambled for an alternative line of work. They found it big time in commercial real estate development, where hotel construction was near the top of the list.

Yet the tsunami of new rooms that materialized during 2004–2008 was not a manifestation of the free market. As in so many other economic sectors in the aftermath of the dot-com bust, the free market had attempted the opposite; that is, to close down the rampant overbuilding of hotels which had occurred in the late 1990s.

But when the Fed cranked up the flow of cheap credit to a fever pitch during the second Greenspan bubble, the monetary central planners succeeded in levitating another spree of malinvestments in a sector already saturated with excess capacity. The supply of new hotel rooms surged from just 30,000 in 2003 to 100,000 in 2006 and hit 200,000 new rooms during the 2008 peak.

This building boom raised nationwide hotel construction spending from a $10 billion annual rate in 2003 to $40 billion by 2008. Developers scrambled to deliver new hotels to tax-advantaged real estate trusts (hotel REITs) and the CMBS (commercial mortgage backed securities) market. These financial investors, in turn, placed rooms by the thousands in brand franchising and hotel management company deals.

The hotel sector provided a stunning example of the manner in which the Fed's financial repression policies fostered a chain of economic deformations that fed upon one another. Artificial consumer demand financed by MEW (mortgage equity withdrawal) goosed leisure travel and therefore hotel revenues and operating profits. This demand surge, in turn, generated a boom in hotel room construction which was funded by cheap debt and tax shelter schemes. The resulting boost to industry growth rates and cash flows then elicited a spree of hotel company LBOs, which extracted billions of CEW (corporate equity withdrawal) that was paid out to stock speculators at the 2006–2008 market top. In this manner, proceeds from millions of home ATMs across the land ended up in the bank accounts of the 1 percent.

Blackstone's LBO of Extended Stay America in March 2004 was archetypical. The purchase price was $3.1 billion, of which less than $500 million was funded by sponsor equity. While "revpar" (revenue per available room) for extended stay hotels had been negative in 2002 and 2003 owing to the capacity glut left over from the 1990s bubble, Blackstone caught the second Greenspan wave perfectly. During 2004, the extended stay segment saw revpar gains of 5 percent, and then it was off to the races with double-digit gains in 2005 and 2006.

At the same time, Extended Stay America added new rooms hand over fist owing to the building boom then under way. When Blackstone exited the deal just thirty-nine months later in June 2007 (on the eve of its own IPO), the chain's room count had grown from 50,000 to 76,000 and revpar by nearly 20 percent. More importantly, mania was running at high tide in the hotel financing markets.

Consequently, Blackstone was able to sell its 680-unit hotel chain for $8 billion, resulting in a $2.1 billion gain or 4X its investment. This was a truly astonishing price which amounted to $105,000 per room, yet these were bare-bones, no service hotels which generated only $35 per night of revenue from their extended-stay customers.

The arithmetic thus underscores the lodging market mania. These ultra-low priced rooms would have generated only about of $3,500 in annual EBITDA after appropriate CapEx reserves for well-worn decade-old hotel rooms. This meant that the buyer's purchase multiple was 30X sustainable free cash flow.

One of the hallmarks of financial manias is that propositions which are perfectly absurd nevertheless get widely embraced by those caught up in the excitement. In this case, one David Lichtenstein, proprietor of Lightstone Group, had been plying the leveraged real estate business since exactly the time that Alan Greenspan had kicked off the era of bubble finance in October 1987. Thus, Lichtenstein was financially teethed on the notion that the Fed had abolished the downside. This sentiment was vividly evident in his 2004 proclamation: "We don't care what analysts say. We will buy anything."

As the Fed's financial party reached its roaring crescendo in June 2007, therefore, he was not shy about publicly declaiming his pleasure at being bagged by a truly absurd purchase price. "There seems to be a feeling on Wall Street that because Blackstone is going public, they want to show what a complete cycle looks like," Lichtenstein rhapsodized, "and we're the lucky beneficiaries of that."

Indeed. Everything about what happened at the June 2007 closing subsequently amounts to a brutal demonstration of the great financial deformation wrought by the nation's central bank. By then the leveraged lending market had finally gone berserk. A consortium of Wall Street underwriters led by Wachovia bank and including Bear Stearns, Bank America, Merrill Lynch, and the other usual suspects loaned $7.4 billion to Lightstone, or 92.5 percent of the purchase price.

In point of fact, each of Extended Stay America's guest rooms embodied approximately $35,000 worth of drywall, plywood, cinderblock, rebar, paint, and labor. Now, however, the deranged financial markets were seeing fit to loan the hotel company's new owners three times their replacement cost—about $97,000 per room to be exact.

Indeed, these no-frills hotel rooms resembled an interconnected trailer park under a single roof; the "rooms" were occupied for an average of twenty days per stay by traveling construction workers and temporary nursing home employees. So the question recurs as to why an investor would mortgage such units at three times their replacement cost.

David Lichtenstein, however, had a ready answer: "I don't know much about the hotel business, but the price was right . . . I also liked the fact that it was a simple business . . . there is no food and beverage, no conventions, no bar mitzvahs. And it only takes one employee for every ten rooms to run these properties."

The ordinary laws of the free market, of course, suggest that if something doesn't cost much to produce, then it isn't worth very much, either. Yet that very truism goes to the heart of the higher order of deformation that was now at work in the mega-LBO market. Operating at the very top of the leveraged buyout pyramid, punters like David Lichtenstein were simply buying call options on the upside of these debt-ridden enterprises for comparatively meager amounts.

Thus, it turns out that underneath the $7.4 billion of debt in the Lightstone deal, the sliver of purported equity was not all it was cracked up to be; that is, it was mostly borrowed money, too. Blackstone itself provided $200 million of "rollover" equity. Consequently, the Lightstone Group had become the controlling shareholder based on a mere $200 million "equity" investment. However, the high rollers at Citibank who were advising Lichtenstein on the deal were apparently of the view that a banker should never say never when it comes to scalping a fee from a customer. Therefore, in return for a $6 million deal fee, they loaned Lichtenstein and his colleagues $120 million so they could fund their $200 million equity commitment.

In short, the Lightstone Group controlled an $8 billion financial edifice based on a cash investment of $80 million; all the rest was borrowed and stuffed into one tier or another of the LBO's rickety capital structure. Moreover, there can be no doubt that Lichtenstein viewed his 1 percent stake as a pure roll of the dice. After the deal cratered, he answered a deposition question about his $200 million "equity" investment by pinning the tail squarely on his bankers: "Like the banks just said blow the damn stuff out . . . we don't care . . . just sell the [equity] paper as fast as you can. Citibank just said pay us as many fees as you can . . . and I said I am getting 95%, 99% financing . . . Okay."

There can also be little doubt as to why Citigroup had been so cavalier in advising its client. It happened that the great financial "supermarket" that Sandy Weill built was doing a little internal "cross-selling." It had been selected to co-lead Blackstone's IPO and thereby obtain a generous helping of the $170 million fee pot that would soon be whacked up among the underwriters. At the same time, its M&A department had snagged Lichtenstein as a buy-side client.

The "synergy" was lost on no one: one arm of the bank found the "mullet" and the other side grabbed the fees. Moreover, Blackstone's exit from its Extended Stay America deal had been a hurry-up affair because it provided a perfect example of its investment prowess that could be showcased in its own IPO road show. Accordingly, its selling memorandum for Extended Stay America issued in February 2007 came complete with what was known in the trade as a "stapled financing."

Specifically, potential buyers were told that a $7 billion debt package had already been arranged through Wachovia and Bear Stearns. In order to complete their bids, therefore, prospective buyers only needed to stand up on their tippy toes and place a modest slice of "equity" on top of the tower of prepackaged debt.

Blackstone's "stapled financing" was surely a sign of the mania. This arrangement also explains why Citibank told Lichtenstein to ignore an independent appraisal he had commissioned which suggested that the company was worth only $5 billion. As far as Citibank was apparently concerned, Lichtenstein was their "mark," not their client, and his job was to get the deal closed fast, not to worry about a mere $3 billion potential overvaluation. As it happened, Lightstone Group signed this massive $8 billion deal on April 12, just fifty-five days after it had received the offering memo. At the other end, the deal closed in early June just five days before Citigroup launched the Blackstone IPO road show. Accordingly, in June 2007 Senator Carter Glass of Virginia was justly rolling in his grave.

LIGHTSTONE'S HORRID STAY AT EXTENDED STAY

When Wachovia and the rest of its syndicate funded the $7.4 billion debt portion of the transaction on a bridge loan basis, they had an analysis from Standard & Poor's which said the company was only worth $4.8 billion. So on the eve of the "fee fest" occasioned by Blackstone's IPO, the Wall Street banks wrote a bridge loan for 150 percent of what even their hirelings at the rating agencies believed Extended Stay America was actually worth.

As indicated, Extended Stay's assets were essentially drywall motel rooms painted in three colors. The reason presumably adult bankers believed such flimsy assets could be leveraged at 150 percent of their ostensible value was that they were in the business of hiding the pea.

Thus, the senior portion of the financing consisted of $4.1 billion of mortgage loans that were dumped into a structured finance pool, or "conduit," known as a commercial mortgage-backed security (CMBS). Then this huge pool of debt was sliced into eighteen different tranches. Six of these tranches were given the highest AAA rating, meaning that the $2.6 billion of mortgage-backed securities issued from this tranche had first call on the cash from interest and principle payments coming into the pool. Below that there were many more tranches, each with a lower claim on the mortgage pool's cash, and therefore a greater risk of loss.

And that was the simple part! The CMBS debt had a direct lien on the hotels in the operating subsidiaries, but there were many more layers—$3.3 billion worth—which did not own anything except the stock of subsidiaries which had already hocked all of their hard assets. This so-called mezzanine or subordinated debt was also sliced into a dozen different layers, and each was subject to mind-boggling complexities with respect to access to cash flow from the hotels.

The details of this capital structure were daunting, but the purpose was crystal clear; it was designed to turn a sow's ear into a silk purse. During boom times these subordinated tranches were saleable to high-yield mutual funds and credit-oriented hedge funds because they were designed to satisfy the hunger for "yield" which had been induced by the Fed's interest rate repression policies. In truth, however, these junk securities were vastly overvalued relative to their embedded risks. So when the US economy weakened and hotel revpar began to head south in 2008 the subordinated tranches plummeted in value.

The sudden, drastic repricing of these subordinated debt tranches, which had been replicated by Wall Street in thousands of so-called "structured finance" deals, was the proximate cause of the September 2008 meltdown. This is powerfully illustrated by the fate of the $7.4 billion Extended

Stay financing, much of which remained stuffed in the Wall Street meth labs until the very end.

Thus, Wachovia still held $1.5 billion of the Extended Stay financing, while Bank America had retained $1.4 billion and Bear Stearns $1.1 billion. But underneath the surface the picture was even worse. Each of the three underwriters of this deal would soon join the ranks of the departed, and one of the reasons was that they had disproportionately retained the bottom-dwelling sludge from their structured finance labs.

In this case, Wachovia's retention included about $1 billion of the lowest-rate mezzanine tranches, and the other two underwriters each had close to $1 billion of this sludge as well. Overall, the three underwriters had retained nearly 85 percent of the $3.3 billion of mezzanine debt issued to fund the Extended Stay deal; it was worth virtually nothing and had proved unsalable even after Cramer issued the "all clear."

Moreover, when the army of nomad workers who occupied the Extended Stay rooms twenty days at a crack were demobilized by the faltering economy in 2008, revpar plummeted by 25 percent. Soon EBITDA was falling drastically below plan, even as it became evident that Blackstone had bagged Lichtenstein with tired and under-maintained hotel rooms that needed far more capital expenditure than provided for in the selling memo that had accompanied the "stapled financing."

Indeed, with debt at nearly $100,000 per room an honest free market interest rate would have required more than $10,000 per room in debt service, or three times the available free cash flow. The Extended Stay deal was thus not even a zombie; it was dead in the water the moment Blackstone's pitiful posse of underwriters trotted out their "stapled financing."

By the time of the Wall Street meltdown it was all over but the shouting, and Lighthouse did file for bankruptcy in June 2009. What the latter process revealed was the true essence of bubble finance. A court-ordered appraisal showed that the hotel company assets were worth just $2.8 billion, or only 35 percent of the $8 billion purchase price.

What this finding meant was that Extended Stay America was not worth even the $4.1 billion of secured mortgage debt which had financed the deal. The entire $3.3 billion in the mezzanine tranches was purely bottled air, and yet it was the latter which had financed Blackstone's famous $2.1 billion payday on the eve of its IPO.

THE ROAD NOT TAKEN:
WHY THE WALL STREET CASINO LIVES ON

Drastically overpriced debt is eventually smacked with painful losses on the free market, but not on a Wall Street served by compliant central bankers.

When the Bernanke Fed bailed out Bear Stearns in March 2008, for example, it was sitting on tens of billions of impaired or worthless assets.

Among this financial sludge was $1.1 billion of the undistributed Extended Stay paper. Accordingly, the taxpayers of America through their central bank became the owners of busted bonds which, on the margin, had funded nearly half of Blackstone's legendary profit on the sale to Lightstone.

In this saga of low-rent hotel rooms the evils of bubble finance are starkly revealed. It demonstrates vividly how the mega-LBO frenzy of the second Greenspan bubble escalated income and wealth to the top 1 percent, or in this case the top 0.0001 percent. But even more importantly it documents why Washington's frantic bailouts after September 15, 2008, were so misguided and counterproductive.

The time was long overdue for a classic liquidation of the massive credit bubble which had built up since the 1980s. A generation of speculators who rode it to the peak needed to be unhorsed once and for all. And it could have been easily achieved: Bernanke only needed to ignore the Cramer rant which echoed throughout the canyons of Wall Street in August 2007 and, instead, order the Fed's open market desk to sit firmly on its hands.

So doing, the Fed would have engaged in the right sort of "accommodation." It would have facilitated Wall Street's desperate need for a financial housecleaning, just as J. P. Morgan did with such sublime effect in October 1907.

By staying out of the Treasury market the Fed would have permitted short-term interest rates to soar, thereby laying low the financial meth labs all along Wall Street. Their toxic inventories would have been dumped into the market at fire sale prices; they would have had no choice because trading desks would have been faced with crushing double-digit funding rates in the repo and wholesale money markets—rates which would have been rising by the hour and threatening to soar to terrifying levels. That is how panics ended in historic times, and that's why speculation did not become deeply embedded and institutionalized as it has in the age of bubble finance.

The result would have been a bonfire of speculative paper that would not have been forgotten for a generation. Every single investment bank, including Goldman, Morgan Stanley, and the embedded hedge funds at JPMorgan, Citibank, and Bank of America would have been rendered instantly insolvent and dismembered under court and FDIC protection. Speculators would have denounced the Greenspan Put for decades to come. No banking institution reckless enough to make $100,000 bridge loans against $35,000 hotel rooms would have reemerged from the conflagration.

Just as importantly, the bonfires would have largely burned out in the canyons of Wall Street. The nonfinancial businesses of Main Street would have been largely unscathed for four principal reasons.

First, after having already massively inflated its debt, from $4 trillion to $11 trillion during the fifteen years ending in 2008, the business sector needed to liquidate borrowings, not go into hock even further. A period of high interest rates and scarce new debt availability would have been economically therapeutic.

Secondly, at that moment in time viable and solvent businesses did not need cheap debt to finance productive assets. Huge sectors of the US economy centered on commercial real estate, retailing, hospitality, and other forms of discretionary consumer spending were already vastly overbuilt. A period of high-cost debt, therefore, would have dramatically reduced the rampant malinvestments of the Greenspan bubbles and forced businesses to fund only high-return projects out of internal cash flow or expensive long-term debt.

Thirdly, high interest rates would have shut down the multitrillion flow of new debt to financial engineering. As previously shown, buybacks, buyouts, and takeovers contribute little to real business productivity and growth of national wealth, and mostly serve to scalp economic rents from Main Street and channel them to the top 1 percent.

Finally, thousands of drastically overleveraged business like Extended Stay America would have been forced into bankruptcy but they would have nevertheless continued to function under court protection. More importantly, they did not need Wall Street to reorganize their finances. Several trillions of business debt that had been incurred to fund LBOs, stock buybacks, and corporate takeovers could have been repudiated by debtors in bankruptcy court and replaced by simplified, equity-based capital structures.

Businesses thus freed from the yoke of Wall Street–originated debt would have emerged from Chapter 11 and have been controlled by the knowledgeable businessmen and skilled employees who had operated them all along. The American economy would thereby have embarked on the road to definancialization. Real economic productivity, investment, innovation, and growth based on honest free enterprise might have again become possible.

Instead, after the Lehman event, the madcap money printing of the Bernanke Fed and the bailout frenzy of the Paulson Treasury Department stopped the Wall Street cleansing in its tracks. The only thing that changed was that the remnants of the "departed"—Bear Stearns, Merrill Lynch, Lehman, Wachovia—were recycled back into the even greater girth of the "reprieved"—Goldman, Morgan Stanley, JPMorgan, Bank of America, Barclays, Citigroup, and Wells Fargo.

The system which finally failed in September 2008 was actually reincarnated in even more destructive aspect. The Bernanke Put was far more insidious than the Greenspan Put because it refused to permit even a 10 percent correction in the stock averages before pumping a new round of juice into Wall Street.

Likewise, the carry trade became an even more one-sided gift to speculators: risk assets could now be funded in the wholesale money markets for virtually nothing, while hedge fund operators were solemnly promised by the monetary central planners that their cost of carry would be frozen at nearly zero for years on end.

BLACKSTONE DOUBLE DIP

But the worst effect was that the Wall Street machinery and principal participants in the financial engineering régime were soon back in business. This cardinal reality was made starkly evident in the court papers issued upon Extended Stay America's discharge from bankruptcy in May 2010. The hotel company's proud new owner was, well, the Blackstone Group. And to underscore that speculators had returned to the scene of the prior strangulation, as it were, its partner in the deal was the John Paulson hedge fund.

The ever gullible financial press was wont to characterize this outcome as a triumph of capitalism; that is, the mobilization of flexible private equity capital to reorganize and recapitalize a failed business enterprise. But that was dead wrong because the Blackstone-Paulson partnership didn't recapitalize anything. What it did, instead, was utilize the same cadre of Wall Street lawyers and bankers to shrink and shuffle the busted debt paper from the Lightstone deal into a new deck of about $3.5 billion of notes, bonds, and preferred stock.

The second Blackstone deal, therefore, brought only trivial amounts of actual fresh equity—a couple hundred million—to the table. The Blackstone-Paulson investors essentially performed the same old trick that had become standard fare before the Wall Street crisis: they bought another call option on a debt-laden enterprise that was leveraged at 10:1.

Whether the resulting 50 percent haircut on the total capitalization, from $8 billion to about $4 billion, was the right value for the 76,000 aging hotel rooms in the Extended Stay portfolio would be determined by real-world events. But the underlying facts were not encouraging: the financial deformations that had led to Extended Stay's boom, crash, and rebirth had produced a giant malinvestment in the overall hotel sector.

In fact, the ultimate indication that the Wall Street playpen known as the US hotel sector is not on the level lies in a startling statistic: there are 13.2 million hotel rooms in the world, and 5.6 million of them are located in the United States. Thus, with 4 percent of the global population we have 42 percent of the hotel rooms.

The American economy is drastically overhoteled in part because a significant swath of its labor force has become nomadic. Some of this may be attributable to new-style traveling tech workers and old-style traveling salesmen. But mainly it is due to a drastic policy-induced deformation. The Fed's massive creation of dollar liabilities drove tradable goods production to the mercantilist "cheap labor" regions of the Asian rice paddies. At the same time, it fueled an orgy of real estate development and construction on the "cheap land" precincts of the sun and sand belts at home.

As previously explained, at least 10 million tradable goods jobs had been off-shored during the Greenspan era, meaning that jobs had become scarce where people used to live (Flint, Michigan). At the same time, the debt-fueled boom in the Sunbelt—health care, retirement communities, resorts and leisure, and endless construction of new housing developments, shopping malls, and other commercial real estate projects—happened on the margin, where people didn't yet live (Ft. Myers, Florida).

Not surprisingly, the extended-stay hotel segment, where business travel accounts for 75 percent of room night demand, grew like Topsy during the two Greenspan bubbles. It provided a way station for nomadic workers and populations in transit. As in the case of all malinvestments, however, the music eventually stops when the speculative bubble which finances them implodes. That has now happened, thereby causing the ranks of nomadic finance, construction, leisure industry, and retail and consumer service workers to significantly diminish.

Accordingly, the extended-stay hotel segment remains overbuilt and overvalued a half decade after new construction peaked. Yet the Fed's ZIRP (zero interest) policy perversely thwarts the free market's curative capacities to punish speculation and liberate assets from the encumbrance of excessive debt. Instead, it perpetuates the "extend and pretend" illusion that the debt is money good because it encumbers an asset that is vastly inflated in value.

ECONOMIC SUFFOCATION BY BERNANKE'S RENTIERS

In effect, Bernanke is the godfather of the debt zombies. His radical interest rate repression campaign has not created much new lending, but it has disabled and overridden the free market's capacity to liquidate bubble-era credit. Instead of taking the drastic debt write-downs which are warranted, banks and other lenders have been enabled to pursue the "extend and pretend" route; that is, extending maturities on debt that can never be repaid while booking it at par because borrowers stay current on interest payments.

The low interest rates on bubble-era debt, as well as post-crisis restructured debt, are laughable by all historic standards. Banks should be reserving heavily against the maturity cliffs ahead, but are not being required to do so owing to the utter folly emanating from the Eccles Building; namely, the Fed's fatuous promise that one day it will be able to "normalize" interest rates without triggering a debt-impairing conflagration on Wall Street and another plunge on Main Street.

So by not taking the deep reserves required, Wall Street banks are (again) reporting phony profits. Indeed, led by JPMorgan they are massively reversing out reserves they had previously taken in order to goose their earnings and levitate the value of executive stock options. And phantom banking profits are only the surface issue.

The real economic problem is that by keeping properties and businesses encumbered with too much restructured and rescheduled zombie debt— as was evident in the so-called restructuring of Extended Stay America by Blackstone and Paulson—free cash flow is siphoned off to pay what are essentially unearned rents. These ill-gotten receipts are collected by Keynes's famous rentiers who nowadays are called PMs (portfolio managers) at fixed-income funds.

Stated differently, bubble-era properties and companies are being bled to death by uneconomic interest payments and thereby precluded from reinvesting in plant, equipment, technology, new products, human resources, and all the other ingredients of sustainability. After a decade as a debt zombie, therefore, the typical commercial property will have lapsed into a state of terminal decay and the typical operating business will have become a hollowed-out cipher.

None of this would have been a surprise to pre-Keynesian-era economists because they knew that credit inflations are tricksters. They fund artificial demand which gives rise to secondary and tertiary waves of additional demand, usually to build new infrastructure and production capacity that ends up redundant when the bubble pops.

This crack-up boom cycle so well known to the ancients was vividly at work in the extended-stay hotel segment. At the peak of the bubble, nomadic workers in construction, finance, and real estate were actually creating part of their own demand; that is, they were filling rooms that justified even more construction. Yet developers couldn't fill up rooms with their own workers indefinitely, nor could the Fed permanently extend the speculative building mania in commercial real estate.

As a result, the nation is now saddled with vastly more capacity—malls, lodging, restaurants, car dealerships, office buildings, movie houses—than can be justified by the sustainable income and spending capacity of the American economy. Ironically, the monetary central planners take this overhang as evidence of insufficient "demand" and therefore a need for more money printing. Like nineteenth century practitioners of the bleeding cure, they single-mindedly press ahead toward the patient's eventual demise.

PART V

SUNDOWN IN AMERICA:
THE END OF FREE MARKETS
AND DEMOCRACY

CHAPTER 27

WILLARD M. ROMNEY AND THE TRUMAN SHOW OF BUBBLE FINANCE

T HE 2012 PRESIDENTIAL ELECTION SIGNALED THE ONSET OF SUN-down in America, and not merely because an avowed big-spending statist won the race. Rather, it's because the Republican candidate proved in words and lifelong deeds that there is no conservative party left in America—at least not one that is willing or able to defend sound money, free markets, and fiscal rectitude. So the drift into the crony capitalist end game will now accelerate, suffocating what remains of free market prosperity and honest political democracy.

Mitt Romney made numerous revelatory choices in his quest for the Oval Office and they unfailingly showed that the old-time conservative economics cannot be revived. Gerry Ford would never have bailed out GM, and Bill Simon would have busted down the door to the Oval Office if his president had even mentioned it. And for good reason. As will be seen in chapter 30, the auto bailout was a frontal assault on the free market: the GOP candidate should have denounced it from the rooftops as an $80 billion theft from innocent taxpayers.

Yet candidate Romney tried to bury the issue. Mumbling a tortured retreat from his 2008 "Let Detroit Go Bankrupt" editorial, he insinuated that his disagreement with Obama was on the bankruptcy venue, not the bailout. The reason that Romney did not take what was a defining issue of our times to the nationwide electorate was obvious enough: his handlers believed that finessing the auto bailout was crucial to Ohio and to the outcome in the electoral college.

And that it why all is lost. The bailout "saved" perhaps 10,000 jobs in Ohio, a figure that represents two-tenths of 1 percent of the 5 million votes cast there. So Romney's de facto flip-flop on the auto bailout was both a profile in cowardice and proof that the Republican political apparatus believes that the party's core free market principle is an electoral loser.

Romney's assault on fiscal rectitude, likewise, would have made Eisenhower shudder and George Humphrey turn apoplectic. The true issue of the 2012 campaign was the exploding national debt, and the true facts were that honest ten-year fiscal projections produced cumulative deficits of $20 trillion. As will be seen in chapter 33, that would be the mathematical result of Republican tax policy and the welfare state–warfare state status quo based on an "unrosy" scenario; that is, a ten-year forecast identical to the US economy's actual performance during the last ten years.

Facing this terminal challenge to fiscal solvency, Mitt Romney choose to double down on the GOP's tax-cut elixir, proposing a 20 percent rate reduction on top of the Bush tax cuts which had already added trillions to the national debt. K Street greeted with mirthful nonchalance his ritual promise to recoup the $5 trillion revenue loss by closing tax "loopholes," duly noting that the candidate did not name a single one of them out loud.

ROMNEY'S RYAN COP-OUT

But Romney's true fiscal dereliction was on the spending side of the budget, where the welfare state and warfare state status quo got a hearty embrace. The proof, oddly enough, was in Romney's adoption of the Ryan budget as his fiscal plan and its author as his running mate. Notwithstanding Democratic arm-waving, the Ryan budget provided that not a single recipient of Social Security or Medicare would face benefit cuts for a decade.

The GOP's fiscal plan of 2012 for all practical purposes, therefore, gave final bipartisan validation to FDR's eighty-year-old mistake in enacting social insurance. So doing, it put the lie to Ryan's pretensions to being the scourge of Big Government. It also revealed that what passed for the GOP anti-spending agenda was a brutal, unprincipled attack on the means-tested safety net, a position that candidate Romney famously and perhaps inadvertently crystallized in his lament about the 47 percent.

The ten-year projection for total domestic spending at election time was about $33 trillion and its internals illuminate why the Ryan budget amounted to a declaration of class war, even if its earnest author was simply trying to come up with a big number for budget "savings." The social insurance core of the welfare state, Social Security and Medicare, account for nearly $19 trillion, or 55 percent, of all projected domestic spending in the next decade. Hiding behind the phony rigmarole of trust funds and insurance argot, Ryan gave social insurance a free pass through 2022, notwithstanding that trillions of this huge expenditure would go to upper-income and wealthy retires who hadn't earned it and didn't need it.

By contrast, means-tested programs including food stamps, Medicaid, Supplemental Security Income, and the earned-income tax credit account for just $7 trillion, or 22 percent, of projected domestic spending under current law. Upon being slammed by Ryan's fiscal meat ax, however, the current law figure would have been cut by 30 percent over the next ten years. This meant that citizens who had (mostly) proved they deserved help from the state and were by definition on the ragged edge of financial survival would take a $2 trillion punch in the chops.

Ryan and his fellow travelers have never presented any evidence of sloppy eligibility criteria or outright cheating to the tune of 30 percent or even 3 percent. Nor have they made any pretense of an effort to selectively repair and strengthen the safety net as we did in the 1981 Reagan entitlement reforms. Instead, Ryan's $2 trillion assault on the means-tested safety net was simply a goal-seeked number: it functioned as a "plug" to affect the appearance of fiscal retrenchment, while being gussied up as a block grant "reform." Under it, states would take over medical, food, and income assistance to the poor, albeit with 30 percent less money.

That was a shameful ruse. No governor was any better equipped to find economies in nursing home costs or emergency room visits than current federal policy makers and administrators. The means-tested safety net is just not an issue of federalism; it's a question of how to design and deliver welfare benefits in a manner that is efficient and fair, that minimizes moral hazard, and most importantly, avoids capture by crony-capitalist vendors.

As seen, Milton Friedman had the right answer, and it involved an all-cash, single-benefit system integrated with the federal income tax, not an arbitrary dump of Washington's most justifiable function on fifty ill-equipped state governments. In truth, the block grant cop-out was the smoking-gun evidence that the Romney-Ryan Republicans had reached a state of intellectual bankruptcy.

SOCIAL INSURANCE AND DEFENSE: ROMNEY'S BIG GOVERNMENT

Indeed, having doubled down on another massive dose of revenue depletion ($5 trillion), Romney was in the same position as the Reagan administration had been in February 1981 when it launched its own giant tax-cut program; namely, it was obligated to make a frontal assault on the social insurance core of the domestic budget to sustain fiscal balance.

Plain and simple, social insurance is the true essence of Washington's "overspending" problem. The $19 trillion slated for it over the next decade is what makes the welfare state too corpulent, and also demonstrates why universal entitlements are offensive to the very idea of a limited state.

But the Romney-Ryan deficit howlers offered no "Schweiker plan" (see chapter 6) or any other measure to stop the massive outflow of Social Security and Medicare benefit payments to affluent retirees. Never had there been a better time to insist on a sweeping means test. After all, affluent social insurance recipients were the very epicenter of voters who believed most passionately that trillion-dollar deficits were a deadly economic threat and who thought voting for Obama was beyond the pale. Indeed, championing a means test for social insurance would have put Romney on the right side of the class war, rather than being postured as wanting to throw grannie out in the snow to fund tax cuts for billionaires.

Yet Romney-Ryan offered a spending cure which was both cowardly and a legislative nonstarter. The proposed $2 trillion in savings over ten years from shredding the means-tested safety net was entirely illusory; as indicated, it depended upon enactment of sweeping block grants that would massively shortchange state and local budgets that were already teetering on fiscal collapse. Needless to say, forty years of history going back to Nixon's abortive "special revenue sharing" reforms demonstrated this kind of lopsided swap within the federal system would never see the light of day. In short, the Romney-Ryan fiscal plan was the ultimate incarnation of the GOP's embrace of free lunch fiscal policy.

And that wasn't all. Candidate Romney also chose to surround himself with neo-con foreign policy advisors, led by the bombastic John Bolton, former Bush ambassador to the UN and warmonger extraordinaire. The Romney national security budget therefore called for spending $800 billion annually in order to sustain and modernize the machinery of invasion and occupation required by the aggressive ambitions of neo-con foreign policy.

In inflation-adjusted dollars the Romney neo-con defense plan thus amounted to 200 percent of Eisenhower's final budget, a plan which had been set against a real nuclear-armed enemy and which had also had been wrapped in a prophetic warning about budget aggrandizement by the military-industrial complex. Had Ike been here today, he would have sent Bolton and his posse of neo-cons packing and put candidate Romney through a heavy remedial education on the limited uses of military power in a world where the United States has no industrial state enemies.

In all, it can be well and truly said that the 2012 election campaign of the Romney-Ryan ticket brought fiscal sundown to America. In what was a "last chance" election to confront the looming fiscal calamity, the purported conservative party served up a potpourri of budgetary flimflam, delusion, and lies. In so doing, it left the American electorate in the dark with respect to the dire challenges and painful austerity which lies ahead. Likewise, the congressional Republicans who survived the Romney defeat had sought no mandate that was remotely geared to fixing the nation's giant fiscal gap. Instead, they merely promised to continue tilting at Big Government windmills and repeating ritual incantations about tax cuts for job creators.

Fiscal governance has thus been reduced to a doomsday machine. With the voice of the old-time fiscal religion terminally silenced, there is no counterpoint to the din of bastardized Keynesianism emanating from both parties; that is, the shibboleth that the US economy is too weak to ask either the "job creators" or the "consumption units," as the case may be on the respective sides of the partisan aisle, to shoulder the taxes needed to pay the government's bills. Indeed, after the November election the initial rounds of the so-called fiscal cliff battle amply demonstrated that Washington is mired in dysfunction and drifting into national insolvency.

ROMNEY'S WALL STREET SHILLS

Candidate Mitt Romney's whiff on the looming fiscal crisis, however, was just a warm up. Even more consequential was his complete failure to grasp that free market capitalism was failing in America because it had been fatally corrupted by two decades of Wall Street coddling by the Fed and nearly four decades of worldwide floating money and central bank monetary inflation. To be sure, he had called for Bernanke's replacement during the primary campaign in order, apparently, to parry Governor Rick Perry's fusillade in the direction of the Eccles Building.

But Romney's choice of his top economic advisor was proof that he was dream-walking in the great financial bubble that had been fostered by the nation's central bankers. According to the headline of a *New York Times* profile, the candidate's "Go-To-Economist" and author of the campaign's official economic platform was one R. Glenn Hubbard, dean of the Columbia Business School, and George W. Bush's chief economic advisor and architect of the 2001–2003 "Bush tax cuts." Not surprisingly, Hubbard was of the opinion that the Wall Street–coddling policies of the Greenspan-Bernanke era had been a roaring success. He suggested that Romney should consider keeping Bernanke on board because he had been a "model technocrat" who was owed a "pat on the back."

As indicated earlier, the single most noxious deformation of bubble finance had been the $5 trillion MEW spree of the nation's household sector. It had been the proximate source of the consumption binge that left American families buried in mortgage debt and the residential housing industry in smoldering ruins.

Yet Hubbard had been an unabashed proponent of MEW. Near the very top of the housing bubble and after gross mortgage financings had hit the freakish level of $5.3 trillion, or 40 percent of GDP, in the spring of 2003,

Hubbard opined that the "revolution in housing finance" which had led to "large increases in mortgage equity withdrawal" had been a salutary development; it was "one reason why consumer spending held up well" during his tenure as chairman of the White House Council of Economic Advisers (CEA).

This is pure Keynesian blather, but Hubbard was not yet done. In an article co-authored in late 2004 with William Dudley, who was then chief economist at Goldman and is now Bernanke's right-hand money printer as president of the New York Fed, he averred that due to the Fed's unleashing of the Wall Street casino there had been a "dramatic decline in the cyclical volatility of housing."

Say again! It is not surprising that Hubbard did not see the most violent collapse of housing in American history looming just around the corner: he was a full-fledged proponent of bubble finance. Accordingly, Hubbard and Dudley had found "100 percent financing to purchase a home" to be a key contributor to the great prosperity purportedly under way at the time. An exasperated blogger rightly tagged this as "the mortgage bankers' equivalent of 'The Anarchist Cookbook'—a recipe for disaster."

Cookbook in hand, however, Hubbard kept candidate Romney firmly planted in the Wall Street–Fed consensus. Consequently, voters did not hear a word about the true menace stalking the land; namely, that their livelihoods, future prospects, and efficacy as citizens of American democracy were under relentless assault from the monetary politburo which inhabits the Eccles Building.

Here was a chance, in the first election after the dust had settled from the Bernanke-Paulson-instigated BlackBerry Panic, to call out the real source of what Romney appropriately called the "failing" American economy. Romney could have blasted financial repression as a gift to Wall Street speculators that undermined honest capital markets, crushed Main Street savers, battered low-and middle-income families with soaring food and energy costs, and enabled the nation to live far beyond it means while putting it in hock to the rest of the world by $8 trillion.

Instead, Romney-Ryan blamed it all on Obama, notwithstanding the inescapable facts—obvious to the overwhelming share of voters—that the terrifying meltdown on Wall Street and the associated sharp plunge of the American economy had occurred on the Republican watch of George W. Bush. So by their silence on the Fed and their defense of failed free lunch fiscal policies, the Romney-Ryan ticket failed to give the electorate a credible reason to abandon an incumbent who drank his Keynesian Kool-Aid straight up. Under the second Obama administration, therefore, big deficits and massive money printing will occur as a matter of policy choice, not simply as the default outcome that was implicit in the half-basked nostrums offered by Romney-Ryan.

Historians may someday wonder how the conservative party failed so badly when the very future of free market capitalism and fiscal solvency were at stake. The short answer would be that after three decades the entire party had become lost in the false world of bubble finance.

In that regard, a considerable share of blame could be assigned to the GOP's final rash of crypto-Keynesian economic advisors like Hubbard and his successor, Greg Mankiw of Harvard, or Ed Lazear of Stanford. As Bush's last CEA chairman, Lazear had insisted in May 2008 that "the data are pretty clear that we are not in a recession." Needless to say, when the Wall Street meltdown struck with cyclonic force a few months later Lazear did not have the foggiest notion of why it happened. He just rolled over and watched Bernanke and Paulson stampede Washington into the BlackBerry Panic.

But ultimately the GOP is the party of businessmen and financiers, and it was they who in Jim Carrey–like fashion had spent decades in a great and artificial financial bubble, the economic equivalent of *The Truman Show*. Accordingly, they did not know why Wall Street collapsed in September 2008 and didn't recognize that the American economy was dangerously leveraged at 3.6X national income. And most especially they did not perceive that the violent booms and busts on Wall Street had been the handiwork of a destructive régime of monetary central planning.

So failing to comprehend the crumbling world outside the bubble, they embraced a content-free revival of Reaganite rhetoric that was a veritable caricature of what Republican governments have actually done. They decried excessive regulation when economic regulation had peaked in the 1970s and had been rolled back ever since. In fact, the only thing of material import which had happened on the regulatory front since the Gipper's time had been the disastrous "deregulation" of banks, licensed wards of the state which had never been free enterprises in the first place.

Republican governments of the Bush era had also brought federal spending to the highest share of GDP since WWII and turned the small surpluses of the Clinton period into a raging torrent of red ink. Self-evidently, after the mad-cap tax cutting of the Bush period the federal tax burden had been reduced to the lowest level in fifty years. In short, the Republican mantra that the nation was overtaxed and overregulated was utterly disconnected from the economic facts, as were its tirades against the deficit.

THE JIM CARREY OF BUBBLE FINANCE

Willard M. Romney did not see this, and for a compelling reason: he was the Jim Carrey of bubble finance. He had made a fortune during a twenty-year career in the studio, riding the wave machines of debt and leveraged speculation enabled and powered up by the Fed. Not surprisingly, Romney mistook the windfall riches garnered in the great hall of bubble finance for the fruits of honest enterprise on the free market, and was therefore blind to the profound monetary and financial disorders of the American economy.

Accordingly, his presidential campaign readily adopted the content-free Reaganite rhetoric against taxes, Big Government, regulation, and deficits. As Romney saw it, there was nothing wrong with the nation's economy which couldn't be fixed by a can-do businessman in the Oval Office who knew what it takes to rejuvenate the "job creators," impose fiscal discipline, and unleash the capitalist energies.

In truth, this was pure political pettifoggery that would fix nothing, but it did underscore why Romney's successful sojourn in the financial bubble had made him uniquely unfit to be the GOP standard-bearer. He had been a big winner because the state and its central banking branch had failed miserably. What was needed was not the unleashing of the battered and impaired remnants of free market capitalism, but a drastic throttling of the state's engines of false prosperity; that is, an end to the madness of the Fed's financial repression and rampage of bond buying coupled with the imposition of taxes on the electorate for every dollar of federal spending that the legislature was unwilling to cut.

A return to sound money policies, of course, would bring ruin to the 1 percent, and years of painful austerity to Main Street. Needless to say, the masses would not have cottoned to such a program, especially if championed by one of the baby boom's biggest lottery winners. More importantly, Wall Street would have gagged and muffled their candidate before he could make a single utterance about cleaning house in the Eccles Building or taxing capital gains at the same rate as wage earners.

In fact, keeping the candidate safely enveloped in a fog of Reaganite rhetoric was exactly what Wall Street–oriented advisors like H. Glenn Hubbard excelled at. After all, the enterprising Professor Hubbard had been paid to investigate the operations of Countrywide Financial, for example, and found them laudatory. So it was plain that he could be counted on to keep the campaign looking with favor on gutting the Volcker Rule, keeping the giant Wall Street banks free from the threat of dismantlement, and empowering the monetary central planners to keep the juices flowing from the Eccles Building.

As seen in earlier chapters, bubble finance created a vast arena of financial engineering in which debt-fueled buyouts, buybacks, and M&A takeovers systematically channeled wealth and income to the very top of the economic ladder. But these windfalls did not foster capitalist growth and wealth creation on the free market; they simply extracted unearned rents from the Wall Street casino, and it was in the leveraged buyout business—where Romney made his fortune—that the most spectacular cases of this capture occurred.

So when all was said and done, Willard "Mitt" Romney was a creature of the great deformation of finance that had been unleashed by the administration in which his father had served as secretary of HUD. History has left few clues about what George Romney thought about Nixon's final destruction of the gold dollar, but his son's business history documents in spades how Nixon's actions eventually destroyed the free market in finance and fostered an unsustainable era of debt-fueled GDP growth and speculation-driven accumulation of wealth by the 1 percent.

That Mitt Romney turned out to be the conservative party's candidate for president in 2012 is ironic in the extreme. As detailed below, Romney's winnings from bubble finance during his years at Bain Capital were so preposterously impossible in an honest free market that it is no wonder that his 2012 campaign amounted to one giant platitude. He honestly thought his experience doing leveraged buyouts could show the way forward to ameliorate the nation's economic ills. In fact, Romney had been an energetic agent of the very financialization process that had generated the economic failures against which he campaigned.

BAIN IN THE BUBBLE

The Bain Capital that Mitt Romney built was a product of the Great Deformation. Like much of Wall Street, it garnered fabulous winnings through leveraged speculation in financial markets which have been perverted and deformed by three decades of money printing by the Fed. So Bain's billions of profits were not rewards for capitalist creation—they were mainly unearned windfalls collected from gambling in markets which were rigged to rise.

That is why Mitt Romney's claim that his essential qualification to be president was grounded in his fifteen years as head of Bain Capital clashed so discordantly with the truth. It was also why Bain's fulsome returns, which averaged more than 50 percent annually during Romney's 1984–1999 tenure, were not evidence that he had learned the true secrets of how to grow the economy and create jobs or that he had been uniquely prepped for the task of restarting the nation's sputtering engines of capitalism.

In fact, Mitt Romney was not a capitalist businessman; like the other LBO kings, he was a master financial speculator who bought, sold, flipped, and stripped businesses, but he did not build enterprises the old-fashioned way:

out of inspiration, perspiration, and a long slog on the free market fostering a new product, service, or process of production. Instead, he had spent his fifteen years raising debt in prodigious amounts on Wall Street so that Bain could purchase the pots and pans and caste-offs of corporate America, leverage them to the hilt, gussy them up as reborn "roll-ups," and then deliver them back to Wall Street for resale—the faster, the better.

This is what Romney's work consisted of during his stint in the Truman Show. It is also the modus operandi of the leveraged buyout business, and in an honest free market economy there wouldn't be much scope for it because it creates little of economic value. But as has been seen, we have a rigged system—a régime of crony capitalism—where the tax code heavily favors debt and capital gains, and the central bank purposefully enables rampant speculation by propping up the price of financial assets and battering down the cost of leveraged finance.

So the vast outpouring of LBOs in recent decades has been the consequence of bad policy, not the product of capitalist enterprise. And I had learned about this firsthand during seventeen years doing leveraged buyouts at one of the pioneering private equity houses, Blackstone, and then my own firm. The whole business was about maximizing debt, extracting cash, cutting head-counts, skimping on capital spending, outsourcing production, and dressing up the deal for the earliest, highest profit exit possible. Occasionally, we did invest in genuine growth companies, but without cheap debt and deep tax subsides, most deals would not make economic sense.

As shown earlier, the waxing and waning of the artificially swollen LBO business has been perfectly correlated with the bubbles and busts emanating from the Fed—so timing is the heart of the business. In that respect, Romney's tenure says it all: it was almost exactly coterminous with the first great Greenspan bubble which crested at the turn of the century and ended in the thundering stock market crash of 2000–2002. The credentials that Romney proffered as evidence of his business acumen, in fact, mainly show that he hung around the basket during the greatest bull market in recorded history. And that's why heralding Romney's record at Bain was so completely perverse. The record was actually all about the utter unfairness of windfall riches obtained under our anti–free market régime of bubble finance.

RIP VAN ROMNEY

When Romney opened the doors to Bain Capital in 1984, the S&P 500 stood at 160. By the time he answered the call to duty in Salt Lake City in early 1999, it had gone parabolic and reached 1260. This meant that had a modern Rip Van Winkle bought the S&P 500 index and held it through the fifteen years in question, the annual return (with dividends) would have been a spectacular 17 percent. Bain did considerably better, of course, but the reason wasn't business acumen.

The secret was leverage, luck, inside baseball, and the peculiar asymmetrical dynamics of the leveraged gambling carried on by private equity shops. As previously demonstrated, LBO funds are invested as equity at the bottom of a company's capital structure, which means that the lenders who provide 80 to 90 percent of the capital have no recourse to the private equity sponsor if deals go bust. Accordingly, LBO funds can lose 1X their money on failed deals, but make 10X or even 50X on the occasional home run. During a period of rising markets, expanding valuation multiples and abundant credit, the opportunity to "average up" the home runs with the 1X losses is considerable; it can generate a spectacular portfolio outcome.

In a nutshell, that's exactly the story of Bain Capital during Mitt Romney's tenure. The *Wall Street Journal* examined seventy-seven significant deals completed during that period based on fund-raising documents from Bain, and the results are a perfect illustration of bull market asymmetry. Overall, Bain generated an impressive $2.5 billion in investor gains on $1.1 billion of investments, but ten of Bain's deals accounted for 75 percent of the investor profits.

Accordingly, Bain's returns on the overwhelming bulk of the deals—sixty-seven out of seventy-seven—were actually lower than what a passive S&P 500 indexer would have earned even without the risk of leverage or paying all the private equity fees. Investor profits amounted to a prosaic .7X the original investment on these deals and, based on its average five-year holding period, the annual return would have computed to about 12 percent, well below the 17 percent average return on the S&P in this period.

By contrast, the ten "home runs" generated profits of $1.8 billion on investments of only $250 million, yielding a spectacular return of 7X investment. Yet it is this handful of home runs which both make the Romney investment legend and also seal the indictment: they show that Bain Capital was nothing more than a vehicle for leveraged speculation that was gifted immeasurably by the Greenspan bubble. It was a fortunate place where leverage got lucky, not a higher form of capitalist endeavor. No training school for presidential aspirants, Bain Capital during Romney's watch was actually the stage set for the Truman Show of bubble finance.

VICTORY FROM THE JAWS OF DEFEAT: HOW BAIN MADE $600 MILLION ON THE WAY TO THE COURTHOUSE DOOR

The startling fact is that *four of the ten Bain Capital "home runs" ended up in bankruptcy,* and for an obvious reason: Bain got its money out at the top of the Greenspan boom in the late 1990s and then these companies hit the wall during the 2000–2002 downturn, weighed down by the massive load of debt Bain had bequeathed them. In fact, nearly $600 million, or one-third, of the profits earned by the home run companies had been extracted from the hide of these four eventual debt zombies.

The most emblematic among them was a roll-up deal focused on down-in-the-mouth department stores and apparel chains that were falling by the wayside in small-town America due to the arrival of Wal-Mart and the big-box retailers. Bain invested $10 million in 1988 and nine years later took out eighteen times its money; that is, a $175 million profit.

Fittingly, Stage Stores Inc. was the last deal underwritten by the Drexel-Milken junk-bond machine before its demise. And the $300 million raised for this incipient LBO was exactly the kind of slush fund that Milken's stable of takeover artists had used to acquire corporate cast-offs and other bedraggled "pots and pans" that got rechristened as "growth" companies.

During the next eight years Bain slogged it out, accumulating about three hundred small Main Street storefronts under such forgettable banners as Royal Palais, Bealls, Fashion Bar, and Stage Stores. Yet the company wasn't making much headway. By 1996 it had paid back none of the Milken debt and was only earning $14 million, exactly what it had generated back in 1992 on half the number of stores.

In the spring of 1997, when Chairman Greenspan decided that "irrational exuberance" was not such a worrisome thing, Bain Capital decided to indulge, too. It caused Stage Stores Inc., which was already publicly traded, to raise $300 million of new junk bonds and used the proceeds to buy a faltering 250-store chain of family clothing stores called C.R. Anthony.

These 12,000-square-foot cracker-box stores sold mid-market shoes, shirts, and dresses right in Wal-Mart's wheelhouse. In hot pursuit of "synergies" Bain promptly rebranded these "Anthony's" stores to the purportedly more compelling banners of its "Stage" and "Bealls" lineup. While the name change did nothing to ward off the grim reaper from Bentonville, it suddenly gave Stage Stores Inc. the "growth" story that Greenspan's bull market craved. Within five months of this ostensibly "transformative" deal and long before the results of the ritual "synergies" and "rebranding" could be determined, the company's stock price had doubled. Bain Capital and its partner, Goldman Sachs, quickly unloaded their shares at the aforementioned eighteen times gain.

As a matter of plain fact, the "transformative" C.R. Anthony deal was a bull-market scam. Almost immediately results headed south. After growing 4 percent during the year of Bain's quick 1997 exit, same-store sales turned to a negative 3 percent in 1998 and negative 7 percent in 1999, and were still falling when Stage Stores Inc. filed for bankruptcy shortly thereafter. The company hemorrhaged $150 million of negative cash flow during 1998–1999; that is, during the two years after Bain and Goldman got out of Dodge City.

Bain Capital subsequently claimed the company was "growing, successful and consistently profitable during the nine years we owned it" but then immediately ran into "operating problems." That was a whopper by any other name but typical of the standard private equity narrative that confuses speculators' timing with real value creation on the free market. The fact is, the bad inventory and vastly overstated assets which took the company down did not suddenly materialize out of the blue during the twenty-four months after Bain's exit: they were actually the result of financial engineering games from the very beginning.

Worse still, the Stage Stores deal embodied all of the hidden leverage that had become par for the course in the era of bubble finance. When the crunch came, the company had no assets to fall back on because Bain had hocked virtually everything; that is, it sold all the company's credit card receivables to a third party and among its 650 stores it owned exactly 3! The capitalized debt embedded in its store leases was nearly $750 million and when added to its disclosed balance sheet debt, the company's true debt of was $1.3 billion, or a devastating twenty-five times its peak year free cash flow.

The bankruptcy forced the closure of about 250, or 40 percent, of the company's stores and the loss of about five thousand jobs. Yet the moral of the Stage Stores saga is not simply that in this instance Bain Capital was a jobs destroyer, not a jobs creator. The larger point is that it is actually a tale of Wall Street speculators toying with Main Street properties in defiance of sound finance: an anti-Schumpeterian project which used state-subsidized debt to milk cash from stores that would not have otherwise survived on the free market.

Bain's acclaimed success with another retailer, Staples, is also not what it is touted to be. Tom Stemberg was a visionary entrepreneur who got $5 million of seed money from Bain in 1986 when Bain was still in the venture capital business; the Milken-style LBO schemes came later. As it happened, Bain exited the Staples deal after only a few years with a $15 million profit, a rounding error in the scheme of things.

Stemberg made Staples a free market success, a relentless generator of efficiency in the retail distribution of office supplies. Yet this honest capitalist efficiency, which benefited millions of customers, was achieved by a rampage of job destruction among tens of thousands Main Street stationery and office supplies stores and other traditional distributors. These now defunct operations could not compete with Staples due to their high labor costs per dollar of sales, including upstream labor expense in the traditional, inefficient wholesale and distribution layers that stood behind Main Street retailers.

Ironically, the thousands of businesses and hundreds of thousands of jobs which Staples eliminated on the way to its current head count of 50,000 part-timers and 90,000 total were the office supply counterparts of Stage Stores Inc. At length, Wal-Mart eliminated the cracker-box stores selling shoes, shirts, and dresses that Bain kept on artificial life support and replaced their jobs with back-of-the-store automation and front-end part timers in its own giant stores. The pointless election-year exercise of counting jobs won and lost owing to these epochal shifts on the free market was obviously irrelevant to the job of being president, but the fact that Bain made $15 million from the winner and $175 million from the loser is evidence that it did not make a fortune all on its own. It had considerable help from the Easy Button at the Fed.

THE $100 MILLION YELLOW PAD

American Pad and Paper (Ampad) was a twenty-bagger; that is, $5 million was invested in 1992 for a $100 million profit; a miraculous outcome for Bain and Romney, but hardly so for the Ampad workers and shareholders left holding the bag when the company bankrupted in 1999 with massive debt. Ampad was the focus of competing narratives in the election, but what it truly represented was neither jobs destroyed or saved—just an exercise in LBO cash stripping that would not occur on an honest free market where the central bank was not in the tank for Wall Street.

Ampad, owned by the giant paper conglomerate Mead Corporation, had plants in fourteen states in the faintly archaic business of making notebooks, envelopes, file folders, and writing tablets, including the eponymous "yellow pad." Not surprisingly, at a time when the Internet and paperless office were taking the world by storm, Mead discovered that Ampad was "not a good fit" and that its sale to Bain Capital was "an early step to increase productivity." So the question recurred as to how spread-sheet-toting suits that Romney sent from Boston could resurrect what deeply experienced executives in Dayton, Ohio, knew to be a value-destroying sunset operation.

The answer was leveraged financial engineering; that is, the roll-up of like and similar pots, pans, and discards for an eventual coming-out party on Wall Street. To this end, Mead perfumed the pig on the way out the door. In conjunction with a sweeping corporate "restructuring" program, thirteen manufacturing and distribution facilities were consolidated into six and a $90 million "restructuring reserve" was established to cover asset write-downs and severance costs for upward of a thousand terminated employees.

So Bain Capital and the division's senior management became the proud owners of a slimmed-down $100 million business that dominated the market for legal-sized yellow pads. Yet even with all of Mead's predi-vestiture elimination of plants and jobs, Ampad's earnings in 1991 (before interest, tax, depreciation, and amortization) amounted to the grand sum of $4.9 million.

Mead also topped up Bain's tiny $5 million equity investment with short-term financing and generous loans to the divested executives, but despite these Band-Aids from a big company trying to rid itself of a loser, the results showed that the suits from Boston had not moved the needle at all. By 1993 earnings had inched up only to $5.1 million, meaning that after eighteen months of effort Bain had come up with only $1 million of value gain at prevailing cash flow multiples.

Accordingly, it determined that yellow pads were not enough and in the summer of 1994 it launched a spree of acquisitions hoping that accordion file folders and business envelopes were the way of the future! The market was held to be large, amounting to some 169 billion envelopes per year, but the snag was they sold for only 1.6 cents each. To make a difference to its profits, therefore, Ampad needed to sell 10–15 billion envelopes a year.

This turned out to be not a problem. Another group of leveraged opera-tors had been at work for nine years consolidating the business-envelope sector under the "Williamhouse" umbrella and had accumulated numer-ous plants and properties. By 1995 the Williamhouse roll-up of envelope makers and distributors had accumulated $150 million of debt, about $250 million of sales, and a modest operating cash flow of about $16 million.

So in November 1995 Bain again rolled the dice on a "transformative" acquisition. It spent $300 million acquiring Williamhouse, assuming all its heavy debt. The purchase price at 18X operating free cash flow was on the far edge of sanity, but once again the putative "synergies" proved com-pelling to Bain's bankers at the Bankers Trust Company. They refinanced all of the huge Williamhouse debts and on top provided an additional loan of $245 million. As it happened, Bain only needed $150 million to buy Williamhouse's stock and pay the deal fees. So it sent its bankers a case of champagne and helped itself to a $60 million dividend in compensation for prospective "synergies" from a day-old merger.

By year-end 1995, Ampad had added envelopes and accordion files to its yellow pad portfolio, but in the process of its frenetic acquisitions Bain had trashed the company's balance sheet. Compared to $45 million of debt at year-end 1994, Ampad by June 2006 had ten times as much debt to service—$460 million!

It therefore desperately needed the promised giant synergies, but, alas, they were not arriving as scheduled. Ampad generated barely enough operating income during the first six months of 1996 to cover its swollen interest payments, causing it to report a negligible five cents per share of net income. Yet since Bain Capital had now harvested a dividend that was twelve times its original investment, it was basically home free, with a call option on either operational miracles or clever marketing and accounting. Not surprisingly, Bain opted for marketing and accounting razzmatazz. In June 1996, it launched an IPO at $15 per share—a truly crazy valuation of 150X its actual annualized earnings during the first half of the year.

The road show had an altogether different spin, however. The IPO boasted "pro forma" financials; that is, not actual sales and profits but "would have been" results. Thus, 1995 pro forma sales of $620 million reflected the full-year impact of its acquisitions, implying that Ampad was a born-again "growth" company. Compared to its actual sales of only $100 million in 1991, it had purportedly been growing at 53 percent annually. The fact that 90 percent of this growth was due to debt-funded acquisitions was presumably to be overlooked.

The magic wand, however, came in the pro forma "adjustments" to earnings. The company had actually reported 1995 operating earnings of a scant $1.5 million and a net loss after interest and taxes, but in a five-page bridge table which was a wonder to behold, the offering prospectus detailed several dozen pro forma "adjustments" that envisaged the newly minted amalgamation of companies, Ampad-Williamhouse-Globe-Weis-Niagara, as a gusher of profits. Its interest costs had tripled, but thanks to "synergies," cost savings, and future operating improvements the $1.5 million of actual 1995 earnings were to be viewed as $57 million of pro forma operating income.

This $57 million result included a lot of chickens which had not yet hatched. For example, $8.5 million of higher operating income was to be from the Niagara Envelope acquisition that had not actually finalized as of the IPO prospectus. Likewise, a savings of $4.5 million was cited from closing Williamhouse's New York City headquarters, even though rent and severance costs several times greater were buried in purchase accounting and would be paid for years to come.

Yet by July 1996, the Greenspan stock market bubble had a goodly head of steam. This meant that Ampad had no trouble selling nearly $250 million of stock based on a prospectus riddled with pro forma adjustments to the point of incomprehensibility, and a "growth" story that strained credulity. Bain Capital was able to sell to credulous IPO punters another $50 million of its stock, bringing its return to over $100 million and the fabled twenty-bagger. Meanwhile, the hedge fund speculators pumped the company's stock to a peak of $26 per share by late summer of 1996, making all the more evident that the Ampad deal was really about speculative mania on Wall Street, not a revival of "old yeller" from the bits and pieces of a dying industry.

The company's combined debt and equity was then being valued at $1.1 billion, or a fantastic 35X the $30 million of operating free cash flow (EBITDA less Capital Expenditure) that Ampad actually posted during 1997. However, within weeks of the IPO and a profits warning, the fast money smelled the rat and followed Bain in scampering off the listing ship. Margins were being squeezed by the superstores faster than the promised synergies could be realized. By early 1999, the stock was delisted and when the company was finally liquidated in bankruptcy shortly thereafter, secured lenders recovered about $100 million and other creditors got zero; that is, the company was worth about 10 percent of its peak valuation.

Once again, the moral of the story is about the ill effects of bad public policy, not just that smarter speculators like Bain bagged the slower-witted. In fact, LBOs are just another way for speculators to make money, but they are dangerous because when they fail they leave needless economic disruption and job losses in their wake. That's why LBOs would be rare in an honest free market; it's only cheap debt, interest deductions, and ludicrously low capital gains taxes which artificially fuel them.

BAIN'S $165 MILLION SCORE ON EXPERIAN: LEVERAGED SPECULATION WITHOUT BREAKING A SWEAT

In September 1996, Bain Capital and some partners bought Experian, the consumer credit reporting division of TRW Inc. for $1.1 billion, but Bain ponied up only $88 million in equity along with a similar amount from partners; all the rest of the funding came from junk bonds and bank loans. *Seven weeks later* they sold it to a British conglomerate for $1.7 billion, producing a $600 million profit on their slim layer of equity capital and after not even enduring the inconvenience of unpacking their brief cases.

Quite obviously, Bain Capital generated zero value before it flipped the property. So the fact that it scalped a sudden and spectacular $165 million windfall gain has nothing to do with investment skill or even trading prowess. Instead, the Experian corporation's $600 million valuation gain in just fifty days smelled like an Inside Job.

That explains how a division put on the auction block by one of the nation's most prominent deal makers, CEO Joseph Gorman, could have been so badly mispriced in the initial sale to Bain Capital and its partners; that is, how they got it for just 65 percent of what the property fetched only months later.

In fact, the original auction had been run by Bear Stearns, and it became evident in March 2008 that Bear Stearns had never been in the client service business; it had been in the brass-knuckled trading business where it used its balance sheet to underwrite and trade immensely profitable "risk assets." Not surprisingly, the private equity houses were the premier source of profits for its trading and capital markets desks, so its "investment bankers" needed little encouragement about where to steer corporate divestiture deals.

In that endeavor they got plenty of help from the inside management of spun-off divisions, who were usually marketed as a "key asset" of the business and eager to participate in the prospective LBO. Thus, Experian's CEO D. Van Skilling and his lieutenants reaped millions from this Wall Street–orchestrated windfall almost before they got new business cards. Oblivious to the irony, however, Skilling defended Bain's instant $165 million profit by insisting "there was never a hint of financial chicanery at all."

He had that upside down. The deal was pure chicanery, but not because the private equity investors were underhanded. It was because they were artificially enabled by the central banking and taxing branches of the state, the true source of this kind of rent-a-company speculation.

THE WESLEY JESSEN HOME RUN:
FAR LESS THAN MEETS THE EYE

Wesley Jessen was a small specialist firm that did reasonably well in cosmetic eye-color lenses and toric lenses to correct astigmatism. In mid-1995, when Schering-Plough Corp put it on the block, Bain Capital bought it for $6 million and reaped a $300 million profit for itself by 1999; that is, it made nearly 50X its investment in the same number of months. On an apples-to-apples basis, however, the company's operating income rose by only 2X during the same period: all the rest of the gain, $275 million to be exact, was due to massive leverage, the Greenspan bubble, and accounting maneuvers that can fairly be called myopic.

Bain employed a hoary old dodge: having its accountants write off every dime of plant, equipment, and intangible know-how, reassigning roughly $40 million to the inventory accounts, and then charging it to income in the immediate two or three quarters. This trick eliminated all future depreciation, thereby magically adding $14 million to the pro forma operating income on Wesley Jessen's $100 million of sales.

Investors were promptly told to ignore the resulting losses, of course, since these inventory charges were "nonrecurring"! In fact, savings from pre-deal "restructuring" actions by the seller plus the accounting magic generated $24 million of freshly minted "operating income" before Bain's turnaround squad even showed up at the company's Des Plaines, Illinois, headquarters. The alleged "turnaround" of Wesley Jessen was thus largely an artifact of Bain's PR machine.

In the fourth quarter of 1996, the company borrowed $70 million to acquire a competitor, Barnes-Hind, from Pilkington plc. Before the ink was dry on the merger contract, Bain filed an IPO prospectus. While Barnes-Hind had an operating loss of $17 million the year before the merger, its results for that period were improved by $23 million owing to Bain's pro forma adjustments, creating the appearance of another dramatic turnaround.

During the twelve months ending at the merger date, the combined companies had actually incurred a net loss of $27 million, but it vanished with the help of $50 million in pre-tax adjustments for merger accounting and prospective savings. So its pro forma earnings took on a decisively improved aura; that is, it would have booked a $14 million profit, or about $0.73 per share.

Not surprisingly, the stock market eagerly scooped up $45 million of new shares at $15, or twenty times these gussied-up earnings, just in time for the Fed to begin a new round of stock market goosing in March 1997. And that proved propitious for Bain. Almost to the day on which its 180-day IPO lockup expired, it sold its first batch of shares in a secondary offering in a now red-hot stock market at a red-hot price that was up 60 percent from the IPO.

Wesley Jessen had not then filed financial statements with even $1 of GAAP net income, but when Bain's underwriters wired the proceeds in August 1997 the selling price was $23.50 per share. That's 52X the $0.43 per share it had paid for the stock twenty-five months earlier. At the end of the day, massive leverage, fancy accounting, and bubble finance, not entrepreneurial prowess, were the source of Bain's fifty-bagger.

THE GREATEST WINDFALL EVER: THE ITALIAN JOB

In November 1997, Bain Capital pulled off a veritable capitalist heist in the socialist redoubts of the Italian yellow pages. On a $17 million investment in the Italian phone book, it took out a profit of $375 million. This was not only a twenty-two-bagger, but for Mitt Romney it was the ultimate in no-sweat riches. According to the company's CEO, Romney's sole involvement was a cameo appearance during a due diligence session: "He came into the room, asked a couple of very sharp questions immediately, shook hands and left." Twenty-eight months later in February 2000, Romney's former colleagues at Bain located him during his tour of duty in Salt Lake City, where they wired his share of the winnings, a reputed $50 million.

Bain and a syndicate of private equity houses were originally brought in as a stalking horse to validate the government's "privatization" machinations. At the time, the key Italian treasury official was one Mario Draghi. His assignment was to get the nation's huge deficit down to a Maastricht treaty–compliant 3 percent, and he elected to do so by means of a rent-a-balance sheet ploy of the type then in favor.

The short story is that Bain and the other investors paid 5X the company's operating income for their shares, and were paid 100X operating income to leave when local circumstances obviated the need for the rental deal. That preposterous multiple expansion accounted for virtually all of Bain's twenty-two-bagger.

In the interim, the dot-com bubble reached it fevered peak, so Italy's lumbering phone book publisher had puffed itself up as a fleet-footed Internet company, claiming to be the next AOL. In the fog of 1999's worldwide financial bubbles, a group of corporate raiders who did not have two nickels to rub together then got control of Italy's storied typewriter maker, Olivetti, and parleyed massive borrowings through that vehicle into control of the Italian phone company.

Now hoist atop a stupendous house of cards, the raiders next went after Italy's gussied-up yellow pages, paying $24 billion, or 180X net income, for a business that was slithering into the sunset. In fact, the exit value reaped by Bain top-ticked Greenspan's NASDAQ bubble in February 2000 and since then has shriveled to the vanishing point. Never have a group of private equity men laughed more heartily on the way to the bank.

The Bain Capital investments here reviewed accounted for $1.4 billion, or 60 percent, of the fund's profits over fifteen years. Four of them ended in bankruptcy; one was an inside job and fast flip; one (Wesley Jessen) was essentially a massive M&A brokerage fee; and the seventh and largest gain, the Italian Job, amounted to a veritable freak of financial nature.

In short, this is a record about a dangerous form of leveraged gambling that has been enabled by the failed central banking and taxing policies of the state. That it had been offered as evidence that Mitt Romney was a deeply experienced capitalist entrepreneur and job creator is surely a testament to the financial deformations of our times.

It is also proof of why 2012 was the sundown election. Mitt Romney was the very apotheosis of bubble finance. By embracing his candidacy and proffering his Bain Capital record as that of a "job creator," the conservative party demonstrated that it no longer had a clue about the cause of the accumulating ills afflicting the nation's economy and deeply unsettling its electorate.

The Republican Party needed to be against everything which made Romney possible; that is, the whole machinery of bubble finance. It needed to denounce the Fed's lunatic bond buying, its destruction of interest rate pricing signals, its pegging and propping of risk assets, its provision of free overnight money to the carry trades, and its trashing of the dollar's external value. Likewise, instead of yammering about tax cuts for the job creators, it needed to attack the deep tax subsidies for debt and capital gains and the false prosperity flowing from massive federal deficits, even if it took new taxes such as on energy or consumption to close the gap.

Finally, it needed to acknowledge that the vast overfinancialization of the American economy and the rampant speculation embodied in Wall Street's financial engineering games were not the natural outcome of the free market. Instead, they are the spoiled fruits of printing press money and chronic fiscal profligacy. These deformations, in turn, had resulted in massive windfalls that had accrued to the top of the income ladder, and most especially to the 1 percent at the very top.

In short, the bubble of opulence at the top of the nation's failing Main Street economy was neither natural nor defensible. Obama sensed it, and offered demagoguery. The Republicans denied it, and offered Romney.

INSIDE THE FINANCIAL BUBBLE: LESSONS LEARNED LATE

I learned these truths the hard way, staring at the prospect of spending my remaining years as a guest in one of Uncle Sam's cell blocks. It turns out that my fraud indictment had been a case of a prosecutor gone wild and all charges were dropped by the government "in the interest of justice." But I had gotten into this pickle not for violating any statute or accounting rule, but because I had plied an LBO trade right to the very edge of sanity.

It thus happened that after twenty years in the financial bubble, prospering as an investment banker and private equity investor, albeit at a much more modest scale than Mitt Romney, I had become as oblivious to the dangers of leveraged speculation as most of Wall Street. Having been the scourge of debt in the public sector, however, my lassitude on the matter was especially telling.

Indeed, it was only after my own crash landing on the shoals of excessive leverage that I came to recognize the Great Deformation. Like most baby boomers playing hard inside the bubble, I simply had not noticed the financial landscape morphing ever deeper into a debt-fueled casino of speculation and rent seeking.

In fact, if you were aggressively engaged inside the financial bubble the music never really stopped. After brief pauses in 1987, 1998, and 2000–2002, the deal-making machinery came roaring back stronger each time; the availability of high-yield debt and other forms of high-risk capital became more abundant and less demanding; and the benchmark interest rate drifted steadily lower, meaning that the valuation of financial assets was lifted ever higher.

As seen in chapters 14 through 26, everything financial got bigger: the size the mortgage market, the girth of Wall Street balance sheets, the magnitude of M&A takeover volumes, the scale of stock buybacks, the AUM of the hedge fund sector, the size of LBOs, and the extent of funds invested in private equity and other alternative asset classes. In short order, financial growth got totally out of synch with the possibilities for growth of real output and wealth.

Thus, even a healthy and balanced free market economy can grow at perhaps 3 percent per year on a sustained basis, or 35 percent in a decade, or 3X in half a century. But as the financial bubble expanded, gains on leveraged deals and various classes of stocks and risk assets frequently grew by 5X, 10X or even 50X in just a few years. The Bain Capital cases cited above were not that unusual.

Most wave riders, including myself, didn't see the disconnect between the modest economic advance during the bubble years and the massive financial advance. A combination of factors including the end of the cold war, the technology and Internet revolutions, the stunning rise of China and East Asia, and the roaring stock markets produced a suspension of disbelief. To see that the Greenspan prosperity was actually a giant, relentlessly inflating financial bubble you had to be thrown off your ride and gain some alternative perspective from being sprawled out on the terrain below.

I was afforded exactly that experience in the spring of 2005 when the largest LBO in my equity fund blew up in bankruptcy, and not just an ordinary one. The company called Collins & Aikman was a supplier to Detroit of automotive interior components such as instrument panels, door panels, and molded floor carpets and was heavily leveraged, with debt at nearly 6X EBITDA. When Ford and General Motors were downgraded to non-investment grade status in May, debt covenants were triggered throughout my company's capital structure and supplier trade credit dried up rapidly.

Collins & Aikman's scramble into bankruptcy was considered unseemly at the time, but it proved to be only a prelude to the eventual unwinding of the entire automotive house of cards in the industry's fiery crash in the fall of 2008. In fact, as detailed in chapter 30, the auto industry had become a daisy chain of debt during the bubble era and that was truly insensible: the auto industry was among the most cyclically violent sectors of the economy, but by the second Greenspan bubble nearly every link in the supply chain, from the giant GM to tiny auto fabric mills, was freighted down with debt, including massive unfunded retirement and medical obligations.

Nevertheless, Collins & Aikman was among the first to splatter and the shock of it caused the company's board to demand my resignation as CEO, even though I had personally organized the company from a series of M&A deals, had raised its tottering layers of debt, had worked without pay as CEO for nearly two years to salvage it, and was the majority shareholder through my private equity fund. Whether the board acted correctly or not, the bankruptcy filing and my abrupt departure generated a swirl of controversy and scapegoating in Detroit.

It also attracted the attention of the aforementioned prosecutor, an assistant US Attorney (AUSA) in the southern district of New York named Helen Cantwell, who had just come off the drug and murder beat and was apparently hunting for bigger game in the arena of white-collar crime. In short order, AUSA Cantwell, who had never previously led a business case, filed an indictment charging me with violation of an accounting standard that I had never heard of.

It had to do with accounting for supplier rebates, which at the time were a common practice in Detroit. The auto industry's pricing structure was then collapsing under the weight of massive excess capacity funded with way too much debt. Desperate suppliers therefore were offering customers large cash rebates from their lists prices in order to retain business volume and the cash flow to meet their debt service.

Collins & Aikman had paid millions to GM and the other OEMs every quarter to keep them alive, and had in turn put the screws to its own suppliers for cash rebates against their invoice prices. Sensibly, my company had booked the massive outflow of cash rebates to the OEMs each quarter as a current-period expense, and the rebate payments from suppliers as current-period income.

This was the practice and pattern of the entire auto industry's supply chain as it descended into the fires of deflation and insolvency. As we struggled to pay the company's crushing debt, it never occurred to me that this symmetrical and industrywide practice was not kosher.

Blessed with no training or experience in business, accounting, finance, and the tottering auto sector, the big-game-hunting AUSA found this to be a violation of a pending accounting standard called EITF 02-16. The block letters meant that it was an "emerging" rather than a settled standard and that the profession was still divided, but Cantwell was certain that Collins

& Aikman's rebate accounting practices were criminal violations ordered by me.

Put in mind of what Samuel Johnson once said about the gallows, I found that a criminal indictment did, indeed, concentrate my mind. At least it did so long enough to prove to the top US attorney that in 15 million pages of discovery there was not a shred of evidence that anyone at Collins & Aikman had violated EITF 02-16 or even heard of it.

By then Cantwell had already fled the courthouse for a berth in a top-drawer white-collar defense firm for good reason: she had brought a groundless indictment that now had to be withdrawn by the mighty Southern District of New York. When the charges were withdrawn, the case was also dropped against eight other employees of my company whose lives, needless to say, had been ruined by a badge-toting prosecutor trying to leapfrog up a legal career path. Needless to say, the case also attracted the usual quota of class action lawsuits and piling on by the SEC. All of these cases were settled for $7 million in nuisance money without any trial or any denial or admission of wrongdoing in any of the venues involved.

Yet during a multiyear battle to prove there was nothing wrong with Collins & Aikman's accounting, I had extensive occasion to delve into every nook and cranny of its balance sheet and other financial statements and come face to face with the debt monster I had created in this case, and had been doing in the LBO business as a general practice for years.

Stated simply, the company had no shock absorbers because every imaginable asset had been hocked and every dime of even quasi-discretionary expense had been cut. Thus, all of the receivables had been sold to GE Capital or to "fast pay" lenders who discounted future payments from shipments to the Big Three. Nearly all of the equipment including multimillion-dollar plastic molding machines in eighty worldwide manufacturing plants had been sold for cash and leased back, creating mandatory rental payments just like regular debt. Trade credit from suppliers had been pushed to the breaking point, and the balance sheet itself was freighted down with several different bank revolvers, a half dozen flavors of junk bonds, tax-exempt economic development bonds, and other debt exotica.

And yet Collins & Aikman was typical, if not conservative. It had started out as an M&A roll-up of interior component suppliers in 2001 with leverage at 3.8X EBITDA, a ratio which was exceedingly modest by the standards of the LBO blow-off phase in 2006–2007. But the problem was that as the auto industry's deflationary crisis intensified, the whole supply chain descended into an orgy of price cutting and for an overpowering reason: the fixed cost of debt service was so great that any business that produced "variable contribution" to debt service was the object of ferocious competition, even if the return on plant capital and corporate overhead was negative.

As price cutting intensified in this manner, cost cutting followed right behind. Auto companies all the way up the chain to and including GM were literally throwing their future down the drain in order to generate cash in the present period, and head-count reduction was the go-to angle of first resort. In the case of Collins & Aikman, we had started with 32,000 employers and were down to 20,000 or so based on the same $4 billion annual volume of business when the crash finally came.

I had actually moved into the CEO suite in Detroit in order to be expense-cutter-in-chief because I thought I knew how to do it and my fund had hundreds of millions invested in the company. What I learned was that one day at a time, the debt monster can cause rational executives to devour their own enterprise.

We started by getting rid of long-term expenses like marketing, R&D, new business development, information services, and human resource people, and then any and every frill including employee cafeterias, lawn care services, and weekend heating. Yet as the pricing and revenue deflated, even that wasn't enough and so soon pensions were slashed, 401k matching was eliminated, bonuses were terminated, employee health-care cost sharing was drastically increased, cell phones were curtailed and expense accounts cut to the bone, and much more.

But the debt kept rising and pricing and cash flow kept falling. So then it got really serious. The sales force was gutted, the company's well-regarded engineering ranks were drastically pruned, assistant plant managers were eliminated, and more than half of all executives making more than $100,000 per year were terminated and their jobs assigned to those who remained. By April 2005, the company had been picked to the bones and was an accident waiting to happen. In short order it did.

In my early days in the LBO business I had taken to speech making about the wondrous efficiency and productivity-generating powers of debt. During most of the years at Blackstone and my own fund I went to quarterly board meetings and harassed managers about the need to cut more and "restructure" faster. In the final days at Collins & Aikman I had become a desperate ax wielder, red in financial tooth and claw from sacrifices made to the monster of debt.

Only in exile did I see that Collins & Aikman was not simply a one-off accident or case of bad timing, but that it was an economic deformation that would never have occurred on the free market. Its mountains of debt and off-balance sheet leverage had been raised right in the heart of Wall

Street via syndications led by JPMorgan, Credit Suisse, Deutsche Bank, GE Capital, and many more. They had been able to distribute this toxic paper to hundreds of banks, CLOs, high-yield mutual funds, pension managers, insurance companies, and just plain speculators because in the world of bubble finance economic risk was badly underpriced and high-yield paper was drastically overowned.

In the end, upward of $100 billion of losses were absorbed by investors in auto sector equities and debt when the house of cards collapsed in the bankruptcy of every major Detroit company save for Ford and Johnson Controls. This should have been the lesson of a lifetime, a thundering wake-up call that cheap debt, the Greenspan-Bernanke Put, the huge tax bias for debt, and capital gains are a mortal threat to free market capitalism. They generate behaviors which ultimately destroy enterprises and wealth, even as speculators like myself, Mitt Romney, and the rest of the LBO kings and hedge fund complex extract windfall rents along the way.

But the canaries which fluttered briefly in the mine shaft in September 2008 just dropped dead. That's all. As will be seen in chapter 30, the auto industry was on fire with speculative windfall gains within months of the horrid bailout of GM and the Fed's shift to all-out money printing in March 2009. So the Truman Show of bubble finance has entered yet another season. After the failed election of 2012 and the conservative party's embrace of a standard-bearer who was actually a member of the cast, there is nothing to stop the final triumph of crony capitalism.

Sundown now comes to America because sound money, free markets, and fiscal rectitude have no champions in the political arena. The very antithesis of bubble finance, they are anathema to the Wall Street machinery of speculation and rent seeking which insouciantly demands more debt and more money printing to keep the fatal game going.

CHAPTER 28

BONFIRES OF FOLLY

Bernanke's False Depression Call and
the $800 Billion Obama Stimulus

T HE BLACKBERRY PANIC OF 2008 WAS INDUCED BY TWO MEN, BEN
Bernanke and Hank Paulson, who were in the wrong high office at
the worst possible time. Bernanke, like Greenspan, was weak and
no match for the furies that came screaming out of the canyons of Wall
Street when the great financial bubble, decades in the making, violently exploded during the Lehman failure. Paulson, in fact, was one of the furies
and single-handedly neutered the GOP for its final capitulation to fiscal
folly.

Under the circumstances, Bernanke was the more dangerous, and his
stint as monetary commissar made the maestro look good by comparison.
Even after Greenspan surrendered his gold standard virginity in the political
fleshpots of Washington, he had remained a numbers-crunching monetary
experimentalist. Most certainly, he would have paused in September 2008
to ascertain why the financial system was suddenly in apparent meltdown.

By contrast, Professor Ben Bernanke was a doctrinaire academic who
"knew" what was happening. Except what he knew was dead wrong. So in
becoming yoked to Bernanke's calamitous error the nation was victim of a
terrible fluke.

Virtually no one in the nation's capital had initially viewed the sinking
stock market averages and collapsing CDOs which greeted officialdom on
the morning of September 15, 2008, as a flashback to 1930–1933. Reasonably informed observers understood that the market had closed the previous Friday only 10 percent lower than where it had been in January 2007
before the subprime trouble started, and that by comparison the stock
market meltdowns of 1987 and 2000–2001 had been far more severe—three
to four times more severe.

Perforce, these two more recent crashes were far more pertinent to the
contemporary financial system than that of 1929, and neither had led to a

depression or even a significant recession. The nation's economy, in fact, kept on growing for several years after the 30 percent stock collapse on Black Monday in 1987, and suffered only a minor hiccup during 2001–2002 in the wake of an even larger decline in the stock averages.

So Bernanke's depression mongering was on its face reckless and inexcusable, and leaves no doubt about his culpability for the fear-driven fiscal mania that soon enveloped Washington. Indeed, not one in a thousand of the politicians, policy players, and cronies who inhabited the nation's capital were in mind of the Great Depression on the morning of the Lehman event.

The threat of the Great Depression 2.0, and the madcap doubling of the Fed's balance sheet from $900 billion to $1.8 trillion during the next seven weeks, got interjected into the discourse only because Bernanke claimed to be a scholar of those seminal events. Ironically, Ben Bernanke, the full-fledged Keynesian, invoked the moral authority of Milton Friedman, the implacable anti-Keynesian, to sanction his case.

Within nine months, the empirical data would prove that what was actually happening on September 15 didn't remotely resemble the circumstances after the 1929 crash, and that the idea the nation was threatened by the Great Depression 2.0 was specious nonsense. But by then it was too late. Even if the evidence could have been properly interpreted, the nation's political system had already gone off its rails.

The folk memory of the Great Depression had been in deep hibernation, but Bernanke's invocation of it in the context of tumbling financial markets and the hysteria surrounding the passage of TARP brought it roaring out of the remote caves of financial history. The impact was incendiary; it was a full-throated cry of "Fire" in Washington's crowded theater of special interest plunder and statist projects of economic stimulus and social uplift.

The city's plodding policy machinery was electrified. The urgent project of stopping the Great Depression 2.0 was the legislative equivalent of suspending the fiscal and economic rules. Opening the floodgates to any and all measures of intervention and bailout, Bernanke's depression bugaboo thus installed crony capitalism as the conclusive algorithm of American governance.

The danger to free markets and political democracy was overwhelming. Depression fighting triggered a great doubling down by all of Washington's policy factions: monetarists, Keynesians, and Republican tax cutters alike. They all scrambled to implement more of the same when, in truth, the financial crisis was a repudiation of these very doctrines: monetarism had produced serial bubbles and had ruined capital markets; tax cutting had generated massive public debt and deep subsidies for leveraged speculation; and Keynesianism had remained an all-purpose excuse for government spending and fiscal profligacy. Now the nation's bedraggled economy would get massive doses of all three of these poisonous medications.

MORE HOUSING BAILOUTS:
THE DISASTER WHICH WON'T QUIT

In truth, the American economy was already booby-trapped with deformations that had resulted from the application of these doctrines. The housing sector was in ruins, for example, because it had been battered by endless ministrations of the state, all of which had the purpose of overriding honest housing prices and free market choices about whether to rent or own, spend, or save, live in big houses or small, and accumulate home equity or cash it out.

As previously reviewed, Fannie and Freddie, the Federal Reserve, the tax code, and Wall Street had all conspired to preternaturally jack up housing prices by 180 percent between 1994 and 2007, thereby paving the way for a thundering crash that since then has wiped out upward of four-fifths of the bubble-era gain in many leading markets. Yet, in stubborn denial that any lesson had been learned and spurred on by Bernanke's depression bugaboo, post-crisis policy has degenerated into a mindless scramble to prop up the remnants.

Lack of homeowner skin in the game was the indelible lesson of the subprime fiasco, but the Federal Housing Administration (FHA) was soon wheeled onto the battlefield with a massively ramped-up mortgage insurance program based on up to 97 percent loan-to-value ratios (LTV). Consequently, FHA insurance exploded from $300 billion to more than $1 trillion during the four years ending in June 2011, dragging the nation's taxpayers once again directly into harm's way.

With virtually no down payment cushion, FHA insured mortgages quickly lapsed into "negative equity" as housing prices continued to fall throughout the period. An American Enterprise Institute (AEI) study recently estimated that more than half of FHA mortgages are "underwater," meaning that as the American economy continues to flounder, borrowers will send back the keys and default rates will soar.

In fact, already nearly 17 percent of FHA's 7.6 million borrowers are delinquent, and this rate will continue to rise as the giant recent tranches of new mortgages go sour. Accordingly, the AEI study projects that the FHA fund will require a $50 billion taxpayer infusion—a prospect that is not only appalling, but also demonstrates the unrelenting hold of crony capitalism on public policy.

It is now blindingly evident that big down payments are essential to a healthy mortgage market. Even the boneheads who control congressional housing policy would not willingly embrace FHA's 97 percent LTV policy if they were not indentured to the National Association of Realtors, the mortgage bankers, the home builders, the Appraisal Institute, and the rest of the housing lobby.

Similarly, the shock stemming from the failure of Fannie and Freddie in September 2008 and the quarter-trillion-dollar price tag for its nationalization have not slowed down the government-sponsored enterprise (GSE) racket at all. In a desperate gambit to prop up housing prices, Washington nearly doubled the lending limit for qualified mortgages to $730,000. So, instead of winding down the GSEs, Washington insinuated them even more deeply into home finance. They accounted for 70 percent of all mortgages by 2011, a figure which rises to 97 percent when all government programs including FHA and Veterans Administration are considered.

There was also the home-buyers' tax credit scam, another brainchild of the Bush administration and a noisy anti–Big Government Republican senator from Georgia, Johnny Isakson. This boondoggle was utterly stupid as a policy matter, but in that benighted state it perfectly illustrates the end game of crony capitalism: it is a place where eventually there is no plausible public purpose at all. Special interest lobbies simply conduct naked raids on the treasury. In this case, the real estate brokers and home builders secured an $8,000 per household tax credit for so-called "first-time" buyers in a desperate attempt to stimulate churn in a housing market that was otherwise dead as a doornail.

In the end, $30 billion was spent during 2009 and 2010, at a time when the federal deficit was soaring above $1 trillion, while the ranks of the poor mushroomed due to the Great Recession. Still, there was no effort to target inherently scarce federal dollars by a means test. Instead, the policy was "come one and all" for taxpayers with family incomes up to $250,000.

It is hard to think of a more capricious use of public money than to gift $8,000 to a $150,000 household, for example, that had been a serial house flipper but had wisely stayed out of the market for thirty-six months, thereby qualifying as a "first time" buyer. Beyond that, 90 percent of the 4 million taxpayers who claimed the tax credit bought existing homes, meaning that the credit directly stimulated only a tiny amount of new construction and jobs.

In fact, the program amounted to a giant, random reshuffle of the capital gains being scalped from the existing US housing stock. The evidence clearly shows that the expiration of the tax credit on a date certain caused housing transactions to be pulled forward and crest as the deadline approached. For instance, the monthly sales rate for existing homes soared from a rock-bottom recession level of 4.3 million (annualized rate) before the tax credit incepted to a peak of nearly 7 million prior to the original November 2009 deadline, and then fell back to the recession bottom after the tax credit's final expiration.

So it might be fairly asked why $30 billion was wasted fiddling the existing housing stock turnover rate by a few months. But that would be the easy question. This artificial acceleration of housing demand also caused a temporary pause in the downward housing price correction. So when the tax credit expired the plunge resumed, meaning that last wave of proud new home buyers it had "incentivized" was instantly underwater.

This whack-a-mole effect was especially pronounced in the lower tier of the housing market. Between mid-2010 (when the final extension expired) and December 2011, housing prices in the bottom one-third of the market dropped by 20 percent in Minneapolis, 30 percent in Chicago, and 50 percent in Atlanta. Lower-end households who got lured into home ownership via the tax credit thus ended up taking it in the chops yet again.

In the boundary case of Atlanta, the decline could have amounted to $40,000 for a lower-end home purchased during the last month of the tax credit. In short, attempting to levitate the housing market in the midst of an unprecedented and unavoidably deep price correction, government intervention only arbitrarily reshuffled the deck chairs, and probably ended up luring the least financially capable households into harm's way.

Worse still, the housing lobby once again found it could bully through the Congress a raid on the treasury that on its face was implausible, but which generated as much GOP support as Democratic. Debt-free home owners and renters once more saw their less prudent neighbors get a big Washington handout.

Not least, the legions of hustlers who prowl for federal goodies were also strikingly emboldened. The subsequent fraud investigations show that the credit was claimed by 75,000 taxpayers who weren't eligible, 19,000 who didn't actually even buy a house, 1,200 that already had a home as guests of the US prison system, 500 who were minor children, 3 who were dogs, and 1 who was a four-year-old.

HOW THE FED MANGLED HOUSING EVEN MORE

The Bernanke Fed made all of these affronts to fairness and consistency seem trivial. In its money-printing madness after Lehman, the Fed has not only purchased $1 trillion in outright Treasury Department debt, but has also accumulated nearly $1 trillion of GSE mortgaged-backed securities and agency debt, or nearly 20 percent of the total outstanding. The purpose has been straightforward; namely, to drive down the yield on mortgages and thereby levitate the moribund housing market.

Yet this blunderbuss maneuver to fix housing prices has backfired miserably. On the one hand, housing prices have remained marooned 30 percent below the peak achieved five years ago, proving that the Fed has levitated nothing. At the same time, it has forced down the yield on thirty-year GSE-guaranteed mortgages from 5.3 percent on the eve of the crisis to 3.3 percent at present, meaning that a select subset of US home owners have been afforded the opportunity to realize massive windfalls by refinancing their mortgages.

These windfalls, which have a present value of $600 billion, reflect the interest-rate rigging of the state's central banking branch, not an outcome on the free market. The proof of that lies in the nonexistent mortgage yield when taxes and inflation are taken into account. Savers in an honest market would never lend thirty-year mortgage money at 0.7 percent, yet that is the implied real after-tax mortgage yield, given that the consumer price index has increased 2.3 percent annually since the crisis.

Accordingly, the entire 2 percentage point reduction of the nominal mortgage rates engineered by the Fed since September 2008 represents a gift of the state; that is, a noxious and arbitrary transfer from saver-depositors to mortgage debtors. Given the fact that about $5 trillion of mortgages have been refinanced since the crisis, the Fed is essentially conducting a fiscal transfer of $100 billion per year from savers to households that have refinanced, often multiple times. At the same time, the giant survivors in the home mortgage market—JPMorgan Chase, Wells Fargo and Bank of America—have also captured a slice of this windfall via lucrative refinancing fees.

This refinancing binge is non-economic; it would not have happened on the free market. The Fed's money-printing policies therefore, have generated a reallocation of wealth that is mind-boggling in its pure caprice. There are about 50 million households with mortgages, but currently upward of 25 million can't refinance because they are "underwater," or do not have enough positive equity in their homes to cover a down payment and refinancing fees. Accordingly, the serial refinancers have been drawn from the remaining pool of 25 million households which are generally more affluent or still have a decent chunk of embedded equity. Beyond that, the 35 million households which are renters and 25 million who own their homes free and clear have gotten none of the refinancing windfall, but undoubtedly have chipped into the Fed's fiscal transfer pot in their role as deposit account holders.

At the end of the day, a random subset amounting to 15–20 percent of US households has made a killing in the mortgage refinancing game since the financial crisis, and has done so in a manner that embodies the worst features of crony capitalism. Their good fortune came at the expense of society's savers, who had no say whatsoever in this giant wealth transfer; it was effectuated by what amounts to fiscal policy implemented by an unelected central bank in response to overwhelming pressure from Wall Street speculators.

To be sure, Bernanke and his fellow monetary central planners rationalize their capitulation to Wall Street demands through a lame version of Keynesian stimulus. Households will purportedly have more discretionary income after refinancing their mortgages and so will increase their consumption spending, thereby triggering a round of multiplier effects on sales, production, jobs, and income. This might be labeled the MEW-II doctrine. In this version, however, the equity withdrawal occurs on the monthly installment plan (e.g., lower mortgage payments) rather than in a lump sum cash-out.

That the MEW-II doctrine is actually a pitiful fig leaf is evidenced by the stunning $435 billion decline in personal interest income since August 2008. On the eve of the crisis, the GDP accounts clocked interest income at an annual rate of $1,420 billion, but after four years of aggressive financial repression by the Fed the run rate had shrunk to only $985 billion by August 2012. And those figures are in nominal dollars; in real terms, interest income was down by 40 percent. Needless to say, the negative spending multiplier from this draconian reduction in household interest income easily outweighs any gains from lower mortgage payments.

The facts, then, are quite startling. The Fed has now driven mortgage rates lower than they were even during the 1930s. So doing, it has neither levitated housing prices nor triggered Keynesian spending multipliers, even as it has generated massive, random wealth transfers among American households. There is only one possible explanation, therefore, for the Fed's dogged adherence to this mindless policy; namely, that Bernanke made a totally erroneous depression call and then went all-in on money printing. Now the Fed is stuck, hostage to insuperable Wall Street pressures to continue juicing its bloated machinery of speculation.

THE FALSE DEPRESSION CALL
THAT PETRIFIED WASHINGTON

Wall Street's occupation of the third floor of the Treasury Building could not have been more timely or strategic. Decisively empowered by Bernanke's professorial-sounding depression call, the Goldmanite wheeler-dealers and their bully-boy leader essentially declared economic martial law. For the remaining few months of the Bush administration this cabal of error, arrogance, and greed kept the fear of depression palpable in Washington—a mood that the spenders and Keynesians of the in-coming Obama White House were quick to exploit.

Yet, even as their massive $800 billion "stimulus" boondoggle was being enacted in February 2009, the severe but swift inventory correction that incepted the previous fall was flattening out. The US economy actually hit bottom and began a natural cyclical rebound by June 2009. By that point in time, not even the first $75 billion of the stimulus bill—that is, one-half of 1 percent of GDP—had hit the spending stream. As documented below, there had been no economic Armageddon looming at all. The politicians had been turned loose for an orgy of spending and tax cutting that had no justification.

That truth is evident in a vast range of data that make a mockery of Bernanke's depression call. For instance, liquidation of manufacturing inventories is always an early catalyst of business downturn, so it is remarkable that the data for 1981–1982 and 2008–2009 are virtually identical. In constant dollars (2000$), the decline in factory inventories was $60 billion, or 14 percent, in the earlier period and $70 billion, or 15 percent, in the recent downturn.

Needless to say, Paul Volcker did not scare the wits out of Washington with a depression call in 1981–1982. He knew full well that an inventory liquidation of this magnitude had occurred in 1974–1975 without triggering anything remotely resembling a depression; and in any event, the inventory collapse during the Great Depression had been four times greater. Likewise, the decline in actual industrial production had been 17 percent during the current cycle, not even remotely in the same ballpark as the 50 percent decline between the 1929 crash and the July 1932 bottom.

In fact, during the nine months after Lehman's failure there is no trace of depression-scale shocks in any of the economic data. And this interval is a fair test of the underlying, or "pre-policy," path of the US economy because none of the spasm of extraordinary fiscal or monetary stimulus touched off by the Bernanke depression call had yet impacted the data.

Whatever the intent of the monetary politburo in the Eccles Building, for example, its actions had plainly not affected activity rates in the American economy by the end of the June 2009 quarter, the National Bureau of Economic Research's official date for the recession's end. That's because there was no transmission of monetary policy through the credit process, the only real route to the Main Street aggregates of spending and income. In fact, the natural forces of debt liquidation totally overwhelmed the Fed's desperate money printing during this period, explaining why nearly all of the freshly minted deposits it pumped into the dealer markets and banking system flowed right back as excess reserves on deposit at the Fed.

During the nine months after the Wall Street meltdown, therefore, the Main Street economy was on its own. To be sure, zero interest rates and the Fed's alphabet soup of liquidity programs did serve to bail out insolvent banks and speculators and to restart the Wall Street carry trades after the March bottom. But none of the Fed's monetary juice showed up as added spending power in the real economy, as evidenced by the fact that bank business loans declined by 18 percent, consumer credit shrank by about 5 percent, and home mortgages by 2 percent during this period.

Similarly, as indicated above, the Obama stimulus bill had pumped only modest amounts of incremental dollars into the economy by the time the recession was over. The $800 per family tax relief component, for example, amounted to just $15 per week in reduced withholding, and even that did not become operational until well into the second quarter of 2009.

So what happened during this nine-month interval is pretty clearly an indication of the natural business cycle then under way. Yet, even as the economy rolled over, there were several factors breaking its fall that should have been apparent to any reasonably attentive analyst on September 15, 2008. One of the most important was the automatic fiscal stabilizers—unemployment insurance, food stamps, disability benefits, early Social Security retirement, and reduced tax collections—which had been built into the system for decades.

Another was the fact that the United States had become a service economy and therefore was far less inventory intensive. Total business inventories amounted to about 10 percent of GDP in September 2008, a figure dramatically lower than upward of 35 percent in 1929. This meant that the multiplier effect from inventory liquidation would be far less severe and self-fueling.

The reason for this more benign balance sheet condition was straightforward. On the eve of the Great Depression the primary production industries—agriculture, mining, and manufacturing—accounted for more than 70 percent of GDP. These sectors have a long pipeline of crude, intermediate, and finished inventory and therefore exhibit high inventory-to-sales ratios.

By the time of the 2008 financial crisis, however, the primary production sector had become a mere shadow of its former self, amounting to only 17 percent of GDP. When recession hit the American economy, therefore, the downward spiral of inventory liquidation was muted. Aerobics class instructors, for example, experienced modestly reduced paid hours, but unlike factories and mines, fitness centers didn't go dark in order to burn off excessive inventories; they stuck to burning off calories.

In fact, by 2008 China, Australia, and Brazil had become the world's new mining and manufacturing economy; that is, the United States of 1930. When upward of 50 million Chinese migrant workers were sent home from idle factories in late 2008, the villages of China's vast interior became the "Hoovervilles" of the present era. So owing to the fact that inventory and production adjustment took place mainly in the outsourced economies abroad and that the automatic stabilizers were already in place at home, there was no downward lurch in US incomes and spending.

The vast difference between 1930 and 2008 is crystallized in the data on personal consumption expenditure and personal income. When the bottom dropped out of the primary production sector during the Great Depression and took employment and incomes down hard, real PCE subsequently plunged by nearly 20 percent. By contrast, even without any significant Keynesian stimulus during the initial nine months after the September 2008 financial crisis, real PCE declined by only 2 percent.

This order of magnitude difference—that is, only one-tenth the Great Depression era impact—is dispositive. Furthermore, the relative resilience of PCE, which accounts for 70 percent of GDP, should have been easily predicted in September 2008, even under the assumption of no extraordinary policy stimulus. Bernanke's depression call, in fact, was reckless and uninformed.

The reason that PCE remained resilient is that in present times roughly 90 percent of personal income comes from private service industries, government jobs, and transfer payments. As Professor Bernanke made his rounds warning about the Great Depression 2.0, there was absolutely no reason to believe income from these sources would plunge.

In fact, during the next nine months government transfer payments rose by 16 percent, or at an annualized rate of $300 billion, and thereby offset the $275 billion drop in total wage and salary income. Moreover, even this 4.1 percent drop in wage and salary income, the raw material for consumption spending, was highly skewed. On the eve of the crisis, government employee compensation was $1.15 trillion, and not surprisingly it increased at a 2 percent rate during the nine months after the Lehman events; likewise, compensation in the private service sector was $4.2 trillion, and it declined only modestly, at a 3.8 percent annualized rate.

On the other hand, the goods-producing industries—manufacturing, construction, and mining—had been shrinking for decades and therefore posted a total payroll of only $1.2 trillion by the time of the financial crisis. So even though wage income in this sector fell at a steep 12 percent rate during the nine-month period, this drop was a rounding error in the larger scheme of things, amounting to just 1.1 percent of overall personal income.

Ironically, therefore, the long-term structural challenges facing the American economy—the offshoring of goods production and the massive growth of transfer payments and government payrolls not financed by current taxes—functioned as ballast to the Main Street economy in the immediate aftermath of the Wall Street meltdown. Yet none of these structural dynamics were a mystery.

As a plain matter of professional competence, the chairman of the Fed should have known that the vast bulk of wage and salary income no longer came from the inventory-intensive sectors and that consumption spending would be powerfully boosted by automatic transfer payments. There was simply no structural basis for the kind of self-feeding economic free-fall implied in the Great Depression 2.0 horror show that Bernanke pedaled to petrified congressmen.

As it happened, the initial wave of inventory liquidation and labor-shedding triggered by the Wall Street meltdown burned itself out quickly during the first nine months after the Lehman crisis. Thus, business inventories totaled $1.540 trillion in August 2008. While that figure dropped by about $215 billion during the course of the recession, fully $185 billion of the liquidation had occurred by June 2009. Thereafter, business inventories bounced along a bottom of $1.325 trillion from August through December, indicating that the downward momentum of the economy had already dissipated.

The story was similar with nonfarm payrolls. While the recession had technically started months earlier, the jobs count was still 136.8 million as of August 2008. During the subsequent course of the recession, 7.5 million of these jobs were eventually eliminated before the bottom was reached in February 2010. Once again, however, about 6.6 million of this payroll reduction, nearly 90 percent, was completed by June 2009.

During the six months from November through April, job losses averaged 750,000 per month. This heavy labor-shedding cycle occurred because the Wall Street meltdown was the equivalent of an economic punctuation mark; it demarcated that the credit-fueled housing and consumption binge was over. Accordingly, American businesses downsized their payrolls on a one-time basis by about 5 percent, in accordance with the now far less sanguine prospects for the economy—but this did not mark some irrational binge of job destruction that could spiral into depression.

In fact, the labor force adjustment subsided quickly and convincingly. During the May-June period the rate of job loss slowed to 400,000 per month, followed by 250,000 per month in the July-September quarter, and about 135,000 per month in the final quarter of 2009—before the job market stabilized and then began to rebound in early 2010. The adjustment in business spending on equipment and software was even more short-lived: it dropped by 16 percent between the third quarter of 2008 and the first quarter of 2009, and then stabilized during the June quarter before beginning to recover thereafter.

In short, by the end of the second quarter of 2009 the sharp recession triggered by the Wall Street meltdown was all over except for the shouting. There is nothing in the pattern of inventory liquidation or production, consumption, employment, income, or business capital spending that even remotely hints of a self-feeding doomsday scenario. In truth, the Hoovervilles were in Sichuan, Hunan, and Jiangxi Provinces. The chairman of the nation's central bank made a depression call based on errors that the Fed did not make in 1930–1933 and that were, in any event, predicated on a world that no longer even existed in September 2008.

STAMPEDE OF THE FISCAL FOLLIES: THE $800 BILLION OBAMA STIMULUS

I had been part of a new administration that moved way too fast on a grand plan, but the Reagan-era fiscal mishap didn't even remotely compare to the reckless, unspeakable folly represented by the Obama stimulus plan. In exactly twenty-two days from the inauguration, the new administration conceived, drafted, circulated, legislated, and signed into law an $800 billion omnibus package of spending and tax cutting that amounted to nearly 6 percent of GDP.

But the package was not a rational economic plan; it was a fiscal Noah's ark which had welcomed aboard every single pet project of any organization in the nation's capital with a K Street address. Most items were boarded without any policy review or adult supervision, reflecting a rank exercise in political logrolling that had proceeded straight down the gang plank to the bulging decks of the ark.

Indeed, the calamity of the Obama "stimulus" was not merely its massive girth, but also the cynical, helter-skelter process by which the public purse was raided. Nothing like this could have been imagined by even the most wizened Washington power players twelve months earlier. But during the BlackBerry Panic in September-December 2008, the nation's capacity for fiscal governance was eviscerated by Bernanke's depression call and by the frenzied maneuvers of an emotionally unglued and hysteria-gripped treasury secretary.

So by February 2009, when the Keynesian first team had become ensconced in the Washington seats of power, the very idea of hearings, deliberation, and diligent review of fiscal decisions had been suspended; the only thing that mattered was to fling tax cuts and spending "stimulus" toward the economy at breakneck speed and in massive array.

Bernanke's false depression call was thus a gift to K Street that didn't stop giving, and a green light to Capitol Hill politicians to gorge on budgetary giveaways like they had never before imagined. Worse still, the diligent work of decades by fiscal warhorses like Senate Republican Pete Domenici or Democrat Kent Conrad was flushed down the drain in a matter of days.

This unhinged modus operandi undoubtedly accounts for the plenitude of sordid deals that an allegedly "progressive" White House waived through. Thus, home builders were given "refunds" of $15 billion for taxes they had paid during the bubble years; manufacturers got 100 percent first-year tax write-offs for equipment that should have been depreciated over five to fifteen years; crony capitalists got $90 billion for solar, wind, and electric vehicle subsidies under the thin fig leaf of "green energy;" insulation suppliers got a $10 billion handout through tax credits to home owners to improve the thermal efficiency of their own properties; congressmen on the public works committees got $10 billion earmarked for pork-barrel water and reclamation projects in their home districts; the already bloated budget of the Department of Defense was handed $10 billion for facilities it didn't need; and that was only the tip of the iceberg.

The real crime is that the American economy had already bottomed before these projects and the rest of the stimulus programs hit the spending stream. The giant Obama stimulus, therefore, amounted to a naked exercise in borrowing from the future on Uncle Sam's credit card to artificially inflate current spending and income. There was no permanent national wealth gain at all, just a higher mortgage of taxes on future generations.

Since there was no looming depression to forestall, the helter-skelter process and most of the $800 billion substance of the Obama stimulus were a drastic mistake. What was actually happening was that a "new normal" was unfolding; namely, the debt-bloated US economy was undergoing an unavoidable deflation that would actually shrink the size of the nation's economy, and therefore its fiscal carrying capacity.

Accordingly, the stimulus bill was not an "investment" which would jump-start a cyclically stunted economy and thereby pay back the debt later in a Keynesian version of the Laffer curve. In fact, since the American economy had been permanently weakened by its overload of debt, there would be no cyclical "payback" at all—just more permanent federal debt.

DICK CHENEY'S SECRET DEFICITS

That prospect was especially lamentable because the fiscal fundamentals inherited by the Obama White House were actually far worse than they appeared to be. In fact, the massive red ink from the Bush administration's unfinanced wars and tax cuts was only the visible layer of fiscal decay; lurking down below were Dick Cheney's hidden deficits temporarily obscured by the second Greenspan bubble. So the new administration was starting in a much deeper fiscal hole than it imagined, and within two weeks was frantically and recklessly digging itself in deeper.

Cheney had petulantly insisted deficits don't matter during the Bush tenure because the Federal budget was being temporarily flattered by windfall revenues from capital gains, bonus payments, and swollen payrolls and incomes. But these tax revenues were not sustainable once the debt binge ended. Likewise, spending for safety-net programs had unnaturally abated owing to the faux prosperity of the housing and consumption booms. Overall, the pre-crisis deficit was being reported at about $500 billion, but red ink was actually running not far from $1 trillion when the windfalls from the bubble economy were removed from the numbers.

Needless to say, it was exactly those windfall revenue and spending elements which were swiftly erased when the US economy abruptly downshifted during the nine-month adjustment after the Lehman crisis. The Great Recession, therefore, did not generate a temporary swelling of the fiscal deficit, as the Keynesians insisted; it simply uncovered the true structural deficit that had been there all along and that Dick Cheney had fecklessly denied.

The data for realized capital gains and the resulting tax collections cogently illustrate this shift. During the three decades prior to the mid-1990s, realized capital gains averaged about 2 percent of GDP and rarely deviated far from that trend. However, during the first Greenspan bubble realized capital gains soared to about 6 percent of GDP (1998–2000) and then boomed again during the second bubble, reaching nearly 7 percent of GDP in 2007.

The unsustainable financialization and speculation fostered by the Greenspan Fed thus generated a step-change in realized capital gains amounting to about 5 percent of GDP. When the financial bubble reached its peak in 2007, therefore, capital gains realizations soared to nearly $1 trillion, or roughly $650 billion more than the historic trend.

Even at the low 15 percent tax rate, capital gains revenues were artificially swollen, and had reached $140 billion during 2007. Not surprisingly, when the second Greenspan bubble collapsed, these windfall revenues plunged to only about $40 billion in 2009. Likewise, collections of ordinary income and payroll taxes dropped by about $150 billion as inflated commissions, bonuses, and other bubble jobs and incomes disappeared.

Incremental outlays of $250 billion also showed up in the form of a rapid acceleration in Social Security disability and early retirement claims and soaring food stamp and unemployment insurance payouts. None of these impacts were extraordinary and temporary; they reflected the true permanent fiscal cost of current law tax and spending policies once the bubble-era bloat had been purged from the US economy.

So, two powerful realities were obscured by Washington's Great Depression 2.0 panic in February 2009. First, the true run-rate of the federal deficit was already nearly $1 trillion annually. The policy task at hand was to shrink the deficit forthwith because there would be no conventional "cyclical recovery" to automatically alleviate it or justify delaying action into the indefinite future.

Secondly, safety net spending had been structurally increased by upward of $250 billion per year owing to the loss of bubble-era income and jobs and the rising number of human casualties from the failing US economy. This suddenly swollen safety net needed to be reformed to minimize leakage to the non-needy, and the outlays which remained needed to be financed with sustainable tax revenue, not borrowing.

Due to these realities, fiscal discipline, efficiency, and prudence were imperative. There was no fiscal headroom left for boondoggles, scattershot uplift projects, or for income transfers which were not stringently means tested. But spurred on by the depression hysteria, the Obama stimulus went in exactly the opposite direction.

Its $250 billion package of measures to aid families amounted to a helicopter drop, while its $50 billion of incentives to business were a pure grab bag of items harvested by K Street lobbies. Likewise, the massive $250 billion package of Medicaid, education, and other grants to state and local governments was simply an exercise in government finance by credit card. And its $150 billion for infrastructure and energy projects amounted to an excuse for more Keynesian-style deficit finance, not a sensible case for publicly funded investment.

THE OBAMA MONEY DROP: KEYNESIAN FOLLY

While none of these components were appropriate, the stimulus plan's centerpiece—a $250 billion money drop to American households—was especially egregious. It featured a pure handout ranging between $250 and $800 that went to about 140 million income tax filers and 65 million citizens who got checks from Social Security, the Veterans Administration, Supplemental Security Income (SSI), and other benefit programs.

Needless to say, the grandly titled "Making Work Pay" (MWP) portion of this vast largesse had nothing to do with work since it went to income tax filers, whether they worked or not and whether they even owed tax or not.

Likewise, it had virtually no relationship to need: tax filers with incomes up to $200,000 were eligible, or about 95 percent of the population; and among the 65 million entitlement recipients who got "Economic Recovery Payment" (ERP) checks, only the 6 million SSI recipients were even means tested in the first place.

Additionally, about 35 million tax filers got an extra $1,000 per child tax credit on top of the standard allowance. And about 25 million tax filers received an average of $3,000 each based on an especially unique qualification. This $70 billion handout went to taxpayers who had excessively exploited loopholes and would have otherwise been required under current law to pay a minimum tax!

The justification for such indiscriminate handouts by a government already $1 trillion in the red came straight from John Maynard Keynes's current vicar on earth (and White House economic czar), Larry Summers. According to the professor's financial model, American households were not spending enough on goods and services out of their actual faltering incomes. But not to worry. Through MWP and ERP the government would supply them with make-believe income, hoping they would use it buy a lawnmower, flat-screen TV, goose-down comforter, dinner at the Red Lobster, or a new pair of shoes.

The Obama money drop was thus not based on productive effort or need. Instead, it was dispensed to the vast bulk of the citizenry in their capacity as economically robotic "consumption units." Plying "consumers" with deficit-financed handouts was a pointless theft from future taxpayers, but the White House professors insisted there would be a "multiplier" effect and that the money drop was actually an "investment" in economic recovery.

Yet when the Keynesian multipliers didn't show much kick in 2009–2010, the MWP tax credit was simply given a life extension do-over. On Christmas Eve it morphed into a $110 billion "tax holiday" for 2011, providing a 2 percent reduction in payroll tax rates on 165 million workers. Yet, even though the money drop now averaged about $1,000 for a median wage worker, there was still no sign of "escape velocity" from the Keynesian multipliers; real GDP growth in 2011 of 1.8 percent was actually lower than the anemic "recovery" year growth of 2.4 percent recorded in 2010.

Accordingly, the tax holiday was extended again through 2012. And when the predicted hearty cyclical rebound still did not appear, Professor Summers' heirs and assigns (he had fled the White House by then) summoned help from the contrafactual. Peering into a realm visible only to Keynesian true believers, they espied an economy that would have grown even more anemically, save for the $500 billion of MWP, ERP, and payroll tax handouts that had been added to the national debt over 2009–2012 to induce citizens to buy more shoes and soda pops.

In truth, this ever-extendable consumption stimulus was not only futile in the face of a debt deflation, but it also did violence to the progressive policy principles so loudly proclaimed by the Obama White House. As a conventional distributional matter, the payroll tax holiday would have been worth $4,000 to a two-earner household at the top of the payroll tax scale compared to $300 to a minimum wage worker. The payroll tax holiday, therefore, stimulated purchases of several Coach bags by households that didn't need the help and barely a full Wal-Mart shopping cart by those who did.

In the aftermath of the financial crisis, however, there was a far more consequential equity issue; namely, that the Obama money drop was inherently anti-progressive. It wasted the state's now radically diminished balance sheet capacity. In truth, the era of chronic deficit finance triggered by the Reagan Revolution thirty years earlier had taken the national debt from 30 percent to 100 percent of GDP.

Accordingly, it was no longer prudent to borrow in order to fund expensive money drops because there was very little runway left on Uncle Sam's balance sheet. Indeed, the very real risk of a runaway debt service spiral loomed just over the horizon. So Washington faced an unyielding requirement to eliminate current deficits and to target scare federal dollars tightly and unfailingly on the truly needy.

That was the objective reality, but the "progressives" in the Obama White House never got around to discovering it. Petrified by the Bernanke depression call and badly advised by its cadre of antiquated Keynesian professors, it hastily embraced the greatest money dump ever concocted on the banks of the Potomac. The party which claimed to champion the down-and-out and which advised itself to "never let a good crisis go to waste" failed on both counts.

FISCAL FOLLY FROM THE VICAR'S NAPKIN

On the surface, the $160 billion in grants for Medicaid and education programs appeared to be better aligned with needs-based transfers. Yet the fact that these funds might support low income households through classroom instruction or outpatient medical services was only incidental. They still amounted to a deficit-financed money dump in the form of a temporary funding bridge to state and local governments.

The actual objective at hand, once again, was the Keynesian project of borrowing money on Uncle Sam's credit card and pumping "demand" into the American economy. And like most of the stimulus package, this misdirected purpose was taken hostage by powerful special interest groups, thereby immeasurably deepening the nation's fiscal crisis.

The flaw was embodied in the White House's overall predicate; namely, that the Obama stimulus would generate a conventional cyclical rebound. This, in turn, would cause recession-swollen expenditures to decline and the state and local revenues to recover. The $160 billion funding bridge for Medicaid and education would thus be self-liquidating.

This predicate was not remotely accurate or plausible, however. The Medicaid and education funding crisis was structural and permanent, not a transitory artifact of recession. If these expenditures were vitally necessary as a social policy matter they needed to be funded out of taxes, not deficits. By going the latter route, the stimulus package was merely setting up yet another fiscal booby trap that would be lurking a few years down the road.

What happened during the bubble years was that state and local budgets were flattered by windfall revenues from swollen incomes, sales, and property values, and from one-time fees and taxes scalped from bubble hot spots such as new shopping centers and subdivisions. Accordingly, between 1990 and 2008, state and local revenues from their own sources (i.e., not federal grants) more than tripled from $700 billion to nearly $1.9 trillion, thereby raising their revenue take from 12.2 percent to 13.6 percent of GDP.

This gain in the revenue take (percentage) from GDP amounted to $200 billion, but as it happened the education and public welfare spending (mostly Medicaid) burden relative to GDP increased even more. During the same eighteen years, state and local spending for these purposes rose from 6.8 percent of GDP to 8.6 percent. This translated into $250 billion in incremental spending by the bubble peak in 2008, and meant that state and local governments had used up their entire revenue windfall, and then some, just on these items.

It was in this context that the Keynesian vicar in the White House handed Nancy Pelosi and Harry Reid a piece of paper on which was scribbled the simple term "$800 billion." Professor Summers' writ thus rivaled the Laffer napkin as the kind of foolish macroeconomic nostrum that could only incite politicians to spectacular feats of abuse. In this instance, the education lobbies, the nursing home operators, home health agencies, and legions more lined up outside the Speaker's office volunteering to help fill in the blank on Summers' napkin.

As indicated, this $160 billion exercise in filling in the vicar's stimulus target created a giant fiscal trap. On the one hand, a significant portion of the revenue gain from the bubble era has evaporated during the Great Recession. By 2010, for example, the state and local revenue windfall had shrunk by half, to $100 billion.

At the same time, total spending for education and public welfare has continued to rise dramatically, fueled by both growing need and the temporary federal money drop. State and local spending for these functions thus reached 9 percent of GDP by 2010, meaning that the expenditure burden gain relative to the 1990 GDP benchmark was now $300 billion per year.

Needless to say, the resulting gap will generate excruciating pressure for new Washington bailouts and fiscal transfers; that is, for relief of the state and local fiscal gap that was recklessly widened by the Obama stimulus. The original "good crisis" was thus wasted. Facing the evaporation of their bubble-era revenues, state and local governments should have been forced to make hard choices; namely, to raise new taxes to pay for these swollen programs or to enact deep program reforms and spending cuts.

Along the periphery, in fact, some modest instances of that occurred. During 2010, for example, Arizona drastically cut nonclassroom education funding while also approving by statewide referendum a sales tax increase earmarked for education. So doing, it proved that voters were willing to face the music if presented with honest choices.

But that was the great exception. In the main, the vast money drop stemming from the vicar's $800 billion napkin permitted state and local officials to simply kick the can to Washington. They were thereby enabled to avoid the wrath of their own voters or, better still, the need to face down the real culprits behind their fiscal squeeze: the teachers and other municipal unions and the legions of crony capitalist health care providers who feast off the Medicaid program.

Bernanke's spurious depression call thus cast a long shadow of fiscal mayhem. It created a twenty-two-day sprint to fashion a stimulus bill in the new Obama White House that amounted to policy by pandemonium. In that context, the vicar was empowered to launch the giant Keynesian experiment that his Uncles'* textbooks had only pined for decades back.

Once he had scribbled "$800 billion" on the napkin, it meant that the nation's check-writing pen would be handed off to Speaker Nancy Pelosi and Harry Reid. Not surprisingly, they used it to pay off the National Education Association (NEA), the school superintendent's lobby, the textbook publishers, the school construction industry, the special education complex, the preschool providers, and dozens more. For good measure, they

---

*Summers' uncles were Paul Samuelson, who won the Nobel Memorial Prize in Economics in 1970, and Kenneth Arrow, who won the Nobel in 1972.

threw in another $16 billion so that millions of middle-class college students could get their Pell Grant handouts topped up by about $1,000 each. And these money drops only constituted the $100 billion education piece of the bounty.

To be sure, apologists for the Obama stimulus who are of the "progressive" persuasion would undoubtedly insist that even if the NEA and Head Start lobbies have offices on "K Street," they do not belong in the same camp as the mortgage bankers, oil and gas drillers, or private-jet leasing companies. Yet, whether they were doing God's work or lining their own pockets, as the case may be, the NEA's impact on fiscal governance is of the same character as the notorious business lobbies that raid the tax code.

In fact, the Obama stimulus was insidious precisely because it mobilized scores of organized special interest groups that happened to be in the social uplift business to lean hard on Washington for debt-financed fiscal subventions. Whether the $1.22 trillion that state and local governments had spent on education and public welfare in 2008 was squeaky clean and not amenable to reduction, or riddled with excesses and waste and therefore capable of deep cuts was actually not the question at hand.

The truth was that the massive fiscal due bill at issue had been built up over two decades of faux prosperity. The issue in February 2009, therefore, was how the federal system of governance would face up to cutting these programs or raising new taxes to fund them or some combination of both. The overwhelming bulk of these outlays went to permanent programs and clients: school budgets and nursing home patients, not recession-induced caseloads. Accordingly, there was simply no justification for deficit finance of the fiscal gap which emerged when bubble-era revenues fell away.

Yet that's exactly what happened. The $160 billion health and education package was simply an end-run around fifty state constitutions which prohibit deficit finance of ongoing operating budgets. So four years have been lost and the fiscal gap is now greater than ever owing to Washington's endless game of shuffling the fiscal pea from one pod to the next.

But the giant state and local fiscal gap that the Obama stimulus temporarily alleviated is a menacing overhang which will continuously impinge upon the already paralyzed machinery of fiscal governance in Washington. The K Street lobbies mobilized by the vicar's napkin will never stop coming back for second and third helpings.

This is implicit in the truly shocking bottom-line fiscal equation for state and local budgets during 2010, when the Obama stimulus was having its maximum impact. Own-source tax revenue amounted to $1.27 trillion. This was 8.7 percent of GDP, meaning that the state and local tax claim on

GDP had lapsed all the way back to its pre-bubble-era level recorded in 1990.

At the same time, total general government spending (excluding pensions and insurance funds) reached a record level of $2.54 trillion, representing 17.5 percent of GDP. This was a dramatic gain from 1990 when state and local spending had been only 14.3 percent of GDP. So after the two-decade bubble finally collapsed, the state and local tax take had not budged at all, while the overall spending claim had soared by 3.2 percent of GDP—a staggering $475 billion gain.

The point had now been reached where state and local governments were only funding half of their general budgets with broad-based local taxes on income, sales, and property. Half of the balance, or $625 billion, was coming from Washington; that is, from grants and transfers that were drastically swollen by the Obama stimulus.

Furthermore, the balance was being obtained by a mushrooming array of user fees, service charges, permits, licenses, and especially soaring tuition charges at state colleges and universities. In theory, these user-based revenue sources are the preferred way to finance local government services, but they also measure the level of fiscal desperation and instability now embedded in state and local finances.

At the end of the day, the vicar planted a fiscal time bomb. It is evident that state and local officials are failing miserably at the task of raising general tax revenues commensurate with their massive spending commitments, and may be reaching the limits of their political capacity to extract fees and charges. So the pressure on Washington to continue to fill this cavernous fiscal gap will be overwhelming—until the next recession ensues, and then there will be a fiscal catastrophe.

CHAPTER 29

OBAMA'S GREEN
ENERGY CAPERS
Crony Capitalist Larceny

T HE FISCAL NOAH'S ARK ERECTED ON CAPITOL HILL DURING THE
first twenty-two days of the Obama administration contained upward of $60 billion for green energy and was additive to about $30
billion of loan guarantee authority already in place. Yet every dime involved
an unnecessary and inappropriate fleecing of American taxpayers and
constituted a warning sign of the nation's true fiscal peril. Indeed, corporate welfare this egregious, sponsored by a purportedly left-wing White
House and promoted by famous venture investors like John Doerr, virtually
proves that free market capitalism has been abandoned in the United
States.

GREEN ENERGY:
CRONY CAPITALIST LARCENY IN PLAIN SIGHT
Wholly apart from the technological virtues and economic prospects of the
various flavors of green energy—solar, wind, electric-battery cars and
biofuels—that landed a berth on the Obama stimulus ark, there exists an
underlying truth that literally shuts down the debate. The evidence that the
private market is providing prodigious amounts of risk capital to both develop and commercialize new energy technologies is overwhelming. The
"market failure" meme mainly comes from promoters of perpetual "science projects" and from scofflaws peddling technology and entrepreneurial failures.

Indeed, the Obama green energy extravaganza implicates a stunning
case of taking coals to Newcastle. Financialization has done vast harm to
the American economy, but that it has produced the greatest class of speculators and fortune seekers that the world has ever known cannot be gainsaid. What has been true at least since the early 1990s is that there is no

speculative project in any field of commercial endeavor—internet advertising, mobile telecom, social media, online services, conventional retailing, software-based gadgets, and countless more—that cannot attract capital and even a large crowd of momentum-chasing speculators if it is even remotely meritorious or viable.

Indeed, the Obama green energy boondoggle seems to have been flung out of some ideological time warp. It's as if Amory Lovins had come back to the White House to see if Jimmy Carter was still wearing his cardigan sweater and took the opportunity to peddle the virtues of solar power to the new incumbent he found there. In the interim, however, there occurred the saga of First Solar Corporation and dozens like it. These stories are dispositive; they both prove Lovins was a prophet in 1979 and also that the Department of Energy has been a sinkhole of waste ever since.

First Solar was started in the late 1980s by entrepreneurs focused not on exotic science, but on the practical problem of relentlessly driving down the delivered cost of solar power to the point where it would attain so-called "grid parity" and thereby become competitive with conventional fuels. The company's pioneering inventor, Harold McMaster, believed this could not be achieved with the expensive crystalline silicon wafer technology of the day, and so he experimented with various thin-film photovoltaic processes, settling on a cadmium telluride (CdTe) coating on a glass substrate.

By the late 1990s, the venture capital arm of the (Wal-Mart) Walton family became convinced that McMaster was on the right track. So the Waltons bought the company and funded an aggressive plan toward commercialization, launching production in 2002 and reaching a respectable 25 megawatts (MW) of capacity by 2005.

More crucially, First Solar made consistent, impressive strides driving down the cost per watt to below $2 by 2003, and then to $1.20 by 2007, below the $1 barrier in 2011, and to around $.70 at the present time. It is this cost-reduction riff that is the pathway to alternative energy commercialization. First Solar's success with the relatively exotic second-generation technology, cadmium telluride coating, powerfully demonstrates that real entrepreneurs do not need a K Street lobbyist to locate grants for their science or capital for their plants.

Owing to these cost breakthroughs First Solar's thin-film technology took off like a rocket, permitting the company to launch an IPO in late 2006 at a market cap of nearly $2 billion. But then came the dramatic proof that the financial markets are crawling with punters. This reality obliterates the case for a Department of Energy nanny, whether the power-hungry Dr.

James Schlesinger back in 1979 or the befuddled Professor Steven Chu today. To wit, during its first sixteen months as a public company, First Solar's market cap soared from $2 billion to $22 billion.

That amounted to an eleven times gain in almost as many months, and meant that the company would never again be wanting for capital. Nor would it need to lean on taxpayers to build plants and develop and launch products, as have the serial scams which emerged from the Obama stimulus. Indeed, First Solar's manufacturing capacity went parabolic from its 25 MW in 2005, reaching 300 MW in 2007 and 2,400 MW by 2011; that is, a hundred times expansion in seven years. Today, the company has eight thousand employees, $2.8 billion of revenue, and a $6 billion globe-spanning asset base.

Even more telling, its stock price has dropped by nearly 90 percent from its 2008 peak, meaning that the world is so full of punters and speculators that even out-and-out barn-burner successes frequently attract way too much capital and investor confidence. In this case, the Waltons made a killing from their perspicacity as venture capitalists. Yet the market is so rife with speculative capital that short sellers, too, made a fortune on the retraction of First Solar's stock price to an earthbound valuation.

It borders on the criminal to saddle future taxpayers with tens of billions of new debt in order to fund First Solar imitators. In the latter case, even the short sellers made fortunes the honest way—by being at risk. But under the Obama stimulus, the fundamental deal is that insiders get to short the US treasury without taking any risk at all.

That's the lesson of Solyndra which ended up a spectacular $850 million waste of taxpayer dollars (including tax benefits). In fact, however, Solyndra was not that different from First Solar: it had also been developing what it hoped would be an alternative to crystalline silicon cells using an even more exotic copper-indium-gallium-selenide (CIGS) coating and also tubular rather than flat-panel collectors.

The short story is that it did not scramble down the cost curve far enough or fast enough, and was left high and dry in 2011 when Chinese solar producers flooded the market with what had become dramatically cheaper conventional silicon panels. Yet whereas First Solar achieved dramatic cost reductions first, and then built up manufacturing capacity incrementally with several dozen conventional fabrication sites around the world, Solyndra made a huge role of the dice. Even before its manufacturing process had been proven, it constructed a single giant manufacturing works to produce its exotic thin-film coatings and fabricate its tubular panels.

Needless to say, even the great Wall Street speculators were unwilling to pony up $500 million for a vast green field plant based on what was still a speculative technology. But the earnest Professor Steven Chu raised the taxpayers' hand for that honor, and a perfectly useless factory was built that has never even opened. Worse still, this never-started factory had cranked up its supply chain full tilt before it had orders or shipments. Accordingly, its subsequent bankruptcy filing showed it had purchased more than one million glass tubes from a lucky firm in Germany called Schott Rohrglas.

It thus turns out that a goodly portion of the half billion dollars of taxpayer money had actually helped to build the German trade surplus: the massive glass tube inventory shipped by Schott Rohrglas to the Solyndra plant in California would have stretched six hundred miles end to end. All of this high-purity glass was now useless, however, and was ordered destroyed by the bankruptcy court to avoid storage costs. In a final insult to injury, the court's disposal order undoubtedly also bolstered China's trade surplus: the fleet of lift trucks used to move these mountains of glass to the dump were made in China.

Still, the full rancid odor of crony capitalism did not materialize until the aftermath. Throwing good money after bad, Professor Chu agreed to subordinate the government's $535 million loan to $75 million of "rescue" money provided by affiliates of George Kaiser, the oil billionaire and Obama fund-raiser who controlled Solyndra. Coming from the oil patch, Kaiser obviously knew a thing or two about tax dodges and operating loss carry-forward schemes.

It now turns out that Kaiser and his cronies were more than happy to have the factory dismantled because as the senior creditor they ended up with the tax NOLs (net operating losses). The latter are worth about $350 million and can be used in one of Kaiser's profitable businesses, perhaps shielding oil production profits. In other words, by essentially "shorting" Uncle Sam, George Kaiser stands to harvest a 4.6 times return on his sham investment to "rescue" the company.

The obvious point is that the punters who bid up First Solar's market cap to $22 billion had no clue about whether the correct route to thin-film solar was CdTe or CIGS. Professor Chu apparently knew all about that topic. But his knowledge was irrelevant because the issue was the pace of manufacturing cost reduction per watt, not the science of photovoltaics.

Likewise, the firm's outlook for profitable survival was embedded in the quarterly path of orders, shipments, margins, and working capital ratios—the very thing that financial markets, even speculative ones, are designed to assess. By contrast, the Department of Energy apparently failed to notice that something was radically amiss with a 500,000-square-foot factory which had no output, shipments, or even orders, but was stacked with six hundred miles' worth of glass tube inventory. It is no wonder the CEO of Solyndra referred to the company's White House sponsors as "the Bank of Washington."

The case of First Solar versus Solyndra makes clear why the whole green energy program is a pointless waste. Each had a thin-film route to grid parity, but the entrepreneur behind the former attracted gobs of speculative capital, while the promoter behind the latter bagged White House staffers looking for ways to quickly spend down the vicar's $800 billion. Indeed, given that the CdTe route had already been a resounding marketplace success, having the taxpayers put up $850 million for its first cousin, CIGS, amounts to grand larceny, crony capitalist style.

FISKER AND TESLA: GREEN VANITIES OF THE BILLIONAIRES

The solar boondoggles are modest compared to the crony capitalist capers in the electric vehicle (EV) sector. Here the Obama administration has guaranteed loans of $530 million for Fisker Automotive and $465 million for Tesla Motors and provided $270 million in stimulus money for a company called A123 that makes electric vehicle batteries. The first two of these are essentially failing vanity projects of Silicon Valley billionaires that are now being bailed out by the taxpayers for no discernible reason. The third has already filed for bankruptcy, taking the taxpayers down the drain with them.

The US treasury was put in harm's way in all three of these cases not simply to boost the debatable concept of electric-battery vehicles. The global automotive industry is already rife with efforts in that direction by incumbent car companies including the Toyota Prius, the Nissan Leaf, the Chevy Volt, the upcoming (2013) Ford Escape electric vehicle, and countless more.

Instead, the big bucks from Washington are being used to prop up billion-dollar bids by venture capitalists to create totally new car companies. Yet unless you believe in tin-foil hat theories about Detroit buying up all the patents on magic carburetors which get a hundred miles per gallon, the last industry that needs start-up companies fostered by government is autos. In fact, the global automobile industry is hungry for new product markets owing to its vast overcapacity and is endowed with all of the engineering and manufacturing competence that could ever be needed to bring electric cars to market—that is, if consumers wanted to buy them.

Since gasoline still sells at 1973 prices in real terms, however, there remains only a tiny market for hybrid and electric vehicles. Thus, notwithstanding approximately $1.2 billion of venture capital funding, mainly from Kleiner Perkins Caufield & Byers, Fisker Automotive is literally going down in flames: in addition to massive financial losses, many of the five hundred gasoline-electric hybrid cars it has actually sold have ended in fiery destruction in their owners' driveways. Indeed, the folly of Washington's Fisker caper could not have been more poignant than when Hurricane Sandy hit the New Jersey docks with its vast storm surge; more than a dozen Fisker cars ignited and burned to rubble when washed over by seawater.

Given the $100,000 price tag for these vehicles, however, the story is not really about any hardship suffered by the credulous buyers of the Fisker Karma. The actual hardship will soon fall on the taxpayers because the underlying deal stinks to high heaven. It seems that Silicon Valley's leading venture capital firm had a failing auto start-up and Vice President Joe Biden had a failed GM auto plant in his home state of Delaware. Kleiner Perkins's chief green energy maven and major Obama fund-raiser, John Doerr, therefore arranged a deal.

In return for the aforementioned $530 million from Uncle Sam, Doerr and his purportedly Republican partner Ray Lane would present a new business plan to Henrik Fisker, the intrepid designer-entrepreneur behind their start-up auto company. Flush with vast new money from Washington, the struggling Fisker Automotive would develop a second version of its electric vehicle—a "people's car" that could retail for a mere $50,000—and build it in Joe Biden's empty auto plant.

While the vice president thought this was a swell solution and duly cut the ribbon at the plant's reopening, Fisker was not the most likely man for the job of building a people's car in Newark, Delaware. In fact, before becoming an electric vehicle tycoon, he had been a famous designer of ultra-luxury vehicles including the 2005 Aston Martin DB9 Volante. The latter carried a price tag of $250,000 and was built by hand in what is essentially an automotive museum in the United Kingdom.

Nevertheless, pending the development of a people's car to be called the Atlantic, Fisker got a $170 million installment from the Department of Energy to complete the design, engineering, tooling, and manufacturing launch of the $100,000 per copy Karma. After repeated delays, the first Karma was delivered to the company's launch customer (and investor) Leonardo DiCaprio, but it is surely the case that the green crusader–actor had not calculated the full carbon footprint of the Karma when it arrived at his Beverly Hills estate.

In fact, the vehicle had been assembled in Finland based on an aluminum frame that was manufactured in Norway and an interior cabin that was made by automotive giant Magna International of Canada, and sent to Finland for final assembly. Moreover, the heart of the vehicle, the electric battery power train, was also shipped back to Finland after it was made by A123, based in Waltham, Massachusetts.

The latter was both an investor in Fisker and also a recipient of $260 million of Obama stimulus money. A few months after DiCaprio got his car, A123 filed for bankruptcy under a cloud, some of which emanated from the fiery demise of batteries it had installed in the five hundred or so Karmas which had been actually delivered to customers.

So the carbon footprint from its far-flung supply chain is considerable, given that all of these components are shuttled to Finland and back. But that's not the half of the Karma's severely challenged claims to being green. One of the great truths of the modern economy is that central-station electric power is grossly inefficient as a thermal matter, with less than 30 percent of the BTUs delivered to plant boilers actually ending up as useful work in homes and factories. Therefore, the fuel efficiency of electric-battery cars can only be fairly measured on a so-called "wells-to-wheels" basis, thereby taking account of the vast thermal losses at power plants and distribution grids from the hydrocarbon fuels originally consumed.

It turns out that the Karma gets nineteen miles per gallon on a wells-to-wheels basis; that is, it has worse fuel economy than the Ford Explorer. So the question recurs as to why public money is being used to fund toys for rich people and to bail out the approximate $1.2 billion that has been invested in Fisker by Kleiner Perkins, Al Gore, and Qatar Holdings, among numerous well-endowed others.

THE PEOPLE'S CAR FROM GOLDMAN SACHS

To be sure, electric vehicles are the red-hot flavor of the month, even on Wall Street. That explains how Goldman Sachs got into the act, too, bringing to market in April 2010 the IPO of the Fisker Automotive clone called Tesla Motors. The latter also makes high-end electric-battery vehicles and was created by another billionaire venture capitalist who has also been a serial harvester of the Washington money tree, one Elon Musk. Indeed, so incestuous is the plot that Musk hired Henrik Fisker in one of the latter's earlier ventures to perform design work on an electric vehicle, then sued him for design theft when Fisker launched his own EV venture.

Not surprisingly, the ostensible reason Tesla got its very own $465 million loan guarantee from the DOE was to perform exactly the same gambit as Fisker. Tesla had developed a $110,000 electric vehicle called the Roadster, and so the taxpayer money was supposed to help it develop a people's car called the Model S which would retail at $55,000 before the $7,500 electric vehicle buyers' tax credit that Uncle Sam also had on offer.

Not surprisingly, Tesla has stumbled bringing its people's car to market just like Fisker has. In fact, Fisker is so far behind that even the DOE has had to freeze its funding; the company has fired the few workers who had been hanging around Joe Biden's empty car plant and now suggests the Atlantic may not appear until 2015, if ever.

Yet the Tesla stumble is the more egregious because it was brought to the public market by Goldman and its billionaire promoter in an utterly cynical manner as an upside call on the US treasury. As it happened, Tesla had lost in excess of half a billion dollars building and selling about two thousand Roadsters, not withstanding their $110,000 sticker price and well-advertised celebrity owners like George Clooney.

So with the company at death's door by late 2008, Elon Musk had to publicly confess that the long-promised high-volume S Model was a pipe dream and suspended development; that is, until Tesla could get on Uncle Sam's life-support system by obtaining the massive DOE funding needed to develop the "people's car" version of his electric battery vehicle. Not surprisingly, the Obama administration had no trouble believing that the world needed another car company, and that a true believer in the green gospel like Musk could bring a volume production vehicle to market.

In June 2009, Tesla got its $465 million in federal money and proceeded to plow it into the development of the S Model and funding of a corporate ramp job designed to suggest a muscular business with orders and factory production capability. To that end, it promoted advance sales through $5,000 deposits which conveniently could be recovered from $10,000 worth of federal and California electric vehicle tax credits.

This was cash-out financing for the prosperous classes. Not surprisingly, the company has booked about 10,000 orders and upward of $100 million of customer cash via this backdoor infusion from the IRS.

It also used $40 million of its federal loan in May 2010 to purchase the cavernous but shuttered General Motors–Toyota assembly plant in Fremont, California—approximately one mile from the Solyndra plant, as it turned out. The Potemkin village aspect here lies in the fact that the Freemont plant had assembled upward of 250,000 cars per year in its salad days compared to scheduled S Model production of less than 3,000 vehicles in 2012.

But a bulging order book, even if an artifact of EV tax credits, was exactly what Goldman needed to pump the Tesla story. So the IPO at $17 per share was launched in June 2010, just one month after the company acquired its taxpayer-financed manufacturing plant. After rising 40 percent the first day, Tesla became a favorite rabbit of the momo chasers, and spurred by breathless "research" from Goldman and other Wall Street firms, the stock price reached $35 by later 2010 and has cycled around that level since. In short, Tesla has been valued at about $3.5 billion by the stock market on the strength of the S Model hype and the simulacrum of a company propped up by Uncle Sam's $465 million loan and EV tax credits.

The company's SEC filings leave little doubt that it is the humble taxpayers of America who have fueled Elon Musk's pretensions of grandeur. During the eighteen quarters since January 2008, Tesla has booked $500 million of revenues, but has racked up $750 million of net losses and nearly $1 billion of negative operating cash flow. Not surprisingly, in October 2012 Tesla got a delay from DOE on its loan repayment obligations and a waiver on its debt covenants. So as Tesla circles the drain, it is essentially following the playbook that had been used by its former next-door neighbor, Solyndra.

It goes without saying that Tesla would have been Chapter 11 bait years ago without the $465 million federal loan, and will likely end up there anyway. Yet the question recurs as to why the public purse was opened to this scam in the first place. After all, the S Model has turned out to be a high-end luxury sports sedan which will retail with normal customer options for at least $75,000. Like all EVs, its environmental benefits are dubious at best. Unlike most of its more stodgy competitors, however, it does accelerate from 0 to 60 mph in 4.4 seconds.

In truth, the historic boundary between the free market and the state has been eradicated, and therefore anything which can be peddled by crony capitalists like Musk and Doerr in the name of social uplift is fair game. In this instance, the Obama administration adopted the entirely capricious goal of one million electric vehicles on the road by 2015 and had the dollars to throw at it, thanks to the bipartisan fiscal follies that have now become firmly entrenched.

While much of the funding for this misguided effort came from the Obama stimulus, the fact is that $20 billion came from the Bush administration's Advanced Technology Vehicles Manufacturing Loan Program. This was the source of the loan guarantees for both Fisker and Tesla and, more importantly, also provided the political cover.

Thus these EV boondoggles were not really Obama's green energy waste; these were "Republican loans" and had been applied for during the Bush administration under a program which it had embraced. Indeed, Fisker's lead director, Ray Lane, claimed to be a Bush-supporting Republican benefactor, and dismissed as "silly" the notion that an automotive company could be started without government aid.

He was correct on that point, although the idea that the government should be starting car companies, in a world drowning in auto capacity, was apparently not yet a well-known part of the Republican creed. So whether acknowledged or not, it was the Bush White House which paved the way for the abomination of Fisker and Tesla.

That a megalomaniacal promoter like Elon Musk could walk off with half a billion in taxpayer money, blow it in less than four years, and make himself the toast of Hollywood in the process is powerful evidence that the putative conservative party has vacated the ramparts of the US Treasury Department. The latter now stands politically helpless in the face of whatever flavor-of-the-month projects crony capitalist raiders happen to be promoting.

THE GREEN ENERGY DOG WHICH DIDN'T BARK

At the end of the day, Tesla and Fisker did not have much to do with real conservation. That is evident in the policy dog that didn't bark; namely, a rip-snorting increase in the gasoline tax. To be sure, it is not evident that dragging BTUs through the roundabout path of the electric power grid would really alter the carbon footprint of the typical auto's 10,000 vehicle miles per year. Yet if reduced gasoline consumption is the policy objective, a European scale fuel tax, say, $4 per gallon, would cut US consumption by upward of 3 million barrels per day, or about 35 percent.

In fact, it turns out that Secretary Steven Chu spent nearly as much time disavowing his earlier support for a stiff gasoline tax as he did handing out subventions to crony capitalists of the green energy persuasion. And that symbolizes the problem in a nutshell.

The virtue of a high energy tax is that it harnesses the pricing mechanism silently, efficiently, and relentlessly to the task of altering behaviors throughout the nooks and crannies of the entire Main Street economy. That would be especially true if the tax were levied broadly as a variable level on petroleum imports. Using that mechanism, policy could permanently fix a minimum domestic price floor at, say, a $125 per barrel equivalent by raising or lowering the levy to capture the difference between the floor and the world price.

Henceforth, every consumer and producer in the domestic economy would react as they saw fit to the rule of one price: $125 per barrel of liquid hydrocarbon equivalents, always and everywhere. Thousands of entrepreneurs would be thereupon unleashed to conserve liquid petroleum BTUs whenever investments, from insulation to solar panels to electric vehicles, were profitable under the floor price. Likewise, consumers might decide to buy smaller cars with fewer features and less powerful engines under a guaranteed, permanent régime of high fuel prices. They might even choose to live in smaller houses or locate closer to work or make day trips by light rail.

By the same token, there would be no possible excuse for government subsidies and loan guarantees to encourage energy production or for the myriad oil and gas tax breaks now in place. With a permanent price floor, the message of the marketplace would be "Drill, baby, drill" wherever it was economic, including the cost of regulatory compliance. The big bucks would go to petroleum engineers and geophysicists, not K Street lobbies.

It goes without saying that there is a ferocious bipartisan consensus against a variable petroleum levy; that is, against drafting the marketplace to accomplish conservation goals set by the state, if goals must be set at all. Such a régime would put the energy branch of crony capitalism out of business. It would allow the state to sit back with its feet up on a stool, and to abolish its congressional committees on energy and its busy-body departments and agencies which ceaselessly meddle in markets and waste societal resources. Most importantly, it would remove the energy sector from the checklist of spending options next time Washington gets out the stimulus napkin.

THE MYTH OF INSUFFICIENT PUBLIC INVESTMENT

The massive green energy subsidies and tax credits contained in the Obama stimulus patently defy the fact that unlimited speculative capital is available for any alternate energy technology that appears even remotely viable. But there is a reason for this disconnect; namely, the false progressive narrative that the ills of the American economy are owing to too little "public investment."

The Obama stimulus thus contained $85 billion for public infrastructure investments that turned out to be not so "shovel ready" as first advertised. Rather than being a fault, however, the big delay in executing these projects was the smoking gun; that is, proof that most of the public investment agenda had nothing to do with the long-term growth and productivity of the American economy, but was just an excuse to fill up the vicar's $800 billion deficit spending napkin.

The project list speaks for itself. It included $4.2 billion to repair and modernize Department of Defense facilities, $200 million for a new Homeland Security headquarters, $280 million for wildlife refuges and fish hatcheries, $500 million for Bureau of Indian Affairs infrastructure projects, $500 million for wildfire prevention, $650 million for the Forest Service, $750 million for the National Park Service, $750 million for federal buildings, and $4.6 billion for Army Corps of Engineers water projects—

something even Jimmy Carter found to be a net loss to the nation's economy more than three decades ago.

Some of these expenditures might well improve public amenities, but none of this involves productive capital investment. And none were so urgent as to require deficit finance, and self-evidently none of these and dozens of similar items straight from the congressional logrolling fest had anything to do with enhancing the long-term growth capacity of the American economy. So the progressive mantra that public investment had been an important feature of the Obama stimulus boiled down to about $30 billion for highways and bridges and $20 billion for assorted rail and mass transit projects. Behind this modest curtain, however, lies the truth about the "public investment" thesis; namely, that there is nothing there.

The federal government and the states spend about $150 billion each year on highways, roads, and bridges and that is actually too much, not too little. At about 1 percent of GDP these highway outlays are fully in line with postwar averages, so there has been no policy "neglect," Republican or otherwise. But even this normal level of spending does not stimulate economic efficiency and growth but harms it: less than half of this $150 billion total is financed with user fees and gasoline taxes. This means that two classes of users, suburban commuters and long-haul trucking, are heavily subsidized by general taxpayers.

Ironically, progressives are always complaining that not enough freight moves by rail nor enough people by mass transit. Yet the stimulus bill poured $30 billion of general fund financing into the very system that biases transportation toward trucks and one-passenger car trips.

Beyond that, there is no evidence the nation's highway system is in disrepair. Outside local street and road disgraces in a few big cities like New York—where available funds are squandered on union and contractor corruption and absurdly inflated wage rates and work rules—the nation's highway system has not deteriorated from its five-decade standard condition. Indeed, the freight-hauling routes on the interstate highways—the only portion of the system that can significantly impact measured productivity in the GDP accounts—are in better shape than ever before.

In truth, with today's E-Z Pass technology all significant highways, interchanges, secondary roads, and bridges could be funded with user charges. It is virtually certain that such a system would lead to improved transportation system efficiency and arguably an enhancement of national economic productivity. It is also certain that aggregate spending for highways would fall, not rise, because uneconomic use of the highway system, especially the wear and tear on highway surfaces caused by heavy trucks, would be sharply curtailed. Indeed, use of time-of-day pricing on congested urban freeways would also expand "effective capacity" dramatically by flattening out traffic loads.

Like everything else in the Obama stimulus, the $30 billion of highway money thus amounted to "borrow and spend," not productive public investment. More often than not, stimulus money went to surface repair of roads that didn't need it, or replacement of rural bridges that have virtually no traffic, or the construction of new highway interchanges that will reconnect sparsely trafficked secondary roads out in the countryside. Pyramid building would have accomplished the same thing.

The real pyramid building in the Obama stimulus, of course, was the $20 billion or so for transit and light rail. Forty-five years of mucking around with the abomination known as Amtrak proves that cross-country passenger rail can never be economically viable because it cannot compete with air travel.

Presently, every single ticket sold on the Sunset Limited from New Orleans to Los Angeles, for example, requires a $500 subsidy—more than coach airfares on the same route. Indeed, Amtrak's long-distance routes account for only 15 percent of its passengers but 80 percent of its red ink; that is, about $1 billion in annual subsidies go to 4 million citizens who patronize Amtrak's hopelessly uneconomic long-distance routes. These windfalls are dispensed without regard to ability to pay, but the intended beneficiaries are not the passengers anyway; the subsidies are meant to keep overpaid, feather-bedded union jobs on the Amtrak payroll.

The only potentially viable part of the public rail dream relates to dense urban corridors between large and nearby urban centers: Philadelphia and New York City or Los Angeles and San Francisco. Yet if there is one truism about interurban light rail it is that it must be paid for by direct users and regional transit authorities from local taxation.

This stems from the fact that the productivity benefits to business travelers in reduced travel time are modest, if even measurable. On the other hand, the potential to overbuild, overschedule, and overman these systems to the benefit of land speculators, developers, construction contractors, railcar suppliers, transit unions, and leisure travelers is enormous, most especially when much or all of the cost consists of other taxpayers' money.

Federal funding of interurban rail like the dozen projects started in the stimulus bill, therefore, is a sure-fire recipe for waste of scarce fiscal resources and reduced national productivity. This truth has been proven decisively by forty years of federal operating and capital subsidies for local mass transit. Time and again, systems have been overbuilt, money-losing lines have stayed open, transit union workers have gotten way overpaid, and local politicians have been encouraged to demagogue for more service and lower fares, and to demand Washington make up the shortfalls.

From an economic equity viewpoint, the argument for federal funding of regional light rail is especially perverse. Most of it would be built in the highest income regions of the United States—California and the Eastern Seaboard—and paid for by taxpayers in the lower income and less densely populated interior. Worse still, this redistribution of fiscal resources from the poorer regions to the richer areas would incite still another giant Washington logrolling system.

Indeed, chronic battles over tens of billions in regional transit funding would only further dissipate the nation's capacity for fiscal governance, even as it undermined efficiency, accountability, and care in the local management and operation of these systems. Federal funding of regional rail is thus not a productive form of public investment. It is merely another excuse for deficit spending, and another opportunity for K Street to prosper at the expense of the innocent public.

REACTIONARY WELFARE, PROGRESSIVE STYLE

At the end of the day, the Obama stimulus bill was a massively wasteful and unaffordable tribute to the textbooks written long ago and in a different time by the vicar's uncles. Yet the stampede on Capitol Hill and K Street to fill in the blanks on the stimulus napkin caused Washington to give short shrift to the true and urgent task under the circumstances; namely, the need to shore up and refocus the social safety net.

Four years after the crisis, median family income has fallen by 10 percent in real terms. Likewise, as documented in chapter 31, the number of full-time breadwinner jobs in the US economy is still down by 5 million; that is, it is more than 8 percent below its late 2007 level. In short, the Main Street economy has been failing for years, and now the massive debt deflation under way will aggravate that condition enormously, leaving millions of citizens to depend upon intermittent employment in low-paying part-time jobs or to fall back on family, friends, charity, or nothing at all.

Yet the total amount of funding for means-tested assistance in the Obama stimulus was just $28 billion, or 3.5 percent, of the $800 billion package. Funding for unneeded bridges, interchanges, and road repair got more money than the combined total for food stamps, the earned income tax credit, and federal grants for public assistance and WIC (the health and nutrition program for women, infants, and children). This outcome was telling because it demonstrates that trapped in its Keynesian fog, the nation's so-called progressive party cannot see that the overwhelming task of national governance for years to come will be tending and funding the safety net. The challenge will be to systematically and forthrightly address the swelling level of human needs, but to do so in a manner that is stringently targeted on means-tested programs and which does not encourage dependency and freeloading.

In fact, however, the de facto policy of the Obama stimulus and subsequent renewals has been to throw money at non-means-tested programs, particularly extended unemployment benefits and Social Security disability. Since September 2008, approximately $300 billion has been spent on unemployment insurance benefits but upward of one-third of that has gone to affluent workers laid off from jobs in finance, real estate, and other white-collar occupations or to two-earner families with high combined incomes. At the same time, there can be no doubt that ninety-nine weeks of benefits have been a deterrent to reemployment, even if in part-time jobs or lower-paying positions.

Likewise, since the official end of the recession in June 2009 there have been 3.5 million new cases on the disability benefits rolls, a figure which towers over the 200,000 breadwinner jobs restored during that period, and which is nearly double the caseload growth rate prior to the crisis. In short, the disability benefit has become a backdoor safety net, and in the process is encouraging millions of desperate citizens to abuse the program and become permanent dependents of the state.

Rather than retargeting resources through the earned income tax credit (EITC) or converting food stamps into a proper means-tested cash transfer system, however, the progressive policy agenda remains ensnared in a time warp; it digs Uncle Sam ever deeper into debt with stimulus boondoggles, and even justifies massive supplemental funding for grossly inefficient social insurance programs as a stimulus to consumer demand. Yet in the context of today's crisis of fiscal solvency, these measures to bolster the macroeconomy rather than transfer societal resources directly to needy citizens and families are reactionary.

The old-time New Deal–like initiatives revived by Bernanke's false depression call, in fact, have mobilized special interest lobbies to feast at the public trough like never before. Consequently, Washington has been dragged ever deeper into fiscal paralysis and incapacity to perform functions that are actually needed, such as funding an adequate national safety net. Worse still, all these misbegotten depression-fighting measures have destroyed what remained of an honest fiscal culture.

CHAPTER 30

THE END OF FREE MARKETS
The Rampages of Crony Capitalism
in the Auto Belt

THE BAILOUT OF CHRYSLER AND GENERAL MOTORS (GM) WAS UT-terly unnecessary and did not save any auto jobs; it just reshuffled them from rising plants in right-to-work (red) states to dying plants in the UAW (blue) states. But the auto bailouts were more than just another policy error which emerged from the BlackBerry Panic. They were, in fact, the final crushing blow to free market capitalism.

The auto bailouts corrupted political discourse beyond repair, elevating official mendacity and crony capitalist deceit to a new level. And as Washington plunged into a sweeping rearrangement of both the nation's largest industry and its financial overlay, it was a Republican administration which led the bailout bandwagon, thereby leaving the public purse vulnerable to crony capitalist raids for the permanent future.

The auto bailout was initiated by the nation's bailout crazed de facto president, Hank Paulson, based on the specious claim that a million jobs would be lost from an industry which, according to the Bureau of Labor Statistics (BLS), employed only 750,000 workers. At the time it was self-evident that the real issue was job allocation, not job loss. Up to half of this BLS figure for manufacturing jobs in the "motor vehicle and parts" industry was in the new auto belt of Kentucky, Tennessee, Mississippi, Alabama, Georgia, and South Carolina. It was absolutely the case that the auto OEMs involved—Toyota, Nissan, Hyundai, BMW, and Mercedes-Benz—would have gained sales and jobs had Chrysler and GM been allowed to meet their maker in bankruptcy court.

So the bipartisan embrace of the auto bailout changed everything. The pieces and parts of the national economy would now become fair game for a perpetual Washington food fight. Yet a government which is responsible for every bob and weave of the entire national economy will quickly succumb to pure crony capitalism, a régime which cannot avoid eventual fiscal insolvency and the destruction of any semblance of a free market economy.

Most importantly, it means a fatal corruption of political democracy. Ironically, President Obama did not earn reelection in 2012. He bought a second term with taxpayer dollars in the auto precincts of Ohio, Michigan, and Wisconsin, and did so under the cover of a GOP-endorsed bailout. But the terrible lies about the bailout's necessity, repeated over and over by the Democratic campaign, constituted far more than partisan cant. In fact, they represented the fundamental confusion about economic events and conditions which have arisen from the Fed's destructive régime of financial repression and financial markets manipulation.

THE HOARY LEGENDS OF THE GM BAILOUT

The hoary urban legend that General Motors could not get a debtor in possession loan (DIP) at the time of the Wall Street meltdown is a dramatic illustration of the ill effects from the Fed's destruction of interest rate price signals. True enough, GM could not get bankruptcy financing at 5 percent. But under the conditions which existed in December 2008, the job of the free market was to treat financial train wrecks like GM with stringent terms and interest rates commensurate with their risk.

As it happened, however, any memory of the function of free market interest rates among policy makers had long ago vanished. So after the Senate had properly rejected aid to Detroit, Paulson struck again, on the apparent theory that if GM couldn't get cheap financing fair and square in the marketplace, then it was the taxpayer's job to step into the breach.

As he himself made clear in his own telling of the episode, GM was never asked to scour the earth for DIP financing, even if available terms were onerous. In fact, Secretary Paulson never even asked GM to prove that it had tried.

For all practical purposes the US Treasury Department, armed with the massive firepower and open-ended authority of TARP, had staged an economic coup d'état. Paulson had just returned from a ten-day trip to China where he had been mesmerized by the miracles of Red Capitalism, and was not about to see the stock market in general, and Goldman's stock in particular, take another beating.

Never mind that GM was a veritable fount of corporate incompetence and long-standing financial scams, and that it could no longer dodge the harsh and messy resolution of the marketplace and bankruptcy courts. The US economy was now being run by the writ of a "can do" power tripper who had no clue that deal making Wall Street style was a frightfully dangerous way to make public policy, and a lethal blow to the integrity and resilience of free market capitalism.

So without the benefit of any analysis whatsoever, the hapless lame duck in the Oval Office wolfed down a hot dog for lunch while his treasury secretary instructed him to "sign here" on a $13 billion TARP check to GM. It thus transpired that the most important test of free market capitalism in modern times was cancelled for the ephemeral reason that the treasury secretary did not want the stock market to open the next morning—Friday, December 12, 2008—on a down note.

Paulson's rendition of this Rubicon moment is downright embarrassing in its myopic lack of perspective. If the Bush administration didn't rescue Detroit from its own folly, "the GOP risked being labeled the party of Herbert Hoover," he prattled on, implying that the nation's taxpayers existed for the political convenience of the party in power.

Worse still, Paulson's memoir reveals a neurotically obsessed and self-appointed economic czar who had unilaterally suspended any and all free market rules until further notice. Washington would take over the auto industry for the stunningly superficial reason that the country was "in the midst of a financial crisis and deepening recession." Accordingly, it would be inconvenient for GM to "declare bankruptcy [because] they would be doing so without advance planning or adequate financing for an orderly restructuring."

From that moment on there was no turning back—not just from the GM loan but, more profoundly, from a permanent régime of bailout capitalism. The TARP funds allegedly provided GM with a three-month bridge loan, yet once the Bush White House blinked it was a foregone conclusion that GM would not get an honest DIP loan and that the TARP funds would become a "bridge" to a full-scale federal intervention.

The eventual, rule-shattering $50 billion bailout of a single company, which had only 62,000 US hourly workers, was thus set in motion by a Republican administration stumbling around in a spree of seat-of-the-pants interventionism. Only after the fact did the perpetrators and beneficiaries of this horrid abuse of state power invent the pretext that GM's continued existence was threatened by a total shutdown of the financial markets.

That was unspeakably false. Even a moment of calm reflection would have revealed to Paulson and his posse that GM had massive amounts of pledgeable assets. Accordingly, it needed to be told in no uncertain terms never to bring its tin cup to Washington again, but instead to market its massive collateral pool to potential DIP loan investors anywhere on the planet, no matter how unpalatable the terms and interest cost might be to the moguls in Detroit.

Such a mission would have readily succeeded because at the end of 2007, General Motors reported a giant pile of assets worth nearly $150 billion on a book-value basis. While this total was offset by an equal amount of liabilities—mainly debt, retirement obligations, and trade payables—the whole point of the US bankruptcy code under exactly this circumstance is to permit a new court-protected lender to "prime" any and all of these existing liabilities.

Stated differently, any DIP lender would have had first dibs on the entire $150 billion asset litter. This included a first lien on billions' worth of machines and tools, trucking fleets, massive factories and industrial sites, foreign subsidiaries in Brazil and China that were worth billions, brands such as Cadillac and Chevy that had not yet been ruined by generations of incompetent management at GM (despite their best efforts), and much, much more.

None of GM's financial liabilities mattered to a DIP lender—not lawsuits by injured dealers, not the contract-waving UAW labor bosses at Solidarity House, not the underfunded pensions that would be dumped on Uncle Sam, not the $25 billion that GM owed suppliers, and certainly not the $45 billion in long-term debt that GM owed to banks and bond fund managers who unaccountably still held its clearly worthless paper. In short, all of these claimants would have gotten in line behind a DIP lender had GM been forced into ordinary Chapter 11 where it belonged.

$100 BILLION OF FROZEN LIABILITIES:
WHY GM DIDN'T NEED UNCLE SAM'S CREDIT CARD

In fact, GM didn't need a taxpayer bailout at all. The real meaning of the incantation that GM couldn't get a DIP loan is that it could not get one with single-digit interest rates, and appropriately so. General Motors was a colossal dinosaur owing to self-inflicted harm over decades. After the turn of the century, its financial statements had "shoot me" written all over them.

There is no other possible way to explain the company's staggering losses: $85 billion during the five years ending in 2008. Indeed, losses of this magnitude were almost incomprehensible, since GM's worldwide sales during that period were just shy of $1 trillion. Yet these monster sales totals, which represented the cumulative shipment of more than 35 million cars and trucks, could not even remotely cover GM's massive costs and endless write-offs.

Accordingly, its financial crisis was not owing to a temporary plunge of auto sales in the fall of 2008. GM's problem was terminal, and could only be solved through a massive downsizing and dismemberment under regular-way Chapter 11. As will be seen, to conduct an extended, court-protected campaign of cost restructuring and asset liquidation, GM actually needed only a modest-sized DIP loan—one that could have been readily obtained at an interest rate commensurate with the risk, say, 15 percent or even 25 percent.

This was true because the Detroit auto business had a dirty secret. The latter was never disclosed by President Obama's so-called auto task force when it inherited Paulson's bridge; namely, that in the context of bankruptcy protection, GM did not need much fresh cash (i.e., a huge DIP loan) to operate a reduced cohort of viable plants and car lines. The Big Three business model, in fact, was to pay suppliers slowly and collect from dealers fast, thereby generating a huge float of working cash.

Indeed, GM's vast complex of suppliers was the industrial equivalent of indentured servants: their factories were filled with GM-owned tools, and in the short run billions' worth of supplier production lines were useless without these tools and GM parts orders. Accordingly, GM was able to delay payment to its suppliers for parts and materials for forty-five days after GM was invoiced, in effect using its supplier base as a $25 billion payables "bank" to finance its production cycle.

At the same time, GM North America generally had only about $5 billion of receivables because it collected from dealers within days of delivery, leaving the GM treasury with a net $20 billion piggy bank to fund its operations. The fact that it burned through this massive cash hoard near the end of 2008 was a measure of its total dysfunction, not proof that it needed a loan from taxpayers.

Upon a bankruptcy filing, this favorable payables-receivables float would have been rapidly regenerated because all of GM's pre-petition obligations, including the claims and invoices of suppliers, would have been frozen. Accordingly, any serious DIP lender would have seen that GM was readily capable of floating its own boat, once it was freed of contractual debts and cash-burning plants.

Indeed, GM was insolvent precisely because it had accumulated too many fixed contractual obligations—the very thing bankruptcy was designed to alleviate. In addition to its $45 billion of bank loans and bonds, for example, it also owed $55 billion for retiree health care, pension liabilities, and similar obligations.

Nothing could have been more obvious than the fact that this $100 billion of bad debts would be put on the chopping block. Any bankruptcy judge worth his salt could have cut that number to $40 billion or $15 billion or whatever figure a viable post-bankruptcy enterprise could support.

The "hit" for these bad debts was strictly the business of GM's unions, employees, and lenders who had made bad bargains for decades, not the taxpayers of America who were innocent bystanders. Moreover, while the court was working toward an equitable shrinkage of this mountain of bad debt, payments would be stayed and the DIP loan would be spent on revenue-producing operations.

The fact that a $100 billion liabilities freeze was available through the regular bankruptcy process just plain destroys the spurious claim that only Uncle Sam was rich enough to keep General Motors operating. Indeed, absent the cash drain of the frozen liabilities and closed factories that would have been enabled by Chapter 11, GM's remaining needs for operating cash were so strikingly small that the Washington operatives running the bailout did not dare disclose this truth to the public.

At the end of 2008, for example, the company's US operations consisted of forty-seven power-train, stamping, and assembly plants which employed 62,000 hourly workers and produced product for eight different vehicle brands. Under an honest bankruptcy process, all of these metrics would have been dramatically downsized. In truth, GM has only three viable brands—Chevy, Cadillac, and GMC Trucks—and needed only a handful of plants to produce them.

In a steady-state 15 million unit US light-vehicle market, therefore, a properly downsized and three-brand GM might have profitably retained a 15 percent market share. This means that it would need to source about 2.3 million light vehicles per year—about 1.8 million from its best US plants along with about 500,000 from the efficient plants it operates in Mexico and Canada.

Based on the North American industry benchmarks published in the annual *Harbour Report*, the startling truth is that GM could produce its downsized vehicle requirements in eight US assembly plants and in an equal number of power-train and stamping facilities. That means it would need sixteen US-based plants, not forty-seven. This drastically downsized production complex, in turn, would have required a total of only 25,000 hourly employees, assuming productivity levels of about twenty-five man-hours per vehicle that were already being achieved in the company's best operations.

Moreover, under a court-supervised process, GM would have paid at most $28 per hour in cash wages. This is so because the vast bulk of the $60 per hour fully loaded cost under the UAW contract was for pensions, health care, supplemental unemployment benefits, and other contractual items which would have been frozen by the court. GM's monthly cash wage bill under a US bankruptcy scenario would have been just $100 million per month.

With a DIP loan of $10 billion, GM could have provisioned a year's worth of hourly wages and still had $9 billion available to strategically liquefy pre-petition supplier payables where necessary to support production. But that's not all. It also could have covered plant operating costs, corporate overhead, marketing, and product development until its natural, large working capital float was regenerated within a few months.

In a free financial market, even under stressed-out conditions like in 2008, there is never a shortage of high-risk investors interested in earning double-digit interest rates on the kind of modest DIP facility that GM actually needed. Their funds would have been used to restart a drastically downsized but viable "GM Lite" while being protected by a $100 billion liability freeze, and collateralized many times over by GM's tens of billions of good assets.

THE GM BAILOUT: QUINTESSENCE OF CRONY CAPITALIST PLUNDER

The entire urban legend about "no DIP and no alternative" to a Washington intervention, therefore, was actually a smoke screen. The "bailout" was really about the transfer of GM's bad debts to the taxpayers, not its need for Uncle Sam's cash during a bankruptcy. And most certainly it did not involve any "need" on the part of the American economy for the company's remnants outside a potentially viable GM Lite; that is, there was no need for thirty redundant plants, 40,000 excess UAW wage workers, and its dead-in-the-water car brands like Pontiac, Hummer, Saturn, and Buick.

If a GM Lite had emerged from regular-way bankruptcy, it's likely that $30 billion of bonds would have been wiped out and that its retiree health-care plans would have been frozen at existing asset levels, not funded eighty cents on the dollar as actually happened. Likewise, the Cadillac-style UAW pension plan would have been terminated with a 25 percent benefit haircut and any remaining funding shortfall paid by the federal Pension Benefit Guaranty Corporation (PBGC).

In this respect, the argument that the bailout saved the PBGC from billions in losses is laughable. The same case could be made for rescuing every single company that files for bankruptcy if it has an insured pension plan. What the bailout actually saved was a UAW pension benefit plan that was so rich no auto company on the free market could actually afford it.

In the same manner, the bank group led by JPMorgan would have taken a severe haircut on their $6 billion loan facility, and suppliers would have eaten some of their pre-petition payables. Similarly, redundant workers at several dozen closed GM plants would have gotten the same unemployment insurance benefits as all other American workers. The company-paid layer on top—the so-called supplemental benefits that provided 95 percent of take-home pay—would have been cut off by bankruptcy.

The ills of crony capitalism are not limited to economic inefficiency and the dead-weight costs of propping up uncompetitive companies, however. The even greater societal evil lies in the inequities: the "impressing" of innocent taxpayers into funding bad debts and economic privileges that often far exceed what rank-and-file citizens can obtain in the private market and from public programs such as unemployment insurance.

Needless to say, Republicans had no basis to support the auto bailout except rank opportunism. In voting twice for the auto bailout, Congressman Paul Ryan's conclusion that the GM's Janesville, Wisconsin, plant deserved a better fate than the verdict of the free market was dispositive.

Yet it is the progressive Democrats who were the most hypocritical. At a time when they deemed that a generous ninety-nine weeks of extended unemployment payments was good enough for 10 million unemployed American workers, the Obama White House singled out 60,000 aristocrats of labor for the extra-special privileges of the state.

The sheer facts of the North American auto industry make clear that in bailing out GM, the fundamental purpose of the Obama White House was the crass political objective of payback to the UAW. As indicated above, the bailout did not save a single net job; it just altered the allocation of automotive sales, production, and jobs among companies and regions.

The claim that the entire auto industry was at risk and that the nation faced the loss of more than a million jobs is plain stupid propaganda. Worse still, the pro-industry shills who issued it, such as the Center for Automotive Research, actually received substantial funding from taxpayers.

In truth, the North American auto industry was at the time swamped in excess capacity—a reality punctuated by the plunge of capacity utilization to just 27 percent at the January 2009 bottom. And it remains amply supplied even after nearly 3 million units of capacity have been shuttered. On a three-shift basis and with activation of mothballed plants, there are still 22 million units of light-vehicle assembly capacity in North America, but no economic scenario in which sustainable demand for NAFTA (North American Free Trade Agreement)-built cars and light trucks would exceed 16–17 million units.

At the end of the day, the GM bailout was about whacking up the wage bill between plants north and south of the Mason-Dixon Line. Under steady-state conditions the wage bill for the power-train, stamping, and assembly operations of US OEMs is about $15 billion, representing around

300 million man-hours at a fully loaded average cost of $50 per hour. This flows from the basic math of auto sales, output, and productivity.

Because of the deep-seated brand preferences and buying behavior of the American consumer, it can be easily stipulated that imports will capture 20–25 percent of the US market, as they have for several decades. Accordingly, assuming a steady-state US demand of 15 million light vehicles, about 3.5 million vehicles will be imports and 11.5 million will be sourced in North American plants, including about 10 million units from the US assembly plants operated by a dozen NAFTA-based auto OEMs (the other 1.5 million units would be sourced in Canada and Mexico).

From these facts of auto industry life, the political food fight over the auto wage bill can be seen as the stark, straightforward battle it was. Senator Richard Shelby of Alabama fought for the free market and the twenty-seven newer, more efficient auto assembly complexes mainly in the South. Ron Bloom, the labor bosses' designated hitter on the White House auto task force, fought for the fifty older, high-cost UAW-organized plants in the north.

When the dust settled after GM's whirlwind forty-day faux bankruptcy, several billions of the national auto wage bill had been arbitrarily shuffled from Senator Shelby's side of the line to Ron Bloom's. Had nature been allowed to take its course, GM Lite would have emerged from bankruptcy with 25,000 hourly jobs, representing about 45 million annual man-hours. Owing to the White House political fix, however, GM ended 2011 with 48,000 US hourly jobs, representing about 85 million man-hours. At $60 per hour, the 40 million man-hour difference made for a lot of UAW political gratitude—about $2.5 billion worth to be exact.

HOW THE FREE MARKET WAS LOST
AND THE 2012 ELECTION WON

Yet even this stupendous figure does not capture the full measure of gratitude the Obama administration paid to the UAW. None of GM's "bad debts" related to labor issues were canceled or even significantly hair cut—not pensions, not retiree health care, not wages. Auto czar Steve Rattner removed all doubt when he later told the Detroit Economics Club, "We did not ask any UAW member to take a cut in their pay."

Needless to say, this capricious $2.5 billion shuffle of wages from the plants of one region to those of another generated no public welfare benefits whatsoever. American consumers will not buy one more car because of the bailout, even if they are presented with about 600,000 more vehicles (i.e., reflecting GM's current 19 percent market share rather than 15 percent) coming out of GM plants and the same amount less coming out of Ford, Toyota, Nissan, Honda, and Hyundai plants.

Likewise, there are approximately 20,000 auto dealers in the United States and they, too, experienced not a whit's gain in volume—only a shuffle among brands. In fact, all the usual suspects trotted out by bailout apologists fit this same template. Everything claimed as a "benefit" from the bailout—from higher payroll checks to increased electrical power purchases, plant maintenance contracts, hazardous waste hauling volume, local taxes, and more contributions to the United Way—amount to nothing more than a reshuffling of these expenditures among approximately two dozen counties within the United States that host the major auto OEM complexes.

During the two years after the bailouts, auto sales recovered smartly from the 9–10 million unit panic lows of late 2008 to a 13–15 million unit level after mid-2010. However, this natural but modest rebound in final sales had a bullwhip effect on production of parts and finished vehicles, because the auto industry's supply chain had been virtually depleted of inventory during the first half of 2009. In fact, never before in peacetime history had the automotive supply chain's cupboard been this bare. Accordingly, the ballyhooed "booming" production of 2010–2011 was actually just an aggressive one-time fill of this depleted inventory pipeline.

Not surprisingly, in the midst of this inventory refill in November 2010, Wall Street triumphantly brought GM public at a nosebleed valuation. The fast money then bid up even higher during the next few months, so that at its early 2011 peak GM was valued at $60 billion.

Needless to say, that wasn't the real thing—the White House auto task force had not sprinkled GM with fairy dust. Instead, Detroit's lumbering dinosaur was temporarily minting profits by restuffing its dealer channel with a new round of excessive inventories and burying some of its running costs in the massive cookie jar of "fresh start" accounting reserves created upon its bankruptcy exit. Likewise, money printing by central banks the world over had engineered a short-lived auto rebound that had staunched GM's losses in Europe and generated sales and profits boomlets at its operations in Brazil and China.

By the end of 2012, however, GM's miraculous recovery was all over except the shouting. Stuffed dealer lots in the United States put the clamps on production and profit in North America. At the same time, GM's European operations plunged into multibillion-dollar losses, Brazil headed south, and the bulging profits out of China were rapidly vanishing as red capitalism entered its hard landing phase.

The White House's forty-day rinse cycle had cured nothing. But it did produce a temporary rebound that was perfectly feathered into a completion date of November 6, 2012. Pure and simple, the leading edge of President Obama's reelection was in the General Motors (and Chrysler) precincts of Ohio.

The pro-bailout triumphalists who celebrated GM's post-IPO surge because they didn't recognize a Wall Street ramp job when they saw one will now receive a stinging rebuke. GM is heading for a relapse into red ink, and its now vastly diminished market cap has already shed much of its post-IPO value.

What happened between mid-2009 and mid-2012, therefore, was not a miracle in Motown; it was just another lamentable episode of crony capitalism on parade. Wall Street fixers—first Secretary Paulson and then auto czar Steve Rattner—had wantonly eviscerated the curative mechanisms of the free market. The outcome was "winners" picked by Washington and "losers" who didn't even know what hit them; that is, taxpayers who had to foot the bill and competitors from whom the bailsters stole the business.

In this respect, Chrysler had also been kept alive when there was no earthly reason for it in a North American market already served by seventeen different global suppliers. Any number of them would have gladly purchased its only viable components, the Jeep franchise and Dodge Ram trucks, but none would have been interested in its rundown UAW-controlled car plants.

Indeed, the wage bill at the latter plants was about $1.5 billion, meaning that from the artificially resuscitated parts of GM and Chrysler combined, the auto task force had gifted the UAW with a wage bill of about $4 billion that would otherwise have gone to workers at the North American plants of Hyundai, Toyota, Honda, Ford, BMW, and six other OEMs. By the same token, the auto task force did not add one dollar of sales or one job to the supplier base; it just spun the roulette wheel on the available business, shifting the mix to parts plants in the rust belt from those in the mid-South.

Nevertheless, even this arbitrary tampering with the auto supply base came at a large price. The unmistakable message of the bailout was that the auto OEMs are also in that privileged class of "too big to fail." Even more importantly, it demonstrated unequivocally that the White House is for sale and, therefore, that the nation's fiscal solvency and free market economy have been mortally compromised.

THE AUTO BAILOUT LOBBY: BORN AND BRED IN THE ECCLES BUILDING

Self-evidently, it was not the car company executives who famously brought their tin cups to Washington in Gulfstream jets that pulled off the auto bailouts. Nor could this blatant heist have been accomplished even by the assembled might of the UAW alone. In truth, the auto bailouts happened because the entire auto supply chain—from toolmakers and parts suppliers to vehicle haulers and car dealers—was up to its eyebrows in debt.

The era of bubble finance had left this vast swath of the US economy massively leveraged and therefore vulnerable to a cascade of bankruptcies and harsh downsizings in the event of a material decline in car sales. Consequently, when new car sales temporarily plummeted in the weeks after the Lehman failure, the level of desperation across the entire auto chain was palpable, and especially so among car dealers.

There was nothing about the sheet metal moving business that wasn't immersed in debt. Dealers had hocked their showrooms and had borrowed nearly 100 percent of the wholesale value of cars on their lots through floor plan loans. Likewise, they were utterly dependent upon loans and lease financing, much of it with deep embedded losses, to support their retail customers. All of this was the handiwork of the Greenspan-Bernanke Fed's financial repression policies and the resulting destruction of honest price signals in the lending markets.

Not surprisingly, the nation's 20,000 auto dealers and the 2 million job holders reported by the BLS for "motor vehicle and parts dealers" were not about to acquiesce to the harsh justice of the free market—not after Wall Street's ten giant banks had lined up in Hank Paulson's office on October 10 to receive checks for $10 billion to $25 billion each. And so a mighty caravan of car dealers figuratively descended upon Washington demanding an auto bailout. Leading the pack was the nation's largest car dealer, a giant pyramid of debt called AutoNation and its shrill, crony capitalist CEO, Mike Jackson.

The desperate circumstances of publicly traded AutoNation in October 2008 were not only indicative of the plight of the entire auto dealer sector, but also were a microcosm of the financial deformations that had been visited upon much of domestic business by the explosion of borrowing after 1994. In the final analysis, what became "bailout nation" when the lucre from TARP and the Fed's alphabet soup of credit lines was spread far and wide had actually been born and bred during the Fed's two-decade-long régime of bubble finance.

AutoNation had followed the usual script during this period, beginning with an M&A spree in the latter 1990s which assembled more than two hundred car dealerships representing the entire spectrum of domestic and imported brands. Built on a diet of heavy debt, the company sold about $20 billion of new and used cars annually, from a $2 billion vehicle inventory financed by "floor plan" loans, and sported brand new showrooms and lots financed either with operating leases or balance sheet debt.

Based on debt and M&A deals, AutoNation's sales grew explosively, rising from $5 billion in 1996 to $20 billion in 1999, but already it was an accident waiting to happen. In typical fashion, AutoNation massively overpaid and overinvested in its dealerships, and was therefore eventually required to take a giant $1.8 billion write-down of goodwill and franchise assets in 2008. As a result, during the six-year period between 2005 and 2011 when it sold $85 billion worth of cars, parts, and service, its cumulative net income of just $50 million amounted to a rounding error. In other words, all of the positive net income it booked during the period was cancelled out by the value destruction represented by its huge asset write-offs.

MIKE JACKSON: CRONY CAPITALIST PITCHMAN

Not surprisingly, AutoNation's longtime CEO, Mike Jackson, has been a pitchman for every raid on the US Treasury that the auto industry has concocted, including the bailouts in 2008–2009 and the absurd waste of taxpayer money called "cash for clunkers" in 2010. During October 2008 especially, Jackson gave voice to a hysterical view on the potential impact of the Wall Street meltdown on the auto industry and Main Street generally.

Sitting on $4 billion of debt at the end of 2007, AutoNation could not afford even a brief slump in the rate of car sales. Its entire inventory of cars was hocked to floor plan lenders, and the real estate and showrooms from which its two hundred dealerships operated were also each encumbered with multi-million debt obligations.

So when the new car sales rate plunged to about 10 million units for a few weeks after the Lehman events, Jackson raced around in Chicken Little fashion yelling that the sky was falling. The reality, however, is that it was an apparent air pocket in auto sales that wasn't real.

In another of the great deformations engendered by the Fed's cheap-money campaigns, the new car sales rate had been vastly inflated for more than a decade. Indeed, the 16–17 million SAAR (seasonally adjusted annual rate) that the industry and AutoNation desperately depended upon included 3–4 million units that were literally being stuffed into the economy with cheap debt.

The most egregious aspect of this was the 40 percent of auto loans that went to subprime borrowers, most of whom couldn't afford new cars in the first place and would soon default in large numbers. But the market distortions actually extended to the entire auto financing system. Millions of new cars were sold each year on lease, for example, but the "residuals" assumed at the end of typical three-to five-year leases were way too high.

This meant that monthly rental rates were artificially low and deeply subsidized.

Likewise, car loans which traditionally had three- to four-year maturities had been steadily extended to upward of seven years. This caused loss rates to soar, since cars depreciated far faster than loan balances were repaid. Yet auto lenders were able to absorb these losses without charging punitive interest rates to their customers because their funding costs were effectively subsidized by the Fed.

In the same manner, rental fleet companies bought upward of 2 million vehicles per year that sat idle most of the time in airport parking lots. Thanks to high leverage and cheap credit, however, this asset-wasting business model was artificially profitable most of the time, thereby spurring additional uneconomic demand for new vehicles and seconding to auto dealers a steady supply of (lightly) used cars.

In the fall of 2008, this whole house of automotive cards came crashing down. Retail consumers pulled back sharply, but that was a healthy correction because American garages were overparked with too many unaffordable cars bought on cheap credit. Indeed, the number of vehicles per household had soared by 50 percent during the previous two decades, while real incomes had advanced by barely 10 percent. Likewise, subprime auto loans dried up, which was a healthy development, and sales to lease and rental fleets also plummeted because their customer lots were already chockablock with idle vehicles.

The central source of Jackson's hair-on-fire panic, therefore, was that American households finally went on a buying strike in response to the plunging stock market—especially the top 10 percent of households which are the predominate source of demand for luxury vehicles. Not surprisingly, one-third of AutoNation's new car revenues and an even larger share of profits come from luxury brands including Cadillac, Lincoln, Mercedes, BMW, Lexus, Porsche, and Land Rover. Unless the affluent classes could be quickly coaxed back into the showrooms, therefore, Jackson's $4 billion pile of debt would have soon crushed the company's crippled cash flow.

Jackson's subsequent all-out campaign to conscript the American taxpayer into the rescue of the credit-swollen auto sector thus had an obvious purpose; namely, to get buyers of its whole stable of brands back into his empty showrooms. Accordingly, through the auto dealers' associations Jackson became one of the chief cheerleaders for TARP, the auto bailouts, and the Fed's radical program to cut interest rates to zero and pump liquidity directly into the auto finance market.

So it wasn't the hapless production-line workers at GM's Lordstown, Ohio, plant alone that Jackson had in mind when he urged Congress to "hold your nose on principles for the greater good." Likewise, it wasn't just rust belt wage earners he was thinking about when he forecast Armageddon if Congress didn't pass TARP, hysterically warning that the nation would face "a systematic shutdown of the entire US auto industry, millions of jobs lost, a depression and 20 percent unemployment."

The jobs Jackson really wanted rescued were also in Stuttgart, Germany, and Toyota City, Japan, the sources of the high-profit luxury vehicles that actually kept his debt-ridden confederation of Sunbelt auto dealerships solvent. Still, the nauseating hypocrisy of Jackson's agitation for a Detroit bailout did powerfully illuminate the true depth of the deformations stemming from Greenspan's bubble finance.

The truth of the matter was that cheap credit and the Greenspan Put had created a hair-trigger economy, and especially so in the complex and lengthy auto supply chain. Most of the key linkages—suppliers, dealers, fleet customers, retail consumers, even the Detroit Big Three—were so dependent upon massive debt extensions that any interruption in the pace of output and sales threatened calamity.

In effect, the Fed's prosperity management policies have stripped the free enterprise economy of its shock absorbers and capacity to adjust to changed conditions; that is, they have crippled the very features that give markets their vast superiority over state-managed economies. Trying to foster and force prosperity artificially, the central bank has invited the nation's business enterprises to gorge themselves on cheap debt, thereby eviscerating the resilience and flexibility ordinarily possessed by firms on the free market. And it has turned their executives and owners into desperate pleaders for bailouts and state intervention.

CHEAP DEBT: ANOTHER GIFT TO THE 1 PERCENTERS

In this respect, the fundamental financial template of AutoNation vividly illustrates the manner in which Fed policy had turned business enterprises into debt zombies and the Mike Jacksons of American business into bully-boy claimants to government subventions. In a phrase, it isn't so much the devil of statist ideology as it is the demon of debt that makes them do it.

After three years of so-called recovery, for example, AutoNation remained heavily leveraged. During 2011 its total debt of nearly $3.6 billion amounted to 7.2X free cash flow (EBITDA less capital expenditure). Yet, notwithstanding this mountain of debt and the extreme risk implied by its high leverage ratio, the company's entire after-tax interest expense was just $68 million. Obviously, a massively leveraged company in a highly volatile and cyclical industry like auto sales could not borrow at this microscopic 1.9 percent annual rate on an honest free market.

In fact, an enterprise bearing that much credit risk would likely pay a free market interest rate on the order of 10 percent, and under a neutral tax code it wouldn't be deductible. The mathematical implication is that virtually all of the profits that AutoNation has posted since the 2008 crisis do not reflect earnings on the free market, but essentially measure the absurdly cheap after-tax cost of debt under current government policies.

This kind of policy-induced windfall is especially perverse because it fuels precisely the kind of financial engineering games previously described. In this case, AutoNation's stock is 67 percent owned by two hedge funds and management insiders. Accordingly, during 2009–2011 they used the taxpayer-financed reprieve of the auto bailout not to pay down debt and get out of harm's way but, perversely, to amp the company's leverage even higher in order to fund massive share buybacks.

During those three years alone, the company spent $1.2 billion on share repurchases, or nearly double its net income, notwithstanding that the latter was itself entirely an artifact of cheap debt. But this feckless raid on its own treasury accomplished the intended purpose: the share count was reduced by 20 percent, thereby goosing per share earnings, even as the maneuver added heavily to the company's existing debt burden.

Not surprisingly, Jackson was a frequent guest on financial TV, castigating opponents of the auto bailout and cheerleading the Fed's money-printing campaign while touting an earnings rebound which was completely phony; that is, it was mainly an artifact of massive share buybacks. AutoNation's fiscal 2011 net income, in fact, was down 43 percent from 2005.

Still, on the strength of the share buybacks, the company's stock price quadrupled from a post-crisis low of $10 per share to nearly $40 per share by the end of 2011. Once again, its hedge fund owners and option-holding insiders made a killing from this orchestrated stock market ramp.

Indeed, this miracle of a booming stock price in the face of performance failure was essentially a gift of state policy to the 1 percenters. Under the honest free market interest rate (10 percent) and neutral tax policy scenario referenced above, AutoNation would have earned the grand sum of $0.20 per share in 2011. The hedge fund scalpers who had climbed on board after the auto sector bailout were thus winning huge because the stock was being valued at 200X its true economic earnings.

The AutoNation scam was repeated again and again in the aftermath of the bailouts. Businesses should have been belatedly cleaning up their balance sheets in order to preclude another perilous squeeze like the one in late 2008. Instead, insiders and their Wall Street accomplices plundered balance sheets further to fund record share buybacks and other financial engineering games.

Indeed, too many of the nation's CEOs have embraced the same corrosive crony capitalism as practiced by Mike Jackson; that is, they have become financial TV pitchmen for stocks medicated by buybacks and cheap money. At the same time, they insist almost without exception that full-throttle state action to goose the economy after the Lehman crisis was justified to prevent an economic Armageddon.

Needless to say, if the American economy really stood that close to the economic abyss in September 2008, the fact that not one net dime of free cash flow has been applied to business debt reduction in the four years since the Lehman event begs for explanation. In fact, the US business sector balance sheets carried $11.8 trillion of debt at the end of 2012—$600 billion more than when Jackson and others were braying that the sky had fallen.

This astonishing truth has materialized for one overwhelming reason: corporate CEOs have not reduced their debt because they are being given profoundly false signals by the Fed's obsessive pursuit of financial repression. Indeed, after-tax interest rates are so stupidly low that executives have come to believe that it would actually be foolish to pay down their debt.

The Fed's destruction of market-pricing signals for both investment-grade and high-yield corporate debt has also tranquilized top financial managers with respect to refinancing risk. The middle and long end of the yield curve has been so brutally flattened by the central bank bond buying that it has triggered the greatest rally in corporate debt prices ever recorded. Accordingly, there has been a corporate refinancing boom that is as far off the charts as was the home mortgage "refi" boom of 2002–2006.

In the United States alone, issuance of investment-grade and high-yield bonds during 2010–2012 totaled $3.2 trillion, or 40 percent more than was issued during the comparable period of the last business recovery (2003–2005). Moreover, since the overwhelming purpose of this record issuance during the current cycle was to refinance existing debt, business executives have learned a profoundly dangerous lesson: that debt carries no risk and that "extend and pretend" is a perpetual option.

Likewise, the Wall Street "risk on" casino fostered by the Bernanke Fed has severely compounded the debt propensity of corporate CEOs. Every time cash flow is applied to share buybacks and other financial engineering maneuvers, hedge fund speculators reward them with higher share prices and more valuable stock options. In Pavlovian fashion, therefore, American business leaders bang the lever again and again, whenever they can allocate cash flow to financial engineering or borrow more to fund it.

Accordingly, the American economy has not alleviated one bit the hair-trigger condition that spawned the Mike Jackson–style panic and the resultant bailout and money-printing sprees of late 2008. In fact, the Fed's announced policy to retain ZIRP for six full years—through the middle of 2015 as of this writing—almost guarantees that the free market is only a few short years away from total suffocation under a crony capitalist–style statist régime.

The fatal driver is the fact that the collective memory of free market interest rates is being extinguished and along with it the political will to tolerate them. Yet if interest rates are not allowed to periodically soar in order to purge financial deformations, like AutoNation and General Motors were in September 2008, one-sided markets and reckless gamblers will run unchecked. Eventually, the latter will mortgage and deplete the entire economic system in an irreversible descent into financialization. Along the way, petulant crony capitalists like Mike Jackson will continue to extract billions in ill-gotten rents.

CHAPTER 31

NO RECOVERY
ON MAIN STREET

AFTER THE US ECONOMY LIQUIDATED EXCESS INVENTORY AND labor and hit its natural bottom in June 2009, it embarked upon a halting but wholly unnatural "recovery." The artificial prolongation of the Bush tax cuts, the 2 percent payroll tax abatement and the spend-out of the Obama stimulus pilfered several trillions from future taxpayers in order to gift America's present day "consumption units" with the wherewithal to buy more shoes and soda pop.

But there has been no recovery of the Main Street economy where it counts; that is, no revival of breadwinner jobs and earned incomes on the free market. What we have once again is faux prosperity. In fact, the current Bernanke Bubble is an even sketchier version of the last one and consists essentially of the deliberate and relentless reflation of financial asset prices.

In practice, this amounts to a monetary version of "trickle down" economics. By September 2012, personal consumption expenditure (PCE) was up by $1.2 trillion from the prior peak, representing a modest 2.2 percent per year (0.6 percent after inflation) gain from the level of late 2007. Yet half of this gain—more than $600 billion—reflected the massive growth of government transfer payments, and much of the rebound which did occur in private consumption spending was concentrated in the top 10–20 percent of households. In short, the Fed's financial repression policies enabled Uncle Sam to fund transfer payments for the bottom rungs of society at virtually no carry cost on the debt, while they juiced the top rungs with a wealth effects tonic that boosted spending at Nordstrom's and Coach.

The Fed's post-Lehman money printing spree has thus failed to revive Main Street, but it has ignited yet another round of rampant speculation in the risk asset classes. Accordingly, the net worth of the 1 percent is temporarily back to the pre-crisis status quo ante. Needless to say, successful speculation in the fast money complex is not a sign of honest economic recovery: it merely marks the prelude to another spectacular meltdown in the canyons of Wall Street next time the music stops.

DEFORMATION OF THE JOBS MARKET:
THE ECLIPSE OF BREADWINNERS

The precarious foundation of the Bernanke Bubble is starkly evident in the internal composition of the jobs numbers. At the time the US economy peaked in December 2007, there were 71.8 million "breadwinner" jobs in construction, manufacturing, white-collar professions, government, and full-time private services. These jobs accounted for more than half of the nation's 138 million total payroll and on average paid about $50,000 per year—just enough to support a family.

Breadwinner jobs also generated more than 65 percent of earned wage and salary income and are thus the foundation of the Main Street economy. Yet after a brutal 5.6 million loss of breadwinner jobs during the Great Recession, a startling fact stands out: less than 4 percent of that loss had been recovered after 40 months of so-called recovery.

The 3 million jobs recovered since the recession ended in June 2009, in fact, have been entirely concentrated in the two far more marginal categories that comprise the balance of the national payroll. More than half of the recovery (1.6 million jobs) occurred in what is essentially the "part-time economy." It presently includes 36.4 million jobs in retail, hotels, restaurants, shoe-shine stands, and temporary help agencies where average annualized compensation was only $19,000. This vast swath of the jobs economy—27 percent of the total—is thus comprised of entry level, second earner, and episodic jobs that enable their holders to barely scrape by.

The balance of the pick-up (1.1 million jobs) was in the HES Complex, which consists of 30.7 million jobs in health, education, and social services. Average compensation is slightly better at about $35,000 annually and this category has grown steadily for years. Its increasingly salient disability, however, is that it is almost entirely dependent on government spending and tax subsidies, and thus faces the headwind of the nation's growing fiscal insolvency.

When viewed in this three category framework, the nation's job picture reveals a lopsided aspect that thoroughly belies the headline claims of recovery. A healthy Main Street economy self-evidently depends upon growth in breadwinner jobs, but there has been none, even during the bubble years before the financial crisis. The Bureau of Labor Statistics (BLS) reported 71.8 million breadwinner jobs in January 2000, yet seven years later in December 2007—after the huge boom in housing, real estate, household consumption, and the stock market—the number was still exactly 71.8 million.

The faux prosperity of the Fed's bubble finance is thus starkly evident. This is the single most important metric of Main Street economic health, and not only had there been zero new breadwinner jobs on a peak-to-peak basis, but that alarming fact had been completely ignored by the smugly confident monetary politburo.

Alas, the latter was blithely tracking a feedback loop of its own making. Flooding Wall Street with easy money, it saw the stock averages soar and pronounced itself pleased with the resulting "wealth effects." Turning the nation's homes into debt-dispensing ATMs, it witnessed a household consumption spree and marveled that the "incoming" macroeconomic data was better than expected. That these deformations were mistaken for prosperity and sustainable economic growth gives witness to the everlasting folly of the monetary doctrines now in vogue in the Eccles Building.

To be sure, nominal GDP did grow by 40 percent, or about $4 trillion, between 2000 and 2007. Yet there should be no mystery as to how it happened. As has been noted, total debt outstanding grew by $20 trillion during that same period. The American economy was thus being pushed forward by a bow wave of debt, not pulled higher by rising productivity and earned income.

Indeed, the modest gain of 7.5 million jobs during those seven years reflected exactly this debt-driven dynamic and explains why none of these job gains were in the breadwinner categories. Instead, about 2.5 million were accounted for by the part-time economy jobs described above. On an income-equivalent basis these were actually "40 percent jobs" because they represented an average of twenty-five hours per week and paid $14 per hour, compared to a standard forty-hour work week and a national average wage rate of $22 per hour. Thus, spending their trillions of MEW windfalls at malls, bars, restaurants, vacation spots, and athletic clubs, homeowners and the prosperous classes, in effect, temporarily hired the renters and the increasing legions of marginal workers left behind.

Likewise, another 5 million jobs were generated in the HES (health, education, and social services) complex. Here the job count grew by 20 percent, but it was mainly due to the fact that the sector's paymasters—government budgets and tax-preferred employer health plans—were temporarily flush.

As shown below, however, these, too, were "debt-push" jobs that paid modest wages. While the steady 2.6 percent annual growth of HES jobs during the second Greenspan Bubble did flatter the monthly employment "print," it was possible only so long as government and health plans could keep spending at rates far higher than the growth rate of the national economy.

THE CRASH AND NONRECOVERY
OF BREADWINNER JOBS

The Wall Street meltdown of September 2008 accelerated the recessionary forces already in motion, causing a total job loss of 7.3 million between the December 2007 peak and the end of the recession in June 2009. That the Fed's bubble finance had camouflaged the failing internals of the American economy then became starkly apparent. Nearly three-fourths of this reduction was accounted for by the above mentioned loss of 5.6 million breadwinner jobs; that is, nearly 8 percent of their pre-recession total.

That devastating hit left the nation with only 66.2 million prime jobs and set the clock back to the level of early 1998. This is an astonishing fact: before any of the Greenspan-Bernanke maneuvers to coddle Wall Street and pump up the wealth effects elixir—that is, the 1998 LTCM bailout, the 2001–2003 rate-cutting panic, the August 2007 Bernanke Put, and the Fed's post-Lehman tripling of its balance sheet—*there were more breadwinner jobs than there are today.*

Since the BlackBerry Panic the Fed has relentlessly pumped freshly minted cash into the bank accounts of the twenty-one government bond dealers. Not surprisingly, therefore, there has been a jarringly divergent outcome between Wall Street and Main Street.

By September 2012, the S&P 500 was up by 115 percent from its recession lows and had recovered all of its losses from the peak of the second Greenspan bubble. By contrast, only 200,000 of the 5.6 million lost breadwinner jobs had been recovered by that same point in time.

To be sure, the Fed's Wall Street shills breathlessly reported the improved jobs "print" every month, picking and choosing starting and ending points and using continuously revised and seasonally maladjusted data to support that illusion. Yet the fundamentals with respect to breadwinner jobs could not be obfuscated.

On the eve of the 2012 election, for example, there were 18.3 million jobs in the goods-producing sectors: manufacturing, mining, and construction. These core sectors of the productive economy had taken a beating during the Great Recession, shedding 3.5 million jobs, or 15 percent. Yet after three and a half years of so-called recovery, the jobs count in the goods-producing sectors had not rebounded in the slightest; it had actually declined slightly from the 18.5 million jobs recorded at the end of the recession in June 2009.

Likewise, there were 7.8 million jobs in finance, insurance, and real estate, meaning virtually no gain from the 7.7 million jobs at the end of the recession. As to lawyers, accountants, engineers, architects, and computer designers, there was no pick-up there, either: the 5 million jobs counted by the BLS in September 2012 barely exceeded the 4.8 million recorded in June 2009; and in the information industries—publishing, broadcasting, telecommunications, motion pictures, and music—the data had slightly deteriorated, with the 2.8 million jobs posted in June 2009 slipping to 2.6 million in the month before the 2012 election.

Similarly, the 10 million jobs in transportation and wholesale distribution in September 2012 had changed hardly a tad from June 2009. Finally, the other heavy-duty category of breadwinner jobs—that is, government employment (outside of education) where average compensation exceeds $65,000 annually—had actually gone south. The 11 million of these high-paying jobs on the eve of the 2012 election had shrunk by more than 4 percent since the recession ended in June 2009. In short, after forty months of "recovery" there was virtually no change in every category of breadwinner jobs that had been slammed by the Great Recession.

THE "BORN AGAIN" JOBS SCAM

These data are extremely important. They belie the sunny paint-by-numbers jobs picture peddled by the Fed to distract the public from the fact that monetary policy is all about fueling the speculative urges of Wall Street, not the economic health of Main Street. This obfuscation is especially true with respect to the aforementioned headline gain of 3 million jobs. Never told is the fact that the majority of these, as indicated above, were part-time jobs in bars, restaurants, retail emporiums, and temporary employment agencies.

That fully 55 percent of the rebound has been in low-paying, part-time jobs not only illuminates the phony nature of the Fed's so-called recovery, but it also comes with a news flash; namely, every one of these 1.6 million new part-time "jobs" had already been "created" once before. During the second Greenspan bubble the part-time job count had risen from 34.7 million in early 2000 to 37.2 million in December 2007. In still another episode of Charlie Brown and Lucy, however, the football had been moved backward during the Great Recession. By June 2009, in fact, the part-time job count had tumbled all the way back to its turn of the century starting point at 34.7 million.

What happened by election eve of 2012, therefore, was nothing more than a partial retracement. At that point the BLS reported 36.4 million part-time jobs, meaning that after three and a half years of "recovery" just 60 percent of the gain from the 2000–2007 bubble had been recouped. These were self-evidently "born again" jobs, but in a display of astounding cynicism the Bernanke Fed claimed to be meeting its statutory mandate to promote maximum employment.

The larger truth is that when these job rebirths are set aside there isn't much left. The part-time job sector has gained an average of just 11,000 authentically new jobs per month during the twelve years between early 2000 and September 2012, thereby contributing hardly a drop in the bucket relative to the working-age population growth at 150,000 per month.

In fact, this "born again" syndrome actually applies to the entire non-farm payroll, and the modest rebound it has registered since the recession officially ended in June 2009. As shown by the data, the Greenspan-Bernanke policy was the monetary equivalent of a Billy Graham crusade: the same jobs got "saved" over and over.

Thus, there had been 130.8 million total jobs in January 2000, and this figure had reached 138.0 million by the December 2007 peak. The Great Recession sent the jobs count tumbling all the way back to the starting point, actually dipping slightly lower to 130.6 million by June 2009.

Then, after forty months of "recovery," the BLS reported 133.5 million nonfarm payroll jobs for September 2012. The Bernanke bubble had thus "recreated" only 40 percent of the jobs that had been "created" by the Greenspan bubble the first time around.   .

That the Bernanke bubble policies have not recouped even half of the total payroll gains that the Fed had already previously counted is still another testament to the sham nature of the "recovery." When the Fed's pump-and-dump cycling of the macro-economy is set aside, it becomes starkly evident that the American economy has been nearly bereft of sustained job growth. *For the entire twelve-year period since early 2000, it has generated a net gain of only 18,000 jobs per month, a figure that is just one-eighth of the labor force growth rate.*

The reason for this anemic figure on total payroll growth is that the great expanse of the nation's economy outside of the HES complex has been a jobs disaster area. Alongside the rounding-error growth in the part-time sector, the 66.4 million breadwinner jobs in September 2012 represented a drastic shrinkage from the approximate 72 million jobs in that category recorded in January 2000. This was the smoking gun: the prime breadwinner jobs market has been shrinking by a net of 35,000 jobs per month for more than twelve years!

Indeed, the tiny gain of 5,000 breadwinner jobs per month since June 2009 means that it would take 90 years to recoup the 5.6 million such jobs lost during the recession; that is, it would take until the twenty-second century to get back to the job count that existed at the end of the twentieth century! The absurdity of it surely puts paid to the notion that a conventional business recovery is underway.

Indeed, it is only the utterly politicized calculation of the "unemploy-ment rate" that disguises the jobless nature of the rebound. Upward of 8 million working-age Americans were no longer classified as being in the labor force due to purely arbitrary counting rules. In fact, the unemploy-ment rate on the eve of the 2012 election would have posted at about 13 percent based on the same labor force participation rate as January 2000, and would have clocked closer to 20 percent if further adjusted for the drastic shift from full-time to part-time employment.

THE HES COMPLEX:
BONANZA OF DEBT-FINANCED JOBS

The HES complex accounted for 1.1 million, or just under 40 percent of the 3 million jobs recovered after the recession bottomed. These were actually new jobs not born-again ones, meaning that the only true post-recession employment growth was embodied in the 27,000 per month gain of HES jobs. And that figure, in turn, represents the continuation of a long estab-lished trend. During the seven years ending in December 2007, about 4.7 million HES jobs were created, or about 50,000 per month. That trend con-tinued right through the Great Recession. While part-time and breadwin-ner jobs disappeared by the millions, the HES complex hardly skipped a beat, generating new jobs at a rate of 35,000 per month right through the eighteen-month shakeout.

A larger theme thus emerges. When the Fed went fully in the tank for Wall Street around the turn of the century, its excuse was that financial re-pression was a necessary tool to comply with the "maximum employment" component of its dual mandate. But that is a smoke screen to justify the Fed's levitation of risk assets and continuous coddling of Wall Street spec-ulators.

The actual jobs data show that if the monetary central planners have been trying to create jobs through the roundabout method of "wealth ef-fects," they ought to be profoundly embarrassed by their incompetence. The only thing that has happened on the "job creation" front over the last decade is a massive expansion of the bedpan and diploma mill brigade; that is, employment in nursing homes, hospitals, home health agencies, and for-profit colleges. Indeed, the HES complex accounts for the totality of American job creation since the late 1990s.

Some details on the internals of the HES complex provide needed per-spective. In September 2012, for example, there were 6.4 million jobs in ambulatory health care alone; that is, physicians' offices, outpatient care centers, and home health agencies. That was more jobs than in the nation's entire construction industry (5.5 million) and far exceeded nondurable goods manufacturing including food, beverages, paper, chemicals, plastics, and petroleum products (4.5 million).

On top of these ambulatory care jobs there were 8 million in hospitals and nursing homes and nearly 14 million in education from kindergarten through university. In all, the 30.7 million jobs posted for the HES complex on 2012 election eve represented a 27 percent expansion of the job count from when George W. Bush took the oath in January 2000 promising to rejuvenate capitalist prosperity.

Health and education are important social and economic functions, but their role as the sum and substance of the nation's jobs machine also engenders obvious questions of sustainability and financeability. The 6.5 million new jobs in the HES complex since January 2000, in fact, amounted to 2.3X the total number of new payroll jobs over the past twelve and three-quarter years.

What was lurking behind this anomalous trend was the pull of financing from the state, not the flourishing of enterprise and invention on the free market. Direct government financing of medical entitlements and private business outlays spurred by deep tax subsides (i.e., tax excludable employer health benefits) accounted for virtually all of the HES sector growth. These fiscal inputs, in turn, largely represented borrowed funds.

Federal spending for Medicare and Medicaid, for example, had grown from $300 billion in 2000 to $800 billion by 2012, or nearly double the rate of nominal GDP growth. Having gone from a modest surplus to a $1.2 trillion deficit during the same twelve-year time frame, it was evident that the robust growth of federal health spending and the consequent bonanza of new jobs, on the margin, had been deficit financed.

In fact, had the federal health-care boom been financed properly out of current taxation there would have been an offsetting reduction in demand elsewhere in the American economy, meaning less output and jobs in those sectors. The same was true of the single most important category of education spending: the job count in nonpublic higher education had risen by nearly 45 percent during the twelve-year period, and there was no doubt whatsoever as to the source. During this same interval student debt outstanding had exploded from $150 billion to $1 trillion, meaning that the for-profit diploma mills became flush with tuition revenues and soaring payrolls.

Again, had the huge expansion of higher education been funded out of family income and taxes rather than new public debt, there would have been an offsetting reduction elsewhere in the economy. Households would have had less to spend on, say, restaurant meals or mall visits or home improvement projects.

So the Fed's cover story that it was busy fostering job growth is even more specious than it initially appears. What was actually happening was that Washington's fiscal machinery financed 42,000 new jobs per month in the rapidly expanding HES complex during the last twelve years. Since the Fed and other central banks were "open to buy" unlimited federal debt at inordinately low, pegged yields, fiscal financing of the HES complex did not crowd out other current spending; it just burdened future taxpayers.

From a paint-by-numbers perspective, these HES gains were just enough to offset the 35,000 breadwinner jobs lost each month during the same twelve years. Yet since all jobs are not created equal, there can be little doubt that this statistical swap left the Main Street economy badly impaired in terms of income-earning capacity and the true ingredients of economic prosperity.

This juxtaposition has especially adverse implications for future economic growth because there are virtually no productivity gains in the health and education sectors. Instead, health and education output in the GDP accounts is essentially a reflection of inputs, and labor is the preponderant constituent of the latter. The heavy flow of labor into the HES complex thus drags down average productivity and sharply dilutes the overall growth capacity of the American economy.

At bottom, the fundamental thrust of bubble finance has been a tidal shift of economic activity and employment to the HES complex. The Fed's dollar trashing and massive balance sheet expansion (that is, bond buying) has enabled fiscal financing to a nearly unlimited extent; this surge of artificially financed demand, in turn, has drafted millions of jobs into the HES complex that would otherwise not exist.

This channeling of economic activity to the HES complex camouflaged a reality that was never hinted at in any of the triumphal pronunciations by the monetary politburo; namely, that the payroll of the American economy has been shrinking outside of the HES complex for more than a decade. But indeed it has. In January 2000 there were 106.6 million jobs in the American economy outside of the HES complex, but by September 2012 that figure had shrunk to 102.8 million.

For all practical purposes, therefore, a decade of Fed money printing and Wall Street coddling has hollowed out the Main Street economy, backfilling it with fiscally financed expansion of the HES complex. Needless to say, the health sector does not create new wealth; it consumes it. And given the vast public monopolies which dominate most of education, the net returns in that sector are debatable as well. In any event, with the federal government now coming hard upon the limits of Peak Debt, a continuation of the last decade's faux prosperity centered on robust expansion of the HES complex is virtually impossible.

BORROWED RECOVERY ON BORROWED TIME

The Fed's post-crisis money-printing polices gifted Wall Street speculators, as intended, but they also delivered an utterly botched recovery on Main Street. The latter was thinly disguised by an uptick in the conventional cyclical markers: purported "green shoots" like jobs, consumer spending, and inventory rebuilding. Wall Street economists touted this smorgasbord of traditional signposts, contending that even if halting and subpar they added up to another conventional business cycle recovery.

Nothing could have been further from the truth. Beneath the paint-by-numbers simulacrum of recovery espied by Wall Street was a drastic lapse into "borrow and spend" that was a veritable affront to economic rationality. By September 2012, the American economy was fifty-seven months past the late 2007 peak, but there was no rejuvenation of its capitalist engines—just a tenuous bounce in the spending accounts that was plainly unsustainable and unhealthy.

Personal consumption expenditures, as indicated, had risen by $1.2 trillion during that five-year period. Yet $625 billion, or half of this modest gain in PCE—the preponderant 70 percent sector of the GDP—had been financed with transfer payments. This was literally off the historical charts: transfer payments had never previously financed even 20 percent of the five-year gain in PCE after a cyclical top.

Worse still, the sources of consumption spending outside of these government subventions were equally cockeyed. Another $330 billion came from wage and salary disbursements from the service sector, consisting heavily of fiscally driven gains in the HES complex. Thus, behind the tepid expansion of consumption—averaging just 2.4 percent annually in nominal terms during the five years—was a massive amount of federal borrowing, not an organic recovery of incomes.

Indicative of the flagging condition of incomes is the data for wage and salary disbursements to workers in the breadwinner economy. At the peak of the second Greenspan bubble in December 2007, these jobs generated about $3.4 trillion of annualized wages and salaries. Five years later that figure was only marginally higher, having risen by just $70 billion. In other words, wage and salary disbursements in these core sectors of the American economy had amounted to only 6 percent of the $1.2 trillion gain in consumption spending, and had actually shrunk by 7 percent after adjustment for inflation.

Likewise, there had also been only a trivial gain of $25 billion over that five-year period in the other major source of private income; namely, the $3.4 trillion accounted for by proprietors' profits, rental incomes, and interest and dividends. These accounts were also down by about 8 percent in real terms, a five-year shrinkage that had never before occurred in the postwar era.

The $7 trillion core of the American economy's income ledger has thus plateaued. The sum of proprietor's profits, rents, and financial income plus breadwinner wages rose by a trivial 1.4 percent during the five years after the December 2007 bubble peak, and has accounted for less than 8 percent of the PCE growth during that span.

This, too, was freakishly off the historical charts, as is evident in the comparable figures for the five years after the late 2000 cycle peak. During that period these same core income components grew by $1 trillion, not $100 billion, and they accounted for 50 percent of the gain in PCE, not 8 percent. In short, the historical income-based recovery of consumption spending had now been replaced by a modest rebound coming mainly from the fiscally supported periphery.

The American economy was thus still in a debt-push mode, but was losing traction rapidly. During the five-year period ending in September 2012, and notwithstanding the massive fiscal medication after the Wall Street meltdown, PCE grew at only a 0.7 percent annual rate after accounting for inflation. This was a sharp fall from the 3 percent annual rate during the preceding five-year period, and the source of this deceleration was not hard to identify; namely, there was no more MEW; the home ATMs had gone dark.

Not surprisingly, the failure of core income components to recover was echoed in other key macroeconomic performance variables. As indicated previously, fixed business investment in plant, equipment, and software is the sine qua non for long-term economic growth and health, but the anemic rebound that began after June 2009 had already rolled over by the third quarter of 2012.

This was a startling development because it meant that capital spending was now retreating even though it was still 7 percent below its peak of five years earlier in constant dollars. Needless to say, there was no historical parallel. Five years after the 1981 peak, for example, real fixed business investment was up by 11 percent and even after the modest 2001–2002 downturn real business investment rose by 5 percent during the next half decade.

MAIN STREET IN THE FED'S POTEMKIN VILLAGE

Five years into the Bernanke bubble the Main Street economy was still languishing. In all of the previous postwar cycles the prior top had been substantially exceeded sixty months later, but this time there had been no gains in breadwinner jobs, business investment, or the core components of national income. Even the consumption accounts were stagnant. They appeared to have gained new ground only because they had been puffed up with borrowings from future taxpayers that had been intermediated through transfer payments and expansion of the HES complex.

To be sure, the latter had been enough to trigger a spurt of inventory replenishment, especially in sectors like autos where a drastic liquidation had occurred in late 2008 and early 2009. In turn, that fueled an associated boost to rehiring and capital stock replacement. Yet the vicar himself was at a loss to explain the tepid multiplier effects from the initial rounds of restocking goods and variable labor, lamenting that a newly invented condition called "escape velocity" seemingly remained just out of grasp.

The reason the Main Street economy refused to follow the Keynesian script, however, could not be found in the texts of the master or any of the vicar's uncles. The Keynesian catechism has no conception that balance sheets matter, yet Main Street America is flat broke, and that is the primary thing which matters. In fact, half of the nation's households have virtually no cash savings and live paycheck to paycheck (or government check), and most of the remainder are still too indebted to revert to borrowing and spending beyond their current stagnant and often precarious paychecks.

The simple reality is that the household balance sheet is still way over-leveraged, and for the first time in the postwar Keynesian era this leverage ratio is being forced down on a secular basis, thereby permanently restricting the rate of consumer spending. It goes without saying that this dynamic is the inverse of all previous postwar cycles.

The long-standing Wall Street mantra held that the American consumer is endlessly resilient and always able to bounce back into the malls. In truth, however, that was just another way of saying that consumers were willing to spend all they could borrow. That was the essence of Keynesian policy, including the Reagan tax cuts.

At the 1981 peak, for example, the household leverage ratio (household credit market debt divided by wage and salary income) was 105 percent, but this had risen to 117 percent five years later as the economy rebounded and interest rates fell. Likewise, households cranked up their leverage still further during the 1990–1995 cycle, causing the ratio to rise from 130 percent to 147 percent. Then during the five years after the 2000 peak, households took on mortgage and credit card debt with reckless abandon, pushing the leverage ratio from 165 percent to 190 percent, and finally topping out at 205 percent in 2007.

So the fundamental history of post-1970 business cycles is that household leverage was being stair-stepped radically upward. Indeed, that was the true foundation of the endlessly resilient American consumer. Yet according to Stein's law, any trend which is unsustainable tends to stop, and that is exactly what has finally happened.

When the second Greenspan bubble burst, household mortgages, credit cards, car loans, and the like amounted to more than two years' worth of wages. That lamentable condition would have shocked any prudent banker in 1970, and it finally shocked most American debtors when both Wall Street and Main Street buckled violently in the final months of 2008. This trauma brought the reversal of a thirty-five-year trend of steadily increasing household leverage—a turnabout which fundamentally slackened the expansion capacity of the nation's consumption-driven economy.

In an exercise that is just plain perverse, however, the Fed's zero interest rate policies have given households exactly the wrong signal. The effect of radical interest rate repression has been to eliminate the sting of excessive debt by reducing the interest carry on current obligations. The natural impulse of households to sharply curtail consumption and materially reduce debt under current circumstances has thus been vitiated.

By contrast, had the free market been allowed to work its will, interest rates would have likely soared, causing a dramatic escalation of defaults as well as prudentially driven voluntary pay downs of debt. In that manner excess debt would have been dramatically liquidated, and the economy would have been given a chance to "reset" on a healthy basis.

Not surprisingly, since Fed policy has had the opposite aim only modest deleveraging has occurred, and even that has been concentrated in foreclosures on the worst of the subprime home and auto loans. Thus, by mid-2012 the household sector still had just under $13 trillion of credit market debt outstanding, amounting to nearly 190 percent of wage and salary income.

It is perhaps a tribute to our debt-besotted age that most Keynesian economists, whether in the hire of Wall Street or simply enthralled by doctrine, have interpreted this modest rollback as evidence that the household sector has substantially repaired its balance sheet. Under this happy scenario households were said to be on the verge of a new spree of borrowing and spending, meaning that the deleveraging crisis was over and that the American economy would soon regain its former gait.

But why is that plausible when the household leverage ratio is still nearly double its pre-1980 norm? Surely that earlier marker has some validity, given the overwhelming evidence that the US economy performed far better during the golden era after 1954 than it has during the last two decades of explosive debt growth. In fact, Keynesians are drastically misinterpreting the situation with respect to household leverage because they have been lulled into the financial repression trap.

As a result of the Fed's yield pegging, the interest carry on household debt is artificially low, thereby generating far less liquidation and financial distress than would an equivalent burden of debt financed at much higher free market interest rates. Yet to accept the current situation as benign is also to deny that interest rates will ever normalize. The implication is that Bernanke has invented the free lunch after all—zero rates forever.

Implicitly, then, Wall Street economists are financial repression deniers. Their favorite statistical chestnut, in fact, dramatically underscores this delusion. The so-called debt service to DPI (disposable personal income) ratio has fallen sharply, from a peak of 14 percent to about 11 percent by September 2012. This is held to be a signal that "escape velocity" will be achieved any day now because the American consumer will soon become his or her former free-spending self.

The two things profoundly wrong with that ratio, however, are the numerator and the denominator! In a normalized financial environment, the interest carry cost of current household debt would be 50 percent to 100 percent higher than at present. At the same time, the disposable income denominator is not nearly what it's cracked up to be. It doesn't measure ability to pay, as implied, because nearly 50 percent of the $1.34 trillion gain in DPI over the last five years is due to transfer payments, and much of the remainder stems from the fiscally swollen HES complex.

So in yet another twist in the endless Keynesian circle of debt and more debt, the household sector is now purportedly ready to borrow again because its debt service-to-DPI ratio has been artificially deflated by deficit financed transfer payments and central bank interest rate repression. In truth, the household sector's trivial amount of deleveraging to date is just the beginning of its corrosive impact on PCE growth and GDP expansion. The nation's households are not even close to having repaired their balance sheets, meaning that the next phase of deleveraging will actually result in a body slam to the Keynesian aggregates.

PEAK DEBT AND THE WAGES OF KEYNESIAN SIN

The proximate cause of this recession waiting to happen is the federal government's unfolding encounter with Peak Debt. The latter is not a magical statistical point such as a federal debt ratio of 100 percent of GDP, but a condition of permanent crisis. From the failed election of 2012 forward, every dollar of additional borrowing will induce new political and financial pressures while every dollar of spending cuts and tax increases will further impair the rate of GDP growth.

The mainstream notion that there is a choice between fiscal austerity and fiscal stimulus is wishful thinking. It does not recognize that owing to the triumph of crony capitalism and printing-press money America has become a failed state fiscally. Deficits and debt have now reached the point where they are too large and too embedded in social, economic, and political realities to be resolved. Accordingly, what passes for fiscal governance will become a political gong show that will make the New Deal contretemps pale by comparison.

What lies ahead is a continuous, mad-cap cycling back and forth—virtually on an odd-even day basis—between deficit cutting and fiscal stimulus to the GDP. Thus, deficit cutting will be in play every twelve months or so in order to purchase enough "conservative" votes to raise the federal debt ceiling by another trillion dollars or so. Yet every upward increment will become harder to pass in the House and Senate, ever the more so as the debt ceiling soon breaks above the $20 trillion mark and begins to soar well above 100 percent of GDP.

The fact is, the great unwashed masses on Main Street know full well that Washington is trifling with national bankruptcy, so the debt ceiling votes have become the one clarifying legislative moment in which they can demand a halt to the madness. Accordingly, the template from the August 2011 debt ceiling crisis will become the recurring framework of fiscal governance: in return for more debt ceiling, the reluctant House and Senate majorities which are finally assembled will get a new package of fiscal restraint in the form of targets, promises, and processes to develop plans to implement budget savings.

Before the ink is even dry on these deficit reduction packages, however, they will become part of the permanent, rolling "fiscal cliff"; that is, a recurrent series of pending tax and spending shocks that would cause negative GDP prints and adverse job reports if implemented. In effect, the Main Street economy will appear to be continuously confronted by the prospect of a "fiscal recession" or a dip in activity because it will be viewed as too weak to absorb the tax increases and spending cuts needed to close the nation's yawning and unshakeable budget gap.

And so short-duration fiscal support measures like the payroll tax holiday and extended unemployment benefits will be enacted on even days in order to bolster a faltering economy. These "stimulus" measures, needless to say, will only exhaust the available debt ceiling headroom and accelerate the next debt crisis.

This impending struggle with Peak Debt, in turn, will unleash a hammer blow to household consumption spending that will be orders of magnitude more severe than was the loss of MEW after 2007. This threat is owing to the fact that the fiscal gong show now unfolding will almost certainly trigger a drastic upward lurch in both the savings rate and the tax rate on household incomes.

These inexorable developments will mark the beginning of the great unwind from decades of borrow and spend. Needless to say, the Keynesian doctors and their Wall Street fellow travelers have not even begun to contemplate the repudiation this will bring to their model of printing-press prosperity.

As detailed below, there will now be relentless tax increases and spending cuts as far as the eye can see. This fiscal sword of Damocles will hang over the American economy on a permanent basis, cutting down to size that great artificially swollen edifice known as the American Consumer Economy once and for all.

One prong of this shift will be a drastic increase in the household savings rate because chronic threat of cutbacks in Social Security and Medicare will finally drive home the need to save for retirement. As indicated earlier, the pre-1980 household savings rate averaged 8.5 percent of disposable personal income at a time when the baby boom was only entering the labor force. Now with 4 million boomers scheduled to reach retirement age each and every year until 2030, the fiscal basis of the New Deal's Faustian bargain on social insurance is certain to buckle.

The resulting continuous debate on actual and potential benefit cutbacks will instill fear throughout the population, even if the actual social insurance cuts are modest, halting, and prospective. Consequently, the savings rate could easily return to the pre-1980 norm or even higher. Yet if the current 3.7 percent savings rate merely reverted to the 8.5 percent historical average, it would extract an incremental $600 billion from DPI.

In the same manner, the crash of bubble finance and desperate Keynesian tax cutting it elicited have resulted in a sharp but unsustainable decline in the rate of taxation on household income. Thus, in late 2007 personal income taxes and employee payroll tax contributions amounted to $2.49 trillion, or 17.5 percent of GDP. On the eve of the 2012 election, however, the direct tax take from household income had actually declined to 15.5 percent of GDP, thereby releasing $300 billion for additional consumption spending.

Needless to say, the era of fiscal reckoning ahead will result in a reversal of this free lunch tax policy at the same time that the savings rate is rebounding. In rough order of magnitude, the combination of these reversals from the current artificial régime of low taxes and low savings could take upward of $1 trillion out of the household consumption stream. And that assumes savings rates and tax rates revert only modestly to the pre-1980 norm.

Nor would this represent some kind of harsh punishment for high living or a reversion to reactionary Hooverite policy. In truth, no viable economy can survive on chronic fiscal deficits nor can it fail to save at a sufficient rate to fund a healthy level of investment in productive capital assets. The blithe assumption to the contrary which animates current policy rests on self-serving clichés such as "deficits don't matter" and the Chinese savings glut.

THE EPIC GENERATIONAL MISTAKE

Dick Cheney's shibboleth is now receiving a brutal comeuppance, however, as the Fed and other central banks reach the outer limits of their capacity to absorb incremental bond issuance. In this respect, it is evident that the crisis of government deficits and debt throughout the developed world—Japan, Europe, and the USA—reflects a common condition.

Sovereign debt everywhere is vastly overvalued owing to monetary repression. Yet that condition is also artificial and unsustainable: the lesson of southern Europe is that sovereign debt will succumb to a violent free fall when and as central bank "price keeping" operations are withdrawn, fail, or even come into doubt.

At the same time, the hoary tale that America's savings function had been outsourced to China and other mercantilist exporters was but a lame invention by the Fed to camouflage its destructive money printing. In truth, the pitifully low US savings rate over the past several decades reflects a colossal financial deformation; namely, a mistaken belief among US households that there was no need to save out of current income, but that they could spend all that came in and then borrow some more.

This epic generational mistake stemmed in large part, as has been seen, from the Fed's serial asset bubbles in stocks and housing, which egregiously misled households about their true wealth; and also from the unwarranted confidence that the nation's vast social insurance benefit distributions could be sustained indefinitely and in full. A crucial pivot point in American financial history has thus arrived because all of these foundational assumptions are about to be invalidated.

Housing asset values have already crashed by 33 percent and have mounted only a tepid recovery. But they will soon undergo another thundering setback when the baby boom retirement army is forced to liquidate millions of empty nests in order to survive financially. Needless to say, the next generation, saddled with $1 trillion of student debts and small earned incomes, will not be open to buy. Since prices inexorably fall in a bidless market there will be nothing to break the decline except an insolvent government.

The social insurance system is now entering an era of permanent funding crisis and chronic political turmoil. And, as detailed in chapter 32, the Bernanke stock market bubble is heading for a thundering meltdown which will vastly eclipse that of September 2008. So what lies ahead is endemic fiscal crisis, wrenching financial market dislocations, and relentlessly rising fear about financial security on Main Street.

All of this will cause household behavior to change fundamentally; that is, it will lay low America's vaunted "consumption units." Indeed, the coming sharp rise in tax rates and savings rates will cause a drastic hit to consumption spending even if these adjustments take several years to unfold. For example, if a $1 trillion increase in household savings and taxes is rolled in over five years, it would reduce the nation's $11.1 trillion level of PCE by nearly 2.5 percent annually in nominal terms. For a half decade running, therefore, the central component of GDP could be reduced by 5 percent annually in real terms (assuming 2–3 percent inflation).

Needless to say, recidivist Keynesians and their supply-side fellow travelers will propose "economic growth" as the way out of this emerging economic box canyon of higher taxes and higher savings. But their fiscal panaceas of lower taxes or higher spending will be powerfully thwarted because these measures require extensive balance sheet runway—that is, short- and medium-term deficits—that no longer exists.

To be sure, advocates of fiscal stimulus will claim growth multipliers based on one or another set of "goal-seeked" statistical manipulations. But unless they want to sign up to Art Laffer's magic napkin, none of the policy measures available will be close to 100 percent self-financing. Given a 20 percent marginal Federal tax take, for example, fiscal stimulus measures would need to generate a 5X GDP multiplier in order to break even. And that is the profound dilemma of peak fiscal debt: there is no remaining headroom in the national debt for policy makers to gamble with play money stolen from future taxpayers.

So the American economy faces a long twilight of no growth, rising taxes, and brutally intensifying fiscal conflict. These are the wages of five decades of Keynesian sin—the price of abandoning the financial discipline achieved by Dwight Eisenhower and William McChesney Martin during the mid-twentieth century's golden age.

CHAPTER 32

THE BERNANKE BUBBLE
Last Gift to the 1 Percent

AS DETAILED IN CHAPTER 31, EVEN THE TEPID POST-2008 RECOVERY was not what it was cracked up to be, especially with respect to the Wall Street presumption that the American consumer would once again function as the engine of GDP growth. It goes without saying, in fact, that the precarious plight of the Main Street consumer has been obfuscated by the manner in which the state's unprecedented fiscal and monetary medications have distorted the incoming data and economic narrative.

These distortions implicate all rungs of the economic ladder, but are especially egregious with respect to the prosperous classes. In fact, a wealth-effects driven mini-boom in upper-end consumption has contributed immensely to the impression that average consumers are clawing their way back to pre-crisis spending habits. This is not remotely true.

Five years after the top of the second Greenspan bubble (2007), inflation-adjusted retail sales were still down by about 2 percent. This fact alone is unprecedented. By comparison, five years after the 1981 cycle top real retail sales (excluding restaurants) had risen by 20 percent. Likewise, by early 1996 real retail sales were 17 percent higher than they had been five years earlier. And with a fair amount of help from the great MEW raid, constant dollar retail sales in mid-2005 where 13 percent higher than they had been five years earlier at the top of the first Greenspan bubble.

So this cycle is very different, and even then the reported five years' stagnation in real retail sales does not capture the full story of consumer impairment. The divergent performance of Wal-Mart's domestic stores over the last five years compared to Whole Foods points to another crucial dimension; namely, that the averages are being materially inflated by the upbeat trends among the prosperous classes.

For all practical purposes Wal-Mart is a proxy for Main Street America, so it is not surprising that its sales have stagnated since the end of the

Greenspan bubble. Thus, its domestic sales of $226 billion in fiscal 2007 had risen to an inflation-adjusted level of only $235 billion by fiscal 2012, implying real growth of less than 1 percent annually.

By contrast, Whole Foods most surely reflects the prosperous classes given that its customers have an average household income of $80,000, or more than twice the Wal-Mart average. During the same five years, its inflation-adjusted sales rose from $6.5 billion to $10.5 billion, or at a 10 percent annual real rate. Not surprisingly, Whole Foods' stock price has doubled since the second Greenspan bubble, contributing to the Wall Street mantra about consumer resilience.

To be sure, the 10 to 1 growth difference between the two companies involves factors such as the healthy food fad, that go beyond where their respective customers reside on the income ladder. Yet this same sharply contrasting pattern is also evident in the official data on retail sales.

INSIDE RETAIL: LESS FOOD, LESS STUFF

One striking example pertains to grocery store sales. Hidden in the numbers for this core segment is the astonishing fact that inflation-adjusted grocery store sales have fallen by 6 percent since 2007. This is absolutely off the charts, given that real grocery store sales have never fallen at all during any five-year period since 1945. Inflation and food stamps, however, explain why this baleful trend has not been noted by the "consumer is back" touts on Wall Street.

The reported data show a 16 percent sales gain, with grocery store sales rising from $490 billion to $570 billion during the five years ending in August 2012. But that is before adjustment for the 15 percent increase in the food price index during that period—which the Fed chooses to ignore—and, even more importantly, the explosive growth of the food stamp rolls. Tracking the faltering Main Street economy, the latter has soared from 26 million to 47 million recipients since the Greenspan bubble burst. As a result, the food stamp share of grocery store sales increased from 6 percent to 13 percent during the period, or by about $45 billion.

The safety net is absolutely necessary, and apparently no one has informed the monetary politburo that the people can't eat their iPads. Yet what is left after food inflation and the surge in food stamps are set aside is what Main Street households are actually spending in grocery stores out of their own resources. That number was $430 billion in the fall of 2012 (2007$), meaning that households bought $30 billion less of food and groceries in real dollars than they did in 2007. No single figure could better refute the notion that the average American consumer is rebounding or give more effective witness to the actual financial distress among Main Street households.

Nor is it the case that average households have decided to eat less and buy more "stuff" instead. The Census Bureau reports a subcategory of retail sales called GAFO and it includes most basic dry goods and necessities including clothing, shoes, electronics, furniture, furnishings, appliances, sporting goods, stationery supplies, and the like. In the fall of 2007 the sales rate for GAFO was $1.15 trillion, but notwithstanding forty months of recovery from the Great Recession, the sales rate by late 2012 was still down by $75 billion, or nearly 7 percent in inflation-adjusted dollars.

This unprecedented plunge in real GAFO sales is another crucial indicator that the era of shop-until-they-drop consumers is over. After all, the GAFO sales category embodies the very "stuff" that has been relentlessly accumulated in American closets, pantries, garages, living rooms, bedrooms, and kitchens for nearly a half century. Again, the break with prior cycles could not be more dramatic. During the five years after the 1991 downturn, for example, real GAFO sales rose by 18 percent. Likewise, helped along by MEW, it rose by 9 percent during the five years ending in mid-2005.

In the more discretionary categories, the reversal from prior recovery patterns is even more dramatic. Lawn, garden, and hardware sales fell by 18 percent in real terms during the five years after the 2007 peak. Five years after the July 2000 peak, by contrast, sales in this category had risen by nearly 25 percent. In a similar vein, new car sales have fallen by 10 percent in real terms during the last five years compared to nearly a 40 percent gain during the 2000–2005 cycle.

In short, the shopping basket of Main Street households has sprung a giant leak, thereby nullifying the consumer-as-Energizer-bunny predicate underpinning Wall Street's recovery narrative. The four basic retail categories reviewed above—grocery, GAFO, lawn/hardware, and autos—accounted for two-thirds of retail sales, or about $2.7 trillion at the August 2007 top. Five years later constant dollar sales in these four basic segments were $2.45 trillion, meaning that household purchases had declined by a stunning $250 billion, or 9 percent.

This condition defines the post-Keynesian reality now upon the nation, and also hints at the perverse effects of the Bernanke money-printing spree. As indicated, on an inflation-adjusted basis total retail sales fell by 2 percent, or $70 billion, during the five years ended in August 2012. Given the $250 billion drop in the four core categories reviewed above, the implication is that all other retail categories grew by a goodly $170 billion. Not surprisingly, the overwhelming share of this latter figure is accounted for by online sales, which grew from $300 billion to $400 billion in real terms during 2007–2012.

Yet the online retail channel remains heavily the province of the prosperous classes. According to surveys by the National Retail Federation, households with incomes under $50,000 account for only *about 20 percent of online sales, indicating that average consumers have realized only a small share of the e-commerce uplift.* By contrast, nearly 40 percent of online sales were attributable to households with incomes above $100,000.

So in the short run, the Fed's wealth effects policy has delayed the day of reckoning: it has encouraged the top 10–15 percent of households, which own 90 percent of the nation's financial assets and which have benefited from the 115 percent rise in the S&P 500, to resume the consumption party.

TALE OF TWO RETAILER GROUPS

That the consumption party is highly skewed to the top is born out even more dramatically in the sales trends of publicly traded retailers. Their results make it crystal clear that Wall Street's myopic view of the so-called consumer recovery is based on the Fed's gifts to the prosperous classes, not any spending resurgence by the Main Street masses.

The latter do their shopping overwhelmingly at the six remaining discounters and mid-market department store chains—Wal-Mart, Target, Sears, J. C. Penney, Kohl's, and Macy's. This group posted $405 billion in sales in 2007, but by 2012 inflation-adjusted sales had declined by nearly 3 percent to $392 billion. The abrupt change of direction here is remarkable: during the twenty-five years ending in 2007 most of these chains had grown at double-digit rates year in and year out.

After a brief stumble in late 2008 and early 2009, sales at the luxury and high-end retailers continued to power upward, tracking almost perfectly the Bernanke Fed's reflation of the stock market and risk assets. Accordingly, sales at Tiffany, Saks, Ralph Lauren, Coach, lululemon, Michael Kors, and Nordstrom grew by 30 percent after inflation during the five-year period.

The evident contrast between the two retailer groups, however, was not just in their merchandise price points. The more important comparison was in their girth: combined real sales of the luxury and high-end retailers in 2012 were just $33 billion, or 8 percent of the $393 billion turnover reported by the discounters and mid-market chains.

This tale of two retailer groups is laden with implications. It not only shows that the so-called recovery is tenuous and highly skewed to a small slice of the population at the top of the economic ladder, but also that statist economic intervention has now become wildly dysfunctional. Largely based on opulence at the top, Wall Street brays that economic recovery is

under way even as the Main Street economy flounders. But when this wobbly foundation periodically reveals itself, Wall Street petulantly insists that
the state unleash unlimited resources in the form of tax cuts, spending
stimulus, and money printing to keep the simulacrum of recovery alive.

Accordingly, the central banking branch of the state remains hostage to
Wall Street speculators who threaten a hissy fit sell-off unless they are
juiced again and again. Monetary policy has thus become an engine of
reverse Robin Hood redistribution; it flails about implementing quasi-
Keynesian demand–pumping theories that punish Main Street savers,
workers, and businessmen while creating endless opportunities, as shown
below, for speculative gain in the Wall Street casino.

At the same time, Keynesian economists of both parties urged prompt
fiscal action, and the elected politicians obligingly piled on with budget-
busting tax cuts and spending initiatives. The United States thus became
fiscally ungovernable. Washington has been afraid to disturb a purported
economic recovery that is not real or sustainable, and therefore has continued to borrow and spend to keep the macroeconomic "prints" inching
upward. In the long run this will bury the nation in debt, but in the near
term it has been sufficient to keep the stock averages rising and the harvest
of speculative winnings flowing to the top 1 percent.

The breakdown of sound money has now finally generated a cruel end
game. The fiscal and central banking branches of the state have endlessly
bludgeoned the free market, eviscerating its capacity to generate wealth
and growth. This growing economic failure, in turn, generates political demands for state action to stimulate recovery and jobs.

But the machinery of the state has been hijacked by the various Keynesian doctrines of demand stimulus, tax cutting, and money printing. These
are all variations of buy now and pay later—a dangerous maneuver when
the state has run out of balance sheet runway in both its fiscal and monetary branches. Nevertheless, these futile stimulus actions are demanded
and promoted by the crony capitalist lobbies which slipstream on whatever dispensations as can be mustered. At the end of the day, the state
labors mightily, yet only produces recovery for the 1 percent.

THE GREENSPAN AXIOM:
HOW THE FED GIFTS THE 1 PERCENT

The financial market rebound since March 2009 is replete with evidence
that bubble finance leads to a profoundly destructive perversion of free
markets. We are in the Fed's third wealth effects levitation of financial assets
and the resulting gift to adroit speculators has now become crystal clear. In
each cycle the Fed has eventually lost control of the speculative Furies, re-

sulting in a spectacular bust and thumping decline in the price of the most risky asset classes; that is, junk bonds, growth-oriented commodities (e.g., copper), emerging market currencies, commercial real estate, high-beta equities, and endless Wall Street wagers embedded in over-the-counter swaps.

In the bust phase there is a bonfire of losses which are mainly absorbed by slow-footed Main Street investors and their proxies including pension funds, mutual funds, and other institutional fiduciaries. Within the circle of hedge funds and trading houses further losses are absorbed by the most reckless and leveraged punters among them, along with true believers who are too slow to let go of losing trades.

The key feature of the bust phase is that it is short and violent. Approximately 95 percent of the stock market sell-off in 1998, for example, occurred during just four trading days. Likewise, 80 percent of the dot-com-NASDAQ meltdown in 2000 transpired within fifteen weeks. Even more dramatically, 90 percent of the 45 percent sell-off between the Lehman event and the March 2009 bottom occurred during just eight trading days when risk assets were crushed by waves of panicked selling.

Following hard upon the capitulation sell-offs came massive liquidity injections by the Fed and elongated periods of bottom fishing that generated spectacular returns to adroit and usually leveraged speculators. Needless to say, the objects of their speculations were exactly those risk-asset classes which had been taken to the woodshed and beaten to a pulp during the short intervals of panic. In this respect, the violently erratic run over the past decade of the Russell 2000 index of small-cap (mainly) domestic stocks provides a striking example of the manner in which the Fed's arbitrary cycling of the financial markets and the macroeconomy creates fantastical windfalls to the 1 percent.

The Russell 2000 composite index is about as close a proxy for Main Street America's small-business sector as can be found on the public markets. Hundreds of companies in the index have market caps of only $100–$200 million, and the median is just $500 million; only a small slice of the Russell 2000 companies have market caps of over $1 billion, and 95 percent of its composite sales and earnings are US based.

Moreover, a random sample of Russell 2000 company names literally resonates its broad diversity of Main Street business addresses. Covering the waterfront from manufacturing to transportation, retail, banking, and services, it includes Alaska Air, American Axle, Applied Micro Devices, Bank of the Ozarks, and Beaver Homes. Moving down the list there is also Bob Evans Farms, Carmike Cinemas, Freight Car America, Ethan Allen Interiors, James River Coal, Maidenform Brands, Red Robin Gourmet Burgers, and Vanda Pharmaceuticals.

Needless to say, the Russell 2000 index was a winner during the Second Greenspan bubble, rising from 340 at the bottom in October 2002 to 820 exactly five years later at the market peak in October 2007. This amounted to nearly a 20 percent compound return for the 401(k) investor; and for Wall Street speculators employing leverage, options, and advanced market-timing algorithms, returns ranged between 50 and 100 percent annually for a half decade running.

These giant gains did not reflect a Main Street economy which was getting 2.5 times better. As has been seen, this five-year period was one of Fed-engineered faux prosperity where there were no new breadwinner jobs and much inflated consumer spending owing to trillions of MEW. There was also a veritable hemorrhage in the nation's current account with deficits totaling $3 trillion and a corresponding enfeeblement of the tradable goods sector. So, too, the Greenspan bubble period witnessed tepid investment in capital assets outside of commercial real estate, the accumulation of $7 trillion of new household and business debt, and a drastic deterioration of public finances owing to the two Bush wars and tax cuts.

None of this mattered, of course, because the market was trading off the liquidity injections of the Fed, the Greenspan Put, and the daily chatter of economic data "prints" which were falsely spun to suggest a robust and sustainable recovery. Accordingly, when the Lehman event unexpectedly shattered the bubble illusions, the Russell 2000 violently plunged back close to its October 2002 bottom, reaching a level of about 360 on March 9, 2009. This was a thundering 55 percent loss from the pre-crisis peak, but it was not the result of price discovery on the free market.

Instead, it was the consequence of an inside job: the temporary loss of confidence in the Fed's money machine by the inner ring of Wall Street traders and hedge funds. These fast money traders liquidated giant positions with lightning speed, leaving Main Street home gamers and their mutual fund proxies grasping at straws before they could even turn on their trade stations. Indeed, the fast money was quickly on the other side of the trade, pouring into short positions with malice aforethought and quietly duplicating a thousand times over the windfall gains being made on the "big short" in subprime mortgages so famously publicized by financial journalists.

The astounding truth is that nearly all of this ruinous 55 percent decline in the Russell 2000 index occurred during just twelve brutal trading days between the Lehman event and the March 2009 bottom. Worse still, during most of those days the correlation within the index reached 0.95, meaning that two thousand companies with vastly divergent business prospects traded sharply lower in exact lockstep. Laughably, the Nobel Prize for economics had been awarded to nearly a dozen glorified math modelers over the last decades who have espied in such moments the glories of "efficient markets" at work.

This is balderdash. Only a financial system addicted to and whipsawed by central bank money printing can produce such erratic, capricious, and correlated results. What is implicated here is not the doings of the free market but the corruption of free money. For that reason, the Greenspan axiom that financial bubbles can't be prevented but only punctured and then bailed out afterward is downright perverse. Now in its third iteration, this policy is, in fact, the backstage mechanism by which society's income and wealth are being redistributed to the top 1 percent.

It goes without saying that during the Russell 2000 crash the fast money traders did not lose 55 percent—not by a long shot. It was the Main Street "investors" and their proxies—mutual fund managers like Bill Miller—who got fleeced, owing to the naïve belief that they were investing in stocks for the long run and that picking good companies mattered. So the true evil of the Fed's financial bubble-making sits right here: Main Street investors had no clue that their cherished "stock picks" could drop 55 percent in a matter of months because in an honest free market share prices wouldn't inflate to absurd heights in the first place, nor plunge irrationally during a monetary panic afterward.

Main Street investors thus inexorably become "bottom bait" as the fast money feverishly forces bursting bubbles to capitulation lows. Eventually overcome by desperation and fear, these "investors" are the last ones off the boat, selling into the bottom layer of losses and retreating to the sidelines measurably poorer. It is no wonder then that Wall Street has a bad name and that with each round of financial boom and bust fewer and fewer real money investors come back to the casino.

LEVITATION WITH SHADOW BANKING CREDIT, NOT REAL SAVINGS

It doesn't really matter, however, because the liquidity bailout phase of the Fed's bubble finance cycle generates unlimited fuel for the carry trades. Indeed, virtually free short-term money means that stocks and other risk assets can be margined, optioned, and re-hypothecated over and over. Thus, when the fast money regains confidence in the central bank "put" the market can be reflated on shadow banking system credit. Real savings from Main Street households are essentially unnecessary.

During the Bernanke bubble the reflation has been fast, furious, and absurdly unwarranted, as underscored by the phony recovery evidence highlighted above. Yet this time it took the Russell 2000 only twenty-five months to scream past its former high, reaching 850 by early April 2011. This meant that vanilla traders generated 50 percent annual returns during the period, and state-of-the-art hedge funds employing leverage, options, and charting algorithms easily tripled or quadrupled their money.

The data make abundantly clear that in goosing the "risk on" trade the nation's central bank was doing no favors for the Main Street rank and file. The second thundering financial market crash within a decade had been more than enough to keep the home gamers on the sidelines and mutual fund managers begging for investors. During the twenty-five months of the miraculous Bernanke reflation, in fact, domestic equity mutual funds experienced a $200 billion outflow and daily share volume collapsed, especially when robotic HFT (high frequency trading) volume is removed from the figures.

There is not much doubt, therefore, that the overwhelming bulk of the $1.5 trillion gain in the Russell 2000 during the short interval between March 2009 and April 2011 was captured by Wall Street traders and hedge funds. And it is also evident why Wall Street has loudly brayed for more quantitative easing (QE), ZIRP, and other liquidity injections ever since; namely, these massive gains in the index of Main Street businesses represent liquidity-driven momentum trading, not the repricing of a fundamental improvement in small-company profitability.

In fact, the great fiscal contraction ahead owing to Peak Debt means that small-business profits are heading south. The fact that the Russell 2000 was sitting at another all-time high just under 900 in early 2013, was thus striking evidence that the stock market is being massively propped up by speculators counting on the Fed to continue to juice the "risk on" trade.

Needless to say, the 2012 election outcome bolstered hopes for new rounds of money printing and Wall Street coddling from the Eccles Building; that is, the top 1 percent ended up with the best friend they ever had returned to the White House. After all, Bernanke is now Obama's Fed chairman and the open market committee is increasingly populated with raging money printers, like Vice Chairman Janet Yellen, who were appointed by the current White House.

While this is seemingly ironic given that Obama was reelected essentially on a platform of "fairness" for the middle class, that was content-free campaign rhetoric. The true irony is that political progressives are so indentured to Keynesian theories of demand stimulus that they have eagerly turned the nation's central bank over to Wall Street lock, stock, and barrel.

Under this perverse arrangement, the ministerial work of keeping interest rates at zero and Wall Street flooded with fresh cash from massive Fed bond buying is performed by befuddled academics like Bernanke and career policy apparatchiks like Yellen. So in the name of encouraging the people to borrow and spend, these hired hands keep the carry trades well lubricated and generate continuous opportunities for speculators to extract vast economic rents from deformed financial markets.

JUNKYARD OF WINDFALLS

In this respect the Bernanke bubble since September 2008 has been a fantastic moveable feast which conferred upon speculators innumerable opportunities to scalp windfalls from the crash-and-reflation template described above with respect to the Russell 2000. As previously indicated, the junk bond market was an especially egregious case. In May 2008 the $950 billion of junk bonds outstanding traded to a yield of about 10 percent according to the leading (Merrill Lynch) market index, but by the bottom of the financial crash in March 2009 yields had soared to 23 percent.

Since yield is the inverse of price, the implicit meaning is that the outstanding pool of junk bonds had lost roughly half of its market value, or a staggering $450 billion. Needless to say, millions of 401-K investors, who had been flushed into junk bond mutual funds by the Fed's "risk-on" promises, were now being carried off the field on their shields.

Yet while Main Street was still licking its wounds, Wall Street greeted the Fed's announcement of quantitative easing in March 2009 as the equivalent of a horn call at a fox hunt. Speculators flocked into the smoldering ruins of the junk bond market and by the end of 2009 had driven the Merrill index yield all the way back down to 10 percent. This meant that the market value of these busted bonds had doubled in nine months, and that fast-money speculators employing leverage had quadrupled their money, or more.

Self-evidently, the debt-laden companies which had issued these junk bonds hadn't recovered miraculously during that thirty-nine-week interval, but Wall Street confidence in the Bernanke Put had. In fact, the $1.1 trillion QE1 bond-buying campaign announced by the Fed in early 2009 was a powerful signal to Wall Street that the Bernanke reflation would aim to drive up bond prices as well as stocks. Accordingly, junk bond prices continued to soar and by mid-2010 the Merrill index yield had fallen to 7 percent, meaning that leveraged speculators had doubled their money again.

This explains how the Bernanke Fed has showered speculators with windfalls again and again in the various risk asset classes, yet the problem is not merely the unfairness of these massive unearned rents and the resulting further skew of societal wealth to the top 1 percent. In truth, the Fed's radical financial repression policies cause vast economic deformations, even as they generate gratuitous upward redistributions of the wealth. That is because interest rates are the price of money, and the Fed's drastic manipulation of the bond market has caused massive unnatural flows into risky debt—a distortion that has opened even more lucrative post-bubble gambling venues for Wall Street speculators.

Thus, by the end of 2009 Main Street was still struggling to stabilize itself, but junk bonds had been the return champions of the year. So once again, Main Street investors were lured back into the chase for riches. Accordingly, fresh money flowed into high-yield bond funds like never before, totaling a record $35 billion in 2009 at a time when the nation's purported brush with Armageddon was still fresh, and then kept rising to a $100 billion inflow over the four years ending in 2012.

New money needed an outlet, of course, and the result was the greatest boom in junk bond issuance ever recorded. During 2009–2012 approximately $1 trillion of junk bonds were issued, or two times the issuance during the Greenspan reflation of 2003–2006. Even more importantly, about 60 percent of this huge volume was devoted to the refinancing of existing bonds. So this was the mother of all "refi" booms, and it meant that speculators in busted junk bonds were taken out at par or even premiums to book value.

Never before had so much cash been hauled home by speculators—literally hundreds of billions—for so little valued added. Indeed, the junk bond windfall of the past several years has been wanton, but that is not all. It has also facilitated an unprecedented junk bond maturity extension—that is, a can-kicking exercise—that has unleashed, in turn, even greater windfall gains on the more junior preferred stock and common equity securities of these issuers.

Thus, as of December 2010 there were nearly $850 billion of junk bond maturities pending for 2013–2116. This amounted to a so-called maturity cliff that threatened the financial viability of many, if not most, of the "debt zombie" LBOs previously described. Owing to the junk bond refi boom fostered by the Fed, however, by late 2012 the "maturity cliff" had been smashed down to only $375 billion, or by nearly 60 percent.

Accordingly, the day of reckoning has been pushed back toward the end of the current decade. In the meanwhile, however, private equity shops have experienced a massive windfall: the value of their thin slices of equity of these born-again debt zombies have soared, often by 3X and even 10X orders of magnitude. Likewise, a comparable refi boom in commercial real estate has unleashed a similar drastic rebound of what had been underwater equity investments in struggling strip malls and office buildings.

Needless to say, this is bubble finance at work, not sustainable economic recovery. But pending the next financial meltdown it means that the entire arena of busted leverage—junk bonds, leveraged loans, LBO equity, commercial mortgage-backed securities, underwater mall investments, and much more—has given rise to several trillions of windfall gains to adroit speculators. When coupled with 115 percent recovery in the broad equity markets, and 200–400 percent gains in high-beta equities, it can be well and truly said that the Fed has engineered a fulsome recovery—for the top 1 percent.

HOW THE TOP 1 PERCENT FOUND RICHES IN THE AUTO CRASH

One of the great untruths of the 2012 election campaign was the Obama claim that the auto bailout was a great victory for the people. As has been seen, it was actually just a heist by the aristocracy of organized labor whereby 50,000 auto jobs were shifted from south of the Mason-Dixon Line to its north. But it was also much worse than that. In combination, Washington's fiscal bailouts and the Fed's massive gifts to carry traders generated truly obscene speculator profits in the burned-out districts of the auto belt.

Thus, in the case of the GM bailout the only group that gained beyond GM's 48,000 active UAW members and 400,000 retirees was a few dozen suppliers. Crucially, however, the windfalls even here went to financial speculators. The preponderance of auto parts makers were pulled into bankruptcy, so it was the "distressed" paper of their Chapter 11 estates that reaped the gains. As it happened, speculators in the various classes of their busted loans and securities harvested spectacular upsides literally within months of the White House–orchestrated quick rinse bankruptcy of GM.

To be sure, these GM suppliers, who were owed about $15 billion for parts and material, were not victims—they were enablers. They had taken a reckless risk in continuing to extend forty-five days of trade credit to GM, even though it was obvious that GM was burning cash so rapidly a crash landing was only a matter of time.

In the White House's simulacrum of a bankruptcy court, however, most suppliers got paid a hundred cents on the dollar. Their unsecured claims did not rank very high in the contractual hierarchy of creditors, but their lobbying ranks on K Street turned out to be nine-tenths of the law. Once again, the free market's disciplinary mechanism, in the case of the regulation of trade credit, was given short shrift.

As previously described, I had been the principal investor when the $4 billion auto supplier I had put together (on too much leverage) had been taken down a few years before the White House gravy train arrived in Detroit. But I had learned the reason why suppliers foolishly extended GM trade credit long after it was objectively bankrupt. Most of them, including my company, were up to their eyeballs in debt and had no choice except to "extend and pretend" in order to keep enough cash coming in to pay the interest bill.

GM was therefore at the end of a destructive daisy chain of debt that encompassed the entire auto supply base. When the free market's unsparing campaign to clean house was stopped cold on December 12, 2008, the Bush administration struck a more deadly blow at the vitals of free enterprise than simply granting GM a stay of execution until it could be officially bailed out by the statists who had won the election. In fact, a corollary effect of the bailout was the further evisceration of business credit discipline.

While rarely acknowledged, trade credit is the first line of defense against unsound finance in the American business system. At the present time, there is about $2.5 trillion of trade credit outstanding; that is, payables owed to suppliers by their downstream customers. These debts among companies handily exceed the $1.8 trillion of bank loans and commercial paper owed by nonfinancial businesses.

In the general scheme of business credit, suppliers are unsecured lenders while banks rank above them and are secured by liens on fixed and working capital. As a result of this junior status, suppliers ordinarily have powerful incentives to closely monitor the financial health of their customers, and generally do so with far better ground-level knowledge and insight into their customers' circumstances and current industry conditions than do the commercial bankers.

By refusing to ship on forty-five-day credit, suppliers can exert a powerful braking effect on the financial policies of their customers. Indeed, a "run" among trade creditors on a profligate customer like GM can ordinarily be every bit as swift, contagious, and devastating as a proverbial run on a retail bank. This natural mechanism of financial discipline on the free market has been greatly crippled, however, owing to the massive increase in credit market debt during the era of bubble finance.

As previously indicated, nonfinancial business credit grew from $4.5 trillion to $11.5 trillion over the last eighteen years. Accordingly, as suppliers got deeper and deeper in debt to external lenders, their trade creditor's trump card—refusal to ship on forty-five-day terms—lost its efficacy. They could no longer make this threat because they could not afford a disruption in the daily cash flow needed to service their heavy external debt. In a process that was subtle and incremental, therefore, the business credit system became an ever more fragile chain of debtors who could not afford to safeguard their own trade credit exposure.

This breakdown of the business credit chain reached its epitome in the auto supply base that served GM and the other original equipment manufacturers (OEMs). During the fifteen years before Detroit's crash landing in late 2008, the domestic auto space had become a playpen for Wall Street–based financial engineering, including M&A roll-ups, LBOs, and supplier division spin-offs from the Big Three OEMs. The consistent theme behind all of these maneuvers was to pile the debt higher and higher.

The impact was especially insidious in the case of the huge upstream parts division spin-offs from the OEMs, all of which ended up in bankruptcy. The GM spin-off was called Delphi and its $30 billion in annual sales made it the largest auto supplier in the world.

THE ELLIOT GANG AND PLUNDER OF DELPHI

Delphi was comprised of the former parts divisions—radiators, axles, lighting, interiors—that had been spun out of GM in the late 1990s by investment bankers claiming it would make GM look more "focused" and "manageable." In truth, Delphi was a dumping ground for $10 billion of GM's debt, pension, and health-care obligations, as well as dozens of hopelessly unprofitable UAW plants and billions more of hidden liabilities such as parts warrantees.

Not surprisingly, Delphi hit the wall early, entering Chapter 11 in the fall of 2005. That this spin-off company was intended all along to be a financial beast of burden for GM is evident in its reported financials for its prior six years of existence as an independent company. During that period its sales totaled $165 billion, mostly to GM, but it recorded a $6 billion cumulative net loss and generated negative operating free cash flow. Indeed, saddled with $60 per hour UAW labor costs against non-union competition at $15 per hour, it was kept alive only by an intra-industry Ponzi scheme: Delphi floated bad trade credit to GM and GM massively overpaid Delphi for parts.

Needless to say, Delphi was an economic train wreck that had no prospect of honest rehabilitation, but under pressure from GM and the UAW it remained mired in bankruptcy court for the next four years. In the interim it continued to float billions of GM's payables on the strength of its DIP facility, yet was ultimately able to emerge from Chapter 11 only because the White House auto task force saw fit to pump billions of taxpayer money into its corpse as part of the GM bailout.

The first-order effect of this terrible abuse of state power, of course, was a few more $60 per hour UAW jobs in Saginaw, Michigan, and a few less $15 per hour non-union jobs in Tennessee and Alabama. But the real evil of the bailout lay in its rebuke to free market discipline and the powerful message conveyed by the White House fixers that failure in the marketplace no longer mattered. Even complete zombies like Delphi could be spared, so long as crony capitalism was alive and well in Washington.

The self-evident fact is that Delphi should have been liquidated, with its few viable operations auctioned off and its dozens of uncompetitive and obsolete UAW plants shuttered. The billions of trade credit it had foolishly extended to GM should have been written off, not paid in full by the taxpayers (with GM bailout funds). Yet this capricious assault on the free market was only one of the evils that came from the auto bailouts.

After Delphi was unnecessarily resuscitated with what turned out to be $13 billion of taxpayer money, including $5 billion from TARP and $6 billion from the Pension Benefit Guaranty Corp.'s takeover of Delphi's busted pensions, an even more obnoxious turn of events unfolded. A marauding band of hedge fund speculators were able to scalp an astounding $4 billion profit from a company that under the rules of the free market and bankruptcy law would never have seen the light of day after its original Chapter 11 filing. Indeed, just one of the investors, a so-called vulture fund named Elliot Capital, appears to have realized a 4,400 percent gain, or $1.3 billion, on its Delphi investment, which was taken public in an IPO in the fall of 2011.

The particulars of this case, in fact, reek with the stench of crony capitalism. They powerfully illuminate how the Fed's boom and bust cycling of the financial markets wantonly showers ill-gotten wealth on the 1 percent. According to the SEC filings, Elliot Capital picked up its Delphi position for $0.67 per share in the midst of the auto industry collapse and while both GM and Delphi were still in Chapter 11. It had the good fortune to sell stock to the public two years later at $22 per share.

Perforce, what the filings do not disclose is that in the interim Elliot Capital and its confederates had gained control of the Delphi bankruptcy by buying up the so-called fulcrum securities for cents on the dollar. They then threatened to paralyze GM by not shipping certain irreplaceable precision-engineered parts like steering gears, where GM technically owned the tooling but it was physically hostage in Delphi plants.

Needless to say, in a regular way bankruptcy a judge would have come down on the Elliot Gang like a ton of bricks for contempt; a tough judge might have even figuratively put them in shackles. But under the ad hoc rules of crony capitalism, the law counts for little and political hardball is the modus operandi. This meant that the hedge funds were literally able to strongarm the Obama White House into providing the $13 billion bailout to the Delphi estate. Even auto czar Steve Rattner, who was himself busily fleecing the taxpayers, described the hedge fund position as an "extortion demand by the Barbary pirates."

The winnings of the Elliot Gang are an obscene lesson in how crony capitalism and Fed money printing perverts the free market. Without the $13 billion fiscal transfer Delphi would never have emerged from bankruptcy; and without the flood of liquidity from the Eccles Building there would have been no frothy market on which to unload the Delphi IPO.

As it happened, however, the other vultures in the Elliot Gang had a good feed, too. In particular a credit-oriented hedge fund and spin-off from Goldman Sachs called Silver Point gained a $900 million profit from the deal, and this was not an atypical result: it was one of the most adroit speculators in the busted loans and bonds of overleveraged train wrecks miraculously brought back to life by the Fed's flood of fresh money.

Another huge winner was John Paulson's fund. This time its big short was against the American taxpayer and the gain was a reputed $2.6 billion. But the most egregious windfall was the $400 million gain racked up by Third Point Capital. This hedge fund is run by one Daniel Loeb who had been an Obama supporter in 2008, but had since noisily denounced the president for unfairly picking on the 1 percent.

Given the history here this might have put an uninformed observer in mind of biting the hand that feeds you. Except Loeb didn't stop with his supercilious but widely circulated critique of Obama's purported "class war." Instead, he held fund-raisers for Romney and contributed $500,000 to the GOP campaign.

In so doing, Loeb helped clarify why crony capitalism is so noxious and pervasive. It turned out that another winner from the Elliot Gang's 40X return on the carcass of Delphi was an allegedly passionate opponent of the GM bailout; that is, the author of a famously penned *New York Times* op-ed called "Let Detroit Go Bankrupt."

The ease with which the vultures made their billions from this crony capitalist raid on the US treasury is evident in Mitt Romney's $15 million of Delphi winnings. Based on the timing of this saga, it appears they were obtained while Romney was on the chicken dinner circuit honing his anti–Big Government rhetoric for the upcoming presidential campaign. Call it the Detroit Job.

It goes without saying that with friends like these the free market does not need any enemies. More importantly, under the financial repression and Wall Street–coddling policies of the Fed there is no free market left. Instead, it has been supplanted by a continuous and destructive cycle of boom and bust emanating from the monetary depredations of the state's central banking branch.

In the process of inflating stocks, leverage, and speculation to absurd heights, the Fed finally loses control, transforming the financial markets into economic killing fields. Yet in its panicked reflation maneuvers, it then fosters a vulture capitalist harvest of such magnitude as to be unthinkable on the free market. This is the absurd end game of Greenspan's wealth effects monetary policy and specious claim that bubbles can't be seen, but only left to burst. This is how recovery for the 1 percent happens.

LEAR CORPORATION: PRODIGY OF BUBBLE FINANCE

During 2009–2012 the vultures feasted gluttonously in the Fed's killing fields. Indeed, the Delphi abomination was an endlessly repeated template, even within the smoldering ruins of automotive alley. Thus, the miraculous rebirth of Lear Corporation, the poster boy for the auto industry's excursion into bubble finance, was still another case where riches were extracted from the wreckage. Its two-decade sojourn as a leveraged buyout, IPO, M&A machine and stock market wonder was virtually coterminous with the Greenspan bubble era. Thus, Lear Corporation first emerged as a $400 million sales LBO in 1988—with what appeared to be a unique growth model based on just-in-time seat assembly facilities located near auto assembly plants. In return for rapid sales growth from OEM "outsourcing" of seat assembly, Lear accepted razor-thin margins and extended a huge trade credit to the Big Three; that is, it absorbed their working capital and thereby never made any cash profits.

Lear's revenues skyrocketed from this maneuver, however, permitting it to go public in the early 1990s as a "growth company." In addition to continued huge investments in OEM working capital via the expansion of its seat outsourcing business, it also undertook more than $5 billion of acquisitions to "roll up" suppliers of auto interiors and electronics during the next several years. Accordingly, its sales grew like Topsy from $2 billion in 1993 to $10 billion by 1998 and $17 billion by 2004. Not surprisingly, this stupendous growth absorbed every dime of the company's internal cash flow plus a massive buildup of debt to make ends meet.

At that point Lear had generated immense stock market enthusiasm, sporting a market cap of nearly $5 billion and a 10X return to original IPO investors. What it hadn't generated, however, were profits. In fact, during the two decades between 1991 and 2008 Lear Corporation posted $200 billion of sales, but nearly $1 billion of cumulative net losses.

Like so much else during the Greenspan bubbles, the hit-and-run punters who pumped up Lear's market cap to a preposterous $5 billion were long gone when it became evident that the company was worth zero: the only possible valuation for a company that makes no GAAP net income over two decades. In fact, Lear Corporation was a giant wheel-spinning machine which borrowed $3.5 billion to fund acquisitions and open new plants to supply the Big Three. In return for virtually profitless sales it extended them upward of $4 billion of trade credit—borrowing against its own assets and cash flow as it did.

Accordingly, when GM finally hit the wall, Lear became a bug on its windshield. Yet instead of undergoing the brutal downsizing and deep reorganization that its failed business model required, it went through a quick four-month rinse cycle in Chapter 11, only to reemerge largely intact and with its bad debts from GM paid in full by the White House auto task force.

THE BIG FIX IN MOTOWN

It did not take Wall Street speculators long to realize that both the industry and Lear Corporation would emerge quickly from bankruptcy, thanks to the fact that GM, Chrysler, GMAC, and many auto suppliers were being smeared with $80 billion in taxpayer money. So the fact that Lear went into Chapter 11 with $3.6 billion in debt and came out a few months later with only $900 million of debt completely obscures the real story; namely, that speculators made out like bandits from Lear's faux bankruptcy.

By early June 2009, the operational wheels at GM had ground nearly to a halt and Lear's bonds had dropped to twenty-seven cents on the dollar according to trading services at the time. However, vulture speculators aggressively scooped up this so-called distressed debt because by then it was evident that the "fix" was in, and that the "carry cost" of holding a position in Lear's busted bonds was virtually nothing under the Fed's ZIRP policy. Moreover, there were plenty of good reasons to take a flyer notwithstanding the headline noise about the auto industry's dire state.

The heart of the matter was that the Obama White House had by then made it abundantly clear that there would be no house cleaning on Wall Street. The president's desire to make an example of Citigroup by busting it up had been sabotaged by his own advisors. Likewise, Wall Street's new viceroy in the Treasury Building, Secretary Tim Geithner, had already completed his phony "stress tests" that gave most of the big banks a clean bill of health.

Accordingly, the Fed was free to juice the primary bond dealers with unlimited amounts of fresh cash via Treasury bond and GSE paper purchases in order to levitate financial markets. It was thus "risk on" again with respect to asset classes like junk bonds.

Indeed, with each passing month after the March 2009 stock market bottom it became more evident that the Bernanke put was actually a relentless, turbocharged version of the Greenspan original. So there was enormous potential upside from leveraged speculation in Lear's busted bonds and exceedingly limited downside given the rampant crony capitalism embodied in the auto task force.

General Motors was Lear's largest customer by far, as it was the UAW's largest employer. So there was precious little chance that it would be shrunk down to "GM Lite" in the White House bankruptcy process or that Lear's supply contracts would be cancelled. Most importantly, since the White House fixers had already made it clear that GM's trade debts to Lear would be paid in full, the reorganized company did not need to fund itself with a large working capital revolver.

This was crucial because it meant that Lear's entire enterprise value could be wacked up among its pre-petition bank and bond lenders; that is, the available value could be captured by the vultures because its assets didn't need to be pledged to a new working capital lender. Not by coincidence, therefore, Lear announced a "pre-pack" bankruptcy filing almost to the day—July 5, 2009—that GM exited its fast dash through Chapter 11. As is consistent with normal practice, this deal had already been cleared with the company's principal creditors and provided for expected "recovery" rates for each class of creditor.

In the case of bondholders it was about forty cents on the dollar, meaning that speculators were already well in the money. In fact, when Lear Corporation exited its quickie bankruptcy and its stock began trading on November 9, the package given to its bondholders was worth sixty cents on the dollar, meaning that speculators had doubled their money in about 150 days. But the real "fix" was just getting started.

During the next two years, auto sales recovered smartly from the 9–10 million unit panic lows of late 2008 to a 13–15 unit level after mid-2010. However, as previously indicated, this natural but modest rebound in final sales had a bullwhip effect on production of parts and finished vehicles owing to the auto industry's virtually depleted supply chain. Accordingly, with "booming" production, which was actually just an aggressive one-time fill of the inventory pipeline, even a sow's ear could be positioned as a silk purse.

As previously described, Wall Street triumphantly brought GM public at a nosebleed valuation one year later, and Lear's stock price slipstreamed right behind the expanding auto bubble. It thus came to pass that Lear's busted bonds (which had been swapped for stock) were now valued at the equivalent of 130 percent of par value.

In short, speculators had quadrupled their money from the June 2009 low in just twenty months. And that's assuming that Lear's distressed paper had been bought for cash. Had they employed ultra-cheap and readily available portfolio leverage, hedge fund punters would have made ten times their original investment or more.

So the cleansing therapies of the free market were once again denied. Instead, Washington's central banking branch and fiscal authorities implemented their fixes—bailouts and money printing—and thereby supplanted a healthy adjustment process with a corrupt game of speculation.

Twenty months after the June 2009 auto industry bottom, Wall Street speculators were pocketing massive profits on the auto sector's busted bonds and born-again stocks. Yet this was not because a healthy rehabilitation of the industry had been completed; it was because one had, in fact, been prevented.

THE KEYNESIAN END GAME:
RECOVERY FOR THE 1 PERCENT IS OVER

In the aftermath of the 2012 election the "fiscal cliff" came bounding into the picture. It was greeted by Wall Street as a singular event and inconvenient roadblock in the path to continued economic recovery and ever rising stock averages. The potentates of Wall Street—Jamie Dimon of JP-Morgan, Lloyd Blankfein of Goldman Sachs, and countless lesser lights—therefore demanded that it be rectified by means of a "grand bargain." All that was needed was sufficient political will and bipartisan good faith, they brayed in unison. This was a grand delusion.

The Main Street economy was at stall speed, laboring to stay afloat by means of borrowed money and borrowed time. But it was fast running out of time. In fact, it had already entered the zone of Peak Debt, a place where for the first time in forty years most of Washington's actions and even its inactions will cause the Main Street economy to wobble, weaken, and wilt.

In fact, peak debt will cause the Keynesian fiscal thrusters to swing into reverse. Taxes will rise and households will spend less. Federal benefits will be cut and households will also spend less. The military-industrial complex will slowly starve, meaning less weapons production and jobs, and still more shrinkage of household income and spending. Traumatic and repeated debt ceiling crises will recur, causing fear to spread and savings to rise. Accordingly, household consumption will fall further and business caution will intensify even more.

The fiscal cliff is thus not a singular event or fixable condition on the road to a bigger and better national economy. It is the Keynesian end game: the point where both its truth and its inexorable calamity become clear. The truth is that the conservative critique of Keynesian deficits has been wrong all along. It did not recognize that deficit finance would fuel GDP growth because it didn't reckon that the fiscal deficits could be financed with printing-press money at home and abroad and for decades on end.

And so it was not that deficit didn't matter; it was that printing-press money mattered even more. It permitted spending without earning and investment without saving. It resulted in an artificial prosperity erected on a mountain of debt. But in September 2008, it happened that peak debt on the private side was finally encountered, causing a four-decade-long wave of household and business debt accretion to crest and to subsequently roll over. The resulting steep drop in private spending occasioned one final resort to the Keynesian fiscal thrusters; that is, the extension of the Bush tax cuts, the Obama stimulus, the payroll tax holidays, the Noah's ark of short-term spending, and tax stimulus measures.

But now peak debt has also been reached on the public side of the nation's balance sheet. To be sure, the technical ability of the Fed to print money and buy the state's debt has not yet been exhausted. What has lapsed, however, is the political will to keep on borrowing from the public accounts with reckless abandon; that is, to keep pushing the federal debt ceiling through $20 trillion and beyond.

The implication of the warm-up round of the debt ceiling crisis in August of 2011 was that Washington will now become paralyzed by a complete and worsening inability to secure consensus on raising the federal debt ceiling by more than token amounts, and for a good reason: if it were to be pushed higher by the $5–$10 trillion that would be needed to stay on the current path of Keynesian deficits and central bank bond buying, the national debt would become the overwhelming referendum issue of the 2014 election. In that event, the folk wisdom of the electorate would be summoned in a landslide vote against national bankruptcy—an outbreak that could send Democrats specifically and incumbents generally down to massive defeat.

So Washington will struggle to keep the federal debt ceiling on a short leash, while attempting to push, shove, jam, and jimmy as much of the fiscal cliff's expirations and sequesters as possible under the borrowing limit. Yet it will eventually fail because the fiscal cliff has become way too big for the politicians to finesse by means of gimmicks, phony cuts, and short-term deferrals. In fact, it currently amounts to 5 percent of GDP, or $750 billion at a full-year run rate, and is growing.

So true fiscal contraction will now ensue. In a process of budgetary triage, selective tax credits and cuts will be allowed to expire and the most politically vulnerable spending programs will be shortchanged or abandoned altogether. More importantly, the fiscal battle will become all-consuming with short-term fixes, patches, standoffs, negotiations, and showdowns taking on a 24/7 cadence.

Needless to say, this spectacle of paralyzed and dysfunctional fiscal governance will deliver a fatal blow to business and consumer confidence alike. That will trigger, in turn, a rise in cautionary saving by households and a further hoarding of liquidity by business. Accordingly, the phony recovery of 2009–2012 will come to a desultory end and a long twilight of austerity and deflation will inexorably settle in.

It is no wonder, then, that unreconstructed Keynesians like Professor Krugman hate the Federal debt ceiling with a passion. It is the Achilles heel that will finally stop the nation's mad addiction to borrow and spend. So doing, it will also end the recovery party for the 1 percent. When the great fiscal contraction begins to sap even the headline prints on consumption, GDP, and jobs, the Fed's prosperity model will finally be exposed as fraudulent and impotent.

Even if the monetary politburo invents new, more exotic variations of QE and doubles down on money printing still again, there is one condition it cannot survive: a prolonged run of negative prints from the "incoming data." That will shatter confidence on Wall Street and provide daily proof that there is nothing behind the curtain in the Eccles Building except a printing press that has enabled its balance sheet to become stupid big; that is, host to a rising tower of public debt on the left side and a parallel tower of excess bank reserves on the right.

These twin towers haven't levitated the Main Street economy to date and have no prospect of doing so in the future. Indeed, Main Street's simulacrum of recovery since the BlackBerry Panic has been fueled by one-time factors that are now spent: inventory replenishment and massive fiscal stimulus. Accordingly, a new Wall Street panic is inevitable as it becomes clear that the business cycle and profits are heading south on a permanent basis.

This time the sell-off won't be stopped by central bank money printing and an alphabet soup of borrowing lines because the fast money will see that the Fed is impotent in the face of endemic fiscal contraction. Accordingly, they will sell, and sell, and sell. Then the real fiscal crisis will arise. When the bond market crashes in the sell-off, the carry cost of what is already, objectively, a $20 trillion federal debt will soar. When interest rates normalize, say, by 250 basis points, debt service costs will rise by $500 billion; it will bring the final and complete demoralization to Washington.

In November 2012 the people voted for the only real choice they were presented; that is, for paralysis and stalemate. Now it is only a matter of time before the state finally fails as a fiscal entity. It is out of balance sheet runway, yet so overloaded with mandates and missions that it cannot move forward and it cannot move back. Instead, it will become ever more paralyzed and dysfunctional.

The cruel corollary is that free market capitalism cannot help, either. It has been abused, burdened, demoralized, and impaired by decades of central bank money printing and the speculative raids and rent-seeking deformations which it fosters. Now the White House has a vague mandate that the 1 percent should pay more, but it's too late. The coming crash will leave a lot less to tax.

CHAPTER 33

SUNDOWN IN AMERICA
The State-Wreck Ahead

T
HE WAY FORWARD IS SO RADICAL IT CAN'T HAPPEN. IT WOULD NE-
cessitate a sweeping divorce of the state and the market economy.
It would require a renunciation of crony capitalism and its first
cousin: Keynesian economics in all its forms. The state would also need to
get out of the economic uplift, bailout, and social insurance business and
drastically shift its focus to managing and funding an effective and affordable means-tested safety net.

Restoring fiscal solvency and free market prosperity would also require
the drastic diminution of the state's bloated machinery of warfare and central banking, meaning that the hurdles to true economic recovery are forbidding. Deep shrinkage of the military-industrial complex, for example,
could happen only upon the wholly unlikely abandonment of the inter-
ventionist foreign policy that nourishes it. Likewise, eliminating the
scourge of the Wall Street casino would require restoration of free market
interest rates and honest price discovery in the stock market; that is to say,
elimination of the Fed's open market bond-buying operations and its
régime of financial repression and risk asset levitation.

Alas, none of these solutions are even remotely possible within our now
fully corrupted constitutional framework. The latter is no longer a system
of democratic choice and governance; it is a tyranny of incumbency and
money politics. As such, it has set in motion a financial doomsday machine
that is inexorably speeding toward national fiscal insolvency and monetary
collapse.

The perpetual fiscal stimulus that attends the two-year congressional
election cycle, and the K Street lobbies and the PAC-centered campaign
funding system which lubricates it, drives the public debt skyward without
respite. Similarly, the Fed has become a self-declared vassal of Wall Street,
meaning that no change in the current destructive policy régime is thinkable because trillions of inflated asset values depend upon its perpetuation.

Eighty years on from the New Deal, therefore, crony capitalism has reached an end-stage metastasis. There is no solution except to drastically deflate the realm of politics and abolish incumbency itself; the machinery of the state and the machinery of reelection have become coterminous. But prying them apart would entail sweeping constitutional surgery: a package of amendments to extend congressional and presidential terms to six years, ban incumbents from reelection, provide public financing of candidates, strictly limit the duration of campaigns (say, eight weeks), and impose a lifetime ban on lobbying by anyone who has been on the legislative or executive payroll.

Only such sweeping constitutional change could cope with the real evil of the current system; namely, the contamination of the entire economic and financial system by a money-driven 24/7 régime of electioneering and hyper-politics. The problem thus is not merely that politicians are bought and paid for by special interests, but also the fact that they are absorbed in plenary debate and maneuvering with respect to every nook and cranny of our $16 trillion national economy. In that respect, Karl Rove's American Crossroads is as problematic as the oilmen's American Petroleum Institute.

Indeed, suffocation of the free market in totally mobilized political struggle is the ultimate evil of the Keynesian predicate. It causes every tick of the unemployment rate and every tenth of the GDP report to trigger waves of political praise, blame, and maneuver. The resulting nonstop partisan sound bites about how "our" plans would make the outcomes better and how "their" policies have made them worse continuously reinforce the presumption in favor of more state action to bolster the economy.

The end stage of this oppressive din is the pompous visage of Karl Rove on Fox News ticking through his white-board list of where the Democrats have failed to create jobs, investment, growth, and happiness throughout the land. The subtext is always the same; namely that "job creators" didn't get a big enough fix of tax cuts and the nation's economy is faltering due to overtaxation. Needless to say, these claims are demonstrably untrue. In fact, investors and entrepreneurs among the top 1 percent have the lightest tax burden since Herbert Hoover. Likewise, the overall federal tax take of 15.2 percent of GDP in 2011 had withered to 1948 levels.

The GOP renunciation of fiscal discipline is thus Keynesian, not fact based. In order to compete with the Democrats it has gone into the state-sponsored growth business. Republicans now effectively concede that prosperity cannot be left to the comings and goings of producers, consumers, and investors on the free market; it must be constantly dialed up through the machinery of the IRS. So Washington has become thoroughly bipartisan in its relentless pursuit of schemes for the state to fix the private economy—a modus operandi which guarantees the bankruptcy of the former and the failure of the latter.

FULL-RETARD ANTEDILUVIAN: THE FORGOTTEN STANDARD OF HONEST PUBLIC FINANCE

It was not always that way. Eighty years ago in the spring of 1932, during the nation's darkest economic hour, Herbert Hoover's Washington intensely debated what used to be the essential duty of government; that is, making its revenue and expenditure accounts balance. So doing, the Hooverites imposed economies on nearly every federal department and implemented a manufacturer's sales tax and other revenue increases before adjourning in June 1932.

These actions are considered full-retard antediluvian in today's "enlightened" times. So the fact that the nation's moribund economy actually leapt from the starting blocks within weeks has been, necessarily, Photoshopped out of the official New Deal portrait. Similarly, the economic golden age of low inflation and solid growth which accompanied Ike's refusal to cut taxes until the budget was balanced and politicians had actually earned the right to dispense them has been airbrushed out of GOP history. Instead, JFK's reluctant capitulation to the deficit financed tax-cut theories of Professor Walter G. Heller has taken its place in the Republican fiscal archives.

Indeed, the memory of Washington's pre-1960 regimen of honest public finance, like the ancients' knowledge that the earth was round, has been extinguished, as it were, by the equivalent of a flat-earth fiscal doctrine. At its core, Keynesian doctrine amounts to the crank notion that public borrowing can create private prosperity by topping up the macroeconomic bathtub with incremental "demand." As detailed in earlier chapters, this doctrine has evolved into numerous confessions which now extend far beyond the orthodox Keynesian catechism.

As we have seen, the Democrats first converted to the new economics version of perpetual deficit finance back in the 1960s. But when the giant Reagan deficits broke out there emerged a revised standard version. It was manifested in the GOP's claim that invisible supply-side "incentives" were responsible for the incremental GDP growth after 1983 that was plainly attributable to the quite visible and massive government borrowing.

Eventually there arose the Karl Rove–*Fox News* variation, and it is no less statist despite all its anti-government arm waving. Its Lafferite predicate is that by not paying its bills, Washington can cause the private economy to grow faster! Like any free lunch panacea, of course, such deficit-driven "growth" will also lead to fiscal and momentary collapse as surely as would the perma-deficits of the Democrat "big spenders."

To be sure, Republicans insist that the magic lies in "incentives" not "deficits," but there is not a modicum of evidence to support the Laffer napkin at the current (moderate) range of marginal income tax rates. So in defiance of every historical tradition of sound public finance, the GOP became hooked on the patent medicine of tax cuts.

After stealing credit for the economic recovery from Volcker's victory over inflation, the so-called conservative party actually became a wellspring of statist schemes and cures for goosing the private economy by turning the tax code into an instrument of economic management. During the last thirty years, therefore, Republican politicians have rarely met a tax cut they couldn't embrace. In the cause of economic stimulus through "incentives" for the prosperous classes, they cut taxes on income, capital gains, dividends, estates, carried interest, machinery investments, small business, green energy, black energy, cow pasture energy, and countless more "stimulants" that K Street had on offer.

The GOP apostasy reached an absurd extreme in the 2012 election, when candidate Romney promised to use his four-year term not to balance the budget, but to stump up 12 million new jobs. Herbert Hoover, who well understood the imperative need to keep the state and the private economy separated by a sturdy fence, was doubtless rolling in his grave. For in proposing $5 trillion in additional deficit-financed tax cuts, the GOP candidate was thoroughly conflating the two realms—promising to improve on the private economy's delivery of jobs and GDP by mortgaging the public sector's balance sheet.

In earlier times, Romney's plan would have been seen as crude pandering: an election-year gambit to relieve current American taxpayers of their duty to pay the cost of the government they had elected. But no longer. Giant fiscal deficits "as far as the eye can see" had been properly viewed as an ominous threat when they unexpectedly flared up in late 1981. By contrast, the allegedly "courageous" Ryan plan for fiscal 2013 did not sweat giant budget deficits for a moment: it did not get around to a balanced budget, even on paper, until a quarter century later.

If there was any doubt that the nation has two fiscal free lunch parties, the wanton profligacy of the George W. Bush era had already removed it. Still, the case was sealed by the sheer farce of the 2012 campaign in which Obama couldn't name any tax he would raise except on the 2 percent, and Mitt Romney couldn't say out loud a single federal program he would cut other than Big Bird's stipend.

When every provision of the tax code and each line item of federal expenditure becomes a "jobs" program, then a condition of dissolute fiscal promiscuity has arrived. Under those circumstances there is no way to restore sound fiscal governance except by means of a constitutional chastity belt; that is, an inflexible balanced budget amendment. And a ban on a commitment of military forces anywhere outside of US borders without explicit authorization of Congress would help, too.

THE EPIC IRONY OF THE KEYNESIAN ERA: FAILURE OF THE SAVIOR STATE

So it now transpires that sundown is descending upon America owing to the failure of the state, not the machinery of capitalism. That is an epic irony. The state has grown by leaps and bounds since the New Deal era precisely because it was presumed to transcend the imperfections and disabilities alleged to inhere in the free market.

Those defects comprised the familiar indictment of laissez-faire. They included destructive swings in the business cycle; structural economic dislocations among regions, industries and communities; and humanitarian failure with respect to the ills of aging, poverty, unemployment, disability, and disadvantage. So the state was given one assignment after another; that is, to counterbalance the business cycle, even out the regions, roll out a giant social insurance blanket, end poverty, house the nation, massively subsidize medical care, prop up old industries like wheat and the merchant marine and foster new ones like wind turbines and electric cars.

In the fullness of time, therefore, the state became corpulent and distended—a savior state that could no longer save the economy and society because it fell victim to its own inherent shortcomings and inefficacies. Taking on too many functions and missions, it became paralyzed by political conflict and decision overload. Swamped with unquenchable demands on the public purse and deepening taxpayer resistance, it became unable to maintain even a semblance of balance between its income and outgo. Exposed to naked raids by powerful organized interest groups and crony capitalists, it lost all pretense that the public interest was distinguishable from private looting. Indeed, the fact that Goldman Sachs got a $1.5 billion tax break in the New Year's Eve fiscal cliff bill, legislation allegedly to save the middle class from tax hikes, is a striking if odorous case.

These evident warts and blemishes, however, remain invisible to the Keynesian touts who peddle risk trades on Wall Street and counsel more fiscal stimulants from Washington. Indeed, having become so inured to the state's modern role as an omnipresent agent of economic fixes and fiscal largesse, they are stunningly blind to the oncoming "state-wreck." Yet the mounting failures of the modern welfare-warfare state are every bit as serious as the ancient defects of the free market. Worse still, the misdeeds once attributed to the robber barons of laissez-faire are small potatoes compared to the depredations and extractions owing to the crony capitalists of the Keynesian era.

THE DEMISE OF GROWTH: THE "STATE-WRECK" AHEAD

The American economy would tumble into a paroxysm of economic contraction and financial market meltdown if its three umbilical cords to the state were severed. That is, the private economy has reached a state of utter dependence upon the central bank's printing press, the bipartisan fiscal régime of perma-deficits, and the military-industrial complex that bolsters what remains of the manufacturing sector.

None of these lifelines are sustainable and each may be nearing its asymptote. But like an end-stage alcoholic who finally drinks himself to death, the system is so dependent upon these dispensations of the state that it will inexorably drift toward catastrophe.

Ironically, the enormity of this danger is obscured by the simulacrum of prosperity that flows from these very dependencies. To take one example, we have seen that half of personal consumption expenditure growth since 2007 has been funded by deficit-financed transfer payments. That's phony growth borrowed from future taxpayers and injected into the economy by the consumption spending of transfer payment recipients.

If these safety net transfer payments were properly paid for by taxing the American public there would be no magical boost to GDP—just a state-commanded reshuffle among the citizenry of already existing income from current production. Accordingly, as indicated in chapter 31, even a modest normalization of the rates of household savings and personal taxation would reduce personal consumption expenditures by $1 trillion, or nearly 10 percent.

Yet that is only the leading edge of the state dependency that now undergirds the American economy. These enormous props include the massive inflation of energy and food commodities spurred by the Fed and its global confederation of money-printing central banks, and the freakish expansion of defense spending in a world where there are no advanced industrial state enemies. Save for these state-induced bubbles, the nation's industrial economy would have been shrinking at an astonishing rate.

Not surprisingly, this reality is not immediately evident in the GDP aggregates which so mesmerize the Keynesian commentariat. Total shipments of manufacturing goods in the early fall of 2000, for example, were $4.3 trillion and had risen to $5.8 trillion by September 2012. This $1.5

trillion pickup seems impressive on the surface but is only marginally respectable, in fact, when the 25 percent gain in the GDP deflator during this period is stripped out.

Coincidently, this cumulative rise in the price level amounted to 2.2 percent per year, or almost exactly what the Bernanke Fed claims to be its ideal inflation target. Yet really? Even with this modestly dishonest rise in the price level, the aggregates are not what they seem to be. In fact, constant dollar-manufacturing shipments rose by just $200 billion (2012$), not $1.5 trillion during the twelve-year period, meaning that most of the nominal dollar gain was Bernanke's wondrous inflation.

Even then, the resulting real growth in manufacturing shipments, at an anemic rate of 0.3 percent annually, might pass for the Greenspanian version of prosperity. According to the theory laid out in his memoirs, the United States doesn't really need to grow its manufacturing output, since the Chinese and other exporters are chronic oversavers and eager to lend vast amounts of their excess savings to high-living Americans so they can buy Chinese manufactures. When the onion is peeled further, however, even that twisted rationalization doesn't wash.

Even as total manufacturing shipments grew by just 4 percent in constant dollars between 2000 and 2012, shipments of real defense goods soared by 41 percent. That contrast alone is damning. Defense output by definition contributes nothing of economic value, and in this instance, the national security purpose for this giant expansion is also exceedingly hard to ascertain.

Indeed, it is now evident that there were never more than a few hundred Al Qaeda; that the invasions of Iraq and Afghanistan were grotesque mistakes and failures; that America's rampaging war machine has generated new enemies throughout the Middle East and near Asia; and that a duly elected "peace president" has barely stopped the military spending momentum, even as he has begun to retract our imperial footprint.

Yet this needless defense bubble is only part of the illusion of growth. Another part stems from the great commodity inflation generated by the Fed and its global convoy of money printing central banks after 2000. In round terms, energy prices rose 100 percent and food prices by 50 percent during this twelve-year period. Accordingly, another huge part of what passes for growth in manufacturing shipments consisted of food and energy inflation in the underlying raw materials, not true gains in manufacturing value-added.

Shipments of food and energy manufactures thus doubled during this period, rising from $1.3 trillion to $2.6 trillion. Yet when the vast inflation in these sectors is stripped out, constant-dollar output expanded by a much more modest 12 percent. And the internals of this $1.3 trillion inflation-swollen pickup are even more revealing.

Upward of $1 trillion, or 80 percent, of this gain represented windfalls to the upstream raw material factors; that is, farmland in Iowa, royalties on the North Slope, and rents to the princes and emirs who occupy the desert redoubts of the Persian Gulf. Under a régime of sound money, by contrast, economies throughout the world—especially those of China and the other BRICs—would have grown much more slowly during this twelve year period. In turn, lower-gear growth would have generated modest relative price gains for scare raw materials, not the elephantine windfalls and virulent commodity inflation that issued from the Eccles Building and the People's Printing Press of China.

At the same time, the fact of this rampant commodity inflation means that the balance of the US manufacturing sector between 2000 and 2012 was downright punk. Thus, constant dollar shipments of non-defense consumer durable goods declined by 17 percent; real shipments of non-defense capital goods dropped by 24 percent; and real output of non-durable goods outside of food and energy shrank by a staggering 25 percent. In short, absent the printing press and war machine the American manufacturing economy would have already tumbled into a ruinous decline.

Indeed, in round aggregate numbers the picture is nothing less than startling. At the turn of the century, the US manufacturing economy outside of defense and the food and energy complex (e.g., "core manufacturing") generated constant-dollar output (2012$) of $5 trillion. After twelve years of the (second) Greenspan bubble and the Bernanke bubble, core manufacturing output had tumbled to $4 trillion. This $1 trillion, or 20 percent, shrinkage in real terms is yet another measure of the big lie which undergirds the current simulacrum of prosperity.

THE FISCAL CLIFF:
WRECKING BALL OF THE KEYNESIAN STATE

The "fiscal cliff" gong show which traumatized the nation at the end of 2012 was rooted in a destructive symbiosis between Wall Street and Washington. It was portrayed by the mainstream media as an impetuous display of partisan strife, petty politics, and willful stubbornness, especially among Tea Party Republicans. But in reality the "fiscal cliff" was a boogieman trumped up by traders who needed a stock market prop and Washington politicians in thrall to the sundry Keynesian doctrines of tax-cutting and spending stimulus.

In truth, nearly every single item that constituted the fiscal cliff was a perfectly appropriate and rational fiscal policy action to reduce the $1.2

trillion federal deficit that persisted menacingly during the fourth year of a business recovery. As has been seen, the expiring $110 billion payroll tax abatement had been a stupid idea from the beginning, and the $300 billion Bush tax cuts for everyone had been unaffordable for more than a decade.

Likewise, the alternative minimum tax rise of $125 billion was only going to hit households which for years had not been paying their fair share of taxes due to loopholes. Most especially, the pending automatic 8 percent cut (sequester) of defense spending was a no-brainer relative to the insane explosion of defense spending from $300 billion under Clinton to $700 billion at present.

Ironically, therefore, there was good reason for Washington's inertia and its inability to fashion a consensus to avert the cliff. The clownish action of the Senate in the wee hours of New Year's morning in enacting a pork-dripping Christmas tree of tax giveaways was an outrage not because of the manner in which it was done, but because it was done at all.

In truth, with the awful specter of "peak debt" lurking around the corner, the $650 billion per year of spending cuts and revenue increases should have been permitted to go forward because they constituted a rare instance in which meaningful long-term deficit reduction could have been obtained without need for legislative action and the impossible, labored maneuvering required to achieve majorities in our current fractured system. In fact, Washington blew an opportunity to sit on its hands while enabling a permanent $4.6 trillion 10-year shrinkage of the deficit, a meaningful downpayment on the urgently needed return to fiscal sobriety. And it could have been done politically. The wild arm-waving about the fiscal cliff that animated Washington and financial TV did not have much resonance with the Main Street electorate; the unwashed public was more or less resigned to taking its lumps.

By contrast, there can be little doubt that the near hysteria was fomented by Wall Street and its organs and shills in financial TV. After decades of getting its way, Wall Street simply presumed it was entitled to any and all actions by Washington that might avert a recession and thereby keep the stock averages high and the "risk-on" trades prospering.

At the same time, official Washington did not have to be coaxed into doing Wall Street's bidding. K Street was automatically mobilized to defend its tax goodies and DOD contracts. Likewise, the ranks of elected politicians were prepared to bang the deficit lever hard, having received decades of house-training on the notion that the US economy should be propped up with fiscal "stimulus" whenever it "underperformed" its full employment potential.

As a practical matter, economic "underperformance" was taken by GOP tax cutters and liberal spenders alike to mean GDP growth of under 3 percent and unemployment over 6 percent. Since the reality of the American economy fell far short of those vestigial benchmarks, politicians reflexively insisted that the state continue to dispense what amounts to economic waste (e.g., unnecessary defense spending) and unaffordable gifts to the middle class (i.e., the Bush tax cuts) so that the private sector could spend and consume beyond its means; that is, avoid a recession that is inevitable because fiscal retrenchment is unavoidable.

It thus happened that needing to avoid a collision with peak debt, Washington kept racing straight toward it, desperately searching for a political consensus to ensure that Uncle Sam would incur a trillion-dollar deficit for the fifth year in a row. Indeed, the definition of enlightened and courageous policy action had taken on a perverse aspect: statesmanship now consisted of cancelling any and all previously enacted policy measures which *would cause too little red ink.*

The symbiosis between Wall Street's petulant Cramerites and Washington's champions of Keynesian tax and spending medications thus came to a flailing and twisted estate. Their bedraggled charge up the $650 billion "fiscal cliff" on behalf of more red ink was in reality a noisy and incoherent repudiation of the very tax increases and spending cuts which they had put into law only a few years earlier to reduce that very same budget deficit. Washington was now not only ensnared in a circular process that would inexorably intensify, but was also slipping into a fatal corruption of the policy discourse that would make fiscal governance increasingly impossible.

The fiscal cliff coverage by the Reuters news service, an unembarrassed megaphone of Wall Street's "recovery" delusions, illustrates the growing incoherence of the fiscal narrative. A news story on the eve of the cliff condemned lawmakers for failing to reach a compromise "to avoid the *harsh* tax increases and government spending cuts scheduled for January 1."

Harsh? The implication was that the foundation of the US economy was just fine, and that borrowing another $1.2 trillion to keep the party going another fiscal year was a no-brainer. All that was needed was for the politicians to summon sufficient courage to uncork some more red ink.

Accordingly, there was not a hint of recognition that 2013 would mark months forty-two through fifty-four of the National Bureau of Economic Research–defined recovery cycle, and that since 1945 the average expansion had lasted only forty-five months. Even a few years earlier, the Keynesian doctors would have recommended weaning the patient from its fiscal ventilator at this late point in the cycle.

In fact, these pending "harsh" fiscal contraction measures were not some gratuitous roadblock that had been erected by enemies or aliens; that is, arbitrary impediments to the American economy's divine right to permanent prosperity, even if borrowed. Instead, they embodied the trap left by years of national fiscal cheating on a grand scale; that is, Washington's pretense that just one more year of fiscal freeloading would be enough to put the American economy back on the road to self-sustaining growth.

THE NEW NORMAL AND THE NEED TO WEAN THE US ECONOMY FROM ITS FISCAL VENTILATOR

As has been seen, that was a terrible delusion. The American economy had been steadily weakening year in and year out since the turn of the century. As indicated, during the past twelve years real GDP growth has averaged an anemic 1.7 percent; there has been zero net new payroll jobs; and the very best gauge of future economic growth prospects—real business investment in plant, equipment and technology—has expanded a barely measurable rate of 0.8 percent annually.

This is the new normal; it is not a temporary fluke or a transient condition related to sunspot cycles. It most certainly does not betray inadequate application of Keynesian tax-cutting and spending medications. Instead, it reflects an economy that has been stunted by the massive debt overhang thirty years in the making and the vast structural damage that resulted from this national LBO equivalent; that is, the offshoring of tradable goods production, the inflation of domestic costs and wages from borrowing $8 trillion from the rest of the world, and the busted investments strewn around the US economic landscape in commercial real estate, retailing, and lodging and leisure, among others.

In the face of peak debt, sustainable and stable public finance requires that the American economy be weaned from its fiscal ventilator regardless of the GDP growth and unemployment stats. The "fiscal cliff" is thus not a one-time event or accident of the fiscal calendar or a bump in the road owing to a stubbornly slow business cycle recovery. Instead, it is now a permanent fiscal condition and signals that the fifty-year Keynesian joy ride is over.

Rather than habitually and incessantly cutting taxes and boosting spending in order to ameliorate the business cycle and goose jobs and GDP, fiscal policy will revert to a protracted conflagration over the dollars and sense of balancing the budget accounts. Peak debt will force this epochal reversal, but the money-driven politics and statist ideologies of Washington have no capacity to make the turn. Summoned by financial necessity to return to the fiscal postulates of Eisenhower, Truman, Henry

Morgenthau Jr., Herbert Hoover, Carter Glass, Calvin Coolidge, and Governor James Cox of Ohio, too, fiscal governance will have a crash landing. Indeed, as signaled by the initial fiscal cliff fiasco of 2012, the state-wreck of the Keynesian era is at hand.

The instrument of the impending demise, the permanent fiscal cliff, is a perverse consequence of Washington's adoption of the ten-year budget cycle. Until now, the latter has quietly functioned to obfuscate a régime of perma-deficits embraced by the Keynesian consensus in Washington and the perma-bulls of Wall Street on the pretext that the American economy was operating below potential.

Yet the device of a ten-year budget is downright devilish. It sanctions heavy-duty fiscal stimulus in the current fiscal year or two to goose economic performance, while proffering the simulacrum of fiscal responsibility in the out-years through prospective policy measures and assumptions which close the budget gap, at least on paper. But it is now evident that this expedient has put fiscal policy on a destructive treadmill: the "out-year" phase of fiscal retrenchment will never come because the combination of peak debt and the next decade's deluge of baby-boom retirements virtually guarantees that the US economy will never attain "escape velocity"; that is, sustained GDP growth above 3 percent and unemployment below 6 percent.

As each new fiscal year approaches, therefore, the nation's politicians, house-trained on the Keynesian predicate nearly to the last man and woman, will discover that their previous out-year deficit reductions are now "harsh" instruments of "fiscal drag" that threaten to prolong the national economy's "underperformance." Yet the food fight over which tax increases or spending cuts to defer, or which new temporary stimulus measures to adopt, will generate thundering partisan conflict and recriminations.

The blaring dissonance and daily dysfunction of the failing Keynesian state, in turn, will further undermine confidence and animal spirits in the remnants of the nation's floundering free market economy. In an awful feedback loop, this will pave the way for another economic performance shortfall and therefore another "fiscal cliff" crisis each and every year as far as the eye can see.

THE $20 TRILLION TOWER OF DEFICITS AHEAD

This syndrome should be obvious enough by now. But what is drastically underestimated is the true, staggering size of the permanent fiscal gap. The intensity and persistence of conflict and dysfunction that this will generate on both ends of Pennsylvania Avenue is not even dimly appreciated by either the politicians or the commentariat. Washington is literally in the grip of a fiscal doomsday machine of its own design.

The starting point for grasping the enormity of the coming fiscal conflagration is a singularly towering number; namely, the $20 trillion of cumulative federal deficits that would occur over the next ten years under the aforementioned "unrosy scenario" (chapter 27) and the tax and spending policies advocated during the 2012 campaign by the Republicans and Democrats, respectively. Needless to say, this scenario will not play out in the real world because it would raise the federal debt to $37 trillion, or 160 percent of GDP, by the end of the period (2022).

The sheer dysfunctionality of fiscal governance, therefore, will be generated by the unending struggle over the tax increases and spending cuts that will be needed to forestall the implicit national insolvency built into the current Keynesian fiscal state; that is, the neocon warfare state, the bipartisan social insurance régime, and the Republican religion of low taxes. Yet the reason this scenario is only dimly perceived by official Washington is that the so-called baseline budget forecasts issued by CBO and OMB are essentially economic fairy tales.

These ten-year fiscal projections assume a return to "normalcy" in macroeconomic performance and therefore drastically understate out-year deficits. For example, the January 2012 CBO ten-year baseline for fiscal 2013–2022 assumed that wage and salary income would grow by 5.2 percent annually and that income and payroll tax collections would reach about 39 percent of these earnings by 2022.

Yet this is unaccountable. During the twelve years since 2000, nominal wage and salary incomes grew by only 3 percent per year, and the income and payroll tax take was just 32 percent in fiscal 2012, even after eliminating the impact of the payroll tax holiday. The potential for a massive downside hit to CBO's long-term revenue outlook is thus self-evident.

Were wages and salaries to grow again at only 3 percent during the next decade, for example, income and payroll tax collections would be lower than the CBO baseline by nearly $700 billion in 2022 owing just to economics. Beyond that, it would take protracted, bloody partisan conflict to raise the revenue take from 32 percent to 39 percent of wages and salaries. This implies a 22 percent, or $700 billion, annual tax policy increase from baseline levels. To realize that gain would require the permanent expiration of every single item that stood on the New Year's Eve fiscal cliff, including the Bush rate cuts on all taxpayers; every one of the business, student, and family tax credits; the lower tax rates on capital gains and dividends; the deferral of the massive leap in AMT collections; and much more.

As it happened, most of these massive revenue drains got permanently extended, meaning that the combination of unrosy scenario economics and these eleventh hour tax changes will produce a massive revenue shortfall from the CBO baseline. What emerged from the first fiscal cliff battle, in fact, was a permanent $500 billion per year tax reduction, meaning that the combination of sober economics and revised tax policy will reduce the CBO revenue baseline by $1.2 trillion per year by 2022. The level of partisan conflict that would be needed to close that gap in the years ahead is almost unimaginable, but owing to the looming approach of peak debt there will be little alternative.

This prospect of ceaseless Washington strife over tax raising is not farfetched. In fact, there has already been a real world demonstration of a ten-year CBO error of this same magnitude. Thus, its ten-year outlook for fiscal 2002–2012 projected that federal revenues would reach $3.5 trillion for the year just ended (fiscal 2012), but the actual result was $2.5 trillion. This 29 percent shortfall is nearly identical to the potential 30 percent shortfall from the current CBO baseline for 2022 reviewed above.

Issued in August 2000, the CBO's then ten-year outlook did not contemplate the GOP-led slash and burn of the tax base that would occur over the coming decade. Nor did it envision that the steadily failing US economy would generate far less taxable income than projected, and far more resort to Keynesian tax-cut stimuli such as the payroll tax holiday and the innumerable corporate tax gimmicks pushed through by K Street lobbyists doing their part to promote "recovery."

So the $1 trillion shortfall in CBO's revenue forecast for 2012 was the product of a double whammy of less growth and more tax cuts. Strikingly, both errors in CBO's decade-ago forecast are virtually certain to be repeated in the current ten-year baseline.

By the same token, a decade back CBO had projected that federal revenues in fiscal 2012 would come in at 20.5 percent of GDP, or nearly identical to the 21 percent of GDP that it is now forecasting for 2022. In fact, actual 2012 receipts came in at only 16 percent of GDP, meaning that about one-third of the $1 trillion revenue shortfall for 2012 was due to economics and the balance was caused by legislative action that depleted the revenue base.

There is a striking difference in CBO's prospective forecasting error this time around, however. Back in August 2000, the federal revenue take was at a historic high of 20.5 percent of GDP. So even though its descent to 15–16 percent of GDP over the next decade caused a large miss compared to the CBO projections, it did provide a Keynesian tailwind to the otherwise tepid rate of GDP growth. Since there was still runway available on Uncle

Sam's balance sheet, deficit-financed tax cuts happily pilfered future GDP from unborn workers and taxpayers.

This time around, however, there will be a ferocious Keynesian headwind. The tax take from GDP is starting at a fifty-year low and then is projected to rise by nearly one-third, to 21 percent of GDP under the CBO baseline for 2022. Needless to say, the battle to wrestle higher taxes through the Congress and the resulting relentless squeeze on the Main Street economy will push the growth of jobs, wages, and GDP sharply downward.

THE EXPLOSIVE COST OF THE WELFARE STATE IN A SUNDOWN ECONOMY

The struggle to extract much higher taxes will also compound the spending-side error factor in the current CBO baseline. The reason is that a weak, tax-burdened national economy will generate far more joblessness, poverty, and economic distress than represented by CBO's wildly optimistic assumptions. Transfer payment spending will thus soar far above its baseline projections.

As indicated, when it comes to excessive optimism, CBO puts Rosy Scenario to shame. The aforementioned ten-year growth rate for annual wages and salaries, for example, amounts to an annual gain of nearly $4.5 trillion by 2022. By contrast, at the actual 3 percent growth rate of the past decade the gain would be only $2.3 trillion. That $2.2 trillion difference is a lot of phantom middle-class income, to say the least.

Likewise, CBO's baseline forecast assumes that 20 million new payroll jobs will be created in the next decade. Unaccountably, the green eye-shades at CBO conjured this cornucopia of jobs when in reality there had been essentially zero growth of non-farm payroll jobs in the last decade. Consequently, there is likely $200 billion annually of higher transfer payments unaccounted for in CBO's rendition of Rosy Scenario.

Again, this potential drastic underestimate would be a replay. CBO projected in its 2002–2012 baseline that entitlement and other mandatory spending during fiscal 2012 would total $1.85 trillion, or 10.8 percent of GDP. It actually came in at $2.1 trillion and 13.2 percent of GDP. While some of this huge $200 billion difference was owing to legislated changes such as Part D Medicare benefits, most of the transfer payment overshoot was due to the much weaker than forecast national economy.

In fact, the full story of the CBO drastic underestimate of mandatory spending lies in the crash of the labor force participation rate. Had it remained unchanged at the 2002 level of 66.5 percent, unemployment would have averaged nearly 12 percent during fiscal 2012 versus the 5 percent that CBO assumed (and 8.3 percent actual average).

What this illustrates is that the headline unemployment rate is largely irrelevant to the cost of federal transfer payments. The real driver is the so-called employment-population ratio; that is, the share of adult citizens holding jobs, even part-time ones. By definition, those not employed are likely to receive unemployment insurance, means-tested welfare such as food stamps, or move into the social insurance system via the disability insurance rolls or early retirement on Social Security.

In fact, this is exactly what happened in the past decade. The employment-population ratio fell from 62.5 percent in 2002 to an average of 58.5 percent during fiscal 2012, meaning that there were 10 million more adults not employed owing to the ratio deterioration. Overall, the number of adult citizens (over sixteen) not employed, including ordinary course retirees, rose from 82 million to 101 million during the period. It was this 19 million rise in the count of citizens not employed that drove the transfer payment share higher, and also caused CBO's baseline projection to drastically underestimate entitlement program costs.

This is virtually certain to happen again. Given the headwinds of higher taxes and higher savings rates, the American economy will be lucky during the next decade to create 7 million new jobs, as measured by the household survey (including part-time jobs). That would be no small achievement, since only 7 million jobs were added to the household survey during the bubble-fueled decade ending in fiscal 2012. Even then, however, the number of adults not employed would rise to 113 million by 2022, a figure dramatically higher than is implicit in the CBO baseline.

In fact, the "hockey stick" syndrome that has recurrently led to excessively optimistic long-term budget forecasts is strikingly evident in the CBO assumptions for disability insurance, unemployment, food stamps, and other means-tested programs. These core safety net programs are projected to decline sharply by 25 percent in real terms. This makes no sense whatsoever, especially in light of the last decade's steep gains.

In constant dollars (2012$), these programs grew from $160 billion in 2002 to $270 billion at present (fiscal 2012), or about 5 percent annually. And the driving force was food stamps, which grew in constant dollars from $25 to $80 billion, and disability insurance, which rose from $90 billion to $140 billion. The caseloads and costs for these programs exploded for a reason which is not going away anytime soon; namely, the American economy is failing and leaving more and more adult citizens with few choices except to lean on the state.

Accordingly, CBO's projected march back down the hill to $200 billion by 2022 for this complex of safety net programs is exceedingly implausible; this is especially so in the face of the aforementioned likelihood that the number of adults not employed will rise by another 12 million. Even a 2 percent real growth rate for these safety net programs from current levels, therefore, would result in $150 billion higher nominal outlays for entitlements by 2022 than in the current CBO baseline.

These trends vivify why the Keynesian state will end in political paralysis and enervating conflict. Indeed, viewed in the big-picture framework this outcome seems certain. On the one hand, the US economy can no longer grow at even close to its historic rate because it is trapped in $54 trillion of debt and a debilitating 3.6X leverage on national income that was accumulated during the Keynesian era of high living.

At the same time, the share of the population not employed is soaring owing to the baby boom's aging and the post-Keynesian economy's inability to create new jobs. Accordingly, the state will be afflicted by insuperable demands on its waning fiscal resources: between 2002 and 2022 it is likely that the number of adult dependents (i.e., not working) will have risen from 82 million to 113 million, or by nearly 40 percent.

It is in this context that the cost of the nation's jerry-built safety net and social insurance system will become painfully oppressive. As the dependent population continues to grow, caseloads and expenses for the above-mentioned safety net programs will rise sharply. There will also be additional spillover into Medicaid and social insurance, especially as retirement-age citizens are forced to fully exploit Social Security and Medicare eligibility. Even a 1–2 percent pickup in caseload or program utilization for these latter programs would generate an extra $50 billion per year in federal outlays, but a much larger overshoot is easily imaginable.

Overall, CBO's Rosy Scenario projects that the social insurance and the means-tested safety net programs will cost $3.5 trillion by 2022, or 14.1 percent of its projected GDP. By contrast, under the unrosy scenario outlined above and with minimal allowance for the CBO's underestimates of dependency, caseloads, and costs, likely outlays for these programs will exceed $3.7 trillion, or 16 percent of GDP; that is, social insurance and the safety net will absorb the entirety of federal revenue that will be obtained under the recently installed "New Year's Day" tax policy before even a dime is spent on national defense, general government, or debt service. Therein lies the conflagration ahead.

WHEN THE NEOCONS GOT THEIR GUNS: ANOTHER CONTRIBUTOR TO THE NATION'S EMPTY TREASURY

The reason that the battle over the permanent fiscal cliff will be unimaginably brutal is that the Republican Party was hijacked by modern imperialists during the Reagan era. As a consequence, the conservative party cannot perform its natural function as watchdog of the public purse because it is constantly seeking legislative action to provision a vast war machine of invasion and occupation. So doing, it acquiesces to liberal demands for butter in order to get the neocons their guns.

Here again lies an apostasy. Robert Taft and Dwight Eisenhower were bitter rivals for the 1952 Republican nomination, but neither of them believed that the US had an imperial responsibility to police the globe. The Eisenhower Minimum was predicated on overwhelming nuclear deterrence directed at the paranoid dictatorship which occupied the Kremlin, but its fiscal cost was modest because it eschewed land wars and the buildup of massive conventional military capacity. In provoking the resignation of the army's top generals, Ike lined up in the tradition of Senator Taft and Herbert Hoover. Taft had rightly argued that a "cavalry in the sky" could keep the nuclear peace while avoiding the massive fiscal drain of a cavalry on the ground with hundreds of forts, depots, and supply lines sprawling the globe.

At the present time, the US hardly needs even a cavalry in the sky since it has no industrial state enemies. So even the Eisenhower Minimum at $425 billion in present-day dollars (constant 2012$) would be an unnecessary luxury. Yet it is here that the neocon takeover of the GOP has been so destructive.

President Bill Clinton had courageously allowed the military-industrial complex to attrite to slightly below the Eisenhower Minimum, as befit the post–Cold War world. His outgoing defense budget was $385 billion in present-day dollars (2012$), but that epochal attrition was stopped cold by the Cheney-Rumsfeld-neocon putsch. Like the Reagan reversal of 1981, the warfare state was given a massive new lease on life.

Thus, by 2012 the national defense cost $700 billion, or nearly 80 percent more in constant dollars than Clinton's perfectly adequate outgoing budget, and that does not include some $50 billion for security assistance and foreign aid that has also grown immensely during the last twelve years. Yet when the Congress stumbled into the accident of a one-time level change of $55 billion per year owing to the automatic sequester, that prospect uncorked a frenzy of clacking about "the sky is falling" from the neocon Republicans, including Romney-Ryan, that would have made Chicken Little proud.

In truth, the DOD sequester would result in constant-dollar defense outlays of about $620 billion in 2022, not even a 10 percent reduction from the current wildly bloated levels which mainly keep the generals and military industrial complex in business but have no rational relationship to national security in the twenty-first century. In fact, the post-sequester budget level would still exceed the Eisenhower Minimum by 50 percent, and it is that startling fact that dramatizes the fiscal infamy that should be accorded the neocons.

In today's world what is expensive is military manpower and hardware; that is, the stuff of massive land and sea forces and the capacity for global intervention, invasion, occupation, and resupply. The half billion dollar per week cost of operating the resupply lines over the Hindu Kush is a dramatic case in point. By contrast, what is increasingly and radically cheaper is silicon, and the cost of standby nuclear deterrence and satellite- and technology-based intelligence gathering.

The Republican Party thus desperately needs an Eisenhower or a Taft to champion flinty-eyed austerity and realism in national security policy. Yet populating the congressional defense committees with acolytes of Cheney and Rumsfeld, it is positioning for an all-out battle to keep the defense budget at the high end of the $620 billion to $700 billion corridor that brackets current policy with and without the sequester. So doing, it will squander the political capital of the conservative party, thereby prolonging and worsening the fiscal cliff rather than showing the way forward. Ironically, the Keynesian state is on the road to failure because the conservative party which is supposed to fight it became enamored with carrier battle groups and cruise missiles and a figment of neocon imagination called the new caliphate of Islam.

THE FISCAL CLIFF AND THE YAWNING GAP BELOW

The current CBO ten-year budget baseline should be thrown on the scrap heap because it is an iterative loop of unwarranted economic optimism and policy assumptions that do not remotely embody the stalemated politics of Washington, a reality made starkly evident during the first battle of the fiscal cliff at year-end 2012. To be sure, I no longer have access to the massive computer models from which the budget forecasts are generated, but I have retained the bitter lessons stemming from the original Rosy Scenario and political imperatives that rule the fiscal course of the nation.

Foremost among these is that long-term budget baselines—five years then and an even more preposterous ten years now—are an utterly destructive device. They turn budget-making into an incoherent and unaccountable numbers game that enables politicians to keep the state large and deep in red ink today, and to pretend that it will shrink and become solvent in the by-and-by. In fact, the fiscal cliff that looms permanently ahead is just an ugly symptom of the stage-four fiscal cancer that has crept into the nation's financial organs under the cover of the ten-year budget.

Needless to say, the Keynesian predicate and the crony capitalist money packs are so thoroughly in control of Washington that there is no chance that the nation's government will adopt an honest budget for the current fiscal year or the next. Instead, it will continue to maximize current year red ink based on eleventh hour crisis action by transient majorities, and roll the nation's massive fiscal gap forward under the cover of meaningless ten-year budget aggregates until the final collapse.

The permanent fiscal cliff, therefore, redounds to the everlasting ignominy of the Keynesian professors, from Heller to Laffer, who introduced the nation's politicians to the witch's brew of deficit finance. In trying to improve upon the people's work on the free market, they unleashed a great deformation; that is, a state which lacked any reason to stop the larceny of the K Street lobbies and the plunder of crony capitalist raiders from General Electric to Goldman Sachs, the cotton growers, the UAW, the timber barons, the ethanol distillers, the venture capital industry, the Medicaid mills, and the scooter chair manufacturers, too.

Nevertheless, a ballpark adjustment of the CBO ten-year baseline underscores why it is too late to turn back from the fiscal cliff and the budgetary abyss which lies below. CBO's January 2012 baseline for total federal spending over the next decade was about $45 trillion. That figure would readily go to $50 trillion, however, under an unrosy scenario and with the entitlement and defense policy positions taken by both parties during the 2012 campaign and at the midnight hour of the first encounter with the fiscal cliff.

About $2 trillion of the extra spending would be due to the drastic shortfall in current estimates of safety net and social insurance spending. Another $2 trillion would be from higher interest expense after removal of the current drastically overestimated revenue in the CBO baseline. And the balance would come from unsequestering defense and discretionary domestic spending as advocated by noisy factions of Republicans and Democrats, respectively.

On the other side of the budget, the CBO ten-year revenue baseline of $41 trillion is sheer illusion. With an unrosy scenario based on the nominal GDP and wage and salary growth rates of the last decade and the post-cliff tax law, ten-year revenues would barely come to $30 trillion. In short, as the nation begins its long and debilitating struggle with the permanent fiscal cliff, there is a $20 trillion fiscal abyss looming ahead.

Undoubtedly, small concessions will be forthcoming from each side, but these are rounding errors relative to the $20 trillion deficit monster lurking behind the CBO smoke screen. If the Democrats were to concede on the so-called chained CPI for the Social Security COLA adjustment, it would save $200 billion over the next decade. Likewise, by conceding to the Clinton-era tax rates on families with incomes above $450,000, Republicans have paved the way for additional revenue inflows of about $600 billion over the next decade. These concessions literally provoked blood in the streets on the respective sides of the partisan aisle, but amount to 1 percent and 2 percent, respectively, of the true fiscal gap.

In truth, only a thorough-going dismantlement of the warfare state and the welfare state would make any real difference. If DOD were throttled back to the Eisenhower Minimum (40 percent cut) and social insurance were drastically means tested to eliminate one-sixth of current Social Security and Medicare benefit costs ($400 billion per year savings), spending by 2022 could be reduced to about $5 trillion annually, or 21.7 percent of GDP. The latter figure undoubtedly amounts to spurious accuracy, but it also happens to be exactly the federal spending share of GDP achieved during Ronald Reagan's second term. With a population nearly forty years older by 2022, the Gipper's benchmark would be a miracle to achieve.

Needless to say, the arrival of peak debt will also mean that revenues would need to be lifted to the vicinity of 21.7 percent of GDP, as well. In round numbers that would amount to a $2 trillion annual tax hike relative to the current Republican gospel of low taxes. In theory, that could be achieved with a 15 percent consumption or value added tax (VAT) on most items which comprise the personal consumption expenditure component of GDP.

In a sundown economy fighting for fiscal solvency VAT is probably the only viable solution. Yet in a political culture contaminated by five decades of Keynesian fiscal profligacy, its prospects would be the same as the Schweiker social insurance reform package of May 1981: it would be voted down 100–0 in the Senate, and in well less than ten days.

THE GANGS OF CRONY CAPITALISM: GRAND FINALE

As the nation struggles with the permanent fiscal cliff and the $20 trillion deficit that lurks below, fiscal politics will degenerate into a blood sport. In that unfortunate arena, the gangs of crony capitalism will fight tooth and nail to preserve their slice of an imperiled pie, thereby disenfranchising even further ordinary taxpayers and citizens who have no voice in the Washington policy auctions. In that context, the military-industrial complex and the housing-mortgage finance complex are only the most obvious combatants, but their powers of preservation merely illustrate the truth about all of the crony capitalist gangs, including the energy boondogglers, the medical care complex, and most especially Wall Street.

The military industrial complex vivifies the problem because today the primary purpose of the DOD budget is to make jobs and prop up the manufacturing economy, not provide national security. Bin Laden is dead, the

Iraq war was lost, the Afghanistan surge has already petered out, and Al Qaeda is down to its last few hundred warriors lurking in the barren redoubts of Yemen, Mali, and Somalia. Yet the defense budget has not yet shed one dollar of spending in real terms from its all-time high under the Cheney-Bush imperium.

As indicated earlier, the markers of irrational perpetuation of senseless military spending are everywhere: the DOD budget continues to modernize M1 battle tanks each year when there is no real need for most of the 9,000 ultra-lethal tracked machines we already have. Likewise, the Pentagon still has 800,000 civilian employees, one for every two members of the uniformed forces. Furthermore, the active armed forces still totals 1.5 million plus 1.1 million reserves, a massive war fighting machine of occupation and invasion that has virtually no defensive purpose at all.

This is why the coming fiscal collapse is so certain. The nation is war weary, it has a peace president, and no enemies with modern military capacity. But the DOD spending cannot be stopped; not in the aggregate and not in the weeds of purposeless tank modernizations and a $250 billion payroll of civilians and soldiers who by and large do not have a justifiable mission.

In the same manner, the vast complex of housing credit agencies and tax subsidies nearly destroyed the nation's residential housing market with a lot of help from the Fed. But five years after the housing crash, Fannie and Freddie have not had a comma of their legislative charters altered, the FHA has massively increased its book of business, and the homeowner's tax subsidies have been taken off the table even before the upcoming campaign to close tax loopholes and broaden the basis has started.

More importantly, the overwhelming share of the home mortgage origination and servicing business is now dominated by four giant banks: JPMorgan, Citigroup, Bank of America, and Wells Fargo. The latter have thus far settled litigation for various fraudulent and predatory practices during the mortgage fiasco years to the tune of nearly $100 billion collectively; but traders have gladly ignored the resulting hit to their balance sheets as a meaningless "one-timer," while the proceeds that didn't go to the lawyers are being used to keep defaulted properties off the market and deadbeat borrowers in their homes. The effect is to dispense unfair windfalls all around and to prevent price discovery from doing its job.

Worse still, the four banks carry on the unproductive business of churning the nation's $10 trillion mortgage pool under the Fed's repression of mortgage rates, scalping handsome profits each and every time the same home is refinanced. Meanwhile, the big Wall Street banks are pumping billions of high-risk loans into the latest new thing in LBO speculation;

namely, leveraged pools of buy-to-rent capital that are now accounting for upward of 50 percent of existing home sales in former distressed markets like Phoenix, Southern California, Las Vegas, and Florida.

One thing is certain: the fast money marauders swooping into former subprime neighborhoods are not setting up shop to become long-term local landlords; they are not buying lawnmowers and provisioning HVAC repair parts. Instead, they are setting up local markets for a price pop, so that they can scalp a gain and leave the hindmost to virtually nonexistent buy-to-occupy first-time and trade-up home owners. In short, between the Fed, the big banks, the home builder and real estate lobbies and Wall Street speculators, there is not a chance that the nation's busted residential housing market can recover a healthy balance and honest pricing.

Instead, residential housing will remain a financial playground where crony capitalist gangs are enabled to extract tens of billions of ill-gotten gains from taxpayers and savers alike. In truth, the housing sector needs drastic reform and a clearing of the decks from the statist deformations of a half century. But with Washington paralyzed and hostage to the permanent fiscal cliff and an economy that is perpetually "weak" and in need of a "housing stimulus," the squeaky wheels of crony capitalism and their K Street agents will get the grease. The nation's giant housing market will remain a den where speculators and the big banks churn and burn, and also a place in the years ahead where financially desperate baby boomers will go to pawn their castles for comparatively meager recompense.

SIREN SONG OF THE ENERGY GANGS

Indeed, as the free market economy becomes steadily weaker, the crony capitalist gangs are even more emboldened to raid the public purse under the cover of boosting jobs and economic recovery. Nowhere is this more salient than in the energy sector where the spurious idea that an expensive barrel of domestic energy is better than a cheaper barrel of imported energy has taken deep hold. Accordingly, both black energy and green energy lobbies are lined up at the public trough prepared to ferociously protect subsidies they already have and pounding the table for more on the grounds that an energy renaissance is under way that can create millions of American jobs. Indeed, the black and green energy gangs are conducting a logrolling operating that will soon make the farm cartels look like pikers.

But the central proposition of the energy gangs is wrong; namely, that there is an oil and gas production renaissance in the United States, and that with enough tax breaks, cheap federal loans, and outright subsidies, it can be extended to an entire Noah's ark of energy flavors. In fact, the recent blip in US oil production is just a swiggle upward on a forty-year trend line of declining output. For all the talk of shale oil production in the Bakken and Texas, US production during 2012 (6.4 million barrels per day) was lower than it was in 1995, and 33 percent lower than in 1970.

As indicated earlier with respect to shale gas, the recent production boomlet is due to ultra-cheap debt capital being drilled on Wall Street thanks to the Fed's destruction of interest rates, not new discoveries or even new technologies such as fracking. The fact is, the "lower 48" is the most drilled-over zone on the planet, having been host to 75 percent of all the oil and gas wells ever drilled in human history. What is left is high-cost, low-grade hydrocarbon deposits, such as oil and gas trapped in shale, which can be extracted only by the brute force of massive material and capital consumption.

This means that the economics don't work unless capital is ultra-cheap and world oil prices stay near $100 per barrel. Accordingly, when the next worldwide recession sets in and oil prices drop to $50 per barrel, the North Dakota shale-oil patch will return to weeds and scrub, just as is already happening in the shale-gas patch where massive reserves that were drilled under the brute force of cheap capital are now deeply underwater at to-day's rock-bottom natural gas prices.

So the siren song of energy independence, now forty years old and reaching back to the foolishness of Nixon's FEA (Federal Energy Administration), is just being replayed at a different octave. While oil and gas output has increased by about a 3-million-barrel-per-day oil equivalent from prior all-time lows, that amounts to just 10 percent of the 28 million barrels of oil and natural gas consumed by the US economy every day, and even these slightly improved levels of production have nothing to do with the jobs problem.

In fact, the total job count in the oil and gas extraction industry is just 195,000, and is up by only 30,000 jobs since the fall of 2008, when Bernanke began pumping ultra-cheap debt into the oil and gas patch by way of Wall Street drilling funds and other vehicles of high-yield speculation. Accordingly, the next bubble bursting may well be the shale bubble, and the next bailout demands will come from the junk oil speculators who have recently moved from the sand belts to the Black Hills.

Meanwhile, $100 billion annually is being wasted on energy tax breaks, subsidies, and credits. All the varieties of black and green energy are noisily lined up under the banner of jobs and growth, but most of the beneficiaries would not survive in an honest free market. Indeed, so desperate are these hothouse energy wards of the state that even the wind farms managed to climb aboard the Christmas tree of tax-cut extenders that passed on New Year's Day 2013. That spoke volumes: the wind is free and the nation is broke, but the crony capitalists of energy plundered on.

THE MEDICAL CARE COMPLEX:
ULTIMATE DEFORMATION OF THE STATE

When it comes to plunder, however, the medical care complex is in a league all by itself. The greatest of all abominations on the free market is employer health insurance, a product that would not exist if it were taxed like other wage income and which is not insurance at all but merely a form of prepayment for health services. Like many of the other deformations which distort the free market, today's giant $200 billion per year tax subsidy for employer health plans was a New Deal special (wartime phase).

Organized labor wanted higher pay, but FDR's wage and price controllers didn't want to break the wage cap visibly, so they invited organized labor to visit the backdoor of the IRS after hours. In some long forgotten conference in 1943, it was decreed that employee wages paid in the form of pre-paid health services were not taxable. The rest was history: so-called employer health insurance plans drove a giant wedge between the higher prices received by doctors and hospitals and the negligible out-of-pocket costs felt by medical service consumers.

In the fullness of time, health-care inflation came to occupy its own perch far above all others. During the last half-century, for example, the consumer price index has risen by 8X, average wages by 10X and hospital costs per day by 40X. Inflation in physician costs, drugs, lab tests, and most other health services has been only slightly less explosive, but the underlying cause is the same: routine health services are not insurable risks because both providers and consumers heavily drive the frequency and cost of service.

In certain extreme demographic strata, for instance, the rate of obesity and diabetes is so high that health coverage amounts to providing arsonists with fire insurance. Likewise, it has long been demonstrated that the incidence of a variety of surgical procedures per 100,000 population is a function of the number of surgeons in the catchment area. In truth, employer-provided health insurance is one of the great deformations of our times, and is no more an honest form of free market insurance than Social Security pensions. Instead, it is a form of tax-subsidized cost pooling in which overutilization, overpricing, and free-riding is endemic.

Were the problem of employer health insurance contained within the mainly middle-class population (about 170 million) covered by such plans there would be serious economic efficiency and equity costs, but these would not be the worst blemishes on the free market: workers would transfer some of their income to doctors and hospitals unnecessarily and health-care resources in general would be drastically overconsumed. But the insuperable problem is the *massive spillover on innocent citizens:* rampant health-care inflation means that much of the non-employer-plan population is eventually priced out of the health-care system, including the poor, the retired, the self-employed, and those with preexisting conditions.

Once again, therefore, one market disturbance by the state begat another. Already by the mid-1960s the poor and elderly were being squeezed, and so Lyndon Johnson succeeded in dramatically updating the New Deal via Medicare and Medicaid. The obvious and well-intended purpose was to effectively supplement the incomes of non-working populations being priced out of the health-care market, but what LBJ inadvertently delivered was the greatest victory for crony capitalism ever imagined.

The giant misfire is that the Johnson plans did not deliver cash to people in need; it delivered the bodies of the poor and elderly to health-care providers and equipped them with pre-paid medical cards requiring minimal out-of-pocket cost sharing. It was the worst of all possible worlds, especially with respect to the larger Medicare program because it put the entire retired population into a cost-averaged pool and laid the expense off on the payroll tax and general revenues (for Part B). Needless to say, use of health-care services thereby became utterly divorced from financing their costs, and in the process two great deformations of the state quickly emerged.

Since there was no means test on Medicare, the entire retired population became a potent political force against any patient cost-sharing measures that might have helped contain the explosion of costs owing to the third-party (i.e., taxpayer) payment system. Thus, Part B premiums for physician's services were initially set at 50 percent of costs and long ago eroded to under 25 percent, raising Medicare outlays by $100 billion annually at current cost levels. Likewise, every serious attempt to raise deductibles or co-pays in Medicare has been buried by the AARP (American Association of Retired Persons) and the other retirement lobbies.

More importantly, Medicare and Medicaid were built on a misbegotten combination of socialism for the beneficiaries and capitalism for the providers. While both programs attempt to regulate providers through utilization controls and reimbursement caps, this cumbersome and bulky bureaucratic machinery fights on an inherently uneven battlefield; that is, the K Street– and PAC-dominated milieu of Washington where virtually every medical specialty, supplier, and type of institutional medical care facility has organized representation.

The proof that Medicare and Medicaid function in the realm of crony capitalism, not market capitalism, is in the pudding. By the time these programs were up and running in 1970, combined Medicare-Medicaid costs (including the state matching share of Medicaid) were $15 billion, or 1 percent of GDP. Thirty years later, the cost had escalated to $375 billion and 5 percent of GDP. Today the combined cost exceeds $1 trillion and will reach $2.4 trillion, or 10.5 percent, of GDP by 2022.

It goes without saying that the medical needs of the elderly and the poor did not escalate by a factor of 9 percent of GDP over the last fifty years. What happened was that the state created massive insurance pools for an uninsurable service, and then invited the medical profession to morph into Washington's greatest crony capitalist lobby. The American Medical Association, for instance, fell on its sword in opposition to Medicare in 1965, but in 2010 it sold its soul in support of Obamacare in exchange for a more doc-friendly control régime, the very thing which will cause the cost of Obamacare to explode in the years ahead.

In fact, Obamacare is the endgame of the seventy years ago carve out (from income taxation) for employer health plans. The combination of giant employer-based health cost pools and the even larger ones run by Medicare and Medicaid have not only driven health inflation skyward, but have also generated a noxious system of price discrimination that would be wholly unnatural on the free market. The so-called big buyers, consisting of large plans and managed-care operations, have extracted ever larger "discounts" (25 to 75 percent) from "rack rates" (i.e., sticker prices) for their plan participants, thereby forcing rack rates higher and higher for everyone else including small employer plans and individual insurance buyers.

Accordingly, the Obama health exchanges came about essentially because another component of the population was flushed out of the system. The self-employed and workers in part-time jobs and small businesses became the third wave of citizens needing state intervention to compensate for the original employer-paid insurance distortion. Their claims arose for the same reason as Medicare and Medicaid; namely, part-time and self-employed America was priced out of the crony capitalist health-care system in the same manner as the elderly and the poor. Yet with eligibility for state-run health exchanges under Obamacare reaching up to $90,000 per family, the cost explosion from still more health-cost averaging of pre-paid plans subsidized by the public purse is virtually unimaginable.

What is clear already, however, is that the crony-capitalist-driven health-care system is devouring the American economy, and the figures which prove it could not be more dispositive. In 1960, national health expenditures amounted to $150 per capita and hardly 5 percent of GDP. By 2000 the figures had grown to $5,000 per capita and 13.8 percent of GDP. Today it is nearly $9,000 per capita and more than 18 percent of GDP.

To be sure, these trends are widely known to the policy wonks, and widely lamented, too. But the backstory is far less noted and is the reason that the Keynesian state in America is headed for inexorable insolvency: namely, as the free market economy continues to fail owing to the burdens of debt, money printing, and fiscal profligacy, more and more of the population will be flushed into the state-funded pools of Medicare, Medicaid, and the Obamacare health exchanges.

As the fiscal crunch intensifies, the crony capitalist gangs which fed on these pools will resist controls and cost containment with a vast mobilization of lobbying power and campaign lucre. It is the ensuing hand-to-hand combat in the corridors of Washington which will further paralyze the fiscal process; and it is the asymmetrical nature of the contest which will ultimately break the state.

SUNDOWN AND THE ENDGAME OF CENTRAL BANKING

Under a régime of sound money the prospect of fiscal deficits of $20 trillion would be unthinkable, nor would the free market be barnacled with crony capitalist coalitions which fatten on the public purse and regulatory powers of the state. Indeed, the potent purgative of free market interest rates would have kept the old prudential fiscal culture alive and provided politicians with the shield they need to impose limits, make trade-offs, and balance the fiscal accounts.

In fact, what elected officials desperately needed over the last several decades were intervals of double-digit interest rate flare-ups, even rates which reached 20 percent. High interest rate episodes are the market signal to politicians that vivify the true cost of deficit finance and thereby give them the reason to say no to tax cuts and spending increases financed with red ink.

Herein lies the real evil of the Greenspan-Bernanke régime of financial repression and wealth effects levitation: it destroyed free market interest rates in the name of monetary central planning and thereby unshackled democratic politicians from the ancient fiscal disciplines. But monetary central planning couldn't work in the long run, while the low administered price of debt turned the nation's budget into a fiscal doomsday machine.

As has been seen, the gold dollar was the true embodiment of sound finance and it was steadily strangled between 1914 and 1971. But even then there was a second-best alternative embodied in the worldview of the Federal Reserve Act framers of 1913. It was something called "mobilization of the discount rate" and was an embodiment of the injunctions of the great English banking theorist Walter Bagehot. While he is usually quoted with respect to his advice that central banks should print money freely in a financial crisis, the qualifying clauses were the more important; namely, that the central bank should lend only against good collateral at a penalty rate of interest.

In a narrow sense, Morgan Stanley could have never brought its $100 billion of junk collateral to the Fed window in late September 2008 under the Bagehot rules. But in the larger sense, had the post-Volcker Fed adopted a mobilized discount rate policy rather than financial repression, the Morgan Stanley garbage heap could never have been created or accumulated: it was an artificial product of low interest rates and the Fed-enabled carry trade. And it was only one case, a symptom, of the financial and fiscal deformations that had spread across the entire system by the time of the BlackBerry Panic. The growing piles of federal debt and the rising heaps of Wall Street–created junk securities arose from the same profoundly misbegotten central bank policy.

Under a mobilized discount rate policy, the deformations of both Wall Street and fiscal policy would not exist. There would have been no monetary central planners to enable them and no monetary politburo to provide puts and other assurances that the nightmare of high interest rates would not be visited upon the leveraged speculators on Wall Street and the fiscal libertines on both ends of Pennsylvania Avenue.

Indeed, under a mobilized discount rate régime there would be no need for an open market committee (FOMC) at the Fed at all. Eligible banks with good collateral would come to the Fed window as a last resort, but would always prefer to obtain overnight funding needs in the interbank market to avoid paying the Bagehot penalty; that is, 200 or 300 basis points above the market. Consequently, in times of credit stress the interbank market rates for short-term funding would flare up sharply, and the Fed's discount rate would soar higher. Continuously resetting higher and higher, it would provide a profound warning to speculators that there will be no mercy on the days of financial reckoning: Greed and recklessness would be laid low.

Accordingly, the job of the Fed would be to do what J. P. Morgan's young men did night after night in the great financier's library during the panic of 1907. They did not pontificate on their intentions for the GDP and the Russell 2000 in the manner of Greenspan and Bernanke but, instead, put on their green eyeshades and examined the nitty-gritty of the balance sheets of supplicants for emergency loans who came to the Morgan Library at Madison Avenue and Thirty-sixth Street. As seen, solvent institutions got liquidity injections; insolvent ones met their maker.

Ironically, Pierpont Morgan's top green eyeshade was Benjamin Strong, who went on to become the first great US central banker as president of the New York Fed in the 1920s. Had Strong stuck to his 1907 role as collateral examiner, the Fed-enabled financial bubbles of the later 1920s would not have happened, nor would there have been the Great Crash of 1929 and its aftermath. Likewise, had Alan Greenspan rejected the perfidious implications of the Humphrey-Hawkins Act and simply declared that sound money under a mobilized discount rate was the surest route to low inflation and full employment, the financial calamities of the present era could have been avoided.

Needless to say, today's wanna-be masters of the universe who populate the monetary politburo would have been cut down to size; their job would have been that of penurious, flinty-eyed bank examiners, who would scour the collateral of supplicants for Fed discount window loans one application at a time. They would have no dog in the stock market hunt. Nor would they care about the latest swiggle in the GDP reports or tick in the unemployment rate. Most assuredly, these humble bank examiners would never pretend to manage the rise of national wealth or the rate at which the people on the free market create new output, savings, investment, and consumption.

Under a mobilized discount rate the cardinal rule of sound finance would have been respected; to wit, no man can borrow unless another man first saves. Accordingly, the free market interest rate would become the honest balancing wheel, undistorted by central bank bond buying and cash injections into the money market. With the freedom to soar when the demand for credit sharply exceeds the supply of savings, free market interest rates would automatically check creation of new credit in the banking system and rehypothecated credit in the shadow banking system.

The reason is straightforward: in a financialized economy, the marginal demand for credit consists of funding for the carry trades in one form or another. Yet this is the very perversion which permits the politicians to carry on with deficits without tears. When the Fed drives overnight money to zero and promises to keep it there through long-dated points on the calendar, it creates a false demand for government bonds.

Much of this false demand is financed in the repo market where fast money traders are happy to harvest the spread on the Fed-managed yield curve. They buy ten-year treasuries at a yield of 180 basis points (1.8 percent) and fund 98 percent of their position with 10-basis-point overnight borrowings—all the while sleeping peacefully because Bernanke has promised that short-term rates will not rise until 2015. This amounts to robbing a bank without criminal liability. Not surprisingly, the banks themselves have gone in for this kind of legalized larceny. Since Bernanke slashed deposit rates to essentially zero, bank holdings of government and agency bonds have nearly doubled, rising from $1.2 trillion to $2 trillion.

Here lies the Great Deformation. Over the last several decades the implicit choice has always been between a régime of free market interest rates and a mobilized discount rate versus a régime of financial repression and unchecked private and public debt creation. The former route would have limited the Fed to the role of "bankers' bank," providing emergency discount loans at market-driven interest rates plus a penalty. The latter route, explicitly chosen by Greenspan and carried to an absurd extreme by the Bernanke Fed, has turned the Fed into a destroyer of honest financial markets, an enabler of financial speculation on a scale never before imagined, and a reallocator of society's income and wealth to the 1 percent.

But worst of all, it has transformed the nation's central bank into the handmaiden of fiscal calamity. Today the US Treasury can borrow money from ninety days out to five years, thereby encompassing most of its issuance, at rates between 10 basis points and 80 basis points. Washington's mega-deficits are thus being funded with essentially free money. The Fed's utterly foolish interest rate repression has stripped the politicians buck naked in the face of the free lunch propensities of the democracy and the raids and plunderings of crony capitalists in a political system where money rules.

Needless to say, the Fed has painted itself and the nation into a dead-end corner. Sundown comes because the Fed dares not let interest rates rise by even a smidgeon, let alone "normalize" or ever again approach something like an honest price for money and debt on the free market. If it did, the vast army of fast-money speculators who have rented Treasury bonds and notes on 98 percent repo would sell in a heartbeat, causing the price of government debt to fall sharply. Then the slower-footed bond fund managers would be forced to liquidate in the face of retail investor redemptions and eventually even banks and insurance companies would panic, selling into a bidless market for government debt and everything tied to it.

Standing at the edge of a financial abyss, the Fed is thus hostage to its own four-decade excursion in money printing and macroeconomic management. It cannot stop buying government debt because it is being front run by a herd of speculators which will turn on a dime unless it keeps buying and pegging the price of Treasury notes and bonds. At the end of 2012, its policy was to buy government and GSE debt outright at a rate of $1 trillion per year, which means that its balance sheet would be $6 trillion by the end of Obama's second term.

THE GLOBAL MONETARY BUBBLE

It won't get that far, however, because there are powerful countervailing forces gathering momentum; namely, a global beggar-thy-neighbor currency depreciation war that will dwarf the conflagrations of the 1930s. As indicated earlier, the Fed has been the lead ship in a convoy of monetary roach motels since the 1970s. Not surprisingly, Bernanke's balance sheet expansion spree during the BlackBerry Panic spread like wildfire.

The top eight central banks, including the ECB, Bank of Japan, and the People's Printing Press of China, had combined balance sheet footings of $5 trillion before the financial storm erupted in 2007. Now they total $15 trillion and are expanding at explosive rates. Following in the footsteps of the Fed's 4X increase in its balance sheet and the embarrassingly blatant spree of money printing by the Bank of England, the practice of buying unwanted sovereign debt has become universal.

The ECB's $1.2 trillion so-called LTRO money-printing operation during late 2011 and 2012 was merely a thinly disguised backdoor means of financing the debt of Spain, Italy, Greece, and others that genuine investors did not want to buy at current interest rates. And the announcement by Japan's new LDP government in late 2012 that the Bank of Japan should print money at whatever rate it may take to bring inflation back to life in a bankrupt economy simply carried the money-printing régime to a new extreme.

But it was the Swiss National Bank which was the ultimate canary in the mine shaft: it has been forced into massive expansion of its balance sheet in order offset the destructive flare-up in its exchange rate owing to flight capital out of the euro zone into the "swissie." Indeed, when the Swiss central bank, the paragon of "hard money" in modern times, is forced into negative interest rates on deposits and an explicit policy of trashing its own money, then the currency wars have started, and there is no turning back.

The new government of Shinzo Abe in Japan has already fired the warning shot on the matter of competitive currency depreciation and the oncoming race to the bottom. Its outright attack on the Fed is epochal, and contrasts dramatically with the actions of the Nakasone government which came to the Plaza Hotel in 1985 to receive the "Texas treatment." Implicitly referring to the "Connally treatment" of a decade earlier, the Japanese statesmen meekly declaimed, "We enjoyed that, may we have another?"

No longer. The Japanese government has buried itself in debt building roads to nowhere and implementing every hoary fiscal stimulus device ever conceived. With government debt at 250 percent of GDP, it now stands not only as a monument to Keynesian folly, but as a potent warning about how thoroughly and swiftly financial discipline has been destroyed by the Fed and its convoy of monetary roach motels.

At a meeting in early 1981, a high-ranking delegation of Japanese financial officials came to the White House to politely and discreetly ascertain whether the Reagan administration really intended to create massive and permanent fiscal deficits. At that point, Japan's niggardly public debt stood at less than 35 percent of GDP and their officials were genuinely astonished that the American government would risk violating every standard of fiscal prudence by implementing big tax cuts without paying for them.

Needless to say, today Japan raises in tax revenue less than 50 percent of what its government spends, and it doesn't dare ask about fiscal prudence. With taxation at levels needed to finance its current spending, Japan's economy of old people and increasingly old industries would sink rapidly into the Pacific. Yet Japan's domestic savings rate has fallen from 18 percent at the time of the aforementioned White House visit to essentially zero today, and its long-running current account surplus is turning sharply and rapidly into deep deficits.

Accordingly, there is no place left to sell the vast outpouring of government debt promised by the new LDP government except at the Bank of Japan. Were Japanese interest rates ever to rise even to 3 percent from the current comically low rates pegged by the Bank of Japan (80 basis points for ten-year notes), the interest cost on Japan's gargantuan debt would absorb every single penny of government revenue. Japan's economy would thus sink into the Pacific by another route.

So the Bank of Japan is also hostage to its sovereign debt, and will print yen faster and faster in stride with the QE-to-infinity posture of the US Fed. The ECB will also have no alternative to rapid money printing, as its constituent national economies shrink into permanent recession under the weight of fiscal austerity policies needed to keep their bloated welfare state budgets afloat. More likely than not, the Germans will revolt in the face of extreme ECB money printing and the euro will blow up, sinking the continent into deeper recession still.

Likewise for China. It goes without saying that this towering edifice—of bank credit, rampant speculation by much of the populace, massive state-financed construction of what amount to pyramids and other unusable public infrastructure and unspeakable corruption—cannot function without its export economy: that's where it earns the real capital to keep going the monumental excesses and imbalance of Communist Party–managed economy.

So China's central bank must keep printing, too, and dares not allow the currency to appreciate much more than the token amounts of recent years in order to keep its export sector above water. Indeed, in a world of honest money much of China's export economy would have never arisen or would have sunk below the waves long ago. And with it, of course, would have gone the whole system of tributary raw materials and intermediate components suppliers that feed on the great Chinese Factory; that is, Australia and Brazil in the former category and South Korea, Japan, Taiwan, Malaysia, and Singapore in the latter.

In short, the world economy is now extended on the far edge of a monetary bubble that has been four decades in the making. The next phase of money printing, however, may be the last because all the major, aging consumer economies of the world are failing; that is, the United States, Europe, and Japan. Accordingly, democratic politics will turn increasingly ugly, strident, and nationalistic in the face of chronic fiscal crisis, recession and quasi-recession, middle-class austerity, and bubble opulence among the 1 percent. It will result in protectionism, currency wars, and anti-capitalist policy interventions, including capital controls, punitive taxation of the "rich" (which few will actually pay), and endless bailouts and boondoggles.

During the final phase of the global monetary bubble, economic growth in the United States will be ground to a halt. As this happens, the $20 trillion of prospective debt now obscured in CBO's rosy scenario will become increasingly visible, causing the fiscal cliff to loom ever more forbidding and unmovable. American politics will consequently become more fractious and paralyzed, and the Keynesian state will inexorably sink into insolvency and failure.

The interim winners from this ordeal will be the gangs of crony capitalism and the opulent 1 percent who thrive off the central bank's money printing. But in the end sundown will descend upon the entire nation—even on the 1 percent.

CHAPTER 34

ANOTHER ROAD
THAT COULD BE TAKEN

T GOES WITHOUT SAYING THAT WHEN HISTORY GETS INTO A DEEP RUT it becomes hard to alter the course of affairs. But even at this late date the sundown scenario could be avoided. The Fed's financial repression and Wall Street–coddling policies could be pronounced a failure and abandoned. Crony capitalism could be put out of business by constitutional writ.

Likewise, the corpulent warfare and welfare states could be put into a constitutional chastity belt and the rule of no spending without equal taxation could be made the modus operandi of a shrunken state. Eventually, the free market could regain its vigor and capacity for wealth creation and, under a régime of sound money and honest finance, the 1 percent could continue to enjoy their opulence by earning it the old-fashioned way; that is, by delivering society inventions and enterprise that expand the economic pie, rather than reallocate it.

The crucial steps that would be needed are few but large. They would never be adopted in today's régime of money politics, fast money speculation, and Keynesian economics, but they can be listed. They are compelling.

1. RESTORE BANKER'S BANK AND SOUND MONEY. The Fed's open market operations and interest rate pegging would be abolished in favor of a mobilized discount rate at a stiff penalty over the money market. Humphrey-Hawkins would be repealed and all other Fed mandates with respect to the macro-economy or equity and debt markets would be rescinded. The Fed has created enough central bank credit for the next thirty years, meaning that it would not need to buy government debt or otherwise monetize securities for the foreseeable future. In reverting to the role of a banker's bank, it would examine collateral presented at the discount window and ensure ultimate liquidity of the banking system, while bringing free market interest rates back into the center of financial markets. With open market purchases eliminated, the FOMC and the 12 regional reserve banks could be abolished: bank applicants for discount loans would mainly transact on-line with the borrowing desk at the Eccles Building. Over the next decade, the natural roll-off of maturing treasury and agency securities would automatically shrink the Fed's balance sheet to the September 15, 2008, level (under $1 trillion), thereby paving the way for a full return to sound money, that is, a gold-backed dollar.

2. ABOLISH DEPOSIT INSURANCE AND LIMIT THE FED DISCOUNT WINDOW TO NARROW DEPOSITORIES. The abomination of deposit insurance would be abolished, and the Fed's discount window would be open only to "new charter" national banks. These charters would be offered to "narrow" depository banks which would take deposits and make loans, but would be banned from trading, underwriting, or agenting any business in securities, derivatives, commodities, or whole loan paper they had not originated. Nor could chartered banks be in the asset management, insurance, or financial advisory business, and they would be required to maintain minimum equity capital ratios of 20 percent or higher, the levels which prevailed before the 1920s. A postal banking system would be set up by the federal government for blue-haired ladies and timid savers who were unwilling to risk putting their savings into uninsured, chartered banks, but they would receive a penalty interest rate below the chartered bank rate to compensate the federal government for use of its balance sheet and credit rating.

3. ADOPT SUPER GLASS-STEAGALL II. The great Wall Street Banks would be put out in the cold to compete as enterprises on the free market without recourse to funding from insured deposits or access to the Fed discount window. Pursuant to the implementation of Glass-Steagall II, the large banks would be forced to divest their deposit banking business, and cap their balance sheets at 1 percent of GDP ($150 billion) for ten years in order to regenerate honest, competitive financial markets and to reduce the risk of crony capitalist recidivism.

4. ABOLISH INCUMBENCY THROUGH AN OMNIBUS AMENDMENT. The US Constitution would be subject to an Omnibus Amendment, a twenty-first-century "reset" to restore viability, honesty, and functionality to democratic governance. Accordingly, the terms of the president and House and Senate members would be set at six years, staggered elections to the Congress would occur every two years, and no incumbent of federal office could stand for reelection. The electoral college would also be abolished, bringing the nation into the modern world of one citizen, one vote.

Federal election campaigns would be funded strictly with public funds and the time for federal campaigns would be limited to two months every other year. No federal campaign money would be available before that designated election period, and it would be illegal to campaign for federal office with private money. Additionally, no former federal office holder would be allowed to lobby and the Citizens United decision would be explicitly overturned and replaced with a ban on election funding and legislative lobbying with corporate or union funds. The overall purpose of the Omnibus Amendment would be to rid the nation of a permanent governing class, and weaken the political parties to the point of their disappearance, as they would have no useful purpose in the citizen-based government provided under the amendment.

5. REQUIRE EACH TWO-YEAR CONGRESS TO BALANCE THE BUDGET. A crucial component of the Omnibus Amendment would be a strict requirement that the federal budget be balanced within the two-year term of each Congress other than under a constitutionally valid declaration of war. Enforceability would be guaranteed by a monthly certification from the secretary of the treasury that the run rate of spending and revenues were on track to achieve the balanced budget requirement over the two-year term. The certification would be signed by the president and the top officers of the Treasury Department, upon Sarbanes-Oxley-type criminal penalties for knowing misrepresentation or willful negligence. In the absence of certification, spending run rates would be automatically cut across the board to the estimated run rate of revenues.

6. END MACROECONOMIC MANAGEMENT AND SEPARATE THE STATE AND THE FREE MARKET. The Keynesian predicate would be abolished by virtue of the Omnibus Amendment. Accordingly, the state would be separated from the free market by a sturdy fence. The outcomes of the latter in terms of wealth, living standards, GDP, jobs, housing starts, and shipments of containerboard would be determined on the free market by the actions of consumers, producers, savers, and investors. If there weren't enough jobs, wage rates would tend to fall until there were enough jobs to balance supply and demand; that is, the free market would be in charge of job creation, not Washington and its crony capitalist gangs.

7. ABOLISH SOCIAL INSURANCE, BAILOUTS, AND ECONOMIC SUBSIDIES. The end of the Keynesian fiscal state would require a fundamental reconstitution of the role and functions of government. The provision of police functions (including most of homeland security) and public goods such as highways, education, and amenities like recreational facilities would revert to state and local governments. Social insurance, bailouts, and other forms of federal economic intervention and subsidization of the free market would be abolished. These changes in the functions of the state and the level of government at which they are carried out would eliminate the fiscally suicidal forces built into the current system, including intergenerational thievery under social insurance and interregional larceny embedded in federal grants in aid and economic subsidy programs.

8. ELIMINATE TEN MAJOR FEDERAL AGENCIES AND DEPARTMENTS. Under this régime, much of the federal government could be abolished including the Departments of Energy, Education, Commerce, Labor, Agriculture, HUD, Homeland Security, the SBA, DOT, and the Ex-Im Bank. Likewise, other Washington venues for crony capitalism would be eliminated by abolishing, for instance, Fannie and Freddie, the FHA, homeowner's tax preferences, and the remainder of the housing goody bag. In the same vein, all forms of energy, black and green, would be put strictly on the free market; Amtrak would sink or swim as a private enterprise; subway commuters or taxpayers in New York City would pay the full fare, not innocent taxpayers in Nebraska; and GE, Caterpillar, and the rest of the corporate freeloaders would be deprived of cheap export financing from the Ex-Im bank.

9. ERECT A STURDY CASH-BASED MEANS-TESTED SAFETY NET AND ABOLISH THE MINIMUM WAGE. Outside of national defense and foreign affairs, the primary function of the federal government would be to maintain a means-tested safety net. The latter would fulfill the humanitarian sentiments held by the electorates in modern urban-industrial societies where extended family support networks no longer exist, while strictly containing the risks of abuse and freeloading by the able bodied and non-needy. This means that social insurance and the rigmarole of trust funds and insurance mythology would be abolished and that any citizen wanting aid from the state would be subject to a strict and intrusive means test, including the spend-down of all assets to some minimum level. Additionally, a work requirement for the able bodied of normal working age would be coupled with the abolition of the minimum wage and the scaling out of transfer payments to the working poor based on an all-in tax rate which rewards work and effort. Finally, all existing programs including housing, food stamps, and Medicare and Medicaid would be converted to cash equivalents, thereby eliminating the provider abuse and the crony capitalist policy and administrative exploitation that are inherent in in-kind programs.

10. ABOLISH HEALTH "INSURANCE" IN ALL ITS FORMS. The replacement of Medicare and Medicaid with cash-based transfer payments would be coupled with the repeal of Obamacare and the elimination of the massive tax subsidies for employer health insurance. So doing, the giant third-party payment deformation would be eliminated from the medical care markets and real consumers would take charge of their own health expenditures, putting providers under the competitive discipline of the free market. The cancerous growth of the medical care complex would be halted and reversed, thereby stifling the ultimate driver of welfare state bankruptcy. Indeed, the free market would rapidly give rise to solutions to all of the problems which have justified the massive incursions of the state: cost of care would be lower; pricing would be nondiscriminatory; and proficient fee-based medical care advisory services would arise to help consumers, especially the elderly and poor, navigate the medical care system and get the largest bang for their buck. The one necessary concession to socialism would be a system of federally licensed catastrophic insurance funds which would automatically cover the means-tested safety-net population regardless of preexisting condition in return for mandatory premiums; these would be withheld from beneficiaries' cash transfer payments and be set by competitive bid.

11. REPLACE THE WARFARE STATE WITH GENUINE NATIONAL DEFENSE. The warfare state would be demobilized and dismantled, with budget resources reduced to the Eisenhower Minimum outside of a declaration of war. Foreign policy would be based on the principle of non-intervention in the internal affairs of all other nations coupled with the Eisenhower policy of massive nuclear retaliation. In other words, the nation's conventional forces would be reduced by perhaps two-thirds and be used solely to shield the continent from conventional military attack; the domestic police forces would be in charge of warding off and controlling terrorist subversion; and any foreign aggressor contemplating a nuclear attack against the United States would know with certainty that the consequence would be incineration of their own nation. At the present time the Eisenhower Minimum would amount to about 2.5 percent of GDP and would more than meet the legitimate defense needs of a nation that is broke and which was never elected policeman of the world in the first place.

12. IMPOSE A 30 PERCENT WEALTH TAX; PAY DOWN THE NATIONAL DEBT TO 30 PERCENT OF GDP. Even if another road were chosen, the debt of the US government would not stop growing due to the built-in deficit momentum until it reached $20 trillion at minimum. But contrary to the present

Keynesian foolishness, national debt of that magnitude is a time bomb on an economy that will struggle for years to reach $20 trillion of GDP, or a 100 percent debt ratio. The reason is that eventually interest rates must normalize or the monetary system will implode in a final orgy of money printing. Normalized interest rate increases of, say, 300–500 basis points under a mobilized discount rate régime at the Fed, in fact, would cause an explosion of budget outlays (up to $1 trillion annually) and a resulting feedback loop into honest debt markets which could not be contained because free market interest rates would rise even further. The prudent solution, therefore, would be to get the federal debt burden back to 30 percent of GDP where it was at the time of the Camp David infamy. That would amount to a $6 trillion debt limit compared to a $20 trillion GDP under an unrosy scenario a half decade or so down the road.

Needless to say, $14 trillion of national debt reduction could never be achieved under any known ordinary fiscal device; it would take a one-time wealth tax, essentially a recapture of part of the windfall wealth gain that has accrued to the top of the economic ladder during the age of bubble finance. Presently, household net worth is about $60 trillion and upward of $45 billion is held by the top 10 percent of households. Accordingly, a 30 percent wealth tax on the upper rungs and payable over perhaps a decade would reduce the national debt to the target 30 percent of GDP. In computing the one-time assessment, the present value of all benefits foregone owing to the cancellation of social insurance for the affluent would be credited against amounts of wealth tax otherwise owing.

13. REPEAL THE SIXTEENTH AMENDMENT; FEED THE BEAST WITH UNIVERSAL TAXES ON CONSUMPTION. Needless to say, the wealth tax and national debt paydown would have to be done as part of a grand social bargain that repealed the Sixteenth Amendment. The ultimate lesson of the Great Deformation is that society cannot starve the beast of the state; it must feed it with current taxes on the people, as would be guaranteed by a balanced budget amendment. But in the modern world income taxes on corporations and affluent households are merely an invitation for crony capitalist lobbies to seek endless loopholes and densification of the tax code with obscurantist hair-splitting over definitions of income, expense, time periods, and categories and flavors of income types.

The only thing which can be fairly and efficiently collected, in truth, is a uniform tax on domestic consumption at the point of sale. More importantly, under a balanced budget amendment taxation of income would ultimately incite true class war and generate punitive barriers to acts of capitalist enterprise. The hideous position of the Obama White House during the first fiscal cliff debate was dispositive: it wanted to defend the entire welfare state, tepidly curtail the warfare state, and collect the revenue necessary to pay for them with higher taxes on just 2 percent of the population! If the other road were to be taken, therefore, the people should be required to feed the beast and the state should extract the necessary revenues through an upcharge on the consumption expenditures of each and every citizen, including those who have submitted to a means test to receive transfer payments from the state.

If another road were taken in this manner, the entire domestic welfare state budget could be reduced from 17.5 percent of GDP last year to a permanent 15 percent, notwithstanding the inexorable march of the baby boomers into old age and the honest limits to economic growth in a revived free market economy. In conjunction with the dismantlement of the warfare state and the paydown of the national debt, this would allow the nation's revenue and spending accounts to be balanced at about 20 percent of GDP. The wealth tax would penalize past accumulations and recapture windfalls, but permit a great reset so that entrepreneurs and job creators in the future would face no income tax at all.

At length, the devastating strife of the fiscal cliff would be quieted. Democracy could function, and the people could pursue their ends and ambitions on a free market liberated from the corruptions of crony capitalism, the unfair windfalls to the 1 percent, and the needless inefficiencies and waste which flow from the Keynesian state and its central banking branch. At the end of the day, the cure for the Great Deformation is to return to sound money and fiscal rectitude, and to correct the great error initiated during the New Deal era; namely, that in pursuing humanitarian purposes the state cannot and need not attempt to manage the business cycle or goose the free market with stimulants for more growth and jobs; nor can it afford the universal entitlements of social insurance.

Instead, its job is to be a trustee for citizens left behind, maintaining a sturdy, fair, and efficient safety net regardless of whether the GDP is rising or falling, or whether unemployment is high or low. And most especially, the work of a citizen government attending to and managing the safety net for fellow citizens would proceed apace without regard to the opinion of Professor Paul Krugman or Art Laffer as to whether the free market was achieving the "potential" output decreed by their deeply flawed models and theories. The proof for that imperative is in the pudding.

NOTE ON SOURCES

It goes without saying that this book is a polemic that does not pretend to marshal the pro and con arguments in an even-handed academic fashion. It contains much original interpretation of financial and public policy events and trends of the last century, even a revisionist framework. The facts and information content that have been used to illustrate and support the themes and interpretations are derived from readily accessible sources in the public domain. Accordingly, the book is not footnoted because my purpose has been to interpret and pattern the facts, not discover or explicate them.

I did not use research assistants in the investigation phase or writing phase of producing the book, so all of the factual material cited is the result of my own searches. I am confident that it is accurate insofar as humanly possible and a fair presentation of the underlying source materials in instances where I have made calculations or extracted quotations. The major sources of the extensive financial and fiscal data cited in the book are listed below, but there are certain presentation devices used throughout the book that should be mentioned here. The factual material in the book is presented to illustrate, frame, or document my themes, but not to detract from the flow of the argument owing to inordinate detail or spurious precision. For that reason, the book is also free of charts and graphs. Since I am dealing with long time spans and underlying trends, I have attempted to round billions and trillions to the nearest "big figure" numbers that are true to the underlying facts at issue but are more digestible than the precise raw figures found in the primary databases. Likewise, most percentage change numbers have been rounded to the nearest whole number, unless the argument depends on greater precision, usually in the case of shorter term trends and rates of change. Finally, I have attempted to make data from the periods prior to the Great Inflation of the 1970s more comparable to contemporary financial magnitudes by translating data into "GDP equivalence" on a present-day scale. For example, nominal GDP was about $100 billion in 1929 compared to $15.7 trillion today. So where appropriate, data in the nominal dollars of the day were factored up by approximately 150X. Thus, stock market margin loans at the 1929 peak totaled in excess of $9 billion in dollars of the day and equivalent to 9 percent of GDP, or $1.5 trillion, in today's GDP scale.

The single most important source of data in the book is the economic researcher's best friend, called "FRED," the acronym for the Federal Reserve Economic Data website maintained by the Federal Reserve Bank of St. Louis. It contains current and historical data, some of it stretching back a half century or longer, from more than 61,000 US and international data series. Due to the user-friendly nature of the site, any of these series are virtually three or four clicks away from most of the macroeconomic data cited in the book. These include GDP and all of its components, price trend data for the CPI, and various deflators, banking, interest rate, and monetary data, as well as all the common series on labor markets, housing, and business activity indicators such as industrial production and retail sales. As one brief example, the book is highly concerned with the huge rise in the PCE (personal consumption expenditure) share of national income over the last four decades as one piece of evidence with respect to the Great Deformation. Any of the book's data on PCE, therefore, can be found by clicking FRED's "National Income and Products Accounts" (NIPA) category, which contains 258 series, several of which provide PCE in real and nominal terms, and all of which can be viewed in graph and raw data form by quarter for any period and sub-period back to 1940. In this regard, an alternative source of the NIPA or GDP account data which are at the center of the book's presentation is an online site maintained by the Bureau of Economic Analysis of the Commerce Department (which produces the GDP data) called "NIPA Interactive." It is also virtually a few clicks away from any of the components, sub-components, and underlying data series which comprise the NIPA database.

This book is also highly focused on the "empty quarter" in the Keynesian worldview; namely, the balance sheets of households, the business sector, financial institutions, governments, and the national economy as a whole. The researcher's (and reader's) best friend on that score is a massive database called the "Z.1" report published by the Federal Reserve and formally called the "Flow of Funds Accounts of the United States." This data has been sorted into consistent form on a quarterly basis going back to 1946, and each quarterly update contains more than a hundred pages of tables that are cross-indexed and fully footed, showing the trends in assets, liabilities, and net worth of the components and aggregates of the US economy, including the balance sheets of the banking system and the Fed. Virtually all of the balance sheet data (other than for individual companies) cited in the book is extracted from the Z.1 reports on the Fed's website.

The book also delves heavily into pre-1945 financial and fiscal history, especially chapters 8–10 on the New Deal and World War II periods. Some of the cited data is contained in the online databases indicated above, but most comes from the two-volume series issued by the Bureau of the Census called *Historical Statistics of the United States, Colonial Times to 1970*. This publication is the historical equivalent of the current-period *Statistical Abstract* also published by the Census Bureau and is the source of virtually 95 percent of the historical macroeconomic, banking, and other financial data cited for pre-1945 periods in the book.

A third preoccupation of the book is federal budget and fiscal trends. Both the OMB and CBO websites contained extensive historical and current budget data, and I have used the former in most instances owing to certain historical affinities. The principal exception is the detailed analysis of the current ten-year CBO budget baseline contained in chapter 33 and referenced elsewhere in the book, including the introduction and chapter 27. That analysis and the cited revenue and expenditure data are based on a CBO report entitled "The Budget and Economic Outlook: Fiscal Years 2012 to 2022" published in January 2012.

The chapters in part 4, "The Age of Bubble Finance," are heavily focused on financial markets and the financial data and stock prices for dozens of individual companies. While there are innumerable public websites for financial data as well as proprietary databases maintained for clients by brokers and advisors, the book utilized YCharts for the purpose of consistency and due to its user-friendly features for virtually all of the company and financial and stock price data cited. YCharts provides ten years of SEC-filed financial statement data for publicly traded companies, along with stock price, PE multiple, market capitalization data, and a large variety of standard financial analysis ratios such as leverage, margins, and growth rates. Supplementary company data was also obtained from the "Market Data" section of the *Wall Street Journal*'s website and a similar database maintained by Yahoo! Finance. More detailed company financial data that drilled deeper than the common categories and ratios contained in the financial websites was obtained directly from SEC-filed 10Ks, 10Qs, and 8-Ks for the cited companies. The aggregate data on stock buybacks, M&A deals, and capital markets activities such as junk bond issuance and IPOs were obtained from the Standard & Poor's website and commonly produced research reports issued by the major Wall Street houses.

Certain chapters also contain a fair amount of specialized economic data, such as chapters 18 and 19, which are focused on housing. In addition to the large macroeconomic databases such as FRED cited above, these chapters also draw upon extensive housing finance data published by Inside Mortgage Finance, the authoritative trade source of industry data such as on the variety of mortgages underwritten during the housing boom, including subprime, alt-A, conforming loans, and all the sub-varieties of these categories.

Likewise, part 1 on the BlackBerry Panic of 2008 supplements the standard public data series with additional, related data on the financial crisis gathered and assembled by the National Commission on the Causes of the Financial and Economic Crisis in the United States, and published in its official report released in January 2011. The extensive data on the banking system cited in chapter 2 was also derived from the Fed's weekly H.8 release called "Assets and Liabilities of Commercial Banks in the United States" and especially from the FDIC's large quarterly production called "Quarterly Banking Profile" and related releases.

Another specialized set of data on the jobs and employment issues presented in detail in chapter 31 is derived from the BLS "Employment Situation" reports, and particularly the extensive historical data series for the "A" tables (household survey data) and the Series "B" tables (establishment survey data for nonfarm payrolls). The three categories presented in chapter 31 referred to as breadwinner jobs, part-time jobs, and the HES complex are a re-sort of the more than one hundred payroll jobs categories contained in the "B" series. Other specialized data series include Commerce Department series on foreign trade and the balance of payments, construction spending, personal income, and its disposition including consumption, savings, and taxes.

Nearly all of the "contemporary" trends, episodes, and events in the post-1970 period cited in the book are based on my own observations and recollections, supplemented by Google searches and books and articles that provide context and details. Events during the Camp David weekend in August 1971 and the Nixon period generally, for instance, were illuminated by Allen J. Matusow's book entitled *Nixon's Economy, Booms, Busts, Dollars, & Votes* (University of Kansas Press, 1998). Likewise, journalistic accounts of contemporary events provided further color and details on various episodes, such as Andrew Ross Sorokin's account of the 2008 financial crisis in *Too Big to Fail* (Viking, 2009) and Ron Suskind's accounts of both the early George W. Bush administration in *The Price of Loyalty* (HarperCollins, 2004) and economic policy making during the first two years of the Obama administration in *Confidence Men* (HarperCollins, 2011). I reviewed literally hundreds of these kinds of journalistic and academic accounts with respect to the "contemporary" period, but the main thrust of chapters focused on events after the 1960s are based on the raw data sources cited above and my own observations and assessments as a contemporary observer and sometime participant in these events.

By contrast, my "historic" period perspective for the era prior to 1970, especially the New Deal and post-WWI period, is derived from a distinctive literature that was mainly published before 1940. Succinctly stated, I do not believe that postwar Keynesian historiography gives a fair, accurate, or insightful picture of what actually happened. It is so biased against pre-Keynesian "sound money" traditions based on gold standard money and balanced budgets that much that is relevant gets air-brushed out of the picture, and actions consistent with earlier sound money traditions are badly misinterpreted, even ridiculed. While the literature published during these times was obviously massive, the following are leading examples of pre-Keynesian books that have informed my views on this "historic" period: *Economics and the Public Welfare* by Benjamin M. Anderson (D. Van Nostrand Company, 1949); *The Theory and Practice of Central Banking* by H. Parker Willis (Harper & Brothers Publishers, 1936); *The Banking Crisis* by Marcus Nadler and Jules I. Boden (Dodd, Mead & Company, 1933); *Prelude to Panic* by Lawrence Sullivan (Statesman Press, 1936); *The Money Muddle* by James P. Warburg (Alfred A. Knopf, 1934); *Banking and the Business Cycle* by C. A. Phillips, T. F. McManus, and R. W. Nelson (Macmillan Company, 1937); *War Debts and World Prosperity* by Harold G. Moulton and Leo Pasvolsky (Brookings Institution, 1932); *Deterioration of the Quality of Foreign Bonds Issued in the United States, 1920–1930* by Ilse Mintz (National Bureau of Economic Research, 1951); *The Liberal Tradition* by Lewis W. Douglas (D. Van Nostrand Company, 1935); *The Twilight of Gold, 1914–1936* by Melchior Palyi (Henry Regency Company, 1972); *The Banking Situation* by H. Parker Willis and John Chapman (Columbia University Press, 1934); *Bankers and Credit* by Hartley Withers (Eveleigh, Nash & Grayson, 1924); *The Course and Phases of the World-Economic Depression* by the League of Nations (Secretariat of the League of Nations, 1931); *After Seven Years* by Raymond Moley (Harper & Brothers, 1939); *Crisis in Agriculture: The Agricultural Adjustment Administration and the New Deal, 1933* by Van L. Perkins (University of California Press, 1969); *Closed and Distressed Banks* by Cyril B. Upham and Edward Lamke (Brookings Institution, 1934); *The Banking Crisis and Recovery Under the Roosevelt Administration* by J. F. T. O'Connor (De Capo Press, 1938); *The Banking Crisis of 1933* by Susan Estabrook Kennedy (University Press of Kentucky, 1973); *The Banking Panics of the Great Depression* by Elmus Wicker (Cambridge University Press, 1996); *World Agriculture and the Depression* by Valdimir P. Timoshenko (University of Michigan, 1933); and *The Crash and Its Aftermath: A History of the Securities Markets in the United States, 1929–1933* by Barrie A. Wigmore (Greenwood Press, 1985).

Finally, I have made extensive use of the memoirs written by the principals who shaped many of the periods and episodes deemed salient in this narrative. Examples include *An Adventure in Constructive Finance* by Carter Glass (Doubleday, Page & Company, 1927); *The Morganthau Diaries, Years of Crisis 1928–1938* edited by John Morton Blum (Houghton Mifflin Company, 1959); *Mandate for Change, 1953–1956* and *Waging Peace, 1956–1961* by Dwight D. Eisenhower (Doubleday & Company, 1963); *Inside the Nixon Administration: The Secret Diary of Arthur Burns, 1969–1974* edited by Robert Ferrell (University Press of Kansas, 2010); *Time for Truth* by William Simon (Reader's Digest Press, 1978); *The Age of Turbulence* by Alan Greenspan (Penguin Books, 2007); and *On the Brink* by Henry M. Paulson, Jr. (Business Plus, 2010).

INDEX

ABOUT THE AUTHOR

© CARYL ENGLANDER

DAVID STOCKMAN was elected as a Michigan congressman in 1976 and joined the Reagan White House in 1981. Serving as budget director, he was one of the key architects of the Reagan Revolution plan to reduce taxes, cut spending, and shrink the role of government. He joined Salomon Brothers in 1985 and later became one of the early partners of the Blackstone Group. During nearly two decades at Blackstone and at a firm he founded, Stockman was a private equity investor. Stockman attended Michigan State University and Harvard Divinity School and then went to Washington as a congressional aide in 1970. He is also the author of the number one bestseller *The Triumph of Politics.*

PublicAffairs is a publishing house founded in 1997. It is a tribute to the standards, values, and flair of three persons who have served as mentors to countless reporters, writers, editors, and book people of all kinds, including me.

I. F. STONE, proprietor of *I. F. Stone's Weekly*, combined a commitment to the First Amendment with entrepreneurial zeal and reporting skill and became one of the great independent journalists in American history. At the age of eighty, Izzy published *The Trial of Socrates*, which was a national bestseller. He wrote the book after he taught himself ancient Greek.

BENJAMIN C. BRADLEE was for nearly thirty years the charismatic editorial leader of *The Washington Post*. It was Ben who gave the *Post* the range and courage to pursue such historic issues as Watergate. He supported his reporters with a tenacity that made them fearless and it is no accident that so many became authors of influential, best-selling books.

ROBERT L. BERNSTEIN, the chief executive of Random House for more than a quarter century, guided one of the nation's premier publishing houses. Bob was personally responsible for many books of political dissent and argument that challenged tyranny around the globe. He is also the founder and longtime chair of Human Rights Watch, one of the most respected human rights organizations in the world.

·   ·   ·

For fifty years, the banner of Public Affairs Press was carried by its owner Morris B. Schnapper, who published Gandhi, Nasser, Toynbee, Truman, and about 1,500 other authors. In 1983, Schnapper was described by *The Washington Post* as "a redoubtable gadfly." His legacy will endure in the books to come.

Peter Osnos, *Founder and Editor-at-Large*